THE SMALL TOWN IN AMERICAN LITERATURE

THE SMALL TOWN
IN
AMERICAN LITERATURE

By

Ima Honaker Herron

HASKELL HOUSE PUBLISHERS Ltd.

Publishers of Scarce Scholarly Books

NEW YORK, N. Y. 10012

1971

First Published 1939

HASKELL HOUSE PUBLISHERS Ltd.
Publishers of Scarce Scholarly Books
280 LAFAYETTE STREET
NEW YORK. N. Y. 10012

Library of Congress Catalog Card Number: 70-92967

Standard Book Number 8383-0980-1

To the Memory of
My Brother
Clarence Ray Herron
(1916-1936)

PREFACE

CONTINUOUSLY from the third quarter of the eighteenth century until the present there has developed a body of native small town literature too large and varied to be ignored by the student of American life and letters. Poetry, fiction of many types, histories, essays, diaries and notebooks, and autobiographies all have mirrored in varying degrees of verisimilitude, social satire, and romantic portrayal the prevailing attitudes toward a widely diversified community life. A survey such as this may serve, therefore, to trace the rather complex progression of the small town and its prototype, the village, through American literature, and, incidentally, to correct the false impression held by some that the literary history of the small town had its beginning in the sensational receptions accorded such modern works of protest as *Spoon River Anthology* and *Main Street*. The present study is a presentation of the literary patterns of American small town life comparable in purpose to earlier and now widely known investigations emphasizing the part played by the city, the frontier, and the prairies in the making of American literature. It has been designed to show through discussions, notes, and bibliographical aids that the little town has long interested many of our best writers, whose art has variously touched small town life, however isolated, in all parts of the nation. Undoubtedly, the portrayals of the American small town in literature represent far more than passing fancy or an occasional revolt from the village.

In selecting the historical-geographical approach as a method best adaptable to a cohesive presentation of the various treatments of the town, I have not been unaware of other acceptable modes of interpretation. Perhaps later investigators may choose to approach the undeniably rich field of small town literature by way of emphasizing agrarian, industrial, intellectual, and other frequently used community themes. In this study such familiar problems, common to small towns in many sections and many decades, appear as an integral part of the regional presentations.

In the preparation of this volume I have incurred so many obligations that to acknowledge the assistance of all who have contributed information, means of information, profitable suggestions, and encouragement would be difficult. While various acknowledgments appear in the text, the notes, and Copyright Acknowledgments, here certain obligations require more personal recognition. I wish especially to accord grateful appreciation to the following for their clarifying judgments and suggestions: Professors Paull F. Baum, Allan H. Gilbert, Clarence Gohdes, and Newman I. White of Duke University, Professor Richard H. Shryock of the University of Pennsylvania, and Professors John O. Beaty, Ernest E. Leisy, and John H. McGinnis, and Messrs. George Bond and Henry Smith, my colleagues at Southern Methodist University. For their many courtesies my thanks are due also to the officials and certain members of various library staffs, particularly to those of the Library of Congress, the Chicago Public Library, the Dallas Public Library, and the following universities: Duke University, Southern Methodist University, the University of Texas, the University of North Carolina, the University of Chicago, Columbia University, Harvard University, Yale University, and the University of Washington. To Mr. David K. Jackson, Duke University Press, and Dr. William S. Hoole, Baylor University, I am indebted for helpful information. I wish to thank Mrs. Miletus Yarbrough for assistance in the compilation of the index and Dr. R. O. Rivera of the Duke University Press for his kindness. I am deeply indebted to my parents for their efforts toward making the task of writing a more pleasant one. Also, I thank Thera P. Herron and Wallace W. Herron, my sister and brother, for their criticisms. Finally, I am most deeply indebted to Professor Jay B. Hubbell of Duke University whose keen interest in American literature was the first to encourage my own. I accord the deepest appreciation to him for his generous and invaluable criticism and words of encouragement given throughout the preparation of this study.

I. H. H.

Southern Methodist University
Dallas, Texas
August 15, 1938

CONTENTS

x CONTENTS

COPYRIGHT ACKNOWLEDGMENTS

For permission to reprint material still in copyright, acknowledgment is made to the following :

The American Mercury, for Mrs. Luis M. Marín's (Muna Lee's) "Electors."

MR. HAMLIN GARLAND, for selections from his *Prairie Folks*, *Crumbling Idols*, and "God's Ravens" from *Main-Travelled Roads* (published by Harper and Brothers).

MR. ARTHUR GUITERMAN, for his rimed review, "Edgar Lee Masters," which first appeared in *The Saturday Review of Literature*.

HARCOURT, BRACE AND COMPANY, for selections from Sinclair Lewis's *Main Street*.

HARPER AND BROTHERS, for the selections from Mark Twain's *Roughing It*, *Life on the Mississippi*, *The Man That Corrupted Hadleyburg*, and *Mark Twain's Autobiography*.

HOUGHTON MIFFLIN COMPANY, for the selections from Thomas Bailey Aldrich ; for the selection from Willa Cather's *My Ántonia;* for the selections from Bret Harte's "The Luck of Roaring Camp" and *Gabriel Conroy;* for the selections from Nathaniel Hawthorne's Custom House Sketch and *The House of the Seven Gables;* for the quotation from Sarah Orne Jewett's *Deephaven;* and for the quotation from Edwin Arlington Robinson's *Captain Craig*.

ALFRED A. KNOPF, INC., for the selection from Carl Van Doren's *Many Minds*.

MRS. LUIS M. MARÍN (Muna Lee), for her "Electors," which first appeared in *The American Mercury*.

THE MACMILLAN COMPANY, for the following selections from Vachel Lindsay's *Collected Poems:* "The Illinois Village," "On the Building of Springfield," "General William Booth Enters into Heaven," and "Abraham Lincoln Walks at Midnight" ; for the quoted matter from Julia Patton's *The English Village;* for the lines from Edwin Arlington Robinson's "New England," included in his *Collected Poems;* for the quoted matter from Carl Van Doren's *Contemporary American Novelists;* and for the selections from William Allen White's *In Our Town*.

INTRODUCTION

THE HISTORY of a nation is only the history of its villages written large." Thus Woodrow Wilson, writing in 1900, reaffirmed
the truth that local history, subordinate only in the sense in
which each leaf in a book is subordinate to the volume itself,
is the ultimate substance of national history. Assuredly, since
colonial days the American village (or small town, as it has
been called more recently) has added to "the great and spreading pattern" of this country variously designed details : "intricate weaving, all the delicate shading, all the nice refinement
of pattern-gold thread mixed with fustian, fine thread laid upon
coarse, shade combined with shade."[1] It is this variety which
has given the actual small town both life and significance and
has made it, in Wilson's words, "a stage upon a far journey"
and "a place the national history has passed through." The
parish records of a country-side, where today there is but
slight vestige of old-fashioned village life, may reveal even in
decaying hamlets matter for drama suggestive of the trend of
national development.

Likewise, literary records reveal an equally rich store of
materials. In English literature a recurrent and variously
used theme is that of the English village and the life connected
with it.[2] From the time when Geoffrey Chaucer marked bills
of lading on "the thronged wharf," the mere contemplation of
which moved William Morris to forget "the spreading of the
hideous town" throughout the "Black Country" of his own industrialized England to ". . . dream of London small and
white and clean, The clear Thames bordered by its gardens
green. . . ," until the modern period of Arnold Bennett's Five
Towns, familiarly known writers of all ranks have pictured the
changing panorama of English village and town life.[3] Similarly, in American literature there has developed continuously,
from the imitative late eighteenth century to the more rebellious

---

[1] *Mere Literature and Other Essays* (Boston, 1900), p. 214.

[2] L. S. Wood and H. L. Burrows in their small anthology, *The Town in Literature*
(London, 1925), show how London and other municipalities have been featured
in English literature. See also Julia Patton, *The English Village* (New York, 1918).

[3] Quotation from William Morris, *The Earthly Paradise*, London, 1923 (1st ed.,
1868-70), p. 3.

twentieth century, a definite village and small town tradition. It is a familiar matter that at first the English tradition was followed closely and that its folkways were transplanted to a new land where literary standards, if they existed at all, were in the making.   Inevitably, however, the English village theme, as reflected in American literature, was transformed gradually by the changing civilization of a pioneer country.   With the rapid growth of American individualism the contrast between both the actual and the fictionalized American village and town and their English prototypes became more and more marked.   Virginia Woolf, English herself, elaborates upon the now accepted fact that clearly the English tradition, formed upon a little country and "ruled all the time, if unconsciously, by the spirit of the past," has long been unable to cope with the vastness of America, with "these prairies, these cornfields, these lonely little groups of men and women scattered at immense distances from each other, these vast industrial cities. . . ."[1]   Such a tradition, springing from old landscapes which for endless summers and springs stirred men's emotions, has failed to interpret the meaning of an undeveloped land with limitless possibilities; with varied climates and scenery; and with a rapidly changing people.   Without doubt, the English tradition, though actually transplanted, has been forced gradually to give way to newer interpretations.   In fact, the literary history of the American town has gained so much in distinctiveness that modern delineations have become more and more differentiated from the literature of the parent stock.

Since pioneer America was naturally a country of small settlements isolated on the seaboard of a vast wilderness, it was but in accordance with human custom that its local historians should be concerned with the minutiae of community activity. As settlement progressed through various frontiers to the era of modern industrialization, first the village, still revealing a kinship with its English prototype, and later the small town, truly an American product, have furnished for numerous writers, great and small, varied backgrounds, characters, and plots for a multiplicity of literary and pseudo-literary compositions. Obviously, although the total drama of fictionalized community life cannot receive complete treatment in one volume, nevertheless, the very richness and widespread use of such literary

[1] "American Fiction," *The Saturday Review of Literature*, II, 3 (Aug. 1, 1925).

materials so significantly delineative of an important phase of American life justify, in the author's opinion, a history of the various trends in the portrayal of the small town in our literature.   In the present survey, which is not intended to be exhaustive, an attempt has been made to trace the literary evolution of the American village and small town through the following distinct stages : first, that of slavish imitation of the English village tradition, especially developed in the literature of New England and the middle colonies during the eighteenth century ; second, that of the changing village patterns produced by the widely extended westward movement ; and, finally, that marked by the growth of standardization, or the development of the urban spirit.[5]   It is to be noted, also, that, in contrast to the extremely full literary histories of the New England and the Western town, the treatment of the Southern town in imaginative literature has been slow in development and comparatively meager in output.   Except for certain humorous treatments of provincial towns, in general, the same trends (the fictionalization of the genteel life of the ante-bellum village and the modernized life of the post-war town) have prevailed in the South as elsewhere.   From a wealth of material the author has selected for analysis both prose (novels, short stories, and, in more limited number, autobiographies, diaries, essays, and dramas) and poetry most representative in literary merit and portrayals of the trends in the literature of the town prevailing throughout each of the stages mentioned above.

Several other considerations remain.   The numerous literary records of the American town, ranging from those picturing the colonial village to the more caustic novels of the *Main Street* era, indicate that community life frequently is interpreted by American writers as crystallizing around certain conventions, which after serving their purpose give way, in turn, to newer standards.   This study, therefore, must not disregard typical conventions and revolts reflected in our literature of the town.   Furthermore, attention will be drawn to another mat-

---

[5] What Howard Mumford Jones says about American culture in general may be associated with the progress of town life.   "The cosmopolitan spirit, the spirit of the frontier, the middle-class spirit—these are . . . fundamental in American culture— as it is expressed up to 1848. '   After that epoch, he says, "a fourth great factor [is added] to a situation growing steadily more complicated, . . . the urban spirit, . . ." (*America and French Culture: 1750-1848*, Chapel Hill, 1927, p. 73).

ter. One of the familiarly known fundamentals in the written expression of the town spirit is that usually, though not always, the really distinctive literary studies of the small community, especially those treating of the colonial background, did not appear until long after the type of life described in novel or story had become a part of the past. Consider, for illustration, the fact that *The Scarlet Letter*, rich in descriptions of early Boston, was written generations after the period of the locale featured. On the other hand, a different treatment appears and reappears in town fiction to show that in later periods the parallel between the actual and imaginative versions grows stronger. For example, the city-ward movement of the rural population in Illinois from 1900 to 1910 resulted in the subsequent decay of many villages in that state.[6] But a few years later (1914-1915) *Spoon River Anthology*, picturing changing town standards, made its serial appearance, thus illustrating that actual community changes and fictional portrayals of these changes often have been contemporaneous. Such has been the trend in town fiction during more recent years. So-called "expounders" like Sherwood Anderson, Sinclair Lewis, and Floyd Dell, all of whom have experienced small town life at first hand, have repeatedly satirized all of the provincial changes they themselves have watched develop.

Finally, what Julia Patton applies to her excellent study of the English village likewise may be considered in a similar study of the American small town. A purely literary investigation would have regard primarily for literary trends and kindred subjects; but such a treatment would miss many of

[6] H. E. Hoagland, "The Movement of Rural Population in Illinois," *The Journal of Political Economy*, XX, 913-927 (Nov., 1912). In addition to Census reports, similar accounts of modern town growth and decline may be found in the following: C. Luther Fry, *A Census Analysis of Middle Atlantic Villages* (New York, 1924), Tables I and II showing population growth and decline from 1900 to 1920 for thirty villages (date from the Fourteenth Census of the United States, Vol. I, Table 51) ; Fry, *A Census Analysis of American Villages* (New York, 1925), a study of the 1920 Census data for one hundred and seventy-seven villages scattered over the United States ; Paul L. Vogt, *An Introduction to Rural Sociology* (New York, 1924), two tables, pp. 376-377, indicating causes for population changes, and R. S. Vaile, ed., *The Small City and Town* (Minneapolis, 1930), showing that though many towns have suffered from improved transportation during the ten years from 1920 to 1930 the changes effected thereby have largely proved advantageous to such communities. A better understanding has been created between people of all classes and various communities. Today "hicks," "hick towns," and "city dudes," and the like are virtually obsolete.

the implications of greatest interest and value in subject matter. For this reason, there is added to this literary history a brief preliminary survey of actual village and small town developments in America.

THE SMALL TOWN IN AMERICAN LITERATURE

CHAPTER I

THE SMALL TOWN IN AMERICA

THE AVERAGE American tourist has driven through the century-marked villages of New England and the middle states, and on through noticeably new oil towns in Oklahoma and Texas. He has caught, as Ruth Suckow points out,

varied glimpses of the spirit of the country in the settled prosperity of the plain frame house of the Middle West and the delicate and forlorn distinction of white Southern houses in a pleasantly dilapidated landscape; in the new settlements of tourist cabins that shelter a huge nomad population; and those deserted mining towns where pack-rats scamper over decaying floors. . . .[1]

In spite of these extravagant differences, however, all of these towns are American, bound together by something strangely homogeneous. Considering these marked varieties, one may well puzzle over the question: "What, after all, is the American small town, or village?" Obviously, any definition applicable to the whole necessarily must be elastic, for throughout our national history the small community has occupied a place of large influence.

In all probability the term "village" will suggest entirely different things to different persons. To some will come remembrances of modest homes and few crossroads stores located in a community without railroad service, but marked by "the charm of a familiar homyness impossible to a large town or city."[2] Julia Patton opens her book, *The English Village*, with an explanation of the American small town as many people like to regard it. She begins:

It may be pretty safely said that all the world loves a village. Everybody feels the charm of a "little town." Not to live in necessarily: one may love it as Newman is said to have loved children, "in idea." But there is something essentially appealing to the village "idea" to which few people are indifferent—something small

[1] "The Folk Idea in American Life," *Scribner's Magazine*, LXXXVIII, 246 (Sept., 1930).
[2] Julia Patton, *The English Village: A Literary Study, 1750-1850*, New York, 1919 (1st ed., 1918), p. 2.

and intimate and endearing. Close to humanity and close to nature is the village, and small enough to be grasped imaginatively
as a city with its vast complex of interests and institutions and
activities can not be.

While the city impresses and excites, arouses admiration and
wonder, commands a passionate loyalty, or kindles a high
ambition, it does not inspire, says Miss Patton, the sort of mood
one feels at the mention of village.

To others "village" is antiquated. They prefer thinking of
a little town with busy ways, and embryonic manufacturing
plant, a Kiwanis club, several brick banks and stores, and a
newly paved main street or square. Others even more cosmopolitan will call to mind "a sleeping community" or a small
center connected with a near-by city by bus or interurban.[3]
Oil boom towns in East Texas and dust-visited places in the
Panhandle, Colorado mining camps, company-owned factory
settlements, beach or lake resorts, and college centers, all bear
the name of village or town. No hard and fast lines of definition can be drawn.

According to the restricted classification listed in the 1920
reports of the United States Census Bureau, the entire population of our country is by residence urban or rural—and this
in spite of the fact that there are scores of incorporated communities of no more than a few hundred people and hundreds
of small towns.[4] True, the small place often is divided between the surrounding country and city, temporarily attached
now to one, now to the other. In the apt characterization of
Paul Douglas, "somewhere between the country and the city
lies that which partakes on a petty scale of the nature of both
--the little town."[5] In many instances the small town is a
sort of middle-man or, to borrow Douglas's term, "a negligible buffer . . . impotent between two mighty neighbors." A
neuter, it shares some of the isolation of the open country and

[3] Vogt, *op. cit.*, p. 356.
[4] *Fifteenth Census of the United States* (Washington, 1930-1931), I, 7: "Urban
areas, as defined by the Census Bureau in recent censuses, have included all
cities and other incorporated places having 2,500 inhabitants or more. For use
in connection with the 1930 census the definition has been slightly modified and
extended so as to include townships and other political subdivisions. . . ." Three
divisions of the population were made, as follows: (1) urban, (2) rural non-farm,
or village population, and (3) rural farm. The rural non-farm includes, in general, all persons outside cities living in places having a population of twenty-five
hundred or more. See also pp. 42 ff., Table XVI.
[5] *The Little Town* (New York, 1927), p. 3.

shows in miniature the manners of the city. On the other hand, a fact sometimes overlooked is that the small town, after all, is a concentrated neighborhood with interests varying in accordance with its location, an important factor noticeable in the literary interpretations of the American town. In most cases the visible unity of the town group of homes and shops is warrant enough for treating the place as a community by itself.

Even though the census fixes a population of twenty-five hundred as the boundary between country and city, size does not always stamp a citizenry as forming a little town or city.[6] This is truly applicable to the small towns described in American literature. Writers differ frequently as to the size of the places sketched. Holyoke, the New England village pictured in Mrs. Stowe's *Oldtown Folks* (1869), is populated by only a few hundred souls; the Gopher Prairie of *Main Street*, on the other hand, is larger and more in keeping with the census report. "Village," therefore, both in actual and literary usage, is something of an outmoded term, and "small town," more modern. Often narrowness of spiritual or intellectual outlook, as is dramatically demonstrated in Harold Frederic's caustic novel, *The Damnation of Theron Ware* (1896), determines the small town classification of a place. Sometimes cities of a hundred thousand people, like Sinclair Lewis's Zenith, are but exaggerated country towns. Twenty-five hundred, however, is the usual town size, and conditions remain on a relatively small scale until a greater upward climb in population is accompanied by a change from village to urban characteristics. Again, some towns, such as communities in parts of the Middle West and the Southwest, are country-minded, and have standards of living adapted to agricultural or kindred pursuits; others, like those in the vicinity of New York or Chicago, are so urban-minded that they are merely extensions of the city.

With this regard any consideration, literary or factual, of the American small town must rest upon the fundamental that towns have various reasons for being. Today, with the existence in the United States of thousands of towns and small cities having a population of less than five thousand, numerous varieties of town types may be found throughout the country. Traveled Americans will not agree with St. John Ervine, who sharply contrasts the dissimilarity of English villages with the

[6] Figures based upon the 1920 Federal Census definition.

sameness of American towns by the criticism that "in America
one village is almost an exact replica of another village."[7]
Furthermore, one does not like to think that a selected town-
builder designed a standard town, and that thousands of them,
machine-made, were dropped at intervals about the country.
Had our critic traveled first through the older village communities of New England and New York and then through
certain sections west of the Mississippi, he would have been
aware, surely, of the contrast between substantial old structures bearing the marks of age and those suggestive of recent
and often hasty construction.   Did he take into consideration
the dissimilarities between the North Central communities
centering around grain elevators and small residential centers
near larger cities?   It may safely be said, regardless of the mis-
conceptions of foreign travelers, like Ervine, G. K. Chesterton,
Count Keyserling, and others, that the small town in modern
America has assumed definite proportions in accordance with
its locality and purposes for existence.[8]   In spite of alarmists,
the American small town assuredly is not in the same class with
Câpek's robots.   In reality, the standardization of the modern
town is largely overrated by foreign travelers and others who
view our community life superficially.   While American towns
may look alike to the traveler who views them casually from
the Pullman coach, in various sections they are found to be
really individual if one stays in them long enough to make an
acquaintance with their people and local customs.   This many
of our best writers of imaginative literature have done.   It is
our purpose to show that our earliest writers viewed the little
places about which they wrote as villages and that the moderns,
reflecting the life of recent times, have pictured small towns.

EARLIER HISTORICAL TRENDS

I.   THE SOUTHERN TOWN

Differentiation, as well as a degree of standardization, of the
town type has come gradually with the progress of American
civilization westward.   It is true that, in spite of the changes
wrought by modern inventions, in some sections of England

---

[7] "American Literature; Now and to Be," *Century Magazine*, CI, 578 (March,
1921).
[8] See Chesterton's estimate of the town as given in *The Golden Book*, p. 33 (June,
1931), and Count Keyserling's criticism in *America Set Free* (New York, 1929),
passim.

and Scotland there still lingers about isolated villages an air of antiquity noticeable even to the casual observer. In some of the valley towns of the Lake country, for instance, the inns with their queer or ageworn signs, the small stone churches, and the narrow streets closely lined with houses suggestive often of scenes in *Quality Street* present a past entirely un-American. In America, however, the Old World village form, transplanted by the Englishman, underwent a disintegration as westward migration continued into the free lands beyond the Atlantic seaboard. The original colonial plantation and the New England village organizations, therefore, have been variously transformed in new regions and new periods.[9] The spread of American settlement, the story of an ever retreating wilderness and a changing frontier, may be taken as a focal point from which may be traced, in brief, the actual backgrounds of community expansion which have furnished ample material for numerous highly varied literary delineations of village and small town life.

The colonizing experiments in America are traceable, in part, to certain changes in rural economy in sixteenth-century England. The rise of the woolen industry was accompanied by the ousting of capable laborers from their holdings by landlords avaricious to the point of seizing the common lands of the villages. Once prosperous communities, therefore, became untenanted and strong and active peasants were transformed into wage-workers, or beggars. This economic change thus created a large group of people ready for an undertaking in colonization.[10] Other factors, including religious discontent and an eagerness for wealth and adventure, gave an impetus to American colonization. Sixteenth-century England was stirred by a new national self-consciousness. Commerce and trade expanded as a result of the adventures of the great sailors ; wealth accumulated ; and a general interest was created in the acquiring of solid material possessions. Exaggerated imaginings regarding the unmeasured wealth of the new lands across the sea aroused many to thoughts of fabulous fortunes and inspired writers like Spenser, even, to praise "fruitfullest Virginia."

[9] Lois Kimball Mathews, *The Expansion of New England* (Boston and New York, 1919), a detailed account of the spread of New England settlement and institutions westward (1620-1865).

[10] Charles A. Beard and Mary R. Beard, *The Rise of American Civilization* (one-vol. ed., New York, 1930), p. 24.

Popular plays, such as Chapman's *Eastward Ho*, written and acted before the settlement of Jamestown, fed the fancies of the day by picturing "Virginia, Earth's only paradise," as a land of rare treasures, a place where "golde is more plentifull there then [than] copper is with us."[11] Such "golden" tales led to the formation of trading companies and aroused the adventurer to dreams of easily won treasure. The London Company, chartered in 1606 and organized for quick profit, found, unfortunately, in its first group of immigrants more "gentlemen" than industrious and sturdy mechanics and laborers. Repeated expeditions brought additional so-called gentlemen and fortune-seekers until Captain John Smith, a member of the third band (1607), demanded in exasperation that the company send men skilled in practical trades : carpenters, husbandmen, and diggers.[12]

In these earliest pioneer days "when a continent undeveloped, potential, menacing loomed above and behind the little settlements of the Atlantic seaboard in vast forests and unmeasured acreage," the settlers, whether in Virginia or New England, had relatively little to do with the wilderness stretching endlessly before them.[13] The first settlements, towns or colonies founded by the seashore or on the banks of a river as an approximation of a compact community, gave then but the vaguest promise of a richly indigenous life. The impractical settlers of Jamestown, interested chiefly in the quick possession of glorified wealth, concerned themselves with commercial rather than agricultural pursuits and still looked to England. At first the seaboard frontier in Virginia, and elsewhere later, was markedly European in traits with its society patterned on European forms modified by the exigencies of a new environment. Later, however, during the seventeenth and eighteenth centuries, the absence of towns eliminated from Southern colonial life much that was essentially English. In a plantation country, where there were but scattered settlements like Williamsburg and Charleston, there could be no true counterpart

---

[11] T. M. Parrot, ed., *The Plays and Poems of George Chapman* (London, 1914), *Eastward Ho*, Act III, sc. iii, l. 25.

[12] Edward Arber, ed., *Travels and Works of Captain John Smith, 1580-1631* (Edinburgh, 1910), II, 444, excerpts from a letter sent by Smith to the Treasurer and Council of the Virginia Company when he was president of Virginia.

[13] Henry Seidel Canby, "The Promise of American Life," *The Saturday Review of Literature*, VII, 301 (Nov. 8, 1930).

of the coffeehouse, the political club, or the literary circle.[14]

Under the earliest circumstances the founding of towns in Virginia was a subsidiary development, a secondary phase born out of sheer necessity rather than out of conscious plan. The beginnings of town life at Jamestown, fraught with every conceivable difficulty, are familiar. On the spot were English adventurers badly prepared for the greater adventure of permanent colonial town-building. In London there was the trading company expectant of ready and profitable returns from the emigrants it had financed. The individual most noteworthy in colonial enterprise was Captain John Smith, whose energies gave to the London Company something more valuable than treasure : a regional map, a sketch of the colony's resources, and sound advice as to the kind of emigrants best suited to the new land. Unfortunately, while Smith attempted to direct the toilsome labor of erecting palisades, the work of helping the sick, and the tricky business of bartering with the Indians, the Company—if one may believe Smith's own accounts—continued to send more and more incompetent colonists, there being among them ". . . thirty-three gentlemen adventurers, twenty one laborers, six tailors, two refiners, two gold-smiths, one gun-smith, one blacksmith, one cooper, one tobacco-pipe maker and one perfumer!" Scornful of the London council's neglect of the colony, Smith, with justifiable sarcasm, wonders whether Richard Belfield, the perfumer, "was sent out to compound sweet scents for these fine gentlemen; we could find no other reason for his coming to us."[15] Such colonists as these, unable to cope with the disadvantages of climate, poor housing, inadequate food, severe illnesses, and savage enemies, were destined to tragic failure during those awful first years on the James River.

After this first conspicuous failure at town establishment, the Company employed various methods to support the foundations of the struggling settlement. Between 1606 and 1624 the Council sent over 5,649 emigrants, only 1,095 of whom were in the colony at the end of the period. Disillusioned, many fled back to England; others perished in Virginia.[16] Liberal

[14] Thomas J. Wertenbaker, *Patrician and Plebeian in Virginia* (New Haven, 1910), p. 109.
[15] Arber, ed., *op. cit.*, II, 928 ; cf. John Ashton, ed., *The Adventures and Discourses of Captain John Smith* (London, 1883), p. 83.
[16] Beard, *op. cit.*, p. 43.

land grants, both to persons willing to risk their lives by emigration to America and to the Company's officers, finally resulted in a social system detrimental to the town mode of colonization. With the eventual discovery of the easily grown tobacco and later the profitable cultivation of cotton, rice, sugar, and indigo, all grown for export, there gradually developed in Virginia and other Southern colonies a type of colonial life which rested upon the plantation as a center, whereas in New England the town became the primary factor. Directors of large tobacco and other holdings, rather than the tradesmen of the town, became the important figures in Southern life.

In spite of all English legal measures Jamestown never became a flourishing center. The lack of town growth was a constant source of anxiety to the first promoters of the colony, for they regarded it as a sign of abnormal conditions.[17]   In addition to frequent directions urging colonial leaders to put an end to the prevailing isolated mode of living, numerous legal acts were passed for the promotion of town centers. During 1638-1639 Sir Francis Wyatt, for instance, was instructed "to draw tradesmen and handicraftmen into towns."[18]   Repeatedly during the seventeenth century English kings urged the establishment of trading towns, potential centers of export for the tobacco and other trade. Such legislation, however, was ineffectual in stimulating interest in the development of an urban society. Instead, acts, like that of Charles II in 1662 providing for the building of a city at Jamestown, merely created a rebellious attitude, the beginnings of an unrest culminating in Bacon's Rebellion (1676). Planters of James City, Charles City, and Surrey keenly resented the acts requiring them to store their tobacco in Jamestown warehouses, structures to be built with taxes levied on their crops.[19]

Certainly the most conspicuous result of the absorption of all activities in plantation "money crops" was the non-existence of a promising town life in early Virginia and adjoining colonies.[20] The whole economic framework of Virginia and her neighbors was founded thus upon the large plantations bordering the

[17] Wertenbaker, op. cit., pp. 42 ff.
[18] Virginia Magazine of History and Biography, XI, 56 (July, 1903).
[19] William Waller Hening, Virginia Laws, Statutes, etc. (Richmond, 1809), II, 192.
[20] P. A. Bruce, Economic History of Virginia in the Seventeenth Century, 1907 (1st ed., 1895) and John Fiske, Old Virginia and Her Neighbors (Boston and New York, 1898), give full accounts of Jamestown and other early Southern settlements.

James, York, Potomac, and Rappahannock rivers, so situated that planters far more easily could have merchant vessels land at their private wharves than they could transfer their tobacco to the Jamestown warehouses. This situation, thinks Wertenbaker, is chiefly responsible for the lack of towns in Virginia during the entire seventeenth century. Not until settlements had spread beyond the deep water region did towns of any size arise.[21] Naturally, the Southern planter, with extensive acreage under his supervision, a code of morals largely his own, and a position of isolation, could cultivate his fields without interference or molestation from outsiders. Though his plantation, really his province and his domain, often possessed the marks of village settlements akin to those on Texas and New Mexico ranches today, it lacked the cohesion and organization of New England settlements, the very essence of town life desired by legislators at Jamestown and later at Williamsburg. Both planters and shipmasters had their way, though assiduous efforts were made through legislation to correct the evil of isolation. Repeatedly special town-building acts were either disregarded or suspended, as Mary E. Wilkins Freeman delineates romantically in *The Heart's Highway: A Romance of Virginia in the Seventeenth Century* (1900); and towns refused to grow.[22]

Thus the spirit of individualism, together with the natural topography of coastwise Virginia, retarded the development of manufactures and prevented the growth of towns. Prior to 1700 the only place in Virginia "to which the name of town could, with any degree of appropriateness, be applied was Jamestown, and even this settlement never rose to a dignity superior to that of a village."[23] At the opening of the eight-

[21] Wertenbaker, *op. cit.*, p. 41. When through expansion it became necessary to bring goods overland to the nearest deep water, shipping centers gradually developed at the "fall line." Then it was that Richmond began its growth (1737-1790).

[22] For full treatment see Wertenbaker, *op. cit.*, pp. 42 ff. and his *The First Americans (1607-1690)*, Vol. II, in the series entitled *A History of American Life* (New York, 1927), chap. ii, "Land and Labor in the Tobacco Colonies"; Bruce, *op. cit.*, Vol. II, chap. xx, "The Town"; Fiske, *op. cit.*, pp. 210 ff.; and Sidney George Fisher, *Men, Women, and Manners in Colonial Times* (Philadelphia and London, 1898), Vol. I, chap. i, "Cavaliers and Tobacco."

[23] In many parts of the South the parish vestry took the place of the town in New England. Virginia was the Southern model as Massachusetts was the Northern. Most of the official business transacted by the New England town was in the South under the jurisdiction of the vestry of a parish, the chief difference being that in Virginia, etc., the settlers did not live in close proximity to each other. Compactness characteristic of the New England village did not exist. The making of contracts for church building, opening of roads, levying of fines, etc., were

eenth century there was hardly a definitely organized village in Virginia, unless one makes the doubtful exception of Williamsburg, then a straggling community to which the seat of government had been removed and in which the College of William and Mary had been established in 1693. Norfolk, founded in 1705, had an exceptional expansion because of its proximity to the timber regions of North Carolina and its trade in sugar, molasses, and rum with the West Indies. During this time of slow town growth in Virginia similar retardation was characteristic along the entire Southern seaboard. In Maryland the little community of Annapolis, later to enjoy a political and social prestige greater than that of its larger commercial rivals, marked one of the highest examples of town life. Even by 1752 Baltimore was a settlement of but twenty-five houses and two hundred people. In North Carolina there were the tiny villages of Wilmington and Edenton. Charleston alone deserved the name of town during this period. It alone offered in the South opportunities for the enjoyment of real town life. To the interior, Georgia, established as a new colony in 1732, was little more than a fur-trading frontier.[24]

It is not to be supposed that Maryland and Virginia were covered only by great plantations such as those glorified later in fiction. Gradually the practice arose, especially in Maryland, of renting some estates and of breaking up others for sale. In these colonies hundreds of petty farmers possessed themselves of small land grants on which they erected unpretentious houses, thus creating a group of distinctly democratic middle-class landowners in the primarily aristocratic provinces of Virginia and Maryland. This system eventually gave rise to a slight town development resulting from the efforts of certain enterprising owners to make money out of the sale of their large holdings. Daniel Dulaney, Annapolis lawyer and holder of an extensive central Maryland acreage, became a promoter and town builder on a large scale through his renting and selling

done by the vestry. In many respects the holding of the county court in the South was the nearest analogy, in colonial days, to a compact town organization. See Edward Eggleston, *The Transit of Civilization from England to America in the Seventeenth Century* (New York, 1909), p. 290.

[24] James Truslow Adams, *Provincial Society (1690-1763)*, Vol. III of *A History of American Life*, p. 202. See also O. P. Chitwood, *A History of Colonial America* (New York, 1931), chap. xxviii, for an account of colonial town growth and customs and *A Century of Population Growth, 1790-1900* (Washington, 1909), for the Census Bureau reports on the first census.

to the Pennsylvania Dutch. In 1745 Dulaney, shrewdly business-like, laid out the town of Frederick.[25] Others, equally eager to acquire additional wealth, tried also this scheme of promoting community development. Richmond had its beginning in 1737 when farsighted William Byrd II advertised a portion of his vast holdings for sale in town lots. These, however, were but sporadic efforts and only a few towns—Annapolis Williamsburg, and Charleston—became really important in the South during the colonial period In these places, as is familiarly known, planters had their town houses in which they entertained distinguished visitors from afar and locally prominent people, all a part of the social picture vividly portrayed in John Esten Cooke's romance of Williamsburg, *The Virginia Comedians* (1854), William Gilmore Simms's novel of Charleston, *The Cassique of Kiawah* (1859), and other fiction.

True, the eighteenth century was marked by a gradual expansion of both social and commercial communication through road-building and town growth along the seaboard, from New England southward, and even slightly inland. For contemporary evidence note the varied accounts of travelers ranging from the lively and intimately delineative *Journal* (1704) of Boston-reared Madam Sarah Kemble Knight to the detailed *A Tour in the United States of America* (1784) meticulously recorded by an itinerant Englishman, J. F. D. Smyth, who traveled much through the South.[26] Some of the latter's impressions of Southern villages are noteworthy in revealing how far the South trailed behind New England and the middle colonies in the building of towns. First of all, Smyth observes that, in general, "the towns are so inconsiderable, that in England they would scarcely acquire the appellation of villages." His impressions, paralleled in other contemporary accounts, are of the prevalence in the South of "planters, store-keepers or persons in trade, and hunters : these last [being] chiefly confined to the back country. . . ." Accustomed to the separate shops of English towns, Smyth considers the Southern store, where various articles are exchanged for tobacco, cotton, furs,

[25] Charles M. Andrews, *Colonial Folkways* (New Haven, 1919), chap. ii, "Town and Country."
[26] See Mrs. Knight's *Journal* as edited by G. P. Winship (Boston, 1920), I, 920, and Smyth, *op. cit.* (2 vols. ; Dublin, 1784). See also Alice Morse Earle, *Stage-Coach and Tavern Days* (New York, 1900), *passim*, and Allan Nevins, ed., *American Social History as Recorded by British Travellers* (New York, 1923).

skins, and butter, a great curiosity.[27] He observingly notes, however, the presence, even in smaller towns, of "some few mechanics, surgeons, lawyers, store-keepers, or persons in the commercial line, and tavern-keepers."

All in all, conditions in the early South were such that few towns flourished until the weakening of the plantation system following the Civil War, when a new regime gave an impetus to town growth. In the Southern states the county was the political unit, fulfilling all the functions of both the county and the town in New England. According to the first census of the United States in 1790, before that date no town in the South had a population of even eight thousand. As we have seen, Charleston, a sort of town-state and a self-contained community by virtue of both its trade with the West Indies, New England, England, and Africa and its social leadership, was the nearest approach to a pre-war center of town life on the seaboard south of Baltimore.[28] Gradually, especially with the influx of new people after the war, Richmond, Atlanta, New Orleans, and other towns increased in size and importance; but, relatively considered, there was a marked paucity of town life in the pre-war stages of Southern life. Until recently, therefore, the literature of the small town in the South has been, by contrast with the exceptionally rich interpretations of other sections, almost negligible.

II.   THE NEW ENGLAND TOWN

In New England the town-building program was reversed: from the beginning Massachusetts settlers and, later, other colonists maintained communities planted on the structural basis of town growth. Life, generally speaking, centered around compact little communities, favorably situated on the coast or along the rivers. While from the first religious and agricultural influences on the development of town life were remarkably strong, other significant factors also determined

[27] Smyth, op. cit., pp. 61 ff. By 1828, however, James Fenimore Cooper was writing thus of New England village stores: ". . . an American village store, in a thriving part of the country, where the settlements are of twenty years' standing, can commonly supply as good an assortment of the manufactures of Europe as a collection of shops in any European country town" (Notions of the Americans, London, 1828, I, 330).
[28] For full discussion of this background see Linda Rhea, Hugh Swinton Legaré (Chapel Hill, 1934), chap. iv, and Thomas R. Waring, The Carolina Low-Country (New York, 1931), pp. 131 ff.: "Charleston: The Capital of the Plantations."

the trend of social and political, as well as spiritual, progression.[29] The elements of self-government, religious liberty, and freehold titles, through the early organization of towns, had full influence and effectual operation. Furthermore, many colonists in Massachusetts and elsewhere, though interested in farming, soon enlarged their activities to include fur-trading, fishing, shipping, and incipient manufactures.[30] More industrious than the so-called indigent "gentlemen" of ill-fated Jamestown, the practical New Englanders combined a knowledge of agriculture and handicrafts which enabled them to organize quickly into villages similar to the village communes they had known in England. Eventually, by buying outright the claims of the original investors, the London merchants, these Northern settlers freed themselves for individual progress.

In early New England local registries were established and the towns held the disposal of land in their own hands. The system of common tillage, adopted in the beginning, was abandoned in favor of individual allotment of land to each family, which, however, had "a home lot right" and "acre right," called "accommodations," in the common meadow, forest, or upland. The custom of an occasional regulation in "field meetings" of the time of planting is suggestive of the intimate relations of the New England settlements to English agricultural villages.[31] Community planting and harvesting, together with trading and other interests previously mentioned, thus gave to the New England town a cohesion entirely lacking in the Jamestown project.

Within a few years after the beginnings of the Plymouth settlement, the Pilgrims through community co-operation had established the foundation for the future villages of New England. In 1630 John Winthrop, arriving in Massachusetts with a considerable company of gentlemen and yeomen, with their families and indentured white servants, adopted the plan of

[29] Joel Parker, "The Origin, Organization, and Influence of the Towns of New England," *Massachusetts Historical Society Proceedings*, first series, IX, 15 (1866-1867). See also Charles Francis Adams, Jr., "Genesis of the Massachusetts Town," *Massachusetts Historical Society Proceedings*, second series, VII, 172 ff. (1891-1892), ; and Anne Bush MacLear, "Early New England Towns," *Studies in History and Public Law*, XXIXX, No. 1 (New York, 1908).

[30] James Truslow Adams, *The Founding of New England* (Boston, 1927), p. 11 (summary of the factors which determined the nature of the New England settlements) and p. 339. Compare with Wertenbaker, *The First Americans*, chap. iii, "The New England Town," pp. 49 ff., and Parker, *loc. cit.*

[31] Eggleston, *op. cit.*, pp. 278 ff.

3

the village community as the most suitable one on which to organize Puritan churches and congregations.[32]   Soon after, town settlements were begun in the Boston, Charlestown, Salem, and neighboring regions.   In time economic factors, the climate, and the soil caused the founders of other New England colonies, related by various ties to the Massachusetts Bay colonists, to follow similar plans.   The line of town expansion was extended gradually down the coast to Connecticut and Long Island, and eventually onward to the shores of New Jersey and Delaware.   Towns multiplied.   In 1636 iconoclastic Roger Williams, with five companions, planted the settlement of Providence on Narragansett Bay.   In 1638 Mrs. Anne Hutchinson was instrumental in the founding of Portsmouth.   Out of other migratory movements came other new towns: Hartford, Windsor, and Wethersfield in the winter of 1635-1636; New Haven at about the same time; and later colonization beyond the Merrimac River.[33]

The New Englander, therefore, in spite of his agricultural interests, usually was not a solitary pioneer type.   True, many established themselves on hill farms and in lonely valleys; but the fact remains that widespread interest was manifested in the building of well-organized towns, where "meeting-houses" and schoolhouses were erected and the town meeting, soon to become a vital factor in local government, was organized.   In fact, so effective became the town meeting that each village produced controversialists given to discoursing on almost any phase of theology or politics.   Note, for example, the long-continued controversy about religious toleration which unorthodox Roger Williams waged from 1644 until 1652 with the Reverend John Cotton.   To Williams's *Bloody Tenent of Persecution for cause of Conscience, discussed in a Conference between Truth and Peace* (1644) came Cotton's answer, *The Bloody Tenent washed and made white in the Blood of the Lamb* (1647).   Next followed Williams's final and cumbersomely entitled reply, *The Bloody Tenent yet More Bloody, by Mr. Cotton's effort to wash it white in the Blood of the Lamb* (1652).

As is evident, the word "town" gradually changed from its earlier meaning of a group of farmers engaged in farming on

[32] Beard, *op. cit.*, pp. 52 ff.
[33] Dorothy Deming, *The Settlement of the Connecticut Towns* (New Haven, 1933), pp. 8 ff.

small holdings to that of a township* existing as a definite political, religious, and social unit. With the increasing need for governmental direction and the growing dominance of the church over both spiritual and temporal affairs, the typical New England village, with its more compact organization, gained power over the township.[34] In time deputies were elected to the legislature from the towns. In Massachusetts where the town early acquired prominence, and elsewhere in adjoining regions various town individuals became differentiated as types from the tillers of the soil. Persons trained in handicrafts, for example, soon became recognized village types. The town offices increased.

The swineherd or hogreeve went through the town blowing an early morning horn, the cowherd, the goatherd, the gooseherd, the shepherd were all present, as needed in various New England towns. There were water bailiffs, . . . drummers to call people to meeting and to make announcements, . . . overseers of chimneys . . . sweepers, perambulators, cutters of staves and corders of wood, firewards and hogwards, and all the half a hundred other occasional officers of the town.[35]

Though some towns kept dogs to fight the wolves and owned cows, each citizen had his right to feed his cows in the common pasture and harvested fields. Tradespeople desiring to settle within a town usually had to bargain for a monopoly with the selectmen or those in charge of "the prudentials" of the place. Often the townspeople helped newcomers in the building of mills, blacksmith shops, and other structures.

Harriet Martineau, well-known English writer, traveling in the United States as late as the 1830's, was so greatly impressed by the history and beauty of New England villages that she devoted a whole chapter of her *Retrospect of Western Travel* to the small communities she visited. Among the things she sketched for her English readers was the usual arrangement of an American pioneer village, planned with heavy palisades; dwellings along one long tree-bordered street, each house being

---

* In most sections outside of New England and New York the township is termed a county.

[34] *A Century of Population Growth, 1790-1900*, p. 20.

[35] Eggleston, *op. cit.*, pp. 281 ff. William R. Bliss, *Colonial Times on Buzzard's Bay* (Boston and New York, 1888), gives a delightful picture of a particular colonial town which is in accord with Eggleston's account.

within its own enclosure and in many cases fortified; and a centrally located "meeting-house," often fortified also.[36]

It should be repeated in summary that in New England the individual relinquished his rights to the town or church, both of which were real functioning bodies. The town idea, therefore, furnished for New England settlements a solidarity lacking in the colonization of the South.

III.   THE MIDDLE COLONIES

Turning to a third center of colonial settlement and expanding culture, we find that fertile lands and other factors induced colonists to establish themselves far and wide in the district from New York and New Jersey to the Potomac. Here in the middle colonies (New York, New Jersey, Pennsylvania, and Delaware) diversified living, varying from the distinctly unified New England system and the isolation of the Southern plantation, had a wide expansion in both Pennsylvania and New York. A many-blooded people, a congenial climate, arable lands, and abundant water power combined to make the diversity of the middle colonies. Dutch, English, Scotch-Irish, Germans, Welsh, and various minor stocks helped to people these states.[37] Further varied by religious creeds, these peoples did not come under the domination of an all-powerful ecclesiastical organization like the New Englanders. New York patrons, the tidewater landlords, and other wealthy people combined with both townsmen and numerous small farmers "to give a distinctive tone to the thinking of the middle colonies that would have been impossible in a society that was regimented into a rigid caste system either by theology or economics."[38]

Though there were many farming groups of both large and petty landowners, all of the settlers of the mid-Atlantic states did not turn to agriculture, for this area became truly a section of both town and country. Excellent coastwise harbors and navigable rivers caused the ready establishment of port towns which soon flourished through trade with Europe and the developing area of the back country. Journeying southward

[36] Martineau, *Retrospect of Western Travel* (London, 1838), II, 78.
[37] Fisher, *op. cit.*, I, 340 ff., "Quaker Prosperity"; cf. Russell Blankenship, *American Literature as an Expression of the National Mind* (New York, 1931), p. 8.
[38] Fisher, *op. cit.*, I, 8.

through these colonies at the close of the seventeenth century
the Puritan—says a modern historian—

must have seen many new and unfamiliar sights. . . . He would
have found himself entirely at home among the towns of Long
Island, Westchester County, and northern New Jersey, and would
have discovered much in the Dutch villages about New York and
up the Hudson that reminded him of the closely grouped houses
and small allotments of his native heath.[39]

Had he stopped, however, to visit such extensive estates as the
Cortlandt manor on the Hudson and the Rensselaer manor to
the north he would have seen thousands of acres lavishly bestowed by governors to favored individuals. He would have
seen a division of land wholly different from that in his own
New England : petty farms surrounding the towns and villages,
on the one hand, and on the other, great estates, "where the
farmers were not freeholders but tenants, and where the proprietors could ride for miles . . . without crossing the boundaries of their own territory."[40]   In New Jersey and Pennsylvania he would have observed a similar type of colonization.
Here the holdings of large proprietors and small, a growing
city like Philadelphia, and many flourishing little villages (frequently based upon the Puritan town system) like Elizabeth,
Newark, and Middletown, would have impressed the traveler
with the growing prosperity, urban and rural, in the middle
colonies.

IV.   BEYOND THE SEABOARD

Early America, says Lewis Mumford, was "a place where
the European could remain more nearly his proper self."[41]
Not for long, however. With the "westward drift" America
became, on the contrary, a country where necessarily the European must be transformed into something different. The restless search, that inevitable tendency which began in the early
eighteenth century to form a westward and southward pushing
frontier, started long before the East was fully occupied. By
1700 the outposts of English civilization had left the tidewater
and moved toward the Alleghenies. By 1750, with wave after

[39] Andrews, *op. cit.*, pp. 28-29.
[40] *Ibid.*
[41] *The Golden Day: A Study in American Literature and Culture* (New York, 1926),
p. 57.

wave of settlers crossing the Alleghenies after the preliminary scouting and road building of the Ohio Company, there had developed even in the valleys and mountains small settlements entirely different from the first line of colonization and its English prototype.[42] "Humanity rippled westward" as late as the nineteenth century until one frontier after another was added to the original, "each hurling back its challenge to those who dared to brave the perils of an unbroken and obdurate wilderness" and "each producing a psychology and a type of living less like the previous one and more decidedly 'American' in its characteristics."[43]

Truly, the fuller streams of persons which poured through the Allegheny passes to the West, as well as the diverging thinner streams which followed the natural courses southward into West Virginia, the western Carolinas, Georgia, Alabama, and Tennessee, illustrate Frederick Jackson Turner's aptly turned phrase, "the fluidity of American life." Thus settlements advanced through Kentucky, Ohio, western New York, Indiana, and Illinois until by the early part of the nineteenth century the vanguard had reached the Mississippi. By way of the Mohawk Valley and the Lakes New Englanders migrated to the middle western regions which after the Civil War expanded greatly with Kansas and Nebraska as nuclear states. Iowa, the Dakotas, and the ranching states were of slower expansion. In spite of Indian hazards, early trails marked the advance to Oregon, Washington, California, and the Southwest. Later, of course, the discovery of gold brought "fierce swirls of humanity" beyond the Rockies.[44]

Geographic factors, therefore, largely determined the pattern of westward migration. The process of Americanization was aided by a succession of frontiers until the form of migration changed with the opening of the last tract of free land in Oklahoma in 1890, an era delineated in Edna Ferber's *Cimarron*, a tale of a frontier town.[45] After the passing of the Indian Ter-

[42] A. M. Schlesinger, *New Viewpoints in American History* (New York, 1922), p. 33.
[43] *Ibid.*, p. 37.
[44] Frederick Jackson Turner, *The Frontier in American History* (New York, 1921), *passim*.
[45] *Ibid.*, p. 9: the successive lines of American frontier movements are given as follows: (1) The "fall line"—the frontier of the seventeenth century; (2) the Alleghenies—the frontier of the eighteenth century; (3) the Mississippi—the frontier of the first quarter of the nineteenth century; (4) the Missouri—the frontier of the middle of the nineteenth century (omitting the California movement); (5) the

ritory homeseekers and adventurers could no longer wander aimlessly westward. With the exhaustion of free land, people were forced to go where they could establish themselves economically. As agriculture declined in relative importance varied industries marked the beginnings of the machine age whose forces since about 1920 have become more and more potent and whose fuller development has been decried by many modern writers. (Eugene O'Neill, for example, in 1927 with his *Marco Millions* and again in 1929 with *Dynamo* satirized both American materialistic aspirations and mechanized living.) True, the stimulating forces of pioneer adventure did not completely vanish, but with the growing influence of industrialism the frontier, in an official sense, weakened and about 1890 practically disappeared. As is pictured vividly in Sherwood Anderson's novel, *Poor White*, an era of dynamic progress had begun. America had passed through her adolescence, and the industrial progress begun since the Civil War had been accompanied by a steady parallel increase in urban population. Town communities, earlier developed from amazingly primitive conditions and often modeled on the New England town system (conformable, of course, to the requirements of various localities), changed into flourishing towns or even great cities. With the increase of commercial interests came the development of towns of some size (Boston, New York, Philadelphia, Baltimore, and others). Along with the more fortunately situated larger towns and cities, hundreds of small towns grew with each frontier until the rise and expansion of Pacific Coast towns marked the last line of geographic progression.[46] Widespread scientific and other educational progression; the added strength of millions of foreigners; the amazing advancement made in every form of communication; and innumerable other changes all have combined to transform America from a relatively small seaboard agricultural country into a nation of thousands of towns and cities. Thus the New England town and its developed industries, the Southern "money crop," the commercial interests of the middle colonies, and the far-reaching westward movement have been fundamentals in the growth of a continuous chain of communities from coast

line of arid lands (approximately the 99th meridian) and the Rocky Mountains —the present (1893) frontier.
[46] *The Fifteenth Census of the United States*, I, 6.

to coast. During more than three hundred years of varied expansion the town—even the small town—has continued to figure vitally in the lives of thousands and thousands of people of numerous transplanted stocks. Through Professor Turner's interpretation we may note, in summary, that

The Indian trade pioneered the way for civilization. . . . The buffalo trail became the trader's "trace"; the trails widened into roads, and the roads into turnpikes, and these in turn were transformed into railroads. . . . The trading posts reached by these trails were on the site of Indian villages which had been placed in positions suggested by nature; and these trading posts, situated so as to command the water systems of the country, have grown into cities.[47]

V.   MODERN TRENDS :   THE SMALL TOWN AT THE CROSSROADS

What of the modern small town? What of the relation of its present characteristics to those of the past? Is the small town of the twentieth century at the crossroads between industrial progress and gradual oblivion? What of the shifting of the rural and town populations as revealed by the 1930 census? These are but indicative of the type of discussion recently centering about the small town.

The literary village or town, as we have indicated, has passed through such stages of depiction as those revealing the provincial village, the midwestern town, and the Main Street type of today; similarly the actual town has undergone social, economic, and other changes. Until the unrest of the Gilded Age the prevailing attitudes and beliefs of the more isolated small townsmen were, to a large degree, analogous to those of earlier periods. At first the life of many a village was marked by adherence to local conventions; then came a wave of individualism—largely the result of the Civil War, the Spanish American War, and much later of the World War—characterized by impulsive departure from custom and the setting up of freer standards of living. Today there is a period of readjustment resulting from the economic depression. Whether this will effect radical changes in the whole village and small town program is a question for the future.[48]

---

[47] *Op. cit.*, p. 14.
[48] Roy Wenzlick, *The Coming Boom in Real Estate* (New York, 1936), gives an optimistic view of economic conditions for the next decade and shows the salutary

Before the appearance of modern improvements on the national horizon the small town in many sections was distinguished by a singularly rural and often melancholy peacefulness. Over many such communities as those described in literature by Sarah Orne Jewett and Mary E. Wilkins Freeman there hung an air of conservatism destructive of the ambitious spirit of youth and yet influencing this spirit to seek adventure and livelihood elsewhere. As late as 1899 Rollin Lynde Hartt could report thus on the simple and bucolic life of a New England village of the time:

> We are an old-fashioned folk in Sweet Auburn—we go to church. We think we ought to; besides we can't help it. . . . To obey the insistent behest of the church is perchance to learn that Jim Asa meditates shingling his barn, . . . or that Deacon Abram has slain his fatted Chester Whites. When the Old Cap'n Anthony homestead had gone up in lamentable flames late one Saturday night, and kept us all awake until morning, I said, "Slender congregation to-day . . ."—wherein I erred. There were more worshippers than usual. They came to talk it over.[49]

Carl Van Doren has painted a later and more critical picture of the traditional American small town as it existed before the "talkies," the automobile, and the radio brought its citizens into an ever increasing contact with the city. Certain critical dispositions, aware of agrarian discontent or given a preference for cities, might now and then, he says, lay disrespectful hands upon the life of the farm; but even these usually hesitated to touch the village, sacred since Goldsmith in spite of Crabbe, sacred since Mrs. Stowe in spite of E. W. Howe and Joseph Kirkland. In those halcyon days, if we are to believe some of the things we have heard and read,

> . . . the village seemed too cozy a microcosm to be disturbed. There it lay in the mind's eye, neat, compact, organized, traditional; the white church with tapering spire, the sober schoolhouse, the smithy of ringing anvil, the corner grocery, the cluster of friendly houses, the venerable parson, the wise physician, the canny squire, the grasping landlord softened or outwitted in the end, the village

effect of these changes upon all phases of American life, including that of the small town. Cf. James M. Williams, *The Expansion of Rural Life* (New York, 1926), *passim*, and *Our Rural Heritage* (New York, 1925), pp. 2 ff.

[49] "A New England Hill Town," *The Atlantic Monthly*, LXXXIII, 561 (April, 1899).

belle, gossip, atheist, idiot, jovial fathers, gentle mothers, merry children, spacious barns, lavish gardens, fragrant summer dawns and comfortable winter evenings.[50]

Such elements were not to be discarded lightly, even by those most observant of the smoke-belching factories dirtying the prettiest streams and the alien-tongued workers whose queer customs were frowned upon by old time villagers.[51]

Lowell's essay on Old Cambridge and Miss Jewett's lament over the decay of the older types of New England village tell of those changes in modes of living which resulted either in the transformation of the isolated village into a town with more industrial contacts or in the complete economic degeneration of the place. Before the 1880's, Miss Jewett maintains, many towns in New England adhered strongly to the conventions of past generations. "Now," she says, "the old traditions have had time to disappear almost entirely even in the most conservative and least changed towns. The true characteristics of American society show themselves more and more distinctly to the westward of New England and come back to it in a tide that steadily sweeps away the old traditions."[52] Even in the eighties, then, a certain element of small town society was fast disappearing, giving place to the new.

The gradual metamorphosis of the peaceful and convention-bound village into the modern small town is associated with the tremendous growth, power, and influence of many forces. Chambers of commerce, boosters' clubs—even the large towns and cities, with their frequently advertised "trade trips," are not immune—, secret societies, labor organizations, women's clubs, conventions of every conceivable sort, parades, state and county fairs, pageants, carnivals, revival meetings, the automobile, the moving picture, the radio, the enormous circulation of magazines like the *Saturday Evening Post, Liberty, Collier's,* the *American Magazine,* and *Life,* the annual vacation exodus to Europe, church dinners, family reunions, pioneer picnics, and

[50] Carl Van Doren, *Contemporary American Novelists* (New York, 1922), "The Revolt from the Village," p. 147.

[51] The incoming of the foreign element is the theme of Edna Ferber's *American Beauty* (1931), a novel picturing the revitalization of Brookfield, Connecticut, by the intermarriage of the remnants of the old aristocracy with the uncouth, but up-and-coming, Poles who have taken over the land.

[52] Sarah Orne Jewett, "From a Mournful Villager," *The Atlantic Monthly,* XLVII, 670 (Nov., 1881).

football rallies—all these give a fairly accurate perspective of modern American town life. In fact, although there are undoubtedly regional variations, as we suggested earlier, nearly every section of the United States possesses in some degree these symbols of standardization, characteristics which have stamped themselves on American life in general.

In view of this interest in organizations it has been said that the basic motive of cultural life in the small town is the social element.[53] Usually the intellectual is pushed into the background. While many study clubs exist, actually there is little demand for the so-called intellectual magazines. (The very fact that such magazines as *The Atlantic Monthly, Harper's, Scribner's,* and *The Saturday Review of Literature* are sent to subscribers in remote towns shows, of course, that there are many exceptions.) Plays with an exclusive appeal to the imagination or the intellect, as a rule, do not meet with public favor, though in the past decade or more the Little Theater movement, radio presentations, certain drama projects sponsored by the government, and the remarkable advance made in collegiate dramatic groups have done much toward educating the people to the point of appreciating drama other than those teeming with primitive emotions or characterized by all the trite devices of hokum.[54] We Americans, however, are a social people and the social atmosphere furnishes the small town a very important *raison d'être.*

One of the most significant tendencies both of small town and city life during more than the last decade is that of the movements of population in all sections of the country. There has been, as the Federal Census reports of 1920 and 1930 both show, such a milling about or shifting of rural and small town populations during the present century that some places have become almost depopulated while others have gained more than a hundred per cent.[55] The majestic pioneer movements

[53] L. R. Reid, "The Small Town," from H. E. Stearns, ed., *Civilization in the United States* (New York, 1922), pp. 285 ff. Cf. Charles W. Ferguson, *Fifty Million Brothers* (New York, 1937), *passim* (a survey of American lodges and clubs).

[54] Kenneth Macgowan, *Footlights across America, etc.* (New York, 1929), traces the influence of the Little Theater movement on American culture.

[55] R. L. Duffus, "A Changing Nation Revealed by the Census," *New York Times,* LXXIX, sec. 9, p. 1 (Aug. 17, 1930). Cf. conditions in the West Texas oil boom towns of 1920 (*The Literary Digest,* LXV, 59-62, April 10, 1920) and those in California recently affected by the new gold rush (*The Literary Digest,* CXVII, 30, March 3, 1934).

are no more; the free lands are gone; the old westward drift has long been broken up.   Instead of the prairie schooner there is the automobile, the "family flivver," now frequently with trailer attached, in which certain nomadic groups laden with their *lares et penates* move about from state to state in search of employment, pleasure, or a place for more or less permanent location.   Under such conditions, especially in a period of general unemployment, the lines of population movement become tangled and uneven.

They take shape only when some new opportunity appears on the horizon, when oil is struck, when automobile manufacturers set out to make a nation of two-car families, when there is a land boom in Florida, when work is begun on some great undertaking like the Boulder Dam, when it is found that dates or cotton can be grown in the Imperial Valley, when the hill people of Tennessee are told that they can live less lonely lives if they will come down to the textile mills in the valley.[56]

In the older interpretation of the phrase, the pioneer era has drawn to a close.   While the gambling spirit of the frontiersman has been revitalized by such retrospective studies as Hamlin Garland's Middle Border series, an actual frontier no longer exists for those discontented wanderers who would seek fortune or livelihood elsewhere.   The years of hope, in the decades after the Civil War, when poor boys—often small town lads—actually did become millionaires[57] and the seemingly boundless prosperity of the early twenties have yielded to years of unrest. As the conditions of economic life, at home and abroad, have become increasingly more complicated a new level of living, associated with industrialism and its difficulties, has supplanted the natural trail-blazing of frontier days.   In the larger cities and manufacturing towns various economic issues have led to open conflict between employer and worker.   Reformers, agitating thousands of workers, have urged, among other things, that in Marxism alone lies the panacea for the national ills.

Truly, since the prosperous twenties the pattern of American life has grown curiously complicated.   Akin to the movements of revolt set in motion in the larger industrial centers and expressed in novels of protest similar reactions, but on a smaller

[56] Granville Hicks, *The Great Tradition* (New York, 1933), p. 164.
[57] V. F. Calverton, *The Liberation of American Literature* (New York, 1932), p. 470.

scale, are felt in many little towns. Discontent with outworn community conventions has been responsible for the changed attitudes among both small town peoples themselves and their critics. Motor transportation over improved highways, rural mail delivery, moving pictures in near-by larger towns, and the broadened view conveyed to both farmers and townspeople by radio, daily newspapers, and farm journal account, to a great extent, for the shifting in rural and small town populations and for the marked change in outlook.[58] While Marxism may be directly applied to both the economic crises and the fiction delineative of the larger manufacturing cities, it may be said to affect the small town, especially where its literature is concerned, but indirectly and sporadically.[59] The present so-called "battle of the village," which has provoked much of the modern small town fiction, is, however, a marked indication not only of the unrest in the country at large, but of the changed attitudes of small town critics. On the surface, perhaps, the simple and monotonous activities of Main Street may tire us ; but the definite impress which small town civilization has left upon native literature should demand our attention.

[58] See Introduction, note 6.
[59] Representative novels wherein labor problems play a part in small town life include Howells's *Annie Kilburn*, Mary E. Wilkins Freeman's *A Portion of Labor*, and Upton Sinclair's *King Coal*.

CHAPTER II

THE EARLY NEW ENGLAND VILLAGE
IN LITERATURE

CONTEMPORARY DELINEATORS

DURING HIS later years, Reverend Timothy Dwight, versatile president of Yale, protested, with asperity, in his voluminous travel notes against a recent belittling *Edinburgh Review* evaluation of the literature he himself, as an active Hartford "wit," had helped create. Dwight grew indignant as he read the caustic declaration publicly announcing that ". . . the destruction of [America's] whole literature would not occasion so much regret as we feel for the loss of a few leaves from an ancient classic!"[1] Hadn't his own *Greenfield Hill* been prophetic of a national literature? Hadn't he labored long "to contribute to the innocent amusement of his countrymen, and to their improvement in manners, and in economical, political, and moral sentiments?" Scotch reviewers were growing too bold and prejudiced!

Fortunately for his own peace of mind, Dwight was not one of those Americans who, opening copies of the *Edinburgh Review* for January, 1820, chanced to note a review—beginning mildly enough—of Adam Seybert's *Statistical Annals of the United States of America*. Notations of new roads and post offices, of increases in population, industry, and the national debt were interesting, but unexciting. Besides, most patriots knew already that the Americans were "a brave, industrious, and acute people." Consequently, they may have read on, with a feeling of pride in the national achievements thus favorably advertised. No wonder, then, that the unexpected and scornful questions of the conclusions dumfounded Brother Jonathan! Indeed? Were Americans mere scribblers? It was unbelievable nonsense that in all "the land of Jonathan," during the thirty or forty years of its independence, its people have done absolutely nothing for scientific, literary, political, or economic advance-

---

[1] *Travels in New-England and New-York* (London, 1823), IV, 312.

ment. Where are the American Foxes, Burkes, Paleys, Malthuses, Byrons, Moores, or Crabbes? In what ways have Americans "blest or delighted mankind by their works, inventions, or examples?" Awful questions from the Edinburgh judgment-seat! Scornful and insulting insinuations! But piqued Americans read on, other damning questions arousing their ire more and more.

In the four quarters of the globe, who reads an American book? Or goes to an American play? Or looks at an American picture or statue? What does the world owe to American physicians and surgeons? What new substances have their chemists discovered? Or what old ones have they analyzed? What new constellations have been discovered by the telescopes of Americans? What have they done in the mathematics? Who drinks out of American glasses? Or eats out of American plates? or wears American coats or gowns? or sleeps in American blankets?[2]

Dwight, dying in 1817, was spared this unrestrained diatribe by which brilliant Sydney Smith in 1820 furthered the "paper war" waged by foreign critics. He missed Smith's caustic advice to American orators and newspaper scribblers "to keep clear of superlatives" and refrain from "laudatory epithets" describing themselves and their countrymen as "the greatest, the most refined, the most enlightened, and the most moral people on earth."

These depreciatory remarks, hurtful to the pride of those uncritically believing in America's greatness, show clearly that even so late as the early nineteenth century the problem of creating a vigorous national literature was a difficult one. Even then hostile foreign criticism akin to Smith's, a lack of ably discriminating native reviewers and of financially successful literary magazines (especially in the South), inadequate provision for copyright laws, high postal rates on newspapers, magazines, and books, a limited reading public, technical difficulties hampering the artistic development of native materials, and a general chauvinistic spirit, set in motion by the Revolution and the War of 1812, were all powerful deterrents working against the progress of an emerging literature.

[2] Sydney Smith, "Review of Adam Seybert's *Statistical Annals of the United States*," *Edinburgh Review*, LXV, 79-80 (Jan., 1820).

In spite of early promoters of American literature, like Benjamin Franklin, at the opening of the nineteenth century our literature in general was but a struggling literature whose writers were searching for stabilizing national and literary ideals. Under these conditions, so sharply criticized by Sydney Smith, the first really significant stage in the literary history of the American town could belong neither to colonial New England, nor, except in a very limited sense, to the eighteenth century. In fact, not until long after the era of first colonization had spent itself did the imaginative literature of the town have even a most humble beginning during the late eighteenth century, when Timothy Dwight, Philip Freneau, and other village lyrists gave evidence in their verse of a slowly growing consciousness of the use of village themes as material prophetic of the national literature they desired.

Even a brief survey of contemporary colonial records, however, shows that the social historian may find reportorial literature of the town in abundance. Discursive accounts of the early New England town and its folkways may be found in numerous contemporary histories, letters, and diaries, materials not truly germane to a literary history of the village. Narratives of the first settling, mainly the work of the immigrants, call to mind *A Description of New England* (1616), wherein Captain John Smith pictures the land with some Elizabethan overstatement, and those first reports from Plymouth, the anonymously published *Mourt's Relation* (1622) and Governor Edward Winslow's *Good News from New England* (1625), a warning to future travelers that Plymouth is lacking in natural plenty. Written to inform English friends of the progress of the Pilgrim settlements, these accounts mirror the daily routine of the men who established the town. In both Governor William Bradford's loosely annalistic *Of Plimoth Plantation* (completed in 1650) and Governor John Winthrop's *Journal*, concerning the Massachusetts Bay Colony, seventeenth-century New England village activities are recorded by two intelligent observers, both English bred. In his satiric *New English Canaan* (1637) Thomas Morton, rebel, lampoons the self-righteous Puritans who condemned the hilarious "revells" at "Ma-re Mount," a frontier establishment years later described fictionally in Hawthorne's "The Maypole of Merry Mount" (published in *The Token*,

1836), in John Lothrop Motley's melodramatic *Merry Mount: A Romance of the Massachusetts Colony* (1849), and more recently in Howard Hanson's modern opera, *Merry Mount*. Other historians, English born but colonially bred, have left lengthy annals of colonial manners at mid-century. Captain Edward Johnson delineates in his *Wonder-working Providence of Zion's Saviour in New England* (1628-1652) the affairs of ordinary colonial townspeople. Nathaniel Morton's *New England's Memorial*, based upon the earlier chronicle of his famous uncle, Governor Bradford, contains further pictures of Plymouth.

From the prolific sermonizing, pamphleteering, and discoursing of the Puritan theologians the social researcher may reconstruct certain phases of colonial town life. Of the numerous works of the great Puritan divines the *Magnalia Christi Americana: or, the Ecclesiastical History of New England* (1702) by zealous Cotton Mather may be cited as discursively delineative of the founding of Massachusetts settlements. Finally, for the humanly interesting minutiae of both town and country life the lay reader, as well as the researcher, may turn with interest, or relief, to the intimate details of Samuel Sewall's *Diary* (1674-1729 ; not published until 1878-1882) and to Madame Knight's previously mentioned lively *Journal of a Journey from Boston to New York in 1704*.

These portrayals, mentioned because of their contemporary revelations of colonial village life, offer substantial historical reporting of the courageous efforts of Englishmen on alien soil to organize habitable little towns along the New England seaboard. Although these works, the crude forerunners of a later literary culture, are the earliest interpretations of the first fringe of communities in New England, it is remembered, when one considers them as the prototypes of the more recently exploited small town, that "the history of literature is one thing, bibliography is quite another thing."[3] In literary history, therefore, these colonial records are significant only in furnishing inspiration for the consciously literary artist of later years, whose work of reshaping and recoloring the materials of history to satisfy the technicalities of fiction has produced in American

---

[3] Charles F. Richardson, *American Literature, 1607-1885* (New York and London, 1887), I, xviii. See also Charles Angoff, *A Literary History of the American People* (New York, 1931), I, 389.

4

literature a definite town type, the New England village.   In
short, these colonial local histories have been the ultimate substance of later literary treatments of the little town.

THE ENGLISH VILLAGE TRANSPLANTED

If earlier anthologies may be relied upon as indices to the
interests of earlier writers, it may be repeated that the town
idea, so pronounced in the actual history of colonial New England and mid-Atlantic states, was first used imaginatively in
American literature of the highly descriptive and didactic verse
of the late eighteenth century.[4]   By this time the necessarily
slow progress of American life had reached a stage stable enough
for people to enjoy the luxuries of a developing culture.   From
about 1700 until the mid-century and later, community life
underwent a remarkable development.   Schools were established ; the first newspapers were printed ; political, religious,
and social ideals were solidified ; libraries were collected, largely
through English and other importations ; and a greater desire
for the amenities of civilization was created.   All of these
things, extending beyond the end of the century, stimulated
an interest in both the reading of foreign literature and the
production of native writings.   At the outbreak of the Revolution the time was ripe for a sudden growth of nationalism, for
the exploitation of the indigenous ; but, while the war itself
brought forth controversial writings in abundance by both
patriot and Tory, most writers were blind to the truthful presentation of materials at hand.   They were active, however, in
the production of an amazing amount of verse, essays, dramas,
and other forms, often mediocre and in close imitation of English and continental models.[5]   Poems about Solomon, Ther-
mopylae, the destruction of Pompeii, human frailty, the sparkling bowl, and the powers of music flourished far more than did
literature realistically delineative of American life.[6]   Verisi-

[4] See Appendix I for notations regarding the paucity of early literature of the
village and small town.
[5] For surveys of literary and other backgrounds see Moses Coit Tyler, *The
Literary History of the American Revolution, 1763-1783* (2 vols., New York, 1897);
The Cambridge History of American Literature (hereinafter cited as *C. H. A. L.*), three-
vol. ed., I, 150 ff. ; Blankenship, *op. cit.*, chap. v ; Thomas Dickinson, *The Making
of American Literature* (New York, 1932), pp. 228 ff. ; and Robert E. Spiller, *The
Roots of American Culture* (New York, 1933), pp. 1-21.   Julia Patton's *The English
Village* affords an excellent discussion of the village in English literature.
[6] Subjects selected from Rufus Wilmot Griswold, *The Poets and Poets of America*
(6th ed., Philadelphia, 1845).

militude was entirely lacking in the Miltonic glorifications and the romantic treatments of American backgrounds.   Imitating the heroic couplets of Pope and Goldsmith or the blank verses of Thomson and Young, American poets wrote prolifically and artificially of provincial greatness, the potentialities of westward expansion, and the enjoyments of solitude.[7]   The pioneer himself was glorified almost beyond recognition.   Among these outpourings, more general and numerous after the Revolution than before, there may be found an occasional description of village life, usually developed in the Goldsmithian style, method, and subject matter.   Generalized descriptions of the village locale, poetic delineations of stock characters, such as local merchants, ministers, and schoolmasters, and particularized scenes of the village church, or churchyard, appear repeatedly in this early imitative literature of the little town.

In a letter dated November 22, 1772, a youthful Princeton graduate—then a rather bored and inexperienced teacher at Somerset Academy, Maryland—confessed, modestly enough, to his classmate, James Madison, in Virginia that he had ". . . printed a poem in New York called the American Village, containing about 450 lines, also a few short pieces added; . . . ."[8] Conscious, perhaps, of his literary apprenticeship, the poet, Philip Freneau, self-described as then almost "twenty-one years of age and already . . . stiff with age," assured Madison that "As to the main poem it is damned by all good and judicious judges—my name is on the title page, this is called vanity by some—. . . ."[9] The poem then so quickly damned, probably through its meagre sale, was not reprinted in later collections during Freneau's lifetime.

Today this earliest known independent publication of youthful Philip Freneau, later to be termed "the first essential poetic spirit in America," is, so far as is now known, the first American village poem to be written by a native poet of exceptional promise.[10] Furthermore, though his period of English imita-

[7] C. H. A. L., I, 162: "Goldsmith reached Americans almost at once, and appeared in nine editions between 1768 and 1791."   See ibid., III, 542, for further references to importations of Milton, Pope, Goldsmith, etc.

[8] Fred Lewis Pattee, ed., The Poems of Philip Freneau, Poet of the American Revolution (Princeton, 1902), I, xxii.

[9] Ibid.

[10] For the history of the first edition of this poem see The American Village: A Poem by Philip Freneau, reprinted in facsimile from the original edition published in New York in 1772, with an introduction by Harry Lyman Roopman and bibliographical data by Victor Hugo Paltsits (Providence, 1906).

tion was but a forerunner to his later original work, Freneau, by his own acknowledgment of a marked indebtedness to *The Traveler* (1764) and *The Deserted Village* (1770), pioneered in transplanting the Goldsmithian village tradition in America. For these reasons this promising Princeton poet is first among early village poets and, though of French Huguenot parentage and himself a New Yorker, is associated in a literary sense with the "Hartford Wits" and other New Englanders who but re-echoed less vigorously in their poems of community life the English adaptations characterizing *The American Village*.

Conventionalized in its couplets and its passages of romantic enthusiasm, *The American Village* but faintly suggests Freneau's later poems of nature and his interpretations of American life. In this longer poem, as well as in "The Farmer's Winter Evening," "The Miserable Life of a Pedagogue" (probably autobiographical), and "Upon a very Ancient Dutch House on Long Island"—all titles of the other poems found in the 1772 edition of *The American Village*—the future spokesman for American patriotism shows a noticeable disregard of the stirring national events then so closely impending.[11] Avowedly influenced by his reading of contemporary English poetry, Freneau in *The American Village* was experimentally applying the English romantic manner to descriptions of scenes and people he knew intimately. To this poetry of rural and village life he added in 1794, the year of *The Columbian Muse*, two more realistic sketches, "The Village Merchant" and "The Country Printer," suggestive of modern small town types. These, together with a few minor descriptions to be mentioned hereinafter, show that Freneau from his own youth in New York, New England, and his teaching days in Maryland actually knew the village life of his own day, but, in spite of occasional foreshadowings of later qualities of satire, humor, sincere human sentiment, and local picturing, followed in the main the English romantic tradition.

In the opening description of *The American Village* Freneau, like Dwight later in his idyllic *Greenfield Hill*, presents a delocalized and conventional picture which might be easily mistaken for Sweet Auburn.

[11] This is also true of Freneau's collegiate poem, "On the Rising Glory of America" (1771; pub. 1772), a metrical dialogue written in collaboration with H. H. Brackenridge for the Princeton commencement of 1771. See Pattee, *op. cit.*, I, 49 ff.

> Where yonder stream divides the fertile plain,
> Made fertile by the labours of the swain;
> And hills and woods high tow'ring o'er the rest,
> Behold a village with fair plenty blest : . . . .

To Freneau this "sweet haunt of peace" was what the Lake Isle of Innisfree was to William Butler Yeats. Unlike modern Carol Kennicott, yearning to escape from Gopher Prairie's dullness, Freneau preferred the peace of "the fairest village of the plain" to the noisy throngs of the city. His small town retreat, pictured in all the conventionality of the eighteenth century, was "a smiling village" and a "rural haunt" where the jaded poet—really the schoolteacher at this period—could romanticize about the noble savages, Caffraro and Colma, whose love story forms more than a third of *The American Village*. Out of sympathy with "the gilded beau and scenes of empty joy," Freneau desired but "to strike the rural lyre" in some such retreat as his American village, where he might

> Describe the village, rising on the green,
> Its harmless people, born to small command,
> Lost in the bosom of this western land.[12]

Freneau's interest in the delineation of America's spreading pattern dates from his collaborated Princeton commencement poem, "The Rising Glory of America." Evidently delighting their audience, Freneau and his co-author classmate (the speaker for the occasion), H. H. Brackenridge, boldly traced in one bombastic ode the past, present, and future of America.[13] Unconcerned with the approaching national crisis, these youthful panegyrists glorified the embryo cities and towns of the country and optimistically declared that "future years of bliss alone remain." This glorified picture of 1771 was a mediocre preparation for Freneau's later poem, "The Rising Empire" (1790), wherein he described in rather realistic detail the widespread development of towns in various states.[14] Pennsylvania is praised because "her gay towns unnumbered shine through all her plains." "Gay Maryland," a fertile country, is extolled for her "historic Annapolis" and "Proud Baltimore that envied commerce draws," a place changed from "some wretched huts"

---

[12] Pattee, *op. cit.*, III, 382 ff.
[13] *Ibid.*, I, xx-xxi.
[14] *Ibid.*, I, 19-20.

to a city "high in renown, [with] her streets and domes arranged." Virginia, mentioned for its earlier fertility, is realistically portrayed as being now a country of impoverished river lands with a few "Mercantile towns, where langour holds her reign."[15]

The scenes and characterizations in "The Village Merchant" and "The Country Printer," though analogous to the more familiar pictures of *The Deserted Village*, are presented with more realistic details and human touches than those in *The American Village*. Freneau here portrays definite village individuals such as those he knew near Mount Pleasant, his New Jersey home, or elsewhere in his travels. His genius for newspapers enabled Freneau to describe an obviously American country printer, his village, and the associations of the place: the arrival of the old-time stagecoach, the activities at the tavern, the mill, and the village shops, and the work of preparing the odd mixture of the editor's page. In fact, the editor might well be Freneau himself. In this poem, published in 1794, twenty-two years after *The American Village*,[16] Freneau, having cast aside his earlier romanticism for the verisimilitude of an American Crabbe, sketches a village printer who might serve as the prototype of E. W. Howe's and William Allen White's more modern studies of small town printers. Here Freneau's poetry, like that of Crabbe, has marked fidelity, freshness of inspiration, and originality of treatment.

On the other hand, his earlier picture of the American village, the romanticized counterpart of numerous agricultural villages then scattered over New England and New York, felt

---

[15] In the *Charleston City Gazette or Daily Advertiser* (Feb. 19, 1790) there appeared a humorously satiric sketch, "Lines of a Tavern at Log-Town, a small place in the Pine Barrens of North Carolina." This dejected town is described with a realism most unusual in the town literature of the period. Here

> . . . no gay fabrics meet the eye,
> Nor painted board, nor barber's pole.

> Thou town of logs! so justly called,
>   In thee who halts at evening's close,
> Not dreams from Jove, but hosts of fleas
>   Shall join to sweeten his repose!

[16] Pattee, *op. cit.*, I, 60 ff., says that "The Country Printer" was published serially in the *National Gazette*, of which Freneau was editor, the first part appearing on December 19, 1791. In 1794 it was issued in pamphlet form with "The Village Merchant," composed during his first year at Princeton. See E. A. and G. L. Duyckinck, *Cyclopaedia of American Literature* (New York, 1885), I, 330-331.

the stronger influence from abroad, and, from point of time, may be termed the immediate American precursor of the conventional post-Revolutionary studies of the New England village.

During the last half of the eighteenth century with the appearance in the provincial capital of Hartford, Connecticut, of the first coterie in American literary history, the so-styled "Hartford Wits," the village theme was employed by an alert group of Yale men. These wits, including John Trumbull, Timothy Dwight, Joel Barlow, and David Humphreys, expressed their attachment to the American cause either in imitative glorifications of the country's potential greatness (already mentioned in connection with Freneau) or in ridicule of flaws in American institutions, as the New England town meeting.

The first New England village poem of any length portrayed neither early Plymouth nor commercial Boston, but a pastoral Connecticut town. A patriotic, yet moralizing, preacher viewed his parish from the top of a Connecticut hill, and, thus inspired, pictured with his characteristic energy the social conditions of his changing country, delved into its history, and prognosticated its future. This was none other than Timothy Dwight, one of the Hartfordians eulogized in 1829 by anthologist Samuel Kettell.[17] After he became pastor at Greenfield, Connecticut, in 1703 Dwight felt inspired to write a discursive poem, *Greenfield Hill*, which, he contended, while composed with no thought for publication might serve for the amusement and enlightenment of his countrymen. Today it is generally dismissed as dull and noticeably subservient to English models, "a medley of echoes" (Milton, Pope, Goldsmith, Thomson, and others) ; in the indiscriminate judgment of Kettell it is a work of maturity showing melody and powers of imagination, "a beautiful counterpart to the masterpieces of Goldsmith."[18]

What Greenfield Hill was in reality could hardly be visualized from this fanciful representation of more than four thousand lines of stilted couplets, blank verse, and other forms.

---

[17] *Specimens of American Poetry with Critical and Biographical Notices* (3 vols., Boston, 1829), I, *passim.* See also *C. H. A. L.*, I, 163 ff. ; Griswold, *op. cit.*, pp. 13-21 ; and W. B. Cairns, *Early American Writers: 1607-1800* (New York, 1924), p. 409.
[18] *Greenfield Hill: A Poem in Seven Parts* (New York, 1794). The poem was written in 1787.

How different from the modern sketches of the small town!
Not a single characteristic of a Gopher Prairie, a Spoon River,
or an Oklahoma Town appears in Dwight's poetized

> Fair Verna! loveliest village of the west;
> Of every joy, and every charm possess'd,
> How pleas'd amid thy varied walks I rove,
> Sweet cheerful walks of innocence, and love,
> And o'er thy smiling prospects cast my eyes,
> And see the seats of peace, and pleasure, rise,
> And hear the voice of Industry resound,
> And marks the smile of Competence, around!
> Hail, happy village![19]

An American Utopia, a poet's dream, this interpretation of a
"sweet smiling village! loveliest of the hills!" certainly shows
no improvement over contemporary English models. Dwight's
"flourishing village," with its groves, fields, and rills, suggests
an ideal village society blessed with every virtue. A place of
"every joy" and "every good," Greenfield Hill is everything
against which George Crabbe, with his passion for truth, protested so vigorously in *The Village* (1780-83). The whole poem
is, indeed, the antithesis of Crabbe's uncompromising picture
of "Village Life, and every care that reigns."

Glorifying the agricultural society of his peaceful Connecticut village, Dwight didactically contrasts its pastoral life with
what he considers the artificial social standards of Europe. In
the Goldsmithian manner he notes:

> No griping landlord here alarms the door,
> To halve, for rent, the poor man's little store.
>
> . . . . . .
>
> Nor in one palace sinks a hundred cots;
> Nor in one manor drowns a thousand lots;
> Nor, on one table, spread for death and pain,
> Devours what would a village well sustain.[20]

---

[19] *Ibid.*, p. 32; also quoted in *The Columbian Muse* (New York, 1794), p. 204,
under the title of "Picture of a New England Village."

[20] Compare Dwight's imitative lines with the more familiar lines from *The
Deserted Village:*

> Ill fares the land, to hastening ills a prey,
> Where wealth accumulates, and men decay:
> Princes and lords may flourish, or may fade:
> A breath can make them, as a breath has made:
> But a bold peasantry, their country's pride,
> When once destroyed, can never be supplied.

A place more perfect than Zona Gale's Friendship Village, this entire town is, in short, the scene of unbelievable enterprise, democracy, economy, and happiness, which, so Dwight repeatedly assures the doubting reader, "may be considered as a general description of the towns and villages of New England; those only excepted, which are either commercial, new or situated on barren soil."[21]   Defensively he concludes: "Morose and gloomy persons, and perhaps some others, may think the description too highly colored."   One cannot truthfully second Dwight's own suggestion that "the patriotic mind will perhaps find much more reason to rejoice in this prospect [that is, the prospect of reading of the past, present, and future of Greenfield Hill], than to regret it."[22]

In a period of post-Revolutionary ballads, songs, and odes there was a parallel interest in the American scene, expressed, alas, too frequently in wearisomely didactic statements, lengthy narratives of battles, and personal eulogies.   From this material Kettell selected his representative American poets, a very small number of whom take their places as Freneau's and Dwight's contemporaries in the delineation of New England and other villages.   To this group belong some of the "Hartford Wits," many of whose poems appeared in 1794 in *The Columbian Muse*, already mentioned.

The most prolific of this chauvinistic group was Colonel David Humphreys (1753-1818), a Yale contemporary of Dwight and Trumbull in 1771 and, according to Kettell, in 1780 a colonel and aide-de-camp to Washington, whom he served as a confidant and friend.[23]   One of the four poets with scriptural names, satirized in some English verses beginning

> David and Jonathan, Joel and Timothy
> Over the water, set up the hymn of thee, etc.,

Humphreys is an example of the transitoriness of literary popularity.[24]   Kettell, for instance, comments upon the great popu-

---

[21] Dwight, *op. cit.*, p. 172.   James Parton, *Topics of the Time* (Boston, 1871), says that in most New England towns of his day there were very few paupers.   "At the time of the first cable celebration, Mr. Cyrus Field, . . . sent orders to his native village in New England that a banquet should be provided at his expense for the paupers of the whole town.   The selectmen sent back word that there were no paupers. . . ." (p. 33).

[22] *Ibid.*

[23] Kettell, *op. cit.*, I, 259; Griswold, *op. cit.*, p. 22.

[24] Griswold, *loc. cit.*

larity, in America and abroad, of his first poem, "An Address to the Armies of the United States of America," written in 1782 in the bustle of camp for the encouragement of his fellow soldiers.

Because of his manifold interests in the greater America of his time Humphreys cannot be primarily styled as a delineator of the village. That he was, however, aware of the place of the village and smaller town in the contemporary scene appears in his poetized references to community life. Unlike Dwight, he does not confine his accounts to the New England village, but, ranging afar, optimistically pictures future town life in the West, in his eyes a land of plenty. Into this new domain the New Englander carries his town system, his churches, and his schools.[25]

> There cities rise, and spiry towns increase,
> With gilded domes and every art of peace.[26]

In "An Elegy on the burning of Fairfield in Connecticut"— written on the spot (1779)—Humphreys describes, in conventional romantic manner, "pleasant Fairfield," one of Dwight's villages, whose tall spires and social halls rose "on th' enraptured sight."[27] Although ranked as one of the literary figures of his own time, Humphreys is negligible as a poet except for his part in popularizing a literary vogue glorifying American greatness, village life included. With Kettell, one may justly complain of the monotony and conventionality of his theme, "the true glory of America."

In M'Fingal (1775),[28] John Trumbull's burlesque epic and extravagant absurdity of Revolutionary popularity, a very

[25] See Mathews, op. cit., passim, for the transplanting of New England customs. James T. Adams, New England in the Republic, 1777-1850 (Boston, 1926), p. 456, indicates the following marks of New England influence on western settlements: the church, the common school, and the town meeting. Parton, op. cit., p. 31, wrote in 1871 : "It is evident that the Yankee system, with modifications, is destined to prevail over the fairest parts of this continent."

[26] Quoted in Kettell, op. cit., I, 268-269 ; in Griswold, op. cit., p. 23 ; and in The Columbian Muse, p. 112. Basil Hall, traveling in New York a little later than this (1827-1829), observed many villages and "in the middle I observed there were always several churches surmounted with spires, painted in some showy color, and giving a certain degree of liveliness or finish to scenes in other respects rude enough." He comments also on the bleakness, or rawness, of these villages. (Quoted from Nevins, American Social History as Recorded by British Travellers, p. 151.)

[27] The Columbian Muse, loc. cit.

[28] Full title : McFingal: A Modern Epic Poem. Canto First, or The Town-Meeting (Philadelphia, 1775).

common phase of New England town life, the town meeting, is mockingly ridiculed in over three thousand Hudibrastic lines. Abounding in burlesque contrasts, exaggerated allusions, and figurative language, this Whiggish satire tells of the events at a Massachusetts town meeting, immediately after the Revolution, when two hostile factions debate the issue of rebellion against the mother country.

> The town, our hero's scene of action,
> Had long been torn by feuds of faction ;
>
> .   .   .   .   .   .
>
> They met, made speeches full long-winded,
> Resolved, protested, and rescinded.[29]

Though often stilted and heavy, Trumbull's lines also show a marked comic force in the parodies of the impassioned Whigs and furious Tories, the latter headed by obdurate Squire M'Fingal, as they argue in council.   Alike victorious in argument and fighting, the Whigs tar and feather stubborn M'Fingal and glue him to the liberty pole until he recants.   Gaining his freedom during the night, M'Fingal calls his Tory followers to a cellar where he tells of a vision he has had of the ultimate victory of the despised Whigs.   Afraid, the cowardly M'Fingal flees to the British for protection.[30]

Various New England ministers, lawyers, and even politicians, not so widely known as the more popular "Hartford Wits," show the continuance of interest in different aspects of the village long after the jingling lines of *M'Fingal* had lost their timeliness.   Enoch Lincoln, a lawyer of Worcester, Massachusetts, and later a governor of Maine, followed the vogue of nationalism by showing in *The Village* how "the dreary wilds . . . to peopled villages are changed."[31]   Unfortunately the poet's flights of fancy carry him—and the reader—far from the village he proposes to paint.   Supposedly the picture of a rural village, Lincoln's poem has, as even Kettell admits, "little

[29] Griswold, *op. cit.*, p. 11.
[30] *Ibid.*, pp. 10-11.   *C. H. A. L.*, I, 173, cites Joseph Stanbury's *Town Meeting*, a satirical ballad, as another illustration of the use of the town meeting in poetry. This I have not seen.
[31] *The Village; A Poem with an Appendix* (Portland, 1816).   Lincoln is criticized by Kettell ; no mention of him is made by Griswold.   In this poem Lincoln proposes

> . . . from the camera of the faithful brain,
> [to] paint the little village of the plain.

which were we to refine our criticism, would pass for downright poetry."[32]   On the other hand, its imitative versification and language, together with its moral and political precepts, show again the strong appeal which the poetry of Goldsmith and Cowper made to eighteenth- and early nineteenth-century American readers and versifiers.   In William Ray's "Village Greatness" (1821) the once popular theme of the ever increasing glory of America appears in a new light.   Ray's humorous character, Jack Fallow, "born amongst the woods," indicates the interests of the day in the rise of the common man.[33]   Also in the lighter vein are the Reverend Thomas G. Fessenden's burlesque of village characters.   The Reverend Samuel Deane of Massachusetts in "The Populous Village" (1826) follows the romantic tradition through his descriptions of the inn and the spired church of a New England village.   More subjective is John Howard Bryant's "My Native Village" (1826), in which the poet, a brother to William Cullan Bryant, praises his boyhood home in Cummington, Massachusetts.[34]

These poets, mostly mediocre and now generally unread, were during their stirring period frequently the chief, and often popular, delineators of American life.   Accepted though they were by Samuel Kettell and others equally indiscriminating, the "Hartford Wits" were severely berated by one of their contemporaries, Fessenden (1771-1837)—mentioned above—a satirist aware of the possibilities of American literature.   Protesting against their un-American ideals, he says, in part,

> . . . they possess a taste too pure
> To relish *native literature;*

> .   .   .   .   .   .

[32] Kettell, *op. cit.*, II, 303.
[33] *Ibid.*, II, 143 contains representative verses, as follows :
> In every country village, where
> Ten chimney smokes perfume the air,
>   Contiguous to a steeple,
> Great gentlefolks are found, a score,
> Who can't associate any more,
>   With common 'country people.'

Also note:
> Jack Fallow, born amongst the woods,
> From rolling logs, now rolls in goods,
>   Enough awhile to dash on—
> Tells negro stories—smokes segars—
> Talks politics—decides on wars—
>   And lives in stylish fashion.

[34] Griswold, *op. cit.*, p. 295.

Connecticut ne'er owned a poet.
Dwight, Trumbull, Humphreys, Alsop, show it,
Anu Hopkins sans-discrimination
All, all are doomed to their damnation![35]

In spite of this phillipic the lengthy writings of these poets and
men of affairs show, with relation to the appearance of the
American village in literature, that the village theme, actually
was used and that the accepted literary view of the little town
was a highly sentimentalized and conventional one.   In the
light of the later literature of the small town these poetic ideal-
izations are faint and pale.   They are significant only as signs
of the times.   For more convincing contemporary pictures of
early village life one must turn to the records of travelers, like
James Fenimore Cooper's *Notions of the Americans* (1828) in
which he says that

New England may justly glory in its villages!   Notwithstanding
the number of detached houses that are everywhere seen, villages
are far from infrequent, and often contain a population of some
two or three thousand.   In space, freshness, an air of neatness and
comfort, they far exceed anything I have ever seen, even in the
mother country.[36]

Harriet Martineau, already mentioned as an early traveler in
America, records that

The villages of New-England are all more or less beautiful. . . .
They have all the graceful sweeping elm ; wide roads overshadowed
with wood ; mounds or levels of a rich verdure ; white churches,
and comfortable and picturesque frame dwellings.[37]

Since by 1790 about eighty-five per cent of the entire New
England population lived in towns of less than three thousand
inhabitants, small communities which nearly always attracted
the attention of note-taking travelers, it is strange that the exploitation of the town theme was so small.[38]   Some of the roots
of national culture were still embedded in English soil.

[35] P. G. Perrin, *The Life and Works of Thomas Green Fessenden* (Orono, Maine,
1925), p. 136.   For references to Fessenden and other Revolutionary writers mentioned in this chapter see also H. M. Ellis, *Joseph Dennie and His Circle, Studies in
English*, No. 3 (University of Texas, 1915), *passim*.
[36] Subtitle : *Picked up by a Traveling Bachelor* (London, 1828), I, 80 ff.   Cf. Frances (Wright) D'Arusmont, *Views of Society and Manners in America* (New York, 1821),
p. 166.
[37] II, 78.   Cf. *ibid.*, II, 91, and Parton, *op. cit.*, p. 48.
[38] For population distribution see, in addition to census reports cited in chap. i,
Adams, *op. cit.*, p. 186.

THE RE-CREATION OF THE PAST

Later studies of the provincial New England town mark the transformation of village literature from a conventional genre, the didactic and sentimental product of an incipient literary culture, into one of distinct verisimilitude which has increased immeasurably with the continued fictionalization of the small town. From the time of Cooper more definitely localized backgrounds and intricate themes began supplanting the pastoral delights and sweet effusions of village poetry. While the romantic tradition flourished far into the nineteenth century and appeared sporadically during more recent years, Arcadian villages, representations of "the consecration and the poet's dream," were succeeded by realistic pictures of historic Boston, Salem village, quaint Portsmouth, and other towns of rich associations with the past.

But the realistic novel came into being late in our literature. Puritan prohibition and a slavish attention to English traditions long retarded the development in America of indigenous fiction.[39] Even after the Revolution, when the novel-reading habit was fostered by the American publishers of English tales, the censure of the moralists continued. Consequently, "native novelists appeared late and apologetically, armed for the most part with the triple plea that the tale was true, the tendency heavenward, and the scene devoutly American."[40] In view of this unfavorable condition, the earliest American fiction yields much the same story of the colonial town as that of the village elegists.[41] The thematic selections of our first novelists show a general neglect of the rich material of the Puritan or Revolutionary village. The romantic and didactic made the wider appeal. Moral and sentimental narratives, Gothic tales featuring a morbid hero, weird Indian stories, and bold seductions

[39] Lillie Deming Loshe, *The Early American Novel* (New York, 1907), chap. i; Carl Van Doren, *The American Novel* (New York, 1921), chap. i; *C. H. A. L.*, I, 284-285.

[40] *C. H. A. L., loc. cit.*

[41] The following bibliographies and guides show either a very meagre listing or a total lack of recorded eighteenth-century village and small town fiction : Loshe, *op. cit.*; Oscar Wegelin, *Early American Plays, 1714-1830* (New York, 1900) (not a single village or small town listed) and *Early American Fiction, 1774-1830* (3d ed., New York, 1929) ; S. L. Whitcomb, *Chronological Outlines of American Literature* (New York, 1894) ; J. Nield, *A Guide to the Best Historical Novels, etc.* (5th ed., New York, 1929) ; E. A. Baker, *A Guide to Historical Fiction* (London, 1914) ; Van Doren, *op. cit.*; and B. M. Fullerton, *Selective Bibliography of American Literature, 1775-1900* (New York, 1936).

were characteristic materials. Of no intrinsic value as imaginative literature, the first fictional representations of the small community are dismissed today as mere signposts along the highway of a town literature. Few in number and weak in interest, these early novels of the town usually portrayed in an incidental and frequently didactic style sentimental love stories set against a village background. As Miss Loshe notes, the first forty years of American fiction produced but two novelists of importance, Charles Brockden Brown and James Fenimore Cooper, both of whom lived outside of New England.

The first quarter of the nineteenth century, therefore, offered nothing, aside from a few pioneer delineations like those of Catharine Maria Sedgwick (1789-1867), toward the permanent enrichment of the weakly established literature of the New England village and town.[42]   Hailed as queen of American letters during her day, praised by Bryant in the *North American Review*, and known abroad through the English and French editions of her novels, this now forgotten lady from the Massachusetts village of Stockbridge depicted in 1822, with her first story, *A New England Tale or Sketches of New England Characters and Manners*, the life of a New England village.[43]   Following this puritanic sketch came *Redwood*, a digressive novel of manners picturing community life in a Vermont village, a Shaker settlement at Hancock, Massachusetts, and a fashionable watering place of the 1820's.[44]   In 1827 appeared *Hope Leslie, or Early Times in Massachusetts*, which apart from its moral purpose, presented the bygone life of village and farm (in Boston and Springfield) with some degree of realism, especially developed in the vivid descriptions of Indian attacks.[45]

I.   HAWTHORNE AND THE COLONIAL TRADITION

It was not until the fifties that Herman Melville could enthusiastically urge :

And now, my countrymen, as an excellent author of your own flesh and blood,—an unimitating, and, perhaps, in his way, an

---

[42] John Bristed in *The Resources of the United States* (1818) commented upon the general paucity of memorable American fiction (Van Doren, *op. cit.*, p. 15). Cf. Sydney Smith, *Edinburgh Review*, LXV, 79-80 (Jan., 1820).

[43] S. C. Beach, *Daughters of the Puritans* (Cambridge, 1905), p. 29. Cf. F. L. Pattee, "Catharine Maria Sedgwick," *American Literature*, X, 101-103 (March, 1938).

[44] Two vols., New York, 1824.   [45] Two vols., New York, I, 85 ff.

inimitable man—whom better can I recommend to you, in the
first place, than Nathaniel Hawthorne. He is one of the new, and
far better generation of your writers. . . . Give not over to future
generations the glad duty of acknowledging him for what he is.
Take that joy to yourself, in your own generation, ...[46]

And well might Melville let his enthusiasm be known, for prior
to the emergence of Hawthorne (1804-1864), observer of the
Puritan past, no American novelist had written primarily for
the sake of art.[47]   There were too many deterrents handicap-
ping the leisurely and pleasant cultivation of an American literature.   Art for art's sake was for the writer fortunately possessed of both genius and money.   Without the latter, or some
substitute, like a lucrative profession, the youthful poet or
novelist, though well endowed, could not hope, as Hawthorne
long did, for success to come to his door.   The country was too
young for the support of such an art.   Another handicap was
that of the ease with which publishers could print American
editions of foreign successes.   Those of Hawthorne's predecessors and contemporaries in fiction who had been successful had
divided interests.   Brown was engaged in legal studies and
magazine editing; Cooper was an opinionated man of affairs;
Melville, a schoolteacher by profession, was, to use Carl Van
Doren's phrase, "a transcendentalist with adventures to re-
count"; Simms, a magazine editor and historian; and Irving
and Poe knew the world of magazine editing and criticism.   It
was an unpromising time for the mere literary man.   Applied
more narrowly to the literature of the town, the criticism is obvious that Hawthorne as a careful re-creator of New England's
colonial past had neither worthy predecessor nor rivaling contemporary.   To be sure, Sylvester Judd's didactic novel, *Margaret*, Longfellow's "prose pastoral" and colorless tale, *Kavanagh*, and his Acadian *Evangeline*, Whittier's *Margaret Smith's
Journal*, and Motley's *Merry Mount*, all appearing between 1845
and 1849, were village studies closely coincident with some of
Hawthorne's work prior to *The Scarlet Letter* (1850).   No one
of these, however, deserves a high place in the annals of American fiction.   Consequently, during the winter months of 1849-
1850, when disappointed by his "political decapitation" he re-

---

[46] *The Apple-Tree Table and Other Sketches*, ed. by Henry Chapin (Princeton,
1922), "Hawthorne and His Mosses," p. 75.
[47] Van Doren, *op. cit.*, p. 77.

sumed work in an upper chamber of the house he and Sophia, his young wife, had taken at 14 Mall Street, Salem, Hawthorne had no well-defined native fictional patterns upon which to model his stories. This was still the period when, as Lowell wrote in reviewing *Kavanagh* for the *North American Review* (July, 1849), "our imaginative writers generally, . . . though they take an American subject, . . . *costume* it in a foreign or antique fashion." Here in this old Salem dwelling, after a prolonged period of literary apprenticeship, Hawthorne, as Scott did for English fiction, evolved from his rich store of colonial materials, from his hours of introspection and brooding upon human destiny, a new type of American fiction.

In producing a book like *The Scarlet Letter* he was, in a sense, a discoverer, a pioneer, instead of the product of a definite literary tendency. He was an explorer in a rich field for historic imagination. The background of Puritan Boston, the truthful portraiture of stern old worthies and other provincial dramatis personae and the probing representation of their habits, recollections, and yearnings were Hawthorne's own discoveries. His work, in fact, so vividly re-creates a remarkable era in the history of New England that his name is said to stand more for his subject than for his treatment of it. Among other things, he is, indeed, the novelist of the New England town. His was a Puritan world and the Puritan character with which Cooper failed to sympathize is the very subject of his discovery, the very essence of his characterizations and scene-painting.[48]

Through inheritance, varied experiences, and prolonged study Hawthorne was for years exposed to the village atmosphere in its varying aspects, past and present.[49] To his inheritance from the ancestral Hawthornes first the curious lad— and, later, the introspective young writer—added his own impressions of town life as he had observed it in countless places : at Sebago Lake, near Raymond, Maine, where his maternal uncle, Robert Manning, lived in comfort, though in a remote district ; at Bowdoin College in provincial Brunswick, a pine-forested and "charmingly secluded retreat" bordering on the Androscoggin River ; in many villages and towns with which

[48] John Erskine, *Leading American Novelists* (New York, 1910), p. 179.
[49] For fuller recent discussion see Lloyd Morris, *The Rebellious Puritan: Portrait of Mr. Hawthorne* (New York, 1927), pp. 5-44, and Newton Arvin, *Hawthorne* (Boston, 1929), chap. i.

he became familiar during his vacation wanderings through New Hampshire, Connecticut, western Massachusetts, and elsewhere; and, finally, in quiet, picturesque Concord, where, as he records in the introduction to *Mosses from an Old Manse*, he and Sophia lived happily, though frugally, in the square, two-storied, gabled parsonage, the Ripley house whose ample grounds extended to the Concord River. Through the generosity of an uncle, the owner of a stage line, young Hawthorne made annual short journeys into rural and village communities near Salem, viewing there both commonplace and picturesque scenes and associating with people of the provincial world of New England, all excellent material for his notebook annotations.[50]   From these excursions Hawthorne secured the raw materials for many of his earlier stories reporting characteristic incidents and scenes of village life.   This early developed interest in reproducing the common aspects of the New England countryside and village gave to Hawthorne's work, especially *The Scarlet Letter*, a sharply defined local quality more nearly akin to the style of the modern novel *démeublé* of Willa Cather or Edith Wharton's *Ethan Frome* than to the meticulously detailed realism of Dickens or Thackeray.

Departing from Bowdoin in the summer of 1825, the twenty-one year old student returned to the ancestral Manning house on Herbert Street, Salem, the home of his childhood where, after the death of her seafaring husband, Elizabeth C. Manning Hawthorne had long lived in strange seclusion.   The young man had no settled purpose in life.   Later he was to write to Stoddard :

It was my fortune or misfortune, just as you please, to have some slender means of supporting myself; and so, on leaving college, in 1825, instead of immediately studying a profession, I sat myself down to consider what pursuit in life I was best fit for.[51]

At first, according to his Bowdoin friend, Horatio Bridge, he

---

[50] Arvin, *The Heart of Hawthorne's Journals* (Boston and New York, 1929), pp. vi-vii, says there is no way of knowing how early Hawthorne began making entries in his journal.   "There i record that the habit of journalizing was first formed in him during his boyhood years in Maine, when he was given a blank notebook on his birthday by an uncle, and urged to use it daily for writing out his thoughts, 'on any and all subjects,' with an eye to the development of a sound prose style." The earliest entries preserved by Mrs. Hawthorne belong to the years 1835 and 1836, so Arvin records.

[51] Julian Hawthorne, *Hawthorne and His Wife* (Boston, 1884), I, 96, letter to Stoddard, 1853.

had plans for entering his Uncle Manning's counting-house, but repugnan· ·: to commercial life was responsible, in part, for his lapsing into a state of partial inaction.[52]   Accordingly, with his mother and sisters Elizabeth and Maria Louisa, he, too, became a part of the peculiarly unsocial household on Herbert Street.   Here in a second floor room, under the eaves, he began a twelve-year period of intellectual solitude.   His routine was unexciting.   Endlessly reading "all sorts of good and good-for-nothing" books he brought home from the Salem Athenaeum ; dreaming for hours among strange fantasies which colored his world of reality ; watching from afar the town life outside his window ; strolling, often after dusk, along the streets and deserted wharves, or out into the country and along the seashore ; and, back in his "Castle Dismal," scribbling (as he termed it) and destroying much that he had written, and, in a modest way, publishing in the *Salem Gazette* and other minor publications an occasional anonymous tale, this "handsomest young man of his day," as his own son was years later to describe him, spent his years of prolonged introspection and literary apprenticeship, always hoping for a fame which passed him by.[53]   Mindful of the historical romances of Scott, he pondered over the colonial traditions of his own people, over the fascinating history of his native Salem, from whose present activities he seemed so strangely remote.   Was not this neglected material the source for a strong native fiction?   Might not he, using the themes of New England, become something more than a mere "fiction-monger"?   With these thoughts, the lonely youth gave his energies to the writing of his *Seven Tales of My Native Land*, stories which he collected and submitted to a dilatory Salem printer, Ferdinand Andrews, whose broken promises about the printing of the manuscript thor-

---

[52] *Personal Recollections of Nathaniel Hawthorne* (New York, 1893), p. 67.
[53] For full details see Julian Hawthorne, *op. cit.*, I, chaps. iii and iv ; Bridge, *op. cit.*, chaps. viii-xi ; Moncure D. Conway, *Life of Nathaniel Hawthorne* (London, 1890), chaps. ii and iii ; James T. Fields, *Yesterdays with Authors* (Boston, 1895, 1st ed., 1871), chap. iii : George P. Lathrop, *A Study of Hawthorne* (Boston, 1876) which contains a list of books drawn by Hawthorne from the Salem Athenaeum ; "Books Read by Hawthorne, 1828-50. From the 'Charge Books' of the Salem Athenaeum," *Essex Institute Historical Collections*, LXVIII, 65-87 (Jan., 1932) ; Arvin, ed., *The Heart of Hawthorne's Journals*, pp. 3, 9, 65, 111, and 128, and *Hawthorne*, pp. 43 ff. ; Randall Stewart, ed., *The American Notebooks by Nathaniel Hawthorne* (New Haven, 1932) ; George E. Woodberry, *Nathaniel Hawthorne* (Boston and New York, 1902), pp. 27 ff. ; Paul Elmer More, "The Solitude of Hawthorne," *Shelburne Essays* (Boston, 1904), I, 22-51 ; and Morris, *op. cit.*, pp. 44 ff.

oughly exasperated him. Harshly censuring Andrews, Hawthorne peremptorily demanded the return of his manuscript
and, according to the ever friendly Bridge, "in a mood half
savage, half despairing" burned the work.[54]

Deeply disappointed, he compared himself to a doomed man
drifting helplessly toward a cataract.[55] Happily his despondent
mood lifted and he continued writing, showing as before a predilection for the use of the past even in some of his simplest
stories. At this time, recalling scenes of his "country college,"
Brunswick, and its vicinity, Hawthorne finished a short novel
sketched during his Bowdoin days. In 1828 this was published,
at his own expense, in Boston under the title of *Fanshawe*. The
tale of a young provincial recluse, socially isolated by his intellectual ideals and strongly resembling Hawthorne himself,
Fanshawe proved a complete failure. So ashamed was Hawthorne of the book and its reception that he destroyed all copies
available.

But his writing of tales and sketches continued and eventually, through the encouragement of Samuel B. Goodrich,* editor of *The Boston Token*, and the more helpful financial assistance of Horatio Bridge, his collected stories (originally called
Provincial Tales) appeared as *Twice-Told Tales* (1837). Many
of these so-called apprenticeship stories, as well as others in
Mosses from an Old Manse (1846), foreshadow the more sustained
village treatments in his novels. Some of these sketches are
but brief vignettes of community scenes and people. Often
the village background is but slightly presented, only that necessary for a sort of theatrical backdrop for the central drama ;
but usually it possesses, however, a semblance of local realism
foreshadowing the more detailed pictures of *The Scarlet Letter*
and *The House of the Seven Gables*. The late Julian Hawthorne
once stated an important principle characterizing his father's
treatment of localities when he said that, while the novelist's in-
stinct for localities was not strongly developed, he possessed,
nevertheless, a keen perception of the picturesque. Always
inclined to retire to his "citadel of inward experience," he
shunned rather than sought to make his outlines and directions
correspond too closely with obvious reality.

[54] *Op. cit.*, pp. 67-68.
[55] *Ibid.*, a part of a letter from Hawthorne to Bridge.
* Moncure D. Conway (*Life of Hawthorne*, London, 1890, p. 43) says that
Goodrich had the reputation of being a "sweater" of young writers.

The intensity with which he could convey the feeling of a place, a character, or a situation, was almost in inverse ratio to its literal resemblance to any material prototype; he was essentially a romancer, . . . [his] was a spiritual world of types, elements, and harmonies, rather than a physical world of accidents, individuals, and technicalities.[56]

While the small town idea presents itself again and again in the *Twice-Told Tales* and *Mosses from an Old Manse*, the true localities of the stories are in the characters themselves, who, secondarily, are reflected in their surroundings.   It is Julian Hawthorne's opinion that, on the whole, the illusion of reality is doubtless greater in his father's later works than in these early tales.   "The substance of the later works," he says, "is wrought out of a wider experience and observation of realities than is the case with the earlier ones."[57]

In these collected stories, the work of "the obscurest man of letters in America," the Puritan village scene, with its religionists, tyrants, and iconoclasts, like Endicott, the hated Andros, and rebellious Morton, furnishes the background for little dramas of religious persecution—from within and without—, foreign political tyranny, and the magic of witchcraft.[58]   "The Gray Champion," a story of austere eloquence and graphic imagination, typifies the hereditary spirit of early Boston— 1688 to be exact—expressing itself against tyrannical Edmund Andros; "The Maypole of Merry Mount" shows how the fantastically garbed mummers and misdoers of Mount Wollaston, probably the first "wild Western" town in American fiction, aroused the wrath of Endicott, "the severest Puritan of all who laid the rock foundation of New England"; "The Gentle Boy" portrays the unrelenting and spiritually misguided Bostonians of 1659 who severely persecuted the Quakers; "Endicott and the Red Cross," with its graphically pictured town scenes and its references to a scarlet letter worn by a young woman, foreshadows *The Scarlet Letter;* and "Young Goodman Brown" reveals the witchcraft practices and Quaker persecutions, favorite subjects with Hawthorne, in Salem village.[59]

[56] "The Salem of Hawthorne," *Century Magazine*, XXVIII, 3 (May, 1884).
[57] *Ibid.*, p. 4.
[58] Quoted matter from the preface (1851), to *Twice-Told Tales*, George P. Lathrop, ed., *Hawthorne's Works* (Riverside ed., Cambridge, 1882), I, 13.   This is the edition to be cited hereinafter.
[59] "Young Goodman Brown" is in *Mosses from an Old Manse;* the others, from the *Twice-Told Tales.*

The changing panorama of New England town life from the old times to that of Hawthorne's own Salem is pictured, sometimes but incidentally, in other stories from these early collections. As is shown in "The Legends of the Province House," Revolutionary New England, as well as the Puritan regime, had a deep fascination for Hawthorne. In this series, however, are pictures of a growing provincial capital rather than those of a colonial village. Thomas Waite's antiquated Province House, in the time of its glory the scene of masquerade balls and other festivities to which thronged Revolutionary society, suggests a community life entirely at variance with that of the wilderness village of *The Scarlet Letter*. Here is the beginning of the predestined "Hub of the Universe." Other chronicles of Lilliput present the ordinary minutiae of New England town life at different periods of its development. Ever fond of lonely little journeyings, Hawthorne, in his stories, shares with his readers the varied community sights he sees, perchance, from a steeple or a stagecoach. With him we listen to the monologue of a garrulous pump ; eavesdrop upon the small talk of wondering parishoners about their strangely veiled minister ; marvel, with gaping villagers, over a tobacco peddler's gossipy report concerning the murder of Squire Higginbotham ; and hear countless other wayside discourses revealing small town affairs. We have choice seats at a tavern, where strolling players lure all except a small band of the faithful from prayer meeting. Finally, as we wander with the story-teller, we do not miss that genial uncle to a whole village, a lean old salt, bent with age, who blows his fish-horn through the streets of Salem.

Between Hawthorne's earlier and later pictures of town life there is a definitely increased quality of growth and grasp of material. The earlier sketches and tales, with their rich, multifarious life, are the promises which are fulfilled in the novels. In *The Scarlet Letter*, a masterly tale of mortal error, and *The House of the Seven Gables* (1851), a sombre narrative of the potency of a curse, Hawthorne reached the final fruitage of his own inheritance of Puritanism.

A true Salemite by virtue of inheritance, Hawthorne early came under the influence of the many historical associations of this familiar center of colonial New England. This he shows in numerous written records, especially in his revealing "Main

Street," an antiquarian picture of the interesting old town, and in his "Night Sketches."[60]   As he confessed again in the famous introductory Custom House sketch, Hawthorne could hardly have escaped writing of the town in which his more civic-minded ancestors had played important roles.   This unbreakable bond with the past of Salem had much to do with his frequent literary use of the colonial tradition.   He says, in part:

This old town of Salem—my native place, though I have dwelt much away from it, both in my boyhood and maturer years— possesses, or did possess, a hold on my affections, the force of which I have never realized during my seasons of actual residence here. Indeed, so far as its physical aspect is concerned, with its flat, unvaried surface, covered chiefly with wooded houses, few or none of which pretend to architectural beauty,—its irregularity, which is neither picturesque nor quaint, but only tame,—its long and lazy street lounging wearisomely through the whole extent of the peninsula, with Gallows Hill and New Guinea at one end, and a view of the almshouse at the other,—such being the features of my native town, it would be quite as reasonable to form an attachment to a disarranged checkerboard.   And yet, though invariably happiest elsewhere, there is within me a feeling for old Salem, which, in lack of a better phrase, I must be content to call affection.   The sentiment is probably assignable to the deep and aged roots which my family has struck into the soil.   It is now nearly two centuries and a quarter since the original Briton, the earliest emigrant of my name, made his appearance in the wild and forest-bordered settlement, which has since become a city.   And here his descendants have been born and died, and have mingled their earthly substance with the soil, until no small portion of it must necessarily be akin to the mortal frame wherewith, for a little while, I walk the streets. In part, therefore, the attachment which I speak of is the mere sensuous sympathy of dust for dust.[61]

Although Salem history was in his mind, as is stated in "Main Street," and though he represents himself as having found the plot material in an upper room of the Salem Custom House, this self-styled "degenerate fellow [who] might as well have

[60] Nina E. Browne, *A Bibliography of Nathaniel Hawthorne* (Boston, and New York, 1905), pp. 69 and 72, says that "Main Street" was first published in Elizabeth P. Peabody's *Aesthetic Papers* (1849), pp. 145-174, and again in the Bohn London edition of *The Snow-Image and Other Tales* (1851).

[61] *Hawthorne's Works*, V, 23 ff.   See Van Wyck Brooks's *The Flowering of New England* (New York, 1936), chap. xi, "Hawthorne in Salem."

been a fiddler" chose mid-seventeenth century Boston as the
period of *The Scarlet Letter*.   Most critics agree that the introductory chapter on Hawthorne's fellow-workers at the Custom
House is one of the few blots upon a unique book.   Written
at the period of Hawthorne's dismissal from office as a result
of political changes, the sketch is a sort of personal expression of his attitude toward both Custom House officials and
certain unfriendly local politicians.   Having, as he says in this
chapter, shaken the dust of the Custom House off his feet, he
shakes off also the dust of Salem and seeks inspiration in the
less intimate past of a Boston environment.

An achievement of art competently and carefully exercised,
The Scarlet Letter has a semblance of reality which gives one an
insight into the social and religious practices of provincial Boston.   Though at first designed as one of a volume of tales, to
be called *Old-Time Legends*, the story was at the timely suggestion of James T. Fields, the Boston publisher, expanded into
a longer work of remarkable artistic economy.[62]   Hawthorne
has managed so skillfully the atmospheric elements of his story
that a sort of historical cast is given to the environment, the
physical setting, and the allegorical symbol.   While the historical coloring lacks the elaboration of detail characteristic of
the modern realism of research, several scenes are lingering
relics of the early days of Massachusetts, when people wore
steeple-crowned hats and sad-colored garments.

At the opening of the story Boston, founded a little more
than ten years, was already a thriving village.   Severely Puritan, the town was governed by sternly religious leaders, still
mindful of the tyranny and sin they had crossed the ocean to
escape.   Some mercy, however, had softened the Puritan interpretation of the Hebraic code stipulating death for an adul-
teress.   Instead of receiving this condemnation, Hester Prynne,
wearing the letter A fashioned in scarlet, must stand upon the
pillory platform.   Here the butt of idle, curious talkers and
self-righteous gazers, she must suffer punishment.   Such is the
motivation for a severely simple story, which is neither a true
romance, an allegory, nor a historical novel, although it has
something of each.   A young wife forgetful of earlier vows to
an elderly husband ; a publicly trusted—and also young—
clergyman forgetful of more than his vows ; a wronged husband,

[62] *Op. cit.*, pp. 48-52.   Cf. Morris, *op. cit.*, pp. 222-228.

left in Amsterdam, but brought forward—these and no more, except the individually unimportant townspeople, who serve much the same purpose as a Greek chorus, form the narrative which Hawthorne lifted out of the region of vulgar scandal of everyday life and confined to a world where moral and spiritual forces fill the stage.[63]

The Scarlet Letter is a drama of moods superimposed upon a background of village life. It is a colonial tale of remorse, sorrow, and despair enfolded between two vividly pictured community scenes : the earlier public execution of the magisterial sentence and, at the close, the public holiday of the election ceremonies. Throughout the village serves merely as a somber background against which is projected, with admirable artistic economy, the story of Hester's and Dimmesdale's sin. These occasional, but graphic, scenes bring pictures of a Puritan community in action against one who has dared violate its moral code. At the beginning stern village leaders, following a rigidly conservative and literal sense of morality, pass judgment upon Hester. The motley crowd gathered on the grass-plot before the prison presents a realistic picture. Pitiless goodwives, stern and bearded men, a grim town-beadle, inquisitorial magistrates, officiating clergymen, a thin-visaged stranger, sailors, and a few Indians stare at "this brazen hussy," the tall lady-like young woman on the scaffold. Such a crowd and the somber background of a "beetle-browed" jail and a menacing scaffold indicate plainly that Hester lived in a town where the attempt was made to bind life too tightly. The curious and condemnatory throng symbolizes conventional standards warring against the individual who dares rise above the community ideal.[64] It is the symbol of the environing Puritan world and of the drab circumstances of life in the village of Boston.

The other important delineation featuring provincial village affairs with detailed elaboration contains a series of scenes laid seven years after Hester's ordeal on the pillory platform.[65] It is an unusual holiday time in the little town : the new Governor

---

[63] Albert Mordell, ed., *Notorious Literary Attacks* (New York, 1926), pp. 129-137, has a reprint of A. C. Coxe's scathing denunciation of *The Scarlet Letter*, first written for the *Church Review* (Jan., 1851). ". . . we honestly believe," protests Coxe, "that *The Scarlet Letter* has already done not a little to degrade our literature, and to encourage social licentiousness : . . . ."
[64] Erskine, *op. cit.*, pp. 246-247.
[65] *The Scarlet Letter*, chaps. xxi, xxii, xxiii.

is to receive his office at the hands of the people, already assembled in the marketplace, on this day the teeming center of the town's business.   Eagerly the different spectators—townspeople in costumes of gray or sable tinge, often enlivened with color ; a party of Indians in their savage finery ; and rough-looking bearded desperadoes from the Spanish Main—await the arrival of the elaborately garbed magistrates.   Before this group marches the Election Day procession : the musicians, the Governor with military escort, the men of civil eminence, and the clergymen.[66]   As in the dramatic opening of the novel, the village stage properties for the closing are slight : a street, a crowded marketplace, a church, a scaffold, and a ship in the harbor, all portrayed with the same economy observed in the earlier pictures of the prison, the pillory, Hester's cottage, and Governor Bellingham's many-gabled and ornamentally plastered mansion.[67]

The Scarlet Letter, in fine, is a story of human passions at work under the rigid social conditions of a definite historical epoch ; it is, in the words of Paul Elmer More, a tale whose true moral "lies in the intertangling of love and hatred working out in four human beings the same primal curse. . . ."[68]   As in Maxwell Anderson's vigorous and stirring tragedy, The Wingless Victory (1936), this is a study of the travail of a man's soul when he is faced with a sudden choice involving dishonor.[69] The plight of Hester and Dimmesdale is suggestive of the misfortune and danger confronting Anderson's Malay princess, the self-sacrificing Oparre, who has given up her native country and risked all she has for love of Nathaniel McQueston, Salem sea captain.   In both novel and drama, therefore, the principal characters suffer insidious whispered comments and feel the invisible fingers of scorn pointed at them by accusing townspeople.

The House of the Seven Gables (1851), written at Lenox in the Berkshire Hills shortly after the success of The Scarlet Letter, differs from the latter in its more richly woven groundwork and its wealth of details, much of which Hawthorne had personally observed in Salem.   Less powerful and unique than

---

[66] The only historical figures in the novel are the two governors, Mistress Hibbins (sister to Bellingham), and John Wilson, the clergyman.   Their connection with the story is unhistorical.

[67] The Scarlet Letter, pp. 70 ff., 104, and 128-129.

[68] Op. cit., I, 33.

[69] The Wingless Victory: A Play in Three Acts (Menasha, Wisconsin, 1936), a vigorous denunciation of provincial narrowness, pictures Salem about the year 1800.

its predecessor, *The House of the Seven Gables* presents a fuller picture of the New England town. Here Salem, a small town center of Puritan traditions until the industrial invasions of the late nineteenth century made it a city of factories spreading around the decaying town with its many-gabled old houses, its dilapidated wharves, deserted warehouses, its cobblestone streets, and other reminders of an earlier maritime prosperity, again appears in Hawthorne's fiction. Even with its characteristic Hawthornesque theme of isolation, this novel, says Henry James, comes nearer being a picture of contemporary life than either *The Scarlet Letter* or *The Blithedale Romance.*[70] Here too must be remembered Julian Hawthorne's opinion that though his father had a fine sense of reality, as the jottings in his *Notebooks* testify, the novelist never strove to render exactly the actual facts of his environment.[71] In a prefatory explanation Hawthorne comments upon the subtitle of his novel, *A Romance*, to the effect that the romantic point of view stressed in the tale lies in the attempt to connect it with a bygone time. In a sense, then, *The House of the Seven Gables* is a sort of legend, prolonging itself from a past epoch down to Hawthorne's own time.

As for the setting, the seven-gabled house which is minutely described, we are told by Hawthorne himself that his design was to avoid assigning an actual locality to the imaginary events of his narrative. Positive contacts with the realities of the moment would prove dangerous to his picture of fancy. Characteristically aloof, Hawthorne did not desire to describe local manners, nor interfere with the characteristics of a town and community for which he cherished a natural regard. In his Preface he declared that he had laid out a street that infringed upon nobody's private rights; that he had built a house of materials long in use for constructing castles in the air; and that he had made personages in the story of his own mixing, all with the hope that *The House of the Seven Gables* would not be a discredit to the venerable town which serves as a background.[72] Thus the Preface suggests the degree in which Salem with its fading grandeur enters into the story of a decadent family. How well Hawthorne has applied his romantic principles to

---

[70] *Hawthorne* (New York, 1879), p. 120.
[71] See *ibid.* for a comparison of the opinions of Julian Hawthorne and James.
[72] *The House of the Seven Gables*, p. 15.

village life may be seen from an examination of the novel itself.

The picture of Salem society, painted with some complexity of detail and variety of coloring, springs from the same descriptive faculty which created the moving panorama of "Main Street." As in *The Scarlet Letter*, the town of this story enters but indirectly into the plot structure. Only when certain rare events occur which affect the community at large does the varied populace come into the foreground; yet these occasional events which bring the people of Salem into direct relation with the ill-fated, shadowy house of Pyncheon furnish an element of literary actuality. Always there is the House itself, which, though the normal activities of Salem continue busily in its neighborhood, contrives to stand, as it has stood two centuries, as a symbol of mystery, of decadence. Rusty and wooden, with its seven acutely peaked gables facing toward various points of the compass, with its huge clustered chimney in the midst, the House stands half-way down a by-street.

> The street is Pyncheon-street; the house is the old Pyncheon-house; and an elm tree, of wide circumference, rooted before the door, is familiar to every townborn child by the title of Pyncheon elm.[73]

Hawthorne's skill has pictured both his own and provincial Salem, a town of odd contrasts between the old and the new. The first glimpse of the entire community is given on the occasion at the completion of the Pyncheon mansion, an imposing place. With richness of detail, Hawthorne revivifies the citizenry of early Salem village. The curious, and perhaps awe-struck, villagers, great and humble, have come to view all the splendors of the house. The pompous lieutenant governor, accompanied by his richly attired lady, the Reverend Mr. Higginson, the elders, the magistrates, and whatever of the aristocracy then present in town and country, together with the plebeian throng, crowd into the mansion, all equally curious to see the wonders and eager to partake of the Pyncheon hospitality.

> Velvet garments, sombre but rich, stiffly plaited ruffs and bands, embroidered gloves, venerable beards, the mien and countenance of authority, made it easy to distinguish the gentlemen of worship

---

[73] *Ibid.*, opening paragraph, in part.

at that period, from the tradesman, with his plodding air, or the laborer, in his leathern jerkin, stealing awe-stricken into the house which he had perhaps helped to build.[74]

This, in part, is Hawthorne's many-faceted picture of provincial Salem before its developing seaport had lapsed into decay and quietude.

With the developing story the scene shifts from provincial Salem to that of a more modern day, a town which does not stand out as an unusual village type. In fact, it resembles many other New England seaport towns of the period. The usual type of a public way lined on either side with the usual village shops; cabs and other vehicles rattling over the cobblestone streets; and forlorn-looking tramps near the customhouse and wharves;

. . . a merchant or two, at the door of the post-office, together with an editor, and a miscellaneous politician, awaiting a dilatory mail; a few visages of retired sea-captains at the window of an insurance office, looking out vacantly at the vacant street, blaspheming at the weather and fretting at the dearth as well of public news as local gossip. . . .

—such is Hawthorne's observation of a later Salem which even then, in the words of Van Wyck Brooks, "like the whole New England sea-coast, bristled with old wives' tales and old men's legends."[75] In spite of its lack of the uncommon, however, the town exerted an influence upon even the ancient and now secluded Pyncheon family, people long possessed of distinctive traits. To a certain extent, the remaining Pyncheons, for all of their peculiarities, partook of the general characteristics of the community in which they dwelt, a town famed "for its frugal, discreet, well-ordered, and home-loving inhabitants, as well as for the somewhat confined scope of its sympathies. . . ."[76] Hawthorne's repeated references to the daily routine of the townspeople show that queer old Hepzibah and unfortunate Clifford lived in an ordinary New England community. For instance, while poor Hepzibah miserably awaited the inevitable moment when she must first open her shop, the town outside

[74] *Ibid.*, pp. 25 and 26.
[75] *Ibid.*, pp. 301 and 302; Brooks, *op. cit.*, p. 212.
[76] Hawthorne, *op. cit.*, p. 36.

. . . appeared to be waking up. A baker's cart had already rat-
tled through the street, chasing away the latest vestige of night's
sanctity with the jingle-jangle of its dissonant bells. A milkman
was distributing the contents of his cans from door to door; and
the harsh peal of a fisherman's conch-shell was heard far off around
the corner.[77]

Hepzibah's little cent-shop itself, similar to scores of others,
which a quarter of a century before Hawthorne's book was
written were conducted by widows and lone women in the
towns and villages of New England, offers another suggestion
of reality. Various village, or town, types stand revealed in
the shop customers: the little girl sent to exchange a skein of
cotton thread; the pale, care-wrinkled and haggard woman;
the crabbed laborer in soiled blue coat; and the bustling, fire-
ruddy housewife, all everyday figures and admirable foils to
out-of-the-world Old Maid Pyncheon. More so than in *The
Scarlet Letter*, the chief persons in this story are strangely solitary
individuals; never do they mingle with the villagers according to the custom of small towns. Only a few times are the
recluses, "that awful-tempered old maid, and that dreadful
Clifford," as misunderstanding neighbors class them, brought
into the town proper. On the occasion of Judge Pyncheon's
fateful visit, for instance, brother and sister in hasty flight leave
the retired and unfashionable neighborhood of their ancestral
home and, as in a dream, take the cars far into the country.
The dreary mansion from which they flee is surrounded by
wooden houses of modern date, usually small and typical of
the most plodding uniformity of common life. In the dusky
interior of the secluded place Hepzibah and Clifford had lived
so long removed from the active commercial life of the more
modern part of town that now the railroad, the omnibus,
and even the water cart impressed Clifford as novelties, as
strange things from the outside world.

If the grotesque old spinster and her enfeebled brother seem
a part of the darkened rooms in which they live, Phoebe, with
her youth and modern efficiency, stands out in rather bold
relief from the somber background of a house that is the very
symbol of antiquity. Then there is the daguerreotypist Holgrave, a young man still more modern than Phoebe, holding

[77] *Ibid.*, p. 58.

the latest opinion, and taking a genial and enthusiastic view of life, even though success has not been his. His lack of family traditions, his democratic stamp, and his depth of experience are sharply opposed to the prejudices and weakened vitality of an aristocratic family of which the gaunt, sallow, and near-sighted Hepzibah is the most heroic representative.

Emphasis upon both the sins and the virtues of Salem's citizens saves Hawthorne's treatment of the town's life from sentimentality. The neighbors' curiosity about the return of Clifford, for instance, reveals Hawthorne's penetrating study of human foibles. Again, Miss Hepzibah's customers represent a variety of townspeople ranging from hungry little Ned Higgins to fussy and imperious housewives. Perhaps the most elaborate, and certainly the most ironical, portrait is that of Judge Pyncheon, the picture of a "superb, full-blown hypocrite, a large-based, full nurtured Pharisee, bland, urbane, impressive," apparently benevolent, but actually hard, gross, ignoble.[78]

When considered as a study of New England village life, *The House of the Seven Gables*, though criticized by one of Hawthorne's most discriminating critics because of its burdensome details, reveals many of the minutiae of speech, manners, and appearances of the exemplary and conventional society of provincial and later Salem.[79] In the latter, the Salem of fading grandeur, there is a foreshadowing of the decaying village as imaginatively pictured later by Sarah Orne Jewett and Mary E. Wilkins Freeman. Pathetic and scowling Hepzibah, the age-worn house, the peculiar equipment of the cent-shop, the customers, young and old, philosophical Uncle Venner, the outer man of Judge Pyncheon, and the modern-minded Holgrave suggest the reality of nineteenth-century Salem.

Hawthorne's other novels, *The Blithedale Romance*, the unfinished *Dr. Grimshawe's Secret*, *Septimius Felton*, and *The Dolliver Romance*, present exceedingly casual portrayals of village life. That they are not so deeply rooted in their environments as *The Scarlet Letter* and *The House of the Seven Gables* is not the fault of their milieu but rather of their author whose chief concern was with the problems of the soul. Though Revolution-

---

[78] The characterization of Judge Pyncheon is a satiric portrait of the Reverend Charles W. Upham, who was instrumental in depriving Hawthorne of his position at the Salem Custom House.

[79] W. C. Brownell, *American Prose Masters* (New York, 1909), p. 95.

ary Concord and Salem of a later date furnish apt enough stages for the mysterious experiments of scholarly Septimius Felton and uncouth Dr. Grimshawe, here, as in his earlier character portrayals, Hawthorne's primary interest is not in the social picture. His characters in these unfinished and remarkably similar romances are abnormal recluses wholly in contrast to the few people introduced with normal village associations, like Robert Hagburn and Rose Garfield in *Septimius Felton*. Just so much of the general community life as is necessary for the setting of these dramas of the soul is presented and no more. Truly, the quiet Salem streets of *The House of the Seven Gables*, the community life of Blithedale, and the village houses, shaded hills, the gossip, and various activities of revolutionary Concord as shown in *Septimius Felton* contribute color, not substance, to each story.[80]

Although critically discredited for his narrowed outlook, the incompleteness of his characters, and the inadequacy of his social picture, Hawthorne, nevertheless, was so predisposed by both heredity and environment to write of the New England of the Puritans that he made this literary material his own. In doing so he produced the first really important imaginative delineations of the New England village.

II. MINOR DELINEATORS

The tradition of the New England village thus portrayed in imaginative literature by Hawthorne also claimed the attention of a number of contemporary novelists. In *Merry Mount* (1849) the historian, John Lothrop Motley (1814-87), disclaiming indebtedness to "The Maypole of Merry Mount," produced a romantic story of colonial convention and revolt.[81] The picturesque scene is the log-hut town of Mount Wollaston (Merry Mount), on the southern side of Massachusetts Bay; the time, the years from 1628 to 1631; and the motivating factions, the lawless followers of "the worshipful Master Morton, Lord of Misrule and Sachem of Merry Mount," pitted against "the bloody psalm singers." Merry Mount, sheltered in an oak grove, is the scene of a round of drinking, smoking, dancing, frantic revelry, ribald jesting, and incessant shouting, Maypole

[80] *Ibid.*, p. 93.
[81] Subtitle: *A Romance of the Massachusetts Colony* (2 vols., Boston and Cambridge, 1849).

celebrations which horrified the near-by Puritans who regarded Morton as the most depraved of sinners.   If not an absorbing story, Merry Mount offers a realistic contrast in colonial communities.

In its presentation of the routine of Puritan life John Greenleaf Whittier's *Margaret Smith's Journal in the Province of Massachusetts Bay, 1678-9* is far more realistic than *The Scarlet Letter*.[82] While the diary is not real, it is, as Whittier suggests in a prefatory note, intended to present "a tolerably lifelike picture of the Past, and introduces us familiarly to the hearths and homes of New England in the seventeenth century."   Told from the point of view of a young English visitor in the home of colonial aristocrats, the *Journal* deals largely with the affairs of well-to-do townsmen, though pictures of humble life and of Indian activities color its pages.   Whittier has recaptured the spirit of the past in his descriptions of customs and individuals who assisted in shaping the new settlements of Boston, Newbury on the Merrimac, and Salem.   Her uncle, Secretary Rawson, being one of the magistrates, Margaret had opportunities of meeting such well-known individuals as Samuel Sewall, Cotton Mather, who impressed her as "a pert, talkative lad," and John Eliot, translator of the Bible in the Indian tongue.   From the diary one gets fleeting impressions of the activities occupying these colonial townsmen.   Farming, fishing, trading with the Indians, and working toward the upbuilding of their growing towns, Margaret's associates were exceedingly busy.   Cornhuskings, weddings, the punishment of unfortunate Quakers, and the hanging of witches furnished occasional entertainment. Interwoven with this account of the land, the people, and their customs is the love story of Rebecca Rawson, Margaret's cousin and colonial belle, who unfortunately married an English rogue parading in Boston as a man of rank.

Like Hawthorne, Henry Wadsworth Longfellow, aside from his years of foreign study and travel, was long exposed to the village atmosphere of New England.   In Portland, Maine, the scene of "My Lost Youth" (1855), in the straggling Brunswick of Hawthorne's college days and later, and in Cambridge, for long years but a small college town, Longfellow lived a sheltered and scholarly life amid amiable and intellectual townspeople. Except, however, for incidental portrayals such as those in the

---

[82] *Prose Works* (Boston, 1866), I, 1-199.

6

sermonic "The Village Blacksmith" and the reminiscent "My
Lost Youth," little of this contemporary town life finds reflec-
tions in his poetry.   Though Longfellow must have liked Cambridge's "calm old trees and the village atmosphere and Washington Allston's paintings and the horse-cars and the crinolines
and the cellar of wine and oratory as an art in itself and stocks
and melodeons and beaver hats and the fireplace as a necessity,"
few of these realistic details of the town life around him are
used as the materials of poetry.[83]   With Hawthorne and Whittier a re-creator of the colonial town, Longfellow also found
abundant materials in the legends and histories of colonial
Massachusetts.   Ever fascinated by Old World beauty and
romance, similarly he was attracted by the traditions of early
New England.

His first lengthy poetic contribution to village literature is,
however, not wholly germane to this study of the American
town.   In *Evangeline: A Tale of Acadie* (1847) the popularly
accepted descriptions of the pastoral village of Grand-Pré give
a romanticist's interpretation of Acadian life.   Here, however,
Longfellow, in picturing the multifarious details of an idyllic
village background of the eighteenth century and its busy, happy people, is a romantic realist.   The kindly village priest,
artisans, farmers, Evangeline Bellefontaine and her lover, Gabriel Lejeunesse (son of Basil, the blacksmith), housewives, and
the intruding English soldiers help in strengthening the verisimilitude of this picture of a secluded village, English by conquest but French in loyalty.

I...riting neither from the Longfellows nor the Wadsworths
(his mother's people) little of Puritanism that was especially
straitening, the poet became no Calvinist.   Instead of rigidly puritanic and outworn creeds Longfellow inherited the
principles of good.[84]   Such deep-rooted principles, reflected in
his poetic repudiations of the harshness and fanaticism of re-
ligiously blinded Puritans, color his attempted dramatic representations of the little towns of Boston and Salem.   A few
weeks after the publication of *The Song of Hiawatha* (1855), at
the insistence of friends that he write a poem on the Puritans

---

[83] Quoted matter from Herbert Gorman, *A Victorian American: Henry Wadsworth Longfellow* (New York, 1926), p. 308.
[84] Howard Mumford Jones, "Longfellow," pp. 109 ff., in John Macy, ed., *American Writers on American Literature* (New York, 1931).

and the Quakers, Longfellow considered the subject to the extent of beginning *The New England Tragedies*, which, however, he soon put aside for work on a lighter poem of Puritan life, *The Courtship of Miles Standish*, finished in 1858.[85] Enlivened by humor, realistic movement, and characterizations, the poem re-creates in a succession of scenes the life of early Plymouth. Dry and unimaginative chronicles of the Puritan come to life in this popularly received tale of a New England courtship. Household life, Indian relations, and individualized characters are outstanding features of his reproduction of the Old Colony days.

In 1868 Longfellow remodeled in verse his long-neglected New England tragedy, *John Endicott*, and added a new story which he called *Giles Corey of the Salem Farms*. Usually conceded to be two dull gloomy plays from Puritan chronicles, these tragedies are developments of Hawthornesque themes, the Quaker persecutions and the witchcraft craze of seventeenth-century Boston and Salem. In *John Endicott* Longfellow repudiates the Puritanic fanaticism which led Governor Endicott and his fellow Bostonians to torture helpless Quakers. In *Giles Corey*, suggestive of Hawthorne's "Young Goodman Brown," the scene shifts to Salem of 1692, where Justice Hawthorne (or Hathorne, as the name was then), relentless forbear of the novelist, persecutes innocent villagers, among them Giles Corey and his wife, for suspected practice of witchcraft. Dramatically poor, both of these closet-dramas re-create in detail the

> Delusions of the days that once have been,
> Witchcraft and wonders of the world unseen,

which stirred colonial townsmen to cruel deeds.[86]

Another of Longfellow's ventures into the literature of the town, a digression from the colonial themes above, is a dull prose romance of a small New England village. Published in 1849 under the title of *Kavanagh: A Tale*, this is the prosy story of a small town schoolmaster, meek but imaginative Mr. Churchill, who fights imaginary battles in which he is always the hero.[87] Yearning to write a great work of art, Churchill

[85] H. E. Scudder, ed., *The Complete Poetical Works of Henry Wadsworth Longfellow* (Cambridge ed., 1895), p. 163.
[86] *The New England Tragedies* (Boston, 1868), p. 101.
[87] Longfellow, *Complete Works* (Boston, 1911), Vol. VIII.

searches vainly through his ponderous books for romance.   In
his frantic search among the themes of the past the tedious
master fails to recognize in the love affairs of his fellow-citizens
richly abundant material.   A picture of rural town life in the
early nineteenth century, *Kavanagh* is so indefinite in plot structure that it is little more than a series of impressions from the
humdrum life of a small New England town.   Among the simple villagers the only discontented and professedly learned person is the dreamer Churchill, a Hawthornesque character.
As in many small town narratives of the period, *Kavanagh* pictures community changes resulting from the building of railroads through heretofore peacefully isolated villages.   According to Lowell's criticism in the *North American Review* (July
1849), *Kavanagh*, in its utter lack of motion and color, is "as
far as it goes, an exact daguerreotype of New England life."
Although its village characters, portrayed "faithfully after
nature," and its "remarkably sweet and touching" story might
have delighted Lowell and his genteel contemporaries, these
selfsame qualities account, in part, for Longfellow's modern
title of Victorian American.

In *Tales of a Wayside Inn* (1863) there are scattered New
England village scenes.   The Poet's tale, "The Birds of Kill-
ingworth," centers around a Connecticut town, where local
problems are settled in the town meeting.   To such assemblies
come the town dignitaries and their lowlier associates : the
Squire, an "august and splendid sight," the austere Parson,
the Preceptor from the Academy, the ponderous Deacon, and
various farmers.   The landlord's tale, "Paul Revere's Ride,"
contains a brief series of eighteenth-century Middlesex village
descriptions.

Recent research by Mr. James T. Hatfield concerning a
prize-winning tale has brought to light an additional Longfellow contribution to village literature.[88]   In 1834, when Longfellow was a young Bowdoin teacher chafing at the small town
code of Brunswick, an unknown George F. Brown, Esq. (really
Longfellow) of Boston won with "The Wondrous Tale of the
Little Man in Gosling Green," a provincial mystery story, a
"Literary Premium" offered by the newly established *The New
Yorker*, then edited by Horace Greeley.   Indicative of Long-

---

[88] "An Unknown Prose Tale by Longfellow," *American Literature*, III, 136 ff.
(May, 1931).   See also *American Literature*, V, 377, note (Jan., 1934).

fellow's restlessness in provincial Brunswick, the "Wondrous Tale" had its origin in the young professor's observations of actual persons in the little college community. The Bungonuck of the story is a Down East village in a drowsy land where "the choice of town clerk and select-men, or some occurrence of equal importance, occasionally arouses the drowsy villagers from their wanted repose, and rakes open anew the ashes of some half-extinguished family feud." Sleepy though it is, the petty world of Bungonuck becomes the scene of "uproar and misrule" on the occasions of visits by puppet shows, wild animal caravans, or "some distinguished foreigner with a hand-organ and chinesco." Its curiosity reached the limit when the mysterious Man in Green came to town. As Mr. Hatfield points out, this provincial tale entitles Longfellow to a significant place among the early nineteenth-century village satirists. The penetrating satire which Longfellow directs against small town curiosity and petty criticism foreshadows the more severe judgments which Mark Twain, more than sixty years later, passed against the shallow citizens of Hadleyburg.

In *A Fable for Critics* (1848) Lowell described a certain curious and individual novel, then current, as "the first Yankee book with the *soul* of Down East in't, and things farther East"; another less charitable critic, writing less than half a century after, anathematized the book as "crude, careless, irrelevant, and at times wearisomely sermonic."[89] This "sublimated Unitarian and American 'Pilgrim's Progress' " was Sylvester Judd's *Margaret*, minutely delineative of New England town life from the close of the Revolution to the early nineteenth century and a forerunner to the slightly later novel of locality.[90] Judd (1813-53) once wrote a fellow Unitarian minister that he proposed in this leisurely novel to denounce "bigotry, cant, pharisaism, and all tolerance." Thus didactically designed, *Margaret*, nevertheless, belongs to the fiction of the New England town by virtue of its detailed picture of a Down East community. With its spired meeting-house, shaded streets and village green, antiquated high-roofed houses, courthouse with adjoining pillory, stocks, and whipping post, its school, its shops, and its tavern, Livingston had all the literary ear-

[89] Richardson, *op. cit.*, II, 392 ; see Duyckinck, *op. cit.*, II, 588 ff., for biographical details.
[90] Subtitle: *A Tale of the Real and the Ideal, Blight and Bloom* (Boston, 1871). First ed., 1845 ; second and revised ed., 1851.

68   THE SMALL TOWN IN AMERICAN LITERATURE

marks of a busy shire town.[91]   Intolerance toward the Quakers, freemasonry celebrations, and magisterial investigations, suggestive of *The Scarlet Letter* of later publication, stir the citizens. In time, revival meetings and Thanksgiving services have to share honors with turkey-shooting, husking bees, military parades, and dancing.[92]   Some of the old traditions, such as observance of certain church regulations, linger on.

If Hawthorne and Whittier re-create the backgrounds of the earliest provincial life, Judd, in this novel and its intended modern sequel, *Richard Edney and the Governor's Family* (1850), pictures rural and town scenes at the transitional period from the eighteenth to the nineteenth century.   Often uneven in construction and wearisomely didactic, Judd's novels possess the merit of recording the neglected materials of ordinary American life.   According to Lowell's estimate, *Margaret* "is the most emphatically American book ever written."   Characteristic of a new country, whose writers were motivated by the feeling that "it was absolutely necessary to our respectability that we should have a literature," the novel is formless and slovenly in construction.   On the other hand, "the scenery, characters, dialect, and incidents mirror New England life as truly as Fresh Pond reflects the sky."   Even the moral, "pointing forward to a new social order, is the intellectual antitype of that restlessness of disposition, and facility of migration which are among our chief idiosyncrasies."[93]

According to literary records, the various Goldsmithian adaptations in poetry and the romantic re-creation of the far distant past in prose fiction represent the dominant trends in the literature of the village prior to the widespread economic changes of the Civil War years and the Gilded Age.   Then new trends in the portrayal of American life were influenced by the rapid changes in national attitudes, the rise of the common man, and the increase of inventions, all of which produced, in actuality, a town life in marked contrast to that of the more or less genteel tradition of pre-war times.   With the introduction of the railroad and the building of highways the secluded and often picturesque New England village, like such

[91] *Ibid.*, pp. 54-55, 175, 182, and 275 ff.
[92] *Ibid.*, p. 29.
[93] Review of *Kavanagh, North American Review*, CXLIV, 209 (July, 1849).

villages elsewhere, either grew into a busy industrial town or, being remote from the main lines of travel, finally degenerated as its best citizens moved cityward. All of these movements introduced into fiction a new type of community.

CHAPTER III

THE NEW ENGLAND VILLAGE IN A NEW LIGHT

WITH ITS EARLY established indigenous population and its close
adherence to the original town system, New England long remained the center of traditions and ideals. Until well into the
nineteenth century its population included "a tacitly recognized upper class, whose social eminence was sometimes described by the word 'quality'."[1] No swift changes materially
altered its social organization. In its towns especially local
hierarchies based upon education, public service, and the generally acknowledged importance of the clergy had developed
from colonial days.[2] The growth of a prosperous mercantile
class in eighteenth-century Boston added further to the main-
tenance of the aristocratic social code. Even country communities had their traditional standards. In small towns, not
unlike Equity, Maine, of Howells's *A Modern Instance*, society
showed some complexity of caste. With the development of
the legal and medical professions the village squire, reinterpreted in Howells's Squire Gaylord, and the doctor were, with
the minister, accepted as persons of local distinction. On the
other hand, certain elements were not of the elect. From the
beginning each New England locality had many plain folks,
who, though seldom attaining positions of high intellectual or
political recognition, added, nevertheless, with their ranks of
small shopkeepers, artisans, and farmers another important
town group. There was also a third element, usually undesirable, the descendants of immigrant servants, whose general
character suggested the "po' whites" of the South or the "poor
whiteys" of straggling settlements to the west of the Mississippi.[3]
As generations passed the predominantly aristocratic population increased its compact and rigid society into a sort of town
life best described in the stories of Harriet Beecher Stowe, Rose

---

[1] Barrett Wendell, *A Literary History of America* (New York, 1900), p. 235.
[2] *Ibid.*, p. 236.
[3] *Ibid.* Robert Louis Stevenson in his *The Silverado Squatters, passim*, refers to
the lower elements of Nevada and California mining camps as "poor whiteys."

Terry Cooke, Sarah Orne Jewett, and other recorders of the New England community.

With the Civil War this system underwent a great change, for, as has been observed repeatedly, the conflict educated America.[4] In the words of Lewis Mumford, the age of pragmatic acquiescence was at hand and the Golden Day of antebellum life rapidly waning.[5] Such a far-reaching sectional clash not only broke the bonds of the age-long isolation and self-sufficiency of the New England community, but it started widespread movements affecting the country at large. Gradually, yet surely, provincialism weakened before a newer force, industrial progress. Thousands of soldiers, heretofore provincial farmers, small townsmen, or untraveled students, suddenly were shifted from their native—and often isolated—locales into strange regions of ever changing scenes and contacts. Whole regiments of young provincials, akin to those presented in Henry Ward Beecher's *Norwood, or Village Life in New England* (1867), swarmed from remote hill towns, prosperous valley towns, ports, and farms throughout New England to the South, a virtually new country to many of them. From Harvard, Amherst, Bowdoin, and elsewhere college graduates, like young Cathcart, hero of *Norwood*, measured themselves with men of the Southern plantations. Although a costly training, the war, nevertheless, enlarged the outlook of many provincials and gave opportunity for the development of many kinds of leadership.[6]

As a natural aftermath of any great conflict, the national restlessness following the disbanding of the armies led to radical changes in social structures everywhere. The war put in motion movements to be felt throughout the country. The industrial changes which Sherwood Anderson in his novel, *Poor White* (1920), describes as taking place in Bidwell, an imaginary town in Ohio, may well be accepted as a picture of the general post-war eagerness for new life and material progress. In Bidwell, as in many actual towns of the period, the old individual-

[4] Fred Lewis Pattee, *A History of American Literature since 1870* (New York, 1915), p. 4. Professor Pattee's entire first chapter, "The Second Discovery of America," and chap. xv, "The Decline of New England," of Professor Wendell's *History* are good brief surveys of the decline, as is also the former's *Side-Lights on American Literature* (New York, 1922), pp. 161 ff.

[5] *The Golden Day* (New York, 1926), pp. 157 ff.

[6] Cf. A. W. Tourgée, *A Fool's Errand* (New York, 1879), *passim*.

istic order was crumbling as "new talk ran through the town."
A new force was being born in American life.

> And all over the country, in the towns, the farm houses, and the
> growing cities of the new country, people stirred and awakened.
> Thought and poetry died or passed as a heritage to feeble fawning
> men who also became servants of the new order. Serious young
> men in Bidwell and in other American towns, whose fathers had
> walked together on moonlight nights along Turner's Pike to talk of
> God, went away to technical schools. . . . From all sides the
> voice of the new age that was to do definite things shouted at them.[7]

As Anderson notes, "wealth seemed to be spurting out of the
very earth." Industry, creeping slowly westward, entered the
coal and iron regions of Pennsylvania and the newly discovered oil and gas fields of Ohio and Indiana. "A madness took
hold of the minds of the people."[8] Villages, like the advantageously located Bidwell, speedily were transformed into boom
towns, to which excursion trains brought hordes of investors.

How did this industrialism, with its westward migrations and
its hastily erected Metropolisvilles, affect New England? What
reflection did it find in the literature of the New England town?
It is little short of ironic that New England's active participation in the slavery struggle should have resulted, by a curious
turn in economic affairs, in the eventual loss of her long-cherished prestige of leadership. Such was the situation when,
following the disbanding of the armies, many New England
villages, small towns, and farming communities suffered from
a veritable exodus of their most progressive folk, usually young
men who, lured by thoughts and talk of new lands and new
fortunes, migrated westward leaving behind them the less spirited types : aged men, impoverished but aristocratic old maids,
and others frequently characterized in the stories of Miss Jewett
and Mrs. Freeman. The formerly self-sufficient Sweet Auburns, Fairmeadows, and Greenfields of New England, established villages with shaded streets and substantial buildings
having the charm of age, were either deserted by their most active and adventurous citizens, or, being advantageously situated, developed into mill towns, as did Salem, Haverhill,
and Lowell, into which surged Irish and other immigrants.

[7] *Poor White* (New York, 1920), p. 64.
[8] *Ibid.*, p. 129.

Thus began the so-called decline of New England, a part of the dying provincialism in all sections of the country. Farms were mortgaged ; the once flourishing shipping trade was dead ; and old families often gave way to newcomers. Industrial progress was in its heyday. Under the influence of the railroads, the frontier movement, the national banks and securities, and other things indicative of an ever widening national horizon, the New England of Emerson's Concord, of Cambridge's Brahmins, and of the Saturday Club of Boston was greatly altered. In short, "the adolescent nation of 1820 to 1860, intellectually imitative and dependent, youthfully uncouth and sensitive to foreign criticism, passed through the *Sturm und Drang* of the Civil War into a newly discovered America, a greater America with industrial potentialities everywhere."[9] Thus, according to the spirit of the times, the immense yielding of new resources was accompanied by marked and varied changes in New England as elsewhere.

As the old eminence of New England and the intellectual hegemony of Boston declined, many once flourishing towns, actual counterparts to Miss Jewett's Deephaven, decayed into quiet villages whose impoverished aristocrats jealously cherished memories of their former prosperity. While prairie lands were being turned into wheat fields and other new regions transformed by the discoveries of mineral wealth, the center of economic development gradually was shifting away from New England. The so-called Renaissance of New England, with its transcendental enthusiasts, its Orphic discoursers, its cultivated professors returned from European study and travel, its urbane essayists, its novelists and poets, declined in importance in the wake of the new order. Furthermore, though various representatives of this earlier group lived until long after the war, henceforth much, but not all, of the indigenous New Englandism was to be exploited by new interpreters using new subjects and new media.

Between the Civil War and the close of the century the older prejudices against the reading and the writing of novels greatly decreased. With the developing cityward movement, many people had a greater interest in and leisure for reading. The widespread talk about current economic, social, religious, and

---

[9] Patter, *A History of American Literature since 1870*, pp. 8-9 ; cf. F. O. Matthiessen, "New England Stories," in John Macy, *op. cit.*, p. 399.

political problems was speedily reflected in fiction throughout the country. Among the different localized treatments of real life there appeared numerous sketches of contemporary New England villages and manufacturing towns. The most realistic of these imaginative delineations have been variously termed *novels of locality, provincial novels,* and *novels of local color.*[10] Resembling in some respects the romantic or historical novel, this type, however, usually portrayed contemporary backgrounds and events rather than those of past history. In addition to these longer portrayals, the short story and sketch were used frequently. As already intimated, the picturesque Yankee village, or town, realistically pictured through typical community figures, characteristic activities, and, not infrequently, local speech, was one of the featured backgrounds of this localized fiction. Frequently delineative of a limited environment, this fiction usually bared the narrowed lives of eccentric and often pathetic characters : cross old maids, emotionally starved girls, talkative sea captains, long retired from active service, queerly developed children, and other examples of human oddities.[11] Sometimes laconically humorous characters relieved the general tone of didacticism or moralizing, the heritage of a Puritan past. With the expansion of the New England town into northern New York and beyond, the field of Yankee fiction also was extended westward, as is evidenced in *David Harum* (1898), Edward Noyes Westcott's popular novel of a shrewd Yankee banker, a small town character, in central New York. Many New England villages, wherein there still lingered a flavor of the vanished years, offered post-war novelists and short story writers ample reminders of the old life mingled with the new. Truly, these interpreters might have reasoned, as has a modern poet, that in such small communities there was "soil for the deepest root."[12]

[10] Dickinson, *op. cit.,* pp. 556 ff.; V. L. Parrington, *The Beginnings of Critical Realism in America, 1860-1920* (New York, 1930), p. 398; Pattee, *op. cit.,* chap. xi and *The Development of the American Short Story* (New York, 1923), chap. xi.

[11] Anon., "Alarming Increase of Old Maids and Bachelors in New England," *Literary Digest,* LXV, 66-70 (April 10, 1920).

[12] Lindley Williams Hubbell, "New England Village," *Harper's Magazine,* CLXIV, 91 (Dec., 1931) :
> Here is soil for the deepest root
> And air for branches to spread ;
> Bins for the gathered fruit,
> And ample bins for the dead.

Compare this poem with the prose description by John Sterling, "New England Villages," *The Atlantic Monthly,* CXXXI, 520 (April, 1923).

Who were these successors to the Brahmins, these interpreters of the custom of the country through their sketches and stories of a village-dotted New England? Three groups are noteworthy. First, the great majority of the recorders of the New England decline were women, some of whom, like Mrs. Stowe, were daughters of clergymen of the older regime, and others, such as Miss Jewett and Mrs. Freeman, were natives of the small towns interpreted in their stories. On the other hand, the second group of small town delineators came from outside the charmed circle of the Brahmins. Among these was a Welsh printer's son, a young Ohioan, William Dean Howells, who was drawn to New England by his veneration for the Cambridge literati. Then there was Thomas Bailey Aldrich, sketcher of his native New Hampshire Portsmouth, whose New York apprenticeship left a metropolitan imprint upon much of his work. Finally, a few members of the Renaissance group (Holmes, Lowell, and others) in novel, essay, and poetry gave a local flavor to their studies of the New England village. These are the chief interpreters of the New England community during the activity-crammed years of the Gilded Age. Amid the unsettled, hurried temper of an age dominated by the attendant wild speculation of a changing frontier and by a new industrialization motivated by the rapid progress of science and invention, these New Englanders viewed in various ways their village and town environments. While some, disregarding the shifting emphasis in literature, clung to older ideals, the overwhelming majority of these recorders gave realistic interpretations of New England life. In so doing they were but abetting the wider development of a new realistic fiction arising from Bret Harte's contemporary successes. For them the New England idyl had ended.

Pioneer Depictors of the Yankee Village

Among the earlier depicters of the localized Yankee village* were two members of a gifted family, Harriet Beecher Stowe (1811-96) and her clergyman brother, Henry Ward Beecher (1813-87), both born at Litchfield, Connecticut, at this period an outstanding intellectual community. In a single novel previously mentioned, *Norwood, or Village Life in New England,*

* For discussion of Seba Smith's Downingville see Appendix II.

Beecher produced a wooden fictional interpretation of a Massachusetts small town. Although he proposed "to give a real view of the inside of a New England town, its brewing thought, its inventiveness, its industry and enterprise, its education and shrewdness and tact,"[13] Beecher, unversed in Hawthorne's architectonic economy, failed in his purpose through his selection of too large a canvas. Lacking the powers of constructing plot and characters, he wandered afar from his village locale. His characters, largely lay figures, move puppet-fashion through artificial actions and philosophical disquisitions prescribed for them by the author. The story moves from the little Connecticut River town of Norwood to college scenes at Amherst, to Boston, to Washington, and the horrors at Bull Run and Gettysburg. The novel abounds in didactic digressions, ludicrous contrasts to the modern treatments of small townsmen. If disregarded as a novel and examined as a series of New England sketches and scenic descriptions, *Norwood* offers the patient reader pictures of a New England community during the Golden Age.

Characterized by better technique than her brother's novel, Mrs. Stowe's New England village fiction is truly imbedded in soil for the deepest root. The product of her maturer years, *The Minister's Wooing* (1859), dealing with scenes in her father's library, *The Pearl of Orr's Island* (1862), *Oldtown Folks* (1869), *Oldtown Fireside Stories* (1872), and *Poganuc People* (1878) portray quiet villages of old New England, scenes, in part, of young Harriet Beecher's earlier literary interests, reflected first in the animated moral tales of *The Mayflower* (1843).[14] Like *Norwood*, Mrs. Stowe's novels occasionally smack too much of the parsonage; sentimentalize about the affairs of the heroine; and show weak plot construction. On the other hand, they present convincing pictures of New England rural and village life, the fruit of what Lowell called "an acquirement of that local truth which is the slow result of unconscious observation."

By 1850 Mrs. Stowe had removed to Brunswick, Maine, where her husband, Calvin E. Stowe, had accepted a position in Bowdoin College. It was here that she wrote *Uncle Tom's*

---

[13] From a letter written (Jan. 3, 1866) by Beecher to Robert Bonner and later prefixed to *Norwood, etc.* (Boston and Chicago, 1895). The novel was first printed serially in the New York *Ledger*, 1867, of which Bonner was editor.

[14] Republished by Harpers in 1849. See *C. H. A. L.*, III, 70, and Duyckinck, *op. cit.*, II, 605.

Cabin (1851) and began in 1857 the composition of both *The Minister's Wooing* and *The Pearl of Orr's Island*. In the former Mrs. Stowe has laid her scenes in the old town of Newport, Rhode Island, during the pre-railroad era. A semihistorical picture of New England habits and traditions, the story deals with puritanical life during the time of Dr. Samuel Hopkins (1721-1803).[15] The town life furnishes a realistic background for the doctor, who is about to marry his pupil, the heroine, when her sailor lover appears. *The Pearl of Orr's Island* is a study of a provincial fishing community in Maine.[16] Though rich in local truth, the story is sentimental.

In her *Oldtown Folks* and *Sam Lawson's Oldtown Fireside Stories* Mrs. Stowe used material furnished by Professor Stowe. "Oldtown" is a reproduction of the Natick of his boyhood, a small place near Boston, now known as South Natick.[17] From frequent visits, made before she began her story, Mrs. Stowe added her own observations to the reports of her husband. "Nearly every character and incident not only in 'Oldtown Folks' but in 'Oldtown Fireside Stories' were familiar to the whole Stowe family, from their having heard of them repeatedly from Professor Stowe's lips, many years before they were committed to writing."[18] Outstanding among numerous New England stories for their fidelity, the Oldtown sketches point toward Mrs. Stowe's alliance with the local colorists. Horace Holyoke, teller of the tales (modeled on Professor Stowe), endeavors to show his "gentle reader" New England "in its *seed bed*, before the hot suns of modern progress had developed its sprouting germs into the great trees of today." Characters, scenes, and incidents, all taken from an older New England, reflect the quiet but intensely individualistic life of a pretty little Massachusetts town as it existed in the ante-railroad times, when, says Holyoke, "our hard, rocky, sterile New England was a sort of Hebrew theocracy, half ultra-democratic republic of little villages." Originally an Indian village, Oldtown at this stage had its spired meeting house; its academy; its tavern whose tall and creaking signpost gave an easy invi-

[15] Boston, 1869.
[16] Full criticism of this and Mrs. Stowe's other local stories appears in Charles Edward Stowe and Lyman Beecher Stowe, *Harriet Beecher Stowe* (Boston and New York, 1911), chap. ix, "Delineator of New England Life and Character."
[17] *Ibid.*, p. 257.
[18] *Ibid.*, p. 258.

tation to the great barrels of beer in the taproom ; its dwellings
housing both dignitaries and common folk; and, finally, its
general store where everything was sold,

> . . . where the post-office was kept, and where was a general ex-
> change of news, as the different farm-wagons stood hitched around
> the door, and their owners spent a leisure moment in discussing
> politics or theology from the top of codfish or mackerel barrels,
> while their wives and daughters were shopping among the dress
> goods and ribbons, ...[19]

Mrs. Stowe's characters, familiar types in the fiction of the
period, in some instances are modeled on actual folk in Natick,
many of them kinspeople of the Stowes.   As in Hawthorne's
stories, most of the names are authentic.   Introduced, among
others, are such typical villagers as a miser and his harsh old
maid sister, Miss Asphyxia ; farmers and artisans ; academy
students ; the leading dignitary, the Reverend Mr. Lothrop,
"of good ministerial blood for generations back" ; his wife,
"formerly a widow of large property, from one of the most
aristocratic families in Boston" ; and, finally, the most unforgettable character in the village, shiftless, yet likeable Sam
Lawson, ne'er-do-well, gossiper, and jack-of-all-trades—when
he needed or wanted a trade.   In her sympathetically and
humorously drawn *Sam Lawson's Oldtown Fireside Stories* Mrs.
Stowe continues her portrayal of the bygone society of Oldtown.[20]   Expressed in Yankee talk, Sam's tales further suggest
the life of an old provincialized village, with its settled order
and its intimacy.   Here are the familiar protagonists of a whole
Yankee village world, people of the same stock, creed, and
education.   In the words of George Eliot, who found pleasure
in *Oldtown Folks*, both books picture "our old-fashioned provincial life, which has its affinities with contemporary life, even
all across the Atlantic."[21]

In the records of Litchfield, Connecticut, where her father,
Lyman Beecher, held a pastorate, Mrs. Stowe found the materials for her serial, *Poganuc People*.   The "Dolly" of the sketches
is Hattie Beecher, whose free and humorous reminiscences create Litchfield anew as Poganuc Centre, a small Puritan county

[19] *Oldtown Folks* (Boston, 1869), p. 2.
[20] Boston, 1872 ; reviewed in *The Atlantic Monthly*, XXIX, 365 (March, 1872).
[21] C. E. Stowe and L. B. Stowe, *op. cit.*, p. 261.

town on the Boston turnpike. Again, the old village life is
reproduced localized against the background of the parsonage, the Litchfield hills, woods, and the Bantum River.   A
simple existence it was, stirred occasionally by locally disturbing conflicts between the aristocratic and stanch Presbyterians
and the newer democratic Episcopal faction.

A pioneer realist in the delineation of the New England
community, Mrs. Stowe is significant for her varied records of
a rapidly obsolescent village life.   Whittier, himself an interpreter of simple folk, praised her as a village realist

> . . . whose vigorous pencil strokes
> Sketched into life her Oldtown Folks,
> Whose fireside stories grave or gay
> In quaint Sam Lawson's vagrant way,
> With old New England's flavor rife,
> Waifs from her rude idyllic life.[22]

Other pioneers in the post-war school of New England fiction
gave occasional sketches of the people and happenings in quiet
rural villages and county towns, the latter being "subject to
the annual incursions of lawyers and such 'thrilling incidents'
as arise from the location of a jail or a court-room within the
limits of any village."[23]

Among the once popular purpose novels of Mrs. Elizabeth
Stuart Phelps Ward (1844-1911) a later work, *Doctor Zay*
(1884), belongs to the fiction of the New England village.
Displaying her usual zeal for arguing a cause, Mrs. Ward
preaches here concerning a young woman's struggle between
the choice of marriage and her medical practice.   With a
lawyer-invalid imported from Beacon Street, the author develops a conventional romance against the background of a
Down East town, whose provinciality "impressed [Waldo
Yorke, the hero] as reminiscences of American novels he had
tried to read and failed at the end of the third chapter."[24]   In
Isaiah and Sarah Butterwell, who "put up visitors," Mrs. Ward
has created two memorable Yankee villagers whose expres-

---

[22] Horace E. Scudder, *The Complete Poetical Works of John Greenleaf Whittier* (Boston and New York, 1894), p. 238, "A Greeting," read at Mrs. Stowe's seventieth
birthday anniversary, June 14, 1882, at Newtonville, Mass.
[23] Rose Terry Cooke, "The Ring Fetter," *The Atlantic Monthly*, IV, 154 (Aug.,
1859).
[24] *Doctor Zay* (Boston and New York, 1899), p. 31.
7

sions of laconic wisdom are the most natural touches in an otherwise conventional romance.

The real pioneer of the New England school of realism was not Mrs. Stowe, who sentimentalized about the past, but a Connecticut villager of humble birth, Rose Terry (later Mrs. Cooke), recorder of New England farm and village life in its prime. Native of a small village near Hartford, Rose Terry (1827-92) after several years of teaching and domestic duties yielded to her literary aspirations. So successful was she in recording the commonplace lives of farm and village folk near her native Hartford that she became, during Lowell's editorship, the leading short story contributor to *The Atlantic Monthly*, for which she wrote thirty stories from the first issue in 1857 to that of June, 1891. It was, then, chiefly as a magazinist that she wrote of the New England town.

In spite of the tragic elements of farm and village life, the small communities of Mrs. Cooke's stories are frequently characterized by activity and youthful buoyancy, unlike the more somber atmosphere of Mrs. Freeman's small town studies. Mrs. Cooke wrote of a village life dominated by sewing societies, sleigh rides, huckleberryings, picnics, family reunions, and other rustic amusements. Sometimes a family feud enlivened a pleasantly humdrum existence, while large family gatherings, like that in "An Old-Fashioned Thanksgiving," afforded much merriment.[25] "Hopson's Choice," for example, describes a merry reunion of the Hopsons in such numbers that the village tavern had to be engaged for the accommodation of the extra guests.[26] In nearly all of Mrs. Cooke's villages (Hop Meadow, Pasco, Sandy Creek, and Westbury) young people, happy in their love affairs, often occupy the foreground, whether the scene be an agricultural village or a fishing town, as in "A Double Thanksgiving."[27]

Frequently, however, Mrs. Cooke shattered the then accepted tradition that a beautiful heroine was an essential to any story. Often the plainest and seemingly the most unromantic of women, usually old maids like Miss Lucinda, who "had a general idea that all men were liars, and that she must be on her guard against their propensity to cheat and annoy

---

[25] *Huckleberries Gathered from the New England Hills* (Boston and New York, 1891), "Grit," pp. 1 ff., and "An Old-Fashioned Thanksgiving," pp. 122 ff.
[26] *Ibid.*, p. 152.   [27] *Ibid.*, p. 227.

a lonely and helpless woman," are the central figures in little dramas of village life.[28]   Mrs. Cooke had few adherents in her reverence for old maids and her interest in plain folks.   Her sympathy for plain women is reflected in her portraits of kind, but eccentric Miss Todd, of that militant "old maid Celye Barnes," and of small, thin, twittering Amanda Hart, a sort of town mouse afraid of the country.[29]

Featuring people with scanty resources, these stories picture, however, not morose and dissatisfied types, but industrious villagers scornful of idleness and the Sam Lawsons in their midst.   With particular emphasis on commonplace activities, a new note at this time, Mrs. Cooke opens one story with an unadorned description of "the great kitchen, where Mrs. Griswold was paring apples and Lizzy straining squash."[30]   She is at her best in portraying older women, ordinary village types ever busy at some duty : village tailoresses, "pretty conside'able helpful" not only at sewing but in spreading better than a local gazette all the current gossip ; old maid schoolteachers ; philanthropic but distractingly outspoken old maids of "means," like "Miny"—short for Hermione—Todd, who dared reprimand village idlers and gossips ; and, finally, faithful daughters who lost their youth taking care of bedridden parents.   In many of these portrayals there is a vein of quiet humor, never a thing apart but closely blended with character and plot.   Especially humorous is Miss Lucinda Ann Manners, a sort of Puritan bluestocking, whose accomplishments isolate her from her less fortunate and more plebeian neighbors.   Her long years of solitude are broken by her acquisition of a pet pig, a ridiculously funny motivating agent in furthering Miss Lucinda's acquaintance with the town's dancing master.   Frequently dialect is humorously employed, as in a retired Yankee sailor's exciting report of the British march on Lexington and Concord.[31]

While her feminine portrayals are superior, Mrs. Cooke has realistically characterized a number of masculine types found in the average New England village of the time.   Mrs. Cooke heartily despised those men, who though unkind to their wives

[28] "Miss Lucinda," *The Atlantic Monthly*, VI, 144 (Aug., 1861).
[29] *Huckleberries, etc.*, pp. 85 ; 284 ; 316.
[30] "Lizzy Griswold's Thanksgiving," *The Atlantic Monthly*, III, 282 (March, 1859).
[31] "Sally Parson's Duty," *The Atlantic Monthly*, I, 31 (Nov., 1857).

and children and dishonest in their business transactions, were upheld by the town because they were "pillars of the church." Irascible and miserly Deacon Everts almost starved his "second," the erstwhile old maid Celye Barnes, even while he preached to her : "I don't mean to drive ye a mite, only, as Scripter says, 'Provoke one another to love and good works'."[32] There are frequent pictures of hypocritical village squires, regular in attendance at church and prayer meeting, but sly in sanding the sugar, watering the rum, and cheating their clerks and debtors. Deacon Flint, whom people regarded merely as a little "near," tricked his wife into signing her property away to him and then, half starving her, quoted Scripture about her "pomperin' " the flesh. When the poor woman, in despair, left home, the church sided with the deacon.[33] Alonzo Jakeway of "Clary's Trial" and Abner Dimock of "The Ring Fetter," the brutal sons of tavernkeepers, after leading questionable lives away from their native villages, return to continue their evil doings among their former townsmen.

In the small towns of this period the church played an important part in the lives of the people. Nonconformers, such as the loveless old maid, "Miny" Todd, who shocked pious Deacon Norton by emphatically refusing to attend weekly prayer-meetings, were considered doomed. Rebellious Celye Barnes even dared to call a narrow-minded minister a "great lummox." Other more pious and orthodox villagers not only quoted the Scriptures on all occasions, but burdened their children with long scriptural names. Fire and brimstone sermons were the rule. Mrs. Walker, for instance, wondered how far you could fetch hardened sinners "inter the kingdom, ef ye couldn't scare 'em out of their seven senses a-shakin' of 'em over the pit, as ye may say."[34]

A bolder realist than Mrs. Stowe, who dealt sentimentally with the more aristocratic social levels of the New England village, Mrs. Cooke sketched the small town with a quiet truth which pictures in detail all the common qualities and eccentricities of the Yankee. Produced while less gifted writers were publishing in *Godey's Lady's Book* and other periodicals

[32] *Huckleberries, etc.*, "How Celia Changed Her Mind," p. 292.
[33] "Mrs. Flint's Married Experience," *Harper's Magazine*, LXII, 79 (Dec., 1880). See also "Squire Paine's Conversion," *Harper's Magazine*, LVI, 608 (March, 1878).
[34] "Amandar," *Harper's Magazine*, LXI, 581 (Sept., 1880).

such trivialities as "Tales of Tattletown" and "The Foreign
Count," or "High Art in Tattletown,"[35]   Rose Terry Cooke's
pictures of the New England village are, except for occasional
conventional and romantic delineations, distinctively suggestive of the vigorous community life to be found in the region
of Hartford before the rapid changes of the war period and
the Gilded Age.

RECORDERS OF THE NEW ENGLAND DECLINE

Among the many new fields of localized backgrounds and
indigenous characters so assiduously exploited by the successors of Harriet Beecher Stowe and Rose Terry Cooke was the
economically changed New England village.   The New England of Oldtown and of Mrs. Cooke's Connecticut villages rapidly became one of tradition only.   The Golden Day was
passing, if not already gone, when in 1869 Alice E. Eliot, then
but nineteen, began sending stories to *The Atlantic Monthly*.[36]
This unknown girl was really Sarah Orne Jewett (1849-1909),
whose later *Atlantic* study, *Deephaven Cronies*—republished in
1877 by Houghton Mifflin as *Deephaven*—records her fictionalized impressions of a decaying harbor town, the once populous inland shipping center of South Berwick, Maine, her
birthplace.

Whereas Mrs. Stowe and Mrs. Cooke had delineated the
town in its pre-war provinciality and prosperity, Miss Jewett's
stories were the first to record the diminished glories of the old
order.   The earliest of a group of writers born in the fifties
and sixties, Miss Jewett wrote observingly of the decaying ports
and hillside agricultural towns of Maine and New Hampshire,
places she knew intimately from her habit of taking long drives
with her father and mentor, Theodore Hermann Jewett, a
country doctor whose practice took him along paths that led
from one farmhouse to another along the Maine coast near
Berwick.   This was the limited locale which Miss Jewett understood as well as Jane Austen knew her English countryside.
As a recent biographer has pointed out, Miss Jewett was
equipped at the beginning of her career with an environment

[35] Alexander Jessup, *Representative American Short Stories* (Boston, 1923), "A List
of Representative American Short Stories," II, 134 ff.
[36] F. O. Matthiessen, *Sarah Orne Jewett* (Boston and New York, 1929), p. 23.

rich in possibilities. What she needed was an exact angle from which to express herself. This she found in allowing "her recollections to rise slowly to consciousness and unfold" the older life of Berwick and other places she knew so well.[37]

Unlike Hamlin Garland, who viewed the expansion of the frontier town, Sarah Orne Jewett watched the decline of South Berwick, even in 1869 an interesting old town. One of "those decaying shipless harbors of Maine," it was the prototype of the Deephaven of her first published book. Inspired by the reading of *Oldtown Folks* and *The Pearl of Orr's Island*, young Sarah Jewett, aware even then of the sentimentality marking Mrs. Stowe's sketches, turned with renewed interest to the scenes of her own town and countryside. Material enough she found in decaying Berwick of her own time and in the legends and yarns heard from old townsmen, sailors, and ship-masters, among them her grandfather, who had seen the town in its prime and had participated actively in its business. These local chroniclers watched, as she did, the speedy vanishing of an old fashion of living as Civil War movements sapped the provincial village life of its former individual character. The early self-sufficiency of Berwick's citizens gradually weakened as the old families were crowded out by immigrants brought in to work in the near-by textile mills. Many of the more aristocratic Berwickians lived in the past, treasuring memories of that golden age when their town and their families had had their share "of those great houses full of handsome furniture, old silver, and beautiful women in French silks, which were, one suspects, not nearly so general in Colonial fact as they have become since in Colonial fiction."[38]

One of the keys to Miss Jewett's portrayal of the New England village is furnished in the following picture of the abandoned port of Deephaven which seemed more like

. . . one of the lazy little English seaside towns than any other. It was not in the least American. There was no excitement about anywhere; there were no manufactories; nobody seemed in the least hurry. . . . I do not know when a house or a new building had been built; the men were farmers, or went outwards in boats, or inwards in fish wagons, ... Sometimes a schooner came to

<hr/>

[37] *Ibid.*, p. 51.
[38] Charles Miner Thompson, "The Art of Miss Jewett," *The Atlantic Monthly*, XCIV, 485 (Oct., 1904).

one of the wharves to load hay or firewood ; but Deephaven used
to be a town of note, rich and busy, as its forsaken warehouses show.[39]

The last statement indicates Miss Jewett's aim of sympathetically picturing the transition from a glorious New England to
one of deserted farmsteads and decaying hamlets.   In this respect her sketches have been compared to Hawthorne's pictures of Salem's deserted wharves.

That Miss Jewett excelled in portraying backgrounds and
characters appears in her self-criticism written to Horace E.
Scudder, her earliest critic :   "It seems to me I can furnish
the theatre, and show you the actors, and the scenery, and the
audience, but there never is any play!"[40]   *Deephaven* well upholds this criticism.   At best, it is a series of descriptions rather
than a well-plotted novel.   In fact, the plot is practically submerged by the characterizations of the people and manners of
a deserted seaport, viewed by one long familiar with the causes
of its decline.   Because of its realism, tinged with slight idealization, *Deephaven* has been termed the American counterpart
of *Cranford*.   Frequent references are made to the town's illustrious past—to the days when there resided within its limits a
rich ship-owner and East India merchant, "whose fame and
magnificence were almost fabulous."   Older citizens proudly
recall the coaches kept by the five first families, the governor's
ball, and other regal entertainments at the great mansion.[41]
Even the lowliest fisherman is so proud of living in Deephaven
that he pities those unfortunates who must live elsewhere.
The Widow Moses, speaking of her misguided nephew, remarks, "I never could see what could 'a' sot him to leave so
many privileges and go way off to Lynn, with all them children too.   Why they lived here no more than a cable's length
from the meetin'-house!"[42]   But the Embargo of 1807 ruined
Deephaven, and since then a sand bar has been steadily filling
the harbor.   Now one got the impression that all the clocks
in Deephaven, and all the people with them, had stopped
years ago.   In spite of its unambitious progress and its utter
lack of modern bustle, Deephaven was not "a stupid, common

[39] *Deephaven* (Boston and New York, 1885), p. 98.   First edition published in
1877 by James R. Osgood & Co.
[40] Matthiessen, *op. cit.*, p. 45.
[41] *Deephaven*, pp. 68 and 69.
[42] *Ibid.*, p. 74.

country town," as an outsider once dared call it; instead, in its old houses one might find the best society, charming manners, and good breeding.[43]

Deephaven, then, was firmly rooted in the past. The house where Kate Lancaster and the narrator spent the summer was the old homestead of a departed relative whose spirit seemed to hang over the place. The conversation was mainly of former prosperity, for the past was more real than the present to the aristocratic villagers who proudly struggled to uphold the traditional dignity of their families. Old sea captains, long since retired from active service, retold the adventures of their youth. Empty wharves and warehouses stood near to remind them of their former commercial activity. The decaying warehouses, the decrepit, though talkative, sailors, the ancient homes standing as memorials to respected families—all these bound the villagers to the past.

Though of the gentry, Miss Jewett wrote many stories about ordinary village and country people, the plain folk she knew from her drives and visits throughout the countryside. One often finds people of quality familiarly mingling with others, but tacitly recognized as socially superior. Representative of Miss Jewett's interpretations of New England village characters, both of the old families (the hereditary aristocracy) and the plainer folks, are the simple stories in *Tales of New England*.[44] As in her other tales, Miss Jewett here depicts only the finer side of New England community life. In fact, from her second *Atlantic* story, "The Shore House," featuring the village background, to her last work in the 1890's Miss Jewett's works are marked by a fineness of style foreign to certain modes of the Gilded Age in which she lived. While her stories, with their roots in the romantic past of old New England towns, reveal the changing life within their limits, they are unsoiled by the corruption of the blatant America of the Tweed and Whiskey Rings, railroad inflation, the 1873 depression, the greed of the "money pirates," and the extravagant, but crude, tastes of the Dreadful Decade. She has chosen, instead, a phase of nineteenth-century life which possesses quietness, pa-

---

[43] *Ibid.*, p. 84.
[44] First published by Houghton, Osgood & Co., 1879; the edition here used appeared in 1894.

tience, self-reliance, and culture behind its privations.   None of the meanness of life appears in her stories.

Fully aware of the pathos of the life she depicts, Miss Jewett frequently enlivens her style with touches of humor.   "The Dulham Ladies" is a diverting account of two old maids, Miss Dobin and Miss Lucinda Dobin, so proud of their aristocratic Boston forbears that they "looked on with increasing dismay at the retrogression in society" in their native Dulham.   The "ladies" regarded less fortunately born neighbors as "a noisy, irreverent mob, an increasing band of marauders who would overthrow all landmarks of the past, all etiquette, and social rank."[45]   In "Miss Tempy's Watchers" dry, shrewd, quick-witted New England villagers are realistically sketched as they hold a wake over a neighbor's body.[46]   Showing the influence of the westward exodus on the short story, "A Native of Winby" treats of the familiar theme of a rich man's return to his native village.[47]

Not only these stories, with their homely but genuine village characters, but others also brought Miss Jewett the name of "a new realist with a camera and a fountain pen."[48]   All of these studies are characterized by the spirit of truth, but none by a finer achievement of the artistic than her most beautifully written collection, *The Country of the Pointed Firs*.   In its structure similar to that of *Deephaven*, this more mature work is a series of sketches—not short stories in the true sense of the form—of the inhabitants of Dunnet, one of the many maritime villages of eastern Maine, a coast town where the "houses made the most of their seaward view, and [where] there was a gayety and determined floweriness in their bits of garden ground ; the small-paned windows in the peaks of their steep gables were like knowing eyes that watched the harbor and the far sea-line beyond, or looked northward all along the shore and its background of spruces and balsam firs."[49]   As in *Deephaven*, the viewpoint is

---

[45] *Ibid.*, p. 37.

[46] *Ibid.*, pp. 77 ff.   "An Only Son," "Marsh Rosmary," and "A Lost Lady," all from *Tales of New England*, present pictures of village life in New England.

[47] *The Atlantic Monthly*, LXVII, 609 (May, 1891) ; in book form in *A Native of Winby, and Other Tales* (Boston and New York, 1893).

[48] Pattee, *American Literature since 1870*, p. 235.

[49] *The Country of the Pointed Firs* (Boston and New York, 1927), p. 1.   First published in 1896 and later in 1925, with a preface by Willa Cather, in *The Best Stories of Sarah Orne Jewett* (Boston and New York, 1925).

that of a summer visitor, who, charmed by its simple people
and quietness of life, returns season after season to this remote
fishing village. From her hostess, Almira Todd, widow and
local herb dealer, the narrator learns all the community history : the curious story of young Joanna whose disappointment
in love transformed her into a recluse ; the love affair of "Al-
miry's" shy brother William, a silent farmer-fisherman ; the
early adventures of Captain Littlepage, now the village oracle ;
and other tales of simple contentment and sorrow.

In these stories and others from additional collections Miss
Jewett tells of an old-time village and farm life which, during
the Gilded Age, was on the decline, a life she viewed in its
milder moods without the sordidness, bleakness, and meanness
of spirit which undoubtedly existed, as her successors show.[50]
A village chronicler, she records with loving care and sympathetic insight into the lives of ordinary New England people
scenes from an idyllic past.   Both a deliberate artist and a
Brahmin, the intimate friend of Mrs. Fields, Aldrich, Howells,
and others of the aristocracy of literature, she held aloof from
the more material and industrialized life of the seventies and
later.   She had, in fact, a quiet scorn for the Irish and French-
Canadian invaders of the jerry-built mill centers near Berwick ;
and, feeling thus, "she clung the more tenaciously to the land
of her memories, where the gentry ruled, where the plain people
respected themselves and their betters, and where vulgar display was unknown."[51]   The "cheap streak" of American life
she abhorred and, in her sketches, ignored.

While Miss Jewett, with her love for the old homogeneous
society, was ignoring the new type of New England townsman
rising in the shadows of the mills, younger and more democratic
realists, alive to the changing times, began in the eighties their
portrayals of later phases of the New England decline.   Among
the most critical delineators of this narrow, and often unlovely,
world was Mary E. Wilkins, later Mrs. Freeman (1852-1930),
who saw in her New England townspeople all the grim and
stark loneliness developed from long years of Puritan repression.   Unlike Miss Jewett, she was not a transitional figure,
but a representative of the literature of unromantic actualities.
Further, she was not a Brahmin.   Hers was a lonely childhood

[50] For a complete bibliography see Matthiessen, *op. cit.*, pp. 153 ff.
[51] Parrington, *The Beginnings of Critical Realism in America*, p. 65.

spent in the narrow environment of Randolph, Massachusetts, and Battleboro, Vermont. These formative years of almost Hawthornesque isolation, spent in a provincial world, prepared Mary Wilkins from the first for her later unromanticized portrayals of the New England town. Living in the warping atmosphere of inherited Puritanism that had lost its earlier vitality, the girl was a part of a social group inbred for generations and narrowly restricted to neighborhood limits.[52]

It has been said that there are two periods in the life of a country when the short story is adapted to the best interpretation of the people : when the country is virgin soil for the novelist and when the soil, in agricultural phase, is worn out.[53] It was this second phase, so early brought to her attention, which later gave Miss Wilkins opportunity to individualize, to discriminate, and to disclose distinctions previously overlooked by village interpreters. The New England of her girlhood was socially impoverished by the Civil War, migrations beyond the Mississippi, and the call of the city. Its small towns and villages were peopled by the conservative, the old, and the helpless, whose lives were deeply marked by a round of petty duties. The best elements had disappeared. In a period of tumultous unrest in the world outside, this village life was a humdrum existence broken by few incidents more exciting than the arrival of the daily stage. As a contemporary correspondent to "The Contributors' Club" of *The Atlantic Monthly* wrote, "though probably no village exists in New England where there are literally no young people, yet in many there are so few left at home as to make life pretty forlorn."[54] Such is the social system reproduced in *A Humble Romance and Other Stories* (1887), *A New England Nun and Other Stories* (1891), *Jane Field* (1893), *Pembroke* (1894), and other works. Influenced by the local color fiction of the eighties, Mrs. Freeman presents in these and other stories uncompromising studies of the outward life and thoughts of provincial New Englanders. Using a severe style delineative of the most intimate details, she writes of their ordinary affairs, their eating and drinking, their simple social activities, their belief and thoughts, both of love and hate, and their local speech.

[52] Pattee, *op. cit.*, p. 236.
[53] Anon., "New England in the Short Story," *The Atlantic Monthly*, LXVII, 845-850 (June, 1891).
[54] "The Village Question," XLIV, 547 (Oct., 1879).

Though the New England village had seemingly been exhausted as material for fiction, Mrs. Freeman, disregarding the free usage of community themes by her immediate predecessors, attempted to bring this life to a new focus : to seek out "that terminal moraine of human specimens which the New England glacial period of puritanism had left in its wake. . . ."[55] Abnormal, narrow characters, the product of too frugal living ; prim and unlovely old maids, romantic at heart ; poorhouse inmates with their pitiful pretensions ; work-worn wives and stubborn husbands ; jobless factory workers ; itinerant preachers ; and even joyless and repressed children—these unfortunates people Mrs. Freeman's hillside farms and provincial villages.   Comparable to certain citizens of Spoon River, many of these villagers lead bleak and lonely lives.   The attributes frequently found among these provincials are the results of decayed Puritanism : abnormal conscience, selfishness, and allegiance to scriptural teachings in their narrowest interpretations.   "Though her characters do not brood much upon the mysteries of sin and death, . . . the pattern of existence into which they are born has been warped and twisted by all the intense introspection of their ancestors."[56]   Here are presented, with unflinching directness of style, many types of country town people, their cadences of speech, their pleasure-starved lives, and their occasional flares of revolt from an exacting social order.

Mrs. Freeman's characters frequently are retarded in their growth by the harsh environment in which they have been placed.   In her small towns poverty and physical suffering often move people to queer actions.   The *leitmotiv* of her first novel, *Jane Field* (1892), emphasizes the mental struggle occasioned by a woman's fear of ill health and the poorhouse.[57] Impoverished and rheumatic Mrs. Jane Field, "an old New England woman, all of whose traditions were purely orthodox," poses as her dead sister that she might inherit money for Lois, her consumptive daughter.   The narrow environing world of two New England villages is presented uncompromisingly in the portraits of stoical Jane Field, the gossipmonger, Mrs. Bab-

---

[55] Pattee, *Side-Lights on American Literature*, p. 184.
[56] Matthiessen, "New England Stories," in John Macy, *op. cit.*, p. 405.
[57] First published in *Harper's Magazine*, LXXXIV (May, 1892)—LXXXV (Nov., 1892) with Howells's *The World of Chance;* excellent pictorial illustrations of village scenes and characters.

cock, and spinster Amanda Pratt.   Likewise *Pembroke* (1894), her second novel, is a study of petty and tragic lives bound by the unending struggle of a narrow daily existence.   Domineering husbands and fathers, long-suffering wives and hapless spinsters, diffident middle-aged suitors, young people inhibited by a strict social code and publicly ostracized for any deviation therefrom, usurious shopkeepers, and other similar types people the village of Pembroke.   The very names of the characters— Caleb, Barnabas, Deborah, and Rebecca—reflect the Calvinistic heritage of these simple, yet tragic, village folk.   Furthermore, in her earliest short stories Mrs. Freeman dwells on the utter futility and the poverty of life in the restricted confines of small towns.   According to the custom of the times, one impoverished, but proud, spinster earned a precarious living by odd bits of work.   After sewing for two weeks on quilts for wealthier townsmen, she found that she had mixed their scraps. Weary and discouraged, she had no peace until she had ripped the quilts apart and repieced the entire pattern.   Only after completing her task did she find that her first assortment had been correct.   Painstakingly she remade the quilts, but in the end fainted for want of food and rest.   Afraid of dying, the poor old woman said, "I wonder ef I'm prepared."[58]   Numerous other delineations tell of similar struggles with poverty or worse difficulties: a pathetic old man, a village Lear, is spurned by his own daughters; Louisa Ellis, the New England nun, sacrifices love for a life of isolation; and a crippled pauper in a village almhouse improvises an imaginary Sister Liddy to brighten her beauty-starved existence.[59]

Such villagers are bound by a rigidly dogmatic moral code. Stern and unrelenting in their own unspotted righteousness, village puritans condemn those who revolt from convention, a frequently recurring theme in Mrs. Freeman's stories.   Even among the spiritually elect prying and gossiping seem more prevalent in these towns than in most small communities, for puritanic consciences banned any amusements more worldly than sewing circles and afternoon teas.   In "Calla-Lilies and Hannah," for example, certain self-righteous villagers felt justified in calumniating the good name of a girl whom they judged

[58] "An Honest Soul" in *A Humble Romance, etc.* (New York, 1899), p. 78; 1st ed., 1887.
[59] *A New England Nun, etc.* (New York, 1891), pp. 1; 81; and 268.

falsely.[60]   The judgment of a choir upon its old maid soprano
is the theme of "A Village Singer."   To this obscure woman,
"kept relentlessly by circumstances in a narrow task, singing
in the village choir had been as much as Italy was to Napoleon.
. . ."[61]   In another village a remnant of early New England
witchcraft is shown in the popular sentiment against a "love-
cracked" peddler of holiday decorations.[62]   In still another
community a provincial congregation is scandalized at the
failure of the widow and daughter of Richard Stone to wear
mourning attire at his funeral.[63]   The gossips fairly buzz.   One
realistic story of small town church rivalry dramatizes an eccentric church member who holds to his vow that until the
present pastor resigns he intends remaining on the church
steps every Sunday.   Relentless wrestling of the mind against
the forces of evil, another favorite theme of Mrs. Freeman,
appears rather humorously in "A New England Prophet,"
wherein an entire village, aroused by the frenzied pronounce-
ments of a local Millerite, prepare through frantic conversions
for the immediate end of the world.[64]

The same dogmatic spirit of the shorter stories finds more
elaborate portrayal in *Madelon: A Novel*, picturing that "black
atmosphere of suspicion and hatred which gathers nowhere
more easily than in a New England town."[65]   Melodramati-
cally motivated, *Madelon*, nevertheless, presents the minutiae
of life in a sheltered nineteenth-century town where even the
slightest incident is enough "to afford a choice bone of gossip
to folk sunken in the monotony and isolation of a Vermont
country village."[66]   Many well-known village types and scenes
in Mrs. Freeman's short stories reappear here : tavern groups ;
gossiping bees ; inquisitive folk who watch eagerly all passengers on the Boston-bound coaches ; courtships, dances, weddings ; and countless other familiar village characters and
scenes.   The episode here used of a girl's public refusal to
marry her fiancé on the occasion of the gathering of the townspeople in her father's parsonage for the wedding is employed

[60] *Ibid.*, p. 99.
[61] *Ibid.*, p. 160.
[62] *Ibid.*, p. 30.
[63] "One Good Time," *Harper's Magazine*, XCIV, 309 (Jan., 1897).
[64] *A Humble Romance*, "A Conflict Ended," p. 383 ; and H. W. Lanier, ed., *The Best Stories of Mary E. Wilkins* (New York, 1927), p. 120.
[65] New York, 1896, p. 334.
[66] *Ibid.*, p. 173.

also, in a slightly different fashion, as the central and gossip-provoking scene in "A Conquest of Humility," one of the stories in *A Humble Romance*. In Ware Centre (the village in *Madelon*) lovers are closely beset by spies on every hand. Men in their lounging places in store and tavern and women at their quilting bees "put their heads together" over the choicest gossip. The whole novel, in short, is a satiric exposure of small town littleness.

Mrs. Freeman's little dramas of the village add to the literary history of the American town not only scores of odd provincial types but a variety of town backgrounds. Up-country communities, villages and decaying towns in secluded and hilly districts; bustling trade and county fair centers; small academy towns, with long-established families directing local society; seashore villages and farm hamlets; and, finally, the recurring background of the factory town, then becoming a common enough sight to Mrs. Freeman and her contemporaries—these suggest the wide variety of small town locales with which Mrs. Freeman has enriched the fiction of the American community. The latter, indicative of the decline of the older Sweet Auburns, serves as the background of the novel, *Jerome: A Poor Man*, an interpretation of New England and rural life in the late nineteenth century when the citizens of two small villages on one of the stagecoach lines into Boston were excited about the rumors of factory and railroad buildings in their communities. The prospect brought forth new talk and speculation from the group at Cyrus Robinson's store, "the nursery of the town, the place where her little commonweal was evolved and nurtured." In one of the most realistic descriptions of the novel Mrs. Freeman shows that this store, heaped high with all the paraphernalia of a New England village, was in a sense the nucleus of the community, the judgment seat of the two villages where "simple citizens formed their simple opinions upon town government and town officials, upon whom they afterwards acted in town meeting." Here local wise men "sat in judgment upon all men who were not within reach of their voices, and upon all crying evils of the time which were too mighty for them to struggle against."[67]

[67] *Jerome: A Poor Man* (New York, 1897), pp. 40-41. The authenticity of Mrs. Freeman's descriptions is substantiated by contemporary town sketches, excellently illustrated, such as Anna C. Brackett, "The Aryan Mark: A New England Town

A small town trade center before the era of industrialism, Robinson's store, with its location near superior water advantages, was in a limited sense a factory. Cyrus not only had interest in a grist-mill and a saw-mill, but, purchasing leather in considerable quantities, he employed local workmen in a great room above the store to cut out rude shoes worn in the countryside. Moreover, the shrewd storekeeper had in his house adjoining the store several spare rooms for the lodging of strangers. Industry is used thematically in occasional short stories, as "Two Old Lovers" with its picture of the transformation of a village into a full-fledged factory town.[68] Factory troubles and unemployment in a small manufacturing town motivate the plot of "The Last Gift." A later novel, *A Portion of Labor*, is a rambling story based upon the problems of capital and labor.[69] A provincial New England factory town is the background for successive portrayals of workers and their underfed families, strikes, and a thinly plotted love affair between a capitalist and one of the girls working in his factory.

Mrs. Freeman's later stories and longer works are replete with varied, though often commonplace and sentimental, pictures of town life in different locales. Most of these show that she is at her best in her small field of the New England town and rural community whose social systems she knew and expressed in artistically simple, yet highly interpretative, sketches of Yankee life. *The People of Our Neighborhood*, for example, lacks the realistic quality of her earlier stories. Suggestive of the seventeenth-century character writings, these sketches indicate that there are more virtues than vices in the neighborhood.[70] Villagers characterized as "the village oracle," "the neat woman," "the good woman," and "the friend of cats," all stereotyped figures, appealed, one supposes, to the *Ladies' Home Journal* readers of the nineties. In another later collection, *Edgewater People* (1918), established village families control community society. Illustrative further of the lack of

---

Meeting," *Harper's Magazine*, LXXXV, 577-585 (Sept., 1892) and Alice Morse Earle, "The New England Meeting House," *The Atlantic Monthly*, LXVII, 191-194 (Feb., 1891). See also the latter's *Stage Coach and Tavern Days, etc.*, *passim*.
    [68] *A Humble Romance, etc.*, p. 25.
    [69] New York, 1901.
    [70] In the *Ladies' Home Journal Library of Fiction*, with Garland's *The Spirit of Sweetwater* (Philadelphia, 1895, '96, '97, and '98).

positive virtues among her later town delineations is the in-
effective picturing of a New Jersey village and a New England
academy town in the novel, *By the Light of the Soul* (1907). As
a depicter of the small town Mrs. Freeman will be remembered
longest for her austere and distinctive pictures of decaying centers of Puritanism, those little upcountry places she knew in
her youth.

Miss Jewett and Mrs. Freeman were by no means the only
recorders of the New England village during and after the
Gilded Age. The last phase of this group's work finds vivid
representation in the community sketches of Alice Brown
(1857-   ), whose literary recognition came so late that she
really felt the influences of the turn of the century. Like her
predecessors, Miss Brown is by birth, education in a New
Hampshire "female seminary," and early work as a teacher
a true New Englander, familiar with the life of New Hampshire
villages and towns. A farmer's daughter, Alice Brown resembled Sarah Jewett in her intimate knowledge of the countryside.   Later, however, when first she adapted herself to Boston life she lost some of her provincial New Englandism and
from afar viewed her native towns and their simple inhabitants
with the glamor of childhood.   Her stories of village life, therefore, are realistic but with the additions of a romantic richness
foreign to the staccato expressions of Mrs. Freeman.   If more
closely akin to Miss Jewett in her more ornate and poetic prose,
Miss Brown uses the village subject matter similar to that of
Mrs. Freeman's earlier stories.

While Miss Brown has written New England village stories
which are true to actual conditions, her contribution to this
field has been meagre in contrast to the fuller work of her
feminine predecessors. In her best early village portrayals,
Meadow Grass (1895) and *Tiverton Tales* (1899), she neither ex-
plores new territory nor adds new village types or themes.
Picturing the village with less austerity than Mrs. Freeman,
she, nevertheless, develops kindred themes : the reaction of villagers toward summer boarders from the city, the meeting of
old lovers long separated, and the blight which has fallen upon
almost manless villages.   Delineative of the repression of certain New England village types, Miss Brown's stories at the
same time portray humble life with more humor than pathos.
Her villagers do not labor under the fear of mortgage fore-
8

closure; nor are their conscientious scruples those of Mrs. Freeman's eccentric and morbid townspeople.

Her best stories center around the isolated villages of Tiverton and Sudleigh, the use of one locality for both *Meadow Grass* and *Tiverton Tales* furnishing unity for a variety of separate sketches presenting dissimilar types of Tivertonians and rival Sudleighans. Against a background of woodland, mountain, and meadow she has projected both humorous and serious village people. Similar materials appear in her *Country Neighbors* (1910) and *Bromley Neighborhood* (1915). Maturing through the years with various experiments in fiction, Alice Brown has never discarded these small town materials. Her matured, deepened insight into the lives of common folk is well illustrated in her novel, *Jeremy Hamlin* (1934), a return to community problems in the dramatic story of an enigmatic dictator of a small New England town.

The school of up-country fictionalists, given to writing of quiet villages and decaying towns, had other exponents in addition to the able delineators already presented. Others, less significant, wrote retrospectively in story and sketch of old towns and customs which were not wholly gone even at the turn of the century. Lacking the vigor and sustained individuality of the major interpreters, a few of these, nevertheless, revealed in their stories the essence of New Englandism. Harriet Prescott Spofford, born (1853) in Calais, Maine, and educated in Derry Village (Londonderry), New Hampshire, gained a certain popularity through contributions to *The Atlantic Monthly* and other magazines and through collections like *The Amber Gods and Other Stories* (1863), all stories reflecting the strife between romance and realism characterizing so large a part of her work. From *The Amber Gods* a few stories ("Circumstance," "Knitting Sale-Socks," and "The South Breaker") "were inspired directly by the familiar New England life she knew in family tradition and in actuality."[71] These and a group of realistic stories—collected in 1920 as *The Elder's People*—picturing the monotonous days in small New England communities place Harriet Prescott Spofford in that circle of nineteenth-century women who wrote understandingly of the everyday affairs and crises in the lives of humble people. Mrs. Annie Trumbull Slosson's Connecticut dialect stories, like

[71] Elizabeth K. Halbeisen, *Harriet Prescott Spofford* (Philadelphia, 1935), p. 76.

Seven Dreamers (1891) and *The Heresy of Mehetabel Clark* (1892), were built around certain grotesque elements of New England life.   In *Davis Folks* (1894) and *Uncle 'Lisha's Shop* (1897) Rowland E. Robinson described the manners and employed the dialect of Vermont.[72]   During this period scores of now forgotten delineators, satisfying popular demand, but adding nothing to the permanent literature of the New England village, overloaded their stories with unsubstantial plots and unoriginal provincial characters.   Thus the New England village literature strengthened by Mrs. Stowe and her able successors dwindled away into transparent plots of village social complications, tragedies, and glorified love stories.[73]

Mention should be made here of Margaret Deland's Pennsylvania village locale, a sort of literary outpost of the New England scene as pictured by Mrs. Stowe and her "female coterie."   At the turn of the century Mrs. Deland's Old Chester was as familiar to readers as Cranford had been earlier. She did for Pennsylvania what Sarah Jewett did for the towns of New England.   She created a small town distinguished from the democratic, all-leveling industrial communities in its neighborhood by its aristocracy of birth, its family pride.   In her novel, *John Ward, Preacher* (1888), and her collections, *Old Chester Tales* (1898), *Dr. Lavender's People* (1903), *Around Old Chester* (1915), and *New Friends in Old Chester* (1924), Mrs. Deland has depicted small towns where ancestry counted for much.   Within her limited provincial area she has written of the village not only in ordinary terms, but also from the standpoint of the less tangible materials of life, the problems of the soul.

Old Chester is the literary counterpart of Manchester, now a part of Pittsburgh but in 1857 a small town where on the twenty-third of February Margaretta Wade Campbell was born. The Upper Chester of the stories corresponds to the industrial town of Allegheny.   Old Chester, like the quiet villages of many New England stories, was a place of traditions, a town peopled by cultured English, Scotch, and Irish families with deep religious prejudices, yet wholesome and kindly ideals.   Self-satisfied,

---

[72] T. Stanton, *A Manual of American Literature* (New York, 1909), p. 228.
[73] Examples of stereotyped plots and characters may be found in Harriet W. Preston's *Is That All?* (1877), Margaret Louise Wood's *A Village Tragedy* (n.d.), and P. Orne's *A Love Story* (1885).   Augusta Larned's *Village Photographs*, however, is a more realistic study of neighborhood relationships.

Old Chester, like Deephaven, "looked down upon the outside world. Not unkindly, . . . but pityingly; and it pursued its contented way, without restlessness, and without aspirations."[74] Here, indeed, was the genteel tradition of New England transplanted to new soil.

The different sketches of the short story collections compose into a single picture, for all the action revolves around Dr. Lavender, venerable rector of Old Chester parish. This beloved latitudinarian, like Dr. Primrose, counsels and reprimands all of the villagers: delicate Miss Maria Wellwood; Oscar King, who lived away from Old Chester "in foreign parts; and no one knows what has gone on;" and numerous others. In her later sketches, as in Masters's *The New Spoon River*, Mrs. Deland has shown that even in a settled community like Old Chester new people appear to take the places occupied by the old.

Closely resembling Mrs. Humphrey Ward's *Robert Elsmere* (1888), *John Ward, Preacher* was a stirring polemical novel of the late eighties. The chief figures, martyrs to their puritanic loyalty to conviction, live, ironically enough, in a secluded Pennsylvania village, which, like Old Chester, rather prided itself on having an atmosphere of leisure and repose.[75] Orthodox John Ward, a young Presbyterian minister, preaches of hell and damnation in the Calvinistic manner. Rather than accept this stern view of the after life, John's wife leaves her home, and their mutual happiness is destroyed.

Such writers as Mrs. Deland and her New England contemporaries have delineated variously a type of small town life now remote, even in thought, from the activities of most modern townspeople. With the progress of the twentieth century the old-fashioned New England village, deeply rooted in the past, has been changed, in actuality and fiction, by a new town order. The Wineburgs, Spoon Rivers, Gopher Prairies, and Oklahoma Towns, with their modern improvements, are more familiar today. "But the value of Sarah Orne Jewett and Mary E. Wilkins is greater than that of simply providing a link with the past. They not only reported life; each of them created, if not a world, at least a countryside of her own,

---

[74] *Old Chester Tales* (New York, 1899), pp. 1-2.
[75] *John Ward, Preacher* (Boston, 1888), p. 1. Compare with Mrs. Humphrey Ward's *Robert Elsmere* (London, 1888).

the permanent endurance of which has enriched the American soil."[76]   In their little towns, even in the stage of their decline, there was truly "soil for the deepest root."

[76] Matthiessen, "New England Stories," p. 413.

CHAPTER IV

THE TOWN, THE BRAHMINS, AND OTHERS

THOUGH MAINLY delineated through fiction, the New England small town, in notable exceptions, has been described in essay and journal. Two historic places, one a village and the other a college town, long the center of the "aristocracy of the intellect," find realistic and sympathetic portrayal in the records of such citizens as Emerson, Thoreau, Lowell, and Higginson. Truly, their rich literary associations with both places have made Concord and Cambridge unique in the annals of the American town.

EMERSON AND CONCORD

In the literary history of the smaller American community few other little towns have contributed so much, both directly and indirectly, to the developing pattern of American life as Concord on the Musketaquid. Exceptionally rich in historical and literary associations Concord today is still a small New England town with a clearly defined tradition. Special communities, as the university center of Chapel Hill in North Carolina or the art colony at picturesque Taos among the mountains of New Mexico, have their particular attractions; but Concord is unique in the richness of its earlier historical and its later literary backgrounds. Even today, long after the period of its greatest contribution to the national life, Concord attracts visitors for no other reason than its intrinsically interesting past. The Revolutionary tavern and ancient dwellings, the monuments, the village common, the homes of its later celebrities—Hawthorne, Emerson, and Alcott—the now deserted, but once talked of School of Philosophy, Thoreau's cairn near "Walden Wave," Sleepy Hollow Cemetery, the quaint meeting-houses, and modern Antiquarian House now containing Emerson's library and Thoreau's possessions invite the stranger to think of the town's past.

It was in this place of rural quiet and personal associations that Ralph Waldo Emerson, lately returned from Europe, established himself as a householder when he was thirty-one.

A pleasant place it was with a wealth of rural scenery.   Its natural beauty, its pleasant connections with the history of the Bulkeleys and the Emersons, and its nearness to Boston made Concord admirably suited to the tastes of its newest citizen. Emerson himself a few months later, after diligent research among the Town Records, praised the town of his choice as worthy of the name it wore.   "I find," he noted, "our annals marked with a uniform good sense.   I find no ridiculous laws, no eavesdropping legislators, no hanging of witches, no ghosts, no whipping of Quakers, no unnatural crimes."[1]

In 1835 after his marriage to Lydia Jackson of Plymouth, Emerson moved from the Old Manse, where in his boyhood he had lived with his grandfather, to the Cambridge Turnpike house, an ample dwelling with a large garden space added later.   Here in this peaceful town of early memories and congenial surroundings Emerson soon took his place as a highly respected citizen.   If one may accept the bucolic picture drawn by Emerson's Socratic neighbor, Amos Bronson Alcott, the Concord of this time might well serve as a prototype of Zona Gale's Friendship Village.   To idealistic Alcott the village was nothing short of a

> Calm vale of comfort, peace, and industry,
>
> .   .   .   .   .
>
> Considerate people, neighborly and free,
> Proud of their monuments, their ancestry,
> Their circling river's quiet loveliness,
> Their noble townsman's fame and history.[2]

Emerson's own *Journals*, his numerous public addresses, and the accounts of his contemporaries, including the records of Thoreau and Alcott, point to the poet's friendly, but dignified, association with the descendants of the early Bulkeleys, Hunts, Hosmers, and others of local prominence.   Among the other Concordians whose lives were intimately bound with Emerson's were his beloved younger brother, Charles Chauncey; Elizabeth Hoar, daughter of Judge Hoar and Charles's fiancée; Henry Thoreau, Harvard graduate and individualist; and Ellery Channing with whom Emerson enjoyed long rambles

---

[1] *Miscellanies*, Vol. XI in the *Complete Works of Ralph Waldo Emerson* (New York, 1903-1904), p. 83.
[2] F. B. Sanborn and W. T. Harris, *Memoirs of A. Bronson Alcott* (Boston, 1893), I, 305.   Alcott wrote his poem when he was eighty-two.

through the near-by woods.   During the many years of Emerson's life in Concord these and innumerable other friends,
chance acquaintances, and visiting celebrities found entertainment in the Turnpike home.

As Van Wyck Brooks expressed it, "Everything in Concord
sang to him."[3] The spirit of the place appealed to his poetic
nature.   The old families, the busy turnpike, the adjacent
woods and fields, meadows and ponds, the mountains in the
distance, the village itself, with its historic common, the Old
Manse, the little rivers, and the "rude bridge" were all of
lasting interest to Emerson.   "If city bred," Alcott once wrote
of Emerson, "he has been for the best part of his life a villager
and countryman.   Only a traveller at times professionally, he
prefers home-keeping ; is a student of the landscape, of mankind, of rugged strength wherever found ; liking plain persons,
plain.ways, plain clothes ; prefers earnest people ; shuns ego-
tists, publicity ; . . . ."[4]

Though, as Emerson wrote,

> Not many men see beauty in the fogs
> Of close, low pine-woods in a river town,

during the 1840's a remarkable group gathered from time to
time in this pleasant place by two rivers.   To be specific,

It was in the year 1845 that a circle of persons of various ages,
and differing very much in everything but sympathies, found themselves in Concord.   Toward the end of the autumn Mr. Emerson
suggested that they should meet every Monday evening through
the winter in his library.   Hawthorne, who then occupied the Old
Manse ; the inflexible Henry Thoreau, . . . then living among the
blackberry-pastures of Walden Pond ; Alcott, then sublimely meditating impossible summer houses in a little house on the Boston
road ; George Bradford, an enthusiastic agriculturist and Brook
Farmer, then an inmate of Mr. Emerson's house, . . . ; a sturdy
farmer-neighbor (Edmund Hosmer), . . . ; two city youths, George
and Burrill Curtis . . . ; and the host himself composed the club.[5]

Thus did George Curtis view his fellow-members of the Symposium and reveal the dignity with which these village intellectuals of the forties delved into the philosophies of Plato and

[3] *Emerson and Others* (New York, 1927), p. 4.
[4] *Concord Days* (Boston, 1888), p. 33.
[5] Sanborn and Harris, *op. cit.*, II, 430.

the Neo-Platonists and argued the problems of their own time.

The minutiae of the life at Concord stand revealed in the many entries about the town in the journals of both Emerson and Thoreau. Emerson not only enjoyed the Symposium evenings, but welcomed the opportunities of observing and conversing with his less intellectual fellow-citizens as he met them casually at the grocery stores, the post-office, the court-house, or the village gossip center, the Mill-Dam mentioned in *Walden*. True, the gossips probably suppressed their raciest stories at the approach of their tall and dignified neighbor, but, nevertheless, Emerson was not averse to meeting here, or on his frequent rambles about the town, citizens and neighboring farmers from whose homely philosophy he often drew inspiration. With his neighbor, Sam Staples, in turn, hostler, bar-keeper, constable, deputy sheriff, jailor, auctioneer, and real estate agent ; Edmund Hosmer, the farmer already mentioned ; and Abel Moore, a farmer-musician, he enjoyed frequent chats. Edward Emerson has written of his father's pleasure in talk-ing with horsemen and stage-drivers, whose "racy vernacular and picturesque brag [he enjoyed] as much as the cautious understatement of the farmer."[6] Unable himself to perform expertly various forms of manual labor, Emerson, nevertheless, admired active people. The fishermen, woodchoppers, and cattle drivers whom he encountered on his country walks ; Napoleon ; and even the Irish kitchen maid, in his own house-hold, who could manage an intractable calf—these he admired for their amazing energy. And yet, small town citizen that he was, Emerson, according to Thoreau, had difficulties with the simple tasks of gardening. "I doubt," reports Thoreau, "if Emerson could trundle a wheelbarrow through the streets, because it would be out of character."[7]

Emerson's pride in the ways of the village were strong. His early alliance with the worthier activities of the township proves him no recluse. In addition to his personal writings and his editorial work for *The Dial*, Emerson earnestly tried to respond to the demands made of him from the time of his appointment as village hog-reeve to his speech at the opening of the Concord Free Library in 1873. He attended town meetings and lis-tened to animated discussions about the building of the Fitch-

[6] *Emerson in Concord* (Boston and New York, 1890), p. 98.
[7] Odell Shepard, ed., *The Heart of Thoreau's Journal* (Boston, 1927), p. 114.

burg Railroad, community farming problems, local educational matters, the annual cattle show, and other small town arguments *ad infinitum*. The village Sham-Fight with its "lively clatter of bells and whooping of all the village boys" ; the drills of the local militia ; and the absorbing theme of apple-culture—all these, as recorded in his *Journals*, heightened his interest in the town. Concord, he felt, though a little town was blessed with honors. From the many famous people who came to the city it received its handful, its share of individuals like Everett, Webster, George Bancroft, Alcott, Garrison, and Phillips, all of whom spoke before village audiences.[8]

Numerous town activities not only interested the poet-philosopher, but were participated in by him. Since Concord was a shire town until 1858, Emerson must have met among the throngs at the different sessions both his fellow-citizens and such heralded visitors as Webster and Everett. Once he observed that "a courthouse is a good place to learn the limits of a man."[9] Even the village band concerts entertained him.[10] As a distinguished townsman, Emerson frequently was invited to represent the community at patriotic and other municipal meetings. Diligently he searched through yellowed town records and visited the Cambridge libraries to secure historical data for use in his now familiar discourses. These speeches, together with his annual appearance before the local lyceum, are indicative of his position in the community. John Albee recounts that

A small farmer of Concord told me proudly that he has heard every one of Emerson's lectures delivered in that town ; and after a moment's hesitation he added, "And I understood 'em too."[11]

On another occasion, that of one of Emerson's lectures on Plato, a literal-minded old lady was displeased with the lecture to the extent of commenting emphatically : ". . . if those old heathens really did such things as Mr. Emerson said they did, the less said about them the better."[12] In general, though certain individuals—including Emerson himself, perhaps—may

---

[8] E. W. Emerson, *op. cit.*, p. 103. This information is to be found in R. W. Emerson's *Journals* for 1843.
[9] R. W. Emerson, *Journals*, Houghton Mifflin ed., III, 468.
[10] *Ibid.*, I, 464.
[11] *Remen brances of Emerson* (New York, 1901), p. 6.
[12] E. W. Emerson, *op. cit.*, p. 148.

have laughed over the caricatures and squibs which the Boston papers and individual jokesters directed at the "Orphic" Alcott and Emerson, lecturer and *Dial* editor, the people of Concord appreciated Emerson's kindly and modest attitude toward them.[13] Certainly they called upon him, rather than the solitary Hawthorne or the more radical Thoreau, to serve as their representative on the great days of the village.

Life in Emerson's Concord was not dull. During 1839 Emerson, then admitted to the Social Circle, made close acquaintances among a group of townsmen whom his reserved manner had heretofore prevented his knowing. Here were twenty-five Concordians, described by Emerson in a letter as "doctor, lawyer, farmer, trader, miller, mechanic, etc. solidest men [who yielded] the solidest gossip."[14] While Emerson's lecture tours frequently interfered with his attending the regular winter meetings, he was for forty-three years a member, the last session he attended being that marking the hundredth year of the existence of the club. Thoreau's amusing account of the Walden Pond Society gives a slant on the village opinion of its great and eccentric men.

> About a month ago, at the post-office, Abel Brooks, who is pretty deaf, sidling up to me, observed in a loud voice which all could hear, "Let me see, your society is pretty large, ain't it?" "Oh, yes, large enough," said I, not knowing what he meant. "There's Stewart belongs to it, and Collier, he's one of them, and Emerson, and my boarder . . . and Channing. . . ." "You mean the *walkers;* don't you?" "Ye-es, I call you the Society. All go to the woods; don't you?"[15]

Thoreau also reports one villager as saying that there were three religious societies in Concord : the Unitarian, the Orthodox, and the Walden Pond Society.

Kind-hearted and hospitable, the Emersons frequently, albeit simply, entertained both townspeople and famous outsiders. Sometimes there were dinner guests ; sometimes Symposium members ; and again, those visitors who became permanent guests. In the Emerson home gathered such individualists as Mrs. Ripley, the great Louis Agassiz, travel-minded Harriet

[13] Sanborn and Harris, *op. cit.*, II, 357-359, including notes.
[14] E. W. Emerson *op. cit.* p. 146.
[15] Shepard, ed., *op. cit.*, p. 268. The entry in Thoreau's *Journal* is dated April 16, 1857.

Martineau, Arthur Hugh Clough, Whitman, the Alcotts, of
course, Thoreau, Hawthorne (rarely), Dr. Channing and his
nephew, Ellery, poet and naturalist, eccentric Aunt Mary
Moody Emerson, Margaret Fuller, Elizabeth Hoar, and Charles
Emerson. In later years there was for Emerson the excitement of going into Boston to attend the Saturday Club, where
for many years during the late fifties and sixties he dined once
a month at the Parker House with the notables : Agassiz, Lowell, Holmes, Longfellow, Judge Hoar, Governor Andrew, Sen-
ator Sumner, and others. On other occasions, in Concord,
there were long discourses with his fellow Transcendentalist,
the peripatetic Alcott, either in the Emerson home or as the
two walked to Walden, to the Virginia Fields (a favorite walk),
or to the Indian Meadows by the riverside. How the two
must have argued, Emerson, perhaps, reading to Alcott the
introductory pages of his new book, *Representative Men*, almost
ready for the press, or Alcott discoursing of Plato, Goethe, or
Swedenborg! Often Thoreau and Ellery Channing joined the
two ; and the talk on nature and mankind continued apace.
This intimacy was not shared with another famous townsman,
Hawthorne, whose "Wayside" home—formerly occupied by
the Alcotts—was across the turnpike from the Emerson dwelling. Edward Emerson observed that whereas his father greatly
admired Hawthorne's fine personality, "the gloomy and uncanny twilight atmosphere of his books was one in which Mr.
Emerson could not breathe, and he could never read far."[16]

With the years there came to Emerson increased honors :
invitations from hostile Harvard to be a member of its Board
of Overseers, to receive a Doctor of Laws degree, and to give
once more the Phi Beta Kappa address. Public lectures
throughout the West made him a nationally known figure.
Such recognition, however, did not alienate him from the villagers with whom he had lived for so many years. To the last
"the Sage of Concord" had their kindly regard.[17] Here in
this old-fashioned, sleepy New England village, with its broad,
rambling streets of wooden houses (standing for the most apart
and overshadowed by leafy trees), its quiet village green, and
its shady graveyards, Emerson lived in a roomy house for al-

[16] *Op. cit.*, p. 108.
[17] *Ibid.*, p. 187.

most fifty years in fellowship with the townfolk.[18]   Here loafing
and inviting his soul, he found pleasure in his home, his town
associations, his work, and his family.   Here today on a small
hill in Sleepy Hollow, itself a natural amphitheater within a
quarter of a mile from the Common, Concord's esteemed townsman and individualist is buried in a cemetery for which he had
made the consecration address.

CHEERFUL YESTERDAYS IN OLD CAMBRIDGE

If from the journals of its great men one may re-create certain bits of the simple life of Concord village, from the essays
and occasional poems of such native-born townsmen as Oliver
Wendell Holmes (1809-94), James Russell Lowell (1819-91),
and Thomas Wentworth Higginson (1823-1911) he may gain
glimpses of a charming New England college town, "one of
the few American towns that may be said to have owed their
very name and existence to the pursuit of letters."[19]   The "Old
Cambridge" of their essays and poems was a place of charm
and culture, sweetness and light, and intimate associations, the
representative of a number of mid-nineteenth century New
England towns boasting a college, an academy or a "female
seminary," several churches, pleasant old homes scattered
along elm-lined streets, and shops around a common.   Possessing a passionate regard for their birthplace, these essayists
in urbane and witty comment and chatty reminiscences show
the individuality and distinction not only of their academic
village, which even in its development as a university center
retained some of its earlier exclusiveness, but of the old families whose histories were long connected with town and college.
Cantabrigians, like natives of many New England towns, often
were proud of their birthrights in a village of such natural
beauty and historic associations.   Among the residents it was
a point of pride that Cambridge could boast of successive groups
of eminent ministers, writers, teachers, doctors, lawyers, and
scientists since the early establishment (1639) of the Glover
printing press in the home of President Dunster of Harvard
helped make the settlement a center of growing cultural interests.[20]   Living long in a village society of cultivated men and

[18] Note the British Edward Dicey's descriptions of Concord in Nevins, ed.,
American Social History as Recorded by British Travellers, p. 403.
[19] Higginson, *Old Cambridge* (New York, 1899), p. 3.
[20] *Ibid.*, pp. 5-6.

women, Lowell, Higginson, and Holmes, to a slighter degree, naturally reveal in their writings this idea of conscious satisfaction which they and their fellow Cantabrigians had in their unusual community.

Continuously a Cantabrigian, Lowell in the essay *Cambridge Thirty Years Ago* shows his deep affection for the Middlesex village and the historic house of his birth, the Elmwood to which he always returned with pleasure. The Cambridge of Lowell's youth was still a village with broad country roads shaded by elms, lindens, and horse-chestnuts; with pastures and orchards, "good roaming grounds for schoolboys"; stately colonial homes, like Elmwood, surrounded by large trees and gardens; the usual village shops; the old First Church, where John Hancock had presided over the First Provincial Congress; and, finally, the red brick college buildings, Lowell's "Muses' factories," which impressed Anthony Trollope, viewing them in 1861, as "very ugly red-brick houses standing here and there without order."[21] As variously pictured by Higginson, Cambridge in the early nineteenth century was a village "of simple habits where wealth counted for little and intellect counted for a great deal"; a place of "refined provincialism, with the good manners and respectable attainments prevailing at that time"; and a community rich in both historic and literary traditions "having the advantages of a college town, not yet a university city."

Old Cambridge, as thus pictured, was in a transition state between the more picturesque life of the Revolution and the growing academic life of the new century. "There were still those in Cambridge who could recall the American Revolution and whose sons enacted the surrender of Cornwallis at every country muster."[22] In the reminiscences of both Lowell and Higginson frequent reminders of the Revolutionary past color the narration. Cambridge boys of the golden age of Lowell's youth had ample opportunity to steep themselves in the early traditions of the region. Everywhere landmarks suggested the past. On their walnutting and chestnutting forays village boys, among them James Lowell and Thomas Higginson, often stopped to transcribe the lengthy and revealing Latin inscriptions on the flat stones of the Cambridge ceme-

---

[21] Nevins, ed., *op. cit.*, pp. 408-410.
[22] Higginson, *op. cit.*, p. 22.

tery, the scene later of Holmes's "The Cambridge Churchyard."
According to Higginson's confession, modern cemeteries never
seemed to him very awe-inspiring,

but the old New England graveyards, especially in college towns,
impressed on the boyish mind not only the dignity of virtue, but
of knowledge ; of this world's honors and grandeur perhaps, but
never of its financial treasures.[23]

Thus inquisitive youth learned about the virtues of former villagers of all social stations, Harvard presidents, ministers, and
town drummers included alike.   "Down in the village" schoolboys and college students—Lowell says they were then called
scholars—were privileged to look with curious regard at aged
survivors of the cocked hat regime as they walked along Brattle
Street and elsewhere : at Mr. Sales, Franco-Spanish scholar who
had cue and hair powder, or at dignified Dr. Popkin, who wore
the last of the cocked hats and carried an umbrella of vast
proportions.[24]   There were other reminders of an earlier Cambridge : family portraits of solemn, tie-wigged ancestors ; local
legends of the march of the redcoats on Lexington and Concord and of provincial soldiers going down Kirkland Street,
where the Higginsons lived, to Bunker Hill ; and tales about
historic Craigie House, Elmwood, and other so-called Tory
mansions, the Washington Elm, and countless things associated
with the past.   Such traditions linked with an almost vanished
past the lives of Holmes, Lowell, Richard and Edmund Dana,
Thatcher and Thomas Higginson, William Story (the Edel-
mann Storg to whom Lowell addressed his *Cambridge Thirty
Years Ago*), and other Cambridge youths.[25]

Lowell gives a charming picture of "the Village" of his youth.
From his mature viewpoint of 1854 he looks back on the little
town of thirty years past as being "essentially an English village, quiet, unspeculative, without enterprise, sufficing to itself,
and only showing such differences from the original type as
the public school and the system of town government might
superinduce."[26]   Though suggestive of English prototypes, Old

[23] *Ibid.*, p. 10.
[24] *Ibid.*, p. 23 and Lowell, *Prose Works* (Riverside ed., Boston and New York,
1899), "Cambridge Thirty Years Ago," I, 97.
[25] Horace E. Scudder, *James Russell Lowell* (Boston and New York, 1901), I, 22.
[26] Lowell, *op. cit.*, pp. 55-56. Cf. Holmes, *The Autocrat of the Breakfast Table*
(New York, 1891), I, ii, 127.

Cambridge was, as Lowell reminds his "dear Storg," a town with a character even while sharing characteristics common to New England villages of the eighteenth and nineteenth centuries. Railways and omnibuses, he notes, "had not rolled flat all little social prominences and peculiarities, making every man as much a citizen everywhere as at home." That oracle of news, the barber, had not yet been silenced by the penny paper. "Everybody knew everybody, and all about everybody, and village wit, whose high 'change was around the little market-house in the town square, had labelled every more marked individuality with nicknames that clung like burs."[27] An established and provincial little place, the town had the usual loafers, topers, proverb-mongers, barber, parsons, and postmaster, "whose tenure was for life." The museum-like barber shop, a place of wonder and delight to young Lowell and his friends ; two grocery stores cluttered with miscellaneous goods and country "*prodooce*"; the two town constables, "stalwart and rubicund," who functioned on public occasions ; the old courthouse on the square; the deserted wharf on the Charles ; the huckleberry pastures near Cambridgeport; and the animated scenes of the muster and the village drama of the "Cornwallis" (amusements in many a New England village whereby the grave and suppressed humor of the Yankees expressed itself in all the wildest vagaries of fun)—these things Lowell vividly recalls thirty years afterwards.

Both Lowell's essays and Higginson's essays and letters picture the college life of the town. These were the "cheerful yesterdays" when, as Edward Everett Hale recalls, literature, rather than athletics or sociology, was the fashion.[28] With its college and private libraries, to say nothing of its subscription and club libraries, Cambridge offered excellent facilities for the encouragement of literature. Lowell and his circle found ample opportunity for literary expression in their editing of *Harvardiana*, secretly sponsored by one of the college clubs.

---

[27] *Ibid.*, p. 58.   Cf. Lowell's village poem, "Fitz Adam's Story" (*Complete Poems*, Boston and New York, 1917, p. 414), for description of changes effected in village life by railroad building.

[28] *James Russell Lowell and His Friends* (Boston and New York, 1899), p. 22. For Higginson's letters and essays see Mary Thatcher Higginson, ed., *Letters and Journals of Thomas Wentworth Higginson, 1846-1906* (Boston, 1921) ; her *Thomas Wentworth Higginson* (Boston, 1914) ; and T. W. Higginson, *Cheerful Yesterdays* (Boston, 1899).

This same youthful group found time also for the Phi Beta Kappa activities; for social entertainment in the gatherings at musicales, dinners, teas, and literary evenings of the Band, an informal organization of congenial young men and women, one of whom was the poetess, Maria White, to whom Lowell became betrothed; and for public performance at the most important yearly function in Cambridge, commencement day, then a holiday preserving all the features of an English country fair.[29] Swimming, skating, hunting, football, baseball, and cricket rounded out the list of youthful activities in Old Cambridge.

According to Higginson, this pleasant town of colonial homes and cultured people might have gone the way of many abortive New England settlements had Harvard College not been established there. Among actual New England villages recorded in literature Cambridge was unique in the pronounced influence of Harvard in creating not merely individual authors and professional leaders, but entire literary families.[30] The Holmes, Lowell, Dana, Channing, and Higginson families all showed "how a literary atmosphere was produced by which the young people of Cambridge were inevitably moulded."[31] Contacts with gifted foreigners, like Agassiz and Clough, access to college and public libraries, and the proximity of the village to the Boston music centers gave the townspeople unusual advantages. In spite of this, some of Lowell's English friends later were under the impression "that the 'Hosea Biglow' dialect was that of Lowell's father (a prominent Unitarian minister in Boston), family and personal circle."[32]

This was the little town by the smooth, meadow-banked Charles whose old village life, typical of that used so often in song and story, is recorded faithfully by its famous townsmen. In these delineations Old Cambridge is a unique village, which "besides possessing the common characteristics of New England towns, had its special flavor from the presence there of the oldest college of New England."[33] To paraphrase Lowell's own words, the Cambridge of his youth was a town of traditions and ennobling associations, as yet untouched by a scram-

[29] Lowell, "Cambridge Thirty Years Ago," p. 79.
[30] Ibid., p. 15.
[31] Ibid., p. 17.
[32] Ibid., p. 28.
[33] Ibid., p. 27.
9

ble of *parvenus*, with a horrible consciousness of shoddy thinking running through politics, manners, art, literature, and religion itself.[34]   In short, even in the picture of Holmes's Professor, who composed a poem on the town of his birth while he was under the influence of chloroform for the extraction of a tooth, Old Cambridge was a delightful town.   Praised alike by natives and outsiders, Cambridge was, according to the Professor,

> —Nicest place that ever was seen—
> Colleges red and Common green,
> Sidewalks brownish with trees between.
> Sweetest spot beneath the skies
> When the Canker-worms don't rise,—
> When the dust, that sometimes flies
> Into your mouth and ears and eyes,
> In a quiet slumber lies, . . .
> A kind of harbor it seems to be
> Facing the flow of a boundless sea.[35]

BRAHMIN NOVELS OF LOCALITY

As we have seen, the peculiar characteristics of the nineteenth-century village scene and character were best described by women, who used chiefly the short story form.   New Englandism was depicted also, both before and after the Civil War, in the novel, largely the work of such Brahmins as Holmes, Higginson, Thomas Bailey Aldrich, and Henry Ward Beecher. Each of these contributing variously toward the novel of locality made some fictionalization of New England villages and towns.   The most realistic interpreter of the town, however, did not belong to the natural intellectual aristocracy of New England.   Proof of the decline of the so-called New England Renaissance and of the literary dominance of native-born New Englanders is found in the emergence of an outsider, William Dean Howells.

In "the weeping fifties," the period when Holmes began the serial publication of *The Professor's Story* in *The Atlantic Monthly* (1859), the romantic school of New England was still dominant, even though startling new notes, most expressive in

---

[34] Lowell, "On a Certain Condescension in Foreigners," *Prose Works*, III, 222.
[35] *The Autocrat of the Breakfast Table*, I, xii, 298.   In October, 1852, Arthur Hugh Clough, who became a friend to Emerson and others, settled in Cambridge.   His *Prose Remains* (London, 1888) records his impressions (for the most part favorable) of Cambridge and its people.

Whitman's *Leaves of Grass* (1855), were appearing in other sections of th country. The New England Brahmins were still recognized leaders, however. But nine years earlier Hawthorne's *The Scarlet Letter* and Emerson's *Representative Men* were gaining attention; in 1852 *Uncle Tom's Cabin* made a tremendous stir; in 1854 *Walden* appeared; in 1857 Lowell became the first editor of *The Atlantic Monthly;* and in the next year Longfellow continued his romantic studies of the past in *The Courtship of Miles Standish.* Holmes was already popular as a wit, a writer of *vers de société,* and a familiar essayist through the *Autocrat* series in the *Atlantic* when he first published *The Professor's Story,* a novel later to be entitled *Elsie Venner: A Romance of Destiny* (1861). This, like Holmes's other "medicated" novels, *The Guardian Angel* (1867) and *A Mortal Antipathy* (1885), has but the thinnest thread of a story. The leisurely method of the essayist is everywhere apparent in these stories with a purpose. While all three deal with New England small town backgrounds, no one is primarily a village novel. Holmes's interest was not in village life per se, but in his medicated arguments : the problems of pre-natal influences in *Elsie Venner* and the abnormal impetuosity of Myrtle Hazard in *The Guardian Angel.*

Holmes's slight village delineations add little to the literary history of the New England town except the Brahmin viewpoint so strongly stressed throughout and the characterization —too often to the point of caricature—of abnormal village people. Certain of his inhibited and sensitive characters might have served as models for Mrs. Freeman's repressed villagers.[36] In *Elsie Venner* the narrator is a professor to whom Bernard Langdon, a Brahmin and a Harvard medical student, has reported the strange case history of Elsie Venner, a village girl whose "volitional aberrations make the thesis of the novel."[37] Digressive and episodic, the story opens with Bernard's first teaching experiences in the "deestric" school of a flourishing inland town, all extraneous matter to the main tale, but delineative of provincial life in a river and agricultural town. The scene of the utter defeat of the local bully at the hands of the new master foreshadows the more familiar scene in *The Hoosier Schoolmaster* (1871). The story proper centers around

[36] Mrs. Freeman was for many years Holmes's secretary.
[37] Chapter I bears the title, "The Brahmin Caste of New England."

Master Langdon's experiences at the "Apollinean Female Institute" in Rockland, a mountain town and the home of the
aristocratic Venners.   In spite of its menacing "maounting,"
with its dangerous Rattlesnake Ledge, "the reigning nightmare
of the inhabitants," Rockland was a pleasant town beautified
by old forest trees, ponds, and brooks and known for its English patterned "mansion-houses," its two-story trim, white-
painted "genteel" dwellings with yards of lilac and syringa
bushes, and its comfortable wooden farmhouses.

Against a typical small town background of social entertainments, sectarian disagreements, school affairs, petty gossiping, and ambitious striving Holmes has built the case of
Elsie, exotic daughter of wealthy Dudley Venner, last of a
leading family.   Misunderstood by most of the narrow-minded,
tale-bearing townspeople, Elsie lives in seclusion, except for
her rare appearances at teas and the institute.   Her hypnotic
snakelike eyes, an eccentric antisocial manner, and her nocturnal wanderings in the woods of the Mountain create for
poor Elsie an unusual reputation.   Except for her associations
with a devoted negress, Sophy, her father, and Richard, her
rascally, but fascinating half-breed cousin, Elsie has no intimate relationships.   People feel uneasy in her presence, as if
she exerted some indefinable mesmeric power over them.
Even Langdon, to whom Elsie is deeply attracted, fails to return the unfortunate girl's affection for him.   Thus, in this
situation of social isolation does Holmes develop the thesis of
pre-natal influences affecting the ruin of a helpless person.
The whole story is motivated by the alien element in Elsie's
nature and the secret of the fascination which looked out of
her cold, glittering eyes.   The close of the novel, dramatically
heightened by the deaths of Elsie and old Sophy, a destructive
storm, and the fall of the threatening ledge, suggest the machinery of a Gothic novel rather than a story whose characters
live in a New England mountain town.

In spite of Holmes's prefatory note, *The Guardian Angel* is a
sequel to *Elsie Venner* only in its treatment of another abnormal
case, that of impetuous Myrtle Hazard, who though born in
the Orient is reared to young womanhood in the New England
home of a puritanic aunt.[38]   A retired professor, residing in
Oxbow Village during his last days, becomes Myrtle's "guar-

[38] First edition by Ticknor and Fields, 1867.

dian angel," as she calls him.[39]   The characters are stereotyped :
a village poet ; two ministers, the really sincere and the hypocritical ; a scheming lawyer ; Professor Gridley ; and the usual
gossips evilly misinterpreting Myrtle's impulsiveness.   Holmes's
last novel, *A Mortal Antipathy*, is the weakest of all and a negligible study of village life.   With its scene in Arrowhead Village, the story tells of Maurice Kirkland, an accomplished
young man who, because of an accident in infancy, has a
marked repugnance for young women.

In 1869, concurrently with *Oldtown Folks* and *Innocents Abroad*,
Higginson's *Malbone: An Oldport Romance*, descriptive of the
society at Newport, Rhode Island, appeared in *The Atlantic
Monthly*, from January to May.   A man of varied culture bred
in the Old Cambridge school, Colonel Higginson romanticizes
about the resort town in which he lived during the sixties.
It was then, as described in a letter of the author to his mother,
a place of "great hotels that looked like Saratoga."[40]   The best
drawn and most popular character in the novel is an outspoken
old resorter, Aunt Jane, who regarded Oldport as "amusing in
summer . . . though the society is nothing but a pack of playing cards.   In the winter it is too dull for young people, and
only suits quiet old women like me, who merely live here to
keep the Ten Commandments and darn their stockings."[41]

As we have noted, everywhere in post-war New England,
even in once busy Oldport, the impress of the past was fading
out ; and many other exponents of the genteel tradition felt,
as did Thomas Bailey Aldrich in 1883, that

> The few old-fashioned men and women—quaint, shrewd, and
> racy of the soil—who linger in little gray homesteads strung along
> the New England roads and byways will shortly cease to exist as a
> class, save in the record of some charming chronicler as Sarah Orne
> Jewett, or Mary Wilkins, on whose sympathetic page they have
> already taken to themselves a remote air, and atmosphere of long-
> kept lavender and penny-royal.[42]

A native of Portsmouth, New Hampshire, the sleepy, old town
of Rivermouth in *The Story of a Bad Boy*, Aldrich (1836-1907),

---

[39] Holmes knew this village while he was teaching at Dartmouth (1838-40).
[40] Higginson, *Letters and Journals*, chap. v, "Newport," p. 224.
[41] *Ibid.*, p. 253.
[42] *From Ponkapog to Pesth and An Old Town by the Sea* (Boston, 1897), p. 272.
An Old Town by the Sea was written in 1883.

like Miss Jewett, was steeped in the older town life of New England.   In spite of a short boyhood sojourn in New Orleans and later journalistic work in New York, a period of association with Bayard Taylor and other self-termed Bohemians, Aldrich was essentially a New England Brahmin who "liked to say that if he was not genuine Boston, he was at least Boston-plated."[43]   Consequently, his portrayals of the town are told from the viewpoint of one whose family associations were of the best.   Even in *The Story of a Bad Boy* Aldrich is the Brahmin writing in delightful fashion about his boyhood escapades in a dignified New England town and in faraway New Orleans. A realistic romancer, he re-creates the past in his quaint and humorous descriptions of secluded New Hampshire and Massachusetts towns which were fast losing their individuality.   Aldrich himself once admitted that his portrayals of town life were early affected by a serious accident connected with the running of the first train—during the late fifties—over the Eastern Road from Boston to Portsmouth.   The accident was unobserved at the time, though occurring in the crowded station at the Portsmouth terminus.   "The catastrophe was followed, though not immediately, by death, and that also, curiously enough, was unobserved. Nevertheless, this initial train, freighted with so many hopes and the Directors of the Road, ran over and killed—LOCAL CHARACTER."[44]   Up to that time Portsmouth had been a very secluded little community, and had "had the courage of its seclusion."   It had proudly existed without thought of outside prejudices and conventions, but now, as in small villages everywhere, the new and broader contacts meant the breaking down of the local quality which had long individualized the town.[45]

This decaying seaport, with its worm-eaten wharves, weather-stained and unoccupied warehouses, and deserted piers vividly suggestive of Deephaven, forms the background for *A Bad Boy* and *An Old Town by the Sea*.   Lacking many of its old landmarks, the town of the sixties and seventies, nevertheless, suggested to the romantic Aldrich its former high maritime spirit —characteristic of Portsmouth even in the War of 1812—when the harbor was dotted with ships bringing merchandise to and

[43] *C. H. A. L.*, III, 35. Cf. Ferris Greenslet, *The Life of Thomas Bailey Aldrich* (Boston and New York, 1908), p. 38.
[44] Aldrich, *op. cit.*, p. 258.
[45] *Ibid.*, pp. 259 ff.

from the Indies and its wharves were crowded with sailors and stevedores staggering under heavy loads. The town was alive in those days. At the windows of counting rooms, now musty, portly merchants, in knee breeches, silver shoe buckles, and plum-colored coats, used to stand watching their ships sail up the Narrows. ". . . the cries of stevedores and the chants of sailors at the windlass used to echo along the shores where all is silence now."[46] Like Salem of *The House of the Seven Gables*, Portsmouth eventually became "the interesting widow of a once lively commerce." In the more beautiful parts of the picturesque town tree-fringed streets, "commodious private dwellings, mostly square white houses, with spacious halls running down the center," old public buildings, many churches and cemeteries gave the early New England stamp to the place. As in Old Cambridge the ancient houses bore marks of their former glory: interiors rich in panelings and wood carvings, bric-a-brac, rare pictures—many of them Copleys—deep windows, spacious halls with handsome staircases, and large open fireplaces, ornamented with Dutch tiles. These were keys to the past, to the exciting days of the Revolution when crowds thronged Stavers Tavern (associated with *The Tales of a Wayside Inn*), eagerly scanned the pages of *The New Hampshire Gazette and Historical Chronicle*, and bowed deferentially to dignified governors and clergymen.

Such was the traditionally rich background of the Rivermouth of Tom Bailey's escapades, a quaint town whose austere puritanism threw the boy's badness into unfair relief. Published in 1869, seven years before *The Adventures of Tom Sawyer*, Aldrich's autobiographical *Story* is the first of many notable and realistic studies of boy life in small towns from New England to the prairies of the Midwest and the river towns along the Mississippi.[47] Tom Bailey, the bad boy, was so termed merely to distinguish him from those "faultless young gentlemen," those unnatural Little Lord Fauntleroys, so heartily despised by Stephen Crane.[48] In truth, Tom was a normal New England boy, "an amiable, impulsive lad, blessed with fine digestive powers, and no hypocrite."[49]

[46] *Ibid.*, p. 184.
[47] See later discussions of boy life in connection with Mark Twain, Stephen Crane, Booth Tarkington, Edgar Lee Masters, and others.
[48] See Crane's *Whilomville Stories*.
[49] *The Works of Thomas Bailey Aldrich* (Boston and New York, 1913), VII, *The Story of a Bad Boy*, Introduction.

In reminiscent mood Aldrich recalls the friends and adventures of his boyhood, spent with his grandparents in Rivermouth (Portsmouth). Most of the sketches are of Tom's experiences at the Temple Grammar School in Rivermouth, of his earlier life in New Orleans, and of his vacation escapades, all of which characterize him as a normal boy akin to the other familiarly known small town boys of fiction, Tom Sawyer, Skeeters Kirby, Penrod Scofield, and the youngsters in Crane's *Whilomville Stories*. Here in quiet Rivermouth lived Tom Bailey and his school cronies, twelve adventurers composing the R. M. C. (a secret order, the Rivermouth Centipedes). Among the many dramatically humorous experiences of this select circle is that of their organizing a theatrical group of which Tom was the manager. Performing in the Bailey carriage house, members of the Rivermouth Theater were successful until a disastrous production of William Tell. In spite of a sudden disbanding of his fellow-actors, Tom "retired from business with no fewer than fifteen hundred pins, after deducting the headless, the pointless, and the crooked pins with which our doorkeeper frequently got stuck!"[50] Illustrative of the small boy's love of adventure is the humorous account of the Fourth of July firing of Rivermouth's decorative 1812 guns. The R. M. C. schemed to startle their fellow-citizens by a midnight firing of the twelve ancient guns which had long decorated the parks of the town. Tom, having been chosen by drawing the fatal paper to fire the battery, performed his task faithfully at midnight when all the town was asleep. With the first booming of the guns and each succeeding explosion the confusion of the rudely awakened townspeople grew greater until half of the male population rushed through the streets wildly asking questions. The town watch turned out to a man and marched off, in admirable order, in the wrong direction. Some thought the town was being bombarded; others feared that the end of the world had come, as the Millerites had predicted. In the meanwhile, amidst continued confusion, Bailey's Battery bellowed away at regular intervals.[51] The human story of Tom's "badness" is rounded out with similar boyish pranks, such as his evasion of Sunday school, his part

[50] *Ibid.*, p. 62.
[51] *Ibid.*, p. 214. In "A Rivermouth Romance," delineative of the period of 1860, Aldrich tells the story of an Irish ne'er-do-well and a servant girl (Aldrich, *Works*, IV, 2,2-319).

in pushing a locally famous stagecoach into a Fourth of July bonfire and in changing the town's street signs, and, finally, his running away to sea.

The Stillwater Tragedy (1880) shows no idealization of village life as do Aldrich's other studies of the small town, but is a dramatically handled story of a murder in a small New England manufacturing town, a commonplace, overgrown village, "with whose rural aspects are curiously blended something of the grimness and the squalor of certain city neighborhoods."[52] Graphic descriptions of the industrial boom following the Civil War, a "disastrous, prosperous time," herald Aldrich's abandonment of his role of spokesman for the genteel school.   Being of comparatively recent date, Stillwater lacked those colonial associations which, "like lavender in an old chest of drawers," prove the saving grace of decaying Rivermouths and Deephavens.   Against a dingy background of factory, workmen's shanties, and cheap taverns, favorite lounging places for the laborers, the mysterious murder of an old miser looms large. Especially realistic is the picture of the reaction of the townspeople to the tragedy within their midst.   Mrs. Freeman might well have written such a vignette as this : "Dragged-looking women, with dishcloth or dustpan in hand, stood in doorways or leaned from windows, talking in subdued voices with neighbors on the curbstone."   In this novel conservative Aldrich steps aside from his themes of refinement and Back Bay culture to join his contemporary realists in breathing "a commonplace, polemic, scientific air."[53]   Still the Brahmin, he shows in this picturing of a mean factory town his full awareness of the lamented

> . . . mighty Zolaistic movement [which] now
> Engrosses us—a miasmatic breath
> Blown from the slums. We paint life as it is,
> The hideous side of it, with careful pains,
> Making a god of the dull Commonplace.[54]

Birthright, youthful associations with various Ohio communities, and later writings portraying frontier society link the name of William Dean Howells with the Midwestern interpreters of the small town.   On the other hand, his literary pas-

---

[52] *The Stillwater Tragedy* (Boston, 1907), p. 38.
[53] *Works*, I, 45, "Realism."
[54] *Ibid.*, II, 94, "At the Funeral of a Minor Poet."

sions, his final separation from the region of his youth, and his eventual meeting with Lowell and other literati introduced Howells into the charmed society he enjoyed during the fullest years of his life.   Because of his use of a wide variety of richly indigenous town materials Howells may be introduced in a double capacity : first, as a Midwesterner who in later life turned, as did Mark Twain, to writing reminiscences of his youth and, next, as a New England novelist who, though not to the country born, produced through his keen observation and understanding truly realistic pictures of New England village communities.

If Aldrich's pictures of history-haunted Portsmouth re-create the golden days of his New England boyhood, Howells's *A Boy's Town*, itself a delightfully humorous and penetrating study written at the close of the Gilded Age, is a reconstruction of Ohio boy life in the forties.   From these sketches and other autobiographical portrayals of Midwestern small town and rural life in *My Year in a Log Cabin* (1893), *New Leaf Mills, A Chronicle* (1913), and *Years of My Youth* (1916) one may learn that Howells (1837-1920), the son of William Cooper Howells, a Swedenborgian printer of Welsh extraction, spent his boyhood in the Ohio towns of Martin's Ferry, his birthplace, Hamilton, the scene of *A Boy's Town*, and Dayton, where the elder Howells conducted a newspaper.   There was no romantic "gilt and tinsel" in such a boyhood.   In Hamilton, an overwhelmingly Democratic town, William Cooper Howells had charge of the Whig *Intelligencer*.   Here William, a serious lad at ten years, became a typesetter.[55]   When not working as a compositor or newsboy or engaging in the neighborhood activities of his brothers and friends, he read at every opportunity.   At home his literary passions—later the subject of one of his best known criticisms—were encouraged by his father's fine taste and appreciation of scholarship.   Goldsmith, Cervantes, and Irving became the boy's favorites.

Howells was not, however, so bookishly inclined that he was not a town boy.   "My world," he once wrote of this early period, "was full of boys."[56]   Everywhere in his Boy's Town were lively companions : at school, where William felt the

---

[55] *A Boy's Town* (New York, 1890), p. 7.   In 1840 Hamilton was a place of about three thousand.
[56] *Years of My Youth* (New York, 1916), p. 19.

mockeries of his taunting older fellows; along the rivers and canals, where they enjoyed swimming, hunting, fishing, and foraging in season; and in the fields, where the boy took part in races, football, baseball, and even forbidden fighting. To these lively Ohio lads "life was an experiment which had to be tried in every way that presented itself"; and, as portrayed in *A Boy's Town*, Hamilton during the forties possessed almost unrivaled fitness to be the home of boys. In *Years of My Youth* Howells again refers to the advantageous location of Hamilton. In those days the town, "with its two branches of the Great Miami River and their freshets in spring, and their witchery at all seasons; with its Hydraulic Channels and Reservoirs, its stretch of the Miami Canal and the Canal Basin so fit for swimming in summer and skating in winter," was indeed a boy's paradise.[57] "I doubt," Howells wrote, "if any boy ever lived a gladder time than I lived in Hamilton, Butler County, Ohio."[58] These typical experiences of the "generalized boy," based upon remembrances of the "specialized boy," make *A Boy's Town* one of the sympathetic and natural literary interpretations of normal American small town boyhood.

In the literary records of the American small town life connected with local printing offices has served often as backgrounds for various stories. This is natural enough, for the country town editor, especially in the Midwest, was long an influential individual, "a leader of his people, not a patent-insides recorder of social functions, but a vigorous and independent thinker and writer."[59] Edgar Watson Howe, William Allen White, and Sherwood Anderson, to mention but a few recognized interpreters, have reproduced in essay, short story, and novel various minutiae in the life of the small town printer and his associates. Howells himself, whose irregular schooling was supplemented by home reading and work at the printing shop, says that "at ten years and onward till journalism became my university, the printing-office was mainly my school."[60] The printer appears in a strong personal light in *Years of My Youth*, lengthily descriptive of the village activities which the Howells family enjoyed in Jefferson, a small town in the Western Reserve, where during the fifties William Cooper Howells

[57] *Ibid.*, p. 21.
[58] *Ibid.*, p. 36.
[59] Turner, *The Frontier in American History*, p. 353.
[60] *Years of My Youth*, p. 18.

122 THE SMALL TOWN IN AMERICAN LITERATURE

printed one of his many successive newspapers.[61]   In this community the Howells boys and girls, in spite of their daily tasks at home or at the printing office, found time for dances, games, frolics, sleigh rides, moonlight walks, debating societies, and spelling matches.   The brothers even joined the local cabals at drugstore and tavern.   These were "the days of the County Fair and the Fourths-of-July, and the Christmases rehabilitated from Dickens."

Of this particular village of his youth Howells later recorded that he "came to value it as potential stuff of such fiction as has never yet been written, and never will be by me."[62]   He remained faithful to that avowal only in the narrowed sense. If Howells failed to fictionalize the actual life of Jefferson, he eschewed neither the rich small town material of his native Midwest nor that of his adopted New England.   In his fiction, as in autobiography, Howells put to fine dramatic use the commonplace life of rural districts and small towns from Ohio to Maine.   Broader in the range of his community materials than his Brahmin associates, this transplanted Ohioan was strongly interested in village motives and realities; and, though the metropolitan phase of community life dominates such later novels as *The Rise of Silas Lapham* and *A Hazard of New Fortunes*, small town themes appear repeatedly in his fiction.   Contrasted pictures of isolated Down East villages, quiet summer resorts, suburban life, New England factory settlements, agricultural hamlets, and growing towns of the plains bespeak the catholicity of Howells's taste.

Early years of journalistic writing and political reporting, with occasional poetizing in the manner of Pope and Heine; a four-year consulship in Italy and the record thereof published as *Venetian Life* (1866) and *Italian Journeys* (1867); a brief affiliation with *The Nation* (1865) and, after a few months, with *The Atlantic Monthly* (until 1881) mark Howells's gradual turn toward fiction.   It was not until the seventies that in *Their Wedding Journey, A Chance Acquaintance, Suburban Sketches*, and *The Lady of the Aroostook* he began his long and earnest fight for the new and advancing realism.   In 1882 the publication of *A Modern Instance* gave Howells outstanding rank in the school of realism

---

[61] *Ibid.*, pp. 80-107.   Cf. Mildred Howells, ed., *Life in Letters of William Dean Howells* (Garden City, 1931), I, 7 ff.
[62] *Years of My Youth*, p. 105.

already pioneered by Edward Eggleston, E. W. Howe, and Joseph Kirkland.

His large output of fiction shows that intellectually and emotionally Howells was native to the soil, and though widely he ranged he remained a conscious American.[63] However barren his pages may be of great emotional climaxes, they always bring the reader face to face with the actual. In spite of modern criticism regarding his quiet reticences, his obtrusive morality, his optimism, and his distaste for the uglier phases of life, Howells's small town studies, whether of the West or New England, possess a homely American reality characteristic of most of his fiction. Said to be too respectably commonplace, tedious, and flavorless to suit more advanced modern tastes, his fiction has been variously classified as tales of the New England decline and the last records of the genteel tradition ; Victorian narratives ; and the forerunner of modern sociological stories.[64] There is truth in these criticisms, but it is true, also, that no imprisoning orthodoxies whitewash the verisimilitude of his village interpretations. His fidelity of observation allowed no indulgences in the mawkish sentimentality current in the pre-war and even later fiction. His pictures of quiet villages and small towns lack the bizarre sensationalism characterizing many contemporary stories spiced with glamorous, yet false, scenes. Howells chose to study average American communities "populated with hard-working citizens, not with excessively handsome gangsters and libertine women."[65] Refusing to adopt cheap clichés, he persistently confined his interpretations to normal conditions in the communities he knew most thoroughly. Hamlin Garland, characterizing Howells's ability to record the lives of ordinary men and women, notes that he discovers originality of theme not in what people do in times of fire and murder, but in their everyday lives, in their calm moments. He avoids artificial plots, villains, and heroes.[66] For this ability to create stories as racy of the soil as the New England conscience itself Howells deserves classification as one of the most able post-war interpreters of the New England town.

While later he became dissatisfied with the narrowed out-

[63] Parrington, *The Beginnings of Critical Realism in America*, p. 241.
[64] Hamlin Garland, "Howells" in Macy, ed., *op. cit.*, p. 293.
[65] *Ibid.*, p. 295.
[66] *Ibid.*

look of the Brahmins, Howells turned in his earlier treatments of small towns to the New England locale. In *Suburban Sketches* (1871) the local scenes and characters of the horse-car era in Cambridge are pictured with realism. Sometimes casually dismissed as "another travel novel," the slightly later *The Lady of the Aroostook* should live by virtue of its penetrating study of South Bradfield. In the opening portion, enriched by a wealth of matter delineative of the existence of New England villagers, their habits of thought, their speech peculiarities, and other inimitable minutiae, Howells draws his first full-sketched scenes of upcountry village life. A recent critic, in concluding his praise of the novelist's "pictorial embodiments that defy obliteration," calls attention to the unforgettable values of such minutiae as the parlor lamp of pea-green glass and red woolen wick decorating Miss Maria's center-table.[67]

The Lady of the Aroostook is not so much the study of a Massachusetts small town as it is that of certain small town figures suddenly taken from their provincial environment to a foreign and more complex world without. Lydia Blood, a mill village schoolteacher, untutored in the ways of sophisticated society, is taken unexpectedly from her small town associations to Venice, where she becomes "a lady" in spite of her provincial upbringing. Throughout the book, when the locale is far from South Bradfield, the actions and sayings of Lydia, though newly veneered and polished, reveal the small town from which she came. Notwithstanding his intruding moral that Lydia represents "the true gentility of democracy as opposed to the snobbery of a superficially Europeanized society," Howells produces a realistic picture of a Yankee hill-town of the late nineteenth century. Lydia is the instrument for his teaching that "a lady is a lady anywhere." Other characters (Deacon Latham, Lydia's grandfather, who had "the nervous restlessness of age when out of its wonted place"; Aunt Maria, typically provincial in her curiosity about village funerals and other happenings; the clergyman; and the stagecoach driver) are forceful reminders that South Bradfield is an isolated New England village, shut off from the world in the winter because of the heavy snows and gayer in the summer when boarders arrive from the city. Like many New England towns of the

    [67] Delmar Gross Cooke, *William Dean Howells: A Critical Study* (New York, 1922), p. 179.

period, it was a lifeless place because of the cityward exodus
which has furnished the storyteller many a plot. Lydia, too,
was aware of this situation and she often pondered about the
decrepitude of so many of the villagers. She mused :

> Their children have gone away ; they don't seem to live ; they
> are just staying. When I first came there I was a little girl. One
> day I went into the grave-yard and counted the stones ; there were
> three times as many as there were living persons in the village.[68]

The eighties, the period of Howe's *The Story of a Country Town*,
Kirkland's *Zury*, and other grimly realistic novels, mark not
only Howells's great decade as a novelist, but his best portrayals
of small town backgrounds. In *Dr. Breen's Practice* (1881) the
daily routine in a quiet seaside resort concerns inquisitive and
talkative guests, mostly old maids and widows who make every
triviality matter for their veranda gossiping bees. Small talk
takes on new life with the arrival of a pretty girl, in her late
twenties, who shocks the Victorian veranda brigade by her
announcement that she is a physician. A leisurely and insignificant plot unfortunately weakens this admirably presented hotel world. Similar to the earlier *Doctor Zay*, this later
story of a small town woman physician ends according to the
romantic formula : the young doctor marries and abandons her
profession.

In *A Modern Instance* (1882) Howells's delineations of both
ordinary people and their everyday environment are masterly.
With this realistic study of deterioration of character a deeper
note appears in his work. Dramatizing a modern instance of
young love, marriage, growing distrust, and eventual divorce,
this novel portrays also not only the externals of upcountry
village life during the sixties and seventies, but literary and
journalistic Boston as well. Life in Equity, Maine—in the
White Mountains—moved in the ordinary provincial manner
of the time, the marks of interest being church affairs, business
routine, and a limited social activity. Citizens like that Yankee
of the Yankees, the shrewd village lawyer, Squire Gaylord ; his
faded acquiescent wife ; the humorous philosopher of a near-
by logging camp ; and other native townsmen were well content with Equity's long High Street, its large, square white

---

[68] *The Lady of the Aroostook* (Boston and New York), p. 106. First published in
Boston in 1879.

houses typical of many upper New England villages, its simply styled academy, its hotel, churches, and shops. It was not so with selfish Bartley Hubbard, culture-veneered graduate of a small Down East college, who came to Equity to edit a paper. Then there was Marcia Gaylord, "the most fascinating and full-blooded of Howells's heroines," whom Bartley married.[69] Of the well-chosen minor village scenes and characters which fill out the outline of this small town tragedy, one of the most realistic is that of the printing office force suggestive of the novelist's own early experiences. Another excellent provincial theme, later fully dramatized in *The Rise of Silas Lapham*, grows out of the natural descriptions of the Bostonian Hallecks, newly rich from the father's leather business. Anxious though the children are to cultivate city-born socialites, they fail in their efforts to change the lifelong habits of their parents, who "had come to the city simple and good young village people, and simple and good they had remained." (Just so did Bartley and Marcia, like Lydia Blood, retain their provincial manners even after their residence in Boston.) The novel's primary interest, however, is that of the matrimonial wreck of the young Hubbards, which reaches its highest emotional scene in an Indiana courtroom, where the Squire pleads for his daughter. Here the tragedy of the old man's broken fatherhood presents one of the most poignant scenes in the story. In this revelation of ordinary townspeople Howells is American in scene and portraiture.

Annie Kilburn (1888) is a development of an overworked small town theme, the unexpected return of a prodigal villager. Briefly, this laboriously developed plot tells of wealthy Annie Kilburn, a village aristocrat who returns after a long Italian sojourn to find her native Hatboro transformed into a factory settlement and a summer resort whose citizens are at odds with the original villagers. In delineating the contrast between old Hatboro and the new, Howells shows his kinship with the feminine recorders of the New England decline. He traces the modernization of what once was really an old-fashioned New England village into a sprawling American town, wherein at least a third of the people were raw foreigners or rawly extracted natives.[70] A socialistic note appears in scenes where Howells dallies with the problem of social amelioration for the

[69] Cooke, *op. cit.*, p. 243.   [70] *Annie Kilburn; A Novel* (New York, 1891), p. 117.

laboring Irish, French Canadians, and Italians, as yet unaccepted by the earlier Hatborians.   In *The Quality of Mercy* (1892) Hatboro appears as the provincial stage for a dramatic psychological study of a disgraced capitalist.   When outwardly honest Northwick, local mill official, mysteriously disappears with corporation funds, his daughters, stranded in gossipy Hatboro, are hounded by newspaper reporters and openly snubbed by malicious townspeople.   Here frankly outspoken as the social critic, Howells denounces an unlicensed press, rigid social conventions, and small town narrowness.

The last phase of Howells's interpretation of the small town is marked by his return for inspiration to the materials of his native Midwest.   *The Kentons* (1902) is the story of a typical leading family in an average, though pleasant, Ohio country town.   In the semi-autobiographical *New Leaf Mills* (1913) Howells portrays a pioneer Ohio Valley mill community, hardly to be dignified by the name of town.   It was a place where "a fierce religiosity, choosing between salvation and perdition, was the spiritual life which an open atheist here and there sweepingly denied."[71]   Brush arbor meetings, baptisms, spelling matches, huskings and apple-peelings, house and barn raisings, quiltings, and shooting matches, attended by old and young, enlivened an otherwise drab existence.   *The Leatherwood God* (1916), motivated by the religiosity to be found in the frontier towns described by Howe, Kirkland, and other early realists, is another full account of Midwestern village life. The remotely situated settlers of Leatherwood Creek gave little thought to the industrial problems which then agitated older sections of the country.   Living in the midst of a simple antebellum civilization, these frontier folk found their chief emotional expurgation in an intensely felt religion.   Similar to Squire Gaylord is shrewd Matthew Braile, homely philosopher, genial agnostic, and justice of the peace at Leatherwood.   Plot interest centers around a persuasive evangelist whom the simple native exhorters set up as a god.   The whole novel shows a town in the making.

Recently characterized as "the most pathetic figure in [the] post-war gallery," and a timid realist who tightly hugged the limitations of the contemporary scene,[72] Howells, nevertheless,

[71] *New Leaf Mills* (New York, 1913), p. 22; cf. *Years of My Youth*, p. 44.
[72] Mumford, *The Golden Day*, pp. 167 and 170.
    10

fits into the literary history of the New England small town as
an able interpreter who, though by birth and youthful experiences a complete Midwesterner, turned eastward for most of
his fictional materials.   He was a Brahmin by adoption.

"This Barren Age of Ours"

Throughout America during the late nineteenth century
movements set in motion by the Civil War were reshaping
community standards.   Everywhere life was adjusting itself.
The older provincial world, static and peaceful, steadily dis-
integrated under almost crushing impacts and quickly vanished as the Gilded Age became an Age of Guilt.[73]   Bribery
and graft in state and municipal politics ; deepening struggles
between capital and labor ; growing nepotism in insurance and
other circles ; quantity production abetted by widespread advertising and chain store developments ; exposures of national
scandals involving people in positions of high trust ; the ad-
mission of new states (Oklahoma, New Mexico, and Arizona)
and the expansion of the frontier to the coast ; the urbanization of population and an increasing complexity of living ; and
great changes in the means of transportation—all radically
affected our national outlook.[74]   Materialism developed apace
in city, town, and country, even while Bryan rebelled against
the crucifixion of mankind on a cross of gold.   In England
Americans became known as "claimants for the Biggest in
Everything."[75]   In literature, as in actual life, the end of a
period had come, a swiftly changing era of culmination, "an
equinox between two creative periods, a moment of pause, of
sterility, and Indian summer, silent, hectic with colors, dreamy
with the past, yet alive with mighty gathering forces."[76]   The
old order was attacked, but, at the turn of the century, not
entirely obliterated by the emergence of new forces.

Dominated by the mid-century Brahmins, the older order of
literature, uninvigorated by the new, still was in control.
Lowell, Holmes, Mrs. Stowe, Whittier, Melville, and others

[73] Harry Hartwick, *The Foreground of American Fiction* (New York, 1934), p. 203.
[74] For full details see Pattee, *The New American Literature* (New York, 1930),
pp. 33 ff. ; Holbrook Jackson, *The Eighteen Nineties* (New York, 1922) ; Thomas
Beer, *The Mauve Decade* (Garden City, 1926) ; and Mark Sullivan, *Our Times* (New
York, 1927), II and III.
[75] Alan Bott, *This Was England; Manners and Customs of the Ancient Victorians*
(Garden City, 1931), p. 177.
[76] Pattee, *op. cit.*, "Fin De Siècle."

lived until the early nineties; Howells and Higginson were among those who lived in the new century. As Professor Pattee has noted, with swansongs of the "masters" in each season's lists, American literature continued to flourish in quantity.[77] In quality it was at low ebb. The most popular poetic voices of the age were weak, giving expression to nicely phrased sentiments or verses in polished, but shallow, French forms. In 1895 American readers of Tennyson's popular poetry could turn also to Howells's *Stops of Various Quills*, *Songs of Vagabondia* by Hovey and Carman, and the widely quoted verses of James Whitcomb Riley and Eugene Field. In fiction a devitalized Brahminism and the restrained realism of the Howells regime still held sway, while young Stephen Crane, impoverished in the New York slums, was observing the sordid life he fictionalized in *Maggie: A Girl of the Streets* (1893). While the same insurgent's *The Red Badge of Courage* was puzzling irritated and "genteel" critics before becoming a best seller in 1896, American publishers were turning to England for importations. Even here, however, the conservatives, dominated by the Brahmin tradition, were cautious. Foreign novels, such as Hardy's *Jude the Obscure* which appeared in *Harper's*, often were boldly cut to suit the Victorian taste of many magazine readers. The same public for which Gilder of *The Century* "purified" Mark Twain's manuscripts denounced *Jude the Obscure* as "degenerate" and "rotten," but delighted in the stories of Miss Jewett, F. Marion Crawford, and Frank R. Stockton. It was the era of such popular importations as *Quo Vadis*, *Sentimental Tommy*, and Stevenson's *Vailima Letters*.

Eventually, however, rebellious youth trampled upon long dominant conservatism. Here and there native insurgents made tiny rifts in "this changeless glimmer of dead gray." Harold Frederic's naturalistic small town novel, *The Damnation of Theron Ware* (1896), labeled in England so "dangerous" that it was published inoffensively as *Illumination*, made its author one of the insurgent realists, in America at least, of the *fin de siècle* decadence. Slowly outworn conventions crumpled with the appearance of the new and original work of Garland, Tarkington, Norris, Dreiser, Edith Wharton, Ellen Glasgow, and others. Chicago aspired to become the new literary center as the "yellow nineties" merged into the new century.

[77] *Ibid.*, p. 15.

In 1896, with the appearance of a slender book, "printed for the author" and "dedicated to any man, woman, or critic who will cut the edges of it," an unusual new poet arrived, but without fanfare. This small, but now significant, volume was *The Torrent and the Night Before*, the first book of Edwin Arlington Robinson, a village-born and bred New Englander wonderfully gifted with the powers of reading and recording life. Voicing the same indignation later expressed by Masters's Petit the Poet, young Robinson denounced the flourishing versifiers of the "mauve decade" and earnestly declared the need of a new generation when he pled :

> Oh for a poet—for a beacon bright
> To rift this changeless glimmer of dead gray ;
> To spirit back the Muses, long astray,
> And flush Parnassus with a newer light ;
> To put these little sonnet-men to flight
> Who fashion, in a shrewd mechanic way,
> Songs without souls, that flicker for a day,
> To vanish in irrevocable night.
>
> What does it mean, this barren age of ours?
> Here are the men, the women, and the flowers,
> The seasons and the sunset as before.
> What does it mean? Shall there not one arise,
> To wrench one banner from the western skies,
> And mark it with his name forevermore?[78]

Like many of his predecessors in the interpretation of the New England town, Robinson early lived in a village community. He was born, December 22, 1869, in Head Tide, Maine, a picturesque, custom-bound village on the Sheep-scott River, some miles east of the Kennebec.[79] When the poet was but a child his father, Edward Robinson, the grain merchant, left this old-fashioned village for the old-fashioned town of Gardiner (originally Gardinerstown), on the Cobbossee, which flashes and foams into the Kennebec. Amy Lowell has described in some detail the English appearance of the town,

[78] "Sonnet," first published in *The Critic*, Nov. 24, 1894 ; later included in *The Torrent and the Night Before* (Gardiner, Maine, 1896), p. 12. See C. B. Hogan, *A Bibliography of Edwin Arlington Robinson* (New York, 1936), p. 219.
[79] Amy Lowell, *Tendencies in Modern American Poetry* (New York, 1917), p. 10. Clifton Johnson, *New England and Its Neighbors* (New York, 1924), "Down in Maine," pp. 196 ff., describes illustratively the old village life here suggested by Miss Lowell.   For biographical details see Hermann Hagedorn, *Edwin Arlington Robinson* (New York, 1938).

a leisurely place boasting of a grey stone Tudor mansion, a sort of manor house—supposedly the "Great House" later pictured by the poet—once the center of local social affairs.[80] This little town of Gardiner, Robinson himself has said, "may be responsible in a shadowy way, for Tilbury Town" of his poetry.[81]

In 1897, after a few years at Harvard (1891-93) and a precarious sojourn in New York, Edwin Robinson, working with quiet certainty among the conflicting forces of his confused era, published his second collection, *The Children of the Night*, containing some of his most memorable portraits of Tilbury Town citizens. A definite departure from all earlier romantic village poetry, these compact portraitures are likewise significant as the beginning of an adventure of discovery.[82] Seventeen years before *Spoon River Anthology* Robinson, with his intense curiosity about human nature, was discovering in the provincial life of his native towns the content and method of realistic narrative and character portrayal. Unlike his "literary" contemporaries, he turned to the supposedly unpoetic matter of village failures, idealists, suicides, and other defeated citizens encountered in one's common experiences in hamlet and town. He saw drama in the story of man's insufficiency to cope with a too powerful fate. Wordsworthian in his use of the natural cadences of speech, Robinson effected a significant, but at the time little noticed, innovation in American poetic methods. Marked, in part, by the objectivity of his later poetry, this early group of village portraits deals with materials distinctively of our country and our time. Intensely

[80] In her autobiographical *Stepping Westward* (New York, 1913, p. 240) Mrs. Laura E. Richards, daughter of Julia Ward Howe and resident of Gardiner for more than half a century, comments thus concerning Miss Lowell's comparison of Oaklands (the Gardiner mansion about a mile from the town) to an English manor house : "I have seen lately an account of Gardiner and Oaklands which amused me." To Mrs. Richards, whose family life was closely bound with that of the Gardiners, the town was "not merely a pretty river town, to be viewed with approval by the motorist; not merely a thriving community with churches, schools, factories, and whatever else thrift connotes ; but a place of character and quality all its own" (*op. cit.*, p. 335). Settled by the sturdy Gardiners, the town even today is characterized by "a certain toughness of fibre, a certain unwillingness to bend."

See also Esther Vinson, "Tilbury Town," *The Saturday Review of Literature*, XL, 632 (April 20, 1935), and George St. Clair, "E. A. Robinson and Tilbury Town," *The New Mexico Quarterly*, IV, 95-107 (May 1934).

[81] Richards, *op. cit.*, p. 383.

[82] Lloyd Morris, *The Poetry of Edwin Arlington Robinson* (Garden City, 1923), p. 13.

dramatic, Robinson, even in these early poems, ponders over the problems of the individual and, employing sudden gestures, reveals in a flash moments of choice in which a complete past is harvested.[83]   Certainly, these early distinctive and frequently ironical individualizations of the people of Tilbury reveal Robinson's far-reaching break with tradition.   He himself, though unheralded, was "a beacon bright."

Of Tilbury Town itself we see little, for the poet's interests, like those of Browning with whom he has been compared, early were connected with the passionate feelings and ambitions of his characters.   In *The Children of the Night* Robinson's "meditative ramblings through human character and passions" produced sketches of town folk whose inner conflicts foreshadowed the twisted lives of Spoon River.   Here are subtle revelations of disappointment, frustrated ambition, self-misunderstanding in gentle souls, and nerveless self-indulgence in moral wretches.[84] Here are scenes and characters from an amazingly lifelike, but imaginary, community.   Among the sympathetic, shrewd, yet detached, introductions to plain people, everyday folk as familiar in Oklahoma Town as in Tilbury, are those to John Evereldown, a skirt-crazed reprobate who follows the women wherever they call; "a loveless exile," miserly Aaron Stark; genial Cliff Klingenhagen, a host who drank wormwood; Reuben Bright, grief-stricken butcher; incisively sketched Richard Cory who "put a bullet through his head"; lovelorn Luke Havergal; and melancholy-faced Charles Carville, misunderstood in life.[85]   Frequently, as in "Richard Cory," Robinson delineates a character by showing its effect upon various associates.   Again, as in "Luke Havergal," he uses the inferential method of suggesting through the character some mystery or unusual story.

Occasionally in this first collection Robinson's carefully chosen lines picture decaying or deserted villages where there is little but the ghosts of things:

> No life, no love, no children, and no men;
> And over the forgotten place there clings

[83] *Ibid.*, p. 20.
[84] Charles Cestre, *An Introduction to Edwin Arlington Robinson* (New York, 1930), p. 120.
[85] Robinson, *Collected Poems* (New York, 1922); *The Children of the Night* (1890-1897), pp. 71 ff.

The strange and unrememorable light
That is in dreams.[86]

In a few poems the poet views the towns of his boyhood as he saw them in after years. Stagnating communities they are where the town clerks, once young bloods whom the women called fair, have degenerated into "a shop-worn brotherhood" and the once popular tavern has become an unsightly place whose rank weeds, torn curtains, and broken windows bespeak the decay of many a New England village of the time.[87]   The same thought, suggesting the old homes of Deephaven, finds simple, but revealing, expression in "The House on the Hill," a brief tragedy of decline in staid Tilbury Town.[88]

Robinson's preoccupation with humanity is elsewhere apparent.   In later volumes, *Captain Craig* (1902), *The Town Down the River* (1910), *The Three Taverns* (1920), and *Avon's Harvest* (1921), his predilection for village types again is seen in his use of Tilbury Town themes.   Here, as in *The Children of the Night*, he has used his gift of transmutation.   He has not put the people of Head Tide and Gardiner directly into his sketches and ballads, but in Flammonde, Bewick Finzer, Miniver Cheevy, and others has created realistic townsmen who might well have walked the streets of actual towns.   Though he turned in *Merlin*, *Lancelot*, and *Tristram* to the picturesque settings and romantic characters of a legendary past, in all of his village sketches, set against the background of the New England country rich in traditions and individual types, Robinson proved himself broadly American.

Often Robinson's keen observation discovered what Amy Lowell described as "success through failure."   In homely village individuals like Captain Craig the poet saw a wealth of material for psychological and emotional studies, for moral and intellectual interpretations rich in the elements of human interest.   The wearisome philosophical rambles and letters with which Captain Craig, wanderer and mendicant, reveals his mental attitudes and peculiarities of conscience to his Tilbury benefactors illustrate Robinson's tendency to carry this interest too far.   Supposedly the story of an aged beggar who went

---

[86] *Ibid.*, "The Dead Village," p. 88.
[87] *Ibid.*, "The Clerks," p. 90, and "The Tavern," p. 93.
[88] Mrs. Richards, *op. cit.*, p. 382, says that Robinson denied that this was Oaklands.

"patch-clad through the streets, weak, dizzy, chilled, and half-starved" until he was befriended by several young men, including the poet, the poem does not deal so much with Tilbury Town as with the philosophies of the poet himself. The old captain serves admirably, though at times wearisomely, as the poet's spokesman. Blank verse sketches of Craig, self-styled iconoclast, sage-errant, and humorist at large, of the poet, Killigrew, Plunket, and Morgan, his friends; glimpses of the snug room at "The Chrysalis," where the group smoked before a roaring beech fire with little care for the cold rain outside; and the scenes in the old captain's bedroom show Robinson the master realist.

Like many provincial New Englanders, Tilbury people still adhered to the puritanic principles of cant and bigotry, a spirit with which Robinson had no sympathy. Tilbury Town rejected the old captain simply because he was "a son of Bohemia and disciple of Epicurus." There was, says Robinson, "a false note in the Tilbury tune."

> They found it more melodious to shout
> Right on, with unmolested adoration,
> To keep the tune as it has always been,
> To trust in God, and let the Captain starve.[89]

Social superiority again is given a rap in the sketch of foreign-born Flammonde whose unfamiliarity with local prejudices throws into sharp relief certain town characters so beset by their own narrowness that they are ever ready to create scandal.[90] An artist in the art of living, Flammonde,

> With firm address and foreign air,
> With news of nations in his talk
> And something royal in his walk,

came from afar to Tilbury Town. A perfect gentleman, able to know men and probe into their deeper natures, Flammonde caused small talk and scandal among the villagers. His careless elegance and ease of manner disturbed them. His indulgent geniality was a foil to their native harshness. An unpuritanic sketch, drawn with humor, is "Mr. Flood's Party," the story of old Eben Flood, who came from his mountainside

---

[89] *Collected Poems* (1922), *Captain Craig*, p. 114.
[90] *Ibid.*, "Flammonde" from *The Man Against the Sky* (1916), pp. 3 ff.

home above the village to buy a jug of ale.[91]   Tilbury people
must have looked askance at that abortive poet and dreamer
of dreams, Miniver Cheevy.   Born out of his time, Miniver
lamented the vulgarity of his own time and longed for the picturesqueness and romance of the days of chivalry.[92]

In these and other penetrating sketches Robinson has added
a new approach to the interpretation of American townspeople.
Avoiding treatment of the spectacular and the sensational, he
has developed a psychological type of village drama in concentrated   narrative,   dramatic   monologue,   and   dialogue.
Though in the Tilbury sketches he denies nothing of his New
England legacy, Robinson, nevertheless, has employed his materials with a literary independence vitalized by the modern
spirit.   Years ago—long before his death in 1935—the poet
put "the little sonnet-men to flight," when he began his uncompromising presentation of the repressed folk of his native
towns and countryside, a tradition-bound region where, in the
words of Robinson himself, "the wind is always north-north-
east"; where passion is "a soilure of the wits"; where

> Joy shivers in the corner where she knits
> And Conscience always has the rocking-chair,
> Cheerful as when she tortured into fits
> The first cat that ever was killed by Care.[93]

So full and varied have been the treatments of the New England town in literature that today a sort of literary exhaustion
seems to have put its blight on the region.   Even before the
World War the soil of literary New England, though covering
a wide area, already had been "harried and curried, raked,
screened, sifted and resifted, sowed and reaped, realized and
idealized to the point of exhaustive monotony."[94]   In more
recent years the widespread interest of writers and readers in
other small town materials has caused New England to be less
favored than newer regional fields in the Midwest, the Southwest, and, more recently, the South.   While the Tilbury sketch-

---

[91] *Ibid.*, "Mr. Flood's Party" from *Avon's Harvest, etc.* (1921), p. 573.
[92] *Ibid.*, "Miniver Cheevy" from *The Town Down The River* (1910), p. 247.
[93] *Collected Poems* (New York, 1937), "New England" from *Dionysus in Doubt*
(1925), p. 900.   Other treatments of the New England small town found in later
poems included in the 1937 collection are "Haunted House," p. 870: "A Man
in Our Town," p. 886; "Mortmain," pp. 889 ff.; and *The Man Who Died Twice*,
pp. 921 ff.
[94] John Curtis Underwood, *Literature and Insurgency* (New York, 1914), p. 88.

es are the most significantly artistic among the poetic interpretations of the New England village, comparatively few modern novelists have been intrigued by the long-used provincial
life of this older section.   Suggestive of new and broader attitudes toward the once all-important New England town is the
fact that four of its significant modern interpreters were born
elsewhere; a fifth, a native Cape Codder and the author of
more than thirty New England novels, is either unmentioned,
or merely listed by name and a few works, in the most widely
accepted modern discussions of American literature.   The
former glory of the New England town has faded.*   Except
for guerilla attacks, the war against the village has been waged
on other grounds.

Dorothy Canfield Fisher, daughter of a university president,
was born in 1879 at Lawrence, Kansas.   With unusual advantages of education and travel, she developed through the
years broad sympathies and made friends with many nationalities.   Thus fortunately endowed, Mrs. Fisher in 1907, after
her marriage, came to live in an old house on the side of one
of the Green Mountains, near the village of Arlington, Vermont.   Here she has entered easily into the spirit of New England lives and has developed "a clear-headed, hearty New
England Americanism."[95]

Termed "a clever dramatizer of the obvious," Mrs. Fisher
has not become one of the insurgents against the disturbing
ugliness, cultural poverty, prejudices, and blatant vulgarity of
the modern small town.[96]   Instead, seemingly she has been
unruffled by the bitter fight of her contemporaries against the
"village virus."   Believing that community fellowship breeds a
fine artistic spirit, Mrs. Fisher has contented herself with making friendly observations and developing theses of family relationships, education, and social exactions connected with the
life of certain villages and isolated farm communities of Vermont.   Like her predecessors, she, too, has delineated the New
England of abandoned farmhouses and quiet villages.   In
"Old Man Warner," for example, she notes that after the war
"only the older men returned to the Arnold Hollow settlement

---

* Since the above was written Thornton Wilder's *Our Town* (picturing a New
Hampshire town) has been named the Pulitzer Prize play for 1938.   See Chapter
X.
  [95] Overton, *The Women Who Make Our Novels*, p. 301.
  [96] F. L. Allen, *Only Yesterday* (New York, 1931), p. 229.

to go on cultivating their steep, rocky farms.   The younger
ones set off for the West."[97]   "Adeste Fidelis!" tells of the pathetically ineffectual efforts of a loyal old village woman to
hold migrating townspeople by continuing church services with
but two faithful members, by keeping the library open after
there was no one left to read the books, and by providing a
teacher when only six children could be found in the whole
district.[98]   The new industrial towns took the Vermonters as
they did Mrs. Freeman's villagers.   Others departed because of
loneliness and educational disadvantages.   Left behind were
the Mehitables—New England Lulu Betts—whose greatest adventures in life came from their winning first prizes on laboriously made quilts and counterpanes at county fairs.[99]

While Mrs. Fisher saw the barrenness and provinciality of
such village lives, she also observed the neighborliness of the
people and the beauty of the scenery.   The quiet life of her
Vermont village is not the repressed existence of a Freeman
community.   Even village gossip is taken freely as evidence
of the interest of citizens in their fellows, an interest which accounts for their ignorance of metropolitan culture.   In *Rough-
Hewn* (1922) two expatriates, stranded in Rome, are lured back
to Vermont by thoughts of the "folksy" ways of their native
Ashley, an old-fashioned village remembered for its "long line
of splendid, splendid elms" and white houses.[100]   The town
fool of Hillsboro, the scene of many of Mrs. Fisher's stories,
sums up the attitude of contentment which most of his fellow
villagers have toward their uneventful lives.   When asked "For
Mercy's sake, what do you people *do* all the time, away off up
here, and so far from everything?" the fool answered in astonishment, "*Do?* Why, we jes' *live!*"[101]   Fully aware of the narrow ways of Hillsboro, the novelist has tried to probe the deeper
meaning of provincial life.   Beneath the pettiness she searched
for beauty, love, and sacrifice.   To one who had spent many
months abroad, as Mrs. Fisher has, even the coming of foreigners into Vermont villages is not interpreted as tragedy.
Thrifty, home-loving Italians, hospitable French, and hard-
working Irish are regarded as elements to vitalize the "white-
headed rheumatickers potterin' around."

[97] *Raw Material* (New York, 1923), p. 70.
[98] *Hillsboro People* (New York, 1915), pp. 325 ff.
[99] *Ibid.*, "The Bedquilt," pp. 67 ff.   [100] New York, 1922, p. 404.
[101] *Hillsboro People*, "At the Foot of the Hemlock Mountain," p. 5.

Traditional traits are found in *Hillsboro People, Raw Materials, The Brimming Cup, Rough-Hewn,* and *Bonfire.* In both novel and sketch such familiar New England qualities as restraint, bluntness of manner, and stubbornness are fully exemplified. Unusual, however, is the prominence given the men, often neglected in the provincial fiction of the section. The gay old grandfather in "The Heyday of the Blood," the grim lover in "Flint and Fire," the Puritan preacher and the beauty-loving son in "The Deliverer," the town fool and the town liar in "A Village Munchausen," and others show the variety of Hillsboro men.[102] Unusual also is *Bonfire* (1933), a many-faceted novel of village scandal and violence picturing the drunkards, morons, and other low types of a Vermont mountain settlement and proving that Mrs. Fisher sees more in small town life than sweetness and light. Having a wider interest than dialect and local peculiarities, Mrs. Fisher is broader in her interpretations than Miss Jewett, for she sees both the sordid and the beautiful in New England lives. She has not fathomed the New England soul as has Mrs. Freeman, but she has a broader understanding of human nature and a wider range of subjects.[103]

Another note in the literary interpretation of the tradition-bound New England town is that provoked by outside criticism, a harsher judgment foreshadowed by native realists like Mrs. Freeman. Howells, as an outsider, helped to break down the old provincial wall of the Brahmins. Others, less respectful of the "great" tradition, came in as summer boarders and casual observers and recorded their impressions of the village. Exceptions to such casual, and negligible, recorders, are Edith Newbold Jones Wharton (1862-1937), Louis Bromfield (1896- —), Edna Ferber (1887-—), and Robert Nathan (1894-—), outsiders whose community pictures have marked a new phase in the literary history of the New England town.

There are certain contemporary masterpieces whose scenes, although laid in America and created by Americans, are not closely linked with the great problems of our modern world. One of these, a naturally individual novel, is *Ethan Frome* (1911), Mrs. Wharton's masterly interpretation of the strict New England code. This novelette, together with *Summer*

---

[102] *Ibid.,* pp. 37, 99, 165, and 251.
[103] In *The Squirrel Cage* (New York, 1912), descriptive of an Ohio locale, Mrs. Fisher shows her interest in small town life elsewhere. In *Seasoned Timber* (1939) Mrs. Fisher turns again to Vermont.

(1917), unfolds a tragedy of circumstances far removed from the themes of *The House of Mirth*, *The Custom of the Country*, *The Age of Innocence*, and her other novels dissecting New York's so-called idle-rich class.   In the autobiographical *A Backward Glance* (1934) Mrs. Wharton has confessed that for years before her writing of *Ethan Frome* she "had wanted to draw life as it really was in the derelict mountain villages of New England, a life even in my time, and a thousand-fold more a generation earlier, utterly unlike that seen through the rose-colored spectacles of my predecessors, ..."[104]   Throughout her ten years of residence in Massachusetts Mrs. Wharton had been deeply impressed by the cramped lives of the native element.   As she saw it, rural New England, a no less compact community than her fashionable New York, was bound by the forces of poverty, which repressed its victims more than a social code.   In her sight "the snow-bound villages of Western Massachusetts were still grim places, morally and physically : insanity, incest and slow mental and moral starvation were hidden away behind the paintless wooden housefronts of the long village street, or in the isolated farm-houses on the neighboring hills ; and Emily Brontë would have found as savage tragedies in our remoter valleys as on her Yorkshire moors."[105]

Thus familiar with the aspect, dialect, and mental and moral attitudes of the hill people, Edith Wharton achieved a masterpiece in *Ethan Frome*.   In the bleak Massachusetts community of Starkfield—"from which most of the smart ones get away" —embittered Ethan Frome finds temporary happiness through association with young Mattie Silver, a poor cousin of complaining Zenobia, his wife.   His love for Mattie promises Ethan freedom from a life of almost unbearable sordidness.   But poverty forbids release.   Crippled in an attempt at suicide, Ethan for years is forced to bear the presence in his household of his irritable wife and of the girl whom he loved, now the wreck of her former self.   "Not since Hawthorne has a novelist laid in New England the scene of any tragedy of such power and elevation as this."[106]   Unhampered by local color laws and freed by her knowledge of world society, Mrs. Wharton has given her theme a note of universal tragedy.   She has shown

[104] *A Backward Glance* (New York, 1934), p. 293.
[105] *Ibid.*, p. 294.
[106] Carl and Mark Van Doren, *American and British Literature since 1890* (New York, 1925), p. 67.

how a character, molded by a narrow environment, could not
escape his cheerless situation. With apparent impassivity he
had to bear the life-sentence which circumstances imposed
upon him. The narrator of this tragic tale is an outsider, an
engineer stationed at Starkfield long after Ethan and Mattie
had attempted to escape their despair by guiding their sled into a huge tree at the foot of a dangerous hill. Through the
dramatic recital of local legend the engineer presents that
tragic trio—nagging Zenobia, crippled Ethan, and Mattie—
against the bleak background of decaying Starkfield, an appropriate stage for the gnarled, embittered lives hopelessly
bound to the Frome farmhouse.

Marked by the same literary economy as *Ethan Frome*, *Summer*
likewise deals with "undiluted American material." Young
Charity Royall, like Ethan, challenges the ironclad conventions of a decaying Massachusetts hilltown and is crushed.
The facts of Charity's tragic story are presented with the same
fidelity to truth as are those of Ethan and Mattie. The daughter of a prostitute, Charity is driven to despair by her impoverished life in the "weather-beaten sunburnt village" of West
Dormer. With dramatic and convincing realism Mrs. Wharton bares the tragedy of Charity's existence; of her work in a
musty library, suggestive of the decadence of New England
culture; of her contempt for her foster father, a tippling lawyer; and of her ill-starred associations with a young architect.

In neither of these portrayals of the decaying village does
Mrs. Wharton dally with an ethical thesis. She simply represents human beings as being surrounded by forces quite beyond their own powers to control or defy. In contrast to the
rose-and-lavender pages of some of her predecessors, Mrs.
Wharton's is a picture of the domination of poverty and the
village code.

In 1927 Bromfield, an Ohioan, was awarded the Pulitzer
Prize for his *Early Autumn* (1926), the story of Chicago-born
Olivia McConnel, whose marriage into a once powerful New
England family brought her to an old Georgian house as the
wife of Anson Pentland of Durham Village, near the New
Hampshire foothills. The sleepy peacefulness of the village,
the result of a westward migration of more than half of its
people; its renewed economic vitality through the more recent
building of mills; and the loss of the land by the old families as

incoming, energetic Poles, Czechs, and Irish bought up the mortgaged farms and village property show, bit by bit, how the whole picture of life in the village at large and at the Pentland mansion had come to assume a strange pattern.   Everything had changed from the days when a quiet village of white wooden houses built along High Street was dominated by the pioneer families.   Now "plain columns of ugly stucco bungalows, each filled with its little family of Polish mill-workers" marred the fading beauty of the early elm-shaded houses.

Edna Ferber's *American Beauty* (1931) dramatizes anew the decadence of New England culture.   Primarily the story of the slow degeneration of the Oakes family and its thousand acres of rich farm land through more than two centuries of American life, this novel, abetted by its realistic glimpses of a Connecticut factory town, is significant in its suggestiveness of the breaking of age-old traditions of the New England town and the setting up of new standards of conduct.   Stonefield, rapidly expanding into an ugly factory settlement, and the rich countryside slip gradually from the possession of tight-lipped New Englanders into the hands of a rugged, full-blooded Polish peasantry, an element promising a more virile race of the soil than the unvital native families.

Not long after Sinclair Lewis's first attack against the village Robert Nathan, one of the new romanticists, exposed the pettiness of small town life in a cutting, but unobtrusive, fashion.   A quiet skeptic, Nathan, with something of an ironic touch, often contrasts the ugliness of the actual with a romantic ideal.   Unlike Lewis, he is not aroused so much by provincial dullness as he is by the prejudiced outlook of those villagers who, though petty in their attitude toward less fortunate neighbors, glory in themselves and parade their own righteousness.   *Autumn* (1921), a profoundly ironic tale of a romantic schoolmaster and stupid, unimaginative, grasping townspeople, illustrates what may come from a narrowed environment.   There is Mr. Jeminy, the master, whose peculiar methods of teaching the gospel of happiness arouse the villagers to the point of dismissing the gentle old man after his thirty years of service in Hillsboro.   His detached, dreamy manner, intensified by his frequent reading of Boethius, Plotinus, and other philosophers, cause the more practical townsmen to regard Mr. Jeminy as a befuddled old man, a person apart,

incapable of teaching their children.   Misunderstanding provincials—Mrs. Grumble, for years the master's housekeeper;
long-tongued loungers and male gossips; Miss Beal, the dress-
maker and "as good as a newspaper"; and others—are ironically used as dramatic foils to the disillusioned master.   Completely misunderstood and publicly criticized, Mr. Jeminy, at
last, feels that he has failed in his life-work of teaching his
students something more than plus and minus.   But his practical tradesman and farmer patrons could not understand.
By their cruelty they destroyed the faith of a poetic soul who
sought refuge in headlong flight from the hated, yet dearly
loved, community.   *Autumn* has been effectively termed "an
idyll of loneliness, with a commentary on materialism, done in
simple, wistful language."[107]

In Nathan's earliest novel, *Peter Kindred* (1919), the New
England town is featured in introductory descriptions of Peter's
school life at Phillips Exeter, a school which "stands gravely
to the sun along a wide street of mighty and venerable trees"
in a little New Hampshire town.   It is in *Autumn*, however,
rather than in *Peter Kindred* or the delightful *The Puppet Master*
(1923), that Nathan best affiliates himself with the delineators
of the New England town.   Here, with his whimsicality, subdued irony, quiet satire, and subtle sophistication, Robert
Nathan has given distinction to the fiction of the town.

In the heavily documented literary history of the New England town authors have turned repeatedly to remote upcountry villages, agricultural centers, communities marked by regional peculiarities, and to places of historic interest.   Until
a descendant of seamen more than thirty years ago began describing its life, the Cape Cod region had been neglected in
fiction.   In 1902, when Albert Brandt of New Jersey published
Cape Cod Ballads, Joseph Crosby Lincoln (1870—) added new
localized matter to the bulky materials of the New England
town.   Since his first novel, *Cap'n Eri* (1904), Lincoln has written prolifically concerning the Cape towns and folk, places
and people he has known from boyhood.[108]   His failure to
achieve real distinction in his delineations of the Cape Codders

---

[107] Parrington, *The Beginnings of Critical Realism, etc.*, p. 378.
[108] Lincoln (quoted from Overton, *American Nights Entertainment*, New York,
1923, pp. 333-334) says: I have never knowingly drawn the exact, recognizable
portrait of an individual. . . .   I have endeavored always to be true to type, in
writing of the old deep-sea captain, the coasting skipper, the longshoreman or

lies not in his failure to understand their towns and ways, but in his negligible plots and repeatedly used character types. Further, a prevailing note of optimism brings comparison with the earlier Zona Gale and Booth Tarkington cheerfulness. Lincoln himself admits his preferences for happily united heroes and heroines, for virtue rewarded, and vice punished. In spite of this Richardsonian method, he gives a faithful picturing of Yarmouth, Brewster, Wellmouth Corners, North Ostable, and other villages by the sea as they existed thirty or forty years ago.

These stories of shrewd Yankee seafaring people lack the note of bleakness and repression characteristic of many New England tales. To be sure, there are poorer and foreign elements, especially the "Portygee," in the Cape towns, but there is no prevailing poverty. Wellmouth Corners—in *Head Tide* (1932)—has its quota of retired captains, who had saved much from a profitable India and China trade, shrewd bankers, and politically minded lawyers. Even the penniless hero, from the West, inherits a paying newspaper business and gains the love of a village girl. *Doctor Nye of North Ostable*, as well as *Head Tide*, marks Lincoln as "a genial chronicler" of village political rivalries. Old captains, such as Cap'n Zeb (*The Postmaster*, 1912) and Cap'n Ezra Titcomb (*Partners of the Tide*, 1905), dissatisfied with their inactivity after long years at sea, are among the best and most picturesque of Lincoln's characters. Certain stock characters, however, people his villages : old maids, like Miss Alma Perry, "Four Cornerite of the Four Cornerites"; redoubtable matrons; summer boarders; and "schoolmarms." Such representative works as *Cap'n Eri, Our Village, Fair Harbor*, and *Head Tide*, chronicles of people who do not take life too seriously, portray the seafaring Yankee and Cape Cod village life at the turn of the century and later.

The New England village, changing gradually from its early Arcadian phase into the modernized town, or lapsing into a

the people of the Cape villages. . . . I have made it a rule never to use an expression or idiom I have not heard used by a native of the old colony."

See also Clinton Johnson, *op. cit.*, chap. xiv, "Cape Cod Folks," and Allen Forbes, *Towns of New England, etc.* (commemorating the Tercentenary of the Landing of the Pilgrims), New York, 1921, "Yarmouth, Massachusetts," I, 216. The latter is beautifully illustrated, often with copies of rare prints of early town scenes and people. In this connection see also Henry H. Moore, "A Maine Seacoast Village," *The Outlook*, CXXV, 264 ff. (June 9, 1920), for eight photographs of village scenes.

11

quiet decline, has been rich in its history and familiar by virtue of its many recorders. Established by Englishmen, the
towns of New England bore English names, for the first settlers

> . . . named their rocky farmlands,
> Their hamlets by the sea,
> For the mother-towns that bred them,
> In racial loyalty.

> 'Cambridge, Hartford, Gloucester,
> Hampton, Norwich, Stowe!
> The younger sons looked backward
> And sealed their sonship so.[109]

Such fealty helped to produce a town type which has long enriched American literature.   But the New England dominance
eventually was challenged by those who moved into the free
lands of the West.   New towns and new writers arose even
while loyal New Englanders mourned the decline of their villages.   First, Cooper picturing the New York village, then
the pioneering Kirklands with their studies of frontier settlements, and later Garland, Howe, and Mark Twain introduced
into literature newer towns beyond the pale of New England.
In more recent years the literary map has been dotted with
unromantic names like Gopher Prairie, Winesburg, and Oklahoma Town.   With the South, so long silent in its expressions
of town life, now vocal the New England town might well be,
until new recorders arrive, like Robinson's dead village where
"there is nothing but the ghost of things."   Whether the materials of the New England town have been used "to the verge
of exhaustion—after our prevalent national tendency to penny-
wise and pound-foolish measure in agriculture and other cul-
tures"[110]—is a matter of conjecture.   Once having escaped the
American disease of Growth and Bigness, such towns probably
will not change so radically as to offer wholly new fictional
materials to future interpreters.   One can hardly imagine, as
Bernard De Voto has written, "Concord tattooing its lowlands
with white stakes, calling itself 'Villa Superba : The Sunlight
City of Happy Kiddies and Cheap Labor,' and loosing a thou-

---

[109] Abbie F. Brown, "Names," Forbes, *op. cit.*, p. 224.
[110] Underwood, *loc. cit.*

sand rabid salesmen to barter lots on a Vista Paul Revere or a Boulevarde de ye Olde Inne to its own inhabitants or suckers making the grand tour."[111]

[111] "New England, There She Stands," *Harper's Magazine*, CLXIV, 414 (March, 1932).

CHAPTER V

HEAVENLY DESTINY

And stepping westward seemed to be
A kind of heavenly destiny.—WORDSWORTH.

THE MOST distinctive feature of expansion in New England, as we have noted, was the concentrated type of settlement found in its compactly organized little towns, Puritan in ideas, education, morals, and religion. Established first on an agricultural basis, such towns progressed rapidly to other changes, many motivated by the Revolutionary War, until by the 1790's agriculture had declined in relative significance. The widespread movements in population during the hard times following the Revolution indicated that New Englanders were seeking both new soils and wider opportunities for a livelihood other than those supplied by farming.[1] Although the establishment of mills along the fall lines of rivers brought farm youths into factories and the increase of the shipping industry (1789-92) led to the organization of banks, the building of private fortunes, and other economic changes, extraordinary westward shifts of New England's population came to embrace many classes and grew almost to a mania.

First there went the rustlers and debt-ridden, low in the economic scale ; then the farmers looking for good land at low cost ; and lastly the mechanics and professional men seeking openings in localities of rapidly increasing population. Mingled with these were many sons of families which were well-to-do. . . .[2]

Thus began an influx of New Englanders into the Old West : the western boundaries and back country of New England, the region of Lake Champlain, the Hudson Valley, the Mohawk Valley, the Great Valley of Pennsylvania, the Shenandoah, and the Piedmont. In this manner was opened a great mid-

[1] Turner, *The Rise of the New West* in A. B. Hart, ed., *The American Nation: A History* (New York, 1906), XIV, 3 ; J. T. Adams, *New England in the Republic, 1776-1850* (Boston, 1926), p. 186 ; and P. W. Bidwell, *Rural Economy in New England at the Beginning of the Nineteenth Century* (New Haven, 1916), p. 387.
[2] Adams, *op. cit.*, p. 193. See the recent fictionalization of this in Edwin Lanham's *The Wind Blew West* (New York, 1936).

dle region,[3] "a zone of transition between the east and west, the north and the south," during the late eighteenth and the early nineteenth centuries.[4] In the words of Bryant, the westward-moving settler, no longer traveling as a lone trapper or trader, but with groups, could now look abroad where

> . . . towns shoot up, and fertile realms are tilled ;
> . . . ; [where] the full region leads
> New colonies forth, that toward the western seas
> Spread, like a rapid flame among the autumnal trees.[5]

This frontier progression, however, was not so magically effected as the poet chose to picture it. Added to the usual hardships of migration into new areas, land speculation misled hundreds into selling their New England properties for money to invest in fantastic schemes. At first the Western movement was individualistic, but later capitalists, seizing the opportunity for speculation, organized land companies, set up proprietors and "securing land from Massachusetts or other colonies, like New York, in turn sold their holdings to settlers for townships."[6] Such was the beginning of recurrent speculation to be felt periodically as the frontier extended westward : during the era of readjustment from the close of the War of 1812 to the election of Andrew Jackson (1829), the excitement of the California gold rush, and the post-Civil War movements. Once begun, both westward migration and its attendant speculation continued in spite of current satires calling public attention to the

> Lithographic towns
> In western wilds, where yet unbroken ranks
> Of thrifty beavers build unchartered "banks,"
> And prowling panthers occupy the lots,
> Adorned with churches on the paper plots![7]

Describing her own pioneering experiences in the wilds of Michigan, Mrs. Matilda Kirkland—once praised by Poe— wrote thus in *Western Clearings* (1845) :

The whirl, the fervour, the flutter, the rapidity of step, the sparkling of eyes, the beating of hearts, the striking of hands, the utter

[3] Turner, *The Frontier in American History*, p. 68.
[4] *The Rise of the New West*, p. 28.
[5] *Poetical Works* (New York, 1926), p. 20, "The Ages."
[6] Adams, *op. cit.*, p. 194.
[7] Quoted in Dorothy Dondore, *The Prairie and the Making of Middle America* (Cedar Rapids, 1926), p. 446, from a nineteenth-century satire.

abandon of the hour, were incredible, inconceivable. . . . He
who had no money, begged, borrowed, or stole it; he who had,
thought he made a generous sacrifice, if he lent it at cent per cent.
The tradesman forsook his shop; the farmer his plow; the merchant
his counter; the lawyer his office; nay, the minister his desk, to join
the general chase. . . . The man with one leg, or he that had
none, could at least board a steamer, and make for Chicago, or Mil-
waukee; the strong, the able, but above all, the "enterprising," set
out with his pocket-map and his pocket-compass, to thread the dim
woods, and see with his own eyes. Who would waste time in planting, in building, in hammering iron, in making shoes, when the
path to wealth lay wide and flowery before him? . . . . On they
pressed, with headlong zeal: the silent and pathless forest, the deep
miry marsh, the gloom of night, and the fires of noon, beheld alike
the march of the speculator.[8]

The great majority of the settlements, however, were more
than mere speculators' dreams, more than the paper-plotted
Metropolisvilles which called forth the scorn of Dickens and
Mark Twain. The emigration stream which began in the
1780's continued to flow from New England, along with other
streams from the Middle States, until the overflow carried
settlers beyond New York and Pennsylvania into Ohio, Illinois, and Indiana.[9] In 1824-25, with the completion of the
Erie Canal, the pioneer followed a new route to Michigan,
Wisconsin, and other regions, there to find repeated the same
story of settlement, the chronicle of community expansion in
"an ever-enlarging East and an ever-retreating West."

As the New Englanders migrated away from the seaboard,
they carried into Western lands their ideas and type of social
organization, a matter often recorded by New England annalists and travelers. The New England village type was soon
transplanted, at scattered intervals, throughout the Mohawk
Valley and later in Ohio and other regions. Other types of
towns grew through other channels: through early fur-trading
posts—like those in Irving's *Astoria* and Parkman's *The Oregon
Trail*—where intrepid *coureurs des bois* traded with the Indians;
and through army posts typical of that in Maurice Thompson's *Alice of Old Vincennes*. With the discovery of gold in
California the mining town appeared and ushered in a color-

[8] *Western Clearings* (New York, 1845).
[9] Mathews, *The Expansion of New England*, p. 169.

ful life, a literary lode for Bret Harte, Mark Twain, and others. (In more recent days the reckless life of the mining camps of frontier California and Nevada has been paralleled in the mushroom oil towns of Texas and Oklahoma, all excellent material for fiction.) As settlement expanded in the Mountain West and the Southwest the cattle town—the scene of Garland's romances and Alfred Henry Lewis's Wolfville, Arizona, tales—made its appearance. Finally, throughout the West, hundreds of villages and towns developed in agricultural districts or near rivers and lakes, choice locations for future Detroits, Chicagos, and Buffalos.[10] Thus the nation grew until today there are agricultural towns, manufacturing towns, college towns, lumber towns, fishing towns, boom towns, and countless others, many of which have furnished—and are still furnishing—materials for the creative writer.

Among the many small town annalists who have used materials drawn from such a vast field the recorders of the westward-moving frontier have been far from idle. As Professor Jay B. Hubbell has pointed out, the frontier has contributed both new materials and a new viewpoint to our literature.[11] In the matter of town delineation truly the frontier has caused American writers to discard the overused themes of the New England village for the fresher materials of the West. Since it was part of the first ground of the expansion westward, New York early claimed the attention of community recorders. To these interpretations of town life we turn first. The more complete studies of the Middle Border town and other new settlements in remote regions make another story.

Aside from the novels of James Fenimore Cooper, the earliest treatments of the New York town are significant mainly for their indications of prevailing tendencies. Interest in the New York village, as we have seen, first was expressed as a part of the widespread English influence on American poets. Philip Freneau's eighteenth-century sketches of the American village —already discussed in connection with New England Arcadianism—are significant in showing that the earliest village liter-

---

[10] Adams, *The Epic of America* (Boston, 1931), chap. x, "The End of the Frontier," gives a splendid resumé of national conditions after the Civil War. See also H. O. Rugg, *An Introduction to Problems of American Culture* (New York, 1931), p. 37 and B. H. Clark and R. Nicholson, ed., *The American Scene* (New York, 1930), *passim*.

[11] Norman Foerster, ed., *The Reinterpretation of American Literature* (New York, 1928), p. 44.

ature in New York, as in New England, was imitatively romantic and delocalized. *The American Village*, historically important as the first significant full-fledged village poem in
American literature, has none of the qualities of indigenous
community studies. On the other hand, *The Sketch Book of
Geoffrey Crayon, Gent.* (1819-20), the work of Washington Irving (1783-1859), contains two interpretations of real village
life "while the country was yet a province of Great Britain."
In the colonial folk tales, "Rip Van Winkle" and "The Legend
of Sleepy Hollow"—both advertised as the posthumous writing
of Diedrich Knickerbocker, "an old gentleman of New York,
who was very curious in the Dutch history of the province, and
the manners of the descendants from its primitive settlers"—
Irving has sketched the early village life of Tarry Town and
Sleepy Hollow. While the widely known and humorous legend
of that Yankee eccentric, Master Ichabod Crane, does not deal
primarily with the village scene, it has added to town literature
the name of the market town of Greensburgh, or Tarry Town,
the latter name being given in former days "by the good housewives of the adjacent country, from the inveterate propensity
of their husbands to linger about the village tavern on market
days." The tale of "Rip Van Winkle" pictures in vivid contrast the idyllic pre-revolutionary life in an old Dutch settlement and that of the same community transformed after many
years into a bustling town, whose activities puzzled grizzly
bearded Rip, lately returned from his mysterious sojourn in
the hills. Vividly Irving pictures a feature of village life often
described in provincial literature; namely, the town junto, the
colonial forerunner of the corner grocery and drugstore philosophers of our own time. In this little village lazy Rip, be-
deviled by a termagant wife, frequently escaped from home
to join cronies in "a kind of perpetual club of the sages, philosophers, and other idle personages," which held its sessions
on a bench before a small inn. "Here they used to sit in the
shade through a long lazy summer's day, talking listlessly over
village gossip, or telling endless sleepy stories about nothing."[12]
As a faithful narrative of a quaint Dutch village which vanished in the wake of the busy life of a new republic, "Rip Van
Winkle" may be termed the first popularly received story of
the New York small town. Further, because of its concen-

12 *Selections from Irving's Sketch Book* (New York, 1910), p. 134.

tration on a single major incident, it is often referred to as the first American short story.

Irving's delineations, popular though they have been, cannot be termed more than incidental interpretations of town life. Credit for the first sustained treatment of the New York town—and, incidentally, of the Western town, also—belongs not to Irving, but to Cooper, whose own life history is bound closely to a frontier settlement unique in the literary annals of the American town.

Cooperstown : A Frontier Venture

In 1794 two young English idealists, later to become associated with the great literary movement of their times, broached a peculiarly republican, though woefully impractical, scheme for a settlement in distant America. Much talk of social regeneration resulted in a highly Utopian arrangement for a colony on "the banks of that river in America with the beautiful name—Susquehanna." Stirred with enthusiasm for a type of settlement utterly impracticable, Robert Southey, a Bristol linen-draper's son, and his fellow idealist, Samuel Taylor Coleridge, framed their plans for a "Pantisocracy." Not having suffered the disillusionment of a Martin Chuzzlewit, these young liberals, their imaginations afire, proposed that a cooperative society of twenty-four educated men and women should withdraw from the world to some spot in the backwoods of America where a few hours daily work would provide them with the necessities for a simple life and leave them much freedom for intellectual discourse. The twelve gentlemen who were to found the colony were to acquire wives. In the Fricker sisters of Bristol both of these enthusiasts, as well as their later co-schemer, Robert Lowell, found willing partners. Coleridge must have argued eloquently, for on the fourth of October, 1795, he and Sarah Fricker were married in the Bristol church of St. Mary Redcliffe, where young Chatterton had conceived the Rowley myth. Southey was affianced to Edith, a younger sister, and Lowell married a third. Only one thing was lacking—money! Not a single one of the group had his fund of one hundred and twenty-five pounds calculated to promote the scheme. It was inevitable that hasty impulse should give way to waning enthusiasm. In spite of their lecturing and writing Coleridge and Southey secured neither sufficient recruits nor money.   Quarrels but added to the general lowering of interest.   In short, the Pantisocracy was a signal failure and the valley of the Susquehanna was peopled by more practical men of the frontier than these English dreamers.

During the very same months when the luckless "Pantisocrats" were visualizing a transatlantic retreat the actual frontier of the Susquehanna and the Mohawk was fast being peopled by New Englanders and others who came in the wake of a thrifty young Quaker whose name and family in later days were to be linked with the social and literary annals of New York.   Almost ten years before the impractical Coleridge and his Utopians had talked of the stream which Fenimore Cooper called "the crooked river to which the Atlantic herself extended an arm of welcome," William Cooper, prominent Quaker of Burlington, New Jersey, arrived at the headwaters of the Susquehanna near where George Washington had journeyed two years earlier to chart the waterways of this unsettled and largely unexplored hinterland.[13]   In the autumn of 1785 this William Cooper viewed from the top of Mount Vision—described in *The Pioneers*—unlimited acres of densely wooded country over which he was to have jurisdiction as a sort of landed proprietor. He looked down upon the waters of "Glimmerglass"—Lake Otsego—and saw along its shores the future site of the village his energy was to build, the little town to be known in the course of its history as "Foot of the Lake," "Cooperton," "Cooper's Town," "Otsego"—in the Indian vernacular "a place of friendly meeting"—, and finally as the modern "Cooperstown."

As revealed in his own account, *A Guide in the Wilderness* (1810),[14] this thirty-one year old Quaker proved to be one of the enterprising and persevering men of his time.   Shortly after the Revolution he had become interested in large tracts of land in New York.   Thenceforward until his death (1809) one of his chief occupations seemingly was that of settling his

---

[13] See James Fenimore Cooper, *A Condensed History of Cooperstown* (first printed as *Chronicles of Cooperstown*), ed., S. T. Livermore (Albany, 1862), pp. 14 ff., for a copy of a letter from Washington to the Marquis de Chastellux (1783) with reference to the former's Western trip and his views on the possibilities for "a vast inland navigation of these United States."

[14] The subtitle reads: *The History of the First Settlements in the Western Counties of New York with Useful Instructions to Future Settlers* in a series of letters addressed by Judge Cooper of Cooperstown to William Sampson, Barrister, of New York.

own acres and those he owned jointly with others.   His friend
and correspondent, Irish William Sampson, New York lawyer,
in later years wrote to Judge Cooper praising him for his
achievements :   "Your knowledge has been all practical, all
profitable ; the face of immense tracts of country bears witness
of this, and thousands of living witnesses confirm it."

Why should this wilderness interest such widely differing personalities as the "Pantisocrats," William Cooper, hundreds of
New Englanders, and prominent foreign investors (Necker,
Madame de Staël, and others)?   The history of the early New
York frontier passed through three stages.[15]   First, there was
the fur trading era, lasting from the opening of the seventeenth
century until the outbreak of the border wars.   During these
years the Indians were still the complete possessors of the wilderness.   The second phase (1765-83) saw the Indians drawn
into conflict with the French and English.   The strain of the
fighting was felt by the province of New York long into the
third epoch—from 1783 on—when the whites played the most
significant part in the work of social and economic progress.
As Robert E. Spiller reminds us, the complete colonial conquest
of the country was marked by the opening of the Catskill turnpike in 1802, an improvement which gave added impetus to
the land speculation then attracting hundreds of investors and
settlers, native and foreign, to the domain of New York.

With the close of the French and Indian War, however, settlement suffered a period of stagnation.   French victories encouraged the Iroquois to such hostility that they renewed their
expressions of grievance over the seizure of their lands and the
breach of treaties.   All the influence of Sir William Johnson, royal agent for Indian affairs, was needed to manage these
hostile groups.   Then there was another block in the progress
of settlement.   The country from New York to Lake Champlain and from Albany to Niagara was traversed by armies.[16]
Townbuilding, agriculture, manufacturing, and commerce
were doubly retarded, then, by the ravages of the French and
warring Indians.   Of course, here and there blockhouses and
small forts, the nucleus of hamlets and towns, were built.   Thus
Fort Schuyler (later Utica), erected as early as 1759 at a ford

[15] R. E. Spiller, *Fenimore Cooper, Critic of His Times* (New York, 1931), pp. 1 ff.
Cf. *Home as Found*, chap. xii, for Cooper's statements.
[16] E. H. Roberts, *The Planting and Growth of the Empire State* (Boston, 1887),
pp. 336 ff.

on the Mohawk and known to boatmen and army engineers, was used often as a place of departure for various points.[17]

The economic crisis of the war having passed, new settlers ventured into the Mohawk and Susquehanna valleys and thence on westward. By the time William Cooper, with his gun and fishing rod, arrived on horseback in Cherry Valley the times had changed. Land settlement and speculation were the talk of the day. Cooper's own active furtherance of the settling of the Lake Otsego region finds simple, but forceful, recording in his collected letters to Sampson, *A Guide in the Wilderness*, "a faithful and useful account of the cultivation of the American woods."[18]

In 1785 a hazardous trip of actual exploring through the rough and hilly country of Otsego led Cooper to active planning for a town on the very site where as early as 1612 an Indian village, in all probability visited by Dutch explorers, had existed.[19] With all the foresight and prudence of a successful builder, Cooper selected at the foot of Lake Otsego a site whose natural excellence had long before his day attracted the attention of chance explorers or holders of patents who made the settlement of New York unlike that of the other colonies.[20] In 1761 a Lutheran minister and patentee, John Hartwick, made an abortive attempt at settlement on Lake Otsego. In 1770 there came George Croghan, successor to Sir William Johnson as Indian agent and holder of more than a hundred thousand acres. During these years Indian dangers and invasions by Clinton's troops in 1779 made the region so unsafe for settlers that by the time of William Cooper's arrival in 1785 "the wilderness [had] closed in on the vestiges of the settlement." After his preliminary surveying, Judge Cooper in January, 1786, took possession of about fifty thousand acres, known since as Cooper's Patent, under a deed given by the sheriff of Montgomery County.[21] In May of the same year the Judge opened the sales of forty thousand acres, which, he records in the *Guide*, "in sixteen days were all taken up." Soon after he established

---

[17] *Ibid.*

[18] *A Guide in the Wilderness*, Introduction. The Appendix of this book contains the questions which Sampson propounded to Judge Cooper.

[19] In one of his early letters to Sampson Judge Cooper gives the details of this personal survey of his patent.

[20] James Fenimore Cooper, *The Legends and Traditions of a Northern Country* (New York, 1921), p. 3.

[21] *A Condensed History of Cooperstown*, p. 12.

a store and remained in the community without his family until 1790. The scarcity of food and money; the poor communication with the outside world because of the mountainous, bridgeless, and roadless country; the failure of the first crops; and other difficulties associated with a frontier venture are truthfully chronicled in the *Guide*. The nearest mill was twenty miles away and "not one in twenty had a horse, and the way lay through rapid streams, across swamps or over bogs."[22]

Cooper was no lordly proprietor rivaling the patroons of Albany, Rensselaer, and Westchester counties. According to his own testimony, he resided among the common folk, noting "too clearly how bad their condition was." He erected a storehouse and "during each winter filled it with large quantities of grain, purchased in distant places." A man of business acumen, energy and fairness, he used a co-operative system whereby he established potash works. Lacking sufficient funds for public roads, this energetic Quaker collected people at convenient seasons so that, by joint efforts, they might put bridges over the deep streams and in the cheapest manner make "such roads as suited our then humble purpose."[23] Cooper was, without doubt, a wise community leader, in many respects resembling a Southern planter. Thoughts of roads, canals, churches, schools, and trading facilities were uppermost in his mind as he planned the little town which was to have further delineation at the hands of his famous son. He had the steady mind, sober judgment, fortitude, perseverance, and common sense which he himself described as fitting qualities for a pioneer leader.[24] No Pantisocrat of hasty impulse was he! His success in townbuilding and in developing his patent finds substantiation in the travel notes of "redoubtable Timothy Dwight, ironclad Puritan and Federalist," who writing in 1822 (only nine years after the 1793 setting of *The Pioneers* and eight years after the bursting of the bubble of the Pantisocracy) gave his impressions of the New York frontier. During his Western travels he observed that "a great number of beautiful villages have risen up, as by the power of enchantment: and the road for one hundred and twenty miles is in a sense lined

---

[22] William Cooper, *op. cit.*, p. 8. Cf. *The Pioneers*, Mohawk Ed., p. 238.
[23] *Ibid.*
[24] *Ibid.*, p. 12. In the *Guide*, p. 17, Cooper listed numerous possible trading points or cities of the future. Today at such places are the cities of Buffalo, Utica, Niagara Falls, etc.

by a succession of houses. almost universally neat, and frequently handsome."[25]

Dwight's enthusiastic pictures of middle New York call to mind William Cooper's reiterations in the *Guide* that his own pioneering venture succeeded largely because of his personal supervision of the actual settlement. Ever aware of the conditions of his settlers, Judge Cooper, like Per Hansa in Rölvaag's *Giants in the Earth*, encouraged in every possible way the profitable marketing of raw materials, the use of home manufactures, the most practical cultivation of the land, and the proper handling of the fisheries.[26] National-minded and sagacious, he knew the value of outside associations. As Spiller says, "like Washington, [Cooper] had conceived the Erie Canal project at a time when men of smaller vision were still clearing their own half acres, even though he did not live to see his dreams realized." But what were the larger affairs of the day which, in time, influenced the life of even remote villages?

The years following the British evacuation of New York City on November 25, 1783, were marked by typical post-war changes and adjustments. With the return of the American soldiers to their homes and the subsequent resumption of normal life an impetus was started which brought a pronounced growth to the city.[27] The aspect of life in the whole province changed. People again turned to the problem of local progress so greatly halted by the war. Cooperstown and other frontier towns received recruits from the soldiers of the state and elsewhere who, after the disbanding of the continental army, took up their land bounties and pushed out the line of settlement. French political refugees sought new fortunes in the wilderness and even soldiers from the British army, together with German mercenaries, remained as settlers in the country they had tried to conquer. Others followed and some purchasers of large tracts sold farms to hardy pioneers who by breaking roads and starting homesteads added value to the adjacent wilderness.[28] The incoming multitudes were of such various types, as James Fenimore Cooper shows in *The Pioneers*, that the suggestion has been made that "if New England was Puritan and Virginia

[25] *Travels in New-England and New-York* (London, 1823), III, 531.
[26] William Cooper, *op. cit.*, p. 41.
[27] Roberts, *op. cit.*, pp. 449 ff.
[28] *Ibid.*, p. 450.

Cavalier, and both possibly English, New York was the first to become distinctly American."[29]

The year 1787 was eventful for the little community at the foot of Otsego. Many new settlers, principally from Connecticut, arrived. Most of the land was assigned. Several log houses were built on the site of the village and toward the close of the year William Cooper himself began thinking seriously about removing his family from Burlington to a frontier establishment on Otsego's shores. Accordingly, the second regular dwelling erected was that for the Judge which, built in 1788, was of two stories, with two wings, and a back building added in 1791.[30] (Among the early Cooper papers, so we are informed in the *History of Cooperstown*, was a parchment map or plan for the building of the village. Dated 1788, this map would indicate that it was in this year Cooper seems to have set to work upon the definite formation of a town.) By October, 1790, the town's growth was such that William Cooper felt justified in bringing his family and servants—about fifteen in all—and their belongings to the new home in the wilderness. Here, in his erroneously called manor house, Cooper, the leading citizen of a growing pioneer town, lived in much the same manner as Marmaduke Temple of *The Pioneers*. In short, he was, like the Southern planter, a superior landlord under whose direction the many-sided life of the community prospered.[31]

In many respects the little town on Otsego occupies a very unique place in literature. Perhaps few actual towns, except unusual places like Concord and Cambridge, have had so many varied literary treatments as this picturesque place. There exists today, as we have seen, the founder's practical *Guide*, a first-hand introduction to a town in the making given by one of its makers. Years later the son of this frontiersman wrote a brief social history of the actual village, *Chronicles of Cooperstown*, explaining that "the site of the present village of Cooperstown, is said to have been a favorite place of resort with adjacent savage tribes, from a remote period." In *The Deerslayer* (1841), a tale of Indian warfare, this same "son of

[29] *Ibid.*, p. 454.
[30] Mary Phillips, *James Fenimore Cooper* (New York, 1923), p. 7. Fully illustrated with pictures of early Cooperstown.
[31] The growth of the town is indicated by the fact that by 1795 one of the two papers published west of Albany was the *Otsego Herald*, the other being the *Gazette* at Whitestown (Roberts, *op. cit.*, p. 462).

the frontier" used as a background the wilderness around Lake Otsego (Glimmerglass) during the 1740's. In *The Pioneers* (1823) he re-created discerningly and comprehensively a village frontier of the last years of the eighteenth century, a picture of community evolution based on the novelist's knowledge of real life in Cooperstown. In 1838, after James Fenimore Cooper had lived for years in Europe, Cooperstown again appeared in literature in the social satire, *Home as Found*, in which the author's outlook was that of a returned traveler, so long accustomed to the older social order of foreign cities that his own America and fellow Americans now seemed crude. The "home as found" is Templeton, or Cooperstown, fifty years after the period of *The Pioneers*, satirized as a provincial locality whose citizens look askance at local Europeanized plutocrats. Small town life is described still further in Cooper's social criticism. Scattered throughout his letters, his *Notions of the Americans Picked up by a Travelling Bachelor* (1828), and *The American Democrat* (1838) are glimpses of town life such as Cooper had either heard old settlers describe or had himself experienced at various periods during his life. With such a varied portrayal in fact and fiction Cooperstown occupies an interesting place in the story of the small town as treated by American authors.

In *A Guide in the Wilderness* a real frontiersman, director of landbreakers, wrote for the benefit of future settlers. In straightforward fashion he explained his associations with the advancement of civilization upon the wilderness. There was no glamorous fictionalizing in William Cooper's utilitarian accounts of Otsego's soil, climate, and products. Something of a pragmatist, Cooper presented useful facts. His purpose was to show, for the aid of other investors, why he had succeeded where many had failed. In American literature the son was no less a pioneer than his father was in actual frontiering.

In 1823 James Fenimore Cooper produced one of his most noteworthy novels, a chronicle of the manners and characters of the newly built town among the hills of Otsego. In *The Pioneers* he demonstrated that, in spite of its remoteness and apparent inaccessibility, a thriving community like Templeton could be the scene of a constantly and intrinsically interesting social life. Here, expressing more fully than in some of his surveys his view of the frontier element in American life, Cooper showed how fast events moved in his native village during the days when it progressed rapidly toward the status of a town.[32]

Like Jane Austen, Hardy, and Bennett, Cooper selected all the minutiae of a life with which he was personally familiar. Writing for his own pleasure, Cooper chose for materials his most vivid boyhood recollections. Upon a very realistic background he superimposed a romance of border days. With such an admixture of fact and romance he portrayed the ways of a frontier village, its restless characters hovering "like skirmishers in advance of American civilization." Admittedly, the narrative element proved weak and the heroines unimpressive; but Cooper strengthened the whole fabric by motivating his plot in terms of actual frontier social relationships. He created, or re-created, a strongly realistic frontier background, and brought together some thirty people recognizable as figures closely associated with a new town. He achieved an added note of verisimilitude by modeling the citizenry of Templeton on types as well known to him, "a son of the frontier," as the folk of Egdon Heath were to Thomas Hardy or the middle-class tradesmen of the Five Towns were to Arnold Bennett. But let Cooper characterize his own puppets:

The great proprietor resident on his lands, and giving his name to, instead of receiving it from his estates, as in Europe, is common over the whole of New York. The physician, . . . the pious, self-denying, laborious and ill-paid missionary; the half-educated, litigious, envious, and disreputable lawyer, with his counterpoise, a brother of the profession, of better origin and of better character; the shiftless, bargaining, discontented seller of his "betterments"; the plausible carpenter, and most of the others, are more familiar to all who have ever dwelt in a new country.[33]

Thus is suggested the historicalness of the motley characters who people Templeton: traders, trappers, woodcutters, foreigners, and professional men. The growing town of William Cooper's planning is pictured as having attracted to itself a diversified population. The present examination of *The Pioneers*, therefore, will be made with first consideration to Cooper's picturing the early stages of a small town which he knew intimately.

[32] John F. Ross, *The Social Criticism of Fenimore Cooper* (Berkeley, 1933), p. 47.
[33] *The Pioneers*, Mohawk ed., Introduction.
12

The tale opens, so Cooper carefully notes, in 1793, the seventh year of the establishment of Cooperstown—and presumably of Templeton.[34] To this isolated village come faint echoes of the things and events of the outside world : of Washington's second inaugural address, of Whitney's invention of a cotton gin, of the execution of Louis XVI and the Reign of Terror, and, perhaps, of *The Rights of Man* and *Political Justice;* yet, with all the activity in the larger centers of the country and abroad, life moves forward undisturbed in this Western outpost. Trees are felled, clearings cultivated, rude dwellings and more permanent homes erected, stores and taverns opened, and all the interests of community life developed.

The site of Templeton was picturesque.[35] The country was hilly and densely wooded and the town was located on a little torrent, one of the many sources of the Susquehanna. One first views the town through the eyes of Elizabeth Temple, a border heiress just returning from a Philadelphia school. She notes the incongruous dwellings of the village, the sleigh-filled street along whose sides were piled huge heaps of·logs, the frozen lake, the returning woodcutters, axes on shoulder, passing sleighs, paper-curtained windows, and, at last, the cold, dreary stone walls of Marmaduke Temple's mansion-house.

Repeatedly, as the romance progresses, Cooper reverts to the physical appearance of the town. One sees it at various seasons : as Elizabeth once saw it from the Mansion after a snow storm ; as things appeared at the close of Christmas Day, 1793 ; and as Elizabeth and the weaker Louisa, after the panther episode, looked upon the place "which lay beneath their feet like a picture, with its limpid lake in front, the winding stream along its margin and its hundred chimneys of whitened bricks."[36] Without strained effort at achieving an elaborate pictorial effect, Cooper simply, but realistically, pictures the village dwellings, mostly wooden, at the foot of the lake. Thoughts of William Cooper's careful community plans are suggested by the note that "the whole were grouped in a manner that aped the streets of a city, and were evidently so arranged by the direction of one who looked to the wants of posterity rather than to the conveniences of the present incumbents."[37]

[34] *Ibid.*, pp. 3 and 211.
[35] *Ibid.*, pp. 48 ff.
[36] *Ibid.*, pp. 210 ff., 216, and 319.
[37] *Ibid.*, pp. 29 ff.

An outgrowth of the patroon system of eastern New York, yet different in many aspects, Templeton, in its arrangement of smaller buildings and mansion-house ("towering above all its neighbors"), closely resembled the Southern plantation unit of community organization. The "large, square, and far from uncomfortable" mansion, like the "big house" of a Virginia estate, stood in the midst of a fruit-tree covered enclosure. Around such a semi-manorial setting as this Cooper revolves a conventional love story of a border heiress and a backwoodsman of mysterious birth with the added interest of realistic background and frontier customs.[38]

Though Cooperstown, or Templeton, was a frontier settlement, its social life was not marred by the spirit of lawlessness one might expect in so new a country. Of course, the New Englanders who helped people the town had much to do with the stabilization of affairs. The present James Fenimore Cooper in his *Legends and Traditions of a Northern Country* calls attention to the fact that "the family life at Judge Cooper's home seems to have been most delightful, and the strangers within the village gates evidently grew to love the place and the people residing there."[39] In Judge Cooper's Hall many distinguished visitors, like Talleyrand and Stephen Van Rensselaer, found entertainment. Likewise, in Marmaduke Temple's Mansion, for such it might well be called at this time, both citizens and outsiders were frequent guests. A retired army officer, Monsieur Le Quoi, a French exile, clergymen, and lawyers were among those entertained at the Mansion. In spite of the poor communication with New York, whose society later was satirized in *Home as Found*, these frontier

[38] In an apology for his own country—written in Holland and Switzerland and published in London, 1828—Cooper expressed the following "notion" about Cooperstown: "Cooperstown is the largest place in the county, containing less than fifteen hundred inhabitants, ... The village is neat, better built even than is common in America, which is vastly better (for villages) than any thing of the sort in Europe. . . . . There resided formerly near this village a gentleman who is the reputed author of a series of tales, which were intended to elucidate the history, manners, usages, and scenery of his native country. As curiosity on American subjects had led to their republication in Europe, you may possibly have seen the books. One of them (the 'Pioneers') is said to contain some pretty faithful sketches of certain habits, and even of some individuals who were known among the earlier settlers of this very spot. I cannot pledge myself for the accuracy of this opinion, nor could any one be found here who appeared to possess sufficient information on the subject to confirm it. But, as far as natural objects are concerned, the descriptions are sufficiently exact. . . ." (*Notions of the Americans, etc.* London, 1823, I, 339 ff.)
[39] *Legends and Traditions of a Northern Country*, p. 136.

townspeople found life too full, both with work and lighter entertainment, for prolonged regrets.   It is true that Talleyrand in a poem addressed to Anna Cooper, William's daughter, thus described the real Cooperstown : "Otsego n'est pas gai—mais tout est habitude."   He was pleased, however, with the solitude of the place.   Perhaps this distinguished foreigner, like Marmaduke's friends, also enjoyed the bountiful dinners at the Hall, the walks through the forest, the frequent boating and fishing on Otsego, a ride into the hills to inspect "a sugaring off," and even convivial drinking at the village inns.

For the villagers there were more serious concerns.   The unfolding of the story presents community problems typical of any frontier town.   Often the love story of Elizabeth and the strange young hunter is quite pushed aside by Cooper's concern with community developments : with the plans for an academy, the Masonic celebration, the building of the church, and the betterment of roads.   Templeton was not lacking in ambitious and public-spirited leaders, such as Marmaduke and Richard Jones, who had a natural interest in the forming of a county organization and in political questions, local and national.   In general, the presentation of these interests is unmarked by the later acid touch characterizing the village scenes in *Home as Found.*

The townspeople of *The Pioneers* represent the usual group to be found in frontier towns.   Though the place is young, a diversified citizenry with some pretension toward social grouping exists.   Nearly every major profession is represented.   Dr. Elnathan Todd, "the man of physic," whose mother knew he "was cut out for a doctor . . . for he was forever digging for herbs and tasting all kinds of things that growed about lots" ; Richard Jones, self-appointed man of affairs ; Le Quoi, French storekeeper ; Major Hartmann, who mixed his consonants ; and Benjamin Pump of nautical speech show the various nationalities which Cooper attempted to fit into the American scene.   The two conventional heroines, while not so melodramatic as those of Mrs. Susannah Rowson, are, nevertheless, stock figures.   Briefly characterized, Elizabeth Temple, with her finishing school manners which awe even the loquacious housekeeper, suggests Cooper's own daughters who were educated abroad. Louisa, trusting and yielding by nature, is a "feminine weakling."[40]   While the other two women of the story, Mistress Remarkable Pettibone, inquisitive and resentful housekeeper at the Mansion, and Betty Hollister, cheerful hostess of the "Bold Dragoon," represent a lower social scale, they possess more reality and are less conventionalized.   Ostensibly Cooper's own father was the model for Marmaduke Temple.   With the naming of the officious Doolittle, petty officer that he is ; Indian John, last of the Delawares ; and Natty Bumppo, the hunter, the town register is about complete so far as the major citizens are concerned.   Of Leatherstocking (Bumppo), the most unforgettable character, it has been said that he was "a highly romanticized figure, a solitary seeking escape from the ways of the world, quite as much as a poet and philosopher as a marksman and woodsman, and endowed with all the virtues of the nomad pioneer and with none of his defects."[41]

On April 2, 1823, shortly after the appearance of *The Pioneers*, Richard H. Dana, Sr., wrote to Cooper from Cambridge in praise of the latter's frontiersmen.

You are doing for us what Scott and Miss Edgeworth are doing for their homes.   Living so near to the lives you are describing, being acquainted with people who were actors in them and eye witnesses, and being able from what remains of those days to judge what was their character, your works impress us with all the sincerity of matter of fact. . . .   What a full and true description you have given of a newly settled village in a new country.   Such motley company huddled together, yet all distinctly marked and individual, and everyone as busy as can be, as always is the case in such a place.[42]

True, Cooper's treatment of these frontier men and women occasionally bordered on the conventional and the didactic ; but, after all, *The Pioneers* was a fictional experiment based upon a foundation of reality and written at a time when most of Cooper's contemporaries were creating stereotyped plots and

[40] See Brownell's *American Prose Masters*, pp. 42 ff., for a discussion of Cooper's heroines.   Cf. Lowell's *A Fable for Critics*.
[41] Boynton, *op. cit.*, p. 71.   Cf. Loshe, *The Early American Novel*, p. 89 :   "Leatherstocking himself, a creation of eccentric character in the larger sense, is of course, the most original character in American fiction and the finest, because at once the most human and the most simply poetic, expression of that idealization of the unconventional which had many appearances in fiction since Rousseau invented the primitive virtues."
[42] *Correspondence of James Fenimore Cooper*, I, 90 ff.

wooden, sentimentalized characters. Such titles as Daniel Jackson's *Alonzo and Melissa, or The Unfeeling Father* (1824) and Catherine Hart's *St. Ursula's Convent, or The Nun of Canada* (1824) suggest, by contrast, how American were Cooper's materials.[43]   In large measure Cooper was a literary discoverer exploring in unused fictional fields, then considered impossible.   For this reason, with all of his treatment of the new, Cooper still retained traces of the old and current influences in fiction.   Miss Loshe says that it is largely the presence of his "rather wooden love affairs that gives Cooper the reputation of stiffness among modern novel-readers—yet one does not see how he could have done otherwise."[44]   In following the Scott tradition Cooper often has sacrificed the primary importance of his native and fresh background for a romance of thoroughly conventional lovers.   This is in accord with Balzac's estimate that "if Cooper had succeeded in the painting of character to the same extent that he did in the painting of the phenomena of nature, he would have uttered the last word of our art."[45]

The border life of *The Pioneers*, as already suggested, presented a combination of strenuous activities and such amusements as the people themselves could devise.   Of the latter hunting, fishing, and ice skating on the lake as the seasons permitted, drinking bouts at the "Bold Dragoon," and the shooting of the Christmas turkey suggest a life wholly different from that pictured by the purely realistic delineators of frontier villages.[46]   Under the double influence of Scott and his own contact with frontier realities, Cooper created an American village scene differing as much from Colonel Humphrey's glorified "western Territory"[47] as from the sordidness and stern reality of Joseph Kirkland's *Zury* (1887), with its harsh treatment of a narrow frontier farming community in Illinois.[48]   In Templeton no one grew hardened under the toil of clearing forests and fighting an often losing fight with the wilderness.[49]   On the contrary, Cooper developed the thesis, a favorite one of

[43] Loshe, *op. cit.*, Appendix.   Cf. Lounsbury, *op. cit.*, pp. 90 ff.
[44] *Ibid.*, p. 86.
[45] Lounsbury, *op. cit.*, p. 284.
[46] *The Pioneers*, pp. 448, 259, 218, 141 ff., and 189 respectively.
[47] *The Columbian Muse*, 1794, p. 162.
[48] Subtitle : *The Meanest Man in Spring County: A Novel of Western Life* (Boston and New York, 1887).
[49] In the *Guide* the villagers were mentioned as having suffered from crop failures.   Cf. *The Pioneers*, pp. 237 ff., where Marmaduke describes the very first days of Templeton.

his, that the glories of the wilderness were falling before the successful encroachments of frontiersmen. Both Leatherstocking and Indian John, or Mohegan, symbolize the passing of a socially untrammeled type before the development of community law and social restrictions.

The solid substance of border life in Templeton is suggested by Cooper's picture of general town growth.

The village was alive with business; the artisans increasing in wealth with the prosperity of the country, and each day witnessing some nearer approach to the manners and usages of an old settled town. The man who carried the mail . . . talked much of running a stage, and once or twice during the winter, he was seen taking a single passenger in his cutter, through the snowbanks, towards the Mohawk, along which a regular vehicle glided, semi-weekly, with the velocity of lightning, and under the direction of a knowing whip from the "down countries." Towards spring divers families, who had been into the "old States," to see their relatives, returned, . . . frequently bringing with them whole neighborhoods . . . to make a trial of fortune in the woods.[50]

Marmaduke Temple's peculiar occupations, the literary counterpart of Judge Cooper's interests, caused him "to look far into futurity, in his speculations on the improvements that posterity was to make on his lands."[51] Where his less visionary co-workers saw but a wilderness he visualized "towns, manufactories, bridges, canals, mines, and all other resources of an old country." Through his jurisdiction a county organization with a sheriff and a system of local laws, too soon applied to the old hunter, became a reality.[52] How strangely ironic was the enforcement of the deer-killing law for one who, after all, was not a settler, but a hunter whose home was the wilderness. Even hustling, vain Sheriff Jones and his constables, themselves symbols of the town status of Templeton, were abashed before Leatherstocking's sorrowful protest :

"What would ye with an old and helpless man?" he said. "You've driven God's creatur's from the wilderness, where his providence had put them for his own pleasure ; and you've brought in the troubles and diviltries of the law, where no man was ever known to disturb another. You have driven me, that have lived forty

[50] *The Pioneers*, p. 219. Cf. *ibid.*, p. 234.
[51] *Ibid.*, p. 331.
[52] *Ibid.*, p. 181.

long years of my appointed time in this very spot, from my home
and the shelter of my head, ..."[53]

Templeton, however, had reached such a stage of organized
society that magistrates, warrants, and jails meant more than
the word of a mere hunter wanted for a violation of the law.

Public opinion and idle curiosity were as great in this New
York settlement as in Hawthorne's little New England town
where crowds thronged the streets for a glimpse of Hester
Prynne before the jail.   On the occasion of Natty's trial, one
of the most dramatic events in the annals of early Templeton,
Cooper vividly pictured Templeton as a shire town, "a haven
of justice," to which both horsemen and footmen came "to
hear and to decide the disputes of [their] neighbors."   This
was an exciting and moving time.

By ten o'clock the streets of the village were filled with busy
faces ; some talking of their private concerns, some listening to a
popular expounder of political creeds ; and others gaping in at the
open stores, admiring the finery, examining scythes, axes, and other
such manufactures. . . .   A few women were in the crowd, most
carrying infants, and followed, at a lounging, listless gait, by their
rustic lords and masters.[54]

The increasing social complexities of a frontier town are exemplified in the interest which such makers of tradition, such
steady encroachers upon the great domains of the wilderness,
evinced not only in legal affairs, but in religious and educational
problems as well.   The heated dispute concerning the architec-
ture of the new community church bears close relationship to
problems common even today in many communities.   Primitive
though the society of Templeton was at this early date, differences in religious beliefs led to word battles between Catholics
and Protestants.   In the interim village meetings of every type
were held in the Academy, whose great hall was used variously
for court sessions, balls, and Sunday worship.

Chronicle of provincial town life, *The Pioneers* is, as Lounsbury has suggested, "a moving panorama" of scenes revealing
the interests of frontier townspeople during the late eighteenth
century.   Its fictionalized little town is a symbol of the rapidly
changing society of a new country.   The closing description of

[53] *Ibid.*, pp. 369 ff.
[54] *Ibid.*, pp. 372 ff.

Leatherstocking's departure predicts that the isolated Temple-
tons of 1793 were but the forerunners of new growth to come
with national expansion. They represent the pushing back of
the frontier line. They are the embodiment of a changing
hinterland from which gradually disappeared the picturesque
Leatherstocking type, one who "had gone far towards the setting sun,—the foremost in that band of pioneers who [opened]
the way for the march of the nation across the continent."[55]

After his return from Europe late in 1835, Cooper for years
was so continuously involved in brawls (political, monetary,
and legal) that his character and literary reputation were as-
sailed by vituperative critics who resented the bold and cutting
criticisms of their cosmopolitan countryman. Naturally unwilling to let such invectives pass unchallenged, Cooper took
time amid lawsuits and Cooperstown squabbles "to belabor his
fellow Americans with pamphlets and pronunciamentos, phi-
lippics and pasquinades."[56] To this period belongs an enormous amount of work: *Homeward Bound* and its sequel, *Home
as Found* (1837-38); *The American Democrat, or Hints on the
Social and Civic Relations of the United States of America*—a title
almost as lengthy as the text—(1838); *The Chronicles of Cooperstown* (1838); the *Knickerbocker* review of Lockhart's *Life of Scott*
which brought down the wrath of the critics upon Cooper; the
long naval history in 1839; *The Pathfinder* (1840); and other
novels and letters of argument.

"Cooper," says a modern critic, "was the first American to
write about Americans in a really frank spirit."[57] Ironically
enough in the patriotic *Notions of the Americans* Cooper's John
Cadwallader, a young American traveler, devotes himself to
explaining the merits of his country to an English traveler in
these United States. In many of the works of 1838 and following, however, the earlier tone of apology is replaced by one
of censure and reform. Cooper's further consideration of his
Americana caused a reversal of opinion, both on the part of
the novelist himself and his reading public. Having come to
the belief that democracy as practiced was something of a fraud,
Cooper had launched, in the works named, a vigorous attack
against what he considered the evils of the system.

[55] *Ibid.*, p. 477.
[56] H. L. Mencken, Introduction to *The American Democrat* (New York, 1931).
[57] *Ibid.*

In *The American Democrat*, a sort of handbook for patriots, he tries to explain his position as that of a returned traveler who finds himself a foreigner in his own land.[58]   He deplores the smothering of truth in a country where the speaker of truth *should* be fearless in the face of conflicting opinions.   Seemingly he made a deliberate bid for unpopularity when he boldly stated that his writing was intended to be rather one of "censure than of praise, for its aim is correction."

What connection, one may ask, has this with Cooper's portrayal of small town life?   The story is long and will be retold here only in outline, for both Professors Lounsbury and Spiller have given accounts in fullest detail.   In brief, the wider and harsher criticism of Cooper grew out of a purely local controversy centered around the possession of Three Mile Point, a picnicing ground on Otsego, legally owned by the Coopers, but freely used by Cooperstown citizens.   When Cooper returned to his native village, after a long foreign sojourn, naturally he found many changes upon which he pronounced judgment some time later in his satire, *Home as Found*.   A legal investigation established Cooper's ownership to the erroneously, but long called, public property.   Indignation meetings by the Cooperstown citizens so stirred local feeling against Cooper that, in time, this small town quarrel was echoed in all of the leading papers, many of them political organs, of the state.   Soon the resolutions drawn up against the novelist by his fellow-townsmen and neighbors became the instrument of party squabbling, and Cooper's name and literary reputation suffered.[59]   Cooper won his family claim to Three Mile Point, but lost the good will of the villagers and unintentionally enlarged his small personal difficulty into a national question of the power of the press.

Thoroughly disgusted with village mob action, Cooper decided to write a novel based upon his recent controversy.   It was to be a sort of justification of his own rights.   Finding, however, the Point controversy in itself unsuited to complete fictional adaptation, he fabricated a romance in which the quarrel was but an incident.   The national attention given his libel suits against various newspapers caused him to broaden

[58] *Ibid.*, p. viii.
[59] See Lounsbury, *op. cit.*, pp. 145 ff., for a copy of the resolutions passed by the Cooperstown citizens against Cooper.

the plan of his satire from that of an attack on one small phase of small town life to one on national failings. Accordingly, in 1837 appeared *Homeward Bound*, wherein a group of Americans returning from Europe pass "superior-than-thou" judgments on their less favored countrymen. Members of a self-satisfied and superior family, descendants of the Effinghams of *The Pioneers*, view America through foreign eyes and according to cosmopolitan standards. In this novel, however, the satire is submerged by a tale of adventure, for the sea's fascination for Cooper caused him to create a digressive story of sea piracies. Not so with its sequel, *Home as Found*. Here Cooper gave full vent to his grudges against Cooperstown and the American press. And these views, while often distorted and prejudiced, were never unpatriotic.[60]

Though his primary concern was with the stupid provinciality of the Templetonians, Cooper first attacked New York, which he then regarded as a crude, overgrown town with equally crude and officious social leaders who prided themselves upon having the real culture which could never be theirs. Various phases of New York society are held up for censure. The Effinghams, superior in refinement, quite overshadow less fortunate New Yorkers, provincial in speech, dress, entertainment, homes, and literary aspirations. Cooper is especially scornful in his castigation of the New York literati.[61]

Likewise did Cooper ridicule the men and women of Templeton, in the era about fifty years after the time of *The Pioneers*. Like Cooper himself, the Effinghams—self-appointed critics of their neighbors—return, after a long stay in foreign capitals, to their former Templeton home, the mansion-house of the village. Here the Honorable Mr. Effingham, community dictator, his ultraperfect daughter Eve (called a "Hajji" by her less traveled friends), and Cousin John Effingham, sup-

[60] In the Preface to the first edition of *Home as Found* Cooper argued that: "The governing social evil of America is provincialism; a misfortune that is perhaps inseparable from her situation. . . . That the American nation is a great nation, in some respects the greatest the world ever saw, we hold to be true, and are ready to maintain as any one can be; but we are also ready to concede, that it is very far behind most polished nations in various essentials, and chiefly, that it is lamentably in arrears of its own avowed principles. Perhaps this truth will be found to be the predominant thought, throughout the pages of 'Home as Found'."
[61] For criticism of Cooper's satire directed against the *nouveaux riches* of New York see George A. Dunlap, *The City in the American Novel; 1789-1900* (Philadelphia, 1934), chap. iv, "The Social Life of the City," and chap. v, "The Literary and Artistic Life of the City."

posedly a gentleman and man of the world, preside over a select coterie which from a superior station judges the village and the world at large. "Never," says Lounsbury," was a more bumptious, conceited and disagreeable set of personages created by an author, under the impression that they were the reverse."[62]

With thoughts of the Point agitation and the press attacks still fresh in his memory, Cooper in *Home as Found* divides his characters so that the Effingham aristocrats and their "cultured" friends contrast with the village *hoi polloi*, petty politicians, provincial editors, gossipy women, and others prone to denounce the un-American manners of their aristocratic neighbors. These two factions Cooper would use as instruments with which to launch his attacks upon provincial townsmen and American democracy in general. Unfortunately, as the best Cooper critics have averred, his arguments and characters are not always convincing. The too humanly perfect Eve, for example, could not be taken seriously. It is ironic that the most maligned character, a representative of the pushing American type, proves to be the most effectively pictured person in the novel. In spite of his use as an instrument of satire, "Mr. Aristabulus Bragg, Attorney and Counseller at Law, and the agent for the Templeton estate," possesses the most marked individuality. Aristabulus—satirically conceived, of course— is the boorish American who, above all, has a profound respect for the wish of the majority. He is "a compound of shrewdness, impudence, commonsense, pretension, humility, cleverness, vulgarity, kind-heartedness, duplicity, selfishness, law-honesty, moral fraud, and mother wit, mixed with a smattering of learning and much penetration in practical things."[63] "Monsieur Bragg" is the self-confident democrat whose qualities point him out "for either a member of congress or a deputy sheriff, offices that he is equally ready to fill." To use Cooper's own phrase, Aristabulus was filled with typical American "go-aheadism." He was the prototype of the modern "go-getter."

Home as Found is filled with references to the foibles of a nation still in a very immature and unsettled state of development. As Cooper saw matters, the period was one of inflated prosperity when everyone, including women and clergymen,

---

[62] Lounsbury, *op. cit.*, p. 150.
[63] *Home as Found* (Philadelphia, 1838), I, 17.

dreamed of riches.[64] American land speculation, he pointed
out, was wild~r than that in any other country. Villas, farms,
and even streets and towns "of dimensions and value to suit
purchasers" were on the real estate market.   American society
was ill from lavish use of paper money, gambling, and extravagant indulgence in European credit.   The community, Cooper satirized, "is in the situation of a man who is in the incipient
stages of an exhilarating intoxication, and who keeps pour-
ing down glass after glass, in the idle notion that he is merely
sustaining nature in her ordinary functions."[65]   Furthermore,
as one of the characters affirms, this fancied prosperity and
widespread infatuation, extending from the coast to the ex-
tremest frontiers of the West, might be attributed to "General
Jackson, sir—all that monster's doings."[66] Such national "good
feeling" caused "every avenue of society [to be] thronged with
adventurers, the ephemera of the same widespread spirit of
reckless folly."   Even the more stabilized towns were subject
to periodic mutations.   In the words of John Effingham, com-
mentator on morals and manners, "he who remembers an
American town half a century ago, will see a very different
thing in an American town of today."   In Templeton, for instance, "not only will he meet new faces, but he will find new
feelings, new opinions in the place of traditions that he may
love."[67]   Concerning these national changes Effingham, or
Cooper, argues interminably, even into the second volume
where the talk is of the adventurers one sees "uppermost everywhere; in the government, in your town, in your village, in
the country even.   We are a nation of change."[68]

Cooper is kinder in his treatment of the physical appearance
of Templeton than he is with the provincial ways of its citizens.
He describes at length the beauty of the town and surrounding
country of hills, lakes, and woods.   The place is first seen from
Mount Vision (William Cooper's own vantage point) by the
returning Effinghams.   With its dozen or more streets, neat
dwellings denoting the ease of its inhabitants, and steeples
Templeton was generally beautiful and map-like.   "In England," says Cooper, "Templeton would be termed a small

[64] Ibid., pp. 115, 120, and 188.
[65] Ibid., p. 118.
[66] Ibid., p. 119.
[67] Ibid., pp. 120, 133, and 171.
[68] Ibid., II, 13.

market-town, so far as size was concerned; while in America it was, in common parlance, and legal appellation, styled a village." Neither a place settled under the unnatural excitement of speculation which so upset Cooper, nor the beginnings of a city precociously favored by peculiar advantages of trade, Templeton, at the time of this story, is but "a sober country town, that has advanced steadily, *pari passu* with the surrounding country, and offers a fair specimen of the more regular advancement of the whole nation, in its progress towards civilization."[69]

In Templeton, as in many real small towns, religious criticism bobs up as an ever present point of discussion. Through Aristabulus Bragg the novelist turns ridicule on various local attitudes regarding spiritual matters. Cooper's thrust against American standards finds expression in Bragg's boasting to scornful Eve Effingham that the Templeton churches were business assets, "for any man would be more likely to invest in a place that has five churches, than in a place with but one." Unaware of Eve's secret amusement, Bragg explains that "Methodism [has been] flourishing but little among us since the introduction of the New Lights, who have fairly managed to out-excite them, on every plan they can invent."[70]

Throughout the entire novel Cooper seeks to examine the provincial, as well as the national, scene, without having the thought occur to him that "what set his teeth on edge was the best of all evidences that a new and vigorous national life was in the making in America."[71] Still embittered by personal controversies, Cooper attempts to show how the "inferior" Braggs so fear the voice of the majority that often they deny the truth of an issue. He makes his "superior" Effinghams oppose the encroachments of the mob and maintain their positions as individuals. In "An Aristocrat and a Democrat" Cooper takes the position that those people are the enemies of democracy who "fancy that a democrat can only be one who seeks the level, social, mental, and moral, of the majority, a rule that would at once exclude all men of refinement, education and taste from the class."[72] The expulsion of the village ballplayers from the Effingham grounds and the fear which

[69] *Ibid.*, I, 142 ff.
[70] *Ibid.*, pp. 162 and 166.
[71] Mencken, *op. cit.*, pp. xviii ff.
[72] *The American Democrat*, p. 88.

Bragg showed of the community majority well illustrate Cooper's thinking concerning individual rights. Too often, says
Cooper, the proletariat mistakes *"liberties* for liberty."[73] Too
often men like Bragg and Steadfast Dodge, hypocritical editor,
are "standing candidates for popular favor."

The terse preachments in *The American Democrat* are further
elaborated in *Home as Found*. In the former Cooper says that
". . . we can all perceive the difference between ourselves and
our inferiors, but when it comes to a question of the difference
between us and our superiors, we fail to appreciate merits of
which we have no proper conception."[74] In the novel the
envious townspeople warring against the aristocrats condemned
even their most innocent amusements. Gossipy housewives,
whose views were substantiated by Editor Dodge, were horrified—or pretended to be—over the card playing, dancing, and
constant dining at the Mansion.[75] The Effinghams, on the
other hand, frequently failed to see the position of the villagers.[76]
Cooper, too, tries to justify his own position by the belief that
an individual is "the purest democrat who best maintains his
rights." In the novel Cooper, the social adjuster, too often
forgets that Cooper, the novelist, has a story to tell. This is
particularly noticeable in the second volume, Chapter XII,
where for half a dozen pages he traces the progress of society
in a new country through three stages : first, that of good fellowship and common hazards at the commencement of settlement ; second, that in which society "begins to marshal itself,
and the ordinary passions have sway" over neighborly feeling ;
and, third, the last condition in which "men and things come
within the control of more general and regular laws." Cooper
pictures Templeton at that stage when the old forces conflicted
with the new. To the newly arrived Templetonians the tradi-
tionary interests of the little town meant nothing ; to others
of long residence the legends about the place were held sacred.
Closely in line with his attack on migratory bands is that part
of *Home as Found* which Lounsbury termed the most unfortunate
thing which Cooper ever wrote. The Three Mile Point controversy is carried from the first to the second volume with
strong arguments on the part of Bragg and Dodge to the effect

[73] *Home as Found*, I, 175.
[74] *The American Democrat*, p. 89.
[75] *Home as Found*, II, 19.
[76] *Ibid.*, p. 104.

that the Effinghams will suffer forever should they dare fly in
the face of public opinion.   To this urgent plea the lord of
the mansion pays no heed, for he knows that "Americans are
a set-of-resolution-passing people."[77]

The controversial tone of this story of a town brought Cooper
more than ever into the limelight of criticism.   His democratic
principles, his personal character, and his literary position were
bitterly attacked by many enemies.   During the stress of the
libel suits, in 1842, some self-appointed critic produced a novel
in two volumes called *The Effinghams, or Home as I Found It,* by
the Author of the *Victims of Chancery.*[78]   Thus the "acrid realism" of Cooper's arguments gave him little more than "the
name of a sniffish and unpatriotic fellow, [who] was accused of
all sorts of aristocratic pretensions, immensely obnoxious to the
free citizens of a free and glorious state."[79]   In *A Fable for
Critics* Lowell has accurately described Cooper's position :

> There is one thing in Cooper, I like, too, and that is
> That on manners he lectures his countrymen gratis :
> Not precisely so either, because for a rarity,
> He is paid for his tickets in unpopularity.
> Now he may overcharge his American pictures,
> But you'll grant there's a good deal of truth in his
>   strictures ;
> And I honor the man who is willing to sink
> Half his present repute for the freedom to think,
> And, when he has thought, be his cause strong or weak,
> Will risk t'other half for the freedom to speak,
> Caring naught for what vengeance the mob has in store,
> Let that mob be the upper ten thousand or lower.[80]

Admittedly these works of Cooper offer varied delineations
of the American village and town in native literature.   *The
Pioneers* with its study of frontier community establishment ; the
Chronicles with a factual record of these early settlers, manners,
and events ; and the two sadly distorted novels of social reform
and personal wrangling, in addition to William Cooper's
Guide, have reproduced in literature the varying history of a

[77] *Ibid.,* II, 5.
[78] Lounsbury, *op. cit.,* p. 158.
[79] Mencken, *op. cit.,* Introduction.
[80] H. E. Scudder, ed., *Complete Poetical Works of James Russell Lowell* (Boston and New York, 1917), p. 135.

town dating from the earliest days of expansion in western New York. Such works not only show the usual transformations in the growth of a town, but changes equally as significant in an author's viewpoint toward his material and his public. The frontier venture of *The Pioneers* unfortunately gave way to a venture in reform in *Home as Found.*

THE NEW YORK TOWN IN LATER FICTION

Social discontent, usually attendant upon some national catastrophe such as the labor disturbance and the depression of the nineties, furnished in literature the basis for realism in America.[81] The late eighties and nineties witnessed in various parts of the country—particularly in New England, as we have noted, and in the Midwest—the appearance of local colorists who told of impoverished villagers, toil-marked farmers and their wives, weakened village aristocracy, and other lonely, beauty-starved folk. During this era of maturing realism the prairie towns of the New West, Pennsylvania villages, and the decaying hill and coast towns of New England were featured in short story and novel. In this widespread use of the small community in imaginative literature the New York town did not remain uninterpreted. To be sure, its eighteenth-century spokesmen were few, but the late nineteenth century saw the emergence of a number of realists, who as youths had actually known the backgrounds and people of small towns in New York and New Jersey. It was natural, therefore, that the realistic short stories and novels of such New Yorkers as Harold Frederic (1856-98), Edward Noyes Wescott (1847-98), and Stephen Crane (1871-1900) should prove as telling social documents of their New York villages as the Winesburgs, Spoon Rivers, and Gopher Prairies are of our own century. These and a few others helped promote a newer and more consciously spoken realism than Howells's realism of the commonplace. Among other innovations, they rediscovered the literary materials of New York provincial life. With these not only the realism of the commonplace, but the realism of social discontent and the realism of naturalism were significant.[82]

"A country boy of genius," Harold Frederic was born on a

---

[81] Parrington, "The Development of Realism" in Foerster, ed., *op. cit.*, pp. 140 ff.
[82] *Ibid.*, p. 143.

farm in central New York (near Utica), the scene of some of his fiction.[83]   At twelve, after his father's death, Frederic became "chore boy" to a neighboring farmer in whose home he read all available books and listened to the political and other talk of his elders, provincial folk who frequently became argumentative, not only about Tyron County problems, but about those upsetting the nation at large during the stirring sixties. Later in *The Copperhead* (1893), sketches of the animosities embittering the lives of the stay-at-homes during the Civil War, Frederic made use of these boyhood experiences.   His fictional pictures of a loafing boy, of the excitement of war times in the Valley of New York, and of the Yankee tradition in general are reflective of his early associations.

Shortly after the opening of the Civil War Frederic as a photographer's apprentice was introduced to small town life, where local excitement was slightly different from the even more provincial existence of the farm and crossroads store. Here he had close association with many Yankee types which in his best writing are re-created with a degree of photographic verisimilitude.   Thomas Benton, his photographer employer, served as the model for some of his Yankee characters.   Many of the scenes of his novels portray small town activities : fairs, court sessions, church conferences, funerals, and political rallies.   His vivid pictures of group life, much more forceful than his individual characterizations, offer barbed criticism of late nineteenth-century towns.   His villages (Octavius, Tyre, and Thessaly), like those later denounced by Masters and Lewis, are places of political chicanery, ugliness, joyless existence, and other abominations which Frederic had observed during these early years of hardship and meager education.

During this period of numerous country journals it was nothing unusual for Frederic, at nineteen, to begin a journalistic career as reporter for the Utica *Observer*.   Later progressing to the Albany *Journal* and the New York *Sun*, he became foreign correspondent for the New York *Times*.   Though, as these activities indicate, Frederic's primary interest was in journalism and his novels were written for amusement, he well deserves an important place among the pioneer realists of small town

[83] For biographical details see Warner's *Library of the World's Best Literature*, X, 5971 ; *Who's Who in America, 1897-1916*, p. 260 ; *National Cyclopaedia of American Biography*, V, 358-359 ; and *Dictionary of American Biography*, VII, 7-8.

life. Beginning in 1887 with *Seth's Brother's Wife*, a minutely
descriptive sto. y of the prosaic round of farming life, country
journalism, and elections first published serially in *Scribner's*,
Frederic wrote between that time and 1898 a number of realistic novels and stories in which he rediscovered middle New
York as material for fiction. In these a recurring and often
autobiographical note of semi-frontier hardships and provincial
meanness marks Frederic as a mordantly realistic interpreter
of rural and small town life.

   Seth's Brother's Wife, "as bitter as any tale of the Western
Border,"[84] is an account of sordid provincial life in upper New
York, a work colored by the author's early privations.   Everywhere Seth Fairchild—really the boy Frederic—is beset by the
evils of depression.   The embittered lives of his farming community and the unpromising existence of the farm cause Seth,
like Frederic, to escape to the town.   Here the same petty lives
and grasping ways, set in an environment of political schemes,
make this town an unlovely scene of agricultural life.   There
was no hope for countryside or village.   The Tyre of the novel
is a degenerate town which had seen better days.

   In the noble old time of stage coaches it had been a thriving,
almost bustling place, with mills turning and wares celebrated
through all the section, with a starch factory which literally gave
the name of the town to its product as a standard of excellence,
and with taverns which were rarely left with a vacant room more
than a day at a time.[85]

   But the promise of these days vanished ; the nineteenth century developed a nation of cities ; and they gave "their own
twist to the progress of the age."   Truly this novel presents a
bitter and hopeless picture of mean and vulgar neighborhoods.

   In 1890 appeared *The Lawton Girl*, giving the turmoil of a
small manufacturing town, and *In the Valley*, a tale of the Mohawk Valley during the 1750's.   The background material for
the latter came from Frederic's two great-grandfathers, both
Revolutionary War soldiers who had amused the boy with tales
of Indian raids.   *In the Valley* is a reminiscent story related by
a Dutchman who recalls vividly the days of his youth in the
Mohawk region and in Albany, "the great town of our parts"

   [84] Parrington, *The Beginnings of Critical Realism*, p. 288.
   [85] *Seth's Brother's Wife: A Study of Life in Greater New York* (New York, 1887),
p. 257.   Cf. *ibid.*, pp. 26-27.

during the French and Indian wars. Through Douvw's eyes one sees the early Mohawk Valley settlements, with the beginnings of towns around such focal points as Fort Stanwix and Johnstown; the society of mixed Dutch and English at the growing capital of Albany; the rise of manor houses throughout the valley; and, finally, the fight of the Tories, abetted by the fierce Mohawks, against the valley folk. Though much of the plot is localized in the Mohawk Valley, Albany is vividly pictured as a social and trading center, a frontier settlement fast becoming a town of importance. It was a small capital in the midst of the wilderness, a place still marked by Dutch characteristics. Douvw himself loved "its narrow-gabled houses, with their yellow pressed bricks, and iron girders and high, hospitable stoops, and projecting water-spouts."[86] Everything reminded him of "the dear, brave, good old Holland" he had never seen. How great the town seemed to the quiet Dutch boy from the valley! Amazed, he noticed the oil-lamps set up in the streets; read the weekly paper; and listened to tales about the recent performances of a theatrical band and the fierce sermons which the Dominie preached against such deviltries. He admired the new State House and the palatial manor houses of the aristocratic patroons, where elaborate gatherings were attended by the Van Rensselaers, the Schuylers, the de Lanceys, the Van Cortlandts, and others of high position. He was impressed, too, by the centers where furs, leathers, and lumber were sold and was known to boast of the ships which the townspeople sent to Europe and the West Indies. In his eyes, "no other town in the colonies compared with Albany."

Both Frederic and his brilliant contemporary, Stephen Crane, wrote understandingly of Civil War themes without either's having participated in actual fighting. In addition to *The Copperhead, and Other Stories of the North during the American War*, Frederic wrote other war stories portraying small townsmen, usually stay-at-homes who were in some manner affected by the struggle. The title story of *Marsena, and Other Stories of the Wartime* concerns a New York village coquette, Marsena, who manages to send two of her lovers to the front, where dying on the field, they wake to the irony of their position in realizing

[86] *In the Valley* (New York, 1929; first edition, 1890), p. 186.

that she cares for neither of them.[37] "The Eve of the Fourth,"
told from the viewpoint of the boy Andrew, whose martinet of
a mother forced him to take an inferior place in the gang of
town boys, is an excellent psychological study of boy life in a
small Northern town during this period of stress. A memorable time it was for Andrew and his fellows when the town
crier spread abroad among the townspeople the news that
Vicksburg had fallen. Through Andrew's reporting the reader
shares the exciting news and senses the citizens' wild rejoicing,
subdued only by the sorrow of those receiving notices of loved
ones lost in battle.

The author of other novels, such as *The Market Place* (1898),
Frederic contributed materially to the spreading pattern of
town literature in *The Damnation of Theron Ware* (1896), once
much criticized because of its open attacks on small town religious prejudices and dogmas. The powerfully told tragedy
of a small town Methodist minister and his damnation, this
novel in a broader sense is the study of village social and spiritual standards. Frederic's provincial and dogmatic parishioners view all foreigners and persons of alien belief as barba-
rians.   In Octavius, New York, the Irish and Italian Catholics,
who formed so large a fraction of the population of many of
the cities of the era,[88] were, with a few exceptions, socially insignificant. The Octavian Presbyterians and Methodists, self-
righteous village leaders, regarded the Catholic creed as something "monstrous, unspeakable, hardly imaginable."

Emphasizing such conditions as they existed in a Susquehanna community during the seventies and eighties, *The Damnation of Theron Ware* opens with the graphic picturing of the
closing session of a Methodist annual conference. Eagerly and
anxiously the assembled ministers await the bishop's appoint-
ments. People in the conference town want young Theron
Ware as their new pastor. Great is their disappointment,
therefore, when they "draw from the grab-bag" Brother Abram
G. Tiesdale, a "spindling, rickety, gaunt old man, with a long
horse-like head and vacantly solemn face, who kept one or the

[87] New York, 1894. "Marsena," with "The Cooperhead," "The Eve of the
Fourth," "The War Widow," and "My Aunt Susan," was republished by Scribner's in 1897 as *In the Sixties*. For contemporary praise see W. M. Paine, "A
Century of Stories," *The Dial*, XVII, 332-334 (Dec. 1, 1894).
[88] Leon Kellner, *American Literature* (Garden City, 1915), p. 229.

other of his hands continually fumbling his bony jaw."[89]   Sick
at heart, Theron must go to the unpromising charge of Octavius.

Dolefully Theron and Alice, his sprightly young wife, face
the task of directing a church controlled by unpleasant stewards and an eccentric lawyer, Levi Gorringe.   From Theron's
eventual meeting with Father Forbes, a Catholic priest and a
man of superior culture, dates the deepening of the theme.
Chaos is produced when untrained, though sensitive, Theron
for the first time suddenly is thrown in contact with an individual of a highly cultured and sophisticated nature.   Like his
parents and co-religionists, the unworldly minister had imagined that the Irish were to blame for the drunkenness and
crime of American cities.   Their religion he had regarded as
the source of these evils.   When he accidentally witnesses a
dying Irishman receiving aid from Father Forbes, he becomes
skeptical of his post, his faith, and himself.   His provincial assurance is punctured through his association with Father
Forbes, an agnostic physician, Lidsman, and red-haired Celia
Madden, seductive daughter of a local Irish Catholic manufacturer.

The young minister is fascinated by Celia's beauty and musical talent; she, in turn, is attracted to him by reason of his apparent uprightness.   Theron, absorbed in plans for writing a
life of Abraham and fascinated more and more by Celia, neglects Alice, who turns to Gorringe for comfort.   About this time
the Soulsbys, debt-raisers and sensational evangelists, arrive to
assist with church affairs.   Theron, however, follows Celia to
New York where she, pointing out the degeneration of his
character, spurns him.   In despair and remorse he seeks the
Soulsbys, who nurse him during a long illness.   His redemption occurs when he and Alice are reunited.   Resigning from
the ministry, he begins life anew in Seattle.

By their religion the Octavians are more closely related to
the early seventeenth than to the late nineteenth century.
Their strict view of life, carried out to the minutest detail,
savors of colonial Puritanism.   More than one instance shows
their unbending illiberality.   On one occasion a steward advised Alice to refrain from dressing too elaborately.   She had

[89] *The Damnation of Theron Ware, or Illumination* (Chicago and New York, 1899),
p. 14.

merely worn a simple, flower-trimmed hat with her Sunday costume. The Methodists, Theron's own parishioners, gossip about poor Alice's cooking and countless trivialities. They are angered because Theron buys potatoes from an Irish Catholic. Another steward demands sermons about eternal damnation, fire and brimstone. "Go to the Bible!"—that, notes Frederic, is the first and last resource of Theron's congregation.

Four well-delineated characters stand out in relief from this orthodox community. The first of these is Theron Ware himself, a man of a contradictory nature who vacillates between his religious duty and illicit life. In direct contrast is the Catholic priest, as cultured and urbane as the young minister is socially untutored and self-conscious. Celia Madden represents everything that has been foreign to the simple training of the Wares. She has beauty, wealth, and personality. In pathetic contrast, Alice, a farmer's daughter, has been reared in a poor community.

Said to be the first of modern problem novels, *The Damnation of Theron Ware*, frank in its presentation of provincial religious beliefs, marks another step forward in the development of realistic fiction portraying American town life. It is a pioneer *Main Street*, deemed worthy of ranking "among the most absorbing pieces of fiction ever written by an American."[90]

During Harold Frederic's boyhood a New York schoolgirl, one Caroline Cowles Richards, found pleasure in recording day by day her impressions of certain small town environments in which she lived. Her resultant *Village Life in America* (*1852-1872*) is a mine of information about the nineteenth-century life of the lake towns of Canandaigua, Naples, and Penn Yan, the seminary center of Auburn, and the farming communities of Geneva and East Bloomsfield, all places near the romantic region of *The Deerslayer* and *The Pioneers*.[91]

After their mother's death, Carrie and Anna Richards, daughters of an academy director in Litchfield, Connecticut, come to live with their aged grandparents, Thomas (small town banker) and Abigail Field Beals, pious and leading citizens of Canandaigua. The girls are reared in the simplicity of a refined household dominated by Puritan traditions. In Caro-

[90] Harry Thurston Peck, "Then and Now," *The Bookman*, XXX, 596 (Feb., 1910).
[91] *Village Life in America*, with an introduction by Margaret Sangster (London, 1912).

line's diary—kept from the day she was ten until her wedding
after the Civil War—are recorded childish and later mature
allusions to various customs of the period, to the swift transi-
tions in social standards, the rapid progress of science, and the
reaction of Northerners to the war.   Intensely alive to all the
life about her, Caroline chronicles innumerable happenings
connected with her family and friends.   Her diary gives, furthermore, a faithful record of her impressions of the confusing
time of the war : of her lover's stay in Virginia, Lincoln's speeches and later of his death, her grandmother's association with
the United States Sanitary Commission, and the work she and
her friends did for the relief of Northern soldiers.   Of further
interest is young Caroline's family.   Her grandparents were
closely related to the third wife of Dr. Lyman Beecher.   The
famous Cyrus W. Field, who presented Mrs. Beals with a piece
of the Atlantic cable, was a kinsman.   Her grandfather Richards was for twenty years president of Auburn Theological
Seminary.   Written by a girl reared in a well-to-do family, the
diary, therefore, reflects the life of a cultured group in a better
type of small town of the last century.

Provincial though their environment was, Caroline and her
friends did not find life dull.   Picnics on the lake ; singing
school performances when Anna was "on the top row of the
pyramid of beauty" ; the excitement of having ambrotypes
taken of the Sunday school class ; botanizing trips in near-by
woods and fields ; bargaining for black silk mantillas and summer bonnets ; and the fun of sleigh rides and parties, tableaux,
charades, spiritual seances, literary reviews, musical programs,
and Barnum's Circus featuring the Siamese twins were remembered occasions.   Even though Abram Beals, proud of the an-
tiques in his house, refused to relinquish his candles and sperm
oil lamps for the newer gas lights, he expected Caroline and
Anna to devote a part of their time to reading.   During the
winter evenings the girls joined their grandparents around a
hearth fire and there by the light of "the funniest little sperm
oil lamp" Abigail knitted, while the others read.   Caroline's
reading varied from *The Pilgrim's Progress* to serials in *Harper's
Magazine*.   (She preferred the one "called Little Dorritt, by
Charles Dickens.")   The girls were paid for learning verses in
the Bible and the New England Primer and for reading tales

of "early piety" like *Elizabeth Thornton* or *The Flower and Fruit of Female Piety.*

Aside from their feminine interest in earrings, frizzled hair, hoop skirts and calico dresses bought in New York, in mystic books and autograph albums, Caroline and Anna attended various public entertainments in Canandaigua. Many well-known lecturers came to town: Edward Everett, Susan B. Anthony, who talked to the seminary girls "very plainly about our rights and how we ought to stand up for them," Lyman Beecher, Henry Ward Beecher, and Cyrus W. Field. There were occasional trips to larger places. Once the girls went with a large party of Canandaiguans to Rochester to hear Charles Dickens lecture, and, according to Caroline,

. . . enjoyed it more than I can possibly express. He was quite hoarse and had small bills distributed through the Opera House with the announcement:

MR. CHARLES DICKENS

Begs indulgence for a Severe Cold, but hopes its effects may not be very perceptible after a few minutes' Reading.
Friday, December 27th, 1867.

We brought these notices home with us for souvenirs. He looks exactly like his pictures. It was worth a great deal just to look upon the man who wrote Little Dorritt, David Copperfield, and all the other books, which have delighted us so much. . . . He spoke very appreciatively of his enthusiastic reception in this country and almost apologized for some of the opinions which he published, after his first visit here, twenty-five years ago. He evidently thinks that the United States of America are quite worth while.[92]

For vividness of detail Caroline's impressions of the Canandaigua celebration of Lee's surrender (April 10, 1865) may be compared to Frederic's "The Eve of the Fourth." These lines re-create that exciting Monday:

Bells have rung all day since the news of Lee's surrender. Everybody is wild with excitement. The stores were closed and prayers offered and addresses given on the square. A procession of men, women, children paraded the streets. Some of our most staid and dignified citizens were on a dray ringing bells, waving hats and

[92] *Ibid.*, p. 201.

giving vent to their enthusiasm in most unheard of ways.   In the
evening there was a grand illumination.   A transparency in the
porch of the Congregational church brought out "Hallelujah" in
the brightest light.[93]

Although these are but youthful impressions, they and countless other notes make *Village Life in America* a revelatory personal
document of small town affairs during a period of stirring national changes.

Critically styled "the genius of his generation"[94] chiefly by
virtue of his naturalistic *Maggie: A Girl of the Streets* (1893) and
his great American war story, *The Red Badge of Courage* (1895),
Stephen Crane (1871-1900), misunderstood by many contemporaries, was one of the most gifted interpreters of the late nineteenth-century small town.   While his major interests displayed
his remarkable versatility elsewhere in both fiction and poetry,
Crane contributed much to the imaginative literature of the
town in his sympathetic and realistic studies of child life.   In
1899 readers of *Harper's Magazine* may have been both amused
and, if unduly sensitive, repelled by the frankly expressed *Whilomville Stories*, additions of new literary wealth to Aldrich's and
Mark Twain's more familiar stories of boy life in small towns.
Here "for the first time since Mark Twain's demigod floated
with his lazy slave on the Mississippi, the national child stepped
forward and yelped among the maples and swinging gates of a
little town, unmoral, unadorned, and far from sweet."[95]   Both
the humor and tragedies of boyhood come to life in Crane's
narratives of a lazy New York town.

William Lyon Phelps, who has ranked Crane with Mark
Twain and Booth Tarkington as one of "the greatest diagnosti-
cians of children's diseases," once wrote that "the tales of Whilomville display his playfulness, his humor, his love of children,
his deep sympathy with and his equally deep contempt for that
most brutal of all savage animals, the small boy."[96]

In these illuminating and meticulously developed stories
Crane analyzes both profoundly and gayly boys as individuals
and boys in groups.[97]   Too real, perhaps, for some of Crane's

    [93] *Ibid.*, p. 187.
    [94] Parrington, *The Beginnings of Critical Realism in America*, p. 328.
    [95] Thomas Beer, *Stephen Crane* (New York, 1923), p. 237.
    [96] Wilson Follett, ed., *The Works of Crane* (New York, 1926), V, xi, Introduction
by Phelps.
    [97] *Ibid.*, V, xii.

Victorian readers, Jimmy Trescott, fun-loving son of Whilom-ville's best doctor; Willie Dalzel, a confirmed braggart; and pugnacious Johnny Hedge alarmed their neighborhood and "lied and bragged and shocked ladies dreadfully" with their fights, hunting expeditions, their boisterous performance of "Hold-up Harry, the Terror of the Sierras"—interpreted by a star performer as "the Terror of the Sarahs"—and other escapades rivaling those of Tom Bailey, Tom Sawyer, and Pen-rod Schofield. Among the most human portrayals are those of "Comrade" Jimmy Trescott's trials: his utter humiliation when he was hooted at and cast off by the other children be-cause he took his share of a picnic lunch in a tin pail; his public shame when his unsuccessful Friday afternoon oration convinced the luckless boy that "death amid the flames was preferable to a recital of 'The Charge of the Light Brigade' "; the disastrous conclusion to his attempt at impressing "the little girl who wore the red hood" with his marvelous performances on his new velocipede, the largest in Whilomville; and his ludicrous, yet personally terrifying, firing at a cow which in his fright he mistook for a lynx.[98]

Such small town "kids"—Crane used the term long before its popular acceptance—offer undeniable evidence both of Crane's deep understanding of child psychology and of his complete disgust with the becurled and lace-collared perfection of Mrs. Frances Hodgson Burnett's popular creation. Once he wrote to a friend: "If the Whilomville stories seem like Little Lord Fauntleroy to you, you are demented and I know you are joking, besides."[99] Such an attitude explains Crane's relentless portrayal of small girls. His Burnett-trained readers found something new—and perhaps distasteful—in the esca-pades of "the Angel Child," a petted city vixen who came as a "visitation" upon the helpless Trescotts and by constant drilling, directing, and compelling led Jimmy's gang into wilder and unheard of adventures.

One day in 1897 Harold Frederic, then a London corres-pondent for the *Times*, was a guest at Ravensbrook, Crane's dank villa at Oxted in Surrey.[100] With Sanford Bennett he

---

[98] *Ibid.*, "Shame," p. 73; "Making an Orator," p. 63; "Showin' Off," p. 51; and "Lynx-Hunting," p. 31.
[99] Beer, *op. cit.*, p. 112. Cf. J. N. Beffel, "Fauntleroy Plague," *The Bookman*, LXVI, 135 (April, 1927).
[100] Beer, *op. cit.*, p. 162.

made an audience for Crane's nearly finished and horrible tale of a man who had no face. Finding the story offensive, Frederic advised Crane to destroy the work; Bennett considered it powerful impressionism. "The Monster," as Crane called the tale, was not destroyed and, though refused by *Century*, it remained as proof of its author's powers to expose, in caustic fashion, small town prejudices and popular stupidity.[101] Here again the scene is Whilomville. The emphasis, however is shifted from child life to the tragedy which befell Henry Johnson, negro dandy and hostler for Doctor Trescott. When the Trescott home burned Henry in rescuing young Jimmy so injured himself that ever afterward he was idiotic and faceless. Bound by duty, Doctor Trescott used his best skill in nursing his son's rescuer. His efforts to aid the deformed and terrifying servant—locally termed a monster—brought social ostracism to the doctor and his family. Out of the town's condemnation of the Trescotts Crane developed his main theme of provincial stupidity. Unflattering pictures of contending factions and gossipmongers complete this social parable of an unthinking populace.

Thus, without varnishing the truth, this man, whom his friend Joseph Conrad judged "incapable of affectation of any kind," created in these small town tales sincere, unsentimental portrayals of normal children.[102] Like the Penrod sketches, which appeared fifteen years later, this entire series impresses those having knowledge of town life by the familiar treatment which Crane gives of provincial scenes and characters. The work of one whose boyhood was spent in New York small towns, these sketches are among the most delightfully humorous and truthfully interpretative stories of child life in the literature of the American small town.

About the time that Frederic and Crane were living in England another New Yorker, Edward Noyes Westcott (1847-98), a successful Syracuse banker and nonliterary man, went to Italy for his health. Here to provide diversion during days of invalidism, Westcott began a novel of small town life based on his own experiences and observations. The result was an amazing *coup d'essai*, for though *David Harum: A Story of American Life* (1898) was at first rejected by several publishers eventu-

[101] Follett, ed., *op. cit.*, III, 25 ff.
[102] Beer, *op. cit.*, Introduction written by Joseph Conrad.

ally—after the death of the invalid author—it became an unusually successful best seller.[103]   The original character of David
Harum, shrewd, upstate New York country banker, a genuine and rare type in American literature as indigenous as
Huck Finn and Uncle Remus, quite overshadowed the ex-
istent weaknesses of wooden minor characters, a stereotyped
small town background, and flaws in plot and diction.

David Harum presents the local peculiarities of Homeville, in
central New York.   Here lives the delightfully quaint country
philanthropist, David Harum, whose dry, humorous, and rather illiterately expressed philosophies form the best elements of
a romantic tale centering around the local banking business
and horse trading.   A shopworn plot motif is applied in a new
way.   Here is no romantic featuring of the once popular "success" theme of the country boy who becomes a metropolitan
leader ; instead, Westcott's plot has to do with college-trained
John Lenox, a cultured New York youth who finds happiness
and material advancement as David's assistant in the Homeville Bank.

Though not so ugly as Spoon River or Gopher Prairie, Homeville in the nineties was not an American Dreamthorp.   All
was not roseate.   John's unpleasant experiences in a wooden
shack of a hotel, the Eastern counterpart of Gopher Prairie's
Minniemashie House, introduced him at once to the crudities
of small town life.   Westcott's descriptive details picturing
John's survey of his hotel room foreshadow the realism of Carol
Kennicott's inspection of the outward sordidness of Main Street,
Gopher Prairie, Minnesota :

John surveyed the apartment.   There were two small-paned windows overlooking the street, curtained with bright "Turkey-red"
cotton ; near to one of them a small wood stove and a wood box,
containing some odds and ends of sticks and bits of bark ; a small
chest of drawers, serving as a washstand ; a malicious little looking-
glass ; a basin and ewer holding about two quarts ; an earthenware
mug and soap-dish, the latter containing a thin bit of translucent
soap scented with sassafras ; an ordinary wooden chair and a rock-
ing-chair with rockers of divergent aims ; a yellow wooden bedstead
furnished with a mattress of "excelsior" (calculated to induce early
rising), a dingy white spread, a gray blanket of coarse wool, a pair
of cotton sheets which had too obviously done duty since passing

[103] Pattee, *The New American Literature*, p. 238.   Cf. H. T. Peck, *op. cit.*, p. 595.

through the hand of the laundress, and a pair of flabby little pillows in the same state. . . .[104]

Unromantic also are David's numerous aphoristic statements, suggestive of a Yankee shrewdness. Note :

"Bus'nis is bus'nis" ain't part of the Golden Rule, I allow, but the way it gen'ally runs, fur's I've found out, is "Do unto the other feller the way he'd like to do unto you, an' do it fust."[105]

Written at a period when American fiction was tending more and more to subordinate plot in favor of a realistic portrayal of native life and people, *David Harum*, with such novels as *The Damnation of Theron Ware*, *The Story of a Country Town*, and *Zury*, pointed the way toward the more modern realism of Masters, Lewis, Anderson, and other insurgents. Thus localized realism gradually invaded the strongholds of sentimentality.

"For years," says Professor Pattee, "the David Harum influence was everywhere visible."[106] This is especially evident in a further study of the New York town, in Irving Bacheller's *Eben Holden* (1900), the story of William Brower and old Eben Holden, a farm hand and genial philosopher, the sole survivors of a ruined home in a Vermont village. In the course of the plot the scene shifts to Faraway township—Paradise Valley— and to the small academy towns of Hillsborough and Ogdensburg, New York. Here is a realistic re-creation of antebellum days when Hillsborough and hundreds of other small towns were the scenes of singing schools, public spelling bees, political talk-fests—for the slavery question was then looming large—religious gatherings, horse racing, and exhibitions at the County Fair.[107] Bacheller's Adirondack scenes suggest two earlier minor interpreters of the same country. Philander Deming, a lawyer, published in *The Atlantic Monthly* from 1873 to 1888 a number of unsensational stories about plain country folk whose business affairs occasionally drew them into Albany, the town most frequently described. Deming's chief concern, however, was with rural, rather than town, types. Albion Winegar Tourgée (1838-1905), an Ohioan of varied military,

---

[104] *David Harum, etc.* (New York, 1898), p. 109.
[105] *Ibid.*, p. 184.
[106] Pattee, *op. cit.*, p. 239. Cf. A. B. Maurice, "Irving Bacheller's *Eben Holden*," *The Bookman*, XII, 235 (Nov., 1900).
[107] *Eben Holden* (Boston, 1901), pp. 236-237.

editorial, and legal experience in New York and North Carolina, wrote a series of Reconstruction novels. Perhaps less popular than the once widely read *A Fool's Errand* (1879) is the first novel in the sequence, *Hot Plowshares* (1883), dramatizing pre-war slavery complications in a New York factory town and a New England seminary village.[108] Avowedly a novel of propagandism, *Hot Plowshares* shows the reaction of New York townspeople against what they considered the racial malpractices of Southern plantation owners. In the course of a long-winded and didactic tale of mystery, adventure, and intersectional hatred, one catches glimpses of the Paradise Valley town of Skendoah, eventually to become a mill center, where so early as 1848 the contest between liberty and slavery took on a serious cast.[109]

During the twentieth century the outstanding novelists of the New York scene have chosen metropolitan rather than small town themes. Edith Wharton's novels of New York society, John Dos Passos's *Manhattan Transfer* and his three-decker *U. S. A.* (*The 42nd Parallel*, *1919*, and *The Big Money*), and other studies show the cityward trend in literature.

[108] New York, 1883.
[109] *Ibid.*, p. 356.

CHAPTER VI

EXPOUNDERS OF THE MIDDLE BORDER TOWN

IN 1851 an alert, thirteen-year-old Dutchman, a canal boy, industriously worked up and down the much-traveled Erie Canal wondering anew at the towns and the hundreds of emigrants he saw on each trip. Buffalo, the biggest town he had ever seen, was a marvel to him. Full of sailors, emigrants, waterside characters, ships, and various signs of trade, the town presented a motley sight, almost kaleidoscopic, so constantly changing that even the lad "could see, feel, taste, smell, and hear the West everywhere." Day by day he watched the swelling of the stream of emigration and trade until it became a torrent. Amazed at the quick transformations in the life around him, the boy, village-bred, "thought that all the people in the world had gone crazy to move West. We took families, even neighborhoods, household goods, live stock, and all the time more and more people. They were talking about Ohio, Indiana, Illinois, Michigan, and Wisconsin; and once in a while the word Iowa was heard; and one family astonished us by saying that they were going to Texas." The wide-eyed boy noted, too, that "the Mormons had already made their great migration to Utah, and the Northwestern Trail across the plains to Oregon and California took its quota of gold-seekers every year."[1] Exciting times were these for canal boy Jacob Vandemark, hero of Herbert Quick's dramatic tale of frontier Iowa, as he viewed each day the hopeful or anxious travelers passing through his native New York en route to a Western land of promise.

The experiences of young Vandemark are fictionalized, but they are so steeped in the reality of pioneering that they represent a vital part of the actual drama of the settling of the Midlands, the Southwest, and the Far West, a story familiar to the readers of Turner and his followers. It is also familiar matter that the Erie Canal was but one thoroughfare for settlers bound for the inviting lands of the West. Other streams of migratory people moved by way of the treacherous wilderness trails

[1] *Vandemark's Folly* (New York, 1922), p. 49.

over the Alleghenies from Virginia and the Carolinas into Kentucky's "dark and bloody ground" and thence westward. Some made the long, peril-fraught journey by boat around Cape Horn to the mining settlements of California, lodestones to adventurers from all parts of the older sections of the country. For countless other seekers the Ohio River offered an important highway, while many New Englanders and New Yorkers reached the Ohio and Michigan frontiers by way of the Great Lakes.[2] Along these and other routes came the overflow into the newer country of the Middle Border. It was in this restlessness and confusion of pioneering, with its attendant speculation, that many of the Midland towns had their inception.

In the literature of the West the town has been often and variously pictured. From its first exploration and settlement writers have written of the wilderness, then of the hastily constructed villages, those original "huddles of bare pine structures dumped down on the prairie,"[3] those desolate way stations to the ever promising lands beyond the horizon, and finally of the more stabilized and growing towns (Lexington, Cincinnati, and New Harmony). *Astoria* and *Captain Bonneville* are records of Irving's interests—perhaps mercenary—in the Far West; the Leatherstocking Tales show Cooper's romantic coloring of the frontier material with which he was familiar; and Bryant's poetry reveals clearly his belief in the potential greatness of the vast and beckoning prairies. So early as the eighteenth century an influx of European travelers resulted in all sorts of descriptive records of America and its emerging West.[4] Some, like reformer Fanny Wright D'Arusmont, were impressed by the westward course of empire. Madame D'Arusmont wrote to an English friend:

The increase of population, the encroachment on the wilderness, the birth of settlements, and their growth into towns, surpasses belief, till one has been an eye witness of the miracle, or conversed with those who have been so. It is wonderfully cheering to find yourself in a country which tells only of improvements.[5]

[2] Ralph Rusk, *The Literature of the Middle Western Frontier*, I, 13-78, describes the cultural beginnings of the Midwestern frontier.
[3] Dondore, *op. cit.*, p. 328.
[4] Rusk, *op. cit.*, I, 79-130. "Travel and Observation," and Lane Cooper, "Travellers and Observers, 1763-1846," *C. H. A. L.*, I, 185 ff.
[5] *Views of Society and Manners in America* (New York, 1821), p. 132.

Others not so kind, if not of Johnson's opinion that the Americans were "a race of convicts and ought to be thankful for anything we allow them short of hanging," regarded Americans, especially frontiersmen, as rough, uncouth, and vulgar. Mrs. Frances Trollope in 1828-30 found in Cincinnati, then a frontier town of about twenty thousand people, vulgar surroundings which she in English fashion scorned without considering that the place, though undoubtedly crude, was but one stage in the social evolution of a rapidly changing country. To this censorious social mentor the American frontier meant communities of awkward and uncouth people whose raucous voices, hard faces, whiskey drinking, love for politics, and other inelegancies patently symbolized their utter crudity and ignorance.[6] In her plainly truthful, though hostilely received, criticisms of American manners "sweet Mistress Trollope" attempted the reformation of a society which, without doubt, needed the influence of an older culture. Cordially disliked mainly because she had described as true of the whole country what she had observed in the West, this critical Cincinnati bazaar keeper, like Dickens later in *Martin Chuzzlewit* and *American Notes*, represents the foreign detractor who irritated, yet eventually bettered, the vainglorious American.

Even early native writers of imaginative literature, a number of them pioneers, added their animadversions to the painful strictures of foreign travelers. To some the crude little settlements which they had either helped build or had heard about were but dully commonplace and uninteresting areas upon the surface of the earth; to others these were community centers radiating friendliness and frontier hospitality. Some, especially later critics like plain-spoken E. W. Howe, used the acid touch; others transmuted the naked reality of barren and ugly prairie towns, often dust-swept and lonely, into a finished print tinted "with nice pinks and yellows."[7] If we peep over the shoulders of some of our earlier Middle Western expounders —as Percy H. Boynton has termed them—we may see a vast section dotted at intervals with hastily and economically built villages which nature had "not absorbed into herself with ivy and moss, summer and winter, as in England." It is this

---

[6] *Domestic Manners of the Americans* (New York, 1901), *passim*. (First published in 1832.)

[7] Lewis Bromfield, "An Honest Novel," *The Saturday Review of Literature*, I, 556 (Feb. 28, 1925).

cheapness, this newness, and this ugliness, loosely tied in temporary cohesion, which furnished the materials of provincialism for Edward Eggleston, Joseph Kirkland, E. W. Howe, and other pioneer realists, who, as if following Whitman's urging, did

> Away with old romance!
> Away with novels, plots and plays of foreign courts,
> Away with love-verses sugar'd in rhyme, the intrigues,
>   amours of idlers,[8]

and turned, instead, to picturing bleak lives restricted by the ever binding code of unlovely prairie towns.

THE PIONEER GOES FORTH

As with the New England colonists, there were among the Western frontiersmen those who chose to write in letter, chronicle, and story of their new and undeveloped environments. Outstanding among those who pictured the crude towns of the Midwest were Philadelphia-born James Hall (1793-1868), lawyer and editor of the earliest literary publication in the West, *The Illinois Monthly Magazine* (Vandalia, 1830-32) ; Timothy Flint (1780-1840), a Harvard graduate, missionary-traveler, novelist, and editor of *The Western Monthly Magazine* (Cincinnati, 1833-36) ; and Caroline Matilda Stansbury Kirkland (1801-64), who as "Mrs. Mary Clavers" frequently contributed to magazines and annuals and wrote lively, humorous descriptions of Michigan frontier life.[9]

Romantically inclined and eager for adventure, ex-soldier James Hall, then in his late twenties, went in 1820 to Illinois where he hoped, amid the rough scenes of the frontier, to establish a law practice.   Settling at Shawneetown, a place first opened for settlement in 1812, young Hall became a public prosecutor and editor of the *Illinois Gazette*.[10]   Later as state treasurer Hall went to Vandalia, where he was co-editor of the *Illinois Intelligencer*.[11]   Here he became preëminent among

[8] Emory Holloway, ed., *Leaves of Grass* (Garden City, 1931), "Song of the Exposition," p. 171.
[9] For full discussions see Stanton, *A Manual of American Literature*, pp. 132, 159, and 162 ; Rusk, *op. cit.*, I, 126-127 and 284 ff. ; Dondore, *op. cit.*, pp. 206 ff. and 297 ff. ; J. E. Kirkpatrick, *Timothy Flint, etc.* (Cleveland, 1911), chaps. iv, xii, and xvi ; Duyckinck, *op. cit.*, II, 562 ff. ; and Barrett Wendell, *op. cit.*, Bk. VI, iv.
[10] Duyckinck, *op. cit.*, II, 145 ff.
[11] C. S. Baldwin, *American Short Stories* (New York, 1916), p. 97.

a group of frontier writers through his triple services as projector, editor, and chief contributor of *The Western Souvenir, a Christmas and New Year's Gift* (1829), a frontier annual "written and published in the Western country, by Western men, and . . . chiefly confined to subjects connected with the history and character of the country which gives it birth."[12] Thus was launched a motley series of tolerable verses, sentimental trifles, and historically valuable sketches of the frontier, which though frequently too literary in style revealed close observation of Middle Border life and occasional flashes of humor.

Judge Hall had gained attention earlier through his *Letters from the West*, written in the stereotyped character of a youth traveling for amusement. Begun in 1820 and intended for the *Portfolio*, a periodical edited in Philadelphia since 1801 by John E. Hall, in which some of the letters actually appeared, the entire collection was printed in London in 1828 and advertised as "containing sketches of scenery, manners, and customs; and anecdotes connected with the first settlements of the Western sections of the United States."[13] Scattered accounts in these letters picture insulated frontier towns. Letter X is entitled "Small Town-Manners of the People." Hall was impressed by the lack of curiosity these Illinois villagers displayed toward strangers. This he explains by the frequent arrivals of a great number and variety of people even in isolated posts. Even by 1828, he notes, town building was making rapid progress.

The merchants, who make their annual journies to an eastern city to purchase goods; the innumerable caravans of adventurers, who are daily crowding to the West in search of homes, and the numbers who traverse these interesting regions from motives of curiosity produce a constant succession of visitors of every class of almost every nation.[14]

Hall's account of Shawneetown shows in detail the founding, through sale of public lands, and the subsequent building of a town in the wilderness.[15] Log, frame, and brick houses; stores, already the center of trade; a land office, a post office, and printing shop; a tavern and an independent bank quickly

[12] *The Western Souvenir*, ed. James Hall, n.d. (1829), p. iii.
[13] London, 1828, title-page.
[14] *Ibid.*, p. 170.
[15] *Ibid.*, p. 220.

made Shawneetown a busy frontier settlement. Hall, queerly enough, makes no mention of churches or schools, two institutions most frequently mentioned in the annals of the New England towns.

In his earliest published tales Hall also showed his observation of frontier settlements. One of the best, "The French Village, " a genre study included in the *Western Souvenir*, delineates the fur-trading citizenry of a small, sequestered Mississippi Valley town and their spirited carnival entertainments. Later his stories appeared in collections, the first being the initial issue of *Legends of the West* in 1832.[16] "The sole intention of these tales," wrote Hall for the first edition, "is to convey accurate descriptions of the scenery of the country in which the author resides." Claiming for his tales no other merit than fidelity, Hall founded his fiction "upon incidents which have been witnessed by the author during a long residence in the Western states, or upon traditions preserved by the people, and have received but little artificial embellishment." In the edition of 1853 many tales show that Hall as an industrious practitioner often traveled through a circuit of several counties, where he learned, as did Lincoln, the legends and manners of frontier Illinois, then just admitted into the Union.[17] The Judge thus found an Illinois made up of widely scattered settlements "lying chiefly along the borders of the Mississippi, the Ohio, and Wabash" and peopled largely by settlers from Kentucky, Tennessee, and North Carolina. At that time but thinly settled and with county towns far apart, Illinois could boast of "no hotels, few roads, and fewer bridges."[18] Small towns were the center of the legal activity and, as Hall notes, in a new country like this everybody went to court.

The seats of justice were small villages, mostly mere hamlets, composed of a few log-houses, into which the judge and bar were crowded, with the grand and petit jurors, litigants, witnesses, and, in short, the whole body of the country.[19]

In such surroundings Hall spent twelve years in the practice of his profession and in the observation of the manners of his

[16] Philadelphia, 1832.   [17] New York, 1853. Preface, p. ix.
[18] *Ibid.*, p. x.
[19] *Legends of the West* (Cincinnati, 1857), pp. x-xi. These treatments of village lawyers are comparable to those in Longstreet's more highly humorous *Georgia Scenes* (1835).

associates.   Later he admitted that, like young Walter Scott, he spent hours in searching for adventures rather than in actions at law.[20]   Consequently, the tales comprising *Legends of the West* are rich with pictures of frontier people, customs, and backgrounds.   In "The Seventh Son" is delineated "an obscure town, far in the wilderness," wherein a young doctor, a graduate of an Eastern college, overcomes local superstition and thereby gains the favor of the townspeople; in "A Legend of Carondelet" the experiences of a Yankee college youth who poses as a physician furnish the theme for a story of a Louisiana frontier town; "Harpe's Head" is a horrible tale of border ruffianism in a Kentucky village; "Michel de Coucy," a tale of a Canadian boatman, tells of Fort Chartres in Illinois; and "The Emigrants," an account of an English family seeking new lands in America, contains pictures of small towns and hamlets along the Ohio.[21]

If in his next collection, *The Soldier's Bride and Other Tales* (1833),[22]   Hall failed to expand his Western themes, in *Tales of the Border* (1835) he again turned to the indigenous matter of the *Legends*.[23]   Among these tales are a few sketches of little settlements where, in Hall's words, "a few families far from other civilized communities, enjoyed some of the comforts of society among themselves, and lived in a state approaching that of the social condition."   These stories, though often structurally defective and florid in style, show how a pioneer lawyer, recording the life he often saw in his professional journeyings, became a moving force in the intellectual development of Illinois.   Here, too, are significant records of hitherto unheeded frontier townspeople: of a North Carolinian, who dreaming of building a town in the Western wilderness indulged too much in flattering anticipations of wealth and independence; of Major Obadiah, a shiftless village postmaster; of Uncle Moses, a professional emigrant, who "was *raised* in North Carolina and had regularly emigrated westwardly, once in every three or four years"; and of heartsick villagers whose settlement was depopulated because of the swift changes of the

[20] *Ibid.*, p. ix.
[21] *Ibid.*, 1853 Putnam ed., pp. 293 ; 287 ; 322 ; 98 ; 351 ; and 369 respectively.
[22] *The Soldier's Bride, etc.* (Philadelphia, 1853).   See Rusk, *op. cit.*, I, 280, for analysis.
[23] Philadelphia, 1835.

era.[24] Such are some of the earliest fictionalizations of the Midwest, mildly realistic sketches of men and manners in frontier clearings, invaluable contemporary pictures of embryonic towns in the midst of a wilderness.

Hall was not alone in making the Western frontier a matter of our national literary consciousness. Another able contributor to the *Western Souvenir* and to Middle Border literature was the young missionary, Timothy Flint, whose duties took him along dangerous trails throughout the Mississippi region. The author of several novels delineative of pioneering adventures (*Francis Berrian, or The Mexican Patriot*, 1826, and *George Mason: The Young Backwoodsman*, 1829), Flint best pictures frontier town life in his personal account of his years of itinerant teaching and preaching, *Recollections of the Last Ten Years in the Mississippi Valley* (1826), expressed in a series of letters to the Reverend James Flint, Salem, Massachusetts.[25] Written in simple style, often enlivened by anecdotes, these memoirs reveal, among other minutiae of frontier life, Flint's impressions of the "many thriving villages, that had just risen in the wilderness, and many indications of commencing settlements" along the Ohio and the Mississippi. The record of a keenly observant and educated man, the *Recollections* offer intimate details of life in the frontier settlement of Marietta, Ohio, then "a considerable village," of Cincinnati, "the only place that could properly be called a town, on the course of the Ohio and Mississippi, from Steubenville to Natchez, a distance of fifteen hundred miles," of Kentucky's "many handsome villages," of St. Louis, "a kind of central point" for fur-trading and military outfitting, and of other places in Missouri, Arkansas, and Louisiana.

A third frontier realist whose sketches appeared in the annuals of the thirties and forties was witty Caroline Matilda Kirkland. Born in New York City, Caroline Stansbury moved to western New York on the death of her father, a publisher. Her marriage to William Kirkland, educator and author, took her to Geneva, New York, to Detroit in 1835, and in 1839 to wilderness settlements about sixty miles from the latter city.[26] A good observer with a keen sense of humor, Mrs. Kirkland

[24] *Ibid.*, "A Pioneer's Tale," pp. 33-34; "The Silver Mine, A Tale of Missouri," pp. 157-176; and "The French Village," pp. 116 ff.
[25] Boston, 1826.
[26] *The National Cyclopaedia of American Biography*, V, 356.

wrote such entertaining letters about her emigration that her New York friends, to whom they were addressed, urged her to collect them into a published volume.[27]   In 1839, therefore, there appeared *A New Home—Who'll Follow? or, Glimpses of Western Life* by Mrs. Mary Clavers, an actual settler.[28]   Admittedly influenced by Miss Mitford's village sketches, Mrs. Kirkland was "tempted to set forth [her] little book as . . . a veritable history; an unimpeachable transcript of reality; a rough picture, in detached parts, but pentagraphed from life; a sort of 'Emigrant's Guide'."[29]   In spite of certain acknowledged "glosses, colorings, and lights," *A New Home*, the best of Mrs. Kirkland's works, is historically valuable as a vigorous narrative of frontier life expressed in vivacious and intelligent style.

A New Home wittily describes the perilous "translation" of the Kirklands to the Michigan wilderness out of which was to develop the glorified villages of Tinkerville and Montacute, paper-planned settlements illustrative of " 'the madness of the people' in those days of golden dreams."[30]   Among the speculators who forsook city-planning to content themselves "with planning villages, on the banks of streams which certainly never could be expected to beat navies" were the promoters of the miserable villages in which the Kirklands lived.   With satiric touch Mrs. Kirkland exposes the game by which Detroit speculators gulled hundreds of buyers.

When lots were to be sold, the whole fair dream was splendidly emblazoned on a sheet of super-royal size; things which only floated before the mind's eye of the most sanguine, were portrayed with bewitching minuteness for the delectation of the ordinary observer.   Majestic steamers plied their paddles to and fro upon the river; ladies crowding their decks. . . . Sloops dotted the harbors. . . .   Mills, factories, and light-houses, canals, rail-roads and bridges, all took their appropriate positions.   Then came the advertisements, choicely worded and carefully vague, never setting forth anything which might not come true at some time or other; yet leaving the buyer without excuse if he chose to be taken in.[31]

The Kirklands' journey from Detroit over boggy roads; the

[27] Duyckinck, *op. cit.*, II, 562.
[28] New York, 1839.
[29] Preface to third edition, 1841.
[30] *Ibid.*, p. 7.
[31] *Ibid.*, pp. 48-49.

building of their new home, a log hut; their contacts with backwoods neighbors; their refusal to "buy any amount of stock in the 'Merchants and Manufacturers' Bank of Tinkerville' "; and countless other village affairs are related through intimate descriptions, penetrative characterizations, racy dialect, and a realistic suggestion of frontier manners.

Mrs. Kirkland already was recognized as one of the New York literary set through *A New Home*, contributions to magazines and annuals, and *Forest Life* (1842) when *Western Clearings* appeared in 1845. Mixing both fact and fiction in these sketches, Mrs. Kirkland produced further convincing and vigorous pictures of mushroom Michigan villages. Differing radically from many of her contemporaries who glorified both pioneer and Indian in the popular annuals of the day, Caroline Kirkland with accuracy and humor wrote of the crude towns in which she had experienced the difficulties of pioneering.[32]

In *Western Clearings*, as in *A New Home*, Mrs. Kirkland described with fidelity the land fever which gave impetus to the great migration from all parts of the seaboard states. Recording naturally the life of villages and growing Western towns, she pictured the pioneer inhabitants of such places at work and at play. "Ball at Thram's Huddle" describes the "fast and furious" dancing at a frontier Independence ball; "Love vs Aristocracy" reveals that even in a crude Western town social distinctions may exclude certain citizens from a party given by the richest woman in the community; and "A Forest Fête" sketches vividly a public picnic.[33] Mrs. Kirkland's neighbors were frontier men and women for the most part as realistically pictured as Master William Horner, a sort of Western Ichabod who, she says,

came to our village to keep school when he was about eighteen years of age: tall, lank, straight-sided, and straight-haired, with a mouth of the ·most puckered and solemn kind. His figure and movements were those of a puppet cut out of shingle and jerked by a string; and his address corresponded very well with his appearance. Never did that prim mouth give way before a laugh. A faint and misty smile was the widest departure from its propriety.

---

[32] *Ibid.*, Preface, p. viii: "The papers included in the present collection were all written at the West . . . yet there is reason to believe, after all the efforts of these United States of Alleghania by Magazine and Annual stories, very many of them still remain beyond the pale. . . .'

[33] *Ibid.*, pp. 15-26; 35-56; 27-34 respectively.

. . . Master Horner knew well what belonged to the pedagogical character, ...[34]

Details of slides and lectures over which many of the audience nodded, the spelling school, "the grand exhibition" at the closing of the school year, and sleigh rides indicate that the daily round of activities even in unformed settlements like Montacute was enlivened by entertainment.

Her convincingly accurate and humorous sketches of upstart Michigan settlements show with a certainty that Caroline Kirkland, one of the few early feminine writers escaping the influence of *Godey's Lady's Book* and the gift book craze, probably deserved Poe's praise as "one of our best writers," noted for her wit, verisimilitude, and freshness of style.[35] Her descriptions of heterogeneous village populations, "contriving to live under the pressure of extreme difficulties," are marked by common sense.   While many of her narratives are merely episodic, Mrs. Kirkland's sketches of the rude angularities and false refinements of the backwoods are usually conceded to be the most realistic treatment of the pioneer Western community during the late thirties and early forties.   In this connection Benjamin Drake, author of *Tales and Sketches from the Queen City*, deserves mention for his picture of Western city growth as shown in his sketch "The Queen City," wherein a lonely hunter returning to an early scene of adventure after a lapse of years views in mute astonishment not the virgin forest but a spreading city. "A Kentucky Election" offers a realistic picture of village political excitement.

These were outstanding among those early expounders of the Middle Border who actually viewed the miraculous transformation of forest and prairie land into centers of trade and social association.   From their writings came pictures of the Western town in the making.   It was for their successors to see these same towns, perhaps, solidified into compact village, small town, or city communities whose diverse life has offered through the years fresh materials for the novelist and new viewpoints for the social critic.

[34] *Ibid.*, "The Schoolmaster's Progress."
[35] J. A. Harrison, ed., *The Complete Works of Edgar Allan Poe* (New York, 1902), XV, 84, "The Literati of New York City."

MILITANT REALISTS

If the spirit of adventure and missionary zeal moved Judge Hall and his contemporaries to enter a new country and record its customs and legends, later Middle Border interpreters were moved to expression by different motives. Many Western local colorists of the late eighties and nineties were either concerned with themes of post-frontier life, or, like Hamlin Garland, were back-trailers who wrote of the aridity of life on the plains with a fidelity that startled and offended both East and West. Unlike their predecessors, these latter-day realists did not discover and glorify in literature the scenic beauty of wilderness and prairie. They wrote not of "the Paradise of the West," but with relentless realism and alarming candor portrayed bleakness and hardness of provincial life in village and country. There thus arose a group of Midland realists, including Edward Eggleston, Joseph Kirkland, E. W. Howe, and Garland, who chronicled in short story, novel, and autobiography the difficulties of Western life during their own youths. A life of duress on the soil; the social and emotional curbing of life in bleak provincial towns which stagnated in back-country locations; and the general aridity of life on the plains for those insurgents who looked for truth and beauty— these caught the attention of this second group of interpreters of the Western small town. Sober and often gloomy truthfulness about prairie ways and towns became a dominating note with these newer realists. For a back-trailer like Garland, a student of farm life like Kirkland, or a product of a sordid small town existence like Howe, the glamor of pioneering was gone and the visionary gleam was growing indistinct.

During this era of the spread and growth of prairie towns throughout the West these and other writers were showing in imaginative literature the existence of drama in the smallest localities. As Carl Van Doren aptly notes, many were adding to the annals of America realistic chapters on the influence of the crossroads tavern and corner grocery.

There the neighborhood wits and wise men have regularly come together scanning the national horizon and bringing topics home for local commentary. . . . They have yarned and gossiped; they have turned universal wisdom into the dry vernacular; they have helped popular opinions to be born. . . . As the tavern disappears before prohibition and the corner-grocery before the mail order catalogue, the wits and wise men find new lounging-places, in clubs, in the smoking rooms of railway trains, in all the minor caucuses of ordinary life. But the channels of folk-disquisition, though thus widened, have not greatly shifted.[36]

A most fearless upholder of this tradition was an Indiana circuit-rider, Edward Eggleston (1837-1902), whose fiction made him an outstanding pioneer in the new realism of the eighties. "The day of realism in Western fiction was not fully come until Eggleston appeared as the portrayer of southern Indiana life."[37]   Just as Bret Harte's timely "The Luck of Roaring Camp" (1868) opened a new field and set a new standard for short stories everywhere, so did Eggleston with *The Hoosier Schoolmaster* (1871) determine the fashion for the local color novel and weaken the influence of the domestic-sentimental-pious romance which had dominated fiction during the period from 1850 to 1870.[38] If Harte may be given the honor of the first conception of a vitalized literature of the West, to Eggleston belongs the claim of turning the current of this new literature into realism.[39]

Eggleston prefaced the first edition of *The Hoosier Schoolmaster* with a statement of his attitude toward the fictional use of Western materials.   He confesses, in part :

It has been in my mind since I was a Hoosier boy to do something toward describing life in the back country districts of the Western States.   It used to be a matter of no little jealousy with us, I remember, that the manners, customs, thoughts, and feelings of New England country people filled so large a place in books, while our life, not less interesting, not less romantic, and certainly not less filled with humorous and grotesque material, had no place in literature.   It was as though we were shut out of good society. And, with the single exception of Alice Cary, perhaps, our Western writers did not dare speak of the West otherwise than as the unreal world to which Cooper's lively imagination had given birth.

And Eggleston did do something.   Not only did he picture

---

[36] Carl Van Doren, *Many Minds* (New York, 1924), pp. 34-35.

[37] Rusk, *op. cit.*, I, 283.

[38] Another Indiana writer, John Hay (1838-1905), also influenced the development of local color with his vigorous *Pike County Ballads and Other Pieces* (1871). Pike County, however, is in Illinois.

[39] Pattee, *American Literature since 1870*, p. 98.

isolated rural communities, small Western towns, and provincial people, but he exerted a widespread influence on chroniclers of other sections. *The Hoosier Schoolmaster* and other novels, describing with a strict fidelity the barrenness of life in the Middle West, eventually tended to put the mark of realism on other literature of the region. Howe, Garland, Quick, Masters, and others have dealt unromantically with social conditions in their respective localities. His own fictional theory, as given in the preface to *The Mystery of Metropolisville* (1873), accounts for Eggleston's pictures of homely and often coarse Hoosier manners and communities. A novel, he thought, should be the truest of books, partaking of the nature of both history and art. "It needs to be true to human nature in its permanent and essential qualities, and it should truthfully represent some specific and temporary manifestation of human nature : that is, some form of society." Like Garland's later protest—stated in his *Crumbling Idols*—against American imitation of foreign models, Eggleston's thrust at contemporary literary servility is both timely and forceful. He felt "that the work to be done just now, is to represent the forms and spirit of our own life, and thus free ourselves from habitual imitation of all that is foreign." Writing with this dominant purpose, Eggleston strove to make his stories real contributions to the history of civilization in America.

It was natural that Eggleston frequently should feature in his novels various small town scenes of the Midwest. He was born in the picturesque little Ohio River town of Vevay, Indiana, at that time the political center of Switzerland County, a section peopled largely by the thrifty Swiss realistically featured in *Roxy*.[40] Here the boy had opportunity of knowing not only the Swiss, but many Germans, Scotch, New Englanders, Kentuckians, and the usual "poor-whiteys" of border sections. The Egglestons themselves were of the best family associations, the father, Joseph Cary Eggleston, being a Virginian and an honor graduate of the law school of William and Mary. The mother belonged to a prominent Virginia and Kentucky family. Edward and his brother, George Cary, lived in an atmosphere of books, a direct contrast to the frontier conditions surrounding them. Later in his cross-country travels as

[40] Hamlin Garland, *Roadside Meetings* (New York, 1930), pp. 359-360, contains a reprint of a letter from Eggleston concerning the novel, *Roxy*.

a Methodist circuit rider Edward observed directly the provincial communities and the angularities of Indiana which form the matter of his fiction.

In *The Hoosier Schoolmaster* and his third novel, *The Circuit Rider: A Tale of the Heroic Age*,[41] Eggleston deals but incidentally with the small town.   He is more interested in rural communities.   In the former, however, the village is pictured as the scene of the trials of the young master, Ralph Hartsook.   Incidental pictures of the village school, the minister—a stereotyped figure —Miss Nancy Sawyer, local Good Samaritan, and the poorhouse afford a view of the bleak little town of Lewisburg.

The Mystery of Metropolisville, first published serially in *Hearth and Home* (December, 1872-April, 1873), exposes the speculation and fraud of unscrupulous promoters in a Minnesota town of the fifties "when money was worth five or six per cent a month on bond and mortgage, when corner lots doubled in value over night, and when everybody was frantically trying to swindle everybody else."[42]   Modern interest in the story lies largely in the apt characterization of frontier boom towns and their makers.   Conditions in Metropolisville are best summed up by that homely epitomist, "Whiskey Jim," stage driver and newsmonger :

"A'n't a bed nur a board in the hull city . . . to be had for payin' nur coaxin'. Beds is aces. Houses is trumps. Landlords is high, low, Jack, and the game in ther hands. Looky there! A bran-new set of fools fresh from the factory!"   And he pointed to the old steamboat "Ben Bolt," which was just coming up to the landing with deck and guards black with eager immigrants of all classes.[43]

In this nervous excitement of expansion and speculation is found Eggleston's theme.   The rather irrelevant "mystery" (that of the stealing of a land warrant from the mails) is almost submerged by the novelist's interest in "the growth, the wilting, and the withering of Metropolisville," a process of town life typical of dozens of frontier villages and, according to Eggleston, "the inevitable sequel and retribution of speculative madness."[44]   Characters in the novel are stereotyped, but they

[41] New York, 1874.
[42] *The Mystery of Metropolisville* (New York, 1873), p. 13.
[43] *Ibid.*, p. 18.
[44] *Ibid.*, p. 11.

typify certain conditions during the boom period before the panic of 1857 when the map of the Midwest was dotted with "paper communities," glorified as the towns and cities of the future.

As Eggleston shows, this was a period of wild speculation in land buying; of swindling by oily-tongued dealers; and of the settlement of the Iowa, Minnesota, and adjoining frontiers by all types of settlers.   It was a period of promise, a period of greed intensified by the California gold rush and the craze for town building throughout the West.   Young idealists, educated in the East; picturesque stage drivers and kindred frontier folk; persuasive Mr. Plausaby typifying unctuous-mannered dealers who sold worthless lots to gullible investors; village belles, beaux, and gossips; unscrupulous tavernkeepers; and other boom town figures crowded into Metropolisville, as in its actual counterparts.   Though a flood, a double drowning, fights, love affairs, and a penitentiary scene put the stamp of sentiment and melodrama on the plot, Eggleston succeeds, nevertheless, in creating a boom town such as might have been found by the hundreds during the mid-nineteenth century.   Like many of its neighbors, Metropolisville declined when the railroad was built through an adjoining section.   Speedily the town became little less than a memory.   Main Street changed into a country road, and the plot once set aside as "Depot Ground" became a potato patch.   Likewise the unsettled state of society in which the town grew quickly disappeared.

. . . the land-sharks, the claim speculators, the town proprietors, the trappers, and the stage-drivers have emigrated or have undergone metamorphosis.   The wild excitement of '56 is a tradition hardly credible to those who did not feel its fever.[45]

Roxy (1878) is a study of frontier politics in the county seat of Luzerne, an Ohio River village, during that exciting period when public gatherings were enlivened with cries of

> Hurrah for Harrison and Tyler!
> Beat the Dutch or bust your b'iler![46]

Though one of the oldest towns in the new country, Luzerne possessed neither fine houses not other buildings except "the

[45] *Ibid.*, p. 320.
[46] *Roxy* (New York, 1878), p. 3.

brand-new courthouse with glittering brass ball above the belfry, standing in the treeless, grassless 'public square.'" In the whole community popular education, the butt of outside ridicule, was in its infancy and sectarian strife at its worst. A public election of 1840 with Whigs and Democrats noisily swearing and quarreling at their campaigning and voting presents one of the most vivid scenes. The Whig leaders roasted beeves "to persuade independent voters to listen to arguments on the tariff; they washed down abstruse reasonings about the United States Bank with hard cider; and by good feeling persuaded the citizens to believe in internal improvements."[47] Such were the tactics of shrewd Hoosier politicians, who relied on barbecues, torchlight parades, floats presided over by "a plump Hoosier Goddess of Liberty," drunkenness and fighting to make a rally a success.

Revival meetings provided other local upheavals in a town where a wedding or a funeral was a capital event and matter of universal interest. ("What battles and bankruptcies are to a metropolis, such are marriages and deaths to a village.")

Every one of the fifteen hundred people in the little town knew that there was a revival "going on." Every one of them carried in his head each day a list of those who had "been to the mourner's bench" the night before, and of those who were converted; and everybody knew who had shouted or "taken on" in any way at the meetings.[48]

Great excitement and religious fervor prevailed when old Tom Walters, a notorious drunkard, "got religion." When the young hero, Mark Bonamy, was converted he declared his intention of going as a missionary to Texas. Old-fashioned Methodism thus stirred the most confirmed sinner in Luzerne during that changing period when Indianapolis was but "a straggling muddy village in a heavily wooded morass."[49]

In *The Graysons: A Story of Abraham Lincoln* (1888) Eggleston dramatizes a legendary account of one of Lincoln's court trials.[50] The scene is the prairie town of Moscow, Central Illinois ("Eleynoys"), at the opening of the nineteenth century. Then

[47] *Ibid.*, p. 10.
[48] *Ibid.*, p. 66.
[49] *Ibid.*, p. 73.
[50] In the Preface to the 1888 edition Eggleston states that about 1867 he received the story from one of Lincoln's former neighbors.

but a miniature town, Moscow was the focal point for activities in a newly settled farming section where the events of the outlying communities were closely connected with village affairs. At Wooden and Snyder, General Merchandise Store, town loungers joined with farmers in upholding the traditions of folk disquisition.   Here was a sort of clubroom where, after closing time, the young men of the village were accustomed "to gratify their gregarious propensities."   Here

amid characteristic odors of brown sugar, plug tobacco, vinegar, whiskey, molasses, and the dressed leather of boots and shoes, social intercourse was carried on by a group seated on the top of nail-kegs, the protruding ends of shoe-boxes, and, the counters. . . .   Here were related again all those stock anecdotes which have come down from an antiquity inconceivably remote, ...[51]

The frequency of such assemblies, notes Eggleston, took off something of their zest.   The newcomer or returned traveler, therefore, was always a "heaven-send."   He stirred the stagnant intellect of the village and, for a time, was "the hero of every congregation of idlers."   Even more did a murder and trial arouse the curiosity of all credulous people in town and country.   Using a dramatic trial scene as a central episode, Eggleston vividly portrays the local jail and courthouse and the meagerly furnished, fly-specked dining-room of the tavern, where "Ab'ram" Lincoln, newly fledged lawyer and itinerant, and the judge breakfast before the trial.   This novel, like *Roxy*, exposes the political corruption of a new town whose "custodians of the law" would have sacrificed the life of an innocent boy for the price of votes from a group of nomadic "poor whiteys."   Class conflicts stirred the town.   The poorer settlers, a coarse and discontented element, were ever ready to oppose any member of the "five per cent" class.

Eggleston caught with vividness the spirit of newly made towns scattered over Indiana, Illinois, and Minnesota.   Though occasionally melodramatic, his pictures of frontier towns show "a realism in background and atmosphere that makes the novels real sources of history."[52]   His early poring over the descriptive pages of Taine's *Art in the Netherlands* was not without marked effect on the literary interpretation of the frontier

[51] *The Graysons* (New York, 1915), p. 18.
[52] Pattee, *op. cit.*, p. 98.
    15

town.   As Eggleston confessed to Garland, it was his aim "to
do what the Dutch painters did, paint the homely and grotesque men and women I knew, with artistic truth."[53]

"It was inevitable," says Hamlin Garland in *Roadside Meetings*, "that somewhere in my study of the groups of local colorists in fiction and poetry that I should ask 'Where is the representative of the great Mid-West?'   No one had come to the
support of Eggleston, who was essentially a Hoosier.   The
prairie West had no novelist till a young man named Howe,
editor of the *Globe* in Atchison, Kansas, published 'The Story
of a Country Town' (1883), a singularly gloomy, real yet unreal, narrative written in the tone of weary and hopeless age."[54]
The Mississippi Valley town thus came to further penetrating
expression in Edgar Watson Howe's pitiless picture of that
drab period when the homesteader had become the prairie
townsman.

In his autobiography, *Plain People* (1929), Howe has presented through the medium of a shrewd and waggish philosophy
an intimate picture of Midwestern life during the last eight
decades.   His lively recollections reconstruct a whole past era
in our national development.   Unashamed of his descent from
a long line of plain people, Howe traces his story from his birth,
more than eighty years ago, in Treaty, Indiana, to his boyhood
migration in a covered wagon with his parents, Henry and
Elizabeth Howe, to Missouri, and to his later removal to Atchison, Kansas, where he was long widely known as the author-
publisher of *The Daily Globe* and *E. W. Howe's Monthly* (founded
after his retirement from daily journalism).   *Plain People* is
more than the record of a dominating and unique personality ;
it is a full chronicle of community changes enlivened by talk
of the coming of the first trains through Kansas, backwoods
revivals, the early speeches of Lincoln, Civil War excitement,
anecdotes of small town editors and printers, and many customs now of the past.

A true believer in the potential greatness of American themes,
Howe once wrote that had he

lived in fifty different, widely-separated towns or countries from
1877 to 1929, I do not believe that I would have had better op-

[53] Garland, *op. cit.*, p. 360.
[54] *Ibid.*, p. 94.

portunity to know life or human nature. In every town there is material for the great American novel so long expected, but no one appears to write it.[55]

With such reasoning it is not surprising that the sage of Potato Hill, characterized by his fellow Kansan, William Allen White, as "a plain man who lived a plain life among plain people," should have chosen as the materials for his first novel those of the small town environments he had known during his boyhood and young manhood.

In that original commentary on Kansas town life, *The Story of a Country Town*, a young printer, less than thirty, showed clearly that he was a rebel in advance of his time. This stark and grim book, says Carl Van Doren, "was to the novels of its decade what *Moby Dick* had been to the romances of an earlier decade. It broke a pattern and shouldered its way among the fragments."[56] It departed from the stereotyped novel of sentiment then flourishing. It lacked the traditional glorification of village virtues. Instead, it grimly portrayed the most unpromising of small town living conditions. During the heyday of Mark Twain's Mississippi reminiscences, Thomas Nelson Page's romantic tales of Southern gentry, the Uncle Remus tales, and Riley's sentimental verses, all commentaries on the virtuous or heroic qualities of their particular localities, Howe dared produce an unflattering picture of a bleak, cramped Kansas town. While Miss Jewett was still writing in kindly manner about quiet New England villages Howe was exposing an entirely different order of town life. The Twin Mounds of his story was peopled by the still provincial descendants of actual frontiersmen. With bluntness of language, Howe contemptuously presented the men of his town as overbearing, argumentative, and exacting, yet woefully futile and discontented. In Van Doren's words, "they loafed and waited for miracles to happen." Lacking positive opinions of their own, they were nevertheless full of self-conceit over their petty affairs.

Two or three times a year most of them visited a city a good many miles away, where they spent a good deal of money they

---

[55] *Plain People* (New York, 1929), p. 184.
[56] *Many Minds*, p. 37.

could not afford, to create an impression that they were accustomed
to what they supposed was good society, and where they met men,
who filled their ideas of greatness.[57]

The women led drab, monotonous lives, enlivened by gossip,
revival meetings, and singing conventions.

Such unrelieved realism was truly out of key with the literary
trends of the eighties. It is not strange that Howe's novel
"was sent to one of the leaders in publishing of that day, and
returned. Then it was sent to six or seven others, with like
result, whereupon [he says] 'I decided to print it myself, as
there was a job office attached to my newspaper plant.'"
This, in part, is the story of the first edition of one thousand
copies as Howe himself related it in *Plain People*.[58] Eventually
the book received appraisal especially from William Dean
Howells, who reviewed it in the *Century*, and from Mark Twain
who praised its simple, direct, clear, and yet strong style. In
a letter of praise and advice the latter wrote to Howe : "Your
picture of the arid village life is vivid, and what is more, true.
I know, for I have seen and lived it all."[59] In later years, with
the increasing prominence of the town in imaginative literature,
there has been a revival of interest in this early picture of an
unlovely Kansas town. After all, as Howells early wrote, this
novel "is simply what it calls itself, the story of a country town
in the West, which has so many features in common with
country towns elsewhere that whoever has lived in one may
recognize the grim truth of the picture."[60]

Both the facts of Howe's life and his prefatory statement to
the novel point toward his use of the autobiographical, but he
"considered the book a novel and did not aim at accuracy."
He confesses that "there never was a 'Mateel Shepherd,' a
'Clinton Bragg,' or a 'Jo Erring,' . . . . My father was actually a farmer and a preacher, and bought a weekly paper in a
county seat, . . . but the book is mainly fiction, and so intended. Fairview [Howe's early home] had no mill, and no

[57] *The Story of a Country Town* (Boston, 1884), p. 232.   Originally published in
1883.
[58] The entire twenty-third chapter of this book is devoted to *The Story of a
Country Town*.
[59] Quoted in *Plain People*, p. 212.   *The Story* was praised by authoritative critics
in the *London Saturday Review*, *Edinburgh Review*, *Nation*, *Century*, *Atlantic Monthly*,
and others.   From 1883 to 1900 it ran through thirty editions (*National Cyclopaedia of American Biography*, X, 138).
[60] "Two Notable Novels," *Century Magazine*, XXVIII, 632 (Aug., 1884).

tragedy.''[61]   Certain incidents in his father's life—so Howe admits—were used freely in the characterization of Preacher Westlock.   Every town in which he ever lived afforded Howe some material for his picture of Twin Mounds.   The strength of the book, however, lies in the realization of a whole order of things, rather than in a masterly presentation of individual characters.   In short, *The Story of a Country Town* is the finest realistic picture of the small town produced in America before 1884.   All the facts in the case are faithfully presented.   The happenings, though at times too melodramatic, are logical. No heroic qualities embellish the unadorned homeliness of the background.   Nature is as cheerless as the human life portrayed.   No trace of flattery for the West is found ; but perfectly imaginable American small town conditions of the eighties are reproduced with remarkable candor.   H. E. Scudder, writing for *The Atlantic Monthly* in 1885 shortly after the book's republication by Osgood, noted :

A more dreary waste than the country town which Mr. Howe describes cannot well be imagined.   It appears to have no traditions, even of beauty, and certainly no anticipations of hope.   It is degraded spiritually and mentally.[62]

Here with merciless frankness and acrid humor is revealed the arid village life of the late nineteenth-century Midwest. There is a dual plot, the first dramatizing a stern and apparently zealous Methodist minister, John Westlock, father of the narrator of the story.   Like the author's own father, the minister has an illicit love affair ; deserts his meek wife and his son, Ned ; and years later, after Mrs. Westlock's death, returns in a bitter frame of mind.[63]   The secondary plot, a dreary melodrama suggestive of Dickens, has to do with Jo Erring, an ill-fated miller, who marries Mateel Shepherd, a beautiful girl of the district, only to discover her associations with Clinton Bragg, a reprobate.   Unable to control his jealousy, Jo murders Bragg and is jailed at Twin Mounds.   The story ends in double tragedy with Jo's suicide and Mateel's death.

The town, the background for these tragic events, received

[61] *Plain People*, p. 215.
[62] H. E. Scudder, "Recent Fiction," *The Atlantic Monthly*, LV, 125 (Jan., 1885).
[63] See *Plain People*, pp. 55-57, for Howe's own account of his father's philandering ways.   Cf. pp. 10, 11, 12, 13, 21, 22, 42, 44 ff., 52, and 53 for a more complete character sketch of the elder Howe.

its name from its geographic position. In a valley near the town ran a river. Directly opposite were mounds, a pair of little mountains, where Indians once built signal fires. Twin Mounds, in Ned's eyes, was a mean Kansas town having "a brick courthouse, a stone jail, several wooden stores, a school house, and about six hundred very wicked people." The places of business clustered around the usual square, in the center of which was the courthouse. The stage connected this dull prairie community with the far distant railroad.

Remembering, perhaps, his own youth, Howe has much to say about small town religion. The church at Fairview, the town of his boyhood, he recalled as having been built "on the highest and bleakest point in the county, where the winds are plenty in winter because they are not needed, and scarce in summer for an opposite reason." As with Fairview, the religion of the Twin Mounds people seemed to deepen the natural gloom of an obviously poor community. Westlock, local spiritual dictator, taught that religion was a misery to be endured on earth so that a reward might be enjoyed after death. His own religion would have been unsatisfactory without the fires of hell. (His successor, the Reverend Goode Shepherd, found in religion his vocation and pleasure.) Other citizens spent their idle time on endless discussions or in searching the Bible to find points for disputation. In actuality Twin Mounds was a virtuous community; yet the men invented and spread scandals. They pretended to believe that their associates were libertines and that many of the women lacked virtue. The truth was that "the people watched each other so closely that there was no opportunity to be other than honest and circumspect in this particular, even if they had been differently inclined."[64]

The Story of a Country Town, in spite of the prevailing harshness of its realism, has a few charming things. Youth, with its ardor and fearlessness, is finely exemplified in the ambitions of Jo Erring, who struggles to become worthy of the more cultured Mateel. Occasionally the tone of the book is tempered by romantic qualities: by the use of a dark wood, a mysteriously tolling bell, a chest of curious treasures, hidden identities, and a murder at a ford. Pathos, rather than harshness, is the keynote of the tragedy of Jo and Mateel.

[64] *The Story of a Country Town*, p. 232.

A singular combination of original and conventional elements, the book in itself is remarkable. It is truly a landmark of realism firmly planted in an age of florid, sentimental literature. Often writing in the style of a saga, Howe has achieved his purpose of exposing the sordid life of a prairie town, suggestive not of the teeming frontier, but of an isolated place left in its wake. He has done for the American town what Crabbe did for the English village—painted it "As Truth will paint it and Bards will not."[65]

Howe's second novel appeared in 1885. *The Mystery of the Locks* is the tragic story of Allan Dorris, a young doctor who seeks escape from a mysterious past in the decaying town of Davy's Bend on the Missouri. Establishing himself in a long-deserted mansion, called the Locks because of heavily barred gates and doors, Dorris marries a young organist, the daughter of a local merchant. Again, as in *The Story*, Howe gives a vivid impression of a decayed Midland town, once prosperous, but like many hastily built places, now a failing town by a sluggish river, "which seems to be hurrying away from it, too, like its institutions and its people."[66] All the town's prosperity has gone up the river to a more advantageously located community. The citizens remaining in Davy's Bend are dreamers rather than doers. In their opinion, however, "the town [is] alive with opportunities for profitable investments, but Capital with a mean and dogged indifference, [refuses] to come to Davy's Bend."[67]

While the village characters (a merchant, a hotel clerk, a down-at-the-heels lawyer and sot, the town editor, the young doctor, and others) point definitely toward Howe's personal understanding of provincial Midland types, these are, at the best, conventionally portrayed. Howe's most original touches are in his unforgettable picturing of the decaying river town and in his satiric thrusts at the foibles of his characters, in turn representative of the weakness of mankind. For example, he ridicules thus the little men of Davy's Bend who delight in local newspaper publicity about virtues they do not possess.

So great was the passion for puffery among them that designing men who had heard of it came along quite frequently, and wrote

[65] Carl Van Doren, *The American Novel*, p. 230. Cf. *Many Minds*, pp. 34-49.
[66] *The Mystery of the Locks* (Boston, 1885), p. 1.
[67] *Ibid.*, p. 39.

the people up in special publications. . . . [These gave varying] pages of puffs of the people, at so much per line.[68]

A Moonlight Boy, a Ticknor publication of 1886, resulted from Howe's neglect of advice by Mark Twain and Howells that he should not rush too hastily into print with another book after the success of his *Story*. Neither this work nor *The Mystery of the Locks* has the strength of the first. A poorly developed mystery, *A Moonlight Boy* is the disjointed and weakly motivated life-history of a village foundling, a moonlight boy who became involved in a series of unnatural adventures in New York. Obviously Howe was not so familiarly grounded in the life of a metropolis as in that of bleak Midwestern towns. Even here, however, he does not completely forego the use of a small town locale. The opening and closing scenes are in a small Kansas town, a very ordinary place where the hero once lived as the adopted son of plain villagers.

After *A Man Story* (1889) and *An Ante-Mortem Statement* (1891), a continuation of the story of Jo Erring, Howe devoted his time to the *Globe* and the *Monthly*, to travel and travel sketches, and to aphoristic writing, partly in the *Monthly* and in collections. Through the homely and penetrating philosophies of the *Country Town Sayings: A Collection of Paragraphs from the Atchison Globe* (1911) and *Ventures in Common Sense* (1919) Howe long before his death in the fall of 1937 became widely recognized as a "modernized Franklin of the prairie [coupling] industry and thrift with good behavior and success."[69] When next Howe turned to fiction he brought to his work the observations of a matured and successful man. *The Story of a Country Town* was written before he was thirty; almost forty years later, in *The Anthology of Another Town*, he returned in a new way to the caustic treatment of American small town life.[70]

The *Anthology* is not a story, nor a collection of essays, nor the separate paragraphs of a columnist, but a series of trenchant vignettes of small town characters comparable to those of *The Spoon River Anthology* which appeared but a few years earlier. Though each of the one hundred and fifty items, or "characters," is complete within itself, there is preserved unity in tone,

[68] *Ibid.*, p. 43.
[69] Percy H. Boynton, "Some Expounders of the Middle Border School," *The English Journal*, XIX, 436 (June, 1930).
[70] New York, 1920. Prior to this, however, Howe had published *The Hundred Stories of a Country Town* (1913).

manner, and purpose.   The whole forms a group of penetrating little sketches of the actualities and trivialities of a small
Western town.   Remarkable economy of style is everywhere
apparent.   Unlike *The Story of a Country Town*, it has no romantic embroideries.   It is merely a simple, yet wise, version
of town life, minus all literary furbelows and trivial local color.
The result is "an effect sometimes bald, the accompanying
danger of simplicity carried to a logical conclusion."[71]   Humor,
occasional pathos, and verity indicate the wide range of topics
which Howe knew how to draw from small town materials.

Unlike *The Spoon River Anthology*, Howe's book consists of
anecdotes of the living rather than epitaphs for the village
dead.   As direct and ironic as Poor Richard, Howe produces
little etchings of the dullness of human lives.   Aptly Carl Van
Doren notes that Howe

appears in the book to be—as he is in the flesh—a wise old man
letting his memory run through the town and recalling bits of decent, illuminating gossip.   He is willing to tell a fantastic yarn
with a dry face or to tuck a tragedy in a sentence ; to repeat some
village legend in his own low tones or to puncture some village
bubble with a cynical inquiry.[72]

Here is back-country wisdom earmarked by common sense, the
basis of Howe's philosophy, and expressed in homely aphorisms
suggestive of the humorous sayings of "Josh Billings" and other
"funny men."   Howe needs but a terse comment or two to
expose a villager.   Note :   "We haven't a daily paper in our
town, but really we don't greatly miss one, owing to Mr.
Stevens, the milkman."[73]   Again :   "Sandy McPherson, the
barber, says he charges five dollars for shaving a dead man
because he is compelled to throw away the razor he used.
But how do we know he throws the razor away?"[74]   Here is
another trenchant comment :   "Ben Bradford, known to be a
little gay, says the first time he kissed a woman other than his
wife, he felt as he did when he first began buying of Montgomery, Ward & Co.   But Ben gradually became hardened,
and many say he now trades with Sears-Roebuck, too."[75]

[71] F. E. Schelling, *Appraisements and Asperities, etc.* (New York, 1922), p. 67.
[72] *Contemporary American Novelists*, p. 160.
[73] *The Anthology of Another Town*, p. 133.
[74] *Ibid.*, p. 83.
[75] *Ibid.*, p. 99.

Howe portrays little folkways with wise and neighborly tolerance. While it appeared within a few months of *Main Street, The Anthology of Another Town* is free from malice or uncharitableness. To be sure, the curious townspeople eagerly attend funerals, weddings, and revivals, but, as Howe wisely says, "though we are excited in this town nearly every day because of a rumor that something is likely to happen before night, it usually blows over, and we find there was not a great deal in the talk in the first place."[76] There was no need here of his being humiliated at the mention of these stories as he was, he once confessed, of the earlier *The Moonlight Boy*.[77] What Garland said in praise of *The Story of a Country Town* is applicable to the *Anthology:* "You speak of these people not as one who coldly looks on them as 'picturesque' but in an earnest, sincere tone *as from among them*. Your work has an *indigenous* quality [mainly that of] strong, idiomatic Western prose."[78] Here, as earlier, Howe's straightforwardness as completely destroys sentimental notions about the small town as do the positive indictments of Masters or the satire of Lewis. While his tolerance of the village is herein noticeable, it is evident also that Howe, until the last, was still merciless toward the sweetly idyllic versions of life in small communities.

Another exponent of the crossroads tradition was Joseph Kirkland (1830-94), who as the son of William and Caroline Kirkland had known frontier life in New York, Michigan, and Illinois. During his later years while he was in the midst of a legal career Kirkland carried out a long-cherished purpose of writing a novel of Western rural life. Thus came into being *Zury: The Meanest Man in Spring County* (1887), a sordid and bleak story of the niggardliness of farm and town life in frontier Illinois. The man who later was to advise Hamlin Garland *to tell the truth* in fiction here spares no detail delineative of the plight of the Western farmer in his bootless struggle against the forces of nature and the demands of the money lender. Zury (short for Usury) Prouder, son of a toil-worn Pennsylvania immigrant, continues his father's fight against the stubborn soil. A boyhood of labor and self-denial converts Zury into a thrifty and shrewd, but soul-scarred, farmer, ever bent

---

[76] *Ibid.*, p. 50.
[77] *Plain People*, p. 212.
[78] Garland, *Roadside Meetings*, p. 95.

on acquiring land, stock, and mortgages. In time he grew so parsimonious that his acquaintances declared "he would pinch a dollar bill till the eagle on it squealed."[79] Youthful poverty gradually gave way to hard-won prosperity, but Zury's bitterness of soul became so deeply engrained that his neighbors began to regard him as unfeeling, crabbed, and hard-fisted. Unexpectedly Zury undergoes a remarkable change of heart when he associates with young Anne Sparrow, a "Bostin schoolmarm." His parsimony is so great, however, that he first marries the daughter of a well-to-do farmer before his eventual return in later life to the schoolteacher and his development into a kindly old man.

Primarily a story of a developing personality, *Zury* is further significant for its scenes of frontier town life during the early nineteenth century. When Anne Sparrow, newly arrived from the East, first views the sordidness of Wayback, Illinois, she is afraid of the crudeness and coarseness of the town. She is depressed by the cluster of houses glaring "under the pitiless sunshine, asking in vain for the shadows of trees which had been on the ground before any houses intruded, but which had been unwisely sacrificed, leaving only ugly stumps to show where they had stood."[80] Discouraged, Anne escapes to the tavern only to find the hard bed, flies, and poor service of the usual Western village hotel so boldly denounced by Mrs. Trollope. Anne's bitter experiences later during her "boardin' round" in the crude homes of school patrons; the pitifully small intellectual and social outlets for the Waybackers; and their narrowness of religious and moral beliefs suggest the gloomy realism of *Wuthering Heights* or of Ellen Glasgow's *Barren Ground*. Wayback presented

. . . the extraordinary spectacle of a society without holidays and almost without amusements. (The old "husking-bees" were not in order.) . . . Sociable christenings, of course, there were none. A marriage is often merely a visit to the preacher or to the justice. An afternoon call on a week-day finds the house empty, save one or two busy women and a few unattractive, ill-mannered children; and on Sunday social visiting is sacrilegious. A quilting which Anne attended was ghastly in its dullness.[81]

[79] *Zury: The Meanest Man in Spring County. A Novel of Western Life* (Boston and New York, 1887), p. 65.
[80] *Ibid.*, p. 123.
[81] *Ibid.*, p. 204.

But there always was time for malicious gossip. "Two visits
by one marriageable man to one marriageable woman, plus
one neighbor looking out of window, [amounted] to a reported
engagement in any frontier town. So 'preacher he's a spar-
kin' scule-mom,' was the news in Wayback instanter."[82]

The now familiar story of Western development is introduced with the progress of the narrative and a change in locale.
Anne and her lackadaisical husband, John McVey, leave Wayback for the larger town of Springfield, then a prosperous railroad community. At the end of the story Zury, after experiences as a legislator in Springfield, returns to modernize
Wayback by introducing bathtubs, gas, and better furniture.
Zury is not a great novel, but it is significant as one of the earlier
realistic novels of the unlovely aspects of the frontier town.
Garland early praised it enthusiastically as one of the finest
veritistic novels of the Midwest and stressed the delineation of
the hard lives of mothers and wives of the border, upon whom
fell the heaviest burden of pioneering. Though objecting to
its meticulosity of style, Garland, nevertheless, once wrote that
Zury appealed to him as the best picture of pioneer Illinois life
then written.[83]

In *Zury*, as in *The McVeys* (1888), Joseph Kirkland has dramatized unsparingly and with objective truthfulness the struggle
of farmer and frontier townsman against the almost overpowering forces of hostile nature. The harsh pictures of their
plight re-enforce the sombre theme of *The Story of a Country
Town* and mark Kirkland as one of the pioneer shapers of
Western realism. Without doubt, he achieved his desire—as
set forth in the preface to *Zury*—of making his study "a palpable
imitation of Thomas Hardy's 'Far from the Madding Crowd' "
and reproducing "on American soil, the unflinching realism
. . . of life in actual conflict with the soil itself."

Just prior to 1887, the year of *Zury*, a struggling young student, a back-trailer from a desolate land claim in Dakota, was
in Boston spending long and lonely hours in the public library
in pursuit of a literary culture he most eagerly desired. Other
hours were spent in his cheap room, where he essayed a number of sketches of "those desolate days" on the prairies he had
forsaken, or in making a few wished-for contacts. This am-

[82] *Ibid.*, p. 281.
[83] Garland, *op. cit.*, p. 106.

bitious seeker of "Brahmin culture" was Hamlin Garland, whose first article on Western cornhusking linked his name with a particular phase of the literature of the Middle Border, the trenchant and severe Western fiction of town and country, narrative of protest "concerned with the toil of drab and laborious days." Maturing as a writer during the late eighties and nineties, Garland developed in the literature of the Midland scene the new note heralded by Kirkland, that of the arid life of the pioneer farmer and small townsman of the Midwest, a theme he knew with completeness. Garland was born in 1860 on a half-broken farm in a Wisconsin "coule"; but during his boyhood he migrated with his parents, Richard and Isabel McClintock Garland, to Iowa, where he assisted in all the strenuous labor of converting the prairie into farmland. While still in his teens the future author did a man's work and became accustomed to the privations of border life, all material for his later *A Son of the Middle Border* (1917) and other personal records. Though his schooling was desultory, he graduated from Cedar Valley Seminary, Osage, Iowa. After teaching in Illinois and Dakota and participating in the Dakota land boom, Garland, like Howells, went to Boston, where during days of privation he began his career as a writer. It was at this time, he remarks, that "thinking back into those desolate days [on the prairie], I experienced a singular desire to relive them, painful as they had been, and as I could not do in reality, I was inspired to do so in imagination."[84]

But a new awakening came. Returning to the West for a vacation, Garland visited Kirkland in Chicago under whose tutelage he became keenly alive to the sordid struggle and half-hidden despair of the prairie folk as he observed them anew at his old home in Iowa, his father's farm in Dakota, and his birthplace in Wisconsin. This "epoch-making experience," as he termed his visit, gave Garland a different insight into the life of the prairie farmer and caused him to perceive with "new vision the loneliness and drudgery of farmers' wives." All the glamor of pioneering and all the romantic picturing of frontier farmers, who, like intrepid Richard Garland, rose "to mastery of wind and snow," who went "like soldiers grimly into strife to colonize the plain," were gone. Instead, in town and country, Garland saw in his parents and former neighbors the hard

[84] *Ibid.*, p. 37.

results of days of "restlessness, the grim tribute of grinding labor they exacted, the heart-rending sacrifices of the women who had no choice but to follow their men and slave for them, the unrewarded lives of the rank and file in the pioneering hosts, the repugnance of it all that capped a boyhood on the Middle Border."[85]   Everywhere, as with new eyes, he saw a life of repression, ever unending, for in Garland's own words,

> Yet still they strive!   I see them rise
>   At dawn-light, going forth to toil:
> The same salt sweat has filled my eyes,
>   My feet have trod the self-same soil
> Beneath the snarling plow.[86]

This was what he had tried to forget.   Now he was moved by a new perspective of the plight of the farmer, a new perception of the loneliness and the drudgery of prairie women. Brooding darkly over the problems presented, Garland turned, as he says, in a mood of bitter resentment "to write [immediately after his return to Boston] the stories which later made up the first volume of *Main-Travelled Roads*."   Continued literary effort resulted in the popular Middle Border series which marked their author not only as an uncompromising delineator of the dirt and dust and toil of the farm and the barrenness of prairie towns, but also as an energetic booster of what Professor Pattee has termed "the gospel of western Americanism in art and literature."   All social documents of the Middle West, *Main-Travelled Roads* (1890), *Prairie Folks* (1892), *Rose of Dutcher's Coolly* (1893), *Boy Life on the Prairie* (1899), *Other Main-Travelled Roads* (1910), *A Son of the Middle Border* (1917), *A Daughter of the Middle Border* (1921), *Trail Makers of the Middle Border* (1926), and *Back-Trailers from the Middle Border* (1928), picture the unceasing labor, the futile hopes, and mocking ironies of the restless border society which Garland knew either from actual experience or from the fireside tales of his parents, the McClintocks, and others.

Garland early formed a literary creed to which he unfortunately failed to adhere.   This he published in book form in 1894 as *Crumbling Idols*, a series of twelve rather unrelated essays, a sort of manifesto against the neglect of indigenous ma-

[85] Boynton, *op. cit.*, p. 432.
[86] *Prairie Folks* (Chicago, 1893), p. 5.

terials by American writers. His became "a protesting voice against the smugness of the pastoral writers who told of the delights of the rural scene."[87] Repeating what Whitman had declared years earlier,[88] he wrote that American life had "had only superficial representation in the sketches of the tourist or the reporter; its inner heart has not been touched." In spite of the fact that these essays have been variously described as "pages upon pages of iteration and reiteration," "bellicose, obstreperous, blatant," and "so many explosions of literary jingoism," they indicate something about Garland's literary passions.[89] His insistence upon the use of local color show that by this time he had become an ardent expounder of a regionalism which has marked his best fiction. Alive to the literary potentialities of the life around him, Garland felt that American themes were "crying out to be written." He became a man with a cause, believing in "the mighty pivotal present" and in the living rather than the dead. He found men and women of the Middle West far more dramatic "than the saints and heroes of other countries." His enthusiasm knew no bounds. "It is," he declared, "only to the superficial observer that this country seems colorless and dull; to the veritist it is full of burning interest, greatest possibilities."[90] And Garland himself turned for his best materials to his own "mighty West," then so inadequately treated in novel, drama, and poetry. Very illuminating, however, in connection with the later trend of Garland's romantic realism is the following expression of the veritist's ideal:

> He aims to hasten the age of beauty and peace by delineating the ugliness and warfare of the present, but ever the converse of his picture rises in the mind of the reader. He sighs for a lovelier life. He is tired of warfare and sexualism, and poverty, the mother of Envy.[91]

Whether autobiography or fiction, Garland's most distinctive

---

[87] William Allen White, "Fiction of the Eighties and Nineties," in Macy, ed., *American Writers on American Literature*, p. 390.   John Muir's *My Boyhood and Youth* (Boston, 1913)—especially chap. iii, "Life in a Wisconsin Town," and chap. vi, "The Ploughboy,"—corroborates Garland's realism in *Main-Travelled Roads*.

[88] Preface to the 1855 edition of *Leaves of Grass*.

[89] Anonymous, *The Critic*, XXIII, 213 (Sept. 30, 1893); E. E. Hale, Jr., *The Dial*, XVII, 11 (July 1, 1894); Anonymous, *The Atlantic Monthly*, LXXVI, 840 (Dec., 1895).

[90] *Crumbling Idols* (Chicago, 1894), pp. 14-16.

[91] *Ibid.*, p. 52.

work has to do with essentially the same theme, the ruin of the
golden hopes of the pioneers by burdensome realities. Regardless of endless sacrifice and toil, age found little reward
worth seeking, and youth began looking furtively, or openly,
for avenues of escape. "The whole enterprise of pioneering
had been wasteful of energy and extravagant with life."[92]   In
A Son of the Middle Border, as in his other personal studies, Garland offers convincing records of rural and prairie town life of
the period from about 1865 to 1890.   The Wisconsin lumber
town of Onaluska, in actuality "a rude, rough, little camp
filled with raftsmen, loggers, mill-hands and boomsmen,"
seemed a veritable city to the farm-bred Garland boys.[93]   From
the high plateau on which Onaluska was built they could see
the spires of La Crosse, where steamboats offered connection
with the mysterious world beyond the horizon.

In his later migrations "Dick" Garland, father of Hamlin,
settled near Osage, Iowa, then little more than a small, bleak,
and poor neighborhood center. To imaginative young Hamlin the village was as "a new and shining world, a town world
where circuses, baseball games, and county fairs were events of
almost daily occurrence."[94]   Utterly commonplace to most
people, Osage then seemed mysterious and dangerous to the
farmer's son, for it was the citadel of an alien tribe, "The Town
Boys." With their initiation into the "gang" the Garland brothers thought themselves in the center of the world. Successive
chapters of this autobiography overflow with details of border
town life. A Saturday night brawl, the appearance of the
Garlands at the Sunday services, the Cedar Valley Seminary
with its dreaded "Friday Exercises," Hamlin's participation in
home-talent plays, the conflict between grain buyers and gran-
gers, the coming of an occasional "actor troupe," the Osage
brass band and the baseball team—these and other minutiae
indicate that life in Osage was simple and democratic.   Garland says of the social aspect of prairie town life that there
were "theoretically no social distinctions in Osage, but, after
all, a large house and a two seated carriage counted." The
usual form of entertainment was supplied by circuses, fairs, and
Fourth of July celebrations. To own a covered rig and to

---

[92] Boynton, *loc. cit.*
[93] *A Son of the Middle Border* (New York, 1917), p. 27.
[94] *Ibid.*, p. 173.

take one's sweetheart to the show were the highest forms of affluence and joy.[95]

But Garland was to know other Western towns, for as "day by day the settlement thickened" and "section by section the prairie was blackened by the plow" mushroom towns, little groups of ugly pine structures, and the promise of better land beyond lured adventurous Richard Garland ever onward. Finally at Ordway, in the new land of the Dakotas, Hamlin was to see a boom town, its streets swarming with excited promoters and investors. All talk was of the potential wealth of the unclaimed territory.

Thus in the personal chronicles, *A Son of the Middle Border* and its successors in the series, Garland views retrospectively the life of small settlements associated with his family wanderings; it is in his fiction, however, that he most earnestly protests against prevailing idyllic pictures of rural and town life. He wanted to tell the truth and call attention to the hard lives of the prairie folk. And this he did forcefully in *Main-Travelled Roads, Rose of Dutcher's Coolly,* and *Other Main-Travelled Roads* (some of which had appeared in the earlier *Prairie Folks*). While many of these collected stories describe the farmer, some depict various phases of life in the usual Midland town of the time.

Frequently Garland deals with the old struggle between provincial and cosmopolite. "Up the Coolly" is the poignant story of two brothers, estranged because of the different circumstances of their lives. Howard McLane, a successful actor, returns after a long absence to his boyhood home in a Midwestern coolly. Expecting to find his relatives enjoying rural quiet and peace, Howard, instead, is shocked by the repressed, drudgery-filled lives of his mother and Grant, his younger brother, both forced through meager circumstances to live on a coolly farm beside "a poor and dull and sleepy and squalid" town. Near this miserable town, a drab place almost unrelieved by trees or touches of beauty, Grant, dissatisfied and old before his time, has sacrificed his youth and ambitions to overwork. In "God's Ravens" a city journalist, Robert Bloom, broken in health, returns with his family to the ugly Wisconsin town of his boyhood. The reserve of the Blooms arouses the antipathy of their North Siding neighbors. Robert, disillu-

[95] *Ibid.*, p. 226.
16

sioned by his discovery that village life was not ideal, grows to
hate the townspeople. Their spiritual poverty and prosaic
existence, their gossip and dull jokes become almost unbearable. Bitterly he accuses them :

> Oh, I can't stand these people! They don't know anything.
> They talk every rag of gossip into shreds. 'Taters, fish, hops ; hops,
> fish, 'taters. They've saved and pinched and toiled till their souls
> are pinched and ground away. . . . Talk about the health of the
> village life! It destroys body and soul. It debilitates me. It will
> warp us down to the level of these people.
>
> Their squat little town is a caricature of themselves. Everything
> they touch they belittle. Here they sit while sidewalks rot and
> teams mire in the streets.[96]

Only the crisis of a severe illness could make Robert realize
that sympathy and big-heartedness might exist in such a miserable place.

The cultural poverty of pioneer farm women repeatedly gave
Garland a theme of protest. "A Day's Pleasure" is the pathetic
tale of a farm wife's holiday trip to shadeless Belleplain, a mis-
nomer for a cluster of frame houses and stores on the dry prairie beside a railway station. Against this barren background
is projected the pitiful figure of the tired, dust-bedraggled
woman carrying a dusty, unkempt baby. Wandering forlornly
and aimlessly, up and down the street, she gazes longingly at
the more fortunate women of the town. Embittered at the
contrast between their fashionable demi-trains and her own
faded clothes, she walks on savagely. Unexpectedly—at this
point—a kind woman of the town invites the pathetic farm
woman into her cool, tastefully furnished home. Even a drab
little town, Garland thus admits, may offer a day's pleasure to
the overworked, beauty-starved women of the farm. A similar
motif is employed in "Mrs. Ripley's Trip." Grandma Ripley,
absent for twenty-three years from her native "New Yoark,"
yearns to leave the desolate way station of Cedarville, Iowa,
for the prettier towns of her girlhood. The courage of the
frontier townswoman makes the theme of another grim picture
of life in the coolly country. "A Good Fellow's Wife" dramatizes a woman's part in small town speculation and bank
failure.

[96] *Main-Travelled Roads* (New York, 1899), p. 318.

In *Other Main-Travelled Roads*, with its companion volume "the result of a summer-vacation visit to my old home" in 1887, Garland declares in a prefatory note that "the village life touched upon will be found less forbidding in color" than the condition of the farmer. "Youth and love," he writes, "are able to transform a bleak prairie town into a poem, and to make a barbed-wire lane a highway of romance." Devoted mainly to rural materials, this volume (compiled, as Garland points out, from earlier volumes now out of print) also treats characteristically American prairie towns. Such is the county town of Tyre, Wisconsin, commonplace enough with "the usual main street lined with low brick or wooden stores."[97] Two young book agents, Albert and Jim, find romance in one of its ordinary, but respectable, boardinghouses. Albert, to Jim's disgust, relinquishes his ambitious schemes for a college education in favor of marriage with a pretty, but uneducated, village girl, whose poverty and widowed mother signify, in Jim's words, that "That ends him! He's jumped into a hole and pulled the hole in after him." The background of Tyre again appears in Garland's best known novel, *Rose of Dutcher's Coolly* (1895). The ambitious girl Rose, born and reared to young womanhood in nearby Dutcher's Coolly, is disgusted with the drab town of Tyre and its petty round of life. Its trivialities, unrefinement, and gossips prove as disgusting to Rose as the unloveliness of Gopher Prairie was to affect Carol Kennicott a quarter of a century later. A narrative of "youth and the bright Medusa"—the phrase is Willa Cather's—*Rose of Dutcher's Coolly* recalls many of the experiences of Garland's own career : youth's delight in circuses, the circumscribed life in a Midwestern college, and, finally, days of social success in Chicago. In this and other stories, like "A Fair Exile," Garland graphically describes the poorly lighted and inadequately heated accommodation trains which went "creaking, shrieking, and clattering" through desolate prairie towns.[98] Especially true to life are his passengers and trainmen : small town drummers, poorly clad farmers and their families, an occasional student from Madison, merchants returning from a trip to the city,

[97] "A Stop-Over at Tyre" in *Other Main-Travelled Roads* (New York, 1910), p. 163.
[98] In Willa Cather's *One of Ours* descriptions of accommodation trains, similar to these, have a place in the Nebraska scenes sketched therein. Cf. the Gopher Prairie day coach in *Main Street*.

travelers "going up to Boomtown," brakemen and conductors. These sketches, in part, show that the typical main-travelled road of Garland's youth was "mainly . . . long and weary-ful," with "a home of toil at one end and a dull little town at the other."

In more recent years other realists have examined the earlier Middle Border small town in the uncompromising fashion of Howe, Garland, and their fellow-novelists. Among these is Herbert Quick (1861-1925), who has reported in sober truth-fulness the frontiering experiences of settlers in mid-nineteenth century Iowa. His trilogy, *Vandemark's Folly* (1922), *The Hawk-eye* (1923), and *The Invisible Woman* (1924), is a full and authen-tic chronicling of the usual processes of community expansion : of home finding, ground breaking, town building, and develop-ment into a matured community. Like the best of Garland's stories, these newer novels also are narratives of pioneer hard-ships. In spite, however, of prairie fires, blizzards, droughts, frontier bad men, and speculators, Quick's Iowans eventually triumph. Gradually his drab communities transform them-selves into prairie towns, and then into flourishing county seats or small industrial centers. His pioneer farmers, triumphing at last over the land, become prosperous and often establish themselves and their families as leading citizens in the nearest town. Quick's truthful exploitation of such community changes ranks him with Hamlin Garland as one who has done distinc-tive literary service to the Iowa pioneer.

Vandemark's Folly, acclaimed "the best literary interpretation of pioneer life in Iowa before the Civil War,"[99] is written in the first person with such a note of veracity that many were led into believing it genuine autobiography. To be sure, the narra-tive is the work of one who knew Iowa life through and through, for the Quick family, like the Garlands, came to this Middle Border country before the Civil War. Both Quick and Gar-land, therefore, had their own full memories of pioneer asso-ciations.

As Quick himself said not long before his death, *Vandemark's Folly* represents government as applied to the township ; *The Hawkeye* stands for county affairs ; and *The Invisible Woman* for

[99] Frank L. Mott, "Exponents of the Pioneers," *The Palimpsest*, XI, 62 (Feb., 1930).

state politics.[100] *Vandemark's Folly*, the story of the migration of Jacobus Vandemark from New York to what was later called Vandemark's Township, Monterey County, Iowa, reports with marked realism scenes of New York villages, of the active trade and westward movement along the Erie Canal during the forties, and of the settling of Eastern Iowa. This first novel describes the period when Monterey County was dotted with paper towns, when Eastern prospectors were buying lots from speculators, and when, even in the midst of the land gambling, Monterey Centre was nothing more than a strange cluster of houses on the green prairie, the mere beginning of a village.[101] So early as 1854, however, the diverse elements, later to prove powerful forces in the matured town, moved into the county. The Dutch of the frugal, sturdy type represented by Vandemark, the Scandinavian Thorkelsons, Pennsylvania Dunkards, a few Frenchmen, New Englanders, and scores of others indicated that "the rage for land speculation was sweeping over Iowa like a prairie fire."[102]

The Hawkeye pictures Monterey Centre of the seventies and eighties as a rapidly developing prairie town where many of its citizens handled land deals for numerous farmers, from Ohio and elsewhere, who desired ownership of farm acreage. Herein is portrayed the interest of the Iowa farmer in the Grange movement, a trying period of agrarian agitation which caused Monterey Centre folk to know from bitter experience that

> A chattel mortgage in the West
> Is like a cancer in the breast;
> It eats and eats.[103]

This was particularly applicable to the McConkeys, settlers from Ohio who suffered from poverty and other accumulating ills which, as Garland has shown, embittered farmers throughout the Midwest. Such was the unpromising environment into which Fremont McConkey was born. In spite of grasshopper scourges, cyclones, drouths, and other evils affecting his hapless family, Fremont, always a dreamer, eventually rose

[100] *Ibid.*, p. 63.
[101] *Vandemark's Folly*, p. 210.
[102] *Ibid.*, p. 244.
[103] *The Hawkeye* (New York, 1923), p. 45.

above his people. It was his generation which marked the
change of Monterey Centre, a village, into Monterey, Iowa, a
growing industrial city. Fremont knew the town during its
era of boom. He shared in the general excitement of its second
railway and the subsequent building of machine shops and
roundhouses; he witnessed its increasing social stabilization
and educational progress; and had a keen interest in the new
land sales, an expanding building program, and political agitation which opened a boom period for the whole county.
Possessed of an extraordinary passion for self-betterment and
expression, Fremont became widely known as editor of the
Monterey Journal. Later, as is recorded in *The Hawkeye*, when
a middle-aged man, he wrote intimately of the stirring times
in Iowa when he, a clodhopper dreamer, "grew up" with the
village of Monterey Centre, that tiny nucleus of the great industrial town which recognized Fremont McConkey as editor
and civic leader.

In *The Invisible Woman* the Vandemarks, Thorkelsons, Mc-
Conkeys, and others of the first two novels reappear. By this
time the town has long ago outgrown its village position and
has become "a burgeoning municipality." Now a city of forty
thousand, Monterey seems a place of wonder to country-born
Christina Thorkelson, the child of thrifty Norwegian parents.
Christina's experiences as a stenographer in Monterey form a
part of this last unit of the trilogy. By her day an industrial
city with coal mines, packing houses, insurance companies, and
numerous factories has quite submerged the little frontier village. Thus is completed a realistic chronicle of a typical Midwestern situation of town growth. While Quick's trilogy lacks
the marked artistry of style and the imaginative grasp of Ole
Rölvaag's somber *Giants in the Earth*, nevertheless, it ably helps
preserve one phase of our national past.

The Iowa town of the eighties and later had another interpreter in Alice French (1850-1934), or "Octave Thanet," who,
though Massachusetts-born, may by virtue of her long residence
in Davenport, Iowa, and her local color stories be classed among
the Middle Border realists. Among her numerous and at one
time popular reproductions of characteristic phases of Western
and Southern life such works as *Stories of a Western Town* (1893),
The Heart of Toil (1898), and *The Man of the Hour* (1905) show
her thorough and sympathetic understanding of small town

affairs, especially as she observed them in Davenport and in Arkansas, where she later lived. "Truth," she once wrote, "is what I seek above all things. I want to tell my story as it really is, and describe things and people as they really are."[104] This is the creed applied to her stories of Fairport (a thinly disguised Davenport). Unlike her contemporary Midland realists, she was always little concerned with agrarian unrest or the hardships of frontier townsmen. Her vital interest lay in the growing complexities of industrialized town life. Her town, therefore, having emerged from the pioneer stages, becomes the scene of developing industry. But far more important than her discussion of town locale is Miss French's attitude toward the problems of characterization. In *Stories of a Western Town* her consuming interest concerns people, the owners and employees of a furniture factory and a few others who wander into the situation: Harry Lossing, a rich young manufacturer; Tommy Fitzmaurice, a saloon keeper's son who rises through politics to a place in Congress; Kurt Lieders, a stubborn German master woodcarver; and others. (Often Miss French uses the names of actual citizens in the town.)[105] These Fairport stories picture the workaday routine in an Iowa town as it is viewed by the citizens themselves. Business trials through competition are strongly emphasized. Another collection of Fairport stories, *The Heart of Toil*, ranks Miss French as an outspoken friend of the American workingman—and this in spite of the fact that her father, George Henry French, was a banker, a manufacturer, and at one time president of a railroad. Here are signs of the times: small dramas of capital and labor motivated by strikes, dirty politics, and the routine life of the Fairport iron mills. The labor motif again is thematically important in *The Man of the Hour*, a novel dedicated to "R. T. F. Workingman and Gentleman," Miss French's college-trained brother who entered his father's factory as a day laborer and worked upward by his own merits. This brother in many respects was the prototype of the hero, Johnny Ivan Winslow, son of a New England-born plow manufacturer and an exotic

---

[104] E. F. Harkins and C. H. L. Johnston, *Little Pilgrimages, etc.* (Boston, 1902), p. 168.

[105] For this information I am indebted to Miss Rebecca Sewell of Little Rock, who has been in close communication with the Davenport members of the French family. Miss Sewell's thesis on Miss French's life and works may be found in the Southern Methodist University Library.

Russian princess with socialistic leanings.   After giving away
a fortune during the Pullman strike, Johnny Ivan returns to
Fairport as a laborer in the steel mills, where he rises to an
official position before taking over the factory his own father
had built.   In this novel a more sustained study of Fairport is
given than that of the short stories.   One sees it during the
eighties and later as "an overgrown, delightful town sprawling
among the low hills of the Mississippi Valley."   It is a small
town whose industrial changes are viewed with alarm by its
more conservative pioneer settlers.   Actually, in spite of their
lamentations, Fairport is

. . . a kindly town where every one went to the High School before his lot in life gave him college or work for his daily bread ;
and old acquaintance was not forgot.   Like most middle-western
towns, also, obscure though they may be, it was touched by all the
great issues of the world.[106]

In *The Missionary Sheriff* (1897) the labor question of Fairport
gives way to a moral issue in a country town in Iowa.   Didactic in tone, the six anecdotes comprising the work portray a
man "of sterling worth, sagacity, and Christian zeal" who tries.
to reform the erring citizens of the town.[107]   Miss French, influenced by the times, was herein illustrating in fiction her
stated belief that "it is in the villages and in the country districts that the best of our American citizenship can be found
today, not in the large cities."[108]

More widely known as a romancer, Mrs. Mary Hartwell
Catherwood (1847-1902) was also a delineator of the early
Middle West.   Her novel, *The Spirit of an Illinois Town*, descriptive of the growth of an ordinary prairie town, lacks the
power and scope of the Quick trilogy.   There was nothing
unusual about Trail City's origin or its motley group of citizens.

The prairie was intersected by two railroads, and at their junction, without a single natural advantage, the town sprang up.
Neither lake nor stream, neither old woods nor diversity of hills,

---

[106] *The Man of the Hour* (Indianapolis, 1905), p. 3.
[107] Cf. Annette L. Noble, *In a Country Town* (New York, 1890), a temperance
story centering around the intemperance of a wealthy young man, a visitor in a
small town.
[108] Harkins and Johnston, *op. cit.*, p. 169.

lured man's enterprise to the spot; nothing but the bald rolling prairie, gorgeous if you rode into its distance. . . .[109]

Though "a virgin town . . . still untainted with deep poverty or vice," Trail City was, like the towns of Eggleston's novels, stirred by an intense political spirit.   In brief, this is a story of small town animosity as related by a familiar local character, often found in the fiction of the town, the newspaper editor. Held in the treadmill of a country newspaper business, Sam Peevy acts as a buffer between the community factions.   As Mrs. Catherwood notes, the most characteristic feature of this prairie town is its "Americanness."

As we have seen, a noticeable practice among these earlier and most representative Middle Border writers, from the days of Judge Hall and Caroline Kirkland to later years, is revealed in the unanimity with which they have chosen the pattern of the town.   As expounders of an earlier, but fast changing, frontier these Midlanders, together with Mark Twain, have variously fictionalized the prairie town as it existed from the days of wild speculation and hasty building to the period of stabilization when hundreds of towns, often bleak and unlovely, dotted the plains.

[109] *The Spirit of a Western Town* (Boston, 1897), p. 1.

CHAPTER VII

MARK TWAIN AND THE MISSISSIPPI RIVER TOWN

ON THE thirtieth of November, 1835, the meager population of Florida, in Monroe County, Missouri, was increased by one per cent, for on that day Jane Lampton Clemens gave birth to her fifth child, who was named Samuel, after his grandfather, and Langhorne after his grandfather's benefactor.[1] Florida on the Salt River at that time was an "almost invisible village" whose log houses, rail fences, two stores, two streets, and environing cornfields and forests proclaimed it of the border.[2] With the double failure of navigation schemes for Salt River and Florida's fight for the county seat, John Marshall Clemens, again beset by financial difficulties, moved his family eastward to Hannibal in the adjoining county of Marion. This so-called "loafing, out-at-elbows, down-at-heels, slave-holding town" of the forties and fifties, though proud of its superior size, in contrast to near-by hamlets like Florida,[3] was really little more than a growing village in a Southern-Western community, whose provincial dullness was broken periodically by talk of land sales, speculation about the local railroad routes, and the steamboat traffic on the great river. Environed by prairie, forest, and river, Hannibal, nevertheless, claimed to be a town. "A gentry lived there; it was a port on the Mississippi; houses, even mansions, had displaced such shacks as covered the population of Florida; and one day a railroad would join it to St. Joseph."[4]

Far enough removed from the hazards of newer frontier

[1] Albert Bigelow Paine, ed., *Mark Twain's Autobiography* (New York, 1924), I, 7 and 95.

[2] M. M. Brashear, *Mark Twain, Son of Missouri* (Chapel Hill, 1934), chap. ii, in discussing Mark Twain's pre-Hannibal period describes the promise of Florida's growth through the proposed operations of the Salt River Navigation Company, during the late thirties. Nothing came from these schemes, and Florida remained a village.

[3] Miss Brashear (*ibid.*, pp. 76 ff.) says that in 1839, when the Clemens family moved to the town, Hannibal had a population of about four hundred and fifty, which by the time of John Clemens's death eight years later had increased to about twenty-five hundred. Interest in land speculation, river traffic, and railroad expansion c̟ used Hannibal to have a steady growth from its incorporation in 1838.

[4] Bernard De Voto, *Mark Twain's America* (Boston, 1932), p. 29.

towns to have an easy-going society and prevailing simplicity of life, yet so near the Mississippi as to have contacts with the mysterious river world, Hannibal was an enchanting place for Sam Clemens and his boyhood friends.   The forest and Cardiff Hill beyond the town were perfect backgrounds for games of outlawry and frontier adventures imitative of Robin Hood, the Murrell gang, Captain Kidd, and Daniel Boone.   Then there was Bear Creek for fishing expeditions.   In the town itself enough happened to stir the boyish imagination.   The departure of the triweekly mail coaches for Palmyra, St. Louis, and other points and the arrival of the Mississippi boats were constant sources of interest.   Occasional displays of circuses and menageries; performances by itinerant actors, romantic figures like Sol Smith, Edwin Forrest,[5] and others; fiddlers at corn shuckings or a roof-raising; camp meetings and ballad sing-songs; dancing of jigs and reels, gavottes and boleros, waltzes and polkas; candy pullings and other entertainments brought scores of young and old to the scene.[6]   It was, in many respects, an idyllic time, the seed time for some of the vivid impressions later recorded in *The Adventures of Tom Sawyer*, *Life on the Mississippi*, *The Adventures of Huckleberry Finn*, and *Pudd'nhead Wilson*.

On the other hand, Van Wyck Brooks contends that these impressionable years were not wholly idyllic for such a sensitive lad as Sam Clemens.[7]   The beginning of Mark Twain's lifelong ordeal, he says, dates from these early days in Florida and Hannibal when he was first aware of the drab and tragic social setting into which he had been born, a background reflected in certain scenes of *The Gilded Age*.   In emphasizing the poverty of the country towns in which John and Jane Clemens settled Mr. Brooks would paint a joyless childhood for their children.   "Think," he implores,

. . . of those villages Mark Twain himself has pictured for us, with their shabby, unpainted shacks, dropping with decay, with broken fences, the litter of rusty cans and foul rags, how like the leavings of some vast over-turned scrap-basket, some gigantic garbage-can.[8]

[5] Montrose J. Moses, *The Fabulous Forrest* (Boston, 1929), chap. iii, describes Forrest's pioneer acting in small towns like Hannibal.

[6] De Voto, *op. cit.*, pp. 32 ff.   Cf. Mark Twain's "Jim and the Cats," a ludicrous story of candy pulling.

[7] *The Ordeal of Mark Twain* (New York, 1922), pp. 26 ff.   Cf. Paine, *Mark Twain: A Biography* (New York, 1912), I, 47 ff.

[8] Brooks, *op. cit.*, p. 29.

He theorizes further about the tragic influence on Sam Clemens of the loveless household in which the boy lived; of the unfortunate business investments of "that poor, taciturn, sunstruck failure, John Clemens"; of the "old-fashioned, cast-iron Calvinism" of Mrs. Clemens, a quality later adapted to the portrait of Aunt Polly in *Tom Sawyer;* and of the gambling, drinking, murdering, and mobbing he observed in Hannibal. Then there was the influence, Mr. Brooks notes, of the maltreatment of slaves, a practice recorded later in *Pudd'nhead Wilson.* Although the records of Hannibal life in Mark Twain's writings, autobiographical and fictional, often paint the more sordid side of village life, and, thereby, apparently substantiate the facts of the depressing picture above, one must guard against Mark Twain's use of understatement and overstatement. To be sure, in many Midwestern towns of the same era there was much that was drab and unpleasant. Hannibal probably was no exception.

"Fortunately," so Albert Bigelow Paine records, "there were pleasanter things than these."[9]   In spite of the frequent low water-marks in the family fortunes and the detested restrictions of Sunday and day school, young Sam, until he was twelve, had time for normal enjoyment of occasional picnics, ferry-boat excursions, Fourth of July celebrations, and boyish escapades, many of which are retold in *Tom Sawyer* and *Huckleberry Finn.* Further, in addition to the keen and permanent interest he had in the river, he found delight in roaming through the hills and woods, exploring caves, and swimming in Bear Creek. In short, Sam Clemens grew up in what, though termed "a low-lived little town" by Howells, must have been an outwardly democratic, easy-going river town with certain well-defined social standards, where, as Mark Twain himself recalled,

. . . everybody was poor, but didn't know it. And there were grades of society—people of good family, people of unclassified family, people of no family. Everybody knew everybody, and was affable to everybody, and nobody put on any visible airs; yet the class lines were quite clearly drawn and the familiar social life of each class was restricted to that class. It was a little democracy which was full of liberty, equality, and Fourth of July, and sincerely so, too; yet you perceived that the aristocratic taint was

⁹ *Mark Twain: A Biography,* I, 49.

there.   It was there and nobody found fault with the fact, or ever
stopped to reflect that its presence was an inconsistency.[10]

When he was twelve, however, Sam's more or less carefree
and happy existence was darkened.   In that year, 1847, John
Clemens died, leaving his family with little except his faith in
some Tennessee properties, similar to the barren lands described in *The Gilded Age*.   Equipped with but a desultory
village schooling, young Sam was apprenticed to Joseph P.
Ament, a newcomer who had but recently bought the *Courier*,
a weekly Democrat paper in Hannibal.   Thus working for
"more board than clothes, and not much of either," Sam entered upon the second phase of his village life.   After serving
as a printer's devil for two years, Sam was further initiated
into the mysteries of printing through his association with his
older brother, Orion.[11]   Having formerly worked at the printer's trade in St. Louis, Orion, who "lacked the gift of prosperity in any form," in 1849 established himself, with borrowed
money, as editor of the Hannibal *Journal*.   Sam and Henry,
another brother, were his journeymen.   Following the business failure of the *Journal*, Sam, ever restless, began the traditional vagabond life of the early printer, visiting during his
wanderjahre St. Louis, New York, Philadelphia, New Orleans,
and many scattered smaller places.   A dreamer like his father,
he had visions of discovering great wealth in Brazil and, accordingly, journeyed as far toward South America as New Orleans.   Here finding that no ships would be Brazil-bound for
many months to come, the wanderer abandoned the printer's
trade for the call of the river.

Of the boyhood Hannibal days Paine has recorded :   "It
was the river that meant more to him than all the rest.   Its
charm was permanent.   It was the path of adventure, the gate-
way to the world."[12]   Having early possessed a deep feeling
for the river which swept by his native Hannibal, Sam Clemens
in April, 1857, turned with evident sincerity of purpose toward
his new task of "learning the river" by serving as an apprentice, or "cub pilot," under Horace Bixby, pilot of the steamboat, *Paul Jones*.[13]   The old call of the river, so vividly de-

[10] *Mark Twain's Autobiography*, I, 119-120.
[11] *Ibid.*, I, 85.
[12] *Mark Twain: A Biography, loc. cit.*
[13] *Ibid.*, I, 116 ff.

scribed in *Life on the Mississippi*,[14] was at last fully answered. Sam Clemens had realized his boyhood ambition of becoming a steamboatman. Though his career as a pilot ended with the closing of river traffic in the spring of 1861, it later served a double purpose. The young pilot's close observation of and participation in river life furnished the basis for the richly picturesque background of *Life on the Mississippi* and the novels of Mississippi Valley life. Again, as everyone knows, these experiences suggested the future novelist's nom de plume, "mark twain" being one of the leadsman's calls used in sounding the depth of the ever-shifting channel.

Thus prepared through youthful environment, the occupations of his *wanderjahre*, later observations, and reminiscences, Mark Twain has preserved in literature a colorful epoch and a provincial locale in the lower Mississippi Valley. Just as Hawthorne and others unmistakably convey pictures of the provincial and town life of New England, Clemens portrays the customs and people of an entirely different section—the region of the Mississippi River as it existed during his youth and later. In such books as *The Gilded Age*, *The Adventures of Tom Sawyer*, *Life on the Mississippi*, *The Adventures of Huckleberry Finn*, *Pudd'nhead Wilson*, and *The Man That Corrupted Hadleyburg* Mark Twain has given, in one way or another, varying delineations of the provincial life characteristic mainly of the countryside and small towns he knew along the Mississippi. May we examine these for their presentation of small town ways.

In April of 1873, after the appearance of *Roughing It* a year earlier,[15] *The Gilded Age*, the joint product of Mark Twain and Charles Dudley Warner, was finished.[16] More restrained than *Innocents Abroad* (1869) and less humorous and more satirical than *Roughing It*, this book, containing records of Mark Twain's own youth, his father, and life in Washington and the West, is a satirically styled and penetrating exposé of the rapid overdevelopment of American materialism and of the ultra-optimistic outlook which during the seventies constantly was buoyed up by American Micawbers akin to the inimitable Colonel

[14] See *Life on the Mississippi*, chap. iv, "The Boys' Ambition."
[15] *Roughing It*, picturing life in a far Western mining community, will be discussed later, in Chapter VIII, in connection with Nevada boom towns.
[16] Although the material is similar to that of *The Mystery of Metropolisville*, to Eggleston belongs the credit of prior publication.

Beriah Sellers whose honeyed and smooth speeches gild over the dross of actuality. As the thematically revealing title suggests, this is primarily a novel of the gilded age of wild speculation and extravagant living prior to and following the Civil War. Newspaper sensationalism; "get-rich-quick" exploitation of lands for mines, engineering projects, such as railroad building, and the establishment of countless Metropolisvilles, most of which did not advance beyond the log-cabin stage; the accumulation of fortunes and the growing complexities of national politics fall under the satiric onslaughts of Mark Twain and his collaborator. The widespread feeling of freedom and opportunity best expressed the spirit of the gilded age. To the young American

> . . . the paths of fortune are innumerable and all open; there is invitation in the air and success in all his wide horizon. He is embarrassed which to choose, ... He has no traditions to bind him or guide him, and his impulse is to break away from the occupation his father has followed and make a new way for himself.[17]

In the words of optimistic Colonel Sellers, the West was a great country for ambitious youth. It was "the place for a young fellow of spirit to pick up a fortune, simply pick it up; it's lying round loose here."[18]

In an age of such golden prospects, bold lobbying in Washington, sensational advertising of virgin tracts of Western lands, and widespread investments in worthless bonds, it was natural that hundreds of small settlements, not unlike those of Mark Twain's Napoleon or Hawkeye, Missouri, should flourish for a season and then either pass out of existence or develop by the fortunate building of a railroad through the town. *The Gilded Age*, like *The Mystery of Metropolisville* and Dickens's *Martin Chuzzlewit*, is, among other things, a half-satiric and half-humorous social study of back-country villages and Western boom towns.

Fictionalizing John and Jane Clemens's unfortunate experiences in Jamestown, "in the mountain solitudes of East Tennessee,"[19] Mark Twain opens *The Gilded Age* with a description of "Squire" Hawkins, postmaster at Obedstown, a rubbish lit-

---

[17] *The Gilded Age: A Tale of To-Day* (New York, 1915), I, 132.
[18] *Ibid.*, I, 152.
[19] *Autobiography*, I, 88. Cf. Paine, *Mark Twain: A Biography*, I, 8 and *Mark Twain's Letters*, arranged by Paine (New York, 1917), p. 203.

tered log town in the Knobs of Tennessee where "the mail was monthly, and sometimes amounted to as much as three or four letters at a single delivery." But the westward paths of fortune were open and the Squire, disgusted with his rustic surroundings, decides that he "*will* go to Missouri." The golden tales of Cousin Beriah Sellers prove too alluring and "with an activity and a suddenness that bewildered Obedstown. . . , the Hawkinses . . . flitted out into the great mysterious blank that lay beyond the Knobs of Tennessee."[20] As one follows their westward trek he casually views numerous small towns en route and finally, with the Hawkins family, comes to a halt in frontier Missouri.

Mark Twain and Warner satirize small town life in Missouri during a period of confusion, "when between Unionists and Confederate occupations, sudden maraudings and bushwhackings and raids, individuals escaped observation or comment in actions that would have filled the town with scandal in quiet times."[21] Much of the humor in the various pictures of these Missouri small towns may be found in Colonel Sellers's grandiloquently phrased descriptions of their glories. The chagrin of two adventurous Eastern engineers, expectant of seeing a flourishing town in the wilderness, is fully expressive of the fever of speculation so pointedly satirized in *The Gilded Age*. These young fellows, turning out of their tents, rubbed their eyes and stared about them to see the town·so gloriously pictured by the Colonel. Utterly amazed, they saw before them

. . . a dozen log cabins with stick and mud chimneys, irregularly disposed on either side of a not very well defined road, which did not seem to know its own mind exactly, and, after straggling through the town, wandered off over the rolling prairie in an uncertain way, as if it had started for nowhere and was quite likely to reach its destination. Just as it left the town, however, it was cheered and assisted by a guideboard, upon which was the legend, "10 Mils [*sic*] to Hawkeye."[22]

Such was the Colonel's widely advertised Stone's Landing, on paper an incipient city; in reality, a few huts along a sluggish stream, "Columbus River, *alias* Goose Run," which "if it was widened and deepened, and straightened, and made long

[20] *The Gilded Age*, I, 26.
[21] *Ibid.*, I, 202.
[22] *Ibid.*, I, 193.

enough, it would be one of the finest rivers in the Western country." Had the golden dreams of Colonel Sellers materialized, within a short while the quagmire of Stone's Landing would have been miraculously transformed into a fine city, boasting dwellings, business houses, crowded wharves, and a splendidly situated university. All that was now needed was the consent of Congress to widen the forty-nine mile stretch of the Columbus River (now "some five rods wide in . . . good water") between the Landing and the Missouri River. Such was boomtown logic.

The ephemeral life of many nineteenth-century boom towns often ended abruptly when a rival settlement luckily secured railroad rights. Such was the fate of Stone's Landing. When Hawkeye, having been assured of a railroad, "rose from her fright triumphant and rejoicing," down went Stone's Landing.

One by one, its meager parcel of inhabitants packed up and moved away, ... Town lots were no longer salable, traffic ceased, a deadly lethargy fell upon the place once more, the "Weekly Telegraph" faded into an early grave, the wary tadpole returned from exile, the bullfrog resumed his ancient song, the tranquil turtle sunned his back upon bank and log and drowsed his grateful life away as in the old sweet days of yore.[23]

The Colonel's air castles thus crumbled to ruins as Hawkeye flourished and the Landing became another ghost town, another Metropolisville.[24] His grandiosity had not availed.

From the satire of his first books Mark Twain, in 1874, turned to a romantic treatment of his boyhood and youth in Missouri and along the Mississippi. In the words of a recent critic, Mark Twain in *The Gilded Age* "stood on tiptoe ready to take off on his literary flight. He promised to become the great American satirist, but in the deft touch with which he handled the scenes of his boyhood there was another promise—a promise to turn his back on the satire of *The Gilded Age* and to become the chronicler of a time and a place that had departed with his youth."[25]   In *Life on the Mississippi, Tom Sawyer, Huckle-*

---

[23] *Ibid.,* I, 315.

[24] James Lampton, who figures as Colonel Sellers, always contended that there was great wealth in the Tennessee tract owned by John Clemens. With blazing enthusiasm, he always said, "There's millions in it—millions!" (*Autobiography,* I, 89.) James Lampton was Mark Twain's cousin, prototype for Eschol—later Beriah—Sellers.

[25] Blankenship, *American Literature, etc.,* p. 466.

17

berry Finn, and *Pudd'nhead Wilson* Mark Twain further re-creates the life of small towns along the Mississippi which he knew intimately during his most susceptive years.

The only non-fiction work in the group, *Life on the Mississippi* (1883), is a dramatic revelation of the living pageant spread before the eyes of impressionable Sam Clemens during his years as a steamboatman.[26] A retrospective account of his ways of mastering the difficult business of river piloting, the Mississippi book reveals likewise a cub pilot's keen observation of river customs, his youthful delight in the changing scenes along the banks, and his rapidly enriched knowledge of the varied types of folk, passengers and boatmen, who added color to the drama of an ever moving river life. Our present interest, however, is not in the fascinating life led by a Mississippi boatman, but in the views which Mark Twain has presented of Hannibal, during the forties and fifties typically Southwestern in its drowsy, slaveholding, carefree atmosphere. The most romantic thing about the place was its proximity to the Mississippi, the outlet to the world. "Here the energy of America boiled violently, and here passed, daily, all that St. Petersburg was not. The village slumbered in its sun till smoke was black above the bluffs, and some one cried 'Steamboat a-comin.' "[27] Then the place came to life with a stir and general bustle. No longer was it a sleepy waterside village, for pageantry had come to its wharves. Mark Twain's own picture of the town's awakening is inimitable.

Once a day a cheap, gaudy packet arrived upward from St. Louis, and another downward from Keokuk. Before these events, the day was glorious with expectancy; after them, the day was a dead and empty thing. Not only the boys, but the whole village felt this.

. . . : the white town drowsing in the sunshine of a summer's morning; the streets empty, or pretty nearly so; one or two clerks sitting in front of the Water Street stores, with their splint-bottomed chairs tilted back against the wall, chins on breasts, hats slouched over their faces, asleep—with shingle-shavings enough around to show what broke them down; a sow and a litter of pigs loafing

[26] First written in 1874 and 1875, at the urgency of Howells, then editor of *The Atlantic Monthly*, the book appeared serially as *Old Times on the Mississippi*. In 1883, after Mark Twain had made another trip down the river, the work appeared in revised and expanded form as *Life on the Mississippi*.
[27] De Voto, *op. cit.*, p. 48.

along the sidewalks, doing a good business in watermelon rinds and seeds; two or ·hree lonely little freight piles scattered along the "levee"; a pile of "skids" on the slope-paved wharf, and the fragrant town drunkard asleep in the shadow of them; two or three wood flats at the head of the wharf, but nobody to listen to the peaceful lapping of the wavelets against them; the great Mississippi, . . . rolling its mile-wide tide in the sun; the dense forest on the other side; the "point" above the town, and the "point" below, ... Presently a film of dark smoke appears above one of those remote "points"; instantly a negro drayman, famous for his quick eye and prodigious voice, lifts up the cry "S-t-e-a-m-boat a-comin'!" and the scene changes! The town drunkard stirs, the clerks wake up, a furious clatter of drays follows, every house and store pours out a human contribution, and all in a twinkling the dead town is alive and moving. Drays, carts, men, boys, all go hurrying from many quarters to a common centre, the wharf. Assembled there, the people fasten their eyes upon the coming boat as upon a wonder they were seeing for the first time. And the boat is rather a handsome sight, too . . . ; the captain lifts his hand, a bell rings, the wheels stop; then they turn back, churning the water to foam, and the steamer is at rest. Then such a scramble there is to get aboard, and to get ashore, and to take in freight, and to discharge freight, all at one and the same time; and such a yelling and cursing as the mates facilitate it all with! Ten minutes later the steamer is under way again, ... After ten minutes more the town is dead again, and the town drunkard asleep by the skids once more.[28]

Since Mark Twain was much given to comic exaggeration and understatement, what early Hannibal was in reality cannot be accurately repictured from his works. The lifelike pictures of *Life on the Mississippi*, however, indicate the realities on which the fictionalized village of St. Petersburg was built.

In 1875, with the completion of *The Adventures of Tom Sawyer*, Mark Twain finished the first of a remarkable series of stories founded upon American small town scenes. With lively American boys as protagonists—if such they may be termed—he interpreted the daily life of a picturesque Missouri community in the early nineteenth century. Here are preserved the customs of a small river town of the Mississippi Valley, as Mark Twain remembered them from his early days in somnolent Hannibal. The "poor little shabby village of St. Petersburg," Cardiff Hill beyond and above the town, Jackson's Island, and

[28] *Life on the Mississippi*, pp. 30-31.

the river serve as a background for the natural escapades of Tom Sawyer, Ben Rogers, Huckleberry Finn, and others of the "clan."

As Tom knew it, the village itself, indolent center of an easy-going, slave-holding community, was the abode of common man. The mayor—"for they had a mayor there among other unnecessaries"—the justice of the peace, the stern, irascible schoolmaster, the aged postmaster, the long-winded preacher, the pious Sunday school teacher, lawyer Riverson and other village celebrities, certain domestic characters, like Tom's Aunt Polly, occasional tramps and peddlers, villainous Injun Joe and his confederate, town loafers, including Huck's "pap," the village belle, "followed by a troop of lawn-clad and ribbon-decked young heart-breakers," simpering young clerks proud of their oiled hair and fancy canes, and other villagers, all genuine reproductions of types familiar to Sam Clemens, are introduced as they appeared to a boy.[29] While occasional scenes present some of the figures typical of village descriptions, most of the *Tom Sawyer* creations are more than stock characters. Rather, they resemble members of every real community. Aunt Polly, a female martinet; the Widow Douglass, "fair, smart, and forty, a generous, good-hearted soul and well-to-do, her hill mansion the only palace in the town, and the most hospitable and much the most lavish in the matter of festivities that St. Petersburg could boast"; Tom, a shrewd young rascal; carefree Huck and his shiftless "pap"; Becky Thatcher; and even Willie Mufferson, the Model Boy, "taking as heedful care of his mother as if she were cut glass" are given individual distinction.

Tom Sawyer, in short, records a wide-awake boy's impressions of the democratic life of a bygone day in the little village world of St. Petersburg. The hero, "neither a model of youthful virtues nor a horrible example," is, according to the late Stuart P. Sherman, "distinguished chiefly by pluck, imagination, and vanity, [qualities which make] him leader of a group of average little Missouri rascals running loose in an ordinary small river town and displaying, among other spontaneous impulses, all the 'natural cussedness' of boyhood."[30] The wretched com-

[29] Paine, *Mark Twain: A Biography*, I, 33, 52-55, 61, and 507, mentions similar village types known to Clemens. Cf. *The Adventures of Tom Sawyer*, pp. 47-48.
[30] *C. H. A. L.*, III, 15.

mon school, the pranks of Tom and his fellow scapegraces, their forced attendance at Sabbath school, the endless sermons, the episode of whitewashing the fence, the superstitious faith in charms, the stronghold of the "Avengers" on the pirates' island, and the fear of Injun Joe, all based upon incidents which really happened,[31] show, in part, the literary potentialities of Sam Clemens's boyhood experiences with Tom Blankenship— the original Huck Finn—John Briggs, and Will Owens, schoolboys of Hannibal. Every portion of "this intensely vital narrative" reveals some phase of the unhurried life of St. Petersburg beside the river. As with Aldrich in the slightly earlier *The Story of a Bad Boy*, Mark Twain is here a genuine artist, who, turned aside from his satiric exposure of the foibles and extravagances of Reconstruction, is now drawn by memories of boyhood to a delightful work of romantic pioneering. The mingled romance and reality of the obscure provincial town of his early years flower anew in *Tom Sawyer* and its companion volumes, all emphatic departures from the customary moral tracts and Sunday school fiction of the day.

According to William Lyon Phelps, *The Adventures of Huckleberry Finn* (1884), sequel to *Tom Sawyer*, is a prose epic of American life. In its succession of exciting episodes and its panoramic sweep of scenery this picaresque book does partake of the nature of an epic. While both novels are based upon the author's Hannibal boyhood, in richness of life *Huckleberry Finn* is generally spoken of as surpassing the earlier work. Whereas the latter is restricted by the environment of one indolent village, in "*Huckleberry Finn* the plot, like Mark Twain's imagination, goes voyaging. Five short chapters and Huck leaves his native village for the ampler world of the picaresque."[32] Here unusual characters and extraordinary incidents exhibit various phases of the river life which ever charmed Mark Twain. No longer is the hero a shrewd youngster restrained by the disciplinary restrictions of an orthodox aunt, but a village drunkard's son whose "hard, nonchalant, adventurous adolescence is a more distinctive product of the frontier."[33] Narrated in Huck's own idiom, itself enriched by a number of other dialects, the book reveals the adventure-filled life of a

[31] Paine, *op. cit.*, I, 53.
[32] Carl Van Doren, *The American Novel*, p. 172.
[33] Sherman, *op. cit.*, III, 176.

carefree, but crafty, boy as he drifts aimlessly down the Mississippi on a raft, his only friend being the runaway Negro slave
Jim. On the river Huck finds freedom from the petty re-
straints of St. Petersburg and the Widow Douglass, who, in the
boy's own words, "took me for her son, and allowed she would
sivilize me."

Since the scene of his adventures is the Mississippi Valley at
large rather than St. Petersburg, Huck's story but incidentally
reflects small town life. It is more truly the candid record of
life on and along the great river during the early nineteenth
century. The Widow's attempted reformation of indolent,
freedom-loving Huck; the efforts of the boy's "pap," a worthless loafer and drunkard, to secure Huck's share of the treasure
which he and Tom discovered ; and Huck's miraculous escape
to Jackson's Island—these constitute the chief scenes directly associated with St. Petersburg. Most of the book is pure adventure growing out of Huckleberry's journey on the raft with the
companionable Jim ; his chance participation in the quarrels
of Southern "quality" during an outbreak of the Grangerford-
Shepherdson feud in Kentucky; his unwilling association with
two "regular rapscallions" ; and, finally, the joint attempt of
Huck and Tom Sawyer to free the already liberated Jim.

During the course of his wanderings, Huck, together with
his fellow-adventurers, stops at numerous small, commonplace
towns along the river, where the two "rapscallions" employ
all the arts of trickery to "bamboozle" the natives in shabby
little Pikevilles and Hickvilles. Their scalawaggery appears
in various forms : theatrical hokum, temperance lectures,
swindling schemes, dancing and elocution schools, mesmerizing,
quack doctoring, and fortune telling. Huck's keen observation reveals not only these trickeries, but countless word pictures of gullible or angered villagers and the dirty backwoods
towns in which they lived. The boy's reactions to such unpleasant places find expression in his description of "a one-
horse town in the state of Arkansas." Even to Huck's eyes
Brickville was an uninviting place, with stores and houses "of
all old shackly, dried-up frame concerns that hadn't ever been
painted" and "set up three or four feet above ground on stilts,
so as to be out of reach of the water when the river was over-
flowed."[34] The gardens adjoining the houses produced little

[34] *The Adventures of Huckleberry Finn* (New York, 1912), p. 102.

"but jimpson-weeds, and sunflowers, and ash piles, and old curled up boots and shoes, and pieces of bottles, and rags, and played-out tinware." Dilapidated fences added to the general sordidness of the picture. The one main street of the town, with piles of dry goods boxes in front of the stores, seemed to be the gathering place for numerous loafers who sat on the boxes "all day long, whittling them with their Barlow knives; and chawing tobacco, and gaping and yawning and stretching —a mighty ornery lot." Such loafers were too lazy to care about the boggy streets or the many hogs which "loafed and grunted about everywheres." Sometimes the general lethargy was broken temporarily by the cry of "Hi! *so* boy! sick him, Tige!" Then away a sow would go, "squealing most horrible, with a dog or so swinging to each ear, and three or four dozen more a-coming." Nothing, however, could make the loafers happier than a dog fight, "unless it might be putting turpentine on a stray dog and setting fire to him, or tying a tin pan to his tail and see him run himself to death." Occasionally these indolent, "no-count" folks were stirred to excitement by drunken brawls and the shooting which accompanied them or by circuses and the performances of itinerant players, like those of the "king" and the "duke."

Huck's wanderings brought him to other backwoods towns, obscure places of the most provincial type, often peopled by squatters or down-at-the-heels plantation owners. In them Huck observed gossiping, sallow-faced women, frequently given to snuff taking; straw hatted and calico coated men of the locality; occasional outsiders: river pirates, gamblers, itinerant actors, and other adventurers; and superstitious slaves. Here, far more than in St. Petersburg, villagers of both sexes, probably sufferers from malaria, clay eating, and hookworm, were drowsy and apathetic. They were damned by their provinciality. As Bernard De Voto remarks, the energy of the frontier had departed from them as from the hapless villagers of *The Gilded Age*. Huck had ventured into the country of the Pikes and southward into lower Arkansas in whose villages the frontier had left its wreckage: slothfulness, squalor, unpleasant social relations, and ignorance.

Of further documentary value to the small town historian is *The Tragedy of Pudd'nhead Wilson* (1894), a part of which was issued separately as *Those Extraordinary Twins*. This third Mississippi Valley novel centers around David Wilson, a village lawyer and atheist given to the writing of maxims, and his clever untangling of a puzzling situation. It is the story of two babies, the high-born Tom Driscoll and the slave child "Chambers" (partly white), whose positions are changed by Roxana, mother of the latter. After twenty-three years Wilson, "pudd'nhead" and "lummox," solves this heretofore unsuspected case of mistaken identity through his knowledge of fingerprints. Southern honor, several robberies, a curious pair of twins, the mysterious murder of a judge, and the selling of Roxana down the river offer amazing plot complexities.[35] The main scenes take place in Dawson's Landing, on the Missouri side of the Mississippi, half a day's journey below St. Louis. In 1830 the town consisted of little more than a collection of modest dwellings and a single main street. Although steamboats daily passed up and down the river, "the town was sleepy and comfortable and contented." Old-fashioned gardens in front of the homes, locust-shaded sidewalks, forest-covered hills to the rear of the place, and the river in front, all suggestive of Hannibal—these, and more, are the details which go toward painting the picture of Dawson's Landing.

In *Pudd'nhead Wilson*, as in *The Gilded Age*, Mark Twain exposes conditions which involve criticisms of national policies and social systems. Dawson's Landing is "a slaveholding town, with a rich slaveworked grain and pork country back of it." The place was comparatively young, but fifty years old; yet it boasted of having among its citizens representatives of Virginia aristocracy. York and Percy Driscoll, Pembroke Howard, and Cecil Burleigh Essex pointed proudly to their F. F. V. ancestry. At the opposite end of the social scale were the Negro slaves. A far more undesirable position was that of the mulatto, not wholly a Negro, yet isolated from the society of the whites. Unlike *Huckleberry Finn*, this book depicts the more horrible phase of slavery, emphasis being placed upon the Negro's constant dread of being "sold down the river." Such a practice is poignantly represented in the case of Roxana, mother of the child who usurps the place of the real Tom Driscoll. Tom, really Chambers the slave, needs money to pay his gambling debts. To accomplish his purpose, Tom sells Roxana into slavery, falsely assuring her that she has been bought by

[35] See introductory note to *Those Extraordinary Twins*.

an "up the river" planter. Too late does Roxana realize, by the motion of the boat's wheels, that she has been tricked. She is bound "down the river."

The weakness of *Pudd'nhead Wilson,* as Mark Twain was aware, is to be found in some of the outstanding incidents, such as the absurd episode of the two incredible Italian noblemen campaigning for local offices in a small Missouri town. Again Mark Twain stretched the law of plausibility in handling his central situation, wherein the discovery that master and slave had been exchanged in their cradles is not made until more than twenty years later.   Then it was the village "pudd'nhead" who made the discovery.   In spite of these generally recognized discrepancies, *Pudd'nhead Wilson* illustrates further that Mark Twain had an eye for the realities, unpleasing though they often may be, of small river towns during the slaveholding regime.

If *Pudd'nhead Wilson* is, in part, a grim picture of a slaveholding society, *The Man That Corrupted Hadleyburg* (1898) is a keen arraignment of American character.   The tragic note was struck in *Pudd'nhead Wilson;* in this cynicism predominates. Mark Twain had the same distrust of what the average person thought about religion and morals as he did of what the average American tourist said about the paintings and cathedrals of Europe.   Moved, perhaps, by his hatred of pettiness, greed, and, above all, hypocrisy, Mark Twain in this later story holds up to ridicule a town which boasted of its apparent incorruptibility.   *The Man That Corrupted Hadleyburg,* a product of the same period of philosophic nihilism which resulted in *What is Man?* (1905) and *The Mysterious Stranger* (published in 1916), has been aptly termed "a corrosive apologue on the effects of greed."[36]   It is the story of an all-consuming greed assailing the cherished respectability of the prideful town of Hadleyburg. Written at a time when Mark Twain's fame and position enabled him to brave censorship, this satire shows the author's "deadly temperamental earnestness."[37]   It is an expression of his conviction that the nature of man is corrupt at the root, and that there is no salvation possible for him.   A sardonic study, *The Man That Corrupted Hadleyburg* is a condemnation of the pettiness of man.   The stranger who tempts Hadleyburg

[36] Van Doren, *op. cit.,* p. 182.
[37] Brooks, *op. cit.,* p. 191.

does not corrupt it; he but removes the mask from a town already corrupt and thus demonstrates that there is in that community "none righteous, no not one." As Paine points out, human weakness and rotten moral force are stripped bare and mercilessly jeered at in the marketplace.[38] "Hadleyburg is the world and we are all its citizens."[39] Scornful of self-righteousness, Mark Twain has here conceived the idea of demoralizing not one individual but an entire community. Even the "pillars of society" cannot resist the cheap, glittering temptation of wealth, the same temptation which so often meant the ruin of Colonel Sellers, Washington Hawkins—really Orion Clemens—and Mark Twain himself.

Indefinite as to the time of his story, Mark Twain merely states that it was many years ago. The scene is Hadleyburg, "the most honest and upright town in all the region round about." So unsmirched was the town's reputation that even jealous neighboring communities acknowledge its "honorable supremacy." But an offended stranger, a bitter and revengeful man, decides to corrupt the town by a peculiar test. A heavy sack of gold, with an attached note explaining that a ruined gambler once was given aid and a bit of advice by a citizen of Hadleyburg, is left at the home of the Richardses, the village bank cashier and his wife. This unknown benefactor now is to be rewarded with the contents of the sack, gold weighing more than a hundred and sixty pounds. To prevent fraud the right man must be identified by a prescribed test. He must put in a sealed envelope a statement of the advice he gave the stranger. If this coincides with that contained in a sealed packet within the sack, the gold will thus be awarded to the gambler's benefactor. But the Hadleyburgians, liars and hypocrites at heart, are caught in the trap. Instead of one sealed confession, there are as many as there are supposedly incorruptible citizens in the town. And the sack is found to contain not gold, but gilded lead disks.

A bitter condemnation of hypocrisy, this story, nevertheless, does not lack humor, a humor giving speed to the plot by contrasting situations and characters without further analysis. For example, the "peaceful, holy happiness" enjoyed by the Hadleyburgians before the stranger's advent is at odds with

[38] *Mark Twain: A Biography*, II, 1068-1069.
[39] H. J. Bridges, *As I Was Saying* (Boston, 1910), p. 44.

the universal discontent which followed.   The problem of the
money sack brings about a complete change of affairs in the
heretofore peaceful—and incorruptible—town.   The usual Saturday night bustle of shopping and larking dwindles to noth-
ingness and desolation.

Richards and his old wife sat apart in their little parlor—miserable and thinking.   This was become their evening habit now; the
lifelong habit which preceded it, of reading and knitting, and contented chat, of receiving or paying neighborly calls, was dead and
gone and forgotten, ages ago—two or three weeks ago; nobody
talked now, nobody read, nobody visited—the whole village sat at
home, sighing, worrying, silent.   Trying to guess out that remark.[40]

Humorous also are the glorious visions which the nineteen "first
families," who actually lack wealth, have of their expenditure
of the gold.   These greedy townsmen are no better than the
covetous heirs in Pinero's satire, *The Thunderbolt*.   Like the
British Mortimores and the gold-crazed miners in *Roughing It*,
the Hadleyburgians in their daydreaming "bought land, mortgages, farms, speculative stocks, fine clothes, horses, and various other things. . . ."   Characters, as well as situations, are
in contrast.   Consider the differences between the simple,
honest Richardses and "the little mean, smirking, oily Pinker-
ton," banker and arch-hypocrite.   Strictly observant of the
law of conciseness, Mark Twain in this ironic tale has lam-
pooned the pretensions of leading townsmen and unmasked
their hypocrisy.   In short, the story of Hadleyburg, with its
note of revolt against the false standards of village life, is a
vitriolic forerunner of the more recent protests of Edgar Lee
Masters and his contemporaries.

Characterized by Professor Pattee as "the first man of letters
of any distinction to be born west of the Mississippi,"[41]   Mark
Twain has enriched the literature of the American small town
with two types of vividly drawn delineations.   From his earlier
Roughing It there emerges a many-faceted picture of boom towns
which arose almost magically along the newer frontiers of Nevada and California; from his Mississippi Valley reminiscences
are re-created typical villages of an older frontier.   In both
Mark Twain "incarnates the spirit of an epoch of American

---

[40] *The Man That Corrupted Hadleyburg* (New York, 1910), pp. 20-21.
[41] *American Literature since 1870*, p. 45.

history when the nation, territorially and spiritually enlarged, entered lustily upon new adventures."[42]   Re-creating and preserving many phases of the land and the changing society in which he was born and developed, he is truly "a fulfilled promise of American life."

[42] Sherman, *C. H. A. L.*, III, 1.

Chapter VIII

THE LONG TRAIL: THE FAR WESTERN TOWN

In his peculiarly distinctive account of the ranching frontier, *The Story of the Cowboy*, the late Emerson Hough described the long trails, with their multifold windings, followed by the intrepid plainsmen who established both ranches and towns. With apt analogy he wrote thus:

The braiding of a hundred minor pathways, the Long Trail lay like a vast rope connecting the cattle country of the South with that of the North. Lying loose or coiling, it ran for more than two thousand miles along the eastern edge of the Rocky Mountains, sometimes close in at their feet, again hundreds of miles away across the hard table-lands or the well-flowered prairies. It traversed in a fair line the vast land of Texas, curled over the Indian Nations, over Kansas, Colorado, Nebraska, Wyoming, and Montana, and bent in wide overlapping circles as far west as Utah and Nevada; as far east as Missouri, Iowa, even Illinois; and as far north as the British possessions.[1]

This vast region has furnished fictionalists, good and bad, with varying backgrounds for their interpretations of the soldier, the Indian, the miner, the cowboy, the trapper, the "bad man," and other familiar types of the Far West. Here, in this almost limitless land, during the days before "the edge was worn off the frontier by the grind of the wheels of civilization" life consisted largely of extremes, whether the scene be the wide, unpeopled ranges, mountain trails, or the meager settlements scattered along the watercourses or, later, near the railroad. This was the region, too, which furnished the last line of the frontier before the growing bands of settlers joined the throngs already established in California during the exciting forties and fifties. Further this selfsame area has contributed, in addition to numerous spurious and melodramatic "Wild Westerns" once much in vogue, a small body of town literature which has added further variety to the pattern of American community life. Tiny barren cattle towns ("cow towns" in local parlance),

The Story of the Cowboy (New York, 1919), p. 1.

booming mining towns, ghost towns, remote army posts, often
the nucleus for a later city, and scattered Indian villages were
both the chief types of settlements, except for the ranch communities, along the Long Trail and the source of literary materials for the interpreters of small town affairs in the range
country.   Add to this region and its fictional studies the most
picturesque outpost of advancing frontiers, the California settlements of the forties and fifties and the mining country of
Roughing It, and one has the finished story of the frontier town
as portrayed in American fiction.   Because of its historical
significance through its earlier settlement and subsequent literary exploitation, the Far Western mining town of the Bret
Harte-Mark Twain-Stevenson country should be noted in advance of the ranching country.   It is here, as Professor Turner
points out, that one finds the most distinctive frontier of the
mid-nineteenth century.

THE CALIFORNIA FRONTIER

The California which idealistic Frank Harte first saw during
the days of his youth and journalistic apprenticeship was stimulating to his romantic imagination.   Removing from New
York to Oakland in 1854, but five years after the first gold
rush, the young Argonaut soon found exciting experiences
crowding in on him during his constantly changing career as
teacher, private tutor, druggist's clerk, typesetter in a rural
newspaper office, and an eager witness of the free life of the
mining camps.[2]   He was living in the midst of the flush times
and in a frontier country where the gold discoveries had sent
a sudden tide of adventurers.   In Oakland, then but a village
of several hundred people, or at the nondescript Mexican settlement near Mission San José, thirty miles away, the youth
had the opportunity of seeing a wild, roystering life.   In the
mining camps life was indeed primitive and loose.   Even in
San Francisco the Second Vigilance Committee could not always maintain order.[3]   Brought thus in contact with a new
and vigorous environment, Frank Harte, already romantically

[2] George R. Stewart, *Bret Harte, Argonaut and Exile* (Boston and New York,
1931), p. 43.   Some critics have called Harte "an effeminate 'young squirt' who
never entered the mining camp."   Josiah Royce in his *California* (Boston and
New York, 1886, p. 345) says Harte's tales are examples of "perverse romanticism"
rather than of true realism based upon personal experience of really primitive
conditions.
[3] Stewart, *op. cit.,* p. 40.

influenced by his earlier reading, found fresh literary materials, and using them passed from what has been called an Irving-Hawthorne-Longfellow-Dickens apprenticeship, "step by step by means of magazine and newspaper training in the electric California environment, to final literary form, which is the dramatic blend of romance, of Hugo intensity and melodrama, of California humor, of Dickens sentiment, and of Harte originality."[4] As this apprenticeship lengthened Harte gained a local reputation through his mocking *Condensed Novels*, sketches, and poems published in the *Golden Era* and the *Californian*. Then came the year of 1868 and with it Harte's acceptance of the editorship of a new magazine, *The Overland Monthly*. At last, the jack-of-all-trades had a position of unusual responsibility. With the new position and the success of the first issue of the magazine, July 1, 1868, Harte must have had, according to the belief of his latest biographer, a new realization of the potential literary wealth around him.[5] At any rate, in the August issue the appearance of "The Luck of Roaring Camp" among the contributions made history for the *Overland* and brought both widespread recognition and freshly indigenous material to Bret Harte.

Straggling Western towns with the nomenclature of California: Poker Flat, Red Gulch, Smith's Pocket, Rough and Ready, and Roaring Camp; colorful portraits of gentleman gamblers, daring highwaymen, rough miners, courageous expressmen of the Yuba Bill type, monte-hall operators, dance hall girls, and the more stable element of the mining camps; tales, picaresque and often sentimental, pandering, as Professor Parrington has expressed it, "to the common taste by [the author's] discovering nuggets of pure gold in the dregs and outcasts of the mining camps"—these suggest the extent of Bret Harte's realization of the literary possibilities of California. These indicate further, in barest outline, the pictures which were carried eastward in successive issues of the *Overland* to a public then reading *Oldtown Folks* and other products of the genteel tradition. But this was the period of the late sixties. The leavening process of the war already had broken down many of the barriers of provincialism. In addition, the extension of the Pacific Railroad across the Sierras in 1868, the

---

[4] Pattee, *The Development of the American Short Story*, p. 224.
[5] Stewart, *op. cit.*, p. 165.

glowing reports of returned travelers from the Far West, and the general restlessness of the times were also instrumental in causing people to face westward.   Mark Twain's *The Celebrated Jumping Frog of Calaveras County and Other Sketches* (1867) had already interested Easterners and others everywhere in the bizarre environments of California.   Thus Editor Harte's tales of the mining camps, "The Luck of Roaring Camp," "The Outcasts of Poker Flat," "Tennessee's Partner," and others now widely known, informed readers enamored of the West that even in the most primitive of mining settlements, where life was hard and coarse, the simplest virtues moved the roughest of miners and the most sinful of gamblers to deeds of kindness.   "So," remarks a recent critic, "America awarded these romantic Mexicans, quaint miners, and heartbroken harlots the applause with which it annually welcomes the announcement that hearts are golden after all."[6]   The picturesque names and local speech of Colonel Starbottle, Sandy Morton, the Duchess, Kentuck, Stumpy, M'liss, and others ; the highlights of wicked little towns, lonely valleys, and snow-capped heights of the gold country ; views of unusual foreign types ; and tales of danger added to our literature a popular "Far Western fiction" dramatizing for Eastern readers a romantic and faraway region along the Pacific slope.

The story of Harte's early successes and his subsequent departure from California has been thoroughly developed by his biographers and needs no detailed discussion here.[7]   Of noteworthy significance, however, was the appearance in 1870 of *The Luck of Roaring Camp, and Other Sketches*, a slender volume resulting from the phenomenal success of his *Overland* contributions and the encouragement of Fields, Osgood, and Company, publishers of *The Atlantic Monthly*.   The young editor's countrywide recognition was complete with the immediate success of his humerous poem—also published in the *Overland*—entitled "Plain Language from Truthful James," or, as it was more popularly known, "The Heathen Chinee."   Next, change followed change.   In spite of his position, as writer and editor, in California where a circle of friends and acquaintances (in-

    [6] De Voto, *Mark Twain's America*, p. 162.
    [7] T. Edgar Pemberton, *Bret Harte: A Treatise and a Tribute* (London, 1900), and *The Life of Bret Harte* (New York, 1903) ; H. W. Boynton, *Bret Harte* (New York, 1903) ; Henry C. Merwin, *The Life of Bret Harte* (New York, 1911) ; and Stewart, *op. cit.*

cluding Anton Roman, promoter of the *Overland*, Charles Warren Stoddard, Clarence King, and Mark Twain, then a journalist), Harte felt called to the East. There larger opportunity beckoned. Thus, in 1871, eastward he traveled, passing by in Chicago the editorship of the *Lakeside Monthly* and moving thence to what he considered better centers of culture, to New York, Boston, and Cambridge, where he was fêted by Howells and his associates. In this manner Harte began a lifelong period of exile from the country from which he drew his best materials. Later, with his more distant removal to Europe Harte's exile became complete and his work ever after but fainter reproductions of his original pictures.

A prolific writer, Harte often was little more than "a literary middleman who skillfully purveyed such wares as his eastern readers wanted."[8] On the other hand, his best (and, in this instance, his earlier) creative works were, among other things, something unusually new in the fictional history of the American town. Before 1868, except for Mark Twain's popular "The Jumping Frog," nothing so Western as the tales of Roaring Camp, Red Gulch, or Poker Flat had ever appeared in fiction. Assuredly, frontier speculation and fraud had been featured previously in the sketches made by Judge Hall and his contemporaries of the mushroom towns of the Midwestern prairies and Irving in *Astoria* had produced a tediously drawn account of an actual Far Western trading post. These, however, lacked the Western humor, the picturesqueness, and other qualities of Harte's fiction. His stories, therefore, possessed newness. Literary form, backgrounds, characters, and, in many instances, themes had the merits of originality. The synthetic life of the mining camp and the bawdy town, shocking to some, was here reproduced in fiction for the first time.

Though Californians long criticized the accuracy of his pictures of miners, Harte, as Pattee notes, had the ability to throw over his stories a peculiar atmosphere of locality. For instance, in his one and unsuccessful long novel, *Gabriel Conroy* (1876), Harte produced a sketch—realistic enough in effect—of one of the early California settlements which he frequently used in his short stories. A wooden hotel and temperance house, an express office, several saloons and gambling halls, low, drab-looking houses along a dusty main street, scattered cabins along

[8] Parrington, *The Beginnings of Critical Realism in America*, p. 93.
18

the hillside, freshly hewn stumps, and newly cleared lots—such was One Horse Gulch, Harte's conception of a jerry-built mining town during its short "season of unexampled prosperity." Again, as in this excerpt from "The Outcasts of Poker Flat," Harte often achieved a dominating impression through compressed, but descriptive, paragraphs : "There was a Sabbath lull in the air, which, in a settlement unused to Sabbath influences, looked ominous." With such word economy he could forcefully suggest the atmosphere of a story. Similarly employing carefully chosen details in other stories, Harte described numerous shanty towns, which, if not portrayed with complete historical accuracy, in many ways resembled those once dotting the great valley of Central California, the background of his mining camp narratives.[9] (Now a fertile region, the valley was during the gold rush era a vast untilled plain studded by huge oaks, tall plane trees, and an occasional gigantic redwood, all convincingly described in Harte's stories.)[10]

Harte has been sharply condemned for the melodramatic situations in which he often placed his characters and for the unnatural virtues which on occasion he attributed to the most profligate individuals. But, in spite of his inability to create great characters, he nevertheless, added to the fiction of the small town a new and picturesque citizenry. Even his first portrayals included a wide variety of frontier individuals, many of whom have since become stock figures in dozens of imitative Western tales. Among the men—usually more realistic than Harte's women characters—one finds gentleman gamblers in John Oakhurst and Jack Hamlin ; a pretentious gentleman in Colonel Culpepper Starbottle, who appears repeatedly in short story and novel (i.e., in *Gabriel Conroy*) ; good-hearted loafers and drunkards like Sandy Morton of Red Gulch ; coarse, but too frequently self-sacrificing, miners, such as picturesque Kentuck and Stumpy of Roaring Camp and faithful Chaffee, Tennessee's partner ; and duelists as intrepid as Culpepper Star-

---

[9] Charles Warren Stoddard was impressed by Harte's methods of composition. "One day I found him pacing the floor of his office in the Unitel States Mint ; he was knitting his brows and staring at vacancy,—I wondered why. He was watching and waiting for a word, the right word, the one word of all others to fit into a line of recently written prose. I suggested one ; it would not answer ; it must be a word of two syllables, or the natural rhythm of the sentence would suffer. Thus he perfected his prose" (quoted in Jay B. Hubbell, *American Life in Literature*, New York and London, 1936, II, 130).

[10] Merwin, *op. cit.*, p. 100.

bottle, the Colonel's nephew. Ranchmen and land speculators, boasters and hypocrites, gentlemen and paupers, pick-
swinging Paddies and rice-eating coolies, town boomers and
newspaper editors, vigilantes and drivers of the "Lightning
Express," hardened prospectors and self-sacrificing idealists,
and many others representative of the rugged individualism of
the West people the mushroom towns of the Harte country.
Then there are the border town ministers who try to cope with
the materialism of frontier society. The Protestant clerical
element usually fares but ill in Harte's stories.[11] The oily-
tongued, self-seeking hypocrite, a conventional type, is best
exemplified by the Reverend Joshua McSnagley of "M'liss."
In "A Belle of Canada City" the Reverend Mr. Windibrook,
a jovial, loud-voiced hypocrite, at heart calculating and cold,
is another caricature. The Spanish priest, on the other hand,
frequently appears as a cultivated and polished man.[12] These
individuals, all familiar with the license of the border, largely
determine the character of the mining camps featured so often
in Harte's fiction. Certainly all of them, good and bad, are
representative of an era of reckless exploitation and of individualism gone riot.

Not all of the Harte towns were so womanless as Roaring
Camp. Places like Rough and Ready, Jules, Fiddletown, and
Smith's Pocket boasted of their women. Marked variety may
be noted among these portrayals. The usual boom town of the
fifties and sixties, like that of the Texas oil fields today, had its
dance hall entertainers, women of uncertain reputation: the
Duchess, Mother Shipton, Miggles, and "Nell Montgomery,
the Pearl of the Variety Stage." Even among these there were
paradoxes. The Duchess, one among the unfortunate outcasts of Poker Flat, gave her bastard son to a prudish school-
mistress that he might be removed from the crude environment of a boom town. Nell Montgomery, accustomed to the
low life of the camps, ran away from a dance hall to become the
wife of a pious farmer. Mrs. Conroy, alias Madame Devarges,
alias Grace Conroy, who though at first married to simple
Gabriel Conroy, One Horse Gulch miner, for the purpose of
swindling him out of rich mining property later learns to love
him. Although the frontier settlements of Harte's stories

[11] See Merwin, *ibid.*, pp. 206 ff., for an excellent discussion.
[12] Cf. the cultured Father Forbes in *The Damnation of Theron Ware*, chap. v.

counted among their citizens various types of the unfaithful wife, these towns were not devoid of better women.[13]   When Edgar T. Pemberton, an early biographer of Harte, considered as baseless the late Julian Hawthorne's criticism that "Bret Harte seems not to like women, or respect them,"[14] he no doubt had in mind the latter's numerous portrayals of the better classes.   Among others he may have been thinking of the attractive daughter of "old man Folinsbee," wealthy ranchman near a frontier town; hospitable Mrs. Price, Christmas party hostess for the family of a Rough and Ready miner; or Miss Mary, Red Gulch teacher.[15]

Professor Pattee calls attention to Harte's practices of peopling his towns "with highly individualized types, with picturesque extremes in an abnormal social régime."[16]   Daredevil Yuba Bill, romantically pictured stage driver, and the theatrical Colonel Starbottle are cited as composites rather than actual individuals.   With these and others Harte lapses into what Josiah Royce termed "perverse romanticism."   He stresses strongly marked characteristics, often paradoxical to an extreme.   Concerning the strange assemblage of rough men, waiting anxiously outside Cherokee Sal's cabin at Roaring Camp, it is said that

> The greatest scamp had a Raphael face, with a profusion of blonde hair; Oakhurst, a gambler, had the melancholy air and intellectual abstraction of a Hamlet; the coolest and most courageous man was scarcely over five feet in height, with a soft voice and an embarrassed, timid manner. . . .   The strongest man had but three fingers on his right hand; the best shot had but one eye.[17]

In *Gabriel Conroy* Jack Hamlin, gambler and fugitive from justice, is described thus:

> For the hemorrhage from Jack Hamlin's wound was so great that that gentleman, after a faint attempt to wave his battered hat above his disheveled curls, suddenly succumbed, and lay as cold and senseless and beautiful as a carven Apollo.[18]

[13] Portrayals of unfaithful women are found in "Santa Claus Comes to Simpson's Bar," "An Episode at Fiddletown," and "Tennessee's Partner."
[14] Pemberton, *Bret Harte, etc.*, p. 168.
[15] "The Romance of Madrono Hollow," "Dick Spindler's Christmas," and "The Idyl of Red Gulch" respectively.   (The edition used is the "Argonaut Edition," New York, 1904.)
[16] Pattee, *op. cit.*, p. 238.
[17] "The Luck of Roaring Camp."
[18] *Gabriel Conroy* (Boston and New York, 1903), II, 72.   (First edition, 1876.)

Harte's stories further reveal many customs of trail and town actually in vogue during frontier times. Merwin notes that "at an early date nothing really satisfied the Pioneers unless it was the best of its kind that could be obtained, whether that kind were good or bad."[19] In "Dick Spindler's Family Christmas" the dinner preparations were little short of pretentious for the new mining town of Rough and Ready. The *Weekly Banner* item announcing that "On Christmas evening Richard Spindler, Esq. proposed to entertain his friends and fellow-citizens at an 'at home,' in his own residence" is humorously suggestive of the "easy come-easy go" extremes of frontier society. Again, even at the cost of a great sacrifice, only the best toys could satisfy the rough, but generous, frontiersmen of Simpson's Bar.[20] Often in remote towns theatrical productions, by both strolling players and local performers, provided entertainment for motley crowds.[21] In some communities, in the Harte stories and in actuality, social distinctions were early drawn. Gamblers and courtesans were speedily expelled from Poker Flat, a community smarting from "the loss of several thousand dollars, two valuable horses, and a prominent citizen." One lavish entertainment near Marysville was recorded in the local paper as having no gamblers present.[22] In *Gabriel Conroy* are detailed descriptions of lavish entertainments given not only by newly rich San Franciscans but by lucky miners from One Horse Gulch and other camps. In the Gulch, after the big "silver strike," new buildings, a new hotel—the Grand Conroy—and the extensive foundations of some smelting works quickly replaced the rickety cabins along the hillside. "With these and other evidences of an improvement in public taste, the old baleful title of 'One Horse Gulch' was deemed incongruous. It was proposed to change that name to 'Silveropolis,' there being, in the figurative language of the Gulch, 'more than one horse could draw.'"[23]

Although some have severely condemned while others, equal-

[19] Merwin, *op. cit.*, p. 199.

[20] "How Santa Claus Came to Simpson's Bar."

[21] "An Esmerelda of Rocky Canon" and "M'liss." "The Boom in the 'Calaveras Clarion'" deals with the exhorbitant prices paid for newspaper advertising. See Merwin, *op. cit.*, p. 198, for facts regarding the flourishing of the legitimate drama in California.

[22] Merwin, *op. cit.*, p. 200. As early as 1850 measures were taken to prohibit or restrain gambling.

[23] *Gabriel Conroy*, I, 254.

ly extreme, have highly praised Harte's works, his pictures of
the frontier town unquestionably hold a place of historical significance in the literary chronicle of the Far Western community.   At times overpainted, the best of Harte's stories present
vivid pictures developed with broad strokes and brilliant colors.
Working most effectively with episodic selections of the type of
"The Luck of Roaring Camp," Harte put into fiction a variety
of studies portraying certain phases of a teeming frontier society.
Timely in his presentation of a glamorous material, he early
drew the attention of critics and a curious public to the California gold fields.   Out of such material he produced a new genre
which, regardless of its many weaknesses, interpreted the incredible years of the gold rush, an era replete with thrilling
adventure and rich in inspiring opportunities.   His was an entirely new literature of the small town which pictured the lawlessness of a brief and crowded era.   Humor and sentimentality, impressionism and paradox, realism and romanticism—
these are the keynotes of the Western community portrayals of
Francis Bret Harte, argonaut and exile.

What Walt Whitman once wrote of the "flashing and golden
pageant of California" might be applied, with reservation, to
Robert Louis Stevenson's pictures of the new country he journeyed from afar to see.   The pictorial accounts in *Across the
Plains* (1892), and *The Silverado Squatters* (1893) delineate, in
part, the settlers Whitman saw as

. . . the New arriving, assuming, taking possession,
A swarming and busy race settling and organizing everywhere.[24]

In these fragments of autobiography and travel Stevenson
views the Far West through the eyes of an amateur emigrant,
as he styles himself, who though broken in health writes of his
new experiences with the spirit of a robust adventurer.   Except for occasional glimpses which its invalid author got as he
slowly traveled westward, the first of these travelogues offers
no individualized scenes of small town life along the plains.
There are, however, brief sketches of the miserable way stations,
hardly worthy of being dignified by the name of town, which

[24] Emory Holloway, ed., *Leaves of Grass* (Garden City, 1931), p. 178, "Song of
the Redwood-Tree."

had sprung up along the route of the railroad. Further, there
are realistic portrayals of a California-bound emigrant train,
a crude and comfortless affair, poorly ventilated and packed
with a motley group of adventurers and settlers who were to
help people and build many of the towns then developing on
the Pacific coast. Herein, during the course of a long trip,
Stevenson lived as a fellow-traveler with a part of the "swarming and busy race" which entering California after the period
of the Great Madness were to settle and cultivate its valleys
and hillsides.

The Silverado Squatters, a series of studies based upon Stevenson's sojourn in the California mountains, sketches a different
phase of Western life. Here among the mountains, removed
from the new and growing valley towns, Stevenson lived amid
the ruins of an abandoned camp, a deserted place which finds
unusual description in the writing of a chance visitor. Harte
most frequently recaptures the spirit of earlier, teeming gold
rush years and the period of the first stabilization of town
affairs; Stevenson sees the California mining towns in after
years. By the time he, a health-seeker and foreigner, appeared
in Silverado the boom days had passed and the golden pageant
faded. Agricultural towns, forerunners of small farming centers such as that later depicted in Frank Norris's *The Octopus*,
were rapidly replacing the mushroom mining settlements of
the fifties and sixties. In mining towns, once the scenes of
wild speculation and constant excitement, only empty and half-
decayed buildings were left as mute memorials of former activities. Whole neighborhoods, formerly alive with camps and
villages, were frequently changed into places of sylvan quietness. Such was the fate of Silverado and many of the other
experimentally founded mining towns of northern California.
In the words of Stevenson,

They grow great and prosper by passing occasions; and when the
lode comes to an end, and the miners move elsewhere, the town
remains behind them, like Palmyra in the desert. I suppose there
are, in no country in the world, so many deserted towns as here in
California. . . . Here there would be two thousand souls under
canvas; there one thousand or fifteen hundred ensconced, as if forever, in a town of comfortable houses. But if the luck failed, the
mines petered out; and the army of miners had departed, and left

this quarter of the world to the rattlesnakes and deer and grizzlies, and to the slower but steadier advance of husbandry.[25]

At Silverado, where once had been a lively population, busy hotels, saloons, boardinghouses, and branch stores, Stevenson found a deserted camp occupied only by the family of Rufe the hunter. The "swarming and busy race" of yesteryear had vanished, carting with it most of the movables in Silverado. Such are the records which a foreign observer, arriving on the scene in the nineties, adds to the picturesque history of the California boom town. The next phase of the story of the California town, a chapter but incidentally recorded in literature, is that associated with "the slower but steadier advance of husbandry."

BOOM DAYS IN VIRGINIA CITY

After trailing around for two weeks in the wetness and mud of the hinterland of Hannibal, Missouri, Second Lieutenant Samuel Clemens, erstwhile cub printer and Mississippi pilot, parted company with his group of slightly irregular Confederate calvary. Soldiering, he felt, was not his calling.[26] His unmartial spirit must have found relief when he learned that Orion, his older brother in Keokuk, Iowa, had been appointed secretary of the new Territory of Nevada and "that Brother Sam was invited to go along and act as Secretary of the Secretary without pay for the modest consideration of merely putting up traveling expenses for both of them."[27] Though ten years older than Sam, Orion Clemens, "a dreamer by birth," was willing always to accept the bounties of his younger brother.[28] Accordingly, as Mark Twain later wrote, "Orion and I cleared for that country in the overland coach, I paying the fares, which were pretty heavy, and carrying with me what money I had been able to save. . . ."[29] Thus loaded with about eight hundred dollars in silver coin and "another nui-

[25] *The Silverado Squatters* (New York, 1912), p. 27. Cf. John Muir's description of ghost towns in his "Nevada's Dead Towns," *Steep Trails* (New York, 1918), written in the late seventies.

[26] For full details see Paine, *Mark Twain: A Biography*, I, chap. xxx, "The Soldier," based on details furnished by Ab (A. C.) Grimes, one of the Hannibal "battalion" and later a noted Confederate spy; and Mark Twain's *Private History of a Campaign that Failed*.

[27] W. H. Nelson, "Mark Twain out West," *The Methodist Quarterly Review*, LXXIII, 65 (Jan., 1924).

[28] *Mark Twain's Autobiography*, ed. Paine (New York, 1924), II, 268 and 272.

[29] *Ibid.*, II, 291.

sance, . . . an Unabridged Dictionary," the brothers boarded the "great and swinging stage . . . an imposing cradle on wheels" at St. Joseph, Missouri, for the long, but exciting, trip across the plains. So elated was Sam over leaving the zone of war disturbance and over the prospect of journeying into the faraway country of Nevada that he was eager to undertake the dangerous trip into the desert. Even the "dismally formidable" Mr. George Bemis, their armed fellow-traveler, did not dismay Clemens, for, as he wrote in *Roughing It*, "We jumped into the stage, the driver cracked his whip, and we bowled away and left the States behind us."[30]

It was in July, 1861, that the "poor innocents"—Mark Twain's phrase—began their three weeks trip to Carson City, a journey humorously, vividly described in *Roughing It*. "At noon of the fifth day out," Mark Twain reports, "we arrived at the 'Crossing of the South Platte,' *alias* 'Julesburg,' *alias* 'Overland City,' four hundred and seventy miles from St. Joseph—the strangest, quaintest, funniest frontier town that our untraveled eyes had ever stared at and been astonished with."[31] Transferring to a "mud-wagon," less sumptuous than the coach, the brothers continued their journey across the desert. At last, coated like millers with the dust of the prairies, Sam and Orion arrived in Carson City, the capital of the Nevada Territory, a nondescript place which to these tired travelers at first appeared as "an assemblage of mere white spots in the shadow of a grim range of mountains overlooking it."[32] Once disembarked from the "mud-wagon," the Clemenses saw that Carson City was "a wooden town" with a population of about two thousand adventurers. It was an uninviting place whose tiny white frame stores on main street "were too high to sit down on."

They were packed close together, side by side, as if room were scarce in that mighty plain. The sidewalk was of boards that were more or less loose and inclined to rattle when walked upon. In the middle of the town, opposite the stores, was the "plaza" which is native to all towns beyond the Rocky Mountains—a large, unfenced, level vacancy with a liberty pole in it, and very useful as a place for public auctions, horse trades, mass meetings, and like-

[30] *Roughing It* (New York, 1913), I, 20.
[31] *Ibid.*, I, 58.
[32] *Ibid.*, I, 59.

wise for teamsters to camp in. Two other sides of the plaza were faced by stores, offices, and stables. The rest of Carson City was pretty scattering.[33]

But life in Carson City was not dull. This the newly arrived Clemenses speedily discovered. Immediately after witnessing a shooting match and experiencing all the discomforts of the daily "Washoe Zephyr" (a wind filled with a "soaring dust-drift about the size of the United States set up edgewise"),[34] they knew that their "romantic adventures" had led them to a desert outpost. At once they experienced frontier excitement in a mining town in the midst of a land having sand and sage-brush, a sultry sun and cattle bones, coyotes and tarantulas, desperadoes and land seekers. It was a region of amazing paradox, a country of high altitude, gray alkali, gray sage-brush, buoyant life, spring freshets, and glorious sunsets into which thronged an ever increasing army of seekers, the human drift swept along by every whirlwind of discovery.[35] With the discovery of silver lodes in 1858 the population of "Carson County," up to this time largely Piute, Shoshoni, and Mormon, was increased rapidly by the influx of thousands from California and later from everywhere. The excitement over the discovery of silver in Washoe (the Indian term for Nevada) is unparalleled in the colorful and dramatic history of American frontier towns. By 1859 the great Comstock Lode, the amazing argent bonanza of the West, began to dazzle the world. As dusty caravans brought crowds of weary, but curious, travelers across the desert wastes to Carson City and near-by mining towns, miraculous changes were effected in the region. According to Mark Twain, as the American element gained a majority governmental changes came to pass. "Allegiance to Brigham Young and Utah was renounced and a temporary Territorial government for 'Washoe' was instituted by the citizens. . . .   In due course of time Congress passed a bill to organize 'Nevada Territory,' . . . ."[36] With the spread of rumors about the inexhaustible wealth of what ignorant gold prospectors—bullying H. T. P. Comstock ("Old Pancake"), bibulous James Fennimore or Finney (the "Old Virginny"

[33] *Ibid.*, I, 169-170.
[34] *Ibid.*
[35] See George D. Lyman, *The Saga of the Comstock Lode: Boom Days in Virginia City* (New York, 1934), p. 207, and Paine, *Mark Twain: A Biography*, I, 176.
[36] *Roughing It*, I, 202.

who drunkenly named Virginia City), and a few other early comers—had at first contemptuously termed "that damned blue stuff," numerous caravans of people and animals appeared out of the desert bound for Carson City, Virginia City, Johnstown, or the fast growing settlement in Gold Cañon. Developing from meager settlements of a dozen or more shanties and a score of huts, tents, and dugouts, these and other camps in the shadow of Sun Peak (Mount Davidson later) grew and grew until by 1863 there were forty thousand men on Sun Mountain alone and the mines were turning out from twenty to thirty millions yearly.[37] By the time, then, that Orion and Sam Clemens had established themselves at the so-called ranch of "a worthy French lady by the name of Bridget O'Flannigan, a camp follower of his Excellency the Governor,"[38] and had been accepted by their fourteen fellow-boarders, popularly known as the "Irish Brigade," the mountain roads were jammed with silver-mad people bound for Sun Mountain.

They poured through Sierra passes like pent-up streams that had gotten out of bounds. It was the greatest exodus since the days of '49. . . . The goal of the Washoe crusaders was one lone spot on the flank of a barren mountain a mile and a half above the sea. All the mules, jackasses, and oxen in California grunted their transport up the Sierra. Gamblers and confidence men travelled on priceless thoroughbreds. Some went in coaches, some in stages, a few in covered wagons, but the vast majority travelled on foot.[39]

Everywhere the cry was "Go it Washoe!" Orion and Sam, with thousands of other "boys," had come to "the richest country in the world." They had come to Silverland, where during the strenuous year of 1860 early prospectors had survived the difficulties of snow, avalanches, furious westerly gales, choking alkaline dust, mineralized water, lack of fuel and proper shelter, and the threats of the Piutes.

As the miners "spread along the Comstock range for miles, pitching their tents and establishing their camps wherever wood and water were to be found,"[40] Orion, encouraged by the promise of an eighteen-hundred dollar salary, was trying

[37] Lyman, *op. cit.*, X, "Rush to Washoe, 1859-1863," 60-69.
[38] *Roughing It*, I, 172.
[39] Lyman, *op. cit.*, p. 60.
[40] Dan De Quille (William Wright), *History of the Big Bonanza, etc.* (Hartford, 1877), p. 110.

to attend to his secretarial duties.   Sam, meanwhile, fascinated
by the wonderful new country, concluded to postpone his return to the States.   Free of the routine of piloting and released
from soldiering, he found the keenest pleasure in "wearing a
damaged slouch hat, blue woolen shirt, and pants crammed
into boot-tops, and gloried in the absence of coat, vest, and
braces."[41]   His own job, as he said, was so easy that he had
nothing to do and no salary.   Thus at liberty, he joined several members of the Brigade on a trip to Lake Tahoe.   On
other occasions he watched the display of magnificent horsemanship by picturesquely clad Mexicans in the Carson streets,
where once he was unwittingly "taken in" through his unwise
purchase of a vicious Genuine Mexican Plug.   Often, too, he
found time to listen to glamorous tales of the hidden wealth
of Silverland.   Finally, he was smitten with the silver fever
and, according to his own confession, "succumbed and grew
as frenzied as the craziest."[42]   Fairly inoculated with the disease, he eagerly sought news of the famous Esmeralda mines
and listened to tall tales of the Humboldt, "the most marvelous
of the marvelous discoveries in silver-land."   Eventually going
with one of many tides, Mark got ready for the Humboldt,
whose ranges *The Territorial Enterprise* reported as being "gorged
with the precious ores."   Here, if the *Enterprise* were true, one
might easily find "the true Golgonda."   Clemens was again
"taken in."   Not content with investigating the rich mineral
stores of near-by Gold Hill (in the vicinity of Virginia City),
he and three friends, heavily provisioned, "drove out of Carson on a chilly December afternoon."[43]

In *Roughing It* Mark Twain has recorded that wearisome
journey across the desert to Unionville, Humboldt County, a
miserable town of eleven cabins and a liberty-pole.   Here, full
of dreams of becoming a "gold king," Clemens joined the "beggars' revel" and during two months of winter prospecting became one of the many miners who "swarmed out of town with
the first flush of dawn, and swarmed in again at nightfall laden
with spoil-rocks.   Nothing but rocks."[44]   But everywhere in
Unionville dreams were golden and the talk was of "feet,"
"lucky strikes," and assays.   The big bonanza, however, was

[41] *Roughing It*, I, 181.
[42] *Ibid.*, I, 211.
[43] *Ibid.*, I, 216.
[44] *Ibid.*, I, 234.

not for Clemens and his fellows. Wearily they trekked back to Carson City, their mineral fever still unabated. Forth they went on a second expedition, this time journeying to Aurora in the Esmeralda district, on the edge of California, only to find it in many respects another Unionville. Though there was no lack of excitement in prospecting, Sam Clemens found silver mining at Aurora a hard, long, and dismal task.[45] Burrowing for the coveted ore and the aggravating silver milling proved far too dreary and laborious for him. At last, at a silver mill, where he had secured work at ten dollars a week, he asked for a salary raise. To his employer's question as to how much he wanted, Sam replied that about four hundred thousand dollars a month, and board, was all he could reasonably ask, considering the hard times.[46] Peremptorily dismissed, he again began prospecting. This time his partner was Calvin H. Higbie ("Cal") of California. The ups and downs of their mining experiences are revealed in Sam's urgent letters to Orion begging that he send money or secure him some sort of affiliation with a newspaper. According to Paine, the "Blind Lead" episode in *Roughing It* "is presumably a tale of what *might* have happened—a possibility rather than an actuality."[47] It is, however, vividly true in atmosphere. The two partners' dreams of European trips and mansions on Russian Hill might have been real. As a matter of fact, Sam still lingered around the mines, hoping for the "lucky strike" which never came and devoting much time to the writing of the so-called "Josh" letters to the *Enterprise*. Thus ended the first phase of Sam Clemens's life in the romantic West.

The momentous question of his next move was providentially answered by an unexpected offer which came to Clemens from the chief paper of the Territory, the Virginia City *Daily Territorial Enterprise* (named above), edited by the keenly alert Joseph ("Joe") T. Goodman. Impressed by the "Josh" letters, Goodman felt that the man who wrote them had "something in him." Accordingly, Clemens was asked to join the *Enterprise* staff at the tempting salary of twenty-five dollars a week. Although in debt after his mining failures, Clemens accepted the city editorship of the *Enterprise* only after some debate.[48]

[45] Paine, *Mark Twain: A Biography*, I, 193-203.
[46] *Roughing It*, I, 284.
[47] Paine, *op. cit.*, I, 202.
[48] *Roughing It*, II, 18-19.

With his arrival in Virginia City after walking sixty miles of the way from Esmeralda, Sam, describing himself as "a rusty-looking city editor," began the second phase of his Western career.   As journalist and local humorist he was to play a part in a noisy, turbulent society.

By the time Clemens, or "Josh" as he was then known, became one of the *Enterprise* boys Virginia City was passing rapidly from the first stage of boom-town growth.   Now in its bloom, the ugly town sprawled across the barren slopes of Sun Mountain.   It had, as one writer describes it, become an ant hill with ants hastening toward it from many lanes.   Other settlements were strung "like beads along Gold Canon" and "at night, from the desert, the mountain looked like a monstrous Christmas tree strung with candles."[49]   Six months following Clemens's entry into journalism what he has called "the grand 'flush times' of Silverland began, and . . . continued with unabated splendor for three years."   Meanwhile, the population of Sun Mountain exceeded the growth of any other Sierra town in the same length of time.   Mining shafts, down hundreds of feet, honeycombed the mountain.   In 1863 Joe Goodman, ridiculing one of the many lawsuits for mining titles, entertained Washoe with these *Enterprise* verses descriptive of the largest mines :

> The Ophir, on the Comstock,
>   Was rich as bread and honey.
> The Gould & Curry further south
>   Was raking out the money.
>
> The Savage and the others
>   Had machinery all complete
> When in came the Grosches
>   And nipped all our feet.[50]

Its sidewalks swarming with people and its terraced streets just as crowded with quartz wagons, freighters, and other vehicles, Virginia City impressed Sam Clemens as "the 'livest' town, for its age and population, that America had ever produced."[51]

[49] Lyman, *op. cit.*, p. 92.
[50] Quoted in Lyman, *ibid.*, p. 234.   (See *ibid.*, p. 196.)   Ethan Allen and Hosea Ballou Grosch of Pennsylvania, long unrecognized, were the real discoverers of the Comstock Lode.
[51] *Roughing It*, II, 27.

It is said that Sam would go in his slow way up and down the streets of Carson, talking and listening to stories, and "then stand against a post for hours, just resting, after doing nothing, and letting the picturesque crowds and their strange doings photograph themselves on his brain."[52] What he saw in Carson he found on a grander scale in Virginia. Here the reckless exploitation of the great Comstock Lode, stretching straight through the town from north to south, made money as plentiful as dust. Money-getting schemes and high hopes dominated the actions of the thousands who formed an endless procession along the packed streets or worked in shifts in the hidden city below the mountain. New claims were taken up daily; the sprawling town and all the mountainside were riddled with shafts; and the general belief even in "wildcats" continued strong. The great mines on the Comstock Lode, the Ophir, Gould and Curry, and the Mexican were turning out huge piles of rich rocks daily. Nobody was discouraged. Everybody was excited and optimistic.[53]

As the output of the mines increased stores, saloons, assay offices, lawyers' offices, restaurants, monte and dance halls, flimsy canvas houses for the newcomers and imposing dwellings for Bonanza Kings like illiterate Sammy Bowers and energetic James Graham Fair, and mill buildings, valued at thousands of dollars, all multiplied. A substantial iron-faced building was erected for the Wells Fargo bank and express headquarters. By the fall of 1860 the most luxurious place on Sun Mountain, the International Hotel on "C" Street, was constructed entirely from fine materials laboriously freighted over the Sierras. Its iron-balustraded balconies, billiard parlors, dining- and smoking-rooms, and richly ornamented bar symbolized more than anything else, except the elaborate "Bowers' Mansion," the sudden rise of luxury in Virginia. By 1863 the stately fireproof brick Enterprise Building had been built. In *Roughing It* Mark Twain traces the evolution of Goodman's "poverty-stricken weekly journal, gasping for breath and likely to die," into a great daily, printed by steam. With five editors and twenty-three compositors, a subscription price of sixteen dollars annually, exhorbitant advertising rates, and crowd-

[52] Nelson, *op. cit.*, p. 70; Paine, *Mark Twain: A Biography*, I, 178.
[53] *Roughing It*, II, chaps. ii-iii, *passim.*

ed columns, the *Enterprise* became one of the most powerful
organizations in the community it served.

In *Roughing It* Clemens preserves the frontier spirit which in
these flush times dominated Virginia City and all the region
thereabout.   His pages are rich with sympathetic portrayals
of frontier journalists and the exciting life they led.   Joe Goodman, penetrating critic of the times and owner of the *Enterprise;*
cynical Rollin Daggett; William Wright, known throughout
the Territory as Dan De Quille; and small, but fearless, Steve
Gillis, who delighted in making Sam swear, are some of the
makers of Comstock humor with whom Sam Clemens was intimately associated.   Editorial combats with reporters for the
rival *Union;* unavoidable duelings; deliberately planned hoaxes
which delighted, or angered Washoe; midnight suppers after
the paper was "put out"; attendance upon the current entertainments at Maguire's Opera House and other places of
amusement; and expensive dinners for visiting celebrities like
Artemus Ward suggest, in part, one phase of the teeming life
which Clemens knew intimately.   The scattered references to
desperadoes and the masterly account of the showy funeral
of Buck Fanshaw give a revelation of certain elemental characters found in lusty frontier towns like Virginia City.

Everywhere, during Mark Twain's stay in Virginia, the flush
times held bravely on.   The streets came to hold, in Paine's
phrase, "a congress of nations as only the greed for precious
metal can assemble."   In addition to the "silver nabobs" so
fully presented in *Roughing It*, representatives from many nations gave Virginia's streets a cosmopolitan appearance.[54]   There
were ragged Piutes sullenly regarding the encroachments of the
miners as "bad medicine"; pigtailed Chinese coolies shoulder-
ing huge baskets of wood or laundry; daring Mexican vaqueros
on elaborately saddled horses; members of military squads,
fire companies, and brass bands, all properl; uniformed; heavily bearded miners in blue suits and sturdy boots; French,
German, and other foreign agents or adventurers, all adding
color to the motley groups crowding the sidewalks and streets
day and night.[55]   In Mark Twain's own words, there were

. . . banks, hotels, theaters, "hurdy-gurdy houses," wide-open
gambling palaces, political pow-wows, civic processions, street

[54] *Ibid.*, II, chap. v.   [55] For full discussion see Lyman, *op. cit.*, pp. 196 ff.

fights, murders, inquests, riots, a whiskey mill every fifteen steps, a Board of Alderman, A Mayor, a City Surveyor, a City Engineer, a Chief of the Fire Department, with First, Second, and Third assistants, a Chief of Police, City Marshal, and a large police force, two Boards of Mining Brokers, a dozen breweries, and half a dozen jail and station-houses in full operation, and some talk of building a church.[56]

The splendor of Maguire's attracted throngs of miners and other "boys," including the *Enterprise* staff to whom free tickets were issued. Rough audiences applauded loudly the performances of Lotta Crabtree, Adah Isaacs Menken (the Menken who thrilled her hearers with her interpretation of the title role in *Mazeppa*), Artemus Ward with his popular lecture, "Babes in the Wood," and countless others, famous and otherwise. Money-mad and patriotically stirred people at public auctions held in the various towns along Sun Mountain contributed, according to Mark Twain's estimate, a hundred and fifty thousand dollars in greenbacks for the famous sack of flower which Reuel Gridley of Austin sold in the interest of the United States Sanitary Commission.[57] "Money was wonderfully plenty. The trouble was, not how to get it—but how to spend it, how to lavish it, get rid of it, squander it." One of the earliest nabobs wore six thousand dollars worth of diamonds in his shirt bosom and "swore he was unhappy because he could not spend his money as fast as he made it."[58] Some, like Sammy Bowers and his wife, Eilley Orrum Bowers, erected fine mansions and then went to "Yoorop."[59] Others lavishly spent their "blue stuff" on hetaerae, bold-faced women at the faro tables or in the dance halls. "Birds of Paradise," a recent historian calls them, "decked out in gay dresses, brilliant feathers, and showy jewelry, promenaded slowly up and down 'C' street, proudly displaying vari-colored plumage to rows of ragged, rusty crows who lined the streets with ravenous eyes."[60] Truly, as Mark Twain says, the flush times were in magnificent flower.

Thus associated with the youthful and adventurous spirits on the *Enterprise*, Mark Twain,[61] compositor-pilot-miner-humor-

---

[56] *Roughing It*, II, 27-28.   [57] *Ibid.*, II, 40 ff.   [58] *Ibid.*, II, 48.
[59] C. B. Glasscock, *The Big Bonanza* (Indianapolis, 1931), p. 112.
[60] Lyman, *op. cit.*, p. 198.
[61] Paine, *Mark Twain: A Biography*, I, 222, tells the now familiar story of Clemens's adoption of his nom de plume while he was Goodman's employee.

272   THE SMALL TOWN IN AMERICAN LITERATURE

ist, beheld the enthralling spectacle of a frontier boom town at
the wildest stage of its history. Virginia City was an ugly
place, on a bleak mountainside, crowded with fools of fortune
from all parts of the world; but Mark was completely enraptured.[62] Was he not known, not only in Washoe but all
along the coast, as the author of humorous sketches and extravagant hoaxes which enlivened the *Enterprise?* Did he not receive daily gifts of mining claims from his admirers? Had he
not become a very conspicuous figure at Carson through his
legislative reporting? Further, as the popular Governor of the
"third House," was he not the recipient of a gold watch in-
scribed "Governor Mark Twain"? For Mark Twain this was
truly an era of good feeling and of congenial friendship. As
Bernard De Voto points out, Mark Twain's "ripening personality, the slow drawl of his wit, the splendor of his imagination
drew men after him. He became a Comstock personage, welcomed, deferred to, courted."[63] His youthful exuberance was
in accord with the intense life of this stage of Virginia's history.
Departing for California before the days of the town's decline,
Clemens did not witness the decay of the colorful settlement
whose activities he had enjoyed.[64] *Roughing It*, therefore, contains the record of Washoe's boom days, the era of the big
bonanzas.[65] It is the colorful and humorous chronicle of a
booming frontier community as its author saw it from 1861
until near the end of May, 1864. But the boom days did not
last. By 1865 "barren borrasca had succeeded argent bonanza."[66] With the exhaustion of surface deposits and the water
logging of underground passages, stocks depreciated, mining
companies became deeply involved in lawsuits, and numerous
mines and mills were closed. As the clatter grew less and less,
rumors went abroad that the great Comstock had "played out."
No longer was the air furnace-smoked nor the earth shaken by
the subterranean explosions which Mark Twain vividly describes. "Wildcat" mines were abandoned; men were discharged; and the town, once so crowded, gradually shrank in

[62] De Voto, *op. cit.*, p. 133.
[63] *Ibid.*
[64] In *Roughing It*, II, chap. xiv, Mark Twain recounts the story of his unfortunate
experience at dueling and his subsequent departure from Washoe.
[65] Chapter XIX of the second book contains a graphic description of the decayed mining camps of Tuolumne, California which is highly suggestive of Stevenson's later pictures in *Silverado Squatters*.
[66] Lyman's phrase.

population as its adventurous citizens sought other bonanzas.[67]
But Washoe's decline was not for Mark Twain. It was the
heyday of her flush times to which he did homage and not to
the ghost town that Virginia City later became. For Mark
Twain Sun Mountain had yielded place to Jackass Hill.

THE RANGE COUNTRY

In most parts of the country the busy years after the Civil
War represented an era of transition from an individual, isolated community life to one of standards common to numerous
localities. The range country was in many respects an exception, for in spite of the headlong scramble for rail routes and
subsidies, land and town sites, mineral rights and freight rates,
much of this region, such as the isolated land of Owen Wister's
The Virginian, remained for a while untouched by the forces of
a growing industrialism. Except for the larger towns in the
mining zones, like Denver and Colorado Springs, and in the
cattle-receiving centers, like Kansas City, many of the range
country settlements were, even at the turn of the century, but
small towns set down on the vast prairies.[68] Such inconse-
quential places, however, were not without literary chroniclers.
Hamlin Garland, Emerson Hough, Alfred Henry Lewis, Owen
Wister, and Andy Adams have all written of the cowboy centers in Colorado, Arizona, Wyoming, New Mexico, Kansas,
and Texas. One of the most prolific, but by no means the
most excellent, of these was Garland.

According to one well-known critic, in *They of the High Trails*
(1902) and his later romantic novels Garland "followed the
false light of local color to the Rocky Mountains and began
the series of romantic narratives which . . . interrupted his
true growth and, gradually, his true fame."[69] Such later studies, it is regrettably true, represent an "aftermath of veritism."[70]
For almost twenty years Garland, the former radical, departed
from the publicized themes of his native farm lands and in the
picturesque mountain country apparently forgot "the acrid
dust of controversy," once stirred by his doctrine of truth

---

[67] De Quille, *op. cit.*, chap. lxiii, shows that, in spite of fluctuations of fortune,
milling activities were being carried on with success by some of the mines as late
as the middle seventies.

[68] Cf. Turner, *The Frontier in American History*, p. 9.

[69] Carl Van Doren, *Contemporary American Novelists* (New York, 1922), p. 43.

[70] See Pattee's "The Aftermath of Veritism," an open letter to Garland, in
Tradition and Jazz (New York, 1925).

insistently preached in *Crumbling Idols*. With colors changed, the radical became "a lost leader." His realistic art fell to the level of a weak and monotonous thesis : the stereotyped romantic theme of a love uniting some heroic, uneducated plainsman, or mountaineer, with a girl of superior culture. Outworn formulas thus determined the pattern of plots and characters. In spite of these lapses Garland at times cultivated a limited realism picturing certain isolated settlements of the Mountain West, a region associated with adventurous living even long after many changes had swept across its barriers. Through the prefatory notes to *They of the High Trails*, Garland presents his dramatis personae and picturesque "High Country" locales (the mountain regions of Colorado, Wyoming, Arizona, and New Mexico). Admitting frankly that he is here less of the militant reformer than in his Midwestern stories, Garland, nevertheless, conveys (among other pictures of mountain life) the harsh external realities of isolated towns to be found during the late nineties and the early part of the present century in different sections of the West from Colorado to Wyoming. The drab world of army posts, bleak cattle towns (often a mere cluster of stores, wooden houses, a post-office shack, and a loading platform), gold mining camps, an occasional bad town, and temporary headquarters for engineering projects offsets the romantic tendencies in theme. Even Garland the romanticist disapproves of the fashion of misrepresenting Western towns as "the painted back drops of melodrama, gloomy, fuliginous, hell-litten." He tries instead—too often unsuccessfully—to settle these little frontier towns of his stories with "the sons and daughters of the men and women I had known on the plains and prairies of the Mississippi Valley."[71] Some of his characters, therefore, in spite of his prevailing romanticism, are as real as the toiling farmers and debt-ridden townsmen of the earlier stories. Grubstakers, army officers, ranch owners, cow-bosses, prospectors, trail-tramps, rangers, marshals, gamblers, leaseholders, and storekeepers people the raw towns and wide ranges of Garland's adopted High Country. In the opinion of Carl Van Doren, many of these are formula-created characters ; in that of Theodore Roosevelt, they are "real men and real women," using the vo-

[71] *They of the High Trails* (New York, 1922), Foreword.

cabularies of the Far West and living according to the frontier customs of the country.[72]

Most of these stories are of the open range. A few, however, treat, with some realism, the familiar types of range and mountain country towns. "The Grub Staker," a gold rush tale of the Sierra Blancas, reports the life of the Widow Delaney's cheap boardinghouse in a mountain town. "The Cow Boss," romantically akin in theme to *The Virginian*, exhibits the bleakness of a saloon-marked cattle town. A series of tales about the trail tramp, Tall Ed Kelley—romantic "mounted wanderer, horseman of the restless heart"—takes one from one commonplace, cheap town after another throughout the cattle country. In "Kelley Afoot" he serves for a time as a hostler in a livery stable, the best in Keno City, a double town with one part a sprawling place, "drab, flea-bitten, unkempt, littered with tin cans and old bottles, a collection of saloons, gambling-houses and nameless dives, with a few people—a very few—making an honest living by selling groceries, saddles, and coal-oil."[73] Fort Keno, the other half, was an imitation town, its "spick, span [barracks] in rows, with nicely planted trees and green grass-plots" on the banks of a sluggish river. The scene of "Kelley as Marshall" is Sulphur Springs, Colorado—between piñon-spotted hills—which by 1896 had been several kinds of a bad town : successively, a small liquoring-up place for cattlemen, a land-office, a lumber camp, and a dirty coal town. The theme is trite enough. Tall Ed, now a ranch foreman, is appointed to "clean the old town up" and, as in many familiar Wild Western tales, defies a reckless, lawbreaking gang. Ed's experiences in a rough mining town, where the good luck of the miners brings prosperity to the saloonkeepers, motivate "Partners for a Day."

The novels of Garland's middle period are almost entirely devoid of the dour realism of the Middle Border series. In such romantic tales as *The Spirit of Sweetwater*,* *The Eagle's Heart*, *Her Mountain Lover*, *The Captain of the Gray Horse Troop*, *Hesper: A Romance*, *Money Magic*, *Cavanaugh: Forest Ranger*, and

---

* A novelette appearing in 1898 as a sort of forerunner of a succession of romances written at the beginning of the new century.

[72] Van Doren, *op. cit.*, p. 43 ; Roosevelt, "An Appreciation of Hamlin Garland," appended to the Foreword of *They of the High Trails*.

[73] *They of the High Trails*, p. 97.

The Forester's Daughter stereotyped love themes quite over-shadow the feeble attempts at realistic depiction of locale and the creation of individual character. Except for incidental scenes of military settlements in *The Captain of the Gray Horse Troop* and Colorado mining towns in *Her Mountain Lover* and *Hesper*, these romances offer little positive contribution to the literature of the Western town. Instead, there is monotonous insistence upon thin plots typified by the strained romance in *Her Mountain Lover*. (A crude young American miner, aided by a cultured London girl and his native wit, interests an English financier in his Colorado mine.) *Hesper*, the tale of an untutored Westerner and a cultured, widely traveled girl (the counterpart to the young Londoner in *Her Mountain Lover*), is but a feeble offering of the same theme of *The Virginian* and William Vaughn Moody's *The Great Divide* (1907). *The Spirit of Sweetwater* offers a picture of a Colorado health resort such as a summer boarder might have produced ; *The Eagle's Heart* (1900), the second of the romances, employs a village and its stock characters as nothing more than a backdrop for the commonplace adventures of a commonplace village bad boy. *Money Magic* (1907)* is conspicuous among the romances for its realistic details of the life in a valley farming town during the Cripple Creek gold rush. Forerunners of the Sinclair Lewis pictures—in *Main Street* and *Work of Art*—of ordinary small town hotels are the natural scenes reproduced here of the Golden Eagle Hotel, rendezvous of miners, ranchers, farmers, drummers, traders, barbers, and clerks from near-by stores. Here wealthy Mark Haney, forty-year-old ex-gambler and mine-owner, courts Bertha Gilman, young cigar girl and daughter of the overworked proprietress. Bertha's marriage to Mart, her subsequent dissatisfaction, and her vulgar display of their wealth in Denver expose the shopworn qualities of the tale. *Cavanaugh* has the most sustained representation of small town life appearing in Garland's novels. Something of the verisimilitude of *Main-Travelled Roads* colors the descriptions of Roaring Fork and its people. At best a Western cow town, the place seems cheap, petty, and bald to Lee Virginia, returned escapist, after a long sojourn in the East. (The theme is comparable to that of "Up the Coolly.") Worst of all the ramshackle buildings in the town is the squalid little den of a

* Republished in 1922 as *Mark Haney's Mate*.

hotel, The Wetherford House, half-way managed by Virginia's mother, herself prematurely old, unkempt, and worried. Superimposed upon this realism is the unoriginal love story of Virginia and her heroic lover, Cavanaugh, an English expatriate and forest ranger.

In these tawdry romances the once plain-spoken crusader for social justice is seen worshipping the selfsame crumbling idols which he earlier denounced with vehemence. His most original documents of small town life are those candid, decisive portrayals of his earliest period and his additional commentaries in recent autobiographical records of the Midwestern frontier and other regions, such as *Trail-Makers of the Middle Border* (1926), *Back-Trailers from the Middle Border* (1928), *Roadside Meetings* (1930), and *Companions on the Trail* (1931). These last volumes round out the Middle Border series. In these, as in Garland's first volumes, "lies his best province and here appears his best art."[74] Here Garland shows with new force his ability to impart reality to his reminiscent accounts of the treeless plains of South Dakota, of the aging pioneers of the La Crosse Valley, and of the barren village of Ordway and numerous other small Middle Border towns full of retired farmers and their families. Here, too, are fine studies of actual pioneer conditions in the Midwest, all of documentary significance in the economic and literary history of the Western town. As an annalist of town life, Garland is best remembered for the sordidness and unsparing fidelity to fact with which he has shown vigorously that life in small towns of the older West moved slowly—almost as slowly as that in the decaying seaport villages and little inland towns of New England. Mr. Van Doren was right when he pointed out that the service performed by *Main Street* was, in its fashion, performed many years ago by *Main-Travelled Roads*.[75]

Another Midlander, Emerson Hough, was "preeminently a pioneer, even though he was born after the first great hordes of homeseekers had pushed the frontier into the ocean."[76] A pioneer in the sense that he created a new literature of the West, Hough deserves distinction for his attempts to preserve in fiction "the history of the unsung." It has been said that

[74] Van Doren, *op. cit.*, p. 47.
[75] *Ibid.*, p. 40.
[76] Pauline Grahame, "A Novelist of the Unsung: Emerson Hough," *Palimpsest*, XI, 67 (Feb., 1930).

he elevated "the woman in the sunbonnet to her true place in the sun."[77]   Certainly he purposed to preserve pioneer tradition in his tales of the trail, the cow camp, and the bleak cattle towns used throughout the range country as trading and shipping points.   Though born (1857) on the frontier at Newton, Iowa, and later graduated from the University of Iowa, Hough is associated not with the town literature of his own state but with that of newer frontiers.   Admitted to the bar and located in a tiny New Mexico town, a rough place, "half cow town and half mining camp" between the Rio Grande and the Pecos, Hough had ample time for viewing frontier life and meditating upon literary plots.   Eventually he turned to writing, his first accepted work of this period being "Southwestern Sketches," a series printed in the old *American Field*.[78] After years of disappointment, Hough gained his first actual success in *The Story of the Cowboy* (1897), a series of sketches warmly praised by Theodore Roosevelt.

Herein Hough, as in his later successful novels, *The Covered Wagon* (1922) and *North of 36* (1923), substantially proved his belief in the use of social and historical materials.   While *The Story of the Cowboy* is not pure fiction, its highly descriptive narrative ranks among Hough's writings as his most sustained treatment of the cow town of the Southwest and elsewhere. Scornful of the currently popular "wild West" sensationalism, Hough strove to present typical and actual backgrounds, figures, and customs of the frontier country beyond the Missouri.[79] His *Story of the Cowboy* is not a bare record, not a mere tabulation of the manners of frontier plainsmen, but a living picture of a type often heroic and always invested with an individual interest.   It is a picture also which brings before one the sweep and majesty of the plains during a stirring period.

Among the chapters on various phases of the picturesque life of the plains, the thirteenth ("Society in the Cow Country") describes cow towns, such as Abilene and Wichita in Kansas and Fort Worth village in Texas, as they existed before the

---

[77] *Ibid.*
[78] *Ibid.*, p. 70.
[79] *The Story of the Cowboy*, p. 9: "Description of the Western cattle industry, whether in regard to its features, its characters, or its environments. must be largely a matter of generalization.   The cattle country itself covers a third of the entire territory of the United States."   In his *The Passing of the Frontier* (in *The Chronicles of America*, New Haven, 1921, Vol. XXVI) Hough again uses the material of *The Story of the Cowboy*.

great influx of people from other sections. Here in apt union of actual knowledge and graphic expression Hough reproduces scenes of the "swift and sometime evil blossoming" of cattle towns throughout the vast extent of the ranching country. His is a composite picture of "the little cow towns of the frontier [where] the searcher for vivid things might have found abundance of material." Composed for the most part of a womanless group, the motley population of the usual Western town often consisted of what Hough termed "the flotsam and jetsam of a chaotic flood" : cowboys, half-breeds, gamblers, teamsters, hunters freighters, small storekeepers and tavern owners, petty officials, and dissipated professional men, all part of "an eddy in the troubled stream of Western immigration."[80]

In his particularization of the inhabitants of the typical cow town Hough stresses the versatility of various frontier types. One young and enterprising lawyer in a Western town used a sign which read :

John Jones, Attorney-at-Law. Real Estate and Insurance. Collections promptly attended to at all hours of the day and night. Good Ohio cider for sale at 5 cents a glass.[81]

Among the prominent citizens of such towns there might be the versatile individual who was gambler, farmer, fighter, and schoolteacher all in one. "It was not unusual," Hough writes, "for the justice of the peace to be a barber." In nearly every cow town or mining camp of the West the following were usually to be counted among the citizens : a Jewish merchant who handled the bulk of the business in general supplies ; a sheriff, "quiet, courageous, just, and much respected by his fellowmen" ; a lawyer, frequently something of a personage ; a barber and a druggist who often played the role of dentist and doctor ; an editor who held a certain prestige in political matters ; and other types, such as the saloonkeeper, an occasional man from Leavenworth, cowpunchers from adjoining ranches, wealthy and respected ranchers, and "them girls from Kansas."

Hough recalls also the chief entertainments which enlivened the most remote of the cow towns. News of a ball would bring cowboys from fifty, or more, miles away. On such occasions the entire populace of a town gathered in the largest room in

---

[80] *Ibid.*, p. 238.
[81] *Ibid.*, p. 239.

the community, wherever that might be. Because of the scarcity of feminine partners, no woman, whatever her rank or appearance, was slighted. The Mexican washerwoman, the girls from Kansas, and all other women there assembled were sure of partners for every dance. Other celebrations, attended by people of the most heterogeneous sorts, were in order when the cowmen rode into town with a herd to be shipped. This phase of cow town life is described in the latter half of *North of 36*, Hough's version of the first great drive from the Texas plains to the newly built town of Abilene, Kansas, the nearest shipping point in the late sixties. As Hough pictures it in *The Story of the Cowboy*, "the little cow town of the far-away country, a speck on the great gray plain," was once the background for a very democratic and picturesque society, that of the men of the range and their small town associates.

This free society of the range towns has found further recording in the fiction of Alfred Henry Lewis (1858-1914) and Owen Wister (1860-1938), two observers of the West who became popular during the era of the strenuous life inaugurated by Theodore Roosevelt at the opening of the century. Theirs was the era when a strenuous young school began to rediscover the West. "All at once fiction began to be talked of in terms of 'red blood,' 'men with the bark on,' supermen, and their deeds in the wild areas of actual adventure." Everywhere younger writers like Jack London and Frank Norris were turning to new backgrounds. "No more historical dreamings: the demand was for actuality."[82] During this time of Rooseveltian intensity Lewis, recognizing the fictional possibilities of life on the range, projected his Wolfville series and Wister gained wide popularity with *The Virginian*.

A lawyer and a journalist, Lewis, at twenty-one, abandoned his legal practice in Cleveland for the more romantic occupation of the hobo cowpuncher in the Southwest, then a frontier region which inspired him to write *Wolfville* (1897), *Sandburrs* (1900), *Wolfville Days* (1902), *Wolfville Nights* (1902), *Wolfville Folks* (1908), and *Faro Nell and her Friends* (1913). In these sketches and stories Lewis proved himself one of the pioneers in the interpretation of the range town. He has been termed, like Harte, though less manifestly, the founder of a new school of fiction and the creator of the first authentic portrayal of the

⁸² Pattee, *The New American Literature* (*1890-1930*), p. 105.

hard-riding, hard-living cowboy of the Southwest.[83] In many respects his portrayals of the free, uncertain life of the Arizona cattle country are akin to the sketches of frontier conditions in the Harte stories and *Roughing It*. The humor, frontier idiom, tall tales, and free life depicted in these tales of Arizona show Alfred Lewis's full understanding of the eccentricities of the cowboy as he appeared in town and on the range.[84]

The narrator of the Wolfville tales is a loquacious old cowman, wisely observant of the life around him in the small cattle town of Wolfville, in Tucson (the nearest city), or on his ranch. A homely teller of tales, the Old Cattleman drawls forth his criticisms of the life at Wolfville, a typical cow town of the nineties with its gambling parlors, saloons, rickety hotel, dance halls, and "op'ry house." The counterpart of many cattle towns in the frontier Southwest, Wolfville had a mixed population of cowboys, Mexicans, and Indians whose interests were not wholly confined to the cattle industry. "When I first tracks into Wolfville," so the Old Cattleman's recollections go, "cows is what you might call the leadin' industry, with whiskey an' faro-bank on the side." But with the unearthing of ore, "the mines is opened, an Wolfville's swelled tremendous. We-all even wins a county-seat fight with Red Dog, wherein we puts it all over that ornery hamlet; an' we shorely deals the game for the entire region."[85]

As in Virginia City, there were amusements enough in Wolfville to make life exciting and sometimes uncertain. In the idiomatic words of the Wolfville philosopher,

We visits the Dance Hall; not to dance, sech frivol'ties bein' for younger and less dignified sports. We goes over there more to give our countenance an' endorsements to Hamilton who runs the hurdygurdy, an' who's a mighty proper citizen. We says "How!" to Hamilton, libates, an' mebby watches 'em "balance all," or "swing your partners,' a minute or two an' then proceeds. Then thar's Huggins's Bird Cage Op'ry House, an' now an' then we-all floats

---

[83] Fullerton, *Selective Bibliography of American Literature, 1775-1900*, p. 179. This is later refuted by a statement that Charles Wilkins Webber (1819-56), who came to Texas in 1838, served as a Ranger, and wrote crude, but spirited, stories of the picturesque Southwest, was the true pioneer in the school of "wild West" fiction later established by Lewis (*ibid*, p. 289). See Webber's *Tales of the Southern Border* (New York, 1852). For further material about Lewis see M. G. Boyer, ed., *Arizona in Literature* (Glendale, California, 1934); and *D. A. B.*, XI, 205-206.

[84] See "Some Cowboy Facts," the Introduction to *Wolfville Nights* (New York, 1902).

[85] *Wolfville* (New York, 1897), p. 218.

over thar an' takes in the dramy. But mostly we camps about the
Red Light; the same bein' a common stampin'-ground.[86]

At the post office, the Red Light, and the O. K. Restaurant
the cowman "upholds the hours tellin' tales an' gossipin' about
cattle and killin's, an' other topics common to a cow country."
If the cowboy desired a change of amusement he knew that
he might rely on the stage and his pony "to pull freight with"
when Wolfville life became too pastoral "an' we thirsts for the
meetropolitan gayety of Tucson."[87] Rivalry between dance
hall operators, a Thanksgiving celebration with cowmen from
Red Dog, quarrels with rustlers, excitement and fights over
gambling stakes, funeral services for a Wolfville Buck Fanshaw,
and the cowboys' interest in elections are given "a local habi-
tation and a name" through the narrator's idiomatically
phrased descriptions. Names like Faro Nell, Texas Thompson, Crawfish Jim, Piñon Bill, and Tucson Jennie give a "wild
West" flavor to the Wolfville tales. Lewis, though imitative
a bit of Bret Harte and Mark Twain, has, on the other hand,
preserved in the Wolfville scenes much of the true spirit of
Southwestern cow towns.[88]

It was in 1885 that Owen Wister, on the occasion of a trip to
Wyoming for his health, discovered in the Great Plains frontier a new wonderland and a genuinely appealing pioneer society. After successive trips the transplanted Easterner became an enthusiastic member of the new Western group of
writers. Moved by the encouragement of Howells, who felt
his literary pulse and pronounced it promising, by varied reading from Stevenson, Kipling, and Mérimée, and by continued
vacation wanderings through the Platte Valley and adjoining
regions, Wister began fictionalizing the materials of the cattle
country. After the acceptance by *Harper's* of "How McLean
Came East," he was commissioned to do a series of cowboy
tales. *Red Men and White* (1895), *Lin McLean* (1898), and *The*

[86] "Long Ago on the Rio Grande," *Wolfville Nights*, p. 306.
[87] *Wolfville*, p. 41.
[88] "Wolfville's First Funeral" (*Wolfville*) suggests Fanshaw's funeral in *Roughing
It*, as well as certain phases of "The Outcasts of Poker Flat." The cowboys of
"The Story of Wilkins" and "A Wolfville Foundling" are Southwestern counter-
parts of the big-hearted miners in "The Luck of Roaring Camp," while Old Mon-
te, the stage driver, may have been suggested by Yuba Bill.
   The true spirit of Southwestern cow towns is further preserved in Thomas A.
Janvier's *Santa Fe's Partner, Being Some Memorials of Events in a New Mexican Track-
End Town* (New York, 1907).

Jimmy John Boss (1900) led eventually to the popular *The Virginian* (1902). In all of these Wister, self-styled historical romancer, contrived to preserve the color of a vanished world.

With *The Virginian*, the most popular of Wister's stories of the West, the small town of the Great Plains is moved northward into the sparsely settled region of Wyoming at the close of the last century. Here, deep in cattle land, is Medicine Bow, a "wretched husk of squalor" blotting the endlessly rolling plains of the ranch country. Somber, false-fronted houses, rearing their pitiful masquerade amid a fringe of old tin cans, a diminutive station, two eating-houses, a billiard hall, and a stable place Medicine Bow in the same class with dozens of other cattle towns which once "littered the frontier from the Columbia to the Rio Grande, from the Missouri to the Sierras." These, like Medicine Bow,

. . . lay stark, dotted over a planet of treeless dust, like soiled packs of cards. Each was similar to the next, as one old five-spot of clubs resembles another. Houses, empty bottles, and garbage, they were forever of the same shapeless pattern. More forlorn they were than stale bones. They seemed to have been strewn there by the wind and to be waiting till the wind should come again and blow them away.[89]

Such is Wister's indictment of the monotony of design on which the Western cattle towns usually were patterned. On the other hand, their littleness and foulness were, he says, lessened by the overshadowing immensity and strange beauty of the environing plains and hills. It is this openness of country which appeals most to the romancer in Wister. With its varied descriptions of the open range and its characterizations of assertive frontier types on the ranches within two or three hundred miles of Medicine Bow, *The Virginian* but incidentally contributes toward the literature of the frontier town. The brief Medicine Bow scenes are sufficient, however, to paint the prevailing mode of life in a Wyoming cow town of the nineteenth century. Its primitive society was enlivened periodically by the visits of cowboys, drummers, and, more rarely, an Easterner bold enough to venture into remote, alien country. Boardinghouse hoaxes, gambling, drinking, and shooting, as in Wolfville, were characteristic enough of the place to

[89] *The Virginian: A Horseman of the Plains* (New York, 1902), p. 12.

mark it as distinctly of the frontier. Medicine Bow, for all its meanness and sordidness, typified the self-reliant West where, in the phrasing of the Virginian, no one could be "middling," as in the East, and flourish.

> You've got to deal cyards well; you've got to steal *well;* and if you claim to be quick with your gun you must be quick, for you've a public temptation, and some man will not resist trying to prove he is quicker. You must break all the Commandments *well* in the Western country.[90]

Such was the life re-created in *The Virginian*—the picturesque, free life of the cowpuncher, "the last romantic figure on our soil."[91]

Popular though he has been, Owen Wister has written of the "tough" town in the tradition of the literary man. He is to be thought of as the educated Easterner who chancing to come to the West on a vacation trip remained to describe its fascinating life. To another, however, belongs the credit of having pictured the range country as the cowboy knew it during his danger-fraught days of strenuous herding from the Texas prairies to the valleys of the Platte. But one year after the appearance of *The Virginian* a Texas cowman, Andy Adams— a unique figure until recently undeservedly neglected by literary historians and critics—produced his intimate pictures of the cowpuncher in camp, along the trail, and in town. Adams's story, *The Log of a Cowboy: A Narrative of the Old Trail Days* (1903) is through and through the work of one experienced in the ways of cattlemen. Recently it has been praised as "the only novel of the cattle country destined to become a classic."[92]

For color and naturalness nothing in the fiction of the cattle town surpasses Adams's two chapters (Chapter XIII, "Dodge," and Chapter XVII, "Ogalalla") revealing the cowboy's holiday, at the end of a thousand-mile drive, in wild border towns. As Adams's Georgia-born Texas cowboy experienced it, life in Dodge, Kansas, in 1882, though directed by iron-ruling peace officers, provided for the visiting cowboy full excitement. Enriched by a month's pay, the Texan and his trail buddies "took in the town," from the barbershops, the stores displaying gaudy

[90] *Ibid.*, p. 399.
[91] *Ibid.*, pp. vii-viii. Cf. Walter Webb, *The Great Plains* (New York, 1931), "Literature of the Cattle Kingdom," pp. 455 ff.
[92] Webb, *op. cit.*, p, 456.

clothes, and the Wright House ("at that day a famous hostelry, patronized almost exclusively by the Texas cowmen and cattle buyers") to the Lone Star dance hall, the variety theaters, "and other resorts which, like the wicked, flourish best under darkness." Similar celebrations, described in the idiom of the Old Southwest, await the same group up the trail to the Northwest when they arrive in the valley of the South Platte, where "nestled Ogalalla, the Gomorrah of the cattle trail." As Adams notes, Ogalalla was then a widely known tough town, the rendezvous of Joel Collins, Sam Bass, and other dangerous, boisterous characters. "From amongst its half hundred buildings, no church spire pointed upward, but instead three fourths of its business houses were dance halls, gambling houses, and saloons."[93] With such unlicensed places of amusement, where gambling, drinking, and fighting prevailed and adventuresses of every grade and condition practiced "a careless exposure of their charms," remote Ogalalla was indeed "a town which [had] no night."[94] As a most excellent narrative of the manifold interests of the old trail days *The Log of a Cowboy* deserves a lasting place in the literature of the frontier.

Since the earlier days of national expansion the frontier town has offered varying patterns to the writers of the Middle Border, the Mountain West, and the Far West. New soil, new people, and new customs united in forming a multicolored design for the literature of the frontier town. Crude log towns in the Michigan backwoods and barren settlements on the far-reaching plains; somnolent river towns along an older frontier; tiny cattle towns, mere dots on the widespread range; scattered military posts; and lawless mining camps of the boom days in Colorado, Arizona, Nevada, and California—these are the small town outposts which during the strenuous years of the past century (before the frontier spirit, so long dominant, weakened in the wake of growing industrialism and the pressure of the outside world) were put to literary use by men and women who themselves were often active participants in strange pioneer ventures.

[93] *The Log of a Cowboy* (New York, 1903), p. 259. In 1927 Houghton Mifflin brought out a new edition of this book.
[94] *Ibid.*, p. 261.

CHAPTER IX

"SOUTHERNTOWN" IN BACK COUNTRY AND TIDEWATER

THE DIFFERENCE between the early Southern culture and the Northern was, as we have noted, the result of the difference between their origins and subsequent surroundings. From the very beginning the spirit of the two sections was different and their surrounding conditions were for a long time such as to keep them diverse. In the early South the existence of a flourishing plantation system and the dominance of a so-called "landocracy"* retarded the normal development of towns and cities. Thomas Jefferson probably spoke for his generation of Virginians when he said, "I view great cities as pestilential to the morals, the health and the liberties of man."[1] Agriculture, directly and indirectly, furnished the major share of income ; industrialization, comparatively considered, was slow in development. (Even until more recent times Southern manufacturing has been considered "as largely agrarian manufacturing, physically decentralized and not necessitating an excessive urbanization.")[2] According to A. G. Bradley, so late as the Reconstruction towns had a comparatively small place in Southern economy, except as centers for country business and, on a greater or lesser scale, for tobacco manufacturing and retail trade, largely run by Jews, Irish, or Germans.[3] The early established institutions and traditions of Southern life, therefore, were unfavorable, if not openly antagonistic, not only to the rise of a highly developed urban civilization, but to the establishment of a literary profession as well.

As the literarily unproductive eighteenth century gave way to the nineteenth many Southerners (Poe, Simms, and others) lamented the lack of a literature indigenous to the South. In

---

* This coinage belongs to A. G. Bradley, an Englishman, who lived for ten years in the South.

[1] H. J. Ford, ed., *Writings of Thomas Jefferson*, VII, 459.

[2] H. C. Nixon, "Whither Southern Economy?" from *I'll Take My Stand: The South and the Agrarian Tradition* (New York, 1930), p. 180. See also Edd Winfield Parks, "Southern Towns and Cities," *Culture in the South*, ed. by W. T. Couch (Chapel Hill, 1934), pp. 501-518.

[3] *Other Days* (London, 1913), p. 256.

his glorification of ante-bellum life Thomas Nelson Page pauses long enough to regret the flourishing of oratory, while Southern critics, "who might have shone on the *Edinburgh Review*" and "our writers who might have made an Augustan literature" woefully lacked the needed stimulus of close mental contacts.[4] The paucity of literary productions in the Old South he attributes to the marked absence of cities and the want of publishing houses; the absorption of the intellectual forces of the people of the South by the problems of slavery; the general ambition of Southerners for political distinction; and the lack of a reading public in the South for American authors, "due in part to the conservatism of the Southern people."[5]

With the responsibility for the want of a literature resting not so much with the writers as the environment, it is a natural consequence that, until recent times, the literature of the Southern town has been relatively negligible. During the eighteenth century and well into the nineteenth the only contemporary records of ante-bellum town life in the South were travel accounts and social sketches. Shortly after the Revolution, and even during its progress, America was visited by various Europeans who came with the express purpose of traveling through the country. Germans, English, French, Swedes, and others came to see the wonders of the new country, and often they journeyed with notebook ready. Many of them gave exaggerated observations of scenes, people, and customs which offered themselves incidentally in all parts of the country. In addition to foreign visitors, like John Davis, J. F. D. Smyth, and Harriet Martineau, Johann D. Schoepf, and F. M. Bayard, itinerant actors (Sol Smith and others) and Northern visitors (often tutors who were graduates of the New England colleges and Yankee peddlers) wrote weightily entitled descriptions, including pictures of insignificant Southern villages, frontier hamlets, and the more flourishing towns of Baltimore, Williamsburg, and Charleston.[6]

---

[4] *The Old South Essays Social and Political* (New York, 1896), p. 6.

[5] *Ibid.*, "Authorship in the South before the War," p. 59. Cf. Stark Young, ed., *Southern Treasury of Life and Literature* (New York, 1937), pp. vi-viii. In making the assumption that the Old South showed a lack of literary development, one should, thinks Mr. Young, remember "that the rest of the United States has not done so either."

[6] In addition to Smyth, *op. cit.*, and Martineau, *op. cit.*, these contain occasional pictures of the Southern village: A. J. Morrison, tr., Johann D. Schoepf: *Travels in the Confederation (1784-1794)* (Philadelphia, 1911); John Pope, *A Tour Through*

20

Small town records of another nature, developing before the Civil War, include the humorously realistic sketches of a group of Southern local colorists and frontier humorists, earliest of whom was Augustus Baldwin Longstreet whose popular *Georgia Scenes*, the first of which appeared in the *Southern Recorder* (1832), inaugurated a unique literary movement.[7]   Another pre-war treatment of the Southern town came from a small serious group, including John Pendleton Kennedy, William Gilmore Simms, John Esten Cooke, and a few others who called themselves romantic realists.   Until the time of Ellen Glasgow, the few writers developing after the Civil War adhered rather closely to the humorous and romantic trends mentioned above.   On the whole, both the actual Southern town and its literary counterpart have been of slow and sporadic growth.   The really distinctive treatments did not appear until recent times.   In late years, with the work of T. S. Stribling and others, the much-reported "battle of the village" has been shifting from Midwestern to Southern ground.   At last, the Southern small town has come into the limelight.

VILLAGE SCENES OF THE OLD SOUTHWEST

In the thirties, forties, and fifties, "in the good old times of muster days and quarter racing, before the camp meeting and the barbecue had lost their charm; when men led simple, homely lives, doing their love-making as they did their fighting and their plowing, in a straight line,"[8] there was in the South and Old Southwest (Georgia, Alabama, Mississippi, and Tennessee) a definite, but brief, literary movement manifesting itself in humorous and spontaneous sketches of contemporary life.   During this period, before the Civil War had despoiled earlier traditions, conditions in the South favored the frontier humorist and local colorist.   It is not odd why at this time a school of realistic literature took rise, for the material was at hand and the writers were an integral part of the life they undertook to depict.   Throughout this section, much of which was rustic or pioneer in character, there developed, as Frank-

the *Southern and Western Territories of the United States* (Richmond, 1790); F. M. Bayard, *Voyage dans L'intérieur des États-Unis* (Paris, 1791); and John Davis, *Travels in America during 1798, 1799, 1800, and 1802* (London, 1803).

[7] John D. Wade, *Augustus Baldwin Longstreet: A Study of the Development of Culture in the South* (New York, 1924), p. 384.

[8] Henry Watterson, ed., *Oddities in Southern Life and Character* (Boston, 1883), p. vii.

lin J. Meine has admirably explained, "a picturesque group of humorists who flourished in bar-rooms, on law circuits, on steamboats, and in the wide open spaces. They were not professional humorists, but debonair settlers engaged in various tasks : lawyers, newspaper editors, country gentlemen of family and fortune, doctors, army officers, travellers, actors—who wrote for amusement rather than for gain."[9] Emergent figures, these young men followed not the prevalent traditions of elegant literature by slavishly echoing "Mr. Pope," "Mr. Addison," and "Mr. Steele," but, observing the provincial life about them, seized upon local peculiarities of speech and custom and the incongruities of setting as material for uproarious mirth. Frequently prefatory excuses revealed that the publication of an author's sketches was, according to the custom of the day, purely a concession to the entreaties of friends. Sometimes an unknown young writer, desiring to conceal his authorship, wrote under two signatures.[10] Again, he might make a show of independence, as follows : "Ef yu ain't fond ove the smell ove cracklins, stay outen the kitchen; ef yu is fear'd ove smut, yu needn't climb the chimbley; an' ef the moon hurts yu eyes, don't yu ever look at a Dutch cheese. . . . Ef eny poor misfortinit devil . . . kin fine a laugh, jis' one, sich a laugh as is remembered wif his keerless boyhood, atwixt these yere kivers —then, I'll thank God that I *hes* made a book, an' feel that I hev got my pay in full."[11]

Material for the humorous treatment of character and incident was abundant in various localities : in Middle Georgia, an agricultural country where "no impassable chasm shut off the 'po whites,' completely ostracizing them as was the case in many parts of the Southern states"; in isolated village communities of the Great Smokies; in Alabama and Mississippi of the "flush" times; and elsewhere along and beyond the Mississippi. In village and country at circuit courts, revivals, weddings, infares, quiltings, corn shuckings, fish frys, shooting matches, militia drills, horse races, cock fights, and informal, gossipy gatherings at local doggeries [grocery stores] the daily doings and local life were sufficient to produce anecdotes, community legends, and tall tales and furnish inspiration for hu-

[9] Meine, ed., *Tall Tales of the Southwest* (New York, 1930), pp. xv-xvi.
[10] Longstreet, *Georgia Scenes* (New York, 1897), p. iv. Preface to the first edition (1835).
[11] George W. Harris, *Sut Lovingood* (New York, 1867), pp. x-xi.

morous provincial figures : for shrewd Captain Simon Suggs, whose favorite aphorism was "It is good to be shifty in a new country"—at the expense of others ; Ovid Bolus, Esq., whose "reputation stood higher for lying than for anything else" ; practical jokester, Ned Brace ; Sut Lovingood, "a queer looking, long legged, short bodied, small headed, white haired, hog eyed, funny sort of a genius" ; and Major Joseph Jones, Esq., from Pinesville, Georgia. Such were the rough-and-ready characters created by Southern fun makers whom John D. Wade has described as "the court-jesters of a homogeneous culture," a culture which has crumbled with the entrenchment of cosmopolitanism.[12]

During the thirties, and after, the rapid growth of newspapers and periodicals contributed materially toward this vogue for provincial tales and sketches. Countless anecdotes, character studies marked by a rollicking humor, and exaggerated local stories appeared, often anonymously, in newspaper and magazine and were popular everywhere, in larger towns and villages. "Many a smaller community that boasted a job-print-shop and a young lawyer or printer with an itch to be an editor, supported a local news-sheet featuring humorous sketches. Humorous material was always in demand ; and so the growth of the newspaper encouraged the local humorist."[13]   It was in this fashion that Judge Longstreet, with his initial half-fictitious sketches appearing in a Milledgeville, Georgia, paper, began the series later published on his own press in Augusta, 1835, as *Georgia Scenes, Characters, Incidents, etc. in the First Half-Century of the Republic, By a Native Georgian.*   William Tappan Thompson, associated with Longstreet as a printer for the Augusta *Sentinel,* Johnson J. Hooper, and, later, Joel Chandler Harris also published their stories through their newspaper affiliations. Thus, in much the same manner and about the same years of the Jacksonian era as those unlettered philosophers, peddler

<hr/>

[12] "Southern Humor," Couch, ed., *op. cit.,* p. 623.
[13] Meine, ed., *op. cit.,* p. xxvii.   For special studies in ante-bellum Southern periodicals see A. S. Salley, "Southern Magazines," Charleston *Sunday News* (Aug. 27, 1899) ; E. R. Rogers, *Four Southern Magazines* (Charlottesville, 1902) ; B. B. Minor, *The Southern Literary Messenger, 1834-1864* (Washington and New York, 1905) ; Edwin Mims, "Southern Magazines," *The South in the Building of the Nation* (1909), VII, 21 ff. ; Jay B. Hubbell, "Southern Magazines," Couch, ed., *op. cit.,* pp. 159 ff. ; D. K. Jackson, *Poe and The Southern Literary Messenger* (Richmond, 1934), and *The Contributors and Contributions to The Southern Literary Messenger, 1834 -1864* (Charlottesville, Virginia, 1936) ; and W. S. Hoole, *A Check-List and Finding-List of Charleston Periodicals, 1732-1864* (Durham, 1936).

Sam Slick ("a ring-tailed roarer") and that Down-Easter and yarner, Major Jack Downing, gained popular notice as rustic critics of affairs, in the newspapers and other mediums of the South a new type of local literature was emerging.

As story after story appeared in the Georgia, Alabama, and other newspapers and periodicals, or in William T. Porter's popular humorous journal, the New York *Spirit of the Times* (1831-46), new scenes, newly conceived comic countrymen, local satirists and rustic observers, set up a unique pattern in the literature of Southern village and rural life. In isolated villages and rural sections there was perceived richly varied material possessing interest, if not the values of belles-lettres. In Middle Georgia, for example, life during the thirties and even later has been described as almost archaic in its simplicity. The social unit, as in other pioneer districts, was the trading post, with its nondescript tavern and general merchandise store where liquor was included among the staple supplies.[14] Even slavery existed here in its mildest forms, for the plantations were smaller. The poorer classes, who were treated by their superiors with the confidence and respect that their sturdy independence commanded, were a simple, unlettered folk, full of hardihood, given to doing what they pleased with the King's English, and ever ready for all the fun of quarter racing, target shooting, wrestling matches, talking, and the more formal celebrations of "public days."[15] Georgia of these days was a melting pot lacking the rigid social codes of the great Virginia plantations and the Carolina Low Country, where Williamsburg and Charleston were centers of a gay society whose members clung tenaciously to their family associations and cult of culture. In the midst of the anomalous conditions of Georgian society and of the more turbulent way of life along the newly opened frontier of Mississippi, Arkansas, and Texas, there arose a group of character writers led on by Judge Longstreet in his rude but graphic pictures of his own countryside. Various peoples and dialects for the first time appeared in story, sketch, and tall tale. In addition to Longstreet, other realists, such as Joseph Glover Baldwin, George Washington Harris, Johnson Jones Hooper, and Thompson, all gifted with a lively sense

14 Wade, *op, cit.*, p. 61.
15 Sophie B. Herrick, "Richard Malcolm Johnston," *Century Magazine*, XXXVI, 277 (June, 1888).

of humor and a keen insight into human nature, localized various communities and peculiar types by adapting the most commonplace incidents to stories of the transitory frontier and agricultural life of Georgia, Tennessee, Alabama, Mississippi, and adjoining districts.

Some of these frontier entertainers (Longstreet, Baldwin, Charles H. Smith, creator of Bill Arp, and others) were small town lawyers in a day when the country was so thinly settled that the legal profession was peculiarly unstable.

A bevy of practitioners following the court in its sessions made a peripatetic society for themselves. The scenes in court were sometimes irresistibly funny; the peculiarities of the people, the incongruity of the setting, all supplied material for uproarious mirth in the symposium that followed each day's work.[16]

During these days and nights filled with laugh-provoking court experiences and robust story telling the tales which these men "swapped" admirably developed their natural gifts as raconteurs and made them adept in the fictional adaptation of a dialect familiar to them since childhood. Reminiscences of these circuit lawyers abound in racy anecdotes told from town to town.

Augustus Longstreet easily stands first among these antebellum humorists who have left such inimitable pictures of their contemporary towns and countrysides. He is the forerunner of those later Georgians, Richard Malcolm Johnston and Joel Chandler Harris, whose more polished art was developed after the Civil War. As with most of his contemporaries, with Longstreet literature was a pastime, an enjoyable release from his professional duties as a Middle Georgia lawyer and judge, small town editor, minister, and self-sufficient, energetic man of affairs.

This is the man, the anonymous author of the newly published *Georgia Scenes* whom Poe, in the *Southern Literary Messenger* for March, 1836 (II, 287-292), described and introduced as

. . . a clever fellow, imbued with a spirit of the truest humor, and endowed, moreover, with an exquisitely discriminative and penetrating understanding of *character* in general, and of Southern character in particular.

[16] *Ibid.*, p. 279.

Truly, Longstreet was a part of all the provincial life which he so penetratingly reveals. From his early childhood in the rapidly growing frontier town of Augusta and, later, on a plantation at Edgefield, in the South Carolina country not many miles distant from Augusta, he had a familiar acquaintance with small town and rural folk. A few years later, with his friend, George McDuffie, he was a student at the backwoods school of the Reverend Doctor Moses Waddel at Willington, across the Savannah River in South Carolina a few miles from Augusta. Years later in his didactic novel, *Master William Mitten* (1858), begun when he was president of Centenary College in Louisiana, Longstreet described the oak-shaded community formed by the buildings of the school.[17] Following the way of his neighbor, John C. Calhoun, and other Southern youths of the time, Gus Longstreet went northward to Yale to complete his education. In New England, where at New Haven he was a member of the class of 1813 and at Litchfield, Connecticut, a law student, the youth from Georgia found a town life for whose social activities of dancing, card playing, dramatic entertainment, and other amusements his experience in Augusta had in a measure prepared him.[18] After his return to Augusta in 1814 he was admitted to the bar. Here in a Georgia "now passing a transitory moment as the American frontier" he began a long course of observation and experience through his travels around judicial circuits (courthouse towns boasting of a tavern or two and the scenes of uncommon bustle during court sessions), and, fun loving as he was, enjoyed a general acquaintance with those racy characters which laid the foundation for the broad humor and local tone of the one work by which he is best remembered, *Georgia Scenes*. In this work, with its human oddities, infectious hilarity, and freedom from restraint, Longstreet has preserved the easy rollicking life of frontier Georgia and the borderland of South Carolina as he knew it intimately in the towns and rural communities of Augusta, Milledgeville, Covington, Edgefield, Greensboro, Swainsboro, and elsewhere. Energetic, witty, impulsive, and at home among plain people, Judge Longstreet truly belonged to "a plebian world that approved his plebian qualities" and,

[17] *Op. cit.* (Macon, 1889), pp. 100-102. Cf. O. P. Fitzgerald, *Judge Longstreet: A Life Sketch* (Nashville, 1891), pp. 166-167.
[18] Wade, *op. cit.*, p. 40.

294 THE SMALL TOWN IN AMERICAN LITERATURE

if his *Georgia Scenes* is not polite literature, it is an honest reproduction of a way of life now long past and, as such, is regarded as one of the fountainheads of that humorous Southern realism before Mark Twain.[19]

While some of the nineteen* sketches of the *Georgia Scenes* do not portray town life, all of them are connected by their treatment of various customs peculiar to a closely knit democratic world of farms and smaller plantations, crossroads stores and trading villages, and larger towns like Augusta. Longstreet's interest is in typical town and rural activities, humorous situations, and character portrayals rather than in the meticulous description of the physical background. As Henry Watterson early pointed out, these studies are "the simplest transcriptions of the humorous phases of the life and period embraced by them, done in charcoal, without effort and without pretense. . . ."[20]

Interested himself in the social life of the Lower South, Longstreet frequently centered his sketches around some community gathering where the most intense popular interest prevailed whether the amusement be furnished by Captain Clodpole's local militia, ludicrously unmilitary in company parade, or by the merry business of dancing, in those days "a jovial, heart-stirring, foot-stirring amusement."[21] The more robust elements, in town and country, met their fellows, with whom they swapped jokes and gossip, gambled, engaged in fist fights, got "royally corned," and indulged in horseplay, at tavern and marketplace, race course and target practice field, gander pullings and country "turnouts." The more artificially polite citizens, those whom Longstreet satirizes for pretending to have a culture they could never possess, found satisfaction by at-

* "The Militia Company Drill," says Longstreet, *op. cit.*, p. 196, was written by an observing friend.
[19] Quoted matter from V. L. Parrington, *The Romantic Revolution in America, 1800-1860* (New York, 1927), p. 168.
[20] *Op. cit.*, p. 2.
[21] *Georgia Scenes*, "The Militia Company Drill" and "The Ball," 1897 edition, pp. 196 ff. and 160. Longstreet's early biographer, Bishop Fitzgerald, *op. cit.*, pp. 34-35, says that mention of the Georgia militia brought to old timers memories of fun and frolic, of bloodless war and epauleted glory. "The muster-day was a great day for the patriots who compulsorily and awkwardly marched and countermarched, and mangled the military manuals; for the sellers and drinkers of corn whiskey and hard cider; for the venders and consumers of ginger-cakes; and for the bullies and experts who contended for the championship in fighting, wrestling, running, jumping, and shooting. It was a great day, too, for the politicians who took advantage of the gatherings of the voters in large masses to air their eloquence and solicit popular suffrage."

tracting attention as leaders of jigs and cotillions, self appointed fun-makers at debating societies, crude performers at the wax-works and other amateur theatricals, and entertainers, in the grand manner taught by Madame Piggisqueaki of Philadel-phia, at musical teas.

While there is no sting in his humor, in some of the sketches Longstreet, or his narrator (appearing under the pseudonyms of Hall and Baldwin), is the town's social mentor, either scorn-ful of or amused by artificial, attention-loving beaux and belles, frontier dowagers delighting in chit-chat, wearisomely boastful and indulgent parents, and neglectful wives. There is that artificial pianist and simpering singer, Philadelphia educated Miss Aurelia Emma Theodosia Augusta Crump, whose un-natural warbling reminded Hall of "the squall of a pinched cat."[22] Again, that "charming creature," Miss Evelina Caro-line Smith, affected and finishing-school trained daughter of a prosperous, but almost illiterate, village merchant, suggests Longstreet's occasional tendency for moralizing and his in-debtedness to the eighteenth-century English essayists. Comic character types, further designed to ridicule the pretensions of village "society," are noticeable among the guests at a town ball. Here Mrs. Mushy gossips about Miss Gilt and Mr. Flirt, and the Misses Feedle and Deedle carry on utterly conventional tête-a-têtes with Messrs. Noozle and Boozle.[23]

It is not as an emulator of the moral tone of some of the Addison and Steele essays that Longstreet is at his best. His most original characteristic appears in the extremely humor-ous delineation of the more robust activities already mentioned and in his good natured, but none the less realistic, character drawings of the Ransy Sniffles, Ned Braces, and Bob Durhams, ever present figures at taverns and other gathering places where excitement was in the air. Longstreet had a natural gift for the revelation of local eccentricities. There is keen insight in-to human nature, but no trenchantly biting sarcasm, in his portrayal of Ned Brace, native Georgian and provincial jester who lived "only to amuse himself with his fellow-beings."[24] His "devilabilities" at tavern, church, funeral, and market-place show that humor has been his "besetting sin from youth

[22] *Ibid.*, "The Song," p. 90.
[23] *Ibid.*, "The Ball," *passim*.
[24] *Ibid.*, "The Character of a Native Georgian," p. 34.

up." Clayeater Ransy Sniffle, with a complexion like a corpse, was never happier than "when he was witnessing, fomenting, or talking about a fight." Slyly Ransy "egged on" those bullying gamecocks, Billy Stallings and Bob Durham, into scratching, biting, and gouging encounters which delighted the loafers around Zephaniah Atwater's store. A picture as truly descriptive of a crowd's curiosity and craving for amusement as a painting by Hogarth or Hazlitt's "The Fight" is that of a race in Georgia, where

. . . crowds of persons, of all ages, sexes, conditions, and complexions, were seen moving toward the booths ; some on foot, some on horseback, some in gigs, some in carriages, some in carts, and some in wagons. The carriages (generally filled with well-dressed ladies) arranged themselves about thirty or forty paces from the starting-point, towards the center of the turf. Around these circled many young gentlemen, each riding his prettiest, spurring, and curbing his horse into the most engaging antics, and giving visible token that he thought every eye from the carriages was on him, and every heart overpowered by his horsemanship. As many more plied between the booths and carriages, bearing messages, rumors, apples, oranges, raisins, lemonade and *punch*.[25]

The small towns of *Georgia Scenes*, as unromantically different from Freneau's "rural retreat" as anything could be, bear all the marks of the rough democracy of the back country which flourished not far distant from the planter aristocracy of the seaboard. These are the backgrounds for a semi-primitive society, more Western than Southern, for a boisterously rough and independent population never completely a part of the plantation system, and for all the fighting, roistering, horseplay, and community socializing of frontier days in Middle and Western Georgia. Not far away from these provincial towns, where self-made merchants and other local leaders took pride in their piano-playing daughters and academy-trained sons, where the citizens amused themselves with balls, teas, dinners, and religious and political affairs, there were the country folk, "the 'poor whites,' the most ignorant and yet

[25] *Ibid.*, "The Turf," pp. 207-208. Equally descriptive of a moving, boisterous, coarsely joking Georgia crowd is Longstreet's sketch, "Darby Anvil," first published, according to Wade, in the Augusta *Mirror*, 1839. (Later it was included in *Georgia Scenes, New and Old* which appeared in Fitzgerald, *op. cit.*, pp. 211-241.) Especially f·ank in his exposure of the chicanery of frontier politicians, Longstreet vividly pictures in this sketch a political rally, or barbecue, and a town election.

probably the most well-meaning people in the United States."[26] Though near their fellow Georgians, the townspeople, these crackers "dwelt in log houses, had their water from springs, dressed mostly in homespun, danced lustily on old-fashioned puncheon floors, chewed tobacco, dipped snuff, and drank hard liquor by the quart."[27] Yarning, swearing, fighting frontiersmen, they offered ready material to a circuit-riding lawyer and observant, folk-loving clergyman.

Kindly and humorous, without acerbity of wit, but with the realism of Defoe and Fielding, Longstreet in these sketches, for whose coarseness he made apologies, offers an honest, unglossed criticism of a small town and country life long vanished.[28] Perhaps, as he cautiously prefaced the first edition, these sketches do "consist of nothing more than fanciful *combinations* of *real* incidents and characters"; but, nevertheless, the frank realism of situation, characterization, and dialect has preserved the social records of a sturdy yeomanry, frontier townsmen, clay eaters, clodhoppers, and crackers. For this achievement Longstreet ranks as a pioneer recorder of humor of situation, of local transaction, and of common life in the small towns and farming communities of pre-war Georgia.

His influence on the trend of Southern community literature manifested itself speedily a little more than a decade after the anonymous publication of his own sketches in Georgia newspapers. The popularity of the Augusta edition (1835) of *Georgia Scenes* and of the ten other editions, issued by Harper from 1840 to 1897, influenced the type of frontier studies produced by many Southern imitators. Earliest among these was Ohio-born William Tappan Thompson (1812-82), printer and journalist once associated with Longstreet in editing the Augusta *Sentinel*.[29] After later experiences on other Georgia small town newspapers, Thompson during the early forties won notoriety with a series of humorous sketches, letters writ-

---

[26] Carl Holliday, *A History of Southern Literature* (New York and Washington, 1906), p. 160.
[27] W. F. Taylor, *A History of American Letters* (New York, 1936), p. 221.
[28] Fitzgerald, *op. cit.*, pp. 164-166, cites from Longstreet's own comments concerning the authenticity of characters and backgrounds in the *Georgia Scenes*. In spite of the misapprehension of the public, says Longstreet, "the aim of the author was to supply a chasm in history which has always been overlooked—the manners, customs, amusements, wit, dialect, as they appear in all grades of society to ear and eye witness of them."
[29] W. P. Trent, *Southern Writers* (New York, 1905), pp. 252-253; Wade, *op. cit.*, p. 166; and Napier Wilt, *Some American Humorists* (New York, 1929), pp. 56-57.

ten supposedly by an illiterate villager and thorough rustic, Joseph Jones—dubbed Major because of his position on the local militia drill team.   These were addressed to Thompson, then editor of the *Southern Miscellany*, Madison, Georgia.   These "sketches of rustic life and character," Thompson wrote later, "were written to give variety and local interest to the columns of a Georgia country newspaper."[30]   The original design, he explained, was to portray the Southern cracker, a class of provincial but good people with whom he was closely associated, "with no more exaggeration than was necessary to give distinction to the picture.   For this purpose the local dialect or *patois* peculiar to the rural district of Georgia was employed. . . ."[31] The letters themselves, together with later sketches in collected editions, present a miscellany of rural, small town, and larger town life so closely resembling *Georgia Scenes* as to prove confusing to some contemporary readers.

In the series published in book form as *Major Jones' Courtship* (1840) Major Jones's amusing courtship adventures—developed simply, as Watterson noted, with no obstruction, no plot, no villain—furnish the unifying links for a series of provincial scenes.   Muster drills, tavern activities, religious excitement common to many small towns of the period, the usual community gossip, occasional visits of the townspeople to Macon, "Augusty," Athens, or other larger towns, holiday fun, and countless other realistic features of town life form the material, the homespun stuff, out of which Thompson creates the little community of Pineville, Middle Georgia.

Unique among comic heroes in his frank chatting about his personal affairs, Major Jones, a simple, straightforward, honest Georgia lad, is well-to-do and shrewd, although his education in "grammer" and "retorik" has been neglected.   He has the faculty of making himself ridiculous, especially in his attempts to gain the favor of Miss Mary Stallins, "the darlinest gal in the county."   His own credulity and innocence of his rustic manners add to the fun.   Using the cracker vernacular, the Major writes to editor Thompson about his deep love for Miss Mary and the difficulties of his courting.   Like Longstreet's "high falutin' females," Miss Mary, when newly returned from

---

[30] *Major Jones' Courtship, with other Scenes, Incidents, and Adventures in a Series of Letters by Himself.*   Revised (New York, 1872), p. 4.
[31] *Ibid.*, p. 7.

Wesleyan Female College, disturbs the unsophisticated Major with her high talk.

> Before she went she used to be just as plain as a old shoe, and used to go fishin' and huckleberryin' with us, with nothin' but a calico sunbonnet on, ...

Now she puzzles the Major, for she has the manners of a "schoolmarm" and calls him "Mr. Jones" instead of "jest Joe." He is puzzled, too, by her talk about the pleasant companions she had at Macon. Enlightenment comes only when the Major goes all the way to Macon to attend the Female College commencement exercises—he calls them "the zamminations." Here, while Mary carries the honors of the occasion, Jones learns for the first time that her much talked of "Matthew Matix, Nat Filosophy, Al. Geber, Retric Stronomy, and a whole heap of fellers" were not her city beaux.[32]

In the 1843 Philadelphia edition of *Major Jones' Chronicles of Pineville, embracing Sketches of Georgia* (also issued as *Major Jones' Scenes in Georgia, etc.*) other phases of small town life in Georgia in the early nineteenth century add variety to Major Jones's amatory experiences and show that Thompson, like Longstreet, was a realist who saw in many situations of the commonplace a humorous aspect. Resembling much of the humorous village literature of the pre-war South, these backwoods sketches are deliberately styled with homely idiomatic phrasing and misspelling designed to increase the humor of the content. One of the best-known town sketches, claimed by a recent critic as influencing Mark Twain in the writing of a part of *Huckleberry Finn*, is "The Great Attraction."[33] The circus has come to Pineville! The whole village is in a state of extraordinary excitement and the old and young flock to "the great attraction." "Boss Ankles" treats a trite theme, but furnishes a realistic picture of a small town grocery store, where the usual types of loafers make a rural simpleton the butt of a practical joke by inducing him to smoke a loaded cigar. "The Mystery Revealed" contains a scene familiar to any small townsman, that of loungers and local gossips assembled around the piazza of the village hotel, "to pick their teeth in company, whittle the backs of the split-bottomed chairs, and

[32] *Ibid.*, pp. 20 and 33 ff.
[33] Bernard De Voto, *Mark Twain's America*, p. 254.

discuss the topics of the day." Here the town oracles talk
authoritatively about the price of cotton, the prospects of the
corn crop, and the weather.   Mark Twain's well-known and
vivid description of the somnolence of a Mississippi river town
(*Life on the Mississippi*) comes to mind as one reads Thompson's
story.   When the conversation has reached its lowest mark the
hotel loungers are startled out of their lethargy by the rattling
noise of a buggy, drawn by a jaded horse and driven by two
heavily veiled women.   Since the strange travelers do not stop,
but drive furiously through the town, the idlers believe that
the women are bank robbers from Columbus, who, thus disguised, are making away with their booty.   The suddenly
stirred loafers give a spirited chase, catch the strangers, and,
with great importance, bring them before the local court.   To
the consternation and chagrin of the pursuers, the veiled women
prove to be none other than two of their townsmen, perpe-
trators of a joke upon their gullible fellow-citizens.

These and other less distinctive Pineville representations of
the long continued and variously revised Major Jones's sketches
are faithful, if not literary, transcripts of past conditions and
genuinely humorous genre pictures of Georgia small town life.[34]
In representative quality, both as to the dramatis personae
and the cracker vernacular employed, these studies are genuinely racy of the soil and distinctly Georgian.[35]

In advertising the merits of one of their current popular
books, just out a year, D. Appleton and Company in 1854 released this statement :

These sketches of the "Flush Times" of our own day, personating
our own citizens, are written with entertaining spirit, elegance, and
humor, and cannot fail to contribute to the enjoyment and gratifi-
cation of all readers.[36]

This book was *The Flush Times of Alabama and Mississippi*, parts
of which appeared in 1853 in the *Southern Literary Messenger*, and
the author was Joseph Glover Baldwin (1815-64), a native Vir-

[34] In addition to the earlier Major Jones series Thompson wrote *Major Jones'
Sketches of Travel* (Philadelphia, 1848), travel experiences of the simple Major who
actually ventures far beyond his native village.
[35] Watterson, *op. cit.*, p. 134.
[36] Publisher's advertisement included in *The Flush Times of Alabama and Mississippi: A Series of Sketches* (New York, 1854).   Jennette Tandy, *Crackerbox Philosophers, etc.* (New York, 1925), p. 97, says that in six months after publication
twenty thousand copies of *The Flush Times* were sold.

ginian of good family, who in the mid-thirties "with the scant outfit of a pony, clothing sufficient to fill a pair of saddlebags, and some Virginia bank bills . . . left behind him the red hills of his native Shenandoah Valley home and leisurely pursued his way through Southwest Virginia, East Tennessee, and Alabama to a point in Mississippi where his shortness of funds urged the immediate pitching of his tent."[37] Settling in De Kalb, Kemper County, Mississippi, and later in Gainesville, North Alabama, a busy shipping point on the Tombigbee River, Baldwin made full use of his opportunity to observe the changing panorama of an exciting life in a new country filled with settlers from many parts of the world. He had arrived in the Old Southwest during the "flush times," which he described as "that halycon period ranging from the year of grace 1835 to 1837—that golden era when shinplasters were the sole currency, when bank bills were 'as thick as autumn leaves in Vallambrosa,' and credit was a franchise."[38] The reactions of an adventurous, yet educated, Virginian to all this changing world in which he now sought profitable enterprise are recorded best in his own charcoal sketch of "the reign of humbug and wholesale insanity, just overthrown in time to save the whole country from ruin."

This country was just settling up. Marvelous accounts had gone forth of the fertility of its virgin lands ; and the productions of the soil were commanding a price remunerating to slave labor. . . . Emigrants came flocking in. . . . The new country seemed to be a reservoir, and every road leading to it a vagrant stream of enterprise and adventure. Money, or what passed for money, was the only cheap thing to be had. Every cross-road and every avocation presented an opening, through which a fortune was seen by the adventurer in near perspective.

During this wonderful revolution finance worked upon the principles of a charity hospital. The state banks "were issuing their bills by the sheet." To refuse credit was, perhaps, to be bowie-knifed.

Under this stimulating process prices rose like smoke. Lots in obscure villages were held at city prices ; lands, bought at the mini-

[37] George Mellen, "Joseph Glover Baldwin," in E. A. Alderman and Joel Chandler Harris, *Library of Southern Literature* (New Orleans, 1909), I, 175.
[38] *Flush Times, etc.*, p. 3. Cf. S. A. Link, *Pioneers of Southern Literature* (Nashville, 1900), II, 488.

mum cost of government, were sold at from thirty to forty dollars
per acre, and considered dirt cheap at that.   In short, the country
had got to be a full anti-type of California, in all except the gold.
Society was wholly unorganized, there was no restraining public
opinion, the law was well-nigh powerless, and religion scarcely was
heard of except as furnishing the oaths and technic of profanity.[39]

These were the boom days, as Baldwin knew them, in the
newly made towns of Alabama and Mississippi, raw settlements
where the village "doggeries" were "in full blast" ; gaming and
horse-racing well-patronized amusements ; and murder frequently found to be committed in self-defense.   Prudence gave
way to the riotous carnival of profligacy.   "Larceny grew not
only respectable, but genteel and ruffled in all the pomp of
purple and fine linen."   Felony, dishonesty in public office,
arrogant pretension, unmitigated rowdyism, and bullying in-
solence spread like an epidemic.   The stampede was on.
Paper fortunes multiplied ; houses changed hands ; real estate
see-sawed up as morals went down ; and "men of straw, cor-
pulent with bank bills," strutted along the streets of town and
village.   Shylock himself could not have lived in such towns.
Finally, however, panic came "in the midst of the dance and
frolic. . . .   Men worth a million were insolvent for two millions ; promising young cities marched back again into the
wilderness.   The ambitious town plat was re-annexed to the
plantation, like a country girl from the city.   The frolic was
ended, and what headaches and feverish limbs the next morning!"

This was the short-lived and unrestrained society which produced the models for Baldwin's self-styled "gallery of daubs" :
Ovid Bolus, Esq., a village attorney and "a natural liar, just
as some horses are natural pacers, and some dogs natural
setters" ; that provincial butcher, Steve Higginbotham, "noted
hog thief" ; an old-time lawyer who knew all the gymnastics
of courtroom manners ; stripling lawyers, some thirty or forty
in a single community, ready to swindle any distressed and gullible citizen or to engage in profit-making politics ; an old field
schoolmaster transformed into a conceited and pedantic prosecutor ; and old Judge Sawbridge, "who could tell from smelling
a cork the very region whence the liquor came."[40]   Vigorously

[39] Baldwin, *op. cit.*, "How the Times Served the Virginians, etc.," pp. 79 ff.
[40] *Ibid.*, pp. 3, 20, 21, 52, 106 ff., and 151 ff.

plying their various trades and professions, these are representative of the scoundrels and odd characters of all kinds who flourished for a time in backwoods boom towns ironically called Screamersville, Splitskull, and Rackensack. Scoundrel par excellence among these "flush times" townspeople was Simon Suggs, Jr., Esq., an illiterate lawyer, who, satirically explains Baldwin, "had ancestors," his illustrious father being John J. Hooper's serio-comic, grotesque Captain Simon Suggs of the Tallapoosa Volunteers and his grandfather a "hardshell" Baptist preacher from Georgia.[41]

Most of Baldwin's sketches of small town life center around the bench and the bar. In crudely built courthouses, crowded to capacity with a motley group of noisy spectators, the real issue of a case was often forgotten as a veteran lawyer pitted all his skill and experience against the boldness and youth of a novice. Public interest often reached such a high pitch that the people crowded around the lawyers "and stamped an roared as at a circus."[42] Young lawyers often shared in the wealth of these border towns by joining gamblers in grand swindles. There was also business enough at the circuit courts where town bullies frequently were freed from charges of attacking less influential citizens who had "no weepins"; or Yankee schoolmasters begged protection from assault and battery.

Flush Times, with its original characterization of the hurly-burly of border life in Alabama and Mississippi, like Mrs. Kirkland's *A New Home* (1839), is a worthy forerunner of the post-war pictures of mining camps and other mushroom towns in the Bret Harte stories, Eggleston's *The Mystery of Metropolisville*, and Mark Twain's *Roughing It* and *The Gilded Age*.

Other pre-war followers of the Longstreet tradition produced additional genre pictures of frontier towns, villages, and crossroads communities in the newer, more thinly settled portions of the Lower South and ever widening area of the Southwest through their humorous tales and sketches, which often revolved around a homespun, picturesque hero, and their wildly exaggerated yarns and tall tales retold in character. Usually the village background itself is subordinated in interest to the humorously caricatured experiences of the rustic hero, a famil-

---

[41] *Ibid.*, "Simon Suggs, Jr., Esq., A Legal Biography," pp. 114 ff.
[42] *Ibid.*, "My First Appearance at the Bar," p. 43.

21

iarly local character, like Seba Smith's Major Jack Downing,
ignorant of book learning but natively shrewd.   Belonging to
this literary tradition are genial Johnson Jones Hooper (1815-
63), native North Carolinian, who eagerly migrated to Alabama, where he became influential as a Whig journalist and
lawyer, and that "quiet, rather sombre gentleman," George
Washington Harris (1814-69), a native of Pennsylvania, a
jeweler's apprentice, Tennessee River steamboat captain, political writer, and spinner of newspaper yarns.   Both of these
humorists, familiar with well-known types found in frontier
settlements, reproduced in bold caricature the yarning, lying,
cheating, vainglorious prankster and picaresque hero of the
backwoods.   In all probability these border realists, says Watterson, drew their heroes "from many scraps and odd ends of
individual character to be encountered at the time in the country towns and upon the rural highways of the South."[43]

Hooper's *Some Adventures of Captain Simon Suggs, Late of the
Tallapoosa Volunteers; together with "Taking the Census," and Other
Alabama Sketches, by a Country Editor* has since its Philadelphia
publication in 1845 been considered a masterpiece of lively
provincial humor.   The clever-tongued Alabamian hero, that
"sharp and vulgar, sunny and venal swash-buckler" Simon
Suggs, has often been compared with the picaresque type found
in Fielding and Thackeray.[44]   He is without a virtue, except
his good humor and self-possession.   Dishonest in everything
he attempts, Simon always manages to be the center of attraction.   At a camp meeting he temporarily "gets religion" and
takes charge of the collection box; at his own court trial he
slyly frees himself from gambling charges; and at all other
gatherings in his home village on the Tallapoosa he is a serio-
comic rogue and self-appointed hero, a prototype for Beriah
Sellers.   During the flurry caused by imagined Indian attacks
at the time of the Creek War Simon's none too honest strat-
agems gain him appointment, amidst vociferous shouts from
the gullible townspeople, to the captaincy of the unmilitary
"Tallapoosy Vollantares," raw recruits afterwards known as
the "Forty Thieves."   Even in "Tuskaloosa" Simon, secretly
awed by the citified appearance of the town, boldly enters
gambling parlors frequented by the élite (including members

[43] Watterson, *op. cit.*, p. 40.   Cf. Wilt, *op. cit.*, p. 94.
[44] *Ibid.*

of the legislature) and there through ingenuity and mimicry fleeces the reg.lar patrons, supposedly sophisticated town folk.

". . . a queer looking, long legged, short bodied, small headed, white haired, hog eyed, funny sort of genius" was Sut Lovingood, the previously described Tennessee mountain hero of Harris's *Sut Lovingood: Yarns Spun by A Nat'ral Born Durn'd Fool, Warped and Wove for Public Wear* (1867). Camp meeting sites in isolated rural communities, mountain farms, little traveled and rutted mountain roadways, mean little villages which one sees first as he cuts "acrost the ridge," and, on rare occasion, the larger towns of Knoxville and Lynchburg form the locale of the pranks and hair-raising experiences of the rascally Sut, "a durnder fool nor enybody outside a Assalum, ur Kongriss." Riding on Tearpoke, "a nick tailed, bow necked, long, poor, pale, sorrel horse, half dandy, half devil," or walking along with a rambling uncertain gait, Sut Lovingood nearly always was the center of a crowd of boon companions, mountain villagers "full of fun, foolery, and mean whiskey." Ever ready for rough fun, at the expense of others, Sut was a sort of "local terror," who loved a joke as much as his corn whisky. Once a reward of "ait dullars" was offered "fur the karkus ove a sartin wun sut lovingood, dead ur alive, ur ailin, . . . fur the raisin ove the devil pussonely, an' permiskusly discunfurtin' the wimin very powerful, an' skeerin ove folks generly a heap, an' bustin up a promisin, big warm meetin, and makin the wickid larf, an' wus, insultin ove the passun orful."[45] Sut had turned the meeting into a scene of pandemonium by putting an opened bag, full of lizards, "onder the bottim ove his [the Parson Bullen's] britches-laig." So startled was the evangelist that he stopped preaching "rite in the middil ove the word 'damnation'."

In miscellanies edited by William T. Porter (*The Big Bear of Arkansas*, 1845, and *A Quarter Race in Kentucky and Other Sketches*, 1846) and T. A. Burke (*Polly Peaseblossom's Wedding; and Other Tales*, 1851); autobiographical sketches like Sol Smith's *Theatrical Apprenticeship* (1845) and his *Theatrical Management* (republished, in part, in 1868, from two popular volumes of 1845 and 1855); John Pendleton Kennedy's politically satiric *Annals of Quodlibet* (1850); and other memorials of a bygone day there have been preserved various humorous rep-

[45] *Sut Lovingood*, p. 48.

resentations, other than those previously discussed, of the many oddities of Southern village life and character which in recent years have attracted the attention of modern critics and editors like Jennette Tandy, Constance Rourke, Franklin J. Meine, Napier Wilt, Bernard De Voto, and, more recently, Walter Blair.

The full records of Sol Smith, peripatetic and often penniless actor, printer, and odd job man, and James M. Field's *The Drama in Pokerville* (Philadelphia, 1846) show that, in spite of local prejudice, conflicts with commencement exercises, revivals and camp meetings, with amateurs convinced that they were histrionic, with cranky landlords, gamblers, and others, a company of "traveling artists" nearly always found welcome in the larger towns along the rivers and railroads and the smaller back-country places. Traveling, in good weather and bad, by horseback, coach, wagons, Mississippi River boats, and by train, strolling players, often so important as Edwin Forrest, W. C. Macready, Anna Cora Mowatt, Charles Kean, and others, made their way from town to town throughout the South. Rustic—and usually enthusiastic—audiences delighted in the songs, recitations, tragedies, comedies, and afterpieces which even a mere handful of wandering actors, versatile enough to play many roles on quick notice, presented from improvised stages, frequently lighted by home made candles. The "theaters" were as varied as the communities : tavern ballrooms, dining rooms, and even garrets ; newly built theaters in towns like Mobile, log cabins, Masonic halls, barns, and once, as Sol Smith relates, in an unused building near a graveyard. Sometimes programs, containing unique notices, were provided.

Colonel Mugs, chief constable, will be in attendance to enforce an observance of *etiquette*. The three front benches reserved for ladies. No smoking allowed, save at the windows. Peanuts and Pecans prohibited, save while the curtain is down.[46]

Thus, according to Field,

> doth immortal Shakespeare flourish still—
> First night of a short season in Pokerville.[47]

Kennedy's *Annals of Quodlibet*, published in 1840 as the work

[46] *The Drama in Pokerville*, p. 12.   [47] *Ibid.*, p. 9.

of Schoolmaster Solomon Secondthought, satirizes small town speculation by exposing "the intensity of its political ardors and the absurdity of its excesses."[48] Once pertinent, the issues over which old warriors "dealt mortal blows on each other's sconce" are now quite forgotten.   Indefinitely localized, Quodlibet may be taken for any small, quickly developed town during the era of Jacksonian prosperity when all ambitious folk were turning toward politics as a means of getting wealth and social recognition.   It was the day of oratory, huge political picnics and beer drinking bouts, of unusual prosperity for politicians, and the heyday for Jackson's followers.   In this satiric fictional treatment of the democratic scene Quodlibet passes through a period of unlimited speculation and mushroom growth, expanded through the distribution of treasury notes and the operation of political chicanery designed to hoodwink gullible depositors in the newly established Patriotic Copperplate Bank of Quodlibet.

ROMANTIC REALISTS OF THE OLD SOUTH

While these and other humorous realists dominated the village scene in the pre-war South and local newspapers printed sketches familiar to Southerners the number of men and women capable of the more sustained effort required in novel writing was very small.   Of these, only two or three at the most deserve a place among the leading American novelists.   In the South, as well as in the North, many of the attempts at fiction then current

. . . were mere copies and unintentional burlesques of foreign productions, and possessed no more American flavor than if they had been produced in the jungles of Africa. Lords, dukes, counts, weeping, sentimental ladies, charitable robbers, and other beings largely unknown in America were not infrequently brought into the narrative, while "apt alliteration's artful aid" was often apparent in the wording of the title-page.[49]

Only a few novelists, including Kennedy, William Gilmore Simms, and John Esten Cooke, realized the importance of native materials in the creation of a distinctively American fiction.   Even after the duress of the Civil War highly senti-

---

[48] For fuller discussion of *Quodlibet* see Edward M. Gwathmey, *John Pendleton Kennedy* (New York, 1931), p. 64 and pp. 69-70.
[49] Holliday, *op. cit.*, p. 169.

mentalized stories made an appeal to uncritical readers who evidently delighted in the adventures of a well-born hero with "well-chiselled features" which were "lit up by an eye of tender blue that glanced now and then with a mingled volume of fire and tenderness." "Genteel" readers found much to admire in Byronic heroes so noble as Roland Vernon, hero of *Dolores: A Tale of Disappointment and Distress* (1868). Heir to a South Carolina plantation, Roland is a romantic figure, first introduced thus :

> Crowning his well-shaped head was a crested wealth of golden curls, which now glistened in the sunshine that was creeping through the interwoven boughs overhead ; and these curls were nestling in wavy profusion around a fair and delicately moulded forehead.[50]

Under such restricting, vitiating vogues exceedingly few ante-bellum Southern novelists produced noteworthy treatments of small town backgrounds. Kennedy, Simms, and Cooke, with Robert Montgomery Bird and William Caruthers of lesser importance, are akin in their historical, romantic approach to the study of Southern community life. Abandoning the humorous tale and sketch of their contemporaries, these turned, on occasion, to town scenes frequently, though not always, far removed from the democratic, homespun life of the Georgia, Alabama, and Mississippi back country. In varying degrees all of these novelists were romantic realists who turned seriously to the past history of Kentucky, Maryland, South Carolina, Virginia, and other sections for materials from which to re-create, in full-length novels, town and country life of bygone times. True, their representations are as varied as Bird's scenes of a fortified Kentucky settlement of the 1780's and Cooke's full reproduction of Williamsburg, aristocratic capital of colonial Virginia.

Earliest of these novels of locality is Bird's *Nick of the Woods* (1837).[51] A highly romantic tale of an embryonic town in frontier Kentucky, the novel centers around Indian attacks and the mysterious wandering Quaker, Nathan, variously known as Nick of the Woods and the Jibbenainosay (the Spirit-that-Walks). The bloodiness of the plot speedily sent *Nick of the Woods* through more than twenty editions. As a story of

---

[50] Benjamin Robinson, *op. cit.* (New York, 1868), p. 9.
[51] Subtitle : *The Jibbenainosay: A Tale of Kentucky* (2 vols. ; Philadelphia, 1837).

frontier settlement life this novel, replete with realistic pictures of conflict between settlers and Indians, shows how the tide of emigration became so powerful in Kentucky by the nineties that blockhouses, isolated "stations" or forts in the wilderness, were transformed into growing villages and towns.

Kennedy (1795-1870), Simms (1806-70), and Cooke (1830-36), whose works have been termed the best Southern novels of the ante-bellum period "and indeed among the best written in America prior to the Civil War," likewise wrote the only serious Southern fiction of the time which is still a source of entertainment.

A witty, highly cultured gentleman of Maryland and Virginia parentage, Kennedy repeatedly has been described as "one of the most attractive figures of his generation," "an American Victorian," and "one of the accepted leaders of the Great Whig party, making many addresses and often occupying the same platform with Clay and other great leaders."[52]   For all of his active public services Kennedy was, says Parrington, "a man of letters rather than a lawyer, and if he had eschewed politics and law and stuck to his pen our literature would have been greatly in his debt."[53]

Better known for *Swallow Barn* (1832), the book which gives him a permanent place in American literature, Kennedy also left three novels : a romantic tale of the Revolution, *Horse-Shoe Robinson* (1835), the previously mentioned *Annals of Quodlibet*, and *Rob of the Bowl* (1838).   The latter, subtitled *A Legend of St. Inigoes*, was published anonymously at a time when the author was elected to Congress.[54]   Since the press of political activity gave him no time for labored revision, Kennedy produced in *Rob of the Bowl* a more spontaneous and unified work than *Horse-Shoe Robinson*.   *Rob of the Bowl*, based, so says Gwathmey, upon actual records found in state archives, is a tale of the early and forgotten town of Port St. Mary's, once the capital of the province of Maryland before the removal to Annapolis.   It is a readable, albeit swashbuckling and highly romantic, story of 1681 which recaptures the spirit of old St. Mary's under the proprietorship of the second Lord Baltimore, Cecilius Calvert.   The dangers, problems, jealousies, bitter

[52] Parrington, *op. cit.*, II, 46 ; Link, *op. cit.*, I, 225.
[53] Parrington, *op cit.*, II, 56.
[54] Gwathmey, *op. cit.*, pp. 120-121.

religious feuds, and smuggling of the day make St. Mary's a miniature storm center. Out of the war of intolerance between Protestant and Catholic emerge pictures of life in the little Maryland town, whose port was then a place of considerable activity and gayety. Kennedy's occasional use of stereotyped motivations, like that of the reunion of a long-lost father and son, is offset by his fine ability in presenting the colloquial speech of the town through Garret Weasel, the garrulous inn-keeper, and Dame Dorothy, his tongue-lashing wife.

Much use is made of picaresque adventure. Against the background of the faction-torn town and the surrounding countryside are projected swaggering pirates, one of whom falls in love with the Port Collector's daughter and kidnaps her from her father's house. Then, there are mysterious Rob of the Bowl, occupant of the isolated Wizard's Chapel and con-niver with the piratical fraternity; and all the local aristocracy who frown upon the contrabrand trade of Rob and the smug-glers, but are mystified by reports of witches, and other spirits who dance in fantastic costumes in the haunted chapel.

Simms, leading novelist of the Old South, wrote prolifically from the time of his first novel, *Martin Faber: The Story of a Crim-inal* (1833), until the fifties, when his interest in the slavery question led largely to his abandonment of fiction and to an active participation as pamphleteer and orator in the Southern cause.[55] With his fortunes shattered by the war, Simms died shortly after the conclusion of peace, while trying valiantly to restore his property. While most of his contemporaries in his native and socially restricted Charleston, as elsewhere in the South, thought the cause of Southern letters rested with the orators, humorists, and essayists, Simms early felt that the larg-er defense of the culture of the South depended upon the crea-tion of a literature.[56] Influenced by Cooper's success in ideal-izing native characters and scenes, Simms sought to find in Southern history the rich materials for a distinctive romance. Partisan conflicts during the Revolution; Indian struggles; the danger-fraught adventures of explorers; the daring of border ruffians; and the society of early Charleston gave themes which the imaginative and energetic Simms applied to several series

---

[55] Fullerton, *op. cit.*, p. 246.
[56] Link, *op. cit.*, I, 156; cf. Simms, *Views and Reviews in American Literature* (New York, 1845), ".\mericanism in Literature," *passim.*

of Southern novels. Of these the Border Romances contain the most fully developed village themes. Included in this group and partly descriptive of the same sections treated more lightly in the sketches of Longstreet and others are *Guy Rivers: A Tale of Georgia* (1834), *Richard Hurdis: A Tale of Alabama* (1838), *Border Beagles: A Tale of Mississippi* (1840), *Confession; or The Blind Heart* (1841), *Beauchampe; or The Kentucky Tragedy* (1842), and *Charlemont, or The Pride of the Village* (1856). With these and his colonial revolutionary romances of Southern life Simms "entered the list to represent his section in creative literature against the writers of the North : Irving, Bryant, Longfellow, Cooper, Hawthorne, and even Poe."[57] Apparent in these novels are Simms's keenness of observation of familiar scenes along the border sections of the South, his adaptation of the racy speech used by the actual models of his Porgy and other characters, his love for action, and his use of a vigorous, descriptive prose. In few ante-bellum Southern novels has the small town been so vividly treated as in these Border Romances.

Although *Martin Faber* was his first published novel, Simms, in the 1855 edition of *Guy Rivers* speaks of the 1834 edition of the latter as "the first of my regular novels" and "my first deliberate attempt in prose fiction."[58] Successful from the beginning, *Guy Rivers* is thus described by Professor Trent : "In spite of its stilted style and its wooden characters, there was a bustle and movement about it that interested an uncritical public."[59] The plot, motivated by both love and hate, is marred by sentimentality and bombast, qualities, however, which insured its contemporary success. In spite of the conventionalities of the romance the story vividly portrays the rude, uncertain life of Georgia and Mississippi during the "flush times," a life which Simms knew at first hand. Like several of the later Border Romances, this novel, with its full pictures of a frontier town, presents a series of dramatic adventures motivated by the evil doings of a federation of outlaws led by Edward Creighton, alias Guy Rivers, whose own wild career of political mischief and outlawry affects many innocent of wrongdoing. Formerly a promising Carolina lawyer, Creigh-

[57] W. P. Trent, *William Gilmore Simms* (Boston and New York, 1895), pp. 85 ff. ; Link, *ibid.*, 173.
[58] See introductory letter to C. R. Carroll of South Carolina, to whom Simms dedicated the first edition (New York, 1855), p. 10.
[59] *Op. cit.*, p. 85.

ton murders a judge and is forced into outlawry. Assuming
the name of Rivers and doubly embittered by his loss of position and the love of an heiress, the young lawyer escapes into
thinly settled upper Georgia. Here he becomes the ringleader
of desperadoes who operate, under the name of the Pony Club,
near Chestatee, a river town settled because of its gold mining
possibilities.

Our interest is not in the sentimental love affair developed
nor in the tragic death in prison of the cynical, yet intrepid,
outlaw, but in Simms's pictures of advancing civilization, of
the strife, discontent, and contention found in a frontier place,
where doubtful justice was administered by regulators too often
in accord with the spirit of the mob. Rough woodsmen, restless gold-seeking pioneers, frequently rejected by wholesome
society; "the spendthrift and the indolent, the dreamer and
the outlaw, congregating, though guided by contradictory purposes, in the formation of a common caste"; small farmers, a
few professional people, and tradesmen swarmed the rutted
streets of log-cabined Chestatee or gathered at the Golden Egg,
crudely constructed as were most back-country taverns of the
period. Here villagers and visitors "met their acquaintances,
found society, and obtained news."[60] Because of the wild condition of the country and the absence of civil authority adventurers came from everywhere, far and near, oddly and con-
fusedly jumbled together in a peculiar moral and mental combination.[61] Yankee peddlers, the butt of many jokes, rubbed
elbows with Georgia crackers or state troops sent to quell dis-
turbances at the mines.

In his close, often satiric observations of frontier town life
Simms is an able forerunner of Eggleston and Mark Twain.
Like them, during his early travels he noted that in most Southern and Western towns "the scale by which towns are laid out
is always magnificent. The founders seem to have calculated
usually upon a population of millions; and upon spots and
sporting grounds, measurable by the olympic courses, and the
ancient fields of combat, ... There was no want of room,
no risk of narrow streets and pavements, no deficiency of area

[60] *Guy Rivers*, p. 109. See W. S. Hoole, "A Note on Simms's Visits to the Southwest," *American Literature*, VI, 335 (Nov., 1934).
[61] *Guy Rivers*, p. 61.

in the formation of public squares."[62] Chestatee, scattered and crude, was no exception.

Though in *Richard Hurdis* Simms pictures modes of travel, farming, emigration, all sorts of border ruffianism, and other phases of frontier life, he gives but scant attention to town affairs in Alabama and Mississippi, the shifting locales of his romance. His chief concern is with the bold and cruel operations of an organized band of ruffians, the famous Murrell gang in history, numbering as many, perhaps, as fifteen hundred.[63] The novelist presents but a glimpse of some straggling frontier towns. Tuscaloosa was then but a mere hamlet where the heroes, Richard Hurdis and William Carrington, find dangerous adventure with gamblers, members of the Mystic Confederacy (the Murrell gang). To the young heroes the town seemed "little more than hewn out of the woods. Piles of brick and timber crowded the main, indeed the only street of the place, and denoted the rawness and poverty of the region."[64] They were housed in a tavern filled to overflowing and, regardless of their objections, were forced to share a room with uncouth strangers, for the "landlord was a turbulent sort of savage, who bore down all opposition, and held to his laws."

The third of the Border Romances, *Border Beagles*, dealing again with the Murrell gang, introduces realistic frontier town scenes, more than in *Richard Hurdis* but fewer than in *Guy Rivers*. Here, as elsewhere, Simms's portrayals of frontier types and customs are "deliberately representative, and probably accurate since he was familiar with the society that he portrayed and sought to give an honest delineation."[65] Again another romantic young hero, Lawyer Vernon, is involved as a representative of the Mississippi governor in a scheme to put an end to the unrestrained lawlessness of the Yazoo district. As in *Richard Hurdis*, some of the most dramatic action is motivated by a system of outlawry secretly abetted by outwardly

---

[62] *Ibid.*, p. 63. For a more complete and vivid description see *ibid.*, pp. 60-67.

[63] Hampton M. Jarrell, *William Gilmore Simms: Realistic Romancer*, dissertation still in manuscript, Duke University, 1932, pp. 146 ff., has an excellent discussion of the Murrell gang. Cf. also Mark Twain, *Life on the Mississippi*, pp. 243-247, and H. R. Howard, *The History of Virgil A. Stewart, and His Adventure* (New York, 1836), an account of the capture of Murrell.

[64] *Richard Hurdis* (New York, 1855), p. 120. See also pp. 151, 213-222, and 312-315.

[65] Jarrell, *op. cit.*, p. 159.

law-abiding citizens. Chapter I, "Court Session," pictorial studies of a small Mississippi town during the excitement of court day, offers full proof of Simms's pronounced realism and of his ability, as Trent has said, to transfer to his writing "no little of his own vim and energy to his exciting pages." Unfortunately, his vigorous portrayals of the "saddlebag" and "sulky" lawyers, the sheriff's officers, loquacious small town politicians, swaggering planters and lordly overseers, local bullies, and folks of all conditions who make court day a time to remember in the South and West are overshadowed by a picaresque and at times melodramatic action.

Kentucky offers a setting for a continuation of the Border Romances in *Charlemont* and *Beauchampe*, overdrawn accounts of the once notorious Colonel Sharp-Colonel Beauchamp murder case which, according to Parrington, "deserve no better fate than the rubbish heap." Although written fourteen years earlier, *Beauchampe, or The Kentucky Tragedy* actually is a sequel to *Charlemont, or The Pride of the Village* (1856). In the latter Charlemont, "as lovely a little hamlet as ever promised peace to the weary and discontent," is the frontier village home of Margaret Cooper, an ambitious provincial beauty. While weakly plotted, Margaret's story, one of revolt from a narrow environment, is akin to that of more modern heroines. Proud and disdainful, the girl rebels against the crude interests of her rustic neighbors. A young lawyer, parading as a Methodist convert, inflames Margaret's longing for the world outside Charlemont. His persuasive, cunning arguments prove the girl's undoing and give Simms opportunity for moralizing about the tortures of sin. Melodramatic situations, wooden presentation of town gossips, and the author's didactic tone make *Charlemont* a weak forerunner to *Beauchampe*. Herein the story of Margaret and Stevens (her seducer) shifts to the larger town of Frankfort and is carried to a sensational conclusion involving murder and mystery.

For his romances of the Revolution Simms received contemporary praise for being "thoroughly American in the choice of his subjects, fertile in invention, with descriptive powers, second only to Cooper, and, as a general rule, with a far superior insight into character."[66]   *The Partisan* (1835), with others

---

[66] Press notice from the *Boston Athenaeum* prefacing the revised edition of *The Partisan* (New York, 1870).

in this series, contains pictures of town life deserving far more than passing notice. Primarily a romantic novel of conflict between Southern Tories and Partisans (patriots), *The Partisan* portrays South Carolina small town life in the 1780's. British maneuvers, sudden ambuscades by loyal followers of the Swamp Fox (Francis Marion), murky swamp retreats of indignant, persecuted patriots, intrigue at village taverns, and the wanton destruction of plantations furnish much of the historical matter. Superimposed upon this background of conflict is a carelessly constructed tale of the hazard-filled courtship of Major Singleton, Partisan, and Katherine Walton, plantation heiress.

As Simms himself explains in the preface to the revised edition, the scene of *The Partisan* is laid in and around the town of Dorchester, once prosperous but in the summer of 1834, when revisited by the novelist, utterly decayed.[67] Familiar with the traditions of the old town from his boyhood ramblings and his conversations with "some old inhabitant whose name has not been recorded," Simms was well fitted to re-create from the ruined fort, the decayed, owl-infested church, and the ancient chimney-places a small town once again alive with people. No longer, in his imagination, was Dorchester on the Ashley a mere name—a shadow. Through his detailed descriptions we return

. . . to the time when the village of Dorchester was full of life, and crowded with inhabitants; when the coaches of the wealthy planters of the neighborhood thronged the highway; when the bells from the steeple called to the Sabbath worship; and, when throughout the week, the shops were crowded with buyers, and the busy hammer of the mechanic, and the axe of the laborer, sent up their crowding noises, ...[68]

Then a busy town, with regularly laid out squares and market-place, inns, churches, wharves to which were anchored sloops and schooners, and a fort commanding the river and village alike, Dorchester was inhabited by plantation owners and poor whites, by red-coated soldiers and shopkeepers. It was the center of the hazardous adventure, the thrilling action, so favored by Simms the romancer, and the chief place of meeting for the oddly contrasted loyalists and patriots who give a picar-

---

[67] Trent, *op. cit.*, p. 107, cites the summer of 1834 as the date of Simms's visit.
[68] *The Partisan*, 1870 edition, pp. 18-19.

esque quality to the whole romance. During these perilous times at the high tavern of the village, the "Royal George," were often seen the characters Simms delighted in creating: Humphries, sociable old toper and tavernkeeper; Bella, his coquettish daughter and barmaid; British dragoons with swaggering carriage and flashy uniforms; belligerent countrymen; villagers of all conditions; and, finally, that mountain of a fellow, that South Carolina rice planter and connoisseur of food and drink, the Falstaffian soldier and provincial wit, Porgy.

So interested was Simms in both characters and military action of *The Partisan* that he wrote, after a period of years, two more novels, *Mellichampe: A Legend of the Santee* and *Katherine Walton, or The Rebel of Dorchester*, completing a loosely unified trilogy in which he tried to maintain a sort of historical connection "corresponding with the several transitional periods of the Revolutionary war in South Carolina."[69] The military activities of *The Partisan*, opening with the fall of Charleston and closing with the defeat of the partisan army under Gates at Camden, were continued in *Mellichampe* (1836), but a new love story was developed. Herein "the resolute and hardy patriotism of the scattered bands of patriots who still maintained a predatory warfare against the foe among the swamps and thickets" supplies the historical theme.[70] The region of the Santee, with its wooded hills, valleys, swamps, and plantation areas, takes precedence over the Dorchester scenes of *The Partisan*. Except for an opening account of the partial burning of Dorchester, this romantic tale, with its wilder rural locale, is, says Simms, "rather an episode in the progress of the 'Partisan,' than a continuation of that romance."[71]

Katherine Walton, concluding romance of this trilogy, began to appear in *Godey's Lady's Book* in January, 1850.[72] Although written piecemeal, as were many of Simms's novels, to supply the printer with copy, *Katherine Walton* was the result of painstaking research.[73] At times, without doubt, literature is no document, no exact reproduction of a life long vanished.[74]

[69] Simms, *The Forayers, or The Raid of the Dog-Days* (New York, 1832), Preface.
[70] *Ibid.*
[71] Advertisement to *Mellichampe* (New York, 1864).
[72] Trent, *op. cit.*, p. 191.
[73] *Ibid.* Cf. *Katha ine Walton* (New York, 1882), pp. 3-4.
[74] E. E. Stoll, "Literature No 'Document'," *Modern Language Review*, XIX, 141 (April, 1924).

This novel, however, vividly records the historical romancer's convincing impressions of Charleston society during the crisis when patriots saw their fortunes snatched away and bestowed as favors upon sycophants rallying to the royal cause. *The Partisan* and *Mellichampe* occupied ground in the interior, but *Katherine Walton*, says Simms, "brings us to the city; and a large proportion of the work, and much of its interest, will be found to consist in the delineation of the social world of Charleston, during the Revolutionary period."[75] For the most part, the matter is historical. Even many of the portraits are of real persons and the detailed descriptions of life, manners, and movements, while lacking the freer style and stronger narrative interest of *The Partisan*, have, according to Simms's statement, been drawn from abundant and acceptable sources.

An exciting, but long-vanished, social regime comes to life in the numerous pictures of the loyalist and rebel factions of war-stirred Charleston. Jamaica-loving British colonels and stout, red-faced majors, enriched by the "appropriations" of war; fiery loyalist planters, dowagers, and younger beauties; proudly patriotic rebel ladies; and even disguised partisans mingle at the fashionable balls given in the spacious, illuminated houses and gardens of the town. While intrigue was carried on at tavern and garrison and patriot bands under Marion and Sumter fought for Carolina's liberty, picnics and other parties were attended by "a goodly cavalcade, male and female."[76] Such was Charleston, as Simms imagined it, during a period of ill-endured tyranny. Today the plot of *Katherine Walton* seems cumbersome and romantically strained and some of the characters (especially those of the upper classes) animated mannikins; but the Charleston background ranks with Cooke's delineations of colonial Williamsburg as one of the most complete and realistic ante-bellum portrayals of a Southern seaboard town.

The romantic past of Charleston fascinated Simms, even though his own ambition to intrench himself in local code-bound social circles long was thwarted. Repeatedly his interest in the old town manifested itself in his fictionalization of different periods of its history. In additional Revolutionary

---

[75] *Katharine Walton, loc. cit.*
[76] In *ibid.*, chaps. ii, xx, xxiii, xlii, and xlvi, are devoted entirely to Charleston life.

novels, *The Kinsmen*, later known as *The Scout* (1841), *Woodcraft*
(1854), and *Eutaw* (1856), military operations radiate from
Charleston and Orangeburg (British depot on the Edisto).
Woodcraft, a graphic tale of Lieutenant Porgy's return to his
ruined plantation, admirably describes the lawless conditions
of Carolina after the Revolution.   One sees Charleston on the
eventful day of December 14, 1782.   After an occupation of
almost three years, the British are evacuating the town.   Immediately a season of public thanksgiving, marked by illumi-
nations, receptions, military parades, dancing, and joyful reunions, is opened.[77]   Akin in its romantic movement to Kennedy's *Rob of the Bowl*, Simms's *The Cassique of Kiawah* (1859)
tells of the infant settlement of Charleston (Charles Town)
during the 1780's, when Indian and pirate attacks threatened
the safety of the citizens.   A piratical hero, cherishing a forbidden love, carries contraband merchandise into the small,
but growing, town where even then social cliques enlivened
society with balls and other entertainments.

Because of his numerous interpretations of widely varied
phases of community life and his courage to portray with
marked realism, during a period given to romance, many individualized types of the common run of small town people
Simms ranks high among the few able pioneer delineators of
the small town in the South.

"A study of the ante-bellum novel," says Montrose J. Moses
concerning Southern fiction, "will show it to be largely devoid
of original idea, but full of the historical and local quality."[78]
This is truly applicable to the pre-war town literature of Virginia.   What Simms did in faithful historical portrayal for
Charleston Dr. William A. Caruthers and John Esten Cooke
accomplished similarly for those little seaboard towns of Yorktown, Jamestown, and Williamsburg, whose political, legislative, and social colonial life was exceptionally varied and well
adapted to historical romance.   Though the files of the *Virginia Gazette* contain ample contemporary records of the daily
activities of the colonial past, the fictional interpretations of
these ante-bellum Virginians permit us, if our fancy is alive,

---

[77] *Woodcraft, or Hawks about the Dovecote* (formerly *The Sword and the Distaff*) (New
York, 1882), pp. 31 ff. and 38 ff.
[78] *The Literature of the South* (New York, 1910), p. 253.

to look upon full-length, but often glorified, pictures of Old Dominion folk.

Known variously as "a Virginian among Virginians" and a disciple of Scott and remembered for his spirited colonial romances, Caruthers has left in his *Cavaliers of Virginia, or The Recluse of Jamestown* (1834-35) and *The Knights of the Horseshoe* (1845) some highly colored delineations of Jamestown during Bacon's Rebellion and of Yorktown and Williamsburg during the Spottswood era (*circa* 1714). Herein the local sense, so strongly developed in Simms, is ever present in spite of stereotyped and romantic characters and illogical plot.

Professor Jay B. Hubbell in his *Virginia Life in Fiction* notes that the decade from 1830-1840, when Caruthers began writing, marks an important change in the attitude of Virginians toward the past. It was then, he says, that Virginia novelists "began to rebuild an aristocratic social order like that which Jefferson had overthrown."[79] Even until the end of the century writers persisted in exalting supposed Cavalier ancestors and in creating an aristocratic social background often too glorified to accord perfectly with reality. Among those Virginians more interested in the past than the present was that ardent Southerner and soldier, who served under Lee, John Esten Cooke. Born in Winchester in 1830, when Longstreet was beginning his *Georgia Scenes*, Cooke was a transitional figure who as writer adopted the leisurely manner of the pre-war school. He tried avowedly "to paint the Virginia phase of American society, to do for the Old Dominion what Cooper has done for the Indians, Simms for the Revolutionary drama in South Carolina, Irving for the Dutch Knickerbockers, and Hawthorne for the weird Puritan life of New England."[80]

This aim he realizes in his best remembered novel, *The Virginia Comedians* (1854), a descriptive and romantic picture of the Golden Age of Williamsburg when the town was the capital of a far-flung plantation area. Illustrative of the trend of his fiction, from first to last, this book peoples the imagination with important and other figures who once moved through the ~eets of Williamsburg, crowded the legislative chambers,

---

[79] Jay R. Hubbell, *Virginia Life in Fiction* (Dallas, 1922), pp. 23-24.

[80] See *ibid.*; Holliday, *op. cit.*, p. 276; and John O. Beaty, *John Esten Cooke, Virginian* (New York, 1922), p. 190.

drank convivially at the Raleigh Tavern, or applauded at the New Theater the efforts of Hallam and his English troupers. Showing throughout his delight in description, Cooke preserves innumerable scenes of Williamsburg's colonial social regime when "a splendid society had burst into flower, and was enjoying itself in the sunshine and under the blue skies of the most beautiful of lands."[81]   His emphasis upon the grand assemblies, the crowds flocking to the theater, race course, and cock fight, and the aristocratic visitors in the great manor houses clustering around the Lowland rivers show his delight in old Williamsburg before the Revolution blighted the easy life of planter and townsman.   As he saw it, in town and country life was a pageant: the royal governor went in his coach-and-six to open the House of Burgesses; youths in embroidered waistcoats made love to beauties in curls; the "Apollo" rang with music and the theater on Gloucester Street with applause; and the houses of the planters were full of rejoicing.[82]

Whether Cooke was always true to history is an open question, but, nevertheless, the Williamsburg of this story was indeed a social center for both aristocrats and lesser folk.   Here on special days great crowds attended to business or patronized the various entertainments the town offered.   Restless individuals, resentful of the privileges of their richer neighbors, found the Raleigh a convenient place for political discussions, the offering of duel challenges, and drinking with fellow-grumblers.   When a meeting of the House of Burgesses was three days off, the town already was filled with people,

. . . and on every hand jests and laughter, hearty greetings, the slamming of doors, the rattle of carriages, the clatter of hoofs, the jingle of spurs, and the neighs of horses, gave abundant proof that the joyous season had arrived.   The taverns were filling rapidly, and mine host of the Raleigh was in full activity . . . , running, that is to say toddling; bowing . . . laughing . . . , and calling for his rum, claret, and strong waters.[83]

The gala day had come to Williamsburg.

[81] Cooke, *The Virginia Comedians; or, Old Days in the Old Dominion* (New York, 1854), Preface. Williamsburg never attained a population of over two thousand. For discussion see L. P. Powell, *Historic Towns of the Southern States* (New York, 1900), p. 195; W. B. Blanton, *Medicine in Virginia in the Eighteenth Century* (Richmond, 1931), chap. xvi, "Towns and Town Doctors," pp. 313 ff.; and J. A. Osborne, *Williamsburg in Colonial Times* (Richmond, 1935), Introduction and Part I, "News of the Times."

[82] *The Virginia Comedians, loc. cit.*

[83] *Ibid.*, pp. 208-209. Other important descriptions are those of theatrical ac-

The Virginia Comedians delineates the surface of town and country society under the old Virginia regime when social relationship was one of the joys indulged in by wealthy planters; bold and reckless young blades proud of their caste; foreign-educated colonials affecting London manners and flaunting the latest fashions in the eyes of less fortunate associates; Virginia beauties, as well as middle-class dames; sturdy captains experienced in service abroad; the governor; and others of highest rank. Here, too, appear embittered reformers, shop-keepers, tavern owners, members of Hallam's "Virginia Company of Comedians," and many minor folk belonging to the "Town" during the mid-eighteenth century, all figures needed to make this novel a romantically descriptive cross-section of late colonial town life.

As we have noted, the small town in the ante-bellum South attracted the attention of two sharply contrasted groups of native writers: the border humorists and the historical romancers of the Tidewater. Longstreet and his fellow-humorists of the Lower South, portraying frankly the way of border town life and the back country, were as much influenced by their provincial environments as Kennedy, Cooke, and other socially prominent gentlemen of Virginia and Maryland were by the traditions of the plantation and seaboard capital. Likewise, versatile Simms, through actual observation and research, has preserved in fiction the vanished town life of both the South Carolina back country and seacoast settlements.

Post-War Trends

As illustrated in the work of Kennedy, Simms, Caruthers, and Cooke, the romanticism which began to show itself in America in the late eighteenth century held sway until the 1860's. Then the spreading frontier movements, the Civil War crisis, and the new industrial growth all weakened romanticism, not at once, but gradually and steadily.[84] Step by step in the South, as elsewhere, the emphasis upon local color influenced the change from a romantic to an increasingly more pronounced realistic literary tradition. Cooke himself, writing shortly before his death (1886), acknowledged that "Mr.

tivities, p. 31 and pp. 44-45; the Raleigh Tavern, pp. 65 ff.; the governor's ball, pp. 216 ff.; and the races at Jamestown, pp. 132 ff.

[84] Louis Wann, *The Rise of Realism, 1860-1888* (New York, 1933), pp. 1-17, has a good brief survey of this changing era.

Howells and the other realists have crowded me out of popular regard as a novelist, and have brought the kind of fiction I write into general disfavor."[85] Against the national background of a gilded age newer writers in the South during the seventies and eighties were perceiving in local life abundant and unused material, rich and varied, possessing literary value and interest. Consequently, the cause of local color flourished as the Negro, the mountaineer, the Creole, and other freshly treated types made their appearance in short story and novel. Developing colorful contrasts in manners and dialects, new writers produced work marked oftentimes by accuracy of observation, good portraiture, and even artistic finish. While Cooke considered himself "born too soon, and . . . now too old to learn my trade anew," others did not so appraise their talents. The really distinctive poetry of Henry Timrod (who died in 1867), Paul Hamilton Hayne, Sidney Lanier, and other war poets, the passionate pleas of Henry W. Grady, the editorials of Joel Chandler Harris, and the Reconstruction portrayals of Albion W. Tourgée called attention to the social forces of the changing South, to the new South amid the ruins.

Obviously the interest in realism did not affect all writers. Many, in fact, disregarded the changing literary traditions and even during the confusion of enforced reconstruction continued, like Cooke, faithful to the old standards. In the postwar South, therefore, a retrospective tendency, manifesting itself often in "befo' de war" stories, may be detected in prose fiction. Writers, like Thomas Nelson Page, were influenced by "a realization of changing conditions which threatened to obliterate the characteristics distinguishing the Old South."[86] In the midst of shifting literary evaluations and rapidly changing social and industrial conditions stories of the vanished regime made a bid for popularity, in spite of Howells and others. And during this period, from the close of the Civil War until the Gilded Age had run its course, the literature of the Southern town was sporadic, with nothing especially notable except for the work of a few transitional interpreters.

If Cooke and his contemporary romancers glorified the late colonial years, Francis Hopkinson Smith, Thomas Nelson Page, Mrs. Burton Harrison, Richard Malcolm Johnston, and other

---

[85] Beaty, *op. cit.*, pp. 161-162.
[86] Moses, *op. cit.*, p. 326.

post-bellum storytellers idealized as a Golden Day the years preceding the war. Some of these, born long before the outbreak of hostilities, knew during their impressionable years the happy days of the old order. When, as it has been said of Page, such an individual grew to manhood, his memories of the past were so unconsciously idealized that he could not see it in any other way even when he assumed the role of historian.[87] It was but natural for such Southerners to express the spirit of ante-bellum life which so weakly survived in the new. The plantation, idyllically portrayed in *Swallow Barn* and strongly colored by Caruthers and Cooke, was refashioned by Smith, Page, and their post-war contemporaries in keeping with the trends of a newer day. Forming a part of the newly reshaped tradition was the treatment given the ante-bellum town, often sleepy and bucolic and, like many Southern villages, deriving its name from that of the most prominent family in the vicinity. Nearly always having some association with the plantation gentry, such towns, as yet untouched by industrialism, were, according to the romanticists, the centers of wholesome, gracious living.

Just such community is Francis Hopkinson Smith's Cartersville, a small Virginia town, which, instead of serving as the exact locale of the story, is featured as an aristocratic background for cultured but improvident old Colonel Carter, resident in a Northern city.[88] Here, far away from his beloved Virginia, the Colonel saves himself from many embarrassing financial situations by his Southern code of chivalry and old-fashioned politeness. Following the practices of many of his contemporaries, Smith makes use of a theme, then new but now stereotyped, showing the imprint of the new realism upon romance: the industrialization of Southern properties. The discovery of coal on the Colonel's all but worthless Virginia lands furnishes the small thread of the dramatic narrative in *Colonel Carter*.

Another romancer familiar through experience with antebellum town life is Mrs. Burton Harrison (formerly Constance Cary) of Virginia, whose *Belhaven Tales* (1885) retrospectively present four stories of old Alexandria. Her aim, she says, was to preserve the culture of the quiet grass-grown Potomac town

[87] Hubbell, *op. cit.*, p. 28.
[88] *Colonel Carter of Cartersville* (Boston, 1891).

(first called Belhaven) in which, just prior to the war, might have been noted many marks of colonial days.   Throughout the town old mansions with beautiful echoing rooms, high-walled gardens, and ivy-covered churches bespoke, even during Constance Cary's girlhood, a dignified tradition.   Cobblestone streets, their names smacking of toryism, "prate[d] of figures famed in history." Mrs. Harrison's tales are thus sketched against a background of traditions and memories of a vanished social life, as gay as that of Cooke's Williamsburg, which even after the Civil War made Belhaven "a wholesome brake set upon the rushing wheels of nineteenth-century progress." Unique in its feminine point of view, *Belhaven Tales*, has been aptly compared to *Cranford* and the stories of Jane Austen and, with its full picture of ante-bellum small town life, recognized "as the classic complement to *In Ole Virginia*."[89]

Inheriting more than a century of fine traditions, genuine culture, and the best blood of the Virginia gentry, Thomas Nelson Page, as Professor Edwin Mims emphasizes, was thus by birth, training, and temperament in thorough sympathy with the ante-bellum South.   In the new environment developing around him after the war, Page, though a lawyer by profession, found in literature a means of preserving the best in a civilization which seemed to him "the sweetest, purest, and most beautiful ever lived."[90] Fully aware, especially through his own family's distressing losses, of the widespread changes effected by war and reconstruction, Page tried by means of his stories to prolong the social order which the Pages, Nelsons, and hundreds of others formerly had enjoyed at Roswell (the Page mansion), at the famous Nelson House, Yorktown, once the scene of brilliant assemblies, and at countless other fine houses.

Blending humor and pathos in his tales of the past, Page is primarily the romancer of the plantation.   Occasionally, however, he recaptures the spirit of ante-bellum town life.   Of early Yorktown he once wrote that "it would be difficult to find a fitter illustration of the old colonial Virginia life than that which this little town affords."   In his "Two Colonial Places" Page refers to the old town as "Little York," traces its history

---

[89] Hubbell, *op. cit.*, pp. 29-30.
[90] Edwin Mims, "Thomas Nelson Page," *Southern Writers* (a symposium) (Nashville and Dallas, 1911), II, 121.

from its founding, and gives a romantic picture of the small
settlement during the early dominance of his ancestors, the
Nelsons, long leading townspeople.[91] The earliest houses, the
church, the store which brought golden guineas to the Nelsons,
the custom house, the rude fortifications, and Temple Farm,
where Governor Spottswood held "mimic court" made, as
Salem did to Hawthorne, a strong appeal to Page.

Page's two-volume novel, *Gordon Keith* (1903), devoted in
part to small town life of the Reconstruction, bears the mark
of his romantic method. The book is long, the style prolix,
and the theme now stereotyped. Specifically, it is the biography of a poor, but well-born, Southern boy who makes a precarious living in various small towns and cities of the post-war
South. Though the reader wishes that the hero had had a
lapse of memory, in all of his difficulties Gordon never forgets
that he is a Southern gentleman, the son of a ruined, but cultured, planter. Thoughts of his family associations sustain
him even when he must exist for a season in Gumbolt, a rude
Appalachian mining town stretching crazily up a hillside.
Better done than the complication-loaded plot of Gordon's
rise to fame in New York is Page's realistic account of the transformation of Gumbolt, with the coming of the railroad, from
an isolated, sordid village into a busy town symbolical of the
New South.

George Washington Cable (1844-1925), like Page in *Gordon
Keith*, has a novel of town life during the Reconstruction.
Both novelists protest against the Northern promoter, "the
king of carpetbaggers," who gained a control over natural resources in the South. Page exposes the chicanery of Northern
capitalists who acquired interests in the richly veined Appalachian region. In *John March, Southerner* (1894) Cable also
treats the problems of the carpetbag regime. In a large cotton
section, in the little town of Suez, there are clashes of interest
between Northern investors and profiteers in the building of
railroads, dams, highways, and factories and the highly resentful Southerners. To the dismay of cultured, but war-im-
poverished, citizens certain Reconstruction politicians, abetted
by intruding investors, convert the peaceful little town into a
boom place. Railroads are built, a gigantic realty corporation
formed, mills planned, and brazen half-breeds, ignorant and

[91] *The Old South Essays, etc.*, pp. 182-210.

revengeful but shrewd, are in control of the political factions at the state capital. The old town, battered by the war, is completely submerged by the new industrialism. Thus the romancer finds the cherished plantation life gone and a new urbanized existence flourishing on the site of the old.

Magazine readers of the seventies and eighties reacted favorably toward a long-continued series of rambling, old-fashioned sketches of a post-war Georgia community not far from Augusta and the locale of Longstreet's *Georgia Scenes*. The elderly author, whose knowledge of rural and small town life was rich and broad, was Richard Malcolm Johnston (1822-98), by right of his birth date associated with the Old South and the humorists of the Longstreet period. His late turning from the law and teaching to literary work, when he was almost sixty, made him a contemporary with Page, Cable, and Harris. With his boyhood spent on his father's plantation, Hancock County, Georgia, and in near-by Crawfordville and Powelton, Johnston early began his small town observations. Following a strict instruction under New England and Virginia college graduates at Powelton Academy, the boy entered Mercer University, where again he lived in a village atmosphere.

At the close of the war, after years of legal practice and teaching in Sparta, Augusta, Athens, and other Georgia villages and towns, Johnston moved to Baltimore. Here, as a result of a friendship with Henry C. Turnbull, Jr., editor of *The Southern Magazine*, he submitted for re-printing a few uncopyrighted provincial sketches, previously printed in a Georgia journal. The favorable reception of these by Henry M. Alden of *Harper's*, other critics, and the general public influenced Johnston to continue illustrating characters and scenes among the simple rural folk of his native region as they were during the pre-railroad days of his childhood.[92] In 1871 Johnston gave to the collection made by Turnbull the title *Dukesborough Tales* and adopted the nom de plume of Philemon Perch. With such a beginning, Johnston for more than twenty years contributed Georgia rural and town sketches to *Century*, *The Outlook*, and many other magazines. His novels and collected stories in-

[92] *Autobiography of Colonel Richard Malcolm Johnston* (Washington, 1900), pp. 71 ff. See also C. F. Smith, *Reminiscences and Sketches* (Nashville and Dallas, 1908), chap. ix, "Richard Malcolm Johnston," *passim;* B. S. Hart, *Introduction to Georgia Writers* (Macon, 1929), *passim;* W. A. Webb, "Richard Malcolm Johnston," *Southern Writers*, II, 46-81 ; and Trent, *Southern Writers*, pp. 381-383.

clude *Old Mark Langston* (1884), *Mr. Absalom Billingslea and Other Georgia Folk* (1888), *Widow Guthrie* (1890), *Mr. Billy Downes and His Likes* (1892) and *Old Times in Middle Georgia* (1898), all reminiscent of the author's boyhood and young manhood in Middle Georgia.

First written for personal entertainment and dedicated "to memories of the old times : the grim and rude but hearty old times in Georgia," *Dukesborough Tales, or The Chronicles of Mr. Bill Williams* pictures, in reality, the author's native Powelton, whose fertile region near the Savannah River was peopled by a hardy, democratic folk, humor loving and independent.

> The men of culture and those of wealth, as a general thing, were neighbors of the uncultured, and those with moderate or small property around them, and all were friends with one another ; not only trusting and trusted, but helpful, fond, and often affectionate.[93]

Even the cultured often resorted, through preference, to the use of the dialect of the humbler people.

From his reminiscences of such a democratic social state— the very opposite of Page's brilliant and cultured society— Johnston produced scores of small town scenes and characters which throw light on the intellectual and social development of Middle Georgia. His graphic, humorous portrayals of Dukesborough include many phases of life highly suggestive of Longstreet. As in *Georgia Scenes*, here old times come to life in racy accounts of lawsuits, circuses, weddings, camp meetings, funerals, church trials, musters, and school troubles, all identified with Powelton interests. While every class is faithfully described, the Negro plays a small part both here and in Johnston's other books. Only conventional types, such as the pompous coachman, appear. Realistic description, enlivened by occasional caricatures, is applied to many intensely provincial types known to Johnston in this Middle Georgia ante-bellum town : to garrulous country youths, ambitious to clerk in the village ; stern field schoolmasters and academy teachers ; provincial parsons, modeled, no doubt, upon the elder Johnston, a Baptist preacher ; dames and deacons bickering about free

---

[93] Preface, *Mr. Absalom Billingslea and Other Georgia Folk* (New York, 1888). See also Sophie B. Herrick, *op. cit.*, pp. 276-280, for a fuller discussion of the Middle Georgia folk. C. W. Coleman, Jr., "The Recent Movement in Southern Literature," *Harper's Magazine*, LXXIV, 837-855 (May, 1887), briefly surveys postbellum literary activities in the South.

grace; pompous militia officers; unscrupulous lawyers; comely widows, old maids, and peach-cheeked girls; and timid bachelors. These and other villagers are the pliable instruments employed by Johnston in revealing, with quaint humor but quite without contempt, the provinciality of Dukesborough.

Johnston's love for old associations, old places, and old times qualified all of his work. All of his fiction, especially *Old Mark Langston, Widow Guthrie, Mr. Absalom Billingslea and Other Georgia Folk*, and *Old Times in Middle Georgia*, is essentially reminiscent of the old Georgia village life, which he both idealized and caricatured, but out of which he created community pictures once termed "the truest history of Middle Georgia yet written."[94] More interested in social backgrounds and characterizations than in carefully devised plots, he described with essential accuracy an humble state of small town society which even before his own death had passed away. If Page may be called the preserver of the aristocratic regime, Johnston deserves recognition as a recorder of a life equally as significant in the South, the ante-bellum rural community and small town of Middle Georgia.

The two tendencies dominating the comparatively meager ante-bellum literature of the Southern small town lasted throughout and even beyond the nineteenth century. Along the seaboard, where life was better crystallized, the fascinating histories of Charleston, Jamestown, Williamsburg, and St. Mary's inspired the romancer both before and after the Civil War. As we have seen, in the Lower South and westward to the more sparsely settled regions along the Mississippi popular humorists created border town and back-country scenes unique in American community literature. These sharply contrasted trends, taking on new color as the century advanced, followed no formulas, for throughout America the period was a transitional one with much experimentation in fiction. As the sixties merged into the seventies the traditional fashions of romance and sentimentalism gradually weakened before the advance of a more realistic portrayal of local conditions in life. Toward the end of the century the quieter realism which developed during the eighties was overshadowed by a more harshly rebellious interpretation. About this time, also, highly colored romance, largely historical, became very popular.

[94] C. F. Smith, *op. cit.*, p. 183.

Out of these transitional movements emerged a number of writers who turned for subject matter to the Southern village and growing town. But few of these, however, added fiction of real distinction to the literary history of town life in the South. *Harper's* (November, 1882, through April, 1883) carried the old-fashioned and quietly realistic tale of the upper class in a Southern mountain town in Constance Fennimore Woolson's *For the Major*. Mary Johnston (1870-1936), harking back to the Caruthers-Cooke tradition, re-created colorfully the life of colonial Jamestown in her popular romance, *To Have and to Hold* (1899). Further illustrating the later renewal of popular interest in romance is Owen Wister's *Lady Baltimore* (1906), a delightful comedy of crabbed age and youth. Here, again, is a faithful representation of proud old Charleston. Sparkling dialogue and amusing satire mark Wister's portraits of the town's aristocracy and the scorned "yellow rich." In short, *Lady Baltimore* is an entertaining story of real townspeople who believe in their "hereditary standards mellow with the adherence of generations past."

Continuing the interests of the Longstreet-Johnston school, Joel Chandler Harris (1848-1908) understandingly analyzed various phases of pre-war small town life in the five realistic stories of *Free Joe and Other Georgian Sketches* (1887). His novel, *Gabriel Tolliver: A Story of Reconstruction* (1902), combines romance and realism in its tale of an old Georgia town noted for its long-established and hospitable families. Another native Georgian often associated with Johnston and Harris as a later interpreter of rural life in the South is Will N. Harben (1858-1919), whose realistic style once was highly praised by Howells. Harben's *Northern Georgia Sketches* (1900), together with such novels as *Abner Daniel* (1902), *Pole Baker* (1905), *Ann Boyd* (1906), and *The Cottage of Delight* (1919), are marked by sound, if not powerful, realism. His straightforward sketches of the rough life of farm villages and mountain towns, of plain townspeople and social outcasts foreshadow the sharper and more caustic notes characterizing small town literature after the World War. Likewise realistic are John Uri Lloyd's *Stringtown on the Pike* (1900), a Civil War novel centered in the neutral ground of a Kentucky town near the Ohio; and Ruth McEnery Stuart's collection of seven stories, *In Simpkinsville* (1902), written with marked sympathy for the homely life of a little Arkansas town. A truly descriptive book is E. S. Nadal's *A Virginian Village* (1917), an unsentimental sketch of a Greenbrier County mountain town familiar to the author since his boyhood. Scornful of pre-war Southerners and others whose highly romanticized stories made swans out of geese, Nadal boldly speaks the truth about his native town, portraying with unusual candor a provincial society formed by sturdy Scotch-Irish Presbyterian small farmers and craftsmen rather than by wealthy planters and ladies in stiff brocades.

The efforts of these Southerners, however, were sporadic. Until the century's end no one novelist had emerged from the confusion of transition to voice adequately the changing South, then a region, notes Professor Pattee, with enough untouched material to satisfy a Fielding or a Dickens or a Hardy. James Branch Cabell, seemingly the only younger writer capable of using this wealth, dealt but little with the actual in his Lichfield, but, repudiating the sordid, wearisome facts of daily life, escaped to a fantastically romantic dream-world, to Storisende in Poictesme.[95] It remained for a cultured young Richmond woman, Ellen (Anderson Gholson) Glasgow, to initiate with her first novel, *The Descendant* (1897), the new forthright attack against the oratorical romanticism of a defeated South. Prophetic of later interpretations of her native materials, *The Descendant* marked Miss Glasgow's early interest in the promise of the new order rather than in the glamor of a vanished regime. Here was rich promise of a sustained, deliberate realism subtly revealing the incongruities between the old and the new in the South. From the outset Miss Glasgow's work has expressed her belief in the accurate presentation of historical backgrounds as an approach to the intelligent interpretation of a later Virginia. Such passion for accuracy is evidenced early in her trilogy of historical romances : *The Voice of the People* (1900), *The Battle-Ground* (1902), and *The Romance of a Plain Man* (1909), all tragic novels portraying with power and marked actuality the weakening old regime, the agonies of war and reconstruction, and the emergent South. Built upon the solid foundations of scholarship and honest recognition of "the hardship and struggle imposed by defeat," these novels

---

[95] Pattee, *The New American Literature* (New York, 1930), p. 256. Cf. P. H. Boynton, *Some Contemporary Americans* (Chicago, 1924), chap. ix, "Mr. Cabell Expounds Himself." Note Cabell's presentation of community life in *Cords of Vanity* (1909) and *The Rivet in Grandfather's Neck* (1915).

offer not only a rich social chronicle of Piedmont and seaboard Virginia during stirring times, but also a witty, observing
woman's outlook on post-bellum small town life in her native
state.

Of the novels forming this trilogy, *The Voice of the People*
most adequately shows Miss Glasgow's deep understanding of
the smaller community. An austerely realistic tragedy of the
changes wrought by the new democracy in "blue blood" Virginia, this is the story of a dramatic clash between the upper
and lower strata of society. Tragedy is inevitable when Nicholas (Nick) Burr, a peculiarly ambitious poor white, slowly
forms associations with certain impoverished, but pathetically
proud, aristocrats and neighboring planters of old Kingsborough (Williamsburg). Throughout the uneven course of his
rise to the governorship always Nick is aware of the caste limitations imposed upon him, son of a poor white, by Kingsborough's degenerating aristocrats. Changed through the leveling process of war, the old town still clings to the shreds of
its former gentility. Now a lethargic place of toppling traditions, it is, nevertheless, the seat of once prosperous blue bloods
still adhering stubbornly to cherished codes and quite forgetting that the flourishing center of past generations no longer
exists. Certain old dwellings, the tree-shaded church, and the
historic college buildings still remain, but Gloucester Street,
though "still wide and white and placidly impressed by the
slow passage of Kingsborough feet," is now Main Street. Here
more and more tradesmen, poor whites and free Negroes from
adjoining small farms, and others representative of the new
social order throng when circuit court is in session. In this
story of a poor white hero Miss Glasgow traces with rare genius
the far-reaching influences of the modern spirit upon an ancient town.

Resolutely Miss Glasgow has continued through the years
her realistic treatment of many social themes, none more effective than that of the submergence of a defeated order by the
new economic and industrial rehabilitation of the South. In
rebellion against the affectations of romantic glorifiers, she has
protested repeatedly, with courage and ironic wit, against the
futility and the frustrations of the sheltered life, with its accompanying code of pride. Again and again, from *The Descendant* to *The Sheltered Life* (1932) and other novels, the tragedy

of "diminished grandeur" has intruded itself in her stories. Among such socially revealing studies are occasional treatments of the realities of small town life. Notable among these is her earlier humanitarian novel, *The Ancient Law* (1908), a powerful protest against false social standards. Her hero was, then, a shockingly new type, an ex-convict formerly of good social position. Daniel, newly released from prison, finds the code-bound society of his native aristocratic Botecourt inadequate to heal the wounds in a human soul. Lydia, his genteel wife, is as truly a victim of the sheltered life as he, and evil befalls even his impulsive young daughter when she revolts against the stultifying code. Daniel himself finds release only by social uplift among laborers in the factory town of Tappahannock.

The conflicts between the old and the new in towns the size of Richmond have long been the subject of Miss Glasgow's fiction. In novels such as *The Romance of a Plain Man* (1909), *Virginia* (1913), *The Romantic Comedians* (1926), *They Stooped to Folly* (1929), and *The Sheltered Life* (1932) she examines with rare insight and mingled irony and humor the downfall of the unstable social standards of the mauve decade and later. In a town like her Queenborough, but lately emergent from its pre-war small town state, impoverished First Families, living in faded grandeur, struggle against the almost crushing wealth of newly enriched butchers, machinists, and railroad workers. The socially ambitious sons and daughters of these proletariats storm the very citadels of the old order. They are, as Judge Honeywell of *The Romantic Comedians* reflected, crass representatives of The Age of Pretense, The Age of Hypocrisy, The Age of Asphalt.[96] How, the old Judge wondered gloomily, "was the tyranny of the inferior an advance upon the tyranny of the superior?"[97] In Queenborough, Virginia, as in Midwestern Zenith, the new life was ushering in a triumphant ostentatious democracy tragically affecting the First Families : the Littlepages, the Birdsongs, the Honeywells, and the Archbalds whose own relationships are marred by false loyalties, frustrations, and even cynicism. Steadily the town's long-hallowed genteel tradition weakens before the cynicism and the discontent of the modern acceptance of life. Outmoded

[96] Glasgow, *The Romantic Comedians* (New York, 1926), p. 10.
[97] *Ibid.*

are the Aunt Agathas who once suffered social ostracism—and retired for forty years to back bedrooms—because of youthful indiscretions. Gone are days when all attractive young women used to be shielded from contamination.[98] The older false, if noble, attitudes of not facing life had changed with the times, but not, so far as Judge Honeywell could see, for the better.

Beginning at the century's close as a courageous critic of Southern life, Miss Glasgow, herself closely linked by birth with an aristocratic lineage, has not been moved by a feeling of false allegiance to an outmoded idealism. Brilliantly witty, she early helped form the vanguard of modern writers whose rebellion against the past is now a matter of literary record.[99] Like the "new" biographers, again and again she has brought out the truth about plain folk and cultured—about the hard-working Dorinda Oakleys (of *Barren Ground*) and the genteel Judge Honeywells. Through her brilliant, ironically humorous pictures of the sentimental tradition and her realistic appraisal of the modes and morals of the New South "Southerntown" in modern literature has become a strangely different place from the back-country villages of Middle Georgia and the Williamsburgs, Charlestons, and Cartersvilles of an idealized past. Her strong characterizations of individual folly and economic pressure point the way toward the modern "Southerntown," the creation of Miss Glasgow's younger contemporaries, T. S. Stribling, William Faulkner, Thomas Wolfe, and other social satirists. Their belated participation in the "battle of the village" is another story.

[98] *Ibid.*, p. 165.
[99] Note Herschel Brickell, "The Literary Awakening in the South," *The Bookman*, LXVI, 138-143 (Oct., 1927), and Alan R. Thompson, "The Cult of Cruelty," *The Bookman*, LXXIV, 477-487 (Jan., 1932), a discussion of Faulkner.

CHAPTER X

CRUSADERS AND SKEPTICS

IN SPITE OF certain earlier sporadic revolts against a strong
idealism, it was not until 1915 that the first expression of a
definite and widely noticed revolutionary phase developed in
the literature of the local.   At that time, with the publication
of Edgar Lee Masters's *Spoon River Anthology*, a newer, more
satiric realism in American fiction moved forward, a slow trend
requiring almost five years for its influence to pass thoroughly
from poetry to prose.   Previously, for more than a century,
native writers, generally speaking, had been true to the romantic tradition of the village.   Neither Midwestern agrarian discontent, nor the vast pioneering movements beyond the Mississippi, nor the caustic protest of certain rebels and back
trailers (Kirkland, Howe, Mark Twain, Howells, Garland,
Glasgow, and others) had deterred romantic Easterners and
their followers from their sentimental praise of village "pas-
toralism."   Diligently these romanticists searched out beneath
the quiet surface of American provincial life all evidences of
an indispensable goodness, happiness, democracy, and heroism.   As they saw America, even in the outposts of the Middle
Border, before the World War, many small towns "had developed as living monuments to Puritanism and the pioneer
spirit."[1]   Here, they noted, flourished the gospels of conformity,
thrift, industry, democracy, and boundless optimism, all butts
for the attacks of newly vocal radicals who everywhere were
beginning to look at the town uncompromisingly.   For a while
the old style, dominant since Freneau's *The American Village*,
maintained its strength against the new forces.   All of the
long-established gods of the "villagists" were not at once overthrown.   Stubbornly clinging to the genteel traditions of Tiverton, Deephaven, and Old Chester, their loyal defenders
bravely resisted the almost overwhelming Americanness of a
vigorous emergent order.   Even while a new gospel of realism
was being expounded throughout the Middle Border, the older

[1] Blankenship, *op. cit.*, p. 650.

school continued to produce romantic, sweetly romanticized interpretations of the small town. For some "rosy America" still lived.[2]

The growing antagonism of certain young intellectuals to Puritanism and the Victorian ideals of a smug middle class gradually increased in intensity, but writers like James Whitcomb Riley (Hoosier poet of the bucolic West), Meredith Nicholson, with his elaborate defense of the village in *The Valley of Democracy* (1918), William Allen White, Booth Tarkington, Zona Gale, and others continued idealizing the Midwestern community. Much of their fiction, in contrast to the newly emergent pictures of Masters and others, represented one of two sharply antagonistic attitudes of the first quarter of the century. In poetry and fiction these leaders of this so-called "squeamish and emasculate crusade" saw their country as "America the Beautiful." Dotting its "fruited plains" were countless villages peopled by neighborly, industrious men and women, happy middle-class people "uncursed by poverty and unspoiled by wealth."[3] To them American democracy was "a going concern." According to William Allen White, their chief fear, however, was that the national prosperity might grow into a national folly through the greed for wealth and political power fostered by the boss system.[4] This cognizance of a national evil actually did little, except in the later fictional changes of Tarkington and Zona Gale, toward lessening the earlier glorification of village virtues in the "valley of democracy."

While Riley (1845-1916), native of the country town of Greenfield, Indiana, and the "People's Laureate," belongs with Will Carleton and Eugene Field to an older period, he lived well into the new day and influenced the later literature of the

[2] Henry Seidel Canby in "The Two Americas," from his *Saturday Papers* (1921), excellently describes our confusing country as the modern novelist has seen it. "One," says Mr. Canby, "is the dun America and the other is the rosy America." The first America is a land of prevailing ugliness and dinginess; the second is beautified by "folksy" villages and thriving towns, the homes of a contented, kindly citizenry. But these contrasting pictures, says Mr. Canby, represent states of mind and not the real America, which has both the virtues and the faults of an agricultural country subjected to a metropolized civilization. Cf. Lewis Mumford's powerful argument in *The Culture of Cities* (New York, 1938), "The Insensate Industrial Town," pp. 143 to 221.
[3] Parrington, *The Beginnings of Critical Realism*, pp. 373-374.
[4] *The Old Order Changeth: A View of American Democracy* (New York, 1910), pp. 1 and 21-22.

23

town with his "homely native stuff," his sentiment extolling the virtues of country and small town life, and his humorous dialect. His widespread popularity as a balladist of the homely virtues greatly strengthened the development of the White-Tarkington doctrine of the "beautiful people" and the "folksy" village.

One of the most outspoken apologists for the village who early drew fire from critics of the opposite school is kindly William Allen White (1868—), whose recent collection of editorials, *Forty Years on Main Street* (1937), is truly termed the "saga of an average town." And that town is Emporia, Kansas, White's birthplace, presented in these editorials culled from the files of the *Emporia Gazette* as "the microcosm of Mid-America." A loyal Middle Westerner and widely recognized journalist, White has been, since his purchase of the *Gazette* in 1895, a fearless spokesman for the independence of the small town newspaper. His long close and personal relationship with town and country has made him, like his fellow-Kansan, E. W. Howe, an informed and increasingly influential defender of the West. A product of middle-class Puritan Kansas and a believer in fairness among men, he has announced through editorial and fiction his faith in the basic excellence of the Midwest and its substantial rural and small town life. Since his stirringly caustic "What's the Matter with Kansas?" editorial of August 15, 1896, he has been interested in all problems adding to the material fullness of life in Emporia and his prairie state. As he has grown old with Emporia he has found the town good to him, "charitable," he says, "beyond my deserts, and I have tried to be loyal to the town." On his sixty-fifth birthday he announced editorially that he had "found humanity good with much more that was fine than was false," a discovery in keeping with his belief that "happiness is from the heart out—not from the world in."[5] On the other hand, in *The Old Order Changeth* and his novels, *A Certain Rich Man* (1909) and *In the Heart of a Fool* (1918), he has expressed the fear that industrialism will submerge the older democratic order of village life. To Kansans one of their leading citizens and spokes-

[5] *Forty Years on Main Street* (New York, 1937), pp. 29 and 33; Elizabeth Sergeant, "The Citizen from Emporia," *Century Magazine*, CXIII, 316 (Jan., 1927); and *The Editor and His People*, editorials by Mr. White, selected from the *Emporia Gazette* by Helen O. Mahin (New York, 1914), *passim*.

men, White stands out, it is said, as a builder of a prairie civilization which has gradually assumed the common American shape.[6]

By virtue of his full portrayals in *At the Court of Boyville* (1899) White early joined the ranks of Aldrich, Clemens, Howells, Crane, and others as an understanding interpreter of boy life in small towns. Here the background of the town is of secondary interest. The romance of boyhood (adventures, rivalries, displays of boyish prowess, and even love affairs) makes the primary appeal. The freedom and democracy of boyhood in a small town—a theme often touched upon in the *Gazette* editorials—are set against the restrictions of the city.[7] It is shown that "in a small town, every boy, good or bad, stands among boys on his own merits." Piggy Pennington, king of Boyville, is as real as Crane's Jimmy Trescott or Tarkington's Penrod of a later date.

Maintaining a kindly feeling toward the town, White with *In Our Town* (1906) produced a series of community sketches presented from the viewpoint of an editor in a small Midwestern town at the turn of the century. The newspaper offices, drawn from White's own experiences during the nineties in the *Gazette* office, furnish the background for full-length portraits of the "office gang," the printers and their devils, and the citizens represented in the weekly columns.[8] A friendly spirit rules the community.

Ours is a little town in that part of the country called the West by those who live east of the Alleghanies, and referred to lovingly as "back East" by those who dwell West of the Rockies. It is a country town where, as the song goes, "You know everybody and they all know you," and the country newspaper office is the social clearing-house.[9]

Editorially, for almost half a century, White has been loyal to the good causes of Emporia's Commercial Street, has encour-

[6] *In the Heart of a Fool* (New York, 1918), p. 117.
[7] Cf. *Forty Years on Main Street*, "Thoughts on Kids" and "Real Boys," p. 375 and "The Top Season," p. 376.
[8] In the *Gazette* editorials Editor White long had the habit of writing articles of praise about Emporia's living and dead. His "Old Tom" is a unique tribute to a local ne'er-do-well, a thieving Negro.
[9] *In Our Town* (New York, 1925), p. 3. Cf. *Forty Years on Main Street*, "Beautiful Emporia," p. 378, and "The Glory of June," p. 379.

aged the growth of its College and Normal, and sponsored the cultural development of the community at large.[10]   Likewise, in his fiction he champions wholesome village life and openly scorns the city objector who thinks of all small towns as settled by uncouth "rubes" or "hicks."

Because we live in country towns, where the only car-gongs we hear are on the baker's wagon, and where the horses in the fire department work on the streets, is no reason why city dwellers should assume that we are natives. We have no dialect worth recording. . . . But you will find that all the things advertised in the backs of magazines are in our houses, and that the young men in our towns walking home at midnight, with their coats on their arms, whistle the same popular airs that lovelorn boys are whistling in New York, Portland, San Francisco, or New Orleans. . . . Our girls are those pretty, reliant, well-dressed young women whom you see at the summer resorts from Coronado Beach to Buzzard's Bay.   In the fall and winter these girls fill the colleges of the East and the State universities of the West.   Those wholesome, frank, good-natured people whom you met last winter at the Grand Canyon and who told you of the funny performance of "Uncle Tom's Cabin" in Yiddish at the People's Theatre on the East Side in New York, and insisted that you see the totem pole in Seattle ; and then take a cottage for a month at Catalina Island ; who gave you the tip about [a] quaint little beafsteak chop-house up an alley in Chicago, who told you of [a] second-hand furniture shop in Charleston . . . those people are our leading citizens, who run the bank or the dry goods store or the flour mill.[11]

Our Town counted among its citizens no perverts such as those with whom Masters nine years later peopled Spoon River, but middle-class workers who lived in happy relationship, more or less, with their fellows.   There were, of course, certain village eccentrics and black sheep :   "Mail-Order" Petrie, a miserly codger who refused, even to the extreme of getting a mail-order wife and wishing for a mail-order heaven, to buy from local merchants ; David, a Welsh linotypist, subject to "spells" ; Joe Nevinson, who raided ranches and robbed banks with the Dalton gang ; and "Old Hen," village socialist

<hr/>

[10] See *Forty Years on Main Street*, "An Editor and His Town" (Dec. 4, 1924), pp. 275-276.
[11] *In Our Town*, pp. 7-8. Cf. *Forty Years on Main Street*, *passim*, and the recent novel, *What People Said* (1938), by William L. White, the son of William Allen White, who writes of the "society" group in a Midwestern town, presumably Emporia.

and woman-hater.   Until the arrival of an out-of-town gallant, Our Town—Emporia in embryo—had been a quiet village with a leisure class consisting of "Red Martin, the gambler, the only man in town with nothing to do in the middle of the day; and the black boys who loafed on the south side of the bank building until it was time to deliver the clothes which their wives and mothers had washed."[12]   Beverly Amidon transformed this village peacefulness.   The first man in town who dared wear a flannel suit on the streets, Beverly introduced ping-pong, "tacky" parties, progressive buggy rides, barn dances, and Japanese garden fêtes for the Epworth League. He even tried organizing a polo club, "but the ponies from the delivery wagons that were available after six o'clock did not take training well. . . ."

Like Herbert Quick, White fictionalized the emergence of larger industrial towns from barren settlements having all the rawness of new prairie towns.[13]   In *A Certain Rich Man*, a problem novel, the villager is drawn into the complicated life of a newly industrialized Midland town.   John Barclay and Sycamore Ridge change together as the menace of economic pressure and crass commercialism accompanies the natural growth of the town (from 1857 to 1909).   All of the minutiae of community development are shown : the migration of people to Kansas, the establishment of a nondescript village, and the growth of schools, churches, and commercial centers on the prairie.   In short, as if by some sort of magic, the Sycamore Ridge of the sixties, "a gray smudge of unpainted wooden houses bordering the Santa Fe trail," rapidly became a little city.   In the success of Barclay the author plants the moral that the piling up of millions does not bring happiness.   The city, says White, takes its toll of the village and economic centralization destroys the friendly democracy of the older small town life.[14]

Much of the story of *In the Heart of a Fool* rests upon White's belief that towns, curiously like individuals, take their character largely from their experiences, "laid layer upon layer in

[12] *In Our Town*, p. 72.

[13] White himself watched the development of Emporia from an embryo town to a thriving place of more than twelve thousand (*Forty Years on Main Street*, pp. 37 ff.).

[14] The same idea is enlarged upon in Canby's "Two Americas" and, more recently, Lewis Mumford in his *Culture of Cities* has written at great length upon the effect of centralization upon American life.

their consciousness, as time moves." While these experiences seemingly are forgotten, their results are ineffaceably written into the towns. Harvey was just such a town with its inheritance of a strong New England strain of blood marked by numerous migrations westward from New England into the Mississippi Valley. Even as an infant town—the town of pioneers—it sought instinctively the schoolhouse, the newspaper, orderly government, real estate gambling, and churches.[15] Early in the town's history the cattle trail appeared, the cattle trade flourished, and evil, disorderly times resulted. But the extension of the railroad carried the cattle trail westward and the town languished until the sudden discovery of coal, oil, and gas brought boom days to the community. These were fat years when "it began raining red-wheeled buggies on Sundays, and smart traps drawn by horses harnessed gaudily in white or tan appeared on the streets."[16] Signs of industry's invasion and the disintegration of village ways were everywhere. The boom became a "crass riot of greed" as both early settlers and newcomers gave themselves to an orgy of materialism. Life in Harvey shaped itself into "a vast greedy dream."[17] The democracy of the small town speedily was overshadowed by the growth of social cliques. Huge architectural monstrosities replaced the simpler homes of the pioneer days. The days of the "Haves" (the dwellers on the Hill) and the "Have-Nots" (the factory workers in "the dreary valley of industrialization") had arrived. It was the dawn of the new century, a new day which "brought to Harvey such a plentitude that all night and all day the smelter fires painted the sky" and capitalists profited from the mines while underpaid workers toiled underground and lived in mean, squalid streets.[18]

In this novel, as in *A Certain Rich Man*, White is the idealist whose memories of pioneer days make him reluctant to accept post-war conditions. Bigness and Wealth are antagonistic to his views of happiness and the contentment which he feels may be found in small, friendly places like Our Town (i.e., Em-

---

[15] *In the Heart of a Fool*, p. 63.
[16] Cf. *Forty Years on Main Street*, pp. 16 ff., the editorials "Wanted : a Horse" (April 3, 1906) and "A Grand Old Horse" (Sept. 24, 1912) for White's description of his own horse, Old Tom.
[17] *In the Heart of a Fool*, p. 6.
[18] *Ibid.*, p. 350. See the whole chapter, "The Turn of the Century."

poria). In William Allen White, the son of trail-makers, the small towns of the Middle Border have a loyal, fearless champion.

A "James Whitcomb Riley with a college education, writing fiction instead of verse," Newton Booth Tarkington (1869–), after a seven-year literary apprenticeship, emerged from Indiana in 1889 as another believer in "the friendly village myth." Since then, for more than three decades, his novels praising the virtues of middle-class townsmen, at home and abroad, have gained Tarkington a wide following. Gaining popular success with *The Gentleman from Indiana*, his first novel, Tarkington cut for himself a village pattern which he has used repeatedly in his later stories of "the good dear people" of Indiana towns. In this novel, as in others, the rewards of material success and love are bestowed upon a worthy young hero, sturdy in independence and victorious in his campaigns against local disorders. The conventional plot, akin in theme to *The Hoosier Schoolmaster*, tells the amazingly triumphant story of an upright and youthful college-bred editor in Plattville, a Hoosier hamlet of "folksy" people. This excellent youth puts an end to the local vice ring and rowdiness, restores the village peace of mind, miraculously escapes harm from his enemies, marries the girl of his choice, and is rewarded by his admiring townsmen—"the beautiful people"—by being nominated for Congress. What a model for ambitious Midland youths of the nineties!

After a prolonged period of romantic writings, best represented in *Monsieur Beaucaire* (1900), the gentleman from Indiana began in 1913 a second phase of literary endeavor. Too prone in early years to pander to popular taste, Tarkington now realized the growing importance of realistic trends in literature. Accordingly, he abandoned his romantic genre for the stuff of modern life. Again the village background was his choice. His next stories, the familiar *Penrod* (1914), *Penrod and Sam* (1916), *Seventeen* (1916), and *Clarence* (1919), first given popularity in *The Saturday Evening Post*, call to mind the sort of small town life associated with Mark Twain's masterly portrayal of the bad boy whose "subsequent habitat has usually been the Middle West, where a recognized lineage connects Tom Sawyer and Huckleberry Finn with Mitch Miller and Penrod Schofield and their fellow-conspirators against the

peace of the villagers."[19]   In *Ramsay Milholland* (1919), a sentimental, weakly developed tale of the decade ending with the
World War, the American small town boy is pictured through
the stages of adolescence, college years, and soldierhood. More
recently Tarkington—satirized as "the perennial sophomore"
—has returned to this earlier theme of boyish escapades in
Little Orvie (1934).[20]

Popular with readers, Tarkington has not fared so well with
the critics of these tales of adolescence. Characterized as a
mere reporter, rather than as an understanding interpreter of
his youthful heroes, he has been charged with the superficial
creation of comedy from materials which are not always comic.
He has been censured for winking over the heads of adolescent
Penrod and William Sylvanus Baxter "at men and women
who are able to smile with him at the ridiculous figures which
the youngsters cut" and for parodying a life "which arouses
mirth because it seems so like and yet so unlike the adult life
it parodies."[21]   Others consider his "little monsters" the amusing, spontaneous, and genuine creations of one who knew both
the humor and tragedy of adolescence in a main-street Western
town.[22]

In *The Gentleman from Indiana* and several of his other apprenticeship novels (*The Two Vanrevels* and *The Conquest of Canaan*)
middle-class romance and town politics furnished both plot
and sentimental philosophy. With *The Turmoil* (1915) Tarkington, like Miss French and William Allen White, looked at
the Western town of industry, newly arisen from a prairie village. Here, too, conventionally romantic love stories, commonplace delineations of the newly rich who strive for social
position, and the all too sudden transformation of the hero
from a dreamer and a weakling to a Titan of industry weaken
the really fine portrayals of the evolution of a friendly market
town into a city, the scene of industrial turmoil. Tarkington
shows well how small town burghers, worshiping the new gods
of Bigness and Wealth, themselves either found or lost fortunes.

[19] Carl Van Doren, *Contemporary American Novelists*, p. 9.   Mitch Miller is the
hero of Masters's novel, *Mitch Miller*.
[20] Quotation from Van Doren, *op. cit.*, p. 87.
[21] Carl and Mark Van Doren, *American and British Literature Since 1890* (New
York, 1925), p. 62.
[22] Pattee, *The New American Literature*, pp. 77-78.

This evolutionary process is perhaps best summed up in the words of Sheridan, self-made millionaire :

"You *bet* there's a 'great unrest'!   There ain't any man smart enough to see what it's goin' to do to us in the end, nor what day it's got set to bust loose, but it's frothin' and bubblin' in the boiler . . . the old camp meetin' days are dead and done with."[23]

The evolution of the small town is again the theme in other Tarkington novels.   *The Magnificent Ambersons* (1918) portrays the rapid changes in a Midland town from the seventies to the World War era when big fortunes, says Tarkington, behaved "like an ash-barrel in a cyclone—there wasn't even a dust-heap left to tell where it stood."   Thus it was with the Ambersons, whose magnificence against the homespun background of the small town was as conspicuous as a "brass band at a funeral."[24]   In the years of their glory the Ambersons led the community in styles of dress, social customs, the building of homes, and the direction of business.   Even in a democratic Midland town they constituted something of a small aristocracy.   Such style the town had never seen.   It marveled at the European trips which Major Amberson's wife and daughter enjoyed, gossiped at the Amberson fashion of preparing lettuce salad and eating olives, and gaped at Isabel Amberson's Saint Bernard.   In short, Tarkington's opening chapters colorfully reproduce life at the turn of the century in a small town.

Like hundreds of other towns throughout the country, this town, too, moved forward with the times, its old stock becoming less and less typical and newcomers with energy and business acumen taking their places of community leadership.   In the offspring of German, Jewish, Irish, Italian, and other settlers "a new Midlander—in fact, a new American—was beginning dimly to emerge."[25]   To this new spirit of citizenship the magnificent Ambersons, reared in luxury, were unable to adapt themselves.   Others, with a heritage of labor, rapidly took high places as the town progressed from village to market town to a manufacturing city.   In this downfall of an early

[23] *The Turmoil* (New York, 1915), p. 209.
[24] *The Magnificent Ambersons* (New York, 1918), p. 16.
[25] *Ibid* , p. 388.   For a similar treatment of Midwestern town growth see Louis Bromfield's fully documented novels : *The Green Bay Tree* (1924) and *Possession* (1925).

wealthy and dominating family Tarkington finds his main motif, to which he attaches, as usual, the love story of a persevering and, of course, worthy youth. In *Alice Adams* (1921) and
The Midlander (1924) Tarkington variously uses the same theme
of social changes accompanying small town growth. The
former, more highly praised by discriminating critics than the
earlier Tarkington novels, pictures the small town as the set
stage for the pathetic social struggles of a young Alice Adams,
a romantic, but really clever and pretty, girl who is defeated
by her middle-class environment. Eager to become intimate
with the town's socially élite—those of the "frozen faces," her
brother bitterly calls them—Alice is led into petty deceits to
keep up appearances. Everywhere she is doomed to failure,
for as their old-time acquaintances of village days prosper in
the growing business of the town, the Adamses sink lower in
the social scale. Actually *The Midlander* is little more than a
retelling of *The Turmoil* and *The Magnificent Ambersons*. Like
these, it is the tale of old families, conventional Midlanders
from the earlier days of the community, and of their adjustments to the changing life around them. A slight innovation
in one of the love stories introduces a city wife for one of the
small town philistines. Lena Oliphant, like Sinclair Lewis's
Carol, was unpleasantly critical of the town and its people.
Wholly out of sympathy with the Western attitude toward
materialism, Lena found the town utterly commonplace and
its citizens hopelessly provincial. Her husband's constant
boosting of his real estate ventures and his automobile manufactures convinced her that she had married a madman.[26]
Since he continues dallying with similar characters, plots, and
backgrounds, Tarkington furthers the literature of the town
very little in *Gentle Julia*, *The Plutocrat*, and other Midland
novels.

As writers of the little town both White and Tarkington illustrate what has happened to many extollers of folksiness. Each,
using what one critic has called nice pinks and yellows, began
with glorifications of late nineteenth-century village life. Finally, each, having watched the small town of the Midlands
change with the growth of industry, turned to more realistic

[26] *The Midlander* (New York, 1924), p. 214. Entirely different from his Mid-
land novels is Tarkington's recent *Mr. White, The Red Barn, and Bridewater* (1935).
"The World in the Red Barn" is a powerful story of the circumscribed life in a
New England village.

treatments of the industrialized town and small city. Both, however, have retained earlier traits and, in spite of the appearance of new problems in American fiction, have staunchly defended small town ways and middle-class thinking.

On the other hand, others, responsive to the perplexing changes in our national life, became a part of the spreading restlessness and revolt in the land. Among these was Zona Gale (Mrs. William L. Breese of Portage, Wisconsin),* at one time a saccharine village laureate, but later a turncoat deserting her earlier defense of the village. Beginning her career as a chronicler of the Middle Western town after the style of Miss Mitford, Zona Gale eventually joined the hostile camp of village critics and, equipped with new materials, began in convincing fashion the exposure of small town intellectual aridity. An examination of her first village studies but heightens, through contrast, the tone of her later critical attitude.

Following the negligible work of *Romance Island* (1906) and *The Loves of Pelleas and Etarre* (1907), Miss Gale in 1908 first gained attention from critics with *Friendship Village*, a series of sentimental sketches in which she expressed an idealistic village creed. The intimate associations of little home towns provided motivation not only for *Friendship Village* but likewise for *Friendship Village Love Stories* (1909), *Neighborhood Stories* (1914), *Peace in Friendship Village* (1919), and other stories. The keynote to Miss Gale's earlier attitude appears in her delight in community fellowship. This simple basic emotion, she says in *Friendship Village Love Stories*, is the foundation for her joy in village life. In Friendship Village folk adventured together, "knowing the details of one another's lives, striving a little but companioning far more than striving, kindling to one another's interests instead of practising the faint morality of mere civility."[27] In all of the Friendship series revelations are made of neighborhood intimacies, church affairs, and civic matters. All the young people "keeping company" in the village are discussed in informal colloquies over back fences, at the front gate, and at church socials. Miggy and Peter and other young couples are gossiped about with the usual freedom of the small town by Mis' Toplady, good-hearted· Calliope

* Miss Gale died on December 27, 1938, at the age of sixty-four.
[27] New York, 1909, p. 6. These stories first were published in *Everybody's*, *The American Magazine*, *The Outlook*, *The Woman's Home Companion*, and *The Delineator*.

March, Mis' Sykes, and other interested elders of the village
sisterhood. In short, what one of her villagers termed the
"togetherness" of small town life made a strong appeal to Miss
Gale, who herself was reared in the little town of Portage.[28]

Restricted in theme to the commonplaces of narrow lives,
all the Friendship stories, nevertheless, are happily optimistic
in tone. The busy men and women of the town find time to
enjoy the neighborliness of a limited environment. The village women, especially, are always ready to meet any emer-
gency. Marvels of serenity and capability, they

. . . prepare breakfasts, put up lunches, turn the attention to the
garden, and all, so to speak, with the left hand ; ready at any moment to enter upon the real business of life—to minister to the sick
or bury the dead, or conduct a town meeting or a church supper
or a birth. They have a kind of goddess-like competence, these
women.[29]

Little is said of the village fathers, but one may suppose that
they, too, were both competent and Samaritan-minded. Otherwise, they could not have lived in Friendship, the sweetest of
villages, one, says Carl Van Doren, that should stand "upon
the confectionery shelf of the fiction shop, preserved in thick
syrup. . . ." In all of these stories of secluded, intimate life
Miss Gale varied the same device of "showing how childlike
children are, how sisterly are sisters, how brotherly are brothers, how motherly are mothers, how fatherly are fathers, how
grandmotherly and grandfatherly are grandmothers and grand-
fathers, and how loverly are all true lovers of whatever age,
sex, color, or condition."[30] While Friendship Village, with no
definite location upon the printed map of the world, may once
have been praised as worthy of abiding permanently in the
memories of countless readers, "who in the enjoyment of its
chronicles have been able temporarily to forget the latitude and
longitude of their own personal cares and sorrows," it is really
no haven for the modern escapist.[31] The eternal saccharine
might prove too strong.

Even Miss Gale herself wearied of her own idyllic creed, as

[28] Hamlin Garland gives a glimpse of Miss Gale in her home town in his first
chapter of *Afternoon Neighbors* (New York, 1935).
[29] *Friendship Village Love Stories*, p. 26.
[30] Van Doren, *Contemporary American Novelists*, p. 164.
[31] Frederick Tabor Cooper, *The Bookman*, XXXI, 79 (March, 1910).

her later and more mordant village criticism shows.   The influence of *Spoon River Anthology* marks her complete change of
style in *Birth* (1918), a novel of a small Wisconsin town.[32]
Realistic description, natural characterization, and logical plot
indicate a pronounced deepening of Miss Gale's understanding
of village manners.   Here she has such an assemblage of types
that her *dramatis personae* resemble a living picture of the eighties.   The portrait of Marshall Pitt—a timid little man pitied
by his son and neighbors—gives promise of what Miss Gale
later was to do in *Miss Lulu Bett*.   The heroine's desertion of
her husband and native town in the hope of finding beauty
and pleasure in the city foreshadows *Main Street*.   For the first
time in her recording of inhibited lives Miss Gale, like many
of her Western contemporaries, declared in this novel her
revolt from the village.

In 1920 appeared the novel, *Miss Lulu Bett*, Zona Gale's
most artistic and masterly interpretation of the village type.
A brief, yet definite and realistic, portrayal of uninspired American family life, *Miss Lulu Bett*, like *Birth*, is another study of
inhibition.   The plot, terse and dramatic in every respect,
moves toward the triumphant revolt of a village drudge, who
unexpectedly rebels against her menial position in the household of her silly married sister.   No longer will she be the family scapegoat and slavey.   Into her dull life comes an unconventional marriage with a trifler, who subsequently abandons
her.   Thus her marriage, apparently an escape from her cheerless surroundings, develops Lulu's great tragedy, until, finally,
her release comes through her marriage with the village music-
dealer.   A trivial story of trivial people, *Miss Lulu Bett* is also
a sympathetic study of a kind-hearted, yet pathetic, village
woman.

Terseness of style marks both the depictions of Warbleton,
a dull and petty place, and of the commonplace Deacon family.   By daring to write genuinely dull dialogue, Miss Gale
not only departs from the traditional artificial conversation in
American drama, but ridicules, almost without a word of comment, the affectation of this ordinary household.[33]   Typical
American family conversation serves as the medium for presenting George Herbert Deacon, "the high priest of this elab-

---

[32] Dramatized as *Mister Pitt* (Appleton, 1926).
[33] *Miss Lulu Bett* was dramatized in 1921.

orate banality." and Monona, "the first normal stage child."[34]
Miss Gale's adherence to uninspiring reality violates the traditional rules of the drama.   Above all, she creates ordinary,
dull people.   Mrs. Bett is an old woman who is not sweet and
Monona is a child who is not cute.   Dwight and Ina Deacon
are dull, middle-class villagers, while Lulu is, in the words of
Van Doren, "the symbol of bullied spinsterhood."   The same
uninspired dialogue throughout but intensifies a stultifying atmosphere of monotony and domestic routine.

While more emphasis is placed upon the Deacon household
and the pathos of Lulu's position, the picture of Warbleton is
not dimmed.   The Chautauqua Circle, the popularity of cro-
quet, and a picnic furnish details indicating that "if the Friend-
ships are sweet and dainty, so are they—whether called Warbleton or something less satiric—dull and petty, and they fashion their Deacons no less than their Pelleases and Etarres."[35]

Miss Gale's abandonment of the Friendship formula is further
evidenced in the literary maturity and undeniable artistry distinguishing her later fiction.   *Preface to a Life* (1926) illustrates
both the development of her fictional powers and her further
change in attitude toward small town life.   The revolt indicated in *Birth* and *Miss Lulu Bett* reaches a new stage in this
story of Bernard Mead, a small town businessman.   In sketching Bernard's experiences from his young manhood to his fifty-
second birthday Miss Gale pictures life in the little town of
Pauquette, near Chicago, during the era of 1900 and later.
Like *Main Street*, this is a story of attempted escape from the
village virus.   In youth Bernard wanted to escape the monotony of life in Pauquette by working in Chicago.   At his father's insistence, he remained in the town he despised ; entered
the family lumber business ; and eventually became, to all outward appearances, a fond husband, father, and successful business man.   Through the years Bernard secretly longed for
Alla, with whom he corresponded at rare intervals.   But always he was conscious of his ordeal : the ordeal of being surrounded constantly by too many women within his household.
Finding his love for Alla in opposition to his feeling of family
honor and the small town code, Bernard tried unsuccessfully
to adapt himself to the role of martyr.   Eventually, after a

[34] R. C. Benchley, Foreword to *Miss Lulu Bett* (dramatized version).
[35] Carl Van Doren, *op. cit.*, p. 166.

temporary mental derangement, his outlook became calmer and he ended his long conflict between moral obligation and love with the decision that his life to this point has been but a preface to richer things to come.

This novel, with later stories, such as *Yellow Gentians and Blue* (1927), contains acid sketches of small town characters far different from those of the friendly folk of Friendship Village. Unsavory gossip, hypocrisy, and other kindred marks of repressed lives fill these records sufficiently to place Miss Gale in the newer school emerging during the years following *Spoon River Anthology*. She, too, looked at the village from a new viewpoint, but never with the complete cynicism or utter futility of some of her contemporaries.[36] As the conclusion of *Preface to a Life* suggests, she leaves a little bit of hope in her diagnosis of small town cases.

In Nicholas Vachel Lindsay (1879-1931), poet and idealist, the small town defenders found another ally. A "singer of idealisms once voiced by older democrats of the West," Lindsay drew inspiration from the common people, the farmers and small townsmen of the Middle West whom his contemporaries of the twenties sharply ridiculed or denounced as hopelessly provincial. Preaching a gospel of rural beauty, singing of heroes of the past (Jackson, Lincoln, Roosevelt, Bryan, Barnum, and Booth), and visioning the future in terms of farms and prairie towns, this "minstrel of Springfield" traveled throughout the country exchanging his poems for bread, associating with commoners, and espousing their causes : evangelistic Christianity, prohibition, populism, and socialism.[37] A story-maker for the people, he was not characteristic of modern America. "He never hymned business or mechanical progress or saw happiness in material prosperity."[38] Resisting the false glamor of the cities, Lindsay adhered to what he termed the "new localism" by looking for beauty in his native Midlands. According to the creed announced in *Adventures while Preaching the Gospel of Beauty* (1914), he thought that the things most worth while were to be found in one's own home and neigh-

---

[36] See *Preface to a Life* (New York, 1926), pp. 136 and 148. Cf. Pattee, *op. cit.*, p. 267. In *Faint Perfume* (1923), a tale of martyrdom, there is a partial return to the *Friendship Village* note of optimism.

[37] Cf. Hicks, *The Great Tradition*, p. 239.

[38] Stephen Graham, "Vachel Lindsay," *The Spectator*, No. 5,404, p. 104 (Jan., 1932).

borhood. "We should," he wrote, "make our own home and neighborhood the most democratic, the most beautiful and the holiest in the world." Lindsay, in short, was, during the twenties, a "romantic evangelist of beauty preaching the felicities of an idealized West."[39]   To farmers and villagers throughout the Mississippi Valley and the Southwest he preached, through his hortatory verses, of civic beauty and village improvements, of political and economic fairness, and of virtue and happiness. A romantic idealist in a changing world!

In delineating small town life Lindsay keeps as close to his own district as does Masters. Nearly all of his community descriptions, scattered as they are throughout his writings, portray either his native Springfield, Illinois, or other prairie towns not with sustained and individualized accounts like those in *Spoon River Anthology* or *Main Street*, but with fervent idealism.[40]   Lindsay found inspiration in the pioneer founders of the communities he knew. It was his belief that the strong, fine spirit of the pioneer should continue to dominate, even in the future, the twentieth-century descendants of these heroes of the past. His longest prose work, *The Golden Book of Springfield* (1920), for instance, purports to be a prognostication, or an extended description of the poet's own town as it might appear in 2018. Through the medium of a magical book Lindsay reveals the future state of local politics, religion, and education. In his chronicle he finds place also for praise of Johnny Appleseed, John T. Altgeld, and other neglected heroes. Two sections of his *Collected Poems* (1923), "Home Town" and "Politics," parallel *The Golden Book*.

Of his *Gospel of Beauty* Lindsay says that its three poems form a triad containing in solution his theory of American civilization. The first, eulogizing the farmer, is followed by "The Illinois Village," a picture of the small town contradicting those of Masters and Lewis. Hating industrialism, the poet creates a vision of the future :

---

[39] Cf. Blankenship, *op. cit.*, p. 594.

[40] In a letter to Jessie Rittenhouse, written Christmas Day, 1914, Lindsay wrote that while the *Spoon River Anthology* may seem harsh and cynical to many, "it rouses the same feeling in my soul which caused me to bring out *The Village Magazine*. I feel as though Masters is my big Illinois brother, doing what I have failed to do and wanted to do" (Rittenhouse, *My House of Life*, New York, 1934, p. 308).

> O you who lose the art of hope,
> Whose temples seem to shrine a lie
> Whose sidewalks are but stones of fear,
> Who weep that Liberty must die,
> Turn to the little prairie towns,
> Your higher hope shall yet begin.[41]

He scorns fortune hunters and builders of industrially mad cities. "On the Building of Springfield," the last poem of the triad, contains the earnest plea :

> Let not our town be large, remembering
> That little Athens was the Muses' home,
> That Oxford rules the heart of London still,
> That Florence gave the Renaissance to Rome.[42]

The remainder of the poem is but a reiteration of Lindsay's theory that beautification, religion, and education are the essentials in the upbuilding of a town.

Lindsay cast the emotions which he found in Springfield into a form of poetic expression which he called "the higher vaudeville," a combined singing and speaking of familiar American themes which he popularized through his widely known *The Congo* and "The Kallyope Yell." "General William Booth Enters into Heaven" is both illustrative of his talents and purposes and descriptive of the small town. The poem dramatizes Booth's passage to heaven as it is seen and felt by a Salvation Army sympathizer. Booth, with his brass drum, is pictured as leading a slum crowd to the most impressive place in a Midland town, the courthouse square. Though such a square usually is bleak and frequently dusty, with a brick courthouse in the center, the narrator describes it in splendor, as Booth

> . . . led his queer ones there
> Round and round the mighty court-house square.[43]

Although Lindsay most frequently expressed himself in terms of his home and neighborhood, his Whitmanesque interests also

[41] *Collected Poems* (New York, 1923), p. 72. Cf. Earnest Elmo Calkins, *They Broke the Prairie* (1937), a study of Galesburg, Illinois. Masters, in *Across Spoon River*, p. 349, pictures Lindsay as the Red Cross Knight.
[42] Lindsay, *op. cit.*, p. 74.
[43] *Ibid.*, p. 124.

24

include his state, America, and the world at large. His most
graphic illustration of this is his much quoted "Abraham Lincoln Walks at Midnight," representing Lincoln as pacing the
streets of Springfield in an agony of distress over the World
War.

> It is portentous, and a thing of state
> That here at midnight, in our little town
> A mourning figure walks, and will not rest,
> Near the old court-house pacing up and down.
>
> .   .   .   .   .   .
>
> His head is bowed. He thinks on men and kings.
> Yes, when the sick world cries, how can he sleep?[44]

Here universal interpretation colors a local scene. In his adherence to the theory that poetry can begin at home and that
its form of utterance may be found there, Lindsay added historic Springfield to an ever increasing list of actual towns
featured in American literature.

PROPHETS OF THE NEW AGE

The first years of the twentieth century were not, as village
idealists claimed, years of pastoral delights. Everywhere
change was beginning to be felt. True, in 1900 America as
a country still possessed areas which were of the frontier.
Many prairie villages, just past the early picturesqueness of
two long lines of saloons and stores, had not yet arrived at the
orderliness of established communities. Even the small, flimsily constructed houses suggested transiency. Larger towns,
boasting of a marble Carnegie Library at Second Street, often
had Indian tepees at Tenth.[45] But the evidences of the new life
were everywhere. Already the era of extensive railroad building on the prairies and to the Western mountains had opened.
From Eastern cities, as Stevenson vividly described in *Across
the Plains* (1892), immigrant trains still moved slowly westward,
while in border sections "restless 'sooners' wandered hungrily
about to grab the last opportunities for free land."[46] Even
though in 1900 the American vernacular did not include such
terms as "League of Nations," "income tax," "insulin," or
"radio," this year ushered in a period of growing urbanism,

[44] *Ibid.*, p. 53.
[45] Mark Sullivan, *Our Times, etc.* (New York, 1926), III, 29.
[46] *Ibid.* Cf. Edna Ferber's *Cimarron.*

increased immigration, and unparalleled industrial progress, all of which helped to give the deathblow to the old provincialism which had been slowly dying since the Civil War. With the rapid increase of wealth people continued to turn, as they had done during the extravagant years following the Civil War, toward travel, reading, and art collecting. Indeed, the process begun during the Gilded Age was so accelerated that by "1900 provincialism had little basis in economic fact."[47] As the first decade of the century passed, it was obvious that a new interdependence of formerly separated sections meant the breaking up of the older village isolation and independence. An era of expansion and expansiveness, the day of the average man, had come forth from the industrialism set in motion by the Civil War. As new inventions, with their accompanying social changes, gradually did away with the lingering traditions of Victorian America, hundreds of communities everywhere began to bear the unmistakable stamp of standardization.

Thus the machine age came to Spoon River. And out of this many-sided revolution came a literature of discontent, one phase of which satirized the little town, long a place of genteel traditions, simple folksiness, and, as some saw it, bucolic inertia. Exposed by the searching light of modernity, the small town now appeared far different from the peaceful Victorian villages of the past. Probing and searching, newer critics of the machine age rudely broke into the whited sepulchers and skeletoned closets of townsmen and revealed their secrets to the curious world.

Much of this literature of revolt was the work of men and women, who, ironically enough, were themselves products of the selfsame small town environments which they sharply ridiculed. Disillusioned and pessimistic writers, like Edgar Lee Masters, Sinclair Lewis, Sherwood Anderson, Floyd Dell, and others, all Midwesterners, "denounced the standardization of life in the United States, though that was part of the process which had freed them from provincialism and gentility."[48] Successors to Kirkland, Howe, and Crane of an earlier period, these newcomers (now relegated to the position of a middle generation) were intensely critical. Like young Ellen Glasgow in the

[47] Hicks, *op. cit.*, p. 209.
[48] *Ibid.*, p. 211.

South, they examined searchingly the society which made their
own existence possible and, in poetry and fiction, ruthlessly
exposed the evils they found.   In their various evaluations of
contemporary society these social rebels did not spare the
small town.   In fact, much of their bitterness and scorn was
directed against the evils they found even in remote communities, which, like larger places, were beginning to bear the stamp
of uniformity and dullness.   Nationalistic sentiments, very prevalent during the twenties, the Great God Success, intellectual
mediocrity, and the conventional creed of small townsmen—
these provided pliable tools for the new satirists.   Most of all,
however, these newer critics rebelled, as did Masters first,
against community standardization developing from the

infinite changes, scarcely to be catalogued, [which] resulted from
the passing of the livery stable and the coming of the garage; from
the closing of Beadles Opera House, and the opening of the movie
theatre; from the new type of magazine, not only anonymously
edited but edited by nonentities; and from the fact that everyone
acquired a radio and telephone.[49]

EDGAR LEE MASTERS'S REVOLT FROM THE VILLAGE

It has already been shown that years ago E. W. Howe in
The Story of a Country Town cynically called attention to the
fact that many communities which prided themselves on their
pioneer energy might in reality be little more than dusty corners of futility.   Similarly Mark Twain's *The Man That Corrupted Hadleyburg* showed that meanness, greed, and hypocrisy
might exist in a town celebrated for its incorruptibility.   In
its different vernacular and method *Spoon River Anthology* is a
twentieth-century acknowledgment of hate, dissimulation,
and lust in village life.   A modern corroboration of the neglected testimonies of Howe and Clemens, Masters's poem came
like a bombshell hurled into the group of village idealists.
   In the first years after its publication *Spoon River Anthology*
was both widely read and much discussed.   One contemporary critic, though disgusted with the unflattering pictures and
morbid tone of the *Anthology*, asserted that it might come to
be considered among the great books of American literature.[50]

[49] "The Machine Age Comes to Spoon River," *Today*, April 14, 1934, p. 9.
[50] Amy Lowell, *Tendencies in Modern American Poetry*, p. 139.   Cf. Masters's
comment in *Across Spoon River: An Autobiography* (New York, 1938), p. 348.

Another claimed that the popular reception of the book was due not to poetry, but to the narrative quality of the portraits, abetted by the treatment of sexual complications. He predicted that if *Spoon River* remained as an accepted example of present-day poetry, it would "be a persisting proof of our poetic ineptitude and poverty."[51] Not only were avowed poetry lovers interested, but people who had never cared for a poem became readers of Masters's concisely etched lines. Even its enemies, protesting as they were later to protest against *Winesburg, Ohio* and *Main Street*, acknowledged that the book was unusual. Truly a unique book in the annals of American poetry, the *Anthology* was as much a sensation of its time as *Leaves of Grass* had been in the late fifties. Upholders of the conventional were shocked at its open treatment of sex and its exposure of the immorality which Masters pictured as existing under cover in Spoon River. The sweet singers of the village, the sentimentalists who had long praised the simple, satisfying life of the town, found such ironic transcriptions of community existence unendurable. Quite overlooking the significant fact that many of Masters's pointed criticisms might as well be applied to life elsewhere as to that in the small town of the Middle West, these spokesmen resented what they considered indictments of the small town and its honored citizens. They missed the qualities which more discerning critics found. In their caviling about morals they overlooked the idealism of exemplary portraits like those of Anne Rutledge and Lucinda Matlock. They failed to see that Masters, while ever aware of the unpleasantness of village life, also acknowledged the presence of loyalty, love, and spirituality in the average town and that some of his characters are the happy conquerors of circumstances. Instead, they made a chorus of comment against his morbid pictures of the less pleasing side of community life. While many of the objectors denied the existence of such conditions, others argued that even if the poems were based on actualities such facts had no place in art, or even in print. With their protests, the so-called "Battle of the Village" was begun in earnest.[52]

However familiar it may be to students of American liter-

[51] Clement Wood, *Poets of America* (New York, 1935), p. 173.
[52] This has been widely discussed. For an excellent résumé see Blankenship, *op. cit.*, chap. xxv, "The Battle of the Village," and *Across Spoon River*, pp. 370 and 374.

356   THE SMALL TOWN IN AMERICAN LITERATURE
ature, the history of a book which has been thus both lavishly
praised and sharply attacked deserves retelling here.   As Masters himself recounts in the dedication to *Toward the Gulf*, one
may take, in tracing the successive steps in the development
of this anthology, the year 1909 as a definite starting point.[53]
Prior to this time, however, Masters, who was Kansas-born
(1869), had spent his boyhood in the small towns of Petersburg
and Lewistown, Illinois, in the Lincoln region, where his father,
Hardin W. Masters, was a recognized lawyer and Democrat.
After graduation from the Lewistown High School and study
at Knox College for a while, young Masters studied law in his
father's office ; practised his profession in Lewistown, a county
seat ; and in 1891 went to Chicago, where he became associated
with the law firm of which Clarence Darrow, author of an
iconoclastic village tale, *Farmington*, was a member.   During
his youth Masters dabbled in verse writing and so early as
1898 published *A Book of Verses*, a first book of sixty culled
poems conventionally imitative of Romantic and Victorian
poets.[54]   He continued versifying in this unpromising manner
for many years until, as he says, his friend and frank mentor,
William Marion Reedy, editor of the *St. Louis Mirror*,

. . . pressed upon my attention in June, 1909, the Greek Anthology.   It was from contemplation of its epitaphs that my hand unconsciously strayed to the sketches of "Hod Putt," "Serepta the
Scold" ("Serepta Mason" in the book), "Amanda Barker" ("Amanda" in the book), "Ollie McGee" and "The Unknown," the first
written and the first printed sketches of *The Spoon River Anthology*.
The *Mirror* of May 29th, 1914, is their record.[55]

These American village epitaphs, printed in the *Mirror* from
the early summer of 1914 until January 5, 1915, under the
pseudonym of Webster Ford, marked the inception of an entire series issued by Macmillan within a few months as *Spoon
River Anthology*.   Quoted and parodied during that time in the
country and metropolitan newspapers, the *Anthology* went the

[53] *Toward the Gulf* (New York, 1918), "To William Marion Reedy," pp. vii-xiii.
Cf. *Across Spoon River*, p. 286, for Masters's statement that the germ of *Spoon River*
was formed in 1906.
[54] David Lee Clark, "Edgar Lee Masters Writes the New Poetry and the Old,"
The Dallas Morning News, magazine section, Feb. 17, 1924.
[55] *Toward the Gulf*, p. vii.   Cf. *Across Spoon River*, p. 339.

rounds over the country before it was issued in book form.[56] Masters has also mentioned another factor in the unusual reception accorded the *Anthology*. This was the influence of the newly established *Poetry: A Magazine of Verse*. During 1911 Miss Harriet Monroe of Chicago, poet and art critic, formulated a plan whereby new poets might have a publication medium. Accordingly, a fund was raised to endow a periodical for five years and in October, 1912, *Poetry* made its appearance. During its first years *Poetry* contained many free verse poems, which, Masters asserts, prepared for him the way to Spoon River.[57] Even after years of constant literary failure and constant persistence, Masters still lacked the qualities which characterize the work of a true poet. The free verse of *Poetry* furnished the key to one of the qualities he needed— brevity and freedom from the mechanics of rhyme and meter. The sharp, concise lines of free verse gave him a suitable instrument. This, briefly, is the story of the composition and publication of the *Anthology* which in 1915 created a furore that seems a little ridiculous today.[58]

Even before he sprang into prominence Masters, with his rich background of village and town life, had come to doubt whether American small town conditions were as idyllic as they had been pictured by earlier and even contemporary writers. He had decided that the citizenship of most villages included fools and rogues as well as good and shrewd people. It occured to him, taking his model from the Greek Anthology, to present in a series of poems a complete picture of a small Illinois town as he thought it really should be presented. Reporting in May, 1915, about the finished *Anthology*, Masters described it as

. . . the interwoven history of a whole community, a village, a city, or whatever you like to call it. . . . I had a variety of things in mind in the writing of the anthology. I meant to analyse character, to satirize society, to tell a story, to expose the machinery of life, to present to view a working model of the big world and put it in a window where the passerby could stop and see it run. And I had in mind, too, the creation of beauty and the depiction of our

---

[56] *Toward the Gulf*, p. x.
[57] *Across Spoon River*, pp. 336-339; 345; 346; and 347.
[58] *Ibid.*, p. 340, Masters tells of his completion of *Spoon River* at Spring Lake.

sorrows and hopes, our religious failures, successes, and visions, our poor little lives, rounded by a sleep, in language and figures emotionally tuned to bring all of us together in understanding and affection.[59]

As most readers know, his anthology, deprecating the hypocrisy of the conventional tombstone inscription, purports to be composed of epitaphs in the Spoon River graveyard. The background and key to the entire work, probably suggested by Masters's memories of the deserted cemetery at New Salem, Illinois, are provided in the prologue—"The Hill"—descriptive of the village dead.[60] In most uncompromising terms each buried man and woman—"the weak of will, the strong of arm, the clown, the boozer, the fighter"—is made to speak the truth about himself or herself. Succinctly the villagers speak from the tomb their retrospect of life. Thus is acknowledged the presence of lust, greed, and sordidness, as well as beauty and commendable vitality, in this Midwestern village.[61] The secrets of the entire citizenship are laid bare; few reputations are left undisturbed.

Spoon River Anthology differs from most books in that it possesses neither primary nor secondary characters. Masters has merely pictured a small Midwestern town and the people who inhabit it. Natural emphasis is placed upon the fact that the entire population, and not a few dominating characters, make the town. While the villagers cannot be rigidly classified, Louis Untermeyer suggests a threefold division of them. First, there are those having the power of plain statement, usually heightened by a matter-of-fact humor; there is a disillusioned group, often village misfits; and, finally, there are those who are lifted to a plane of exaltation.[62] To the first class belong Roscoe Purkapile, Mrs. Purkapile, and Russian Sonia; to the second, Editor Whedon, hypocritical journalist, and Daisy Fraser, the town prostitute, whose fines regularly swell the Spoon River school fund. Among the best drawn characters of the last division, those who transcend the hypocrisies of the village, are Doc Hill, a plain country doctor hated by his wife

[59] C. E. Wisewell, "An Interview with Masters," *Current Opinion*, LVIII, 356 (May, 1915). Cf. *Across Spoon River*, p. 342, influence of Turgenev, etc.
[60] *Spoon River Anthology* (New York, 1915), p. 1.
[61] See *Across Spoon River*, pp. 410-413, for Masters's unflattering picture of Lewistown and the surrounding flatlands.
[62] *American Poetry Since 1900* (New York, 1923), p. 115.

but loved by Em Stanton ; Emily Sparks, the old maid teacher ; Lucinda Matlock, mother of twelve children ; and Anne Rutledge, "beloved in life of Abraham Lincoln." Throughout the anthology there are characters representative of the chief types to be found in an American country town. The mere fact that there are two hundred and fourteen of these villagers moved Amy Lowell to remark that the invention of such a large number of names was in itself a feat.[63] As she says, the quality of the *Anthology* stands revealed in these names. Hard, crude, completely local, and uncompromising in their realism, these names throw no glamor over their possessors. There is no subterfuge with fact. Instead of romantic terms there are realistic names : Hannah Armstrong, Archibald Higbie, Faith Matheny, George Trimble, Albert Schirding, and numerous others.

Local realism is an outstanding feature of *Spoon River Anthology*. The realistic picturing of the town as a definite whole suggests that Spoon River is geographically a place. (Petersburg, Lewistown, New Salem, and Hanover, small towns in Illinois intimately known by the youthful Masters, have been variously suggested as the prototype of Spoon River.) Actually, there is no such town—only a river. "And," as Masters notes in his recent autobiography, *Across Spoon River* (1936),

what a river! What a small stream winding its way through flatlands, amid hills that only distance lifts into any beauty, through jungles of weeds and thickets and melancholy cottonwoods. It goes by little towns as ugly and lonely as the tin-roofed hamlets of Kansas.[64]

The citizens seem to be as real as the men and women who, during Masters's youth, crowded the sidewalks and stores of Lewistown on Saturdays and special days. The cemetery, the churches, the shops, and even the courthouse may be visualized. The prevailing American qualities of the cramped, monotonous lives of an ugly little river town show Masters to be an observing poet of the absolute, of the real.

Masters revolts against the stale conventionality of small

[63] Lowell, *op. cit.*, p. 162. Cf. *Across Spoon River*, p. 343. Masters says that he devised names by reconstructing those found in lists of the signers of the Constitution of Illinois and other states.

[64] *Across Spoon River*, p. 411.

town life. In the particular case of Spoon River he is concerned with the general demoralization of the town. He occupies himself with the physical squalor of the community and the low mentality of certain of its citizens, interpretations chiefly based upon impressions of his own beginnings at Lewistown "among a people," he says, "whose flesh and whose vibrations were better calculated to poison, to pervert, and even to kill a sensitive nature."[65]   True, a number of his characters seem removed from the greed and hypocrisy of the majority, but generally Masters pictures the town as fallen both in complacent apathy and sin. His is no delicately tinted picture painted by a sentimental artist. Repeatedly revelation is made of the false standards existing in Spoon River and the country at large. Caustic lines reveal the town's spiritual decay and its adherence to a deceptive decorum, which in concealing its faults almost makes its citizens overlook them. Remembering his boyhood visits to New Salem—the now deserted village, several miles from Petersburg, where Lincoln lived as a young man—Masters makes frequent references to Lincoln and the heroic founders of the town. From an older, stronger generation he takes a standard by which he measures the purposelessness, indolence, and dullness of a town forgetful of its energetic founders.

Masters appears to be more interested in the ironic contrast between *what is believed* and *what is true* about the Spoon River villagers.[66] The most highly respected citizens are made to confess their dissimulation, thus revealing in a sort of postmortem examination that they did not deserve their respectability. In contrast, the most disreputable individuals disclose the amazing fact that their characters were not so tainted as the smug town thought. In telling the actual truth about themselves often husband and wife, or friend and friend, make public heretofore unsuspected crises in their lives. Amanda Barker, for example, proclaims from the dust that, while it was believed that Henry loved her with a husband's love, actually he slew her to gratify his hatred.[67]

As was earlier noted, Masters, even with all his ruthless picturing of ugliness and crime, does not wholly disregard the

[65] *Ibid.*, p. 410.
[66] Van Doren and Van Doren, *op. cit.*, p. 27.
[67] *Spoon River Anthology*, p. 9.

beauty and spirituality that may exist in Spoon River and countless actual towns. Two of his most beautiful and vital characters are Davis and Lucinda Matlock, whose happy married life is truly different from the bitter unhappiness of Benjamin Pantier and his wife. Lucinda, perhaps, gives the key to her happiness in her remark that "It takes life to love life." Again, Anne Rutledge, speaking from the most artistic lyric in the book, throws a sort of glory over the whole village. Her sketch, expressive in Whitmanesque tones of the nation's need for justice, truth, and charity, shows Masters's hostility toward the prevalence in American life of an almost overpowering materialism.[68] With such characters—and scores of others— Masters has created a masterpiece which might well be termed an epic of everyday American life. The pattern is truly a large one—a fact called to mind by the lament of Spoon River's Petit the Poet, who long yearning for themes of epic proportions, suddenly realizes his poetic blindness. Here in the little village beside the Spoon River he is amazed to find all the needed patterns expressive of

> Tragedy, comedy, valor and truth,
> Courage, constancy, heroism, failure—. . . .[69]

Masters has, indeed, an extraordinary range of vision. Though his is a crowded field, teeming with life, he causes some of the happenings of this dull little town to have an almost national significance. The squabbles in the courthouse, the petty feuds, martyrdoms, and occasional exaltations of the townsmen take on, it has been said, an almost epic fire.[70]

Possibly the most severely attacked weakness of *Spoon River* is its preoccupation with crime, disease, and sordidness, pictures of provincial life variously attributed to Masters's close observation of small town ways and his handling of numerous criminal cases. Whatever their origin, the themes of many of the stories center in sex, while others expose the crime of Spoon River. In some instances, as critics have noted repeatedly, Masters does little more than chronicle a series of seductions, liaisons, and perversions. By so doing he often makes his point of view sensual and cruel. Another weakness of the

[68] *Ibid.*, p. 220.
[69] *Ibid.*, p. 89.
[70] Untermeyer, *loc. cit.*

volume is "The Spooniad," an account of local politics told by
Webster Ford, supposedly one of the villagers but actually
Masters himself. It is, says Clement Wood, "a poor parody
of the epic style, lacking both in humor and finish of style."[71]

Since *Spoon River* Masters has continued to write about Illinois, its small towns, its full Lincoln traditions, and its produc-
tive pioneer days. Always he writes without sentimentality,
but in some of his books of poetry with such voluminosity that,
like Wordsworth on occasion, he proves tedious and unpoetic.
In varying measures his later poetry has failed to attain the
vigor and marvelous conciseness of the *Anthology*. *Songs and
Satires* (1916), criticized as "embodying too much satire and
too little song," contains less incisive verse than *The Great Valley*
(1917) with its more varied verse forms and clearer pictures of
the Middle West. Here again Masters seems moved by the
spirit of revolt. Earnestly he again assumes the role of social
exhorter and chider. He looks upon the past unsentimentally
and with marked realism characterizes Lincoln and other
Illinois heroes as conquerors of unpleasant environments. He
sees Lincoln as a backwoodsman and "country lawyer unlettered in the art of states" whose individual superiority and will
to do enabled him to outgrow "a squalid western town."[72]
In another poem, while acknowledging that America has become "an empire of restless vital men and teeming towns,"
Masters deplores the lack of genius in the country at large.[73]
The realistic details of "Gobineau to Tree" suggest the un-
varnished truths of *Spoon River*. As in the earlier book, Masters herein caustically expresses impatience with indolent Illinois townsmen and lackadaisical countrymen, who, unlike
Lincoln, offer no resistance to the forces of environment.
Spiritless, they succumb to the physical ugliness of town and
country; or, if moved to action, take pleasure in drinking,
fighting, and "the orgy of the religious meeting." A defeated,
agued people, they know nothing of inspiration and "of conscious plan to lift the spirit up." The cause of liberty, pleads
Masters as eloquently as Whitman, needs more strong men,
more splendid breeds like the courageous pioneers who made
Illinois and the Midwest.[74] The same local color character-

---

[71] *Op. cit.*, p. 171.
[72] *The Great Valley* (New York, 1916), "Autochthon," p. 40.
[73] *Ibid.*, "Grant and Logan and Our Tears," p. 44.
[74] *Ibid.*, p. 54.

izes other poems of *The Great Valley*, especially the portrait of Old Piery, "a little croaking, mad but harmless waif," once a South Carolina Belle who wandered to Petersburg after the sacking of Columbia. "Cato Braden," the story of a small town editor, is another keen arraignment of dull, narrow Midwestern towns, places described as killing the spirit "as surely as The Island where they cooped up the great Napoleon." "Winston Prairie" and "Will Boyden Lectures" satirize the lack of generosity and the prevalence of political corruption in a prairie town. Thus while *The Great Valley* is not primarily a village tale, much of its poetry touches the life of Midwestern communities. *Toward the Gulf* (1918) is greatly weakened by its lack of poetic fire; *Starved Rock* (1919), with less sarcasm and vulgarity, possesses more genuine poetry. *The Open Sea* (1921) is repetitive and cynical. These treat of the small town only in incidental references. Not until *Domesday Book* (1920) does Masters return with any degree of sustained treatment to the small town.[75]

Ever concerned with the influence of environment on character, Masters, Professor David L. Clark thinks, may well have entitled *Domesday Book*, with its emphasis upon the infinite ramifications of a murder case, *The Spoon River Pathology*. Often compared to *The Ring and the Book*, this is the absorbing, but lengthy, tragi-comedy of Elenor Murray, "whose life was humble and whose death was tragic."[76] The daughter of a ne'er-do-well druggist in a village under the shadow of Starved Rock, Elenor is found dead on the riverbank near the town. Coroner Merival holds an extended inquest, which leads to the exposure and discomfort of numerous people in the community. The varying testimonies of local doctors, ministers, bankers, newspaper men, shopkeepers, relatives, former lovers of Elenor, and innumerable other witnesses marshaled before Merival build up an intensely sordid picture of small town narrowness. Cleanness, high-mindedness, and idealism are noticeably lacking among those who testify. Seemingly the village is devoid of normally happy men and women, for its citizens are dominated by greed, grossness, and cynicism. Even the more normal qualities of the girl Elenor have been crushed,

---

[75] *The Fate of the Jury* (1929) continues the story of *Domesday Book*.
[76] Masters says he wrote his story before he had ever read a line of *The Ring and the Book*.

so the poet argues, by the sordidness of her surroundings.   Hers is the tragedy of one who hungered for self-development, beauty, and richness.   As to the revelation of town life given in the book, one may say with a well-known critic that this may be realism, but it is not reality.   ". . . there is no such cesspool of iniquity in any town in Illinois or elsewhere."[77]

The New Spoon River (1924) is clearly indicative of Masters's continued interest in the Spoon River country of his boyhood in its relation to American life.[78]   If lacking in the more artistically drawn portraits and the ironic contrasts which make the earlier volume notable, The New Spoon River is a larger, fuller study interpretative of the lives of a more highly developed community.   The advent of the automobile and motion pictures, the development of the canning works, the influx of new and foreign people, the electric cars to the city, the increasing power of political grafters, a faster social life, and other factors of modern living have converted the little rural town of the nineties into a ganglion of Chicago.   While some of the older families remain in power, new names appear in the shop signs and on the tombstones in the "Valley of Stillness."   The machine age has come to the

> . . . little town by the river,
> Little town of little hopes.[79]

Spoon River, like towns in all parts of the country, has become a standardized community, a "metropolized" town.   Newer evils have crowded in alongside the gossip, dissimulation, and intellectual sterility of the past.   Expressive of Masters's arraignment of the evils of the present is the satiric confession of Diamandi Viktoria, whose foreign-born parents, searching for liberty, settled in "metropolized Spoon River."   Diamandi, a political opportunist, uses his "gift of gab for liberty" to pocket "quite a roll" while he serves as county treasurer.[80] Such is the new Spoon River, the very antithesis of Zona Gale's kinder estimate of the American town in Portage, Wisconsin and

---

[77] Clark, loc. cit.
[78] See O. W. Firkins, "The Return to Spoon River," The Saturday Review of Literature, I, 178 (Oct. 11, 1924), for the contention that The New Spoon River, with its argumentative tone, is too much of a Mastersville and too little of an objectively pictured Spoon River.   Cf. Across Spoon River, p. 374, for Masters's answer.
[79] The New Spoon River (New York, 1924), p. 100.
[80] Ibid., p. 66.

Other Essays. Her opening description suggests that even so late as 1928 Miss Gale, though ostensibly one of the new realists, had not departed altogether from her earlier ideal of the village.

On one bank of a river it should lie—the town that one means when one says "small town." Homes should border the bank, small lawns, sloping to lilacs and willows.[81]

But in 1924 Masters, voicing his satire through the unflattering words of Ibbetson the plumber, another citizen of modern Spoon River, lamented that this rapidly changing river town should be polluted by ignorance, cruelty, money lust, false . morality, and

> . . . the sewers of hate
> That keep you sick, Spoon River.[82]

In prose Masters has also made some contribution to the literature of the small town, though not to the extent that he has in poetry. *Mitch Miller* (1920), the first novel of a trilogy, presents in "boy lingo" small town life in the Lincoln country during the last half of the nineteenth century. The two protagonists, if they may be thus dignified, are the very boyish Mitch Miller, the precociously imaginative son of a preacher, and Skeeters Kirby (better known as Skeet), the narrator and Mitchie's pal and fellow-adventurer. The story opens with the boys' plotting to visit Tom Sawyer at Hannibal. (Mitch feels sure that there is a real Tom Sawyer. Did he not receive a letter in answer to his note that he and Skeet were coming to Hannibal?) The boy world of these chums, Petersburg in Illinois, is realistically portrayed, though the similarity to Mark Twain's studies is noticeable. Mitch's deep disappointment over parental interference in his love affair with a little neighbor girl recalls the pictures of Tom Sawyer and Becky, as well as those of Penrod Schofield and his love. Descriptions of a "huntin' treasure" expedition, small town theatricals, school and Sunday school escapades, and swimming matches tie up with similar scenes in the Mark Twain sketches. *Skeeters Kirby* (1923), sequel to *Mitch Miller,* continues the story of Skeet's

---

[81] New York, 1928, p. 3. Cf. Garland's picture of Portage in *Afternoon Neighbors*, chap. i.

[82] *The New Spoon River*, p. 38.

life in Midwestern Marshalltown and later in Chicago. *Mirage* (1924), the long-spun-out story of Skeet's later love life, deals with the small town but incidentally in Skeet's memories of his boyhood days in Petersburg and Marshalltown. *Children of the Market Place* (1922) is the fictionalized autobiography of a young Englishman who comes to Jacksonville, Illinois, during the thirties and becomes the close friend of Stephen A. Douglas. Both this novel and *The Nuptial Flight* (1923) portray life in frontier towns. The latter is the tale of two Kentucky families who settle in pioneer Whitehall, Illinois, in 1849.

All in all, Masters's treatment of community life has done much toward withering the sentimental idea that small towns are invariably the scenes of quietude, happiness, industry, and virtue. Arthur Guiterman's rimed review of *Spoon River Anthology* may well be taken as a summary of Masters's stand in the Battle of the Village.

> The glowery castle of E. L. Masters
> Is reared on the jawbones of poetasters;
> Its denizens gloat on the soul's disasters
> With visage as solemn as Zoraster's.
>
> He sees such a ravishing lot of crime,
> Perversion, insanity, slime and grime
> To tell us about, that he has no time
> To put it in meter, much less in rhyme.
>
> Below him, awaiting their resurrection
> From tombs that no longer afford protection,
> Are acres of subjects for keen dissection,
> That being his jovial predilection.[83]

THE REBELLIOUS TWENTIES

The revolt of Masters indicates unmistakably that the village of literature, in response to changing conditions and an increased knowledge and antipathy on the part of many writers, has changed greatly during the years since 1915. Damaged by the keen winds of realism, the village, or town, of fiction in the twenties was no longer the sentimentally pictured little place of idyllic beauty and charmed life. After the World

[83] "Edgar Lee Masters," *The Saturday Review of Literature*, II, 903 (July 3, 1926).

War the present-day small town, emerging from the village of the past, became a modernized place, "the abode of a people whose lives encompassed both happy and sad in a range of experience normal to human life everywhere."[84]

These changes—economic, social, intellectual, and religious —have brought about such limitless literary possibilities that the picture of the American small town has grown steadily in truthfulness, variety, and completeness. Small towns from Minnesota to Texas and from Idaho to Alabama have found their way into fiction and poetry. In some respects the *dramatis personae* of the town have remained the same, though with marked differences in presentation and locale. Such stock figures as the lawyer, frequently treated as a rascal in earlier stories, the benign pastor, the village deacon, the irascible and stern schoolmaster, and the town drunkard have been radically modified to suit a newer social system. With the weakening or disappearance of older themes, experimentation has been made with newer themes and forms, as Masters vigorously demonstrated. Even a casual examination of representative works treating of the American small town reveals that, in many instances, "the older school uncritically delighted in all the village singularities it could discover," while the modern school severely condemns and ridicules all the village conventionalities.[85] Elizabeth Drew, summing up the situation in 1926, considered the revolt of the twenties something far wider than "any special piece of propaganda, or even than that which is presented by the changes in manners and morals which are the inevitable ebb and flow of generations." Her opinion of more than ten years ago—but one applicable to conditions today—was that there existed "a profound and a growing dissatisfaction with the quality of the civilization which is the typical civilization throughout the whole of America."[86]

From this general unrest came a group of rebellious younger writers, products of a changing age whose disciples, in turn, even today keep alive the fires of revolt. For these disillusioned souls the America of the twenties was little more than the Land

[84] Patton, *The English Village*, p. 219.
[85] Van Doren, *op. cit.*, p. 117.
[86] *The Modern Novel* (New York, 1926), p. 140. Cf. Mumford, *The Culture of Cities*, and Storm Jameson, *The Novel in Contemporary Life*, both masterly 1938 reaffirmations.

25

of Bunk peopled by "a vast middleman herd, that dominates the continent, but cannot reduce it to order or decency."[87] In H. L. Mencken's phrase, this country of abundance was the Kingdom of Dollarica whose custodians, cherishing sacred slogans of democracy and patriotism, believed in the good life which flowered in Rotarian conventions.   In Sinclair Lewis's eyes, people everywhere, in small town and city, were falling down and worshiping at the shrine of the Great God Bunk. The *boobus Americanum* (Mencken's discovery) had arrived to dominate the scene in both the Gopher Prairies and the Zeniths.

To many of these insurgents small towns throughout the country offered a comprehensive background for the critical study of the human and social blemishes of American society. Indeed, by their day Main Street was very different in appearance from the older highway.   During the last century, as we have seen, elm-shaded streets, faced by white, gabled houses set in decent lawns and old-fashioned gardens, swept broad and clean through pretty New England villages.   Later another Main Street, rutted and muddy or dusty in season, wound uncertainly among the shacks of Hawkeye and Twin Mounds. Thereafter it was, for a while, broad and peaceful in Friendship Village, Plattville, and "Our Town."   But in its last stretch, its older picturesqueness quite lost, it became lined with drab Gopher Prairies.   Thus, according to the severe critics of the twenties, modern civilization achieved a triumph of uniform ugliness.

In revolt against their material, the writers of the twenties brought further accusations against the small town.   Among other things it stood accused of dull provinciality and intellectual sterility, of economic injustice hardly less flagrant than that of the cities, of political corruption, of social inequality, of moral and ethical instability, of aesthetic starvation, and of a sublime unconsciousness of its sins and an illusion of perfection.   Most of these critics, contemptuous and rebellious, dealt with the society around them as they saw it.   And the pictures they saw were far from pleasant.   Economic menaces in Harvey and Bidwell; political bosses in Sycamore Ridge and social bosses in the Midland towns of *The Magnificent Ambersons*

[87] Parrington, *Sinclair Lewis: Our Own Diogenes* (University of Washington Chapbook, 1927), V, 11-12. (Incorporated in *The Beginnings of Critical Realism in America*, pp. 360-369.)

and *Alice Adams:* furtive sexual immorality in Spoon River and Winesburg; g ssip in Another Town; blatant local pride everywhere; low ethical standards; and cultural deficiency—these are the faults of the town on which the anti-villagists concentrated.

In addition to Mrs. Wharton, Miss Gale, Mrs. Fisher, Robert Nathan, and others earlier mentioned, the most uncompromising of the insurgents, mostly Middle Westerners, include Sherwood Anderson, "corn-fed mystic"; Sinclair Lewis, a contentious Diogenes; Floyd Dell, novelist and critic; Willa Sibert Cather; the E. Haldeman Juliuses; William M. John; Homer Croy; Robert McAlmon; Rupert Hughes; John T. Frederick; Muna Lee (Mrs. Luis Muñoz Marín); and others. These exponents of the school of Masters, critic H. L. Mencken, and *The American Mercury* helped during the twenties to sound the dominant reactionary note against the American small town and all the dull provinciality they thought it symbolized. Products of the age of revolt (1914-1920), these writers determined the trend of the literature of the town during the twenties, an age of cynicism when stress was placed not upon values but upon the folly of them. The spirit of the age was destructive and not constructive.[88]

The homely and finely developed vignettes of *Winesburg, Ohio* (1919) mark Sherwood Anderson as a product of the *Spoon River* period. Akin to many Midlanders in the respect that he originated in the social area he depicts in fiction, Anderson was born (1876) of Scotch-Irish parents in Camden, Ohio. The precarious days of his childhood and adolescence find picturing in *A Story Teller's Story, Tar: A Midwest Childhood* and *Windy McPherson's Son*, all introspective. From these books two fully drawn and contrasted pictures may be selected. The first is that of Anderson's father, an imaginative ex-soldier, who was, in turn, an unsuccessful small town merchant and, finally, a laborer. A born storyteller, he was unreliable but popular. The second portrait is that of his practical wife, the mainstay of the family, hard-working and inclined to silence. *Tar* (1926), fictionalizing the settling of a wandering family in a small Ohio town, is, in reality, a picture of the improvident Andersons. The early scattering of the Moorheads and Tar's

[88] V. F. Calverton, *American Literature at the Crossroads* (University of Washington Chapbook, 1931), XLVIII, 34.

enforced self-support brought the impressionable boy, like the
real Sherwood Anderson, in contact with unpleasant people
and unpleasant places.   A penetrating study, *Tar* is actually
an introspective autobiography and "rural album of coarse
daguerreotypes illustrating the psychology, the manners, the
view of life, the institutions, the personality of an area left behind by a retreating frontier."[89]

While in his teens Anderson, one of a large family, drifted
to Chicago, where he became a laborer.[90]   Following an experience as a soldier during the Spanish-American War, he
restlessly turned from job to job.   He tried both advertising
and, then, the managing of a paint factory in an Ohio town.
Such experiences only served to deepen in Anderson the conviction that he could no longer find happiness in the sort of
life which apparently satisfied his fellow-beings.   His desire
for creative art and beauty was instrumental in turning him
toward writing, where he could discard conformity and grow
through self-expression.   Finally, returning to Chicago, he became associated with Theodore Dreiser, Ben Hecht, and Floyd
Dell, who encouraged his plans for a literary career.   Beginning publication with stories in *The Little Review*, *Seven Arts*,
and *The Dial*, Anderson in 1916, through the material influence
of Dreiser, published *Windy McPherson's Son*.   From that date
until the present Anderson has written prolifically.   Now a
widely known interpreter of the small town and other phases
of American life, Anderson has forsaken the city again for the
life of a small town, Marion, Virginia, where as editor of the
two local papers, one a Republican and the other a Democratic
sheet, he has become intimately associated with restricted community thinking and happenings.

A dreamer and so-called cornfed mystic, Anderson is keenly sensitive.   He broods over the ways of men and women.
He is convinced that only the untrammeled artist is free to tell
the truth.   Filled with indignation at the conventional state
of things, Anderson early brought to his stories a great depth
of sympathetic feeling and original bits of psychological reflection.   In those early days (1910 and following) he deliberately
chose to become a fine craftsman, working honestly with Mid-

[89] Pattee, *op. cit.*, p. 333.
[90] For full biographical details see Harry Hansen, *Midwest Portraits* (New York,
1923), pp. 111 ff.

dle Western village life and fashioning it into form with words which are his tools. As his first stories show, he wanted life and not plot; appropriate language and not literary English; reality, and not Victorian prudishness, in acknowledging the existence of sexual problems. He wanted to search out the passions, the veiled tragedies, the bitter futilities of existence. This he has accomplished in all his studies of the small town, stories in which he has adhered to his own conviction that "Literature is not a means of escape from life; all good works of art take you back into your own life."[91]

A Story Teller's Story (1924) and Tar offer records showing that Anderson's first published novels, Windy McPherson's Son and Marching Men (1917), were the products of the author's probing into the materials of the small town environment of his youth. Both novels have a type of plot frequently found in this study of the small town: an eager, yet bewildered, youth detaches himself from his native towns and finds success elsewhere without arriving at any definite conclusion as to the meaning of life. Sam McPherson and Beaut McGregor, heroes of these novels, gain success; yet each is dissatisfied and searches for some clue to happiness. Largely autobiographical, these are stories of ill-born youths beset by inhibitions. They succeed materially, but fail spiritually. Sam, village-born and of poor parents, does not find ultimate happiness in his dearly bought wealth. Beaut, searching for the imponderable values of life, discovers them neither in the ugly Pennsylvania mining town of his boyhood nor in the larger world of Chicago. Instead, he comes to believe that drunkenness, sex, and hunger are the chief incentives of most men's existence. In these novels Anderson is not misled by the showiness of American prosperity. Probing beneath the surface brilliance, he discovers, in small town and city, the reverse of the stage setting: dirty mining towns where men live like brutes, drinking, beating their wives, and laboring underground; miserable jails; and forbidding factories. These two books, it has been said, reflect the dumb confusion of America, where village peace and stability have departed and the leaven of change is stirring the lump.[92]

[91] George Bond, "Sherwood Anderson Chats at Length about Books and This Changing Age," The Dallas Morning News, magazine section, Oct. 24, 1925.
[92] Van Doren, op. cit., p. 154.

In 1918 and 1919, with *Mid-American Chants* (Whitmanesque in tone) and *Winesburg, Ohio,* Anderson expressed his convictions in verse and short-story form.   In the latter he came into his own, for this work, a psychological study of small town individuals, marks its author as an unusual interpreter of the new America.   Anderson the psychoanalyst is revealed in the methods employed in his naturalistic studies of the Winesburghers.   As suggested in the subtitle to the collection, *Intimate Histories of Everyday People,* Anderson cares little about the behavior of his characters in their outward living.   He is chiefly concerned with their inmost thoughts.   He is Freudian in his attempts to sound the depths of the reason for one's doing things.   *Winesburg, Ohio,* like *The Triumph of the Egg* (1921), *Horses and Men* (1923), and *Death in the Woods* (1933), all containing studies of small town folk, records in a variety of situations the emotional states of people, restless, longing, or wrongly adjusted to the dull routine of life.   Here are people, who seeking fulfilment for their thwarted hopes, do unexpected things; and people who cling tenaciously to old ideals.   No matter how drab or unpleasant these themes may seem on the surface, underneath the simplicity of Anderson's style move the poignant stories of repressed individuals.   Occasional charm and sympathy contrast these tales with the crass reality of *Main Street.*   Unlike Masters and Lewis, Anderson neither bitterly hates nor satirizes the environment from which his people try to escape.   Instead, he seems mystified by it, and broods over it with an intensity which gives his work a haunting tone.[93]

Winesburg, Ohio, especially, is illustrative of this.   Young George Willard, reporter for the *Winesburg Eagle,* on the morning of his departure from the little town of his boyhood has a new conception of his fellow-citizens.   For the first time he becomes aware of the drama stirring beneath the surface of the outwardly humdrum lives of his townsmen.   It is as if he saw, for the first time, that these people whom he has known all of his life are dead, spiritually and morally, even while living in Winesburg.   They lead the lives of sleepwalkers and daydreamers even in the midst of their daily routine.   They are crushed by inhibitions.

[93] Cf. William Faulkner, "Sherwood Anderson," *The Dallas Morning News,* magazine section, April 26, 1925, and Van Doren and Van Doren, *op. cit.,* p. 84.

Like hundreds of young people who go out from their towns into the cities, George, stirred perhaps by his reluctance to leave the familiar haunts of the town, views his neighbors with unusual tenderness. His going, however, gives him a peculiar sense of detachment which causes him to see his associates as "cramped souls, repressed and distorted by the stern customs which have refused them any outlet for the forces working within them."[94] His position as reporter had revealed to George the unusual amidst the commonplace. He had discovered, through his contacts with odd, as well as average, types that the very monotony of life in Winesburg warped the souls of otherwise normal individuals. Having learned secrets about men and women who were but outwardly decorous, George had become aware that the pressure of outward conformity often distorted human spirits into grotesque forms. Even as his train carries him away he begins to feel that his life there has become but a background for his great adventure.

But what of the people left behind in Winesburg? In story after story Anderson, with rare sympathy, reveals the hidden yearnings of varied types of small town individuals : those of a hotel proprietor's unhappy wife, of a strawberry picker, of a middle-aged doctor, of a minister, of a teacher, and of a telephone operator. Each of these portraits is a masterpiece of dramatized insight. A poignant sketch is that of Elizabeth Willard, the reporter's mother, whose longings for adventure were early crushed by an unsympathetic husband.[95] The story of Wing Biddlebaum points out that suspicion and supersensitivity may ruin the career of an ambitious youth.[96] The secret of Wash Williams, an uncouth telegraph operator, centers around his youthful ambitions and his unfortunate marriage to a beautiful girl.[97] These are but a few of the secretly moral outcasts, the libidinous, the morbid, the dreamers, and the eccentrics who inhabit the little Ohio town. Here are human beings condemned to intellectual and moral decrepitude. They struggle mentally, but fail, in most instances, to rise above their surrounding mediocrity.

Anderson's other collections of brief narratives (*The Triumph of the Egg, Horses and Men,* and *Death in the Woods,* already men-

[94] Régis Michaud, *The American Novel To-day* (Boston, 1928), p. 185.
[95] *Winesburg, Ohio* (New York, 1920), "Death."
[96] *Ibid.,* "Hands."
[97] *Ibid.,* "Respectability."

tioned) are marked by his continued analysis of inhibited people, among them small town types, who "stride along talking
to themselves, ponder imponderables, and suddenly break into
tears."[98]   As in *Winesburg, Ohio* and the novels, here also Anderson shows prolonged brooding over the futilities of existence.
In tales like "I Want to Know Why," "The Egg," "Out of
Nowhere into Nothing," and "I'm a Fool" the author shows a
fine faculty for precise observation of small town citizens,
whose inner tumult is in contrast with their commonplace
existence.

In *Poor White* (1920) Anderson seems, according to William
Faulkner, "to get his fingers and toes into the soil, as he does
in 'Winesburg'."   Here again are small town people who answer the compulsions of industrial demands.   Not so composite
a picture of the small community as *Winesburg, Ohio*, this novel
chronicles the transformation of an ordinary village of the mid-
nineteenth century into a manufacturing center.   Anderson
traces the effect of this change upon the villagers.   In so doing
he again resorts to the well-worn device of having "a bewildered
strong man rising from a dull obscurity, successful but unsat-
isfied."   From a "little hole of a town stuck on a mud bank
on the western shore of the Mississippi" comes Hugh McVey,
son of a ne'er-do-well and a victim of inhibitions.   Soon sick-
ening of the ugliness of his environment, the youth, plagued
by visions of greatness, leaves Mudcat Landing.   Eventually
settling in Bidwell, Ohio, Hugh, through his unusual inventive
genius, becomes a part of the new machine age which quickly
transforms Bidwell and its many counterparts from struggling
villages into factory centers.   But quick-growth prosperity ends
in strikes and death.   In the end Hugh, though wealthy and
married to an ambitious woman, feels, as does the typical Anderson protagonist, that his plans for bettering Bidwell and
humanity lead to nothing except blighted hopes.   The road
to truth seems blocked.

Many Marriages (1923) and *Dark Laughter* (1925) further illustrate Anderson's favorite trick of looking under what he calls
the shell of life.   The latter, a weak story based upon psychological analyses, tells of the mental struggles of John Webster,
a washing machine manufacturer in a Wisconsin town, who
at forty feels that he has been missing LIFE.   *Dark Laughter*

---

[98] Hartwic. , *The Foreground of American Fiction*, p. 121.

likewise deals with another "spiritual eruption." In this novel
Bruce Dudley, a factory hand in Old Harbor, Indiana, is the
sensitive dreamer who detaches himself long enough from his
foggy reasonings to run away with his employer's wife. In
these novels seemingly Anderson has given himself the task of
proving and justifying the theories of the psychoanalyst.
Termed the Freudian novelist par excellence, he has here, as
elsewhere, injected a marked autobiographical element. "Daydreaming, double personality, the comedies which the individual plays to himself, the defense and enrichment of one's
'personality picture' " here engage his attention and show his
opposition to the crushing standardization of American life,
especially in the industrial town.[99] John Webster and Bruce
Dudley are products of a world deliberately made ugly by
utilitarianism. Dissatisfied and thwarted in their search for
peace, these two and all of Anderson's characters live in an era
of

> Speed, hurried workmanship, cheap automobiles for cheap men,
> cheap chairs in cheap houses, city apartment houses with shining
> bathroom floors, the Ford, the Twentieth Century Limited, the
> World War, the jazz, the movies.[100]

Tortuous though his mental processes may be, Anderson is
justified by the recent criticism that while others have described
more fully how the common people live, no one has shown so
authoritatively what they feel.[101]

Anderson has long engaged in his search for the baffling
truths of existence. His desires for the unknown have led him
along strange paths : to the mountain quiet of the Ozarks, to
crowded metropolitan centers, to the New Orleans wharves
where he watched Negro stevedores laughing and singing at
their work, and even to Gertrude Stein's Paris salon. It is
not surprising, therefore, that in the late twenties he returned
to the small town. Believing that the small town newspaper
might be used in the struggle against American standardization, he established himself in Marion, Virginia, as the local
editor. Here with his two papers he has continued his struggle
for individualism. Out of this experience has grown *Hello*

---

[99] Cf. Michaud, *op. cit.*, p. 156.
[100] *A Story Teller's Story* (New York, 1924), p. 81.
[101] Hicks, *op. cit.*, p. 230.

Towns! (1929) in which the novelist, according to his own confession, has tried to give a moving picture of a town "lifted right out of reality." Here is a new style for Anderson. Through the editorials and news items selected from his papers and augmented by bits of fictionalized matter Anderson, the editor, presents the drama of an actual small town always unrolling before the eyes.

Although the subject of repeated critical attacks, Sherwood Anderson remains one of the ablest rebels against the code-bound American small town. From his first novel, *Windy McPherson's Son* (1916), until his later study of a Georgia mill town, *Beyond Desire* (1932), continuously he has been a vital part of the creative movement emanating from the unsettled conditions of the first two decades of this century. Steadily observing the life around him—in backwater villages, railroad junctions, large cities, and country—he has worked inwardly interpreting the mental conflicts of repressed villagers and restless townsmen. Defeated men and women, victims of the mechanized order of factory towns; brooding youngsters—dissatisfied Hugh McVeys—warped by the futile life of mean little towns; disillusioned oldsters frustrated by a vicious society; "cracked" Civil War veterans and windy storytellers—these and others are his baffled dreamers struggling pigmy-like against the demands of a crushing world, or settling in apathy in backwater towns. Always—whether using novel short story, Whitmanesque chants, notes, or autobiography—Anderson is fundamentally a psychologist passionately desirous of interpreting the perplexities of the inward life. Like certain Victorian expounders, however, too often he sees a life devoid of both spiritual and material beauty. Everywhere the Andersonian hero is frustrated either by the forces of the machine age or by self-exaggerated inhibitions. Furthermore, Anderson's belief that the standardizing of emotions kills them has led him to sanction unconventionality. It is better, he holds, to be genuine, whatever the cost, than to keep the advantage of conformity. Such has been the nature of his revolt not only against the restrictions of a joyless small town life, but of the standards of American life in general.

Finally, Anderson's independence of literary traditions has enabled him to develop a natural method of story telling, a stream-of-consciousness style well adapted to the revelation of the emotional crises of his characters. Especially successful in achieving marked simplicity of style, Anderson, as he himself acknowledges, owes much to Gertrude Stein's experimentation in original phrasing and careful arrangements and rearrangements of words. The natural expression of much of his fiction—nowhere better illustrated than in his masterly monologue, "I'm a Fool"—is the result of studied experimentation on his part. His artistic achievement, which has left its mark on William Faulkner and other younger novelists, is marred chiefly by his preoccupation with Freudian obsessions and frustrations. His repeated treatment of a noticeably limited segment of life quite blots out his thinking about other phases of American living.[102]

By 1920 the new spirit of satiric radicalism already had waged war upon equally militant conservatives upholding Puritanism and other traditions long established. Journalist H. L. Mencken had started expounding his ideas with characteristic gusto through the Baltimore *Sun*, *The Smart Set*, *The American Mercury*, and his early *Prejudices*. Masters and Anderson had entered the clash between the old and the new and were opposing the evils of the American way of life. Theodore Dreiser had earlier attracted attention by his powerful novels of city life: *Sister Carrie* (1900), *Jennie Gerhardt* (1911), *The Financier* (1912), *The Titan* (1914), and *The Genius* (1915). The time was propitious, therefore, for a newer, bolder attack upon American culture. Hence, the preparations were ready for the singular success of Sinclair Lewis's *Main Street* and its satiric exposure of villages where life "is dullness made God." The popularity of *Main Street* was a sign of nothing less than the awakening of the small towns and villages to the fact that they were no longer regarded as restful havens, but were being ridiculed as the hotbeds of bigotry, as brakes on the wheels of progress. Without doubt, it was "the historical function of *Main Street* to accomplish among the villagers themselves what Edgar Lee Masters had already accomplished in his *Spoon River Anthology* among the literati."[103]

[102] Other works by Anderson include *Sherwood Anderson's Notebook* (1926); *A New Testament* (1927); *Nearer the Grass Roots* (1929); *Alice, and the Lost Novel* (1929); *The American County Fair* (1930); *Perhaps Women* (1931); *Beyond Desire* (1932); *No Swank* (1934); and *Puzzled America* (1935).

[103] Delmar Gross Cooke, "Sinclair Lewis," *The Dallas Morning News*, magazine section, March 8, 1925.

But the beginning of Lewis's revolt against the dull conventionality of small town ways antedates *Main Street*, his first novel to be widely recognized. Long before Lewis became known as the National Champion Castigator he already knew —and scorned—the way of small towns. The son of a small town physician, "Red" Lewis (born February 7, 1885) spent his first eighteen years in Sauk Center, Minnesota, a prairie town situated near a lake in Nicholson's Valley of Democracy "where the old-fashioned, kindly, neighborly, democratic virtues are presumed to thrive in a congenial habitat."[104]   His habits of writing poetry, reading, and walking about the countryside caused neighbors to regard Dr. Lewis's son as a bit queer. After high school he worked for the Sauk Center *Herald;* studied at Oberlin Academy; and, disregarding local warnings, planned to attend an Eastern college. Like other Midland youths before him, Lewis departed for New England —for Yale—to seek the "culture" which had been his dream. After graduation he seriously began a literary apprenticeship and, according to his own testimony, was for eight years (1907-1915) a literary jack-of-all-trades. Janitor-colonist at Upton Sinclair's experimental Helicon Hall, reporter, magazine editor, manuscript reader, steerage and stowaway traveler to Panama, Mexico, Europe, and elsewhere, a free lancer in California with William Rose Benét, and magazine story writer— these are briefly descriptive of his pre-*Main Street* days. Then in 1914 appeared the first of a series of earlier novels which are significant as precursors of Lewis's later attacks on the small town and as records of the maturing genius of America's first Nobel prize-winner in literature.

Our Mr. Wrenn relates the romantic adventures of a gentle man, a meek little bachelor—a sort of Caspar Milquetoast— who spends his free hours reading travel folders and longing for escape from the dull routine of his clerkship. A small and wholly unexpected inheritance enables "Wrennie" to stage a mild revolt by quitting his dull job and taking a cattle boat for England. After a short romantic tramp through Essex with a Bohemian dabbler in art, Wrenn returns to his old work and eventually finds apparent happiness with a salesgirl

---

[104] Parrington, *Our Own Diogenes*, p. 15.   For details about his earlier life see Pattee, *The New American Literature*, p. 339, and William Rose Benét, "The Earlier Lewis," *The Saturday Review of Literature*, X, 421-422 (Jan. 20, 1934).

whom he marries. In the end though "wistfully the exile gazed at his lost kingdom" of foreign travel, he hurried home to play pinochle with Nellie.

As modest and as unimpressive as its hero, *Our Mr. Wrenn* exhibits many characteristics which are traceable to Lewis's own youthful experiences on cattle boats ; to his literary gropings ; and to his keen observation of small town, city, and other types. Amateurish though it is, the novel in several respects foreshadows the more mature work of the later novels. While it is lacking in a background of small town life, this novel presents in embryo several types characteristic of *Main Street* and *Babbitt*. The artist, Istra Nash, with her peculiar romantic attitude ; simple, daydreaming, and even stupid Wrennie ; "Old Goglefogle," hardboiled business man ; and bald-headed Mittyford, Ph.D., a caricature of the American professor abroad, suggest later portraits. In spite of a strained and exaggerated style, Lewis's developing realism and his flair for satiric thrusts appear in the almost photographic picturing of New York boardinghouses, cheap motion picture shows, and offices. Here, too, Lewis makes first use of the American idiom so characteristic of the later novels. While both *Our Mr. Wrenn* and *The Job* (1917) are delineative of metropolitan, rather than small town, backgrounds, each shows that dullness and stupidity may be found in a city office or boardinghouse as often as in the smaller circles of Gopher Prairie and Banjo Crossing. Further, the two main characters, having earlier fled from sordid small towns, find in their city circles the same dull and mean-spirited people.

The Trail of the Hawk: A Comedy of the Seriousness of Life (1915) early shows Lewis's reaction against the intellectual stuffiness of stagnating Midwestern towns. The theme, that of the escape of a restless young American from the Middle Border, develops around Carl Erickson, who grew to manhood in the small prairie town of Joralemon, Minnesota. Carl, a second-generation Norwegian and the son of the village carpenter, was eight years old in 1893 and, therefore, grew up when Victorian ideals dominated society, even in Joralemon. Representative of the new American, Carl constantly was moved by the spirit of revolt, as was young Lewis. First, through the influence of the village atheist (a preliminary delineation of the Gopher Prairie Bjornstam), who talked to the boy of Ingersoll, Marx, and Napoleon, Carl felt moved to disagree with his associates in the stupid little town. Later he enrolls in a near-by narrow denominational college, ironically called Plato College, the prototype for Elmer Gantry's jerkwater alma mater. Here Carl sickens of the dull talks—on the spirit of duty—made by a dull president to dull students. The boy falls into disfavor not only with a prejudiced faculty, but with the provincial students because he openly favors the cause of a young instructor, a Yale graduate, who arouses the ire of the self-righteous community through his discussions in an English class of H. G. Wells and Bernard Shaw. After much wandering in places once visited by Lewis, Carl finally in New York encounters social barriers as narrow as the Joralemon prejudices. Lewis's best satire is directed against the provincial townspeople, both in Joralemon and in the Plato College town, who consistently object to anything out of the ordinary decorous way of life. The objectors to "Bone" Stillman, Carl's radical friend and rural philosopher in Joralemon, share the same fate as the mentally stagnated faculty of Plato College, which in itself was "as earnest and undistinguished, as provincially dull and pathetically human, as a spinster missionary."[105] Small town social snobbery, society reporting in the local paper, and gossip are sharply castigated in the manner of *Main Street*. The patterns for Lewis's later social satires were being slowly designed.

The Job (1917), in spite of its faultiness in plot, is a competent and timely treatment of the American business woman, then newly self-sufficient because of the country's plunge into the World War. The story of a small town girl, Una Golden from Panama, Pennsylvania, who succeeds in New York as a realtor and advertiser, *The Job* foreshadows the social satire of *Ann Vickers* (1933), the study of another feminine rebel. According to William Lyon Phelps, Lewis sees in Una "an intelligent and purposeful feminine will, emerging from the respectable helplessness and hopelessness of girls who married their first choice and 'settled down' in Panama, Pennsylvania—emerging into the beauty of a self-directed life." Here again is a satiric attack against the sentimentalists who still thought of the American village as the sure abode of friendship, honesty, and clean, sweet, marriageable girls, who, once married to their childhood

[105] *The Trail of the Hawk, etc.* (New York, 1915), p. 58.

sweethearts, presumably lived joyously in such a town until death.[106] The unflattering pictures of Panama show the dullness of small town life about 1906. Una, the daughter of a middle-class lawyer, was too alert to find contentment in the petty round of life which Panama afforded. In time she became

. . . frightfully bored! She suddenly hated the town, hated every evening she would have to spend there, reading newspapers and playing cards with her mother, and dreading a call from Mr. Henry Carson. . . .[107]

a widower with catarrh and three children. Rebelling against the hopelessness of affairs in the town, Una finally escaped to the city, where she attended a business college and eventually found work and success among other small town escapists. Primarily a novel of a woman's business slavery, *The Job* is further significant as an early satiric expression of Lewis's condemnation of the small town spirit.

The Innocents: A Story for Lovers (1917) and *Free Air* (1919) are negligible stories. The thin plot of the former tells of the unbelievable experiences of an elderly couple, who, suddenly poverty-stricken, turn to a life of vagabondage. Slight delineation of the small town background appears in the descriptions of the many places they visit from the resort region of Cape Cod to Lippittsville, Indiana. *Free Air*, marking the conclusion of Lewis's apprenticeship, is a bit of yarning about an automobile romance lasting all the way from New York to Seattle. The cross-country trip of the Boltwoods from the East to the Far West gives Lewis a fictional instrument for depicting—in a hurried fashion—various small towns along their route, often ugly prairie towns whose names Claire Boltwood combined "in a lyric so emotion-stirring that it ought, perhaps, to be the national anthem."[108] While Lewis overstretches the rise of the common man thesis in the love tale of socialite Claire and Milt Daggett, a mechanic, he does give promise in his descriptions of characters and drab highway junctions of his *Main Street* village attacks just one year in the offing. Again, in this novel Lewis had opportunity for a comparative study of American small towns.

[106] *Main Street* (New York, 1920), r. 264.
[107] *The Job: An American Novel* (New York, 1917), p. 13.
[108] *Free Air* (New York, 1919), p. 208.

These preliminary attacks on the narrowness, smugness, and intellectual sterility of the small town reached a culmination in *Main Street* (1920), itself the result of six or seven years of preparation. As the author's foreword warns, this novel is not only the comprehensive history of Gopher Prairie, Minnesota, but is also suggestive of "ten thousand towns from Albany to San Diego." It is an indictment of America at large and of a way of life common throughout all sections. The Main Street of the story, says Lewis, is "the continuation of Main Street everywhere."[109]   From East to West there is the same ugliness, the same petty hypocrisies, shoddy culture, self-righteousness, and, above all, the same vitiating dullness. Even in Sauk Center Lewis had viewed at first hand the prototypes of Gopher Prairie's "Bon Ton Store," the "Farmers' National Bank," "Howland and Gould's Grocery," and "Dahl and Oleson's Meat Market." While the names of the characters may vary from place to place, Stanton Coblentz suggests that in a host of towns similar to Sauk Center, or Gopher Prairie, there may be seen the Widow Bogart, outwardly a church member and a Good Influence, piously moralizing and spreading scandal; Dave Dyer, the druggist, repeating year after year the same jokes; and Ezra Stowbody, the pompous banker, posing as an authority on all things human and divine while he forecloses mortgages to inculcate respect for the law.[110]

Primarily *Main Street* is a novel of character and situation rather than one of sustained plot. With the narrative interest subservient to the satiric protest against dullness, only two main figures, Carol Milford Kennicott and her husband, Dr. Will Kennicott, stand out distinctly from the citizenry of the town. The other characters, presented in varying shades of distinctness and ridicule, are representatives of small town types to be found in many sections. In fact, much of the book is given to minutely detailed descriptions of Gopher Prairie's inhabitants, all presented—frequently in caricature—as a commonplace and uninteresting set. Genial, yet blatant, Sam Clark, "dealer in hardware, sporting goods, [and] cream separators"; Dave Dyer, already mentioned, "the guy that put the 'shun' in prescription"; Luke Dawson, a moneylender "with bulging eyes in a milky face"; his wife with "bleached

---

[109] *Main Street* (1920), Foreword.
[110] "Main Street," *The Bookman*, LII, 457 (Jan., 1921).

cheeks, bleached hair, bleached voice, and a bleached manner"; Harry and Juanita Haydock, Rita Simons and Dr. Terry Gould, "the young smart set of Gopher Prairie"—these, together with their associates, people a Midland town, which, as one critic has said, William Allen White would not recognize as his home town. Dull provincials, social parasites, tradesmen, Main Street loafers, and small town leaders are satirized as symbolizing the *genus Americanum*. And that graduate of Blodgett College, Carol the rebel, is little better than the folk to whom she feels superior and has hopes of reforming.

The story itself, now known throughout the world, is a modern version of the time-worn theme of a rebellious heroine. Carol Milford, a city librarian and idealist, comes to drab Gopher Prairie as the bride of good-natured Dr. Kennicott, a well-meaning country physician. Finding only dullness and monotony in the town, Carol revolts against the social pressure that encompasses her. She is depressed by the physical ugliness of the raw prairie town and disgusted by the prejudices, jealousies, and affectations of its people. Spurred on by her college aspirations, she makes herself ridiculous by her determination to "get my hands on one of these prairie towns and make it beautiful." But Gopher Prairie resists Carol's misguided efforts to transform it into the Village Beautiful. Finally, her long smoldering rebellion against the pettiness of her small community breaks out in open revolt and she flees to Washington, only to return, after two years, reluctantly resigned to Gopher Prairie. Her opposition to the forces of conformity has been useless. She is driven back into the group without solving the question of the town's dullness. As in real life, Gopher Prairie remains the same narrow, prosaic, and uninspiring community. What cynical Guy Pollock, the local lawyer, terms the "village virus" has so affected the people that they are devoid of outlook and have resigned themselves to "the humdrum, inevitable tragedy of struggle against inertia."

Lewis has produced the outward life of small town citizens as no other novelist of the century has done, and *Main Street*, as an indictment of provincial dullness, is the worthiest twentieth-century successor to Howe's *The Story of a Country Town*. As he sees it, Main Street is a failure. Standardized life has meant the social devastation not only of Gopher Prairie but of

26

its actual counterparts.   This lack of individuality Lewis presents, through his almost uncanny faculty for unmasking the middle-class mind, with satire, burlesque, and humor, which is sometimes genial, sometimes malicious.   Because of his comic and satiric gifts, he is little concerned with the inner life of townspeople.   Instead, he examines the background of their lives, their houses, schools, churches, clubs, politics, costumes, and diversions.   (Unforgettably satiric is his picture of the Thanatopsis Club which, holding high the banners for cultural progress in Gopher Prairie, determinedly tries to cover the whole field of English poetry in a single meeting.)[111]   Possessed of the arts of mimicry and photographic gifts of accuracy, Lewis reproduces in this problem novel the looks, gestures, and speech of an amazing number of familiar characters.   He seems to understand the conduct of all types of average American citizens.   He is able to forsee their conduct during a given situation.   In the words of Parrington, he "talks easily with Main Street in its own vernacular."   When reproducing American idiom, however, Lewis is again the observing satirist who alters the average level of speech with little touches of exaggeration, if for no other reason than for its eminence of dullness.[112]   Too often ridicule and invective replace realism.

To Lewis, as to Masters, the American small town of the first quarter of the present century presented a definite fictional problem.   The chief interest of *Main Street* is its coping with the flatness and dullness of the small prairie town.   Though Lewis's attack upon the "village virus" may assume an almost Puritanic aspect, though it may not be a fair representation of conditions in all small towns, it has, like *Spoon River*, given a decided impetus to the movement "to escape from sentimentality, from verbiage, from hypocrisy, and to face life and folk, even at the cost of idols and illusions."[113]   *Main Street*, though following *Winesburg, Ohio*, is, indeed, a pioneer work in modern fiction.   Out of the Northern Midwest, "a land of dairy herds and exquisite lakes, of new automobiles and tar-paper shanties and silos like red towers, of clumsy speech and a hope that is

[111] Cf. Edith Wharton's "Xingu," a satire of a small town literary club (the Hillsbridge Lunch Club), which is "taken in" by the cleverness of its most snubbed member.

[112] Van Doren, *op. cit.*, pp. 82-83.

[113] Zona Gale, "Out of Nothing into Somewhere," *The English Journal* (College ed.), XIII, 176 (March, 1924).

boundless," Sinclair Lewis has created a challenging picture, variously termed a satirical masterpiece, a realistic report of town life, a protest against the absorbing poverty of American culture, and the outstanding American social satire of its generation.[114] Everything considered, however, one agrees with Harlan Hatcher that the novel represents "an examination of Gopher Prairie by one who was measuring it by a standard quite alien and unfamiliar to the natives of that village, and his heroine was a college girl educated away from village life and panting for uplift."[115]

Severely criticized as a gopher-village agitator, a born malcontent, a flaying man, and a perfectionist, Lewis since *Main Street* has continued "to work systematically through our sacred American decalogue, smashing one commandment after another."[116] Always, too, he employs the monotonous, but effective, sardonic reportorial style of *Main Street*. Small town dullness, while never forgotten, has yielded first place to broader themes satirically treating of the boastfulness, chicanery, and hypocrisy of the American business man, religious leaders, men of science, political bosses, and hotel officials. More recently he has urged a revolt of parents. But in his exposures of what he considers the larger evils of American society Lewis has found occasion again and again to direct his irrepressible satire against the small town.

Babbitt (1922), a satire upon middle-aged romanticism, narrow conventions, and blatant optimism, is a parallel and coordinate extension, rather than a sequel, of *Main Street*. It is applicable to the study of the small town as a picture of contemporary society in a larger city which still maintains many of the provincial standards of the smaller place. Zenith, the home of George F. Babbitt, a platitude-dispensing, middle-class realtor, is but a magnified Gopher Prairie, symbolizing on a large scale the same dull standardization, the same smugness, and the same superficial culture. In short, *Babbitt*, while primarily the story of a man's unrest, is a comprehensive study,

---

[114] Quoted matter from *Main Street*, p. 24. An amusing parody of *Main Street* may be found in Carolyn Wells's *Ptomaine Street: The Tale of Warble Petticoat* (Philadelphia, 1921). A Pittsburgh waitress marries big Bill Petticoat, a doctor specializing in ptomaine poisoning. They move to Butterfly Center where Warble attempts reforms; to her dismay, she finds in the town an ultramodern and sophisticated social set whose members thrust reforms at the city bride.

[115] *Creating the Modern American Novel* (New York, 1935), p. 119.

[116] Parrington, *Our Own Diogenes*, p. 10.

with caustic notation of detail, of the city's attempt to solve
the problems which it inherited from the small town.

Completely at home in standardized Zenith, George Babbitt, forty-six, state university graduate, father of two children,
and prosperous broker, is a Good Fellow among Good Fellows.
Assuredly the very embodiment of his own wordy definition of
the "Ideal Citizen," Babbitt is "a God-fearing, hustling, successful, two-fisted Regular Guy, who belongs to some church
with pep and piety to it, who belongs to the Boosters or the
Rotarians or the Kiwanis, to the Elks or Moose or Red Men
or Knights of Columbus or any score of organizations of good,
jolly, kidding, laughing, sweating, upstanding, lend-a-handing
Royal Good Fellows, who plays hard and works hard, and
whose answers to his critics is a square-toed boot that'll reach
the grouches and smart alecs to respect the He-man and get
out and root for Uncle Samuel, U. S. A.!"[117]

Carol Kennicott—Régis Michaud, a brilliant foreign critic,
maintains—represents the average American woman ; Babbitt,
the average American man.[118]   Termed one of the few genuinely humorous characters of recent fiction, Babbitt, "industrious, respectable, superficially interested in the church, conventionally moral, unbelievably stupid, and above all exceedingly funny," is made to caricature middle-class America.[119]
In *Main Street* Lewis caustically declares that the climax of
civilization is in the modern town that "thinks not in hoss-
swapping but in cheap motorcars, telephones, ready-made
clothes, silos, alfalfa, kodaks, phonographs, leather-upholstered
Morris chairs, bridge prizes, oil stocks, motion-pictures, land-
deals, unread sets of Mark Twain, and a chaste version of
national politics."[120]   Just as he thus marks the provincial
town with its standardization of mediocrity, Lewis likewise
makes Babbitt a standpatter and a conformist in a larger circle.
Always around him, overwhelming him, the city standardizes
Babbitt, like Mr. Wrenn, in much the same fashion as Gopher
Prairie puts its mark of provincial conformity on Carol.   As
viewed again by Michaud, Babbitt is "conformism incarnate,"
"publicity personified," and "the *homo americanus par excellence*,

[117] *Babbitt* (New York, 1922), p. 188.
[118] *Op. cit.*, p. 135.
[119] Blankenship, *op. cit.*, p. 661.
[120] *Main Street*, p. 264.

the representative average American," comparable to Molière's *bourgeois gentilhomme*.[121]

In the first part of *Arrowsmith* (1925), the thoughtful story of an idealist, Lewis uses for the second time his memories of his father's work as a small town doctor. Like Lewis's other rebels, Martin Arrowsmith, a young genius and scientific researcher dissatisfied with half-truth, experienced a conventional boyhood as the son of a merchant in a Midwestern town. As a youngster, when he was supposed to be watching the office for old "Doc" Vickerson, an easy-going practitioner in Elk Mills, Martin puzzled over the dusty pages of Gray's *Anatomy*. Even then he was determined to become a doctor. Differing, of course, in his superior intellectual capacities, Martin is a more fully realized Carl Erickson who breaks away from the uncongenial small town surroundings which almost stifle him by their dullness. Martin goes to medical college—the University of Winnemac—only to find the school "a mill to turn out men and women who will lead moral lives, play bridge, drive good cars, be enterprising in business, and occasionally mention books, though they are not expected to have time to read them."[122] Here inspired by an immunology specialist, old Max Gottlieb, Martin continues his research only to feel again the deadening influence of the small town. Like Will Kennicott, he marries and becomes a country doctor in Wheatsylvania, North Dakota, the home town of Leora, his self-effacing wife. Always dreaming of devoting his time to research, Martin finds the stupidity and pettiness of Bert Tozer, his brother-in-law, the local jealousies, and the general ignorance of the people unbearable. Gladly he leaves his commonplace surroundings for the larger town of Nautilus in Iowa, where as a health officer he learns that "boosting for better babies is legitimate as long as the milk supply is left alone." Associations with the mountebank and slogan maker, Dr. Almus Pickerbaugh, and later in Chicago with the more sauve charlatans of the Rouncefield Clinic and in New York with the high office seekers at the McGurk Institute bring Martin in contact with greater evils than small town dullness.

In *Arrowsmith*, except for an early outburst, Lewis forgets his ridicule of the small town to turn to a broader field for satire.

---

[121] Michaud, *op. cit.*, p. 144.
[122] *Arrowsmith* (New York, 1925), p. 7.

In his difficult quest for truth Arrowsmith quickly moves through the small town phase of his career. With the comparatively few Wheatsylvania scenes, however, Lewis makes satiric exposures of a mean-spirited little place in the bleak hinterlands of the Dakotas. Nautilus fares little better as a town run by political and social cliques. Luckily Martin escapes his small walled environment only to suffer disillusionment and personal grief in the many-towered city. His struggle, which at last ends in peace and scientific achievement, after all presents the convincing story of idealism in conflict with charlantry.

It is generally conceded that with *Arrowsmith* Lewis closed his best period of work. The qualities which gave significance to *Main Street*, *Babbitt*, and *Arrowsmith* and which placed Lewis in the forefront of the American literati have suddenly vanished. *Mantrap*, *Elmer Gantry*, *The Man Who Knew Coolidge*, *Dodsworth*, *Ann Vickers*, *Work of Art*, *It Can't Happen Here*, *Selected Short Stories*, and *The Prodigal Parents*, all published between 1926 and 1938, are far less convincing and illuminating than his three masterpieces. *Elmer Gantry* (1927), *Ann Vickers* (1933), and *Work of Art* (1934), no one of which is primarily a small town novel, may be cited, however, as additional examples of Lewis's satiric treatments of protagonists who emerge from ugly little towns to attain doubtful success in the world of affairs. The first, a bitterly vituperative study of unscrupulous Elmer Gantry, ecclesiastical hypocrite, bounder, and "salesman of salvation" shows the full force of Lewis's indignation as it is directed against American religious standards. Some of the most vituperative passages reveal scenes of Elmer's boyhood in Paris, Kansas ; his experiences at provincial Terwillinger College and, later, at Mizpah Theological Seminary, Babylon, Minnesota ; and his sensational evangelistic methods in Banjo Crossing, Minnesota, Sautersville, Nebraska, and scores of other small towns throughout the Midlands and elsewhere. *Elmer Gantry*, with its incidental satire against small towns, is obviously the study of a religious hypocrite surcharged with all the vitriolic power at Lewis's command. It represents the most hostile examination of the church in American fiction. Lacking the idealistic theme of *Arrowsmith*, *Ann Vickers* tells of a Great Woman, neurotic Ann Vickers, bent upon her suffragist mission of exposing the horrors of the American prison system and of unmasking morally diseased, bribe-taking officials. Ann's blind search for a fulfilled life, a search beset by disillusionment, graft, chicanery, and moral degradation, had its beginning in the country town of Waubanakee, Illinois. Here Ann, the daughter of the school superintendent, often listened to the town's socialistic cobbler, old Oscar Klebs, who first opened the girl's eyes to the prevalence of social injustice in America. After college graduation Ann, young and rebellious, leaves Waubanakee and old Klebs's Utopian talking for New York, where she begins a long career of welfare work. The remainder of the book, portraying Ann both as reformer and woman, is decidedly below the level of the artistic achievement of *Arrowsmith*.

By the time Lewis published *Work of Art* he had come to be depended upon as the manufacturer of a standard brand : satiric commentary on American life. This story of the rise and fall of a hotel magnate is, like the earlier *The Rise of Silas Lapham*, starkly American. Lewis steadily views his victim and his environment, in small town and city, with a scorn that only at the end threatens to soften to pity. From the opening of the story in 1897 until its close in 1933 the reader gets glimpses of Black Thread Center, a narrow little Connecticut town. Here the American House, in which Myron Weagle (son of the spiritless manager) grew up, is little better than the Minniemashie House in Gopher Prairie or the ugly hotel in Winesburg, Ohio. Myron's rise is true enough for the time : hotel clerk in a larger town ; a better place in New Haven ; and the peak of hostelry achievement—Manhattan management. His fall, too, is typically American. After the failure of his dream hotel and his subsequent financial crash, Myron is again claimed by the small town. This time the small town—commonplace Lemuel, Kansas—is a place of refuge. In this last turn of the story Lewis softens to the point of making a radical departure from his old formula. He has a constructive suggestion, which once he and his tribe scorned. He almost preaches the simple life. Myron at the end is the owner of a tourist camp, and Lewis gives the impression that this return toward the more primitive life from which he and his mannikin sprang is, on the whole, as satisfactory escape as can be made from the labyrinth of mechanized urban complexity.[123]

Whether approving or disapproving of Lewis's technique, the modern reader must concede the significant fact that his best fiction presents documentary evidence of the rebellious twenties, a dissatisfied, post-war generation given over to disillusion. In his varied slashing attacks upon middle-class optimism and smugness in general, Lewis has spared the small town in neither individualized exposure nor in comparative studies, equally as damning. His early revolt from the village has grown to a larger uprising against so many phases of American that he has become the satirist and problem novelist rather than the objective realist. Having clubbed dullness, smugness, and hypocrisy to earth, he brandishes high his cudgels against those innocents who believe that "all American men are tall, handsome, rich, honest, and powerful at golf; that all country towns are filled with kind neighbors who do nothing from day to day save going about being kind to one another; that although American girls may be wild, they change always into perfect wives and mothers; and that, geographically, America is composed solely of New York, which is inhabited entirely by millionaires; of the West, which keeps unchanged all the boisterous heroism of 1870; and of the South, where everyone lives on a plantation perpetually glossy with moonlight and scented with magnolias."[124] Whether he has changed in his attitude toward the gopher-village depends largely upon one's interpretation of *Work of Art*, and the other later novels. Has the age of cynicism, in Lewis's thinking, given way to the age of conviction?

As we have seen, in the history of modern realism the years 1919 and 1920, the era of the Masters-Anderson-Lewis rebellion, are significant dates in that much of the fiction then current bore the earmarks of what has been popularly called "small town stuff." After *Spoon River* realism left its imprint upon every type of small town fiction: upon the social satires of Lewis, the probing psychological studies of Anderson, the

---

[123] The most memorable small town figure of the political satire, *It Can't Happen Here* (1935) is a New England country editor, Doremus Jessup, a victim of a militaristic regime. The town of *The Prodigal Parents* (1938) belongs to the class of Zenith rather than to that of a small town.

[124] *Addresses by Axel Karlfeldt and Sinclair Lewis, on the Occasion of the Award of the Nobel Prize*, p. 11.

short stories of protest by Willa Cather, and other examples of flowering realism. Among the younger writers of the twenties who became associated with the small town realists was Floyd Dell (1887—), another native small townsman, rebel, and individualist who eventually joined the Chicago literary circle, so admirably described in Harry Hansen's *Midwest Portraits*. Born in Barry, Illinois, a small town he fictionalized as Maple, Floyd Dell spent his formative poverty-marked years here and in other towns which likewise became extrinsically significant as the social backgrounds of his fiction. Quincy, Illinois, a river town of about thirty thousand, became Vickly and picturesque Davenport, Iowa—the same Davenport pictured in Octave Thanet's stories—was the model for the Port Royal of Dell's earliest novels to win popular recognition. Thus Dell's beginnings, like those of many of his Midwestern contemporaries, linked his fiction, much of which is autobiographic, with the dreary monotony of life in the small towns of his own boyhood.

Dell's earlier attitude toward the small town differs from that of his more vitriolic contemporaries. Though early termed a "radical" because of his editorial connections with the *Masses* and the *Liberator*, Dell, unlike Lewis, does not show his aversions in expressions of petulant disgust. The small town political and social corruption which provoked Masters to indignant protest gives Dell, a younger contemporary, less concern than the problem of youth's pathetic struggle for adjustment. Gaining popularity in the same post-War era which produced Percy Marks's *The Plastic Age*, Warner Fabian's *Flaming Youth*, and the F. Scott Fitzgerald tales of the jazz age, Floyd Dell championed disturbed youth against restricting social tyrannies. The bewilderment and hopelessness of the younger generation, of the Felix Fays (really the diffident Floyd Dells), whose poetic outlook on life is sadly misunderstood by their more calloused and unthinking small town schoolmates and other associates, prove thematically significant in Dell's early novels of the little town. In his first novel of importance, *Moon-Calf* (1920), Dell neither ridicules nor sentimentalizes about village life. He sympathetically recounts the unconventional career of Felix Fay (obviously a thinly disguised story of the author's own humble beginnings), a young

poet of Maple (actually Barry), Illinois.[125] Concentrating his
efforts upon the portrayal of Felix's delicate susceptibilities
rather than upon the war against the village, Dell traces, without bitter satire or reproach, the steps in the boy's development.   Felix (alias Dell), a dreamer, moons his way through
several Illinois villages and river towns.   With his eyes ever
fixed upon a star, the young hero blunders from one community to another, where he has few adventures more exciting
than his successive discovery of new ideas.   *The Briary Bush*
(1921) is a continuation of the story of Felix's fruitless search
for stability.   Scorned in love by Joyce Tennant, who becomes
the wife of another, Felix grows dissatisfied with his job on the
Port Royal *Record*.   Like the small town reporters in *Winesburg, Ohio* and George Milburn's more recent *Oklahoma Town*,
Felix cannot resist the lure of Chicago and the' great world
beyond.   He feels that the shadow-world of ideas, of theories,
of poetic fancies, amidst which he has moved all his life, is not
enough.   He must live in the real world of which Chicago is
the mighty symbol.   He is tired of being Felix Fay the fool,
the theorist, the poet and imagines himself in Chicago, a
changed person—a young man of action, practical, alert, ruthlessly competitive.[126]   The mental conflict he wages in his
search for another Felix Fay quite different from the moon-
calf is expressed in the words of the old song :

> Oh, the briary-bush
> That pricks my heart so sore!
> If ever I get out of the briary-bush
> I'll never get in any more!

Felix is another small town escapist, representative of the widespread restlessness of youth after the World War.

In *This Mad Ideal* (1925) Dell makes a third penetrating and
unconventional analysis of the progressive mood of modern
youth, but this time he approaches the problem from the feminine viewpoint.   As elsewhere, Dell's rebellion here is not one
of hate.   Like that of *Moon-Calf*, the plot concerns a young
person, Judith Valentine, the orphaned daughter of an actress
and of a black sheep from a respectable New England family,

[125] See Hansen, *op. cit.*, pp. 207-224, for a sympathetic account of Dell's early
career.   Cf. Dell, *Homecoming: An Autobiography* (New York, 1933) for the sources
of many of the autobiographical elements in *Moon-Calf.*
[126] *The Briary Bush* (New York, 1921), p. 4.

who is unable happily to conform to the monotony and narrowness of her community. Consequently Judith, in eagerly searching for a freer and a larger life—a sort of ideal world—and in rebelling against the prejudices of the townspeople, suffers keenly because of their stupid misunderstanding. Individual though the delineation of Judith's mental struggle may be, *This Mad Ideal* is comparable in many ways to other small town novels which have preceded it. The Pompton *Patriot*, its disillusioned editor, once also a seeker for a mad ideal, and its staff, one of whom is Judith, suggest the newspaper background of William Allen White's *In Our Town*. The escape motif, as exemplified in Judith's longing for the poetically beautiful and in her final escape to Boston and New York, is in keeping with the familiar handling of such a theme in *Main Street*. In Pompton, "one of those tiny villages that are like dots on the map of New England," Judith realized that she was hampered by living among provincial people, "subject to folk-influences, compelled by traditional compulsions."[127] Excellent satire directed against the prejudices of small minds appears in the scene where the high-school principal, horrified at finding Judith reading Hardy's *Jude the Obscure*, delivers a chapel sermon on obscene literature. In its satire and character presentation this description equals a similar scene at Carl Erickson's Plato College portrayed in *The Trail of the Hawk*.

Of Dell's other fiction the most satirically delineative of the small town spirit is *Runaway* (1925), another tale of a village escapist, romantic Michael Shenstone, who prefers a life of vagabondage in the Orient to the narrow social standards of a small Midwestern town. With its satirical tone, which tries obviously to be neither too subtle nor too scathing, this novel marks a departure from Dell's usual attitude toward the village. This is the tale of a middle-class and conservative town and its reaction toward the romantic folly of Michael Shenstone, who "had blown into Beaumont one day, a vagabond young reporter, big and breezy." Had he not fallen in love with and won the town beauty from her lawyer-cousin, Michael might have wandered on again within a few months. Eventually, however, he "scandalized the town by putting aside, lightly and wantonly, its best prizes in the game of life—re-

[127] *This Mad Ideal* (New York, 1925), p. 159.

spectability, prosperity and neighborly regard."[128]   After some years of outward conformity to the town standards Michael, ever romantic, revolts against the futility of his life and goes to follow the trail of Marco Polo, without so much as mentioning his plans to his wife and young daughter.   Seventeen years later he returns to find his wife dead and his daughter experiencing a period of revolt similar to his own youthful rebellion, while he himself has come to be traditionally regarded by the good people of Beaumont as the very consummation of evil. The rest of the plot, showing how scapegrace Michael becomes the town idol, is thin.   The importance of the novel lies in its delineations of a narrow society which, at last, put its mark on its one romantic runaway.

An original writer, Floyd Dell has added to the small town of modern fiction a new type of citizen—the youthful dreamer, or seeker of a mad ideal, who feels, like some of Willa Cather's ambitious youths, that a small town envlronment is antagonistic to his cultural development.   While he has written much since the twenties, Dell has not surpassed his earlier pictures of Felix Fay and the lad's hunger for new and stimulating contacts.[129]   With Anderson and Lewis, Dell takes high rank as one of the most significant interpreters of American small town characters during the twenties.

One of the most gifted of modern realists to depict Midwestern small towns and prairies is Willa Sibert Cather (1876—), born of old Virginia stock but through family migration associated from her childhood with Nebraska.   Miss Cather served her literary apprenticeship during the decade before the village insurgents declared open war upon provincial stupidity and false standards of conduct.   A transplanted being, the future novelist educated at the Red Cloud High School and the University of Nebraska (1892-95), early became a part of the West she later fused into her tales of Antonia Shimerda, Alexandra Bergson, and Thea Kronborg.   Even during college days her dream had been literature.   Short sketches of the immigrant families near her father's ranch were done in her

---

[128] *Runaway* (New York, 1925), p. 63.
[129] Dell's other novels include *An Old Man's Folly* (1926), *An Unmarried Father* (1927), *Souvenir* (1929), *Love Without Money* (1931), *Diana Stair* (1932), and *The Golden Spike* (1934), most of which treat of youth's efforts to adjust itself in an unsettled modern world.

English classes.[130]   Graduation, newspaper reporting in Pittsburgh, magazine editing and short story writing in New York, and her discovery by S. S. McClure—these are the steps in her apprenticeship, years of valuable literary contacts and deepening of outlook.

Except for her short stories, to the first of her several literary periods there belongs little which is suggestive of Miss Cather's later realistic portrayals of Midwestern farm and town life. The sweetly lyrical *April Twilights and Other Poems* (1903) contains no mention of the prairie towns featured in her stories and later novels.   Her first novel, *Alexander's Bridge* (written in 1911), shows obviously, to use Miss Cather's own criticism, that the youthful writer "is often more interested in his discoveries about his art than in the homely truths which have been about him from the cradle."[131]   Here, with no foreshadowing of the highly individualized immigrant types of *O Pioneers!* and later novels, sophisticated and educated people move about in Back Bay drawing-rooms and London hotels. To Miss Cather's early period belongs also a collection of short stories, first published as *The Troll Garden* (1905) and later included, in part, in *Youth and the Bright Medusa* (1920).   In these the young writer took her first stand against the village.

Her fortunate meeting with Sarah Orne Jewett in 1912 led Miss Cather, at the former's insistence, to "write the truth and let them (i.e., magazine editors) take it or leave it."[132]   Her second, or thoroughly indigenous, period began with *The Bohemian Girl* (1912) and included *O Pioneers!* (1913), *The Song of the Lark* (1915), and *My Ántonia* (1918), all pictures of a vanished frontier inspired by the associations of Miss Cather's youth.   In these she catches the indomitable spirit of pioneer Nebraskans whose indefatigable energies converted the prairies into wheat lands.   Here are unforgettable accounts of the heroic age of pioneering.   Impressively realistic are the pictures of bitter winters and toil-filled summers ; of the slow adjustments to the new land of the Shimerdas, Cuzaks, and other transplanted foreigners ; of poverty long endured gradually giving place to a dearly bought prosperity ; and of the emer-

[130] Pattee, *op. cit.*, p. 261.
[131] *Alexander's Bridge*, ed. of 1922, pp. vi-vii.
[132] Pattee, *op. cit.*, p. 262. Cf. L. Carroll, "Willa Sibert Cather," *The Bookman*, LIII, 212-216 (May, 1921).

gence of tiny dots of settlements on the Nebraska prairies.

In 1923 with *One of Ours* Miss Cather not only completed her Nebraska cycle but, established in the literary field through a Pulitzer Prize award, began a new period of artistic fulfilment. Since then changing interests have turned her away from tales of humble immigrants who struggle with the elements to other widely varied materials : to those of Colorado small town life, nineteenth-century New Mexico, seventeenth-century Quebec, a professor's life in a college town, and others.   Copiousness of material has been combined with a breadth of sympathy, and maturing artistry has freed the novelist from the conventional style and substance of *Alexander's Bridge*.   Of the more than half dozen volumes published since *One of Ours*, a few deal with small town people, repressed individuals whose stagnating stupidities, malicious gossip, futile aspirations, and timid pieties had early found a limited, but realistic, delineation in Miss Cather's short stories.

In fact, as a recent critic has noted, Miss Cather has never completely departed from her earliest environment, the Western village.[133]   While she has not imitated Masters and Lewis with full-length indictments of Midwestern community life, by no means has she been unaware of the pettiness and ugliness of spirit frequently associated with the village.   Throughout her fiction, from some of *The Troll Garden* stories to the later novels, Miss Cather has looked steadily at the life of the little town and has seen it whole.   Health, courage, a desire for freedom, a will to do—these lift most of Miss Cather's small town protagonists from "the jealous, leveling standards that would reduce all pioneers to jack-of-all-tradeship and general undistinction."[134]   Many of her town folk are heroic characters bravely entering the strife for self-fulfilment,   On the other hand, like her more hostile contemporaries, Miss Cather knew the small town for what it was and pictured it not as the dwelling place of sweetness and light.   On occasion she presented it as the symbol of the passing of the heroic age of the West and its citizens as the weak successors to pioneer "giants in the earth."

While four of the seven stories in *The Troll Garden* are con-

[133] Blankenship, *op. cit.*, p. 677.   Cf. W. F. Taylor, *A History of American Letters*, pp. 357 ff.
[134] Percy H. Boynton, "Willa Cather," *The English Journal* (College ed.), XIII, 379 (June, 1924).

ventional artists' colony stories with metropolitan backgrounds, three point toward Miss Cather's interest in the least laudable aspects of village life long before the outbreak of 1920. "A Wagner Matinée," "The Sculptor's Funeral," and "A Death in the Desert," all later reprinted in *Youth and the Bright Medusa*, early gave promise of Miss Cather's later fully expressed interest in the clash of character and environment. In these, as in other stories from the later collection, ambitious, sensitive youths, misunderstood by provincial relatives and prosaic associates, either escape to find success outside the narrow limits of the town, or, remaining there, beat their luminous wings in vain and are broken by the village code. In each of these stories named there is something of Garland's realism emphasizing toil-hardened village folk, who living apart from the cultural influences of larger places become so starved for beauty that they no longer are capable of appreciating the aesthetic side of life. This appears in modified form in the case of Aunt Georgiana, in her youth a teacher of music in Boston, but whose elopement with a shiftless young man brought her as a bride to a bleak farming community and town in Nebraska. Here for thirty years she slaved so that when finally she returned to the city of her youth and attended a Wagner program by the Boston Symphony she suddenly realized poignantly how much the years of toil had been years of cultural aridity. Katherine Gaylord of "A Death in the Desert" is another arresting figure resembling the gifted artist, Harvey Merrick, of "The Sculptor's Funeral." Katherine, talented pupil and friend of a famous composer, is forced because of tuberculosis to return to the sordid surroundings of her girlhood in a monotonously drab Western town, where she dies. "The Sculptor's Funeral" is Miss Cather's bitterest indictment against the small town and its unappreciativeness of the cultural fineness which belonged to its most maligned son. Her method of delineation is unique as well as forceful. The body of the famous sculptor, Merrick, is brought back to the ugly Kansas town of the artist's repressed boyhood. The drabness of the place, the bickerings and misunderstandings of the utterly provincial citizens—dull souls who misread distinction—and the greatness of the artist himself are uncompromisingly portrayed through the eyes of one of Merrick's young students and admirers, who accompanies the body from the East, and of

of Jim Laird, Sand City's cynical lawyer and boyhood friend of
Merrick, once a promising youth who, pulled down by his village associates, had sunk into the morass of provinciality which
he thoroughly despised.   In stories such as these Miss Cather
shows the degradation of the splendid vitality of her Midwestern frontier.   Its wild freedom and beauty of sky, prairie, and
hills have been ruined, she thinks, by drab towns, characterized by a monotonous standardization, and vulgarly provincial people.[135]

Though in her novels Miss Cather frequently uses rural
settings, she also maintains her original interest in the village.
Even in *The Bohemian Girl* and *O Pioneers!*, primarily novels of
the soil, "in the distance one can hear the village chorus passing judgment on people and incidents."[136]   *The Song of the
Lark*, the story of a village-born singer, young Thea Kronborg,
is another elaborated theme of youth and the bright Medusa.
The daughter of a smugly complacent Swedish preacher and
of a prolific mother, Thea grows up a solitary, but receptive
and eager, girl in the midst of a crowded household in gossipy
Moonstone, Colorado.   She is, however, more fortunate than
most inhibited young men and women.   Under the guidance
of her German music master, the choir leader in the church
where she plays the organ on Sundays, Thea finds expression
through her music.   Finally, her aspirations for self-realiza-
tion lead her from the narrow town to Chicago and elsewhere,
where, after hard struggle, she gains high artistic success.
Her high purpose and her constantly developing character
save Thea from the blighting influences of the town.   *The
Song of the Lark* shows Miss Cather's natural interest in people
whether they be the Moonstone villagers or the operatic folk
of Thea's later days.

Like Thea, some of the other inhibited persons portrayed by
Miss Cather escape from small town bondage; others are not
so fortunate.   Best in scope of the earlier novels is *My Ántonia*,
a retrospective account of a Bohemian girl whose fine courage
causes her to overcome the handicaps of mediocre parentage
and poverty and develop into a triumphant woman.   The
story is related by James Burden, a village escapist and successful lawyer who writes reminiscently of his youthful days in

[135] Van Doren, *op. cit.*, p. 116.
[136] Blankenship, *loc. cit.*

pioneer Nebraska and dwells upon his associations with Ántonia Shimerda, Lina Lingard, and Tiny Soderball, immigrant girls who leave the farm for the exciting freedom of working as hired girls in town. In picturing the position of Ántonia and her fellow-Bohemians in the community of Black Hawk, Jim Burden remembers most of the citizens of this pioneer Nebraska town as people spiritually akin to those of Spoon River, Gopher Prairie, and Winesburg. As in other isolated towns, their gossip saves the marooned folk from utter stagnation. The frail houses of the town impressed Jim as places for the concealment of jealousy, envy, and unhappiness.

The life that went on in them seemed to have been made up of evasions and negations ; shifts to save cooking, to save washing, devices to propitiate the tongue of gossip. This guarded mode of existence was like living under a tyranny. People's speech, their voices, their very glances, became furtive and repressed. Every individual taste, every natural appetite, was bridled by caution. . . . The growing piles of ashes and cinders in the back yards were the only evidence that the wasteful, consuming process of life went on at all.[137]

At times forgetting this drabness Jim, as a high-school student, and his friend, the simple-hearted Bohemian servant girl, find beauty even in Black Hawk. The beauty of the spring, of Western sunsets, and of the snow, the same kind of beauty which so deeply stirred young Thea Kronborg, helps to relieve the monotony of their restricted existence. Finally, in becoming the wife of a good, dull man and the mother of many children Ántonia achieves her ultimate success in life as "the kind of mother to the race of whom Walt Whitman dreamed."[138] The picture of Ántonia Shimerda's contented home life, in contrast with the uglier phases of existence in Black Hawk, is Miss Cather's sympathetic interpretation of an old theme told with consummate art.

One of Ours, appearing shortly after the *Main Street* furor, is the second of the Cather novels having a male protagonist. A war story, the novel deals with a double locale—American and French—and with a Midwestern farm boy's groping for self-fulfilment. Claude Wheeler, a native of the same region

---

[137] *My Ántonia* (New York, 1918), pp. 249-250.
[138] Quoted matter from Hatcher, *op. cit.*, p. 66.

which produced Thea and Antonia, is restlessly stirred by the same yearnings of the spirit and vague dissatisfaction with the unexpected course of his life. His unrest, springing from his desire for richer, fuller experiences, marks every phase of Claude's life : his toil-marked boyhood on his father's farm, his high-school days in the near-by small town of Frankfort, his rudely interrupted college experiences, and, finally, his unfortunate marriage with a prairie Puritan absorbed in her own righteousness. All of his actions are darkened by the joylessness of his outlook. At last, realizing that he has been mismated, Claude sets out from provincial Frankfort "on the crusade to save the world for democracy." His death on a foreign battlefield is an ironic consummation to his life of unfulfilment in his native town.

While the story is, first of all, that of Claude's restlessness and his pitiful efforts to break through the inhibitions of his life, it also portrays, with Miss Cather's usual carefully restrained realism, the boy's associates. The Wheeler family (native New Englanders transformed into frugal pioneers), their Bohemian farm neighbors, and their friends and acquaintances in the near-by town are faithfully sketched. Claude's town associates, including a high-school teacher, his brother who operates a hardware store, and the family of the missionary-minded girl Claude marries, are all familiar and ordinary small town figures. Even among the minor figures Miss Cather finds repressed individuals who resort to different means of forgetting their dull environment: ". . . a lawyer without clients, who read Shakespeare and Dryden all day long in his dusty office ; . . . [and an] effeminate drug clerk, who wrote free verse and 'movie' scenarios, and tended the soda-water fountain."[139]

Conflict between character and environment is also one of the themes of *A Lost Lady* (1923), a novel of restraint portraying the tragedy of Mrs. Marian Forrester, a woman of culture and charm. Unlike the more heroic and triumphant women of the Nebraska novels, the Lost Lady, placed by unfortunate circumstances in a dull isolated Colorado town, is a weakling, a sort of tarnished creature, whose life in a gossipy community is self-defeating. Marian Forrester, unlike Thea or Ántonia, lacks the force of character to battle against adverse circum-

[139] *One of Ours* (New York, 1922), p. 155.

stances : the loss of fortune and the death of her husband.
She is unable to keep herself above the standards of the village.
Though culturally superior to the town gossips, Mrs. Forrester
eventually sinks to their level. After the death of Captain
Forrester, himself a fine figure of Western vitality and honesty,
Marion, the local "great lady," gradually loses caste even in
Sweet Water. Even young Neil Herbert, who had long wor-
shiped Mrs. Forrester as a symbol of exquisite beauty, at last
is bitterly disillusioned when he discovers her disgusting familiarity with a shyster lawyer, vulgar Ivy Peters.

In this tale of character degeneration Miss Cather produces
a restrained, but unflattering, picture of village curiosity. On
the occasion of Captain Forrester's death the housewives of
Sweet Water, really avidly curious busybodies who had never
been invited to the place, fairly swarm into the house on the
hill. Under the pretext of friendliness, they pry into all the
secrets of the house and gossip about Marian's household mis-
management and her clandestine affairs with unscrupulous
Peters. Then, there is Mrs. Beasley, the telephone operator,
characterized as representing all the small-minded, prying
people of Sweet Water. *A Lost Lady* is far more than the tragic
fall of a single weak character. It symbolizes, so Miss Cather
suggests, the tragedy of the passing of the vital older West into
the hands of a newer, a more acquisitive—and less honest—
generation.

The village code operates again in the college town of Hamilton, the stage set for *The Professor's House* (1925), another
novel expressive of frustration. Scholarly Godfrey St. Peter, interested in historical research, is surrounded, ironically enough,
not by scholars of kindred interests, but by jealous colleagues
and a misunderstanding and selfish family. Through their
mutual love for creative work St. Peter and Tom Outland,
a brilliant student, enjoy a stimulating friendship. Tom,
however, dies in France. Shortly before his death he wills to
Rosamond St. Peter, his fiancée, his perfected invention. The
wealth which subsequently comes to the St. Peters destroys
the simplicity of the old life. Deserted by his shallow wife and
their two daughters intent upon their social aspirations, the
professor retreats to his old study where he forgets the disap-
pointing present in his thoughts of Spanish adventurers and
Tom Outland. The real counterparts of Mrs. St. Peter, a

socially ambitious pseudo-intellectual, the daughters, and their commonplace husbands may be found in the average little town.   Here in a small college community is portrayed another conflict between a high-minded, honest character and his shallow associates.

In all of her delineations of the small town, beginning with the earliest stories of *The Troll Garden* and extending to those of her latest collection, *Obscure Destinies* (1932), and her last novel, *Lucy Gayheart* (1935), Miss Cather differs from her contemporary controversialists.   Well aware as she is of all the usual small town faults, she sees more in the little communities of her stories than the petty rivalries and scandals of Spoon River or Gopher Prairie.   As a recent critic points out, "she has gone beyond the village at every point, not to idealize Black Hawk and its thousand prototypes on the western prairies, but to find in the small town and its tributary farming communities experiences and traits confineless by time or locality."[140]   Adhering closely to her critical theory of the well designed novel of restraint (the novel *démeublé*), Miss Cather has selected from her rich materials of Midwestern village life only those best suited to her artistic purposes.[141]   She has, therefore, even while relentlessly exposing the dullness of the prairie town, shown clearly that noble characters, the Harvey Merricks, Ántonia Shimerdas, and Thea Kronborgs, may eventually emerge from their sordid environments to realize, at last, self-fulfilment.   The tragedy of Marian Forrester is that of those weaker souls who cannot resist their restricting environments.

The themes of insurgency popularized by the major village controversialists were developed, to a lesser degree, by other able, but often less prolific, realists of the twenties and even earlier.   Among the satiric novelists who furthered the literature of protest, Upton Sinclair (1878—) pioneered vigorously by preaching the gospel of social justice in a number of important and sensational novels.   As is well known, he early attracted attention through his savage pictures of the Chicago stockyards, of labor conditions, and of the ache of poverty set

[140] Blankenship, *op. cit.*, p. 678.
[141] Willa Cather, "The Novel Déméuble," *The New Republic*, Literary Supplement, XXX, 5-6 (April 12, 1922).   Miss Cather's other novels are not included here because they are not small town studies.

forth in his satiric novel of "Packingtown," *The Jungle* (1906). Believing that a greater degree of happiness is possible to men, Sinclair has written copiously and heatedly in protest against the injustices and malpractices marking many phases of American life. *The Metropolis* (1908), an attack upon the business practices of millionaire New York; *The Moneychangers* (1908), a tale of the panic of 1907; and *Love's Pilgrimage* (1911), based upon the author's own divorce case, are all social satires which once created sensations. In *King Coal: A Novel* (1917) he writes with power, but no artistic finish, of coal mining towns, straggling along a desolate mountain canyon in Colorado, and of the conditions of slavery existing there among the economically enslaved miners, little more than a "file of baboons coming out of a shaft in the gloaming." His powerful plea for social equality and his harsh, unrelieved pictures of the coal towns in this country of lonesome pits quite overshadow the stereotyped plot and the expository style too heavily marked by argot.

The commonplace story is used as an instrument for propaganda. A young American of the upper class, Hal Warner, moved by a great sympathy for the downtrodden and an honest desire to get a first-hand knowledge of labor conditions, takes employment in a mine under an assumed name and disguised as a laborer. Hal's humiliating job as a mule tender, his merciless thrashing in connection with a strike, and other unpleasant experiences furnish the backbone for this story of despotism and class rebellion. Pedro and all the other towns up and down the valley are but squalid places of fear for the miners and their underfed families. The constant dread of gas and explosions in the poorly constructed mines, the dust from the coal, the ill-concealed hate for company "spotters" who carry on a system of espionage to quell outward criticism or disturbance, and the fear of that heavily armed bully, the camp marshal, all make Pedro "a hell of a town." *King Coal*, says Sinclair, was written to expose social hazards in centers of squalor, like Pedro, hazards which otherwise would be screened from the public eye. Here, as in other writings, he appears as a sort of evangelist bitterly indicting the appalling conditions under which wage-earning slaves by the thousands are at the mercy of despotic capitalists. His crusading ardor,

springing from his theory that "All art is propaganda," produces the most satiric exposure of the evils of a mining town
to be found in the fiction of the small town.[142]

Further representative of the growing realism of the period
and of the general prevalence of unflattering small town pictures is *Dust* (1921) by Mr. and Mrs. Haldeman-Julius.   This
is a bitterly ironic story of an early twentieth-century Zury,
whose hard toil in a Kansas mining town and farming community brought long coveted wealth to him, but too late for
his complete enjoyment.   The blasting of Martin Wade's hopes
to perpetuate his name, with the deaths of his wife and son
and the final passing of his accumulated riches into the possession of a woman he never really loved, makes *Dust* a bitter tale.

Another grim reproduction of life in a Midland town appears in John T. Frederick's *Druida* (1923), the sympathetically
told story of a young girl's fight against the low standards of a
farming community and the two towns with which she is associated.   The illegitimate daughter of a mysterious student
posing as a farm hand and of Hilda Horsfell (a farmer's wife),
Druida is superior in mentality and outlook to her Stablesburg
associates.   The harshness of her unfortunate associations, first,
with a gossip-loving and mean-spirited farm village and, later,
with the equally narrow men and women in a near-by college
town is relieved by her happy relationships—all choice morsels
of gossip for her provincial neighbors—with a cultured older
man, a doctor, with a sensitive English professor at the Normal,
and with Bud Madsen, the young farmer she at last marries.
The sordidness of small town hotels, the bigotry and meanness
of small college faculties, the unbridled curiosity of townspeople about any among them who may be slightly different
from the common mold, the struggles of a small town doctor,
old in service but poor in his collections, small town church
services, funerals, annual fairs and races, drummers and the
lady clerks with whom they "carried on"—these are but a few
of the phases of small town life which Frederick condemns.
Like Willa Cather, Frederick also contrasts the physical and
spiritual bleakness of the town with the vastness of the prairies
and the beauty of the environing farm country at various
seasons.

To 1923 belongs Homer Croy's trenchant novel of life in the

<hr />

[142] Quotation from Sinclair, *Mammonart* (New York, 1925), p. 9.   Sinclair's
autobiography, *American Outpost* (1932) pictures him as a sincere humanitarian.

hog and corn belt of Missouri. In *West of the Water Tower*, as in Croy's next novel, *R. F. D. No. 3*, the story of human life stands stark and bare. Both novels are primarily stories of youth's persistent and ultimately unsuccessful effort to break away from a restricted life. Guy Plummer, in *West of the Water Tower*, may have had the necessary qualities for success in a larger field, but he lost his chance because he was diverted by his passion for an inferior girl. The microscopic eye and unfailing memory which brought Junction City, Missouri, to life in the earlier novel are in evidence once more in *R. F. D. No. 3* (1924), the tragedy of an ordinary farm girl, Josie Decker, whose one year at a finishing school deeply dissatisfies her with the farm her father has toiled so hard to keep mortgage-free. Tobacco-stained, dusty, prying Junction City, a commonplace agricultural town, seems a delightful place to country-bred Josie. In the town girls her own age enjoy secret clubs, bridge games, and sorority activities—all forbidden interests to the romantic farm girl. But the dreams she has of social life in Junction and of professional success in Hollywood turn to ashes. After an unfortunate affair with an adventurer, a silo salesman, Josie sees in life little except general barrenness and futility.

During 1924 to the end of the twenties—and even later—the conventions of *Main Street* were steadily applied to the literature of the town. In poetry a brief, but realistic, treatment may be found in a series of eight sonnets, "Mushroom Town," appearing in the first volume of *The American Mercury*.[143] Muna Lee (Mrs. Luis Muñoz Marín), the author, obviously used actual mushroom towns of her native Oklahoma* as models for her vivid descriptions of drugstore, carnival, and revival meeting scenes, all familiar phases of community life known to every Southwestern townsman. In the second sonnet, "Electors," the poet, with fine observational power, has actualized the self-appointed sages one sees and hears even today in the typical Southwestern small town. Note her application of a theme familiar in community fiction to an Oklahoma oil town.

> The drug-store was a club, in whose talk took part
> Tall men, slouch-hatted, neither old nor young—
> Men who had failed elsewhere, and who had wrung

[143] April, 1934, pp. 459-462.
* Mrs. Marín, born in Raymond, Mississippi, attended the University of Oklahoma.

Stakes from scant capital for another start.
Not hopeless men : here was a junction which
Ensured a Harvey Eating House ; next year
Congress would pass the Enabling Act ; right here
Would be a metropolis : they would all be rich.
The consummations meanwhile they awaited
In the drug-store, talking politics till night.
Texans, farmers, and carpet-baggers they hated ;
Feared the negro—"This state should be lily-white,"
And arguments to damn whatever scheme
Were the epithets "Utopia" and "dream."

"August" pictures the treeless streets of an Oklahoma town
baked by the intolerable sun. In "Murderers" and "Mrs.
Hastings" the author bares to the curious reader the unlovelier
side of town life. On the other hand, "Prairie Sky" shows
how the beauty of a Southwestern sunset may transform, as if
by magic, even the ugly shacks and jerry-built houses of mushroom towns. In this connection mention should be made of
the late Clyde Walton Hill's far more kindly view of the Southwestern small town as given in his widely quoted "The Little
Towns of Texas," the most familiar lines of which are :

The little towns of Texas,
    What pretty names they have ;
There's Echo, Garland, Crystal Springs,
    Arcadia, Dawn and Dare,
There's Ingleside and Prairie Home,
    And Bells and Rising Star,
God keep them childlike, restful, clean,
    Pure as the prairies are![144]

Further 1924 and later studies of American small towns con-
vince one that critically minded writers from all parts of the
country were trying "to out-Lewis Lewis." Charles Merz's
Centerville, U. S. A., stories about a variety of small town characters, owes its title to the census report that "there are more
Centervilles in the United States than towns of any other
name." Taking the much overworked "Main Street" town
as his subject, Merz develops his portraits with a ready understanding of the motives and meanings in the lives of ordinary
people. Again imitative of *Main Street* is Emanie Sachs's *Talk*,

[144] First printed in *The Buccaneer*, I, 22 (Sept., 1924) ; reprinted in *The Literary
Digest*, XXCII, 38 (Sept. 27, 1924).

a neither too clever nor scintillating, but essentially honest, novel of social pressure in a Kentucky town.   Neither Merville nor its people—except the heroine—have the vitality of Gopher Prairie and its folk ; but as a satire of social restrictions in a small American town as they combine to wrench the life of a village orphan out of its proper shape *Talk* is an acceptable novel.   Wallace Irwin's *The Golden Bed* is an admirably conceived tale of a thriving river town, presumably in the Midwest. The story opens in 1891 when American townspeople were, as the author says, "still in the feudal age, divided mostly between the Commoners, who did not keep a horse, and the Uncommoners who did."   Vivid and typically American action centers around the contrasted struggles of uneducated Ma Holtz and her two sons, who live near the car barns and the soap factory, and the town's "quality folks," who counted their ancestors "back to the beginning of time and a little beyond."

The Old Home Town (1925) by Rupert Hughes exposes the dull routine of a Mississippi River town.   The stereotyped treatment of the poor-boy-rising-to-fame theme is strengthened a little by the cutting satire directed against small town social dictators.   Bess Streeter Aldrich's popular and kindly pictures of the Midwestern small town (beginning in 1926) give additional evidence that, even during the era of strongest antagonism against the village, all writers were not belittling community virtues.[145]   Anne Parrish's *The Perennial Bachelor* (1925), a study in egotism ; Emile R. Paillou's *Home Town Sketches* (1926), delineative of Boonville, Missouri ; the late Ring (Ringgold Wilmer) Lardner's *The Love Nest and Other Stories* (1926), containing "Haircut," a prose dramatic monologue delivered by a loquacious small town barber ; Robert McAlmon's satiric *Village* (1926) ; William Metrozat John's *Seven Women* (1929), picturing the Southwestern town in a different light ; Lizette Woodworth Reese's *A Victorian Village* (1929) ; and Robert S. and Helen M. Lynd's *Middletown* (1929), a nonfictional sociological survey, are representative of both the many thematic and geographic varieties of small town studies which marked the close of what has been termed recently an "old new era." Miss Reese's autobiographical *A Victorian Village* assures one that, in spite of all the modern sneers at things Victorian, there

---

[145] See Mrs. Aldrich's "Why I Live in a Small Town," *The Ladies' Home Journal*, L, 21 ff. (June, 1933), for an explanation of her village attitude.

was a certain charming leisureliness—conspicuously lacking in
the new Spoon Rivers and Gopher Prairies—in the little village
of Waverly, now an integral part of Baltimore.   On the other
hand, in Robert McAlmon's *Village,* a collection of vivid impressions showing the tragedies of inhibited lives, are deliberately bare, frank, humorless, and objective pictures of an intellectually and socially arid Midwestern town called Wentworth.   Precocious pessimism—even the young boys are cynics
—misanthropy, boredom, and a sentiment of general futility
give the reader numerous impressions of shut-in lives and tragic
attempts at evasions and suppression.[146]   Here is a small town
order which is the very antithesis of that glorified by the school
of sweetness and light.   In Wentworth there is no sign of the
happy average of the 1900's.[147]

William M. John's *Seven Women,* written after the psychological manner of Anderson, consists of seven stories about as many
women who are afraid of telling the truth about themselves
because of the severity of the town's opinion.   Each woman,
outwardly pious but inwardly no better than the worst sinner
in town, is portrayed by a method comparable to the asides
used in the presentation of dual personalities in Eugene
O'Neill's *A Strange Interlude* and Alice Gerstenberg's *Overtones.*
Seven sanctimonious, small-visioned leaders of the Baptist Aid
Society meet at the home of Mrs. Gibbs only to discover that
her maid is having a baby in the woodshed.   These gossips,
all outward models of propriety, unwittingly condemn themselves as they converse in shocked manner about the unfortunate and dying girl.   "This was excitement!   A baby being
born and the mother dying, all during, and right in the house
with, an aid meeting. ... .   Never before was there such a
meeting."[148]   *Seven Women* is truly a departure from the once
popularly fictionalized Southwestern cow town.   The Hope-
ville of the novel is a Colorado Winesburg.

During the twenties and even today the Iowa small town
has been variously identified in fiction.   Much of this treatment has resulted from the literary activities of Iowa's "younger
school," a group stimulated by Professor John T. Frederick,

---

[146] For detailed analysis see Michaud, *op. cit.,* pp. 262-269.
[147] Cf. Brand Whitlock's *The Happy Average* (Indianapolis, 1904), a village tale
described by a contemporary critic as "a most delightful romance . . . as fresh
as the flowers in May."
[148] *Seven Women* (New York, 1929), p. 297.

critic and author of *Druida* previously mentioned, and other instructors at the state university interested in creative writing.[149] Many of these newcomers had their first magazine contributions accepted by *The Midland*, a literary monthly published at Iowa City, or, through the influence of H. L. Mencken, by *The Smart Set* and *The American Mercury*. These younger writers, says Professor Frederick, have tried to represent in literature "all that is racy and authentic in Iowa life." Consequently, there has emerged from Iowa new works of fiction conveying a strong sense, on the part of younger interpreters, of the movement of agricultural and small town life in the state during the last three generations. The new school early found advertisement through John Frederick's excellently developed *Druida* and the sharply attacked first novel of Roger L. Sergel, *Arlie Gelston* (1923), a work in no sense narrowly regional. With primary emphasis on psychological realism, Sergel, an imitator of Dreiser, gives also an accurate presentation of the Iowa landscape and the town of Coon Falls. Carl Van Vechten, born in Cedar Rapids in 1880, did not turn to the writing of fiction until 1922, after he was a recognized music critic. His novel, *The Tattooed Countess* (1924), portrays Maple Valley, Iowa—said to be reminiscent of his native town at the turn of the century—as "a God-forsaken hole full of stupid fools." Neither Sergel's nor Van Vechten's studies of the Iowa town have in any measure the significance in the literature of the American town of those done by two more widely known delineators of Iowa "folks." Let us note the first of these.

So early as 1921 a young Iowan, a minister's daughter who had spent her girlhood in small farming communities in her native state, began contributing to *The Midland* and *The Smart Set* (edited by H. L. Mencken and George Jean Nathan) carefully studied stories showing even then her intimate knowledge of rural and small town Iowans of both German and English stock. It was about this newcomer among Midwestern realists that Mencken encouragingly declared at this time : "I regard Ruth Suckow as the most promising young writer of fiction now visibly at work in America." Miss Suckow early began writing with the authority of a careful observer of the dull, gray monotone which was the life of many of the plain German-

---

[149] Frederick, "The Younger School," *The Palimpsest*, XI, 78-86 (Feb., 1930). Cf. Frank L. Mott, "Iowa Looks at Ruth Suckow," *Wings*, X, 25 (Oct., 1934).

Americans she portrays remarkably well in her first novel, *Country People* (1924) and her collected stories, *Iowa Interiors* (1926).[150] In these, as also in *The Odyssey of a Nice Girl* (1925), *The Bonney Family* (1928), *Cora* (1929), and *The Kramer Girls* (1930), Miss Suckow has succeeded, where many modern realists have failed, in achieving a universal significance in her handling of highly local material.

Ruth Suckow is one with the land and the people about whom she writes. Born (1892) in Hawarden, a typical American small town on the western borders of Iowa, Miss Suckow as the daughter of a Congregational minister had the best possible opportunity of observing small town life. Having lived in ten different Iowa towns and larger places and having traveled widely elsewhere throughout America, she has been advantageously situated to study whatever change of scene there might be in both Iowa community life and small towns in many sections. This association with various localities may account for her objective realism, a quality often varied, however, by her show of intense poetic feeling for the Iowa landscape. While Iowans have objected to the drabness of many of her stories, "the fact is that Miss Suckow is loyal to Iowa. Hers is . . . the accustomed affection which, while it sees faults all too plainly, appreciates too the underlying soundness of the state's character."[151] To be sure, her earlier work did seem to belong to the revolt against the village movement, but it never had the note of intolerance characterizing *Main Street*. In many of her stories she is fair in her judgments of the small town; and in *Cora*, especially, as Frank L. Mott points out, she exhibits "something of that nostalgia for the village which sometimes causes those who have left it behind to idealize it in 'fond recollection.' "

Country People, like Phil Stong's more recent Iowa novel, *State Fair*, exhibits in stark selectivity the interests and life-cycle of simple farming folk, the Kaetterhenrys, whose frugality and hard work enable them to buy land and "get ahead." After years of farm labor August, the head of the family, decides to retire and move to town. It was part of doing well, of succeeding, he thought, but the change really killed him. He became

---

[150] "Uprooted," her first published story appeared in *The Midland* in Feb., 1921.
[151] Mott, *loc. cit.* Cf. Miss Suckow's article on Iowa in *The American Mercury*, IX, 39-45 (Sept., 1926).

helpless and miserable away from the farm. People began to say : "Have you noticed how old Mr. Kaetterhenry's getting to look? He don't seem like the same man he did when they first moved to town." When he died suddenly, after a "stroke," the local paper carried a long, eulogistic obituary and Emma, his wife, had a card of thanks inserted.

In 1925 with *The Odyssey of a Nice Girl* Miss Suckow continued her penetrating and individual analysis of Iowa people. The nice girl, like Miss Cather's unhappy Claude Wheeler in *One of Ours*, is hedged in by forces beyond her control. She has no resistance strong enough to destroy the protecting wall erected by her well-meaning family. The restricted life of farm and village enslave her, in spite of her brief escape to a Boston elocution school. *The Odyssey*, a moving, human story, marks Ruth Suckow as a regionalist who goes beyond the limitations of locale to create a significant study of village-bound youth.

Iowa Interiors bears resemblance to the short stories of Hamlin Garland in their portrayal of the often half-tragic and frustrated lives of commonplace rural folk and small townspeople. In this collection, as in the New England tales of Mrs. Freeman, frequent delineation of older people is noticeable. A long-absent old maid, with purposeless life, who returns to the deserted family home in Spring Valley ; a retired farmer, who, like August Kaetterhenry, moves to town only to find life there unbearable ; a sophisticated and successful writer who comes back to scoff at the shabby town of his youth ; and a village-born millionaire, who has gained eminence, but no happiness, in the world outside—these are representative of the semi-tragic lives presented in *Iowa Interiors*.[152] With photographic art, the result of careful observation, Miss Suckow reproduces in these stories the little towns she has known in central Iowa, places largely settled by retired farmers and resembling each other in general appearance. Spring Valley is such a town, one of "those slow, pretty, leafy towns beside a quiet river, that seemed never to move at all." But, as old settlers sadly noted, it was moving. "In the last ten years it had been growing from a country town to a very small city. People had bridge parties instead of great parties at the Grange." Often

[152] *Iowa Interiors* (New York, 1926), "A Home-Coming," "Retired," and "A Rural Community."

Miss Suckow treats with new art certain themes familiar to readers of the literature of the town. Particularly noticeable is her predilection for themes of failures : of elderly couples either resentful of being pushed aside by youth or ignorantly investing their savings in wild money-making schemes and of people broken in health.[153] In "Home-Coming," "Mame," "Uprooted," "A Rural Community," "Golden Wedding," and "Four Generations" the old homestead theme is presented through various mediums : picnics, golden weddings, and family conclaves. "Mama," "A Rural Community," and "The Top of the Ladder" are other treatments of the now conventional escape of youth from the small town to the larger opportunities of the city. Always, however, Miss Suckow's art moves beyond superficial realism to picture the real middle-class men and women she has met on Iowa's farms and in her villages.

The Bonney Family and *The Kramer Girls*, as well as Miss Suckow's most recent novel, *The Folks* (1934), show in mature interpretation the themes of family life but suggested in some of the short stories. *The Bonney Family* tells, in convincing and homely scenes, of the changes which took place within an undistinguished minister's family after they left the Midwestern town where Brother Bonney had preached for fifteen years to take up residence in the college town of Frampton. The kindly minister working on his sermons ; his wife tired from bending too long over the family darning ; overgrown Warren, always ready for argument ; and Sarah busy at managing the house, all known to the people at Morning Sun, are honestly portrayed. Frampton, a larger community with more intellectual citizens, presents the familiar picture of a prejudiced college community where social cliques and class distinctions, petty in themselves, determine the happiness or unhappiness of newcomers to the town. In describing the adjustments made by the Bonneys Miss Suckow shows a keen understanding and sympathy with the mannish and plain, but intellectual, Sarah and with her awkward, sensitive brother. This is the story of a plain family told with Miss Suckow's unusual ability at presenting ordinary people in the midst of their daily routine.

If in her concern with the drabness of rural scenes and the dull and often unhappy lives of her small town folk Miss Suc-

---

[153] *Ibid.*, "Uprooted" and "An Investment for the Future."

kow may have failed, as one critic thinks, to realize all the rich possibilities of her materials, in her latest novel, *The Folks*, she has artistically woven into the patterns of her earlier work not only the contrasts, colors, and intensities of Iowa life, but many carefully studied realities of the whole country as well.   Here Miss Suckow has bridged the gap in the history of the American small town between the 1920-1930 era, a decade which began in pretense and ended in bewilderment, and the years of the New Deal.   Among the many community novels of today Ruth Suckow's mature story of the Fergusons stands forth because of its full and truthful chronicling of the tragedies and comedies that make up the lives of many Midwestern Americans.   Here she is no mere photographer, but an artist.   No doubt, many readers of this novel have felt all sorts of memories, literary and personal, crowd in : vivid remembrances of other stories of middle-class families and reminiscences of events and people which have actually touched their own lives in small communities.   One feels, somehow, that the citizens of Miss Suckow's little Midwestern town (ironically called Belmond) are the fictional counterparts of his own small town acquaintances.   But *The Folks* is far more than a sharply localized narrative of provincial individuals.   In brief, it is a realistically documental tale of human happiness, petty family difficulties, and deeper suffering so subtly blended as to offer a vital and full fictional record of that changing period in our national history which reaches from the turn of the century through today.

Impressively real, *The Folks* traces in minute detail, at times too digressive, the life-histories of the diverse members of a German-Irish-American family, the Fergusons, who though different in temperament are even in the years of maturity and separation bound together by the early influence of their childhood home in Midwestern Belmond.   Chronicled in six divisions, this family drama treats first of the "old folks," the farmbound parents of Fred and Annie Ferguson, a youngish small town banker and his ambitious, yet conscientious, wife.   Fred and Annie, representatives of a second generation which struggled to keep pace with progress, leave the farm for Belmond, where they, in turn, become the "old folks" as their four children grow to maturity.   Carl, the oldest and a youth of promise, is robbed of inner peace and material success by marriage with a colorless home town girl. Dorothy, the popular younger daughter, whose early marriage to a wealthy suitor awes both family and neighbors, at last has to face the depression in California. Margaret, the introspective and iconoclastic older daughter, is an idealist whose dreams are ever shattered by her contacts with a misunderstanding family and inquisitive neighbors. After deep mental suffering Margaret leaves the despised town for a life of promise in New York. There, rechristened Margot by her Greenwich Village friends, she enjoys a freedom entirely at variance with the limitations imposed upon her by the small town code she so heartily scorned. The story of her reckless transformation into a woman of fascination and complete sophistication is not only a brilliant piece of writing, but something entirely at variance with anything which Miss Suckow has done before. "The Youngest," the record of Bunny, who shocks his parents by his hasty marriage to a strange, elemental Russian, tells also of one who made a break for freedom from the village.

Enhancing her plot interest are Miss Suckow's unsentimental accounts of family and local gatherings and her humanly interesting characters, even to minor figures. Though fully aware of all that is "local and small and actual," Miss Suckow here, as always, is above the long-waged controversy of the small town. Instead, with a strict regard for the truth, she delineates plain rural and small town folk of the Midwest, old men and women who have won their hard fight with the soil, only to be puzzled by the changing times, and their sons and daughters who more readily adapt themselves to the new ways. The final note is expressed by Fred, who in old age suddenly realizes that "the old optimism and trust had come to the edge of an abyss." What lay beyond the awful mists he did not know. Foreshadowing thus the confusion of the depression years, Ruth Suckow brings to a close a penetrating study of middle class life in America.

Iowa small town life is further recorded in the novels of Phil Stong, whose popularly recognized work belongs to the era of the depression and the New Deal, or that of the American "jitters," as one critic has described the confusion of the thirties. In his *State Fair* (1932), *Stranger's Return* (1933), and *Village Tale* (1934) one finds, with a pleasant sense of familiarity, the farm and small town background of Iowa, the same milieu authentically created by Miss Suckow. Full-bodied humor, irrepressible and pervasive, a part of his people's enjoyment of life; a fine pride in the land; an appreciation of material considerations; and amazingly real personalities, who break the farm routine for a glorious week as the state fair, indicate that Phil Stong creates a type of farm life not often found in the so-called sagas of the soil. There is little of grimness, but no lack of convincing delineation and genuinely lusty humor, in *Stranger's Return* and *State Fair*, both primarily farm novels. small agricultural towns are realistically introduced, but merely as picture show and shopping centers for well-to-do farmers and their families in the community.

In *Village Tale* Stong uses for an entirely different sort of novel the idiom he has mastered in *Stranger's Return*, *State Fair*, and some earlier apprenticeship novels. Still the humorist of *State Fair*, Stong in this novel sets forth a deeper view of American life. The cruelties that smolder and flame in the provincial society of Brunswick, Iowa; a man's battle with his neighbors; necessities, pastimes, and rewards as they are distributed in the closely interrelated life of a country town—all these offer evident proof that Phil Stong has felt the influence of the revolt from the village movement. (This may be further noted in *The Rebellion of Lennie Barlow*, his latest novel and another study of the Iowa town.) A village tale motivated by human passions (illicit love, deep-seated hatred, and honest affection), this story involves one by one various people in Brunswick: college-bred Somerville, more prosperous than his fellows and secretly covetous of a neighbor's wife; a young depot agent and village peacemaker; a headstrong girl whose love Somerville does not return; her unscrupulous and cowardly father; ancient Tessie Oosthoek, a happy old sinner; her crony, still more ancient and wise, old Ike Crane; Bolly, a farmer who is killed; and the minor folk of the town. As yet lacking the fine maturity of interpretation possessed by Miss Suckow, Phil Stong, nevertheless, has a talent of a high order for picturing the life of prosperous Iowa farmers and their village neighbors.

More than ten years ago Herschel Brickell was moved to declare that the South—Mencken's "Sahara of the Bozart"— had suddenly burst into flower.[154] This modern literary awak-

---

[154] "The Literary Awakening in the South," *The Bookman*, LXVI, 138-143 (Oct., 1927). Cf. Jay B. Hubbell, "The Decay of the Provinces," *The Sewanee Review*, XXXV, 473-487 (Oct., 1927).

ening, which gained force during the late twenties and early thirties, Mr. Brickell attributed to the new patterns of life wrought by industrial changes ; the leavening process affecting society because of new blood in Southern cities ; the wandering of Southerners of the oldest stock ; and the change in general attitude toward the Negro because of his exodus to Northern industrial centers. At any rate, the South, long comparatively inactive in literature, became vocal. New authors (Stribling, Faulkner, Wolfe, Peterkin, Green, Caldwell, Heyward, young Stuart, and others) began to attract attention by their novels, drama, and poetry. Challenging discussions by eminent scholars and critics (Allen Tate's *Reactionary Essays* and John Crowe Ransom's *The World's Body*, for example) have opened new vistas and offered new viewpoints to those interested in the active movement of Southern thought. Symposiums as provocative as *I'll Take My Stand* (1930) and *Culture in the South* (1934), as well as anthologies like Stark Young's *Southern Treasury*, have turned critical eyes toward many significant phases of Southern culture and industry. Cogent expressions of native opinions in Southern magazines (*The Sewanee Review*, *The Southwest Review*, and others) have reinterpreted debatable questions related to Southern and Southwestern culture, agrarianism, industry, and kindred problems. Such a renaissance, currently notes Professor Donald Davidson, has been given a firmer basis of independence and solidity by the critical acumen of Mr. Ransom, Mr. Tate, and other Southern critics. "They have shown the way to be independent without being 'provincial,' and, if you please, to be 'cosmopolitan' without servile imitation."[155]   In short, Professor Davidson feels that there are in the South today sufficient leadership in critical thought, a sufficiency of artists familiar with the land and the people, and, as noted in the spontaneous work of Jesse Stuart, a source of native exuberance to furnish "the rough equivalent of a national literature." Through the last decade such literary activity has not failed to leave its marks of vitality and independence on the fiction of the Southern town. Consequently, in spite of the number of writers who still find inspiration in community life beyond the Mississippi, during more recent

[155] Donald Davidson, "The South Today : Report on Southern Literature," *The Daily Times Herald* (Dallas, Texas), July 17, 1938, first section, p. 6.

years literary interest in the Midwestern town, long the center of contention, has been deflected by the emergence in fiction of the Southern town. Today Midwestern insurgents may find able cohorts, new battlefields, and different modes of attack in the changing, maturing South.

During the last decade few actively working novelists of the small town, except perhaps Lewis and Miss Suckow, have made such a conspicuous contribution to community literature as T. S. Stribling (1881—). Like many of his predecessors, Stribling is thoroughly familiar with the past and contemporary backgrounds of the communities about which he has written penetrating studies. Born in southern Tennessee, he has spent much time in the Alabama region near Muscle Shoals—Florence, Sheffield, and Tuscumbia—the scene of some of his lucid, provocative pictures of Southern life. With his early novel, *Birthright* (1922), the challenging story of a Harvard-educated mulatto's attempts to improve his people ; *Teeftallow* (1926) and *Bright Metal* (1928), two social satires of shiftless poor whites in Tennessee hill-towns ; his Arkansas small town novel, *Backwater* (1930) ; and his widely acclaimed and attacked trilogy of plantation and town life, *The Forge* (1931), *The Store* (Pulitzer Prize, 1932), and *Unfinished Cathedral* (1934), Stribling has produced, says one critic, "one of the sanest pictures of the South to be presented by a Southern novelist."[156] *Bright Metal* deals with a theme peculiarly fitted to the ironic humor and social comedy which distinguishes not only this but the author's other community studies. The story is told from the point of view of an Eastern girl who has married a Tennessee hillman while he is in the East. Agatha's romantic views of a colorful country marked by ante-bellum glory are quickly dispelled when she sees the hill country as it really is with all the drabness and bigotry which Carol found in Gopher Prairie. With further use of irony Stribling portrays the narrow life of a native hillman in *Teeftallow*. Byron Dickens notes : "Its cruel gossip, its ostracization of the unfortunate, and the hypocrisy and sadistic inhumanity of its mobs he depicts excellently. Yet he offers no remedy, presents no solution for the evils portrayed.

---

[156] Byrom Dickens, "T. S. Stribling and the South," *The Sewanee Review*, XLII, 345 (July-Sept., 1934). Contrast with Robert Penn Warren's hostile criticism of Stribling's liberalism in *The American Review*, Feb., 1934. Cf. Hatcher, *op. cit.*, "Exploiting the Negro," pp. 140-151.

He merely presents characters and conditions as he sees them, glozing over nothing."[157]

The first two novels of the trilogy, the whole being a social history of a Southern white family, the Vaidens, are definitely of the plantation regime.   *The Forge* is devoted to the Civil War and the Reconstruction periods.   The leisurely ante-bellum lives of the Vaidens and their neighbors ; then, during the War, the gallant action of their heroes ; and, finally, the spoilation of their properties are dramatically portrayed.   In *The Store* the scene shifts to the town—Florence—where Miltiades Vaiden, ex-soldier and son of lusty Old Pap Vaiden, recognizing the social revolution effected by the War, opens a store. The former landed aristocrat becomes the tradesman, the shopkeeper who barters with Negroes and works them according to the post-war "sharecrop" system instead of under the older chattel slavery.   The scene of *Unfinished Cathedral* is still Florence, but a larger and more modernized place than the little town of *The Store* and the time is largely of the present.   Always, throughout the trilogy, while Stribling dramatically portrays the Vaidens, "the presence of the Negroes is felt in the house, the yard, the town, all over the South, inextricably woven into the tapestry of wider life of which they are a suppressed part."[158]   As a forthright portrayer of the changing South, especially in its relation to the racial and agrarian problem, T. S. Stribling has produced not only one of the most discussed pictures of the little town in the South, but has made serious criticisms against the old tradition of Southern culture in his chronicling of the degeneration of an established family, the Vaidens, from their earlier affluence to the uncertain present.

Very recently Anthony Buttitta in "William Faulkner : That Writin' Man of Oxford" has given an intimate picture of a naturalistic contemporary of Stribling who has put an ineffaceable mark on the fiction of the Southern small town.

If you ever go to Oxford, Mississippi, and William Faulkner feels like showing you the sights, you won't understand his language unless you've read most of his books, for Oxford is the Jefferson of his many tales and he has attributed to some of its places and landmarks various characters and events of his own invention.   Were

---

[157] Dickens, *loc. cit.*
[158] Hatcher, *op. cit.*, p. 143.

you to start off with Faulkner in the old, quiet court square, with its relics of long porches and balconies of the old South, this is about what he'd say:

"The same courthouse where Temple Drake testified. Christ-mas did his killing in that old house. Lena Grove's baby was born there, too. There's Bayard Sartoris's bank which Byron Snopes robbed. Benbow's place. The house where old Bayard died. Christmas was killed up there. John Satoris's statue and effigy so he could watch his railroad. That's the railroad Colonel Sartoris built. Across the road is Reverend Hightower's place. Up that road near the river Wash Jones killed Sutphen. . . ."[159]

Faulkner, says Mr. Buttitta, has a proprietary interest in Jeff-erson, for the town is his world and he knows every foot of it. It is the Winesburg of the thirties.

By inheritance and experience Faulkner is a part of a small town environment. A member of the old Mississippi family of Falkners, said to be one with the Sartoris family of his novels, William Faulkner was born in New Albany, Mississippi, Sep-tember 25, 1897.[160] His childhood was spent in near-by Ox-ford where he attended high school and later was a special student at the University of Mississippi of which his father, Murry Falkner, was business manager. His great-grandfather, Colonel William C. Falkner, a veteran of the Mexican War and the Civil War, was once popularly known as the author of the sentimental *The White Rose of Memphis*. Joining the Canadian Flying Corps during the War, William Faulkner was transferred to Oxford, England, where he read much in Eliza-bethan literature in the University library; was sent later to France as a lieutenant in the British Royal Air Force; and, like his aviator hero in *Soldiers' Pay*, was injured in a plane crash. Again in America after the Armistice he experienced a period of disquiet, which led to a New Orleans anchorage with Sherwood Anderson, whose influence is marked in his novels. Today, living in a remodeled old plantation house, he mildly interests the people of the community as "that writin' man of Oxford."[161]

Faulkner's pictures of the Mississippi small town, all done in

[159] "William Faulkner: That Writin' Man of Oxford," *The Saturday Review of Literature*, XVIII, 7 (May 21, 1938).
[160] Buttitta says that according to a conflicting report he was born in Riplay, about twenty-five miles away, in October.
[161] See Buttitta, *ibid.*, for full details.

the manner of the new naturalism springing from earlier critical realists (Dreiser, Lewis, and others) and more recently associated with Ernest Hemingway and Robinson Jeffers, the California poet, are developed by themes of suffering and violence. Betrayal, madness, decay, suicide, murder, idiocy, prostitution, and violent mob scenes so overshadow the ordinary life of Jefferson that it has been said his men and women, representatives of an amazingly large pathological range, "are, with few exceptions, twisted shapes in the chaotic wreckage of a mad world."[162]   Throughout his fiction his pictures of contemporary Southern life bear the marks of his morbid naturalism.   A great many of the people of Jefferson, Charleston, and Mottstown are not representative citizens, "the happy average," but eccentric, abnormal, distorted Andersonian individuals, often compared with the characters of Poe and Ambrose Bierce. Crime, insanity, and immorality find a more important place in his practice of "the cult of cruelty" than do the affairs of ordinary citizens.

Faulkner's earliest treatment of the small town, an outgrowth of his war experiences, appears in *Soldiers's Pay* (1926), a first novel recounting the fate of Donald Mahon, a tragically disfigured aviator.   Even while his father, a kindly clergyman, and his shallow sweetheart are adjusting themselves to the news of his death, Donald himself, almost blind and with memory gone, returns to his native Charleston (Georgia). The reaction in the town toward Donald's unexpected and inglorious return makes a startling picture of a war-torn, morally loose, and confused world. After *Mosquitoes*, a sophisticated tale of a yacht party, Faulkner again employed the discharged soldier theme in *Sartoris* (1929). Bayard Sartoris, who also appears in some of Faulkner's short stories, returns to Jefferson with mind unbalanced. His death by an airplane crash but adds a final tragedy to a tale of family degeneration. Here again Faulkner's view of life "is consonant with that of many other moderns and represents broadly speaking a pessimistic scepticism to which morals and aspirations are merely customs and dreams, and the world is an inhuman mechanism."[163]

In the next and matured period of his writing Faulkner repeatedly struck at the fundamental morality of our literature,

[162] Hicks, *op. cit.*, p. 265.
[163] Alan R. Thompson, *op. cit.*, p. 481.

once so highly praised by Bliss Perry.[164] *The Sound and the Fury*
(1929), *As I Lay Dying* (1930), *Sanctuary* (1931), and *Light in
August* (1932), together with certain shorter stories, established
Faulkner as a sort of high priest in the "school of cruelty," as
an experimenter who had a keen eye for the ignoble in human
nature.   Imbeciles, shiftless poor whites and half-breeds,
brawling moonshiners, prostitutes, perverts like the sadistic
Popeye of *Sanctuary*, and others present an ugly view of life, an
uncertain existence dominated by economic unrest and mental
confusion.   Of these *Light in August*, a vigorous book which
Henry S. Canby compares with the post-Hardy books of a
roughly equivalent English life, presents a startlingly vivid
picture of Jefferson, near-by Mottstown, and a decadent
South.   Some may regard the hero, a mulatto foundling named
Joe Christmas, as a shocking figure ; others may see him as an
utterly tragic victim of circumstances.   Joe's early years in an
orphanage, his adoption by a half-crazed fundamentalist and
his hunched, cowed wife, and his long period of vagabondage
"along a thousand savage and lonely streets" form but a frag-
ment of the intricate pattern of a tragic life at last bound to
the town of Jefferson.   His bootlegging and ill-fated association with middle-aged Joanna Burden—the last local descendant of a once vigorous white family—whom he brutally murders, are climaxed in the dramatic burning of the old Burden
house and a wild pursuit by a hate-filled mob which brings
death to Joe.   Uniquely phrased and often highly poetic descriptions merging at times with a stream-of-consciousness style ;
dramatic pictures of crowds of ordinary people along the streets,
at the jail and courthouse, and at the burning of the Burden
mansion ; a skilful use of subplots ; and an amazing ability to
dip far into the past of his characters to reveal painful suffer-
ings of soul and body enable Faulkner to make *Light in August*
a powerful, intense, but at times a repellent, story of the decadent South.

For those desiring but a brief introduction to the Faulknerian methods there are the short story collections, *These
Thirteen* (1931) and *Dr. Martino* (1934).   Here in a few stories
devoted to Mississippi exists in segments the unpleasant small
town world of the novels.   Again Jefferson, always connected
in some manner with the environing farm country, is vividly

[164] *Ibid.*, p. 478.

seen as the home of decaying plantation families like the Sar-
torises, aging judges, politicians, lawyers, college students, the
usual tradesmen and clerks, squabbling farmers, mill hands,
ill-treated Negroes, and countless others who figure again in
the novels.   Probing with power Faulkner, like Anderson and
other Freudians, exposes the moral degeneration and hypocrisy
deforming the lives of the Jeffersonians.   Four stories in *These
Thirteen* ("A Rose for Emily," "Hair," "That Evening Sun,"
and "Dry September") and "Smoke" from *Dr. Martino* picture
the class consciousness, the gossip, and the under-surface hatreds
existing in Jefferson.   "A Rose for Emily" may be taken as
representative of Faulkner's shorter town sketches.   An unpleasant tale, this develops the favorite Faulknerian theme of
the decay of a once aristocratic Jefferson family, whose last
member residing in the old mansion is eccentric, unsocial Emily
Grierson.   Year by year as the neighbors watch the aging of
Miss Emily they gossip about her unusual, secretive manner,
but no one fathoms the truth.   Not until her death, when a
long-closed door to an upper chamber in her house is opened,
do the citizens discover the truth about the mysterious disappearance, years ago, of the one lover they had thought Miss
Emily might have married.   Here in this newly opened and
dust-covered room they see, to their horror, what is left of the
man who had been Emily's suitor forty years ago.

Pylon (1935), a satiric novel about a New Orleans airport
crowd, and *The Unvanquished* (1938), a closely knit story group
again revealing chapters in the history of previously introduced
Jefferson families, complete the list of books upon which Faulkner's reputation rests.*   Even today his work causes debate.
Some think of him as "the *reductio ad absurdum* of American
naturalism" and "the highly conscious architect of plot and
style, working like Poe to freeze the reader's blood."   Others,
like Donald Davidson, regard him as an original free lancer
whose "powerful imagination and close observant eye never
debate a question, but go unhesitatingly to the subject and deal
with it."[165]   Certainly, so far as his Jefferson pictures are concerned, Faulkner, however morbid in his outlook, is, as Davidson maintains, one "whose sensibility is alive to all the dimensions and possibilities of his subject."

---

* Faulkner's *The Wild Palms* has just been published by Random House.
[165] Hartwick, *op. cit.*, pp. 160 and 163 ; Davidson, *op. cit.*, p. 6.

From Asheville, North Carolina, came Thomas Wolfe (1900-1938), one of the most promising and vigorous younger novelists which the South produced during the last decade. In 1920 he graduated from the University of North Carolina, where he was interested in college publications and was one of the original members of Professor Koch's Carolina Playmakers. After receiving the degree of Master of Arts from Harvard in 1923, he began teaching in New York. Climaxing a crowded period of teaching and creative writing (in New York and London), the award in 1930 of a Guggenheim Fellowship gave Wolfe opportunity for travel and writing abroad. Beginning in the mid-twenties he wrote, with an amazing display of energy, the first four of a planned series of six novels, the finished whole to have been entitled *Of Time and the River*.[166] Of this proposed saga of middle-class American life but two novels, *Look Homeward, Angel* (1929) and *Of Time and the River* (1935) have been published. In 1935 also appeared a volume of short stories, *From Death to Morning*.[167] Such cold facts present but the outward picture of the career of a gifted novelist, who died September 15, 1938. Wolfe's own vital account of his artistic struggles is related in his *The Story of a Novel* (originally published in *The Saturday Review of Literature*, December 14 to December 28, 1935). Furthermore, since Wolfe admitted that, like James Joyce, he "wrote about things that I had known, the immediate life and experience that had been familiar to me since childhood," parallels between the author's own background and that of his restless hero, Eugene Gant, offer significant revelations.

In *The Story of a Novel*, frankly confessing that he was neither a professional nor a skilled writer, but one who was on his way "to discovering the line, the structure, and the articulation," Thomas Wolfe described his writing labors as the story "of sweat and pain and despair and partial achievement." Nevertheless, from a strong impelling force within him "that had to write and that finally burst forth and found a channel" came a powerful, richly varied story of a vigorous family, the Gants of Altamont in Catawba (Asheville, North Carolina), and of the unquenchable thirst of the youngest, Eugene, for an

[166] See *Of Time and the River* (New York, 1935), prefatory note and title listing of Wolfe's proposed saga.
[167] See H. M. Jones, "Thomas Wolfe's Short Stories," *The Saturday Review of Literature*, XIII, 13 (Nov. 30, 1935).

all encompassing knowledge. *Look Homeward, Angel,* therefore, presents a sort of cyclorama upon whose gigantic canvas is painted the teeming life of a growing North Carolina resort town during "the great processional of the years" from 1884 to 1920. The rich beauty of the environing hills, the town itself expanding rapidly with economic change, the queerly individualized Pendlands and Gants, and their countless relationships with all classes within the town come to full life in passages ranging from Whitmanesque cataloguing and sentimental introspection to vigorous, colorful prose and poetic chants.

This first novel is devoted largely to the sharp conflicts of temperament within the Gant family. Oliver Gant, a moody stonecutter, given to periodic tirades and drinking bouts ; Eliza Pentland Gant, his acquisitive wife who nagged her boys about learning "the value of a dollar or you'll never have a roof to call your own" ; and their curiosly contrasted children, the most sensitive of whom was Eugene (a butt for constant teasing), are real people in a Southern town. The yearnings and secret desires of all this strange family make the strong undercurrents of the whole novel. Oliver, at times coarsely Rabelaisian, yearns for "the lost and stricken thing in him which he could never find." Eliza thinks, "with a strange meditative hunger," about acquiring property. Ben, "looking, looking from door to door," seeks an elusive peace. Strongest of all is Eugene's unescapable hungering for some obscure cosmos alien to his own uncongenial environment. This Faustian yearning he carries always within him, even beyond Altamont to his university life and the bewildering world outside.

In March, 1935, a part of a huge pile of manuscript—the result of five years of incessant writing and cutting—appeared as *Of Time and the River: A Legend of Man's Hunger in His Youth.* Eugene Gant, here the central figure throughout, still is a bewildered youth beset by strange doubts which distort his view of life. He is a provincial Dr. Faustus hungering to devour the entire body of human experience. Restlessness and blind gropings cloud his life through Harvard, in New York, and abroad. In England, far from his native Altamont, Eugene finds a sort of peace—a temporary release from his furious wanderings—in his mental explorations back to his childhood. In his writing the youth tries to purge himself of the awful feeling of "naked homelessness, rootlessness, and loneliness" which had made his exile miserable.

In his *Story of a Novel* Thomas Wolfe spoke with unusual frankness concerning his limitations. With the critics he, too, criticized his own vast canvas, too frequently overpainted with extraneous scenes. He, too, was aware that much material in his novels of "the river of youth" and of time immutable might be considered "great chants on death and sleep," Whitmanesque voicings of countless sense impressions drawn, as he said, "not only from the concrete, material record of man's ordered memory, but [from] all the things he scarcely dares to think he has remembered." While this passionate desire fully to explore his materials led Wolfe into errors of design, his pictures of a young man's confused life in a Southern town and the larger world of his wanderings take high rank among the memorable creations in recent fiction.

Set in full motion by Lewis and other insurgents of the twenties, the vogue for cataloguing endlessly the follies, inadequacies, and fallacies of contemporary society has not yet lost its force in the literature of the town. O. W. Firkins's lament about an undepicted America seems hardly applicable to the richly varied literary history of the American town.[168] Today, after many generations of community writers have either glorified, ridiculed, or honestly depicted the town, older writers and newcomers continue interpreting it anew in accordance with earlier principles or the demands of a modern and confused era. Fiction, rather than poetry, has been the popular form for most recent town literature and, generally speaking, the realistic approach has prevailed. Adhering more or less to previous patterns, minor novelists have recently produced other interpretations of the Southern town. Hazel Scott Nugent's *The Stumbling Stone* (1934) is a tradition-bound story of old Carterville and its historic Carter mansion. Bruce Manning employs familiar "small town stuff" in *Party Wire* (1934): the tale of a small Southern town whose people find release from boredom by listening eagerly over a party line to their neighbors' conversation. Unique in its presentation from a child's viewpoint, Julia T. Yenni's *Never Say Goodbye* (1937) tells of a large family in a little Southern town. Josephine Johnson, author of *Now in November* (Pulitzer Prize novel for 1935), has

[168] "Undepicted America," *Yale Review*, XX, 140-150 (Sept., 1930).

written in *Jordanstown* (1937), a deeply moving story of the social injustice prevailing in Jordanstown, "a town poised on the borderland between North and South." Willie Snow Ethridge has attracted critical attention with two novels, *As I Live and Breathe* (1937), which gives new life to commonplace community activities, and *Mingled Yarn* (1938), the complicated story of labor conflicts in a Georgia cotton mill town.

Writers like E. A. Heath, author of *The Affairs at Tideways* (1932), a tale of murder in a village; James G. Cozzens in *The Last Adam* (1933), a crowded story of a Connecticut town; Eugene O'Neill in *Ah, Wilderness!* (1933), a sentimental comedy of adolescent youth in another Connecticut town; Louise A. Kent in *The Terrace* (1934) telling of village aristocrats; Mary Ellen Chase, author of *Mary Peters* (1934), a vivid delineation of a Maine coast town recalling Miss Jewett's tales; John DeMeyer who also uses Maine local color in *Village Tale* (1938); and Barbara B. Stevens, recording in *The Strongest Son* (1938) Massachusetts small town life, offer evidence that the problems of the New England town, however much exploited, may again prove rich material for fiction.

The Midwestern and Far Western towns, though repeatedly portrayed in literature, still offer material in both their past and present aspects. Note Glenway Wescott's realistic *Good-Bye Wisconsin* (really a product of the twenties) and his other stories of the region he knew as a boy; Ivan Beede's *Prairie Women* (1930), a series of obscure dramas exposing the strife and bitterness hidden beneath the surface of a workaday existence; Meridel Le Sueur's "Corn Village" (1931), a picture of certain Midwestern villages as "yet the waste and ashes of pioneering"; Nard Jones's *Oregon Detour* (1932); Helen Hull's *Heat Lightning* (1932), disposing of the notion that things stagnate in small places, and her *Morning Shows the Day* (1934), reporting the passing yesterdays; Mateel Howe Farnham's *Great Riches* (1934), the tale of a Kansas town described in a style suggestive of the same shrewd philosophy of her father, E. W. Howe; Vardis Fisher's *In Tragic Life* and other of his introspective novels which give incidentally unflattering pictures of small towns among the Antelope Hills in Idaho; George D. Snell's *The Great Adam* (1934), also a tale of Idaho, telling of the downfall of a small town banker, who built in a farming district a miniature kingdom for himself; Mildred Walker's

Fireweed (1934), the story of a second generation in a Michigan lumber town. which flourished briefly, like fireweed, after the giants of the forests had passed on; Sterling North's remarkably effective novels of Wisconsin, *Plowing on Sunday* (1934) and *Night Outlasts the Whippoorwill* (1936), really fine sketches of prosperous Brailsford Junction from 1913 to the hysteria of the World War; and, finally, Jack O'Connor's realistic *Boom Town* (1938), the story of an Arizona ghost town. Not until recently has the rich mine of small town material associated with the Chautauqua movement been effectively applied to fiction. Gay McLaren's autobiographical *Morally We Roll Along* (1938) and Thomas W. Duncan's novel, *O, Chautauqua* (1935), recreate in personal sketch and fiction a small town society which has almost vanished. Sidney Coe Howard's play, *Alien Corn* (1933), satirizing the provinciality of a small Midland college town, treats the old theme of artists among the Philistines. Howard's *The Late Christopher Bean* (1933) is the adaptation of a French play (*Prenez Garde à la Peinture*) to a New England town setting. Unique in their portrayals of Negro life in the small town—a slightly exploited theme as treated from the viewpoint of gifted Negro writers—are Langston Hughes's *Not Without Laughter* (1930) and Claude McKay's *Gingertown* (1932). Included in current village portrayals are Edwin V. Mitchell's fond recollections of a Michigan village, *American Village*, and Elizabeth Bacon's humorous sketches of a Texas community, *Search the Scriptures, or What Happened When the Circus Came to Town*. Some may see a new trend in community literature in two biographies of towns. Earnest Elmo Calkins in *They Broke the Prairie* (1937) gives a memorable picture of Galesburg, Illinois, a "pious, teetotal, abolition town," from its early settlement on the windswept prairie to the thriving city of 1937. Harold Sinclair's *American Years* (1938), an extraordinary departure from the field of historical fiction, offers another vivid panorama of this country's growth as shown through the chronicle of Everton, Illinois, from its beginnings in 1830 to the Civil War when it was a sizable county seat.

A loud echo of the noise of the fight against the small town is heard in the Oklahoma stories of George Milburn. In *Oklahoma Town* (1931) Milburn writes of the daily happenings of his community both as he has observed them and as he has listened to "old-timers" boastfully spin tall tales of the Indian

Territory.   Milburn shows complete familiarity with the Oklahoma idiom and keen observation of the minutiae of town life. Sometimes the lives he portrays are twisted, grotesque, and tragic ; sometimes homely and often unfruitful ; and again normally happy.   *No More Trumpets, and Other Stories* (1933), another array of warped and mediocre personalities found among Oklahomans and Texans, and his first novel, *Catalogue* (1937), give proof that George Milburn abundantly deserves the acclaim for which he made a strong bid in *Oklahoma Town.* James Gray's *Shoulder the Sky* (1935) tells, in the manner of *Main Street,* about the struggles of a young doctor and his wife in a sordid Minnesota town.   Lee Shippey's *Where Nothing Ever Happens* (1935), sketches of the personalities that mold events in a village, reveals beneath the serene surface of existence in Ourville currents of jealousy, intrigue, and jealousy, themes treated to the point of monotony in small town fiction.   Bradda Field's *Small Town* (1932), sketching a Canadian town ; Robert Marshall's *Arctic Village* (1933), a community analysis after the manner of *Middletown;* and Melvin Levy's *The Last Pioneers* (1934), convincingly reconstructing an open town of the Pacific Northwest during its boom time, illustrate the recent expansion of the small town field outside the States.

Even today the small town of fiction, from all outward indications, seems entrenched behind popular and critical favor. Currently, New England and the Middle West again are in the literary foreground in two widely recognized studies of the small town.   The successful stage run of Thornton Wilder's experimental three-act drama, *Our Town,* and its winning a Pulitzer award for 1938 have made the simple life of Grover's Corners, New Hampshire, familiar to hundreds of theatergoers and readers.   William L. White as the son of William Allen White represents the voice of a second generation expressing itself about the town.   His first novel, *What People Said,* is a sort of *Middletown* translated into action and dialogue for the portrayal of a backstage view of the political and financial scandals in Athena, Oklarada.   A level-headed, level-voiced study, *What People Said* transfers to the plane of drama the philistine vices and virtues of a Midwestern town.

Chapter XI

A GLANCE BACKWARD

Literature," once wrote E. E. Stoll, "is, of course, not life, neither history nor material for history, but a scroll where are traced and charactered the unfettered thoughts of writer and reader, a life within life, fancy somewhat at odds with life."[1] In the final evaluation of the "life within life" evoked by the full body of small town literature in America, one is not unmindful of Professor Stoll's dictum that literature is no document for real life. The agreement between the literary painting and the actual town, it has been found in this study, has varied from the beginning according to the taste of the times and the outlook, or approach, of individual authors. In fact, the American small town literary pattern, first cut by eighteenth-century idealists, is comparable in its constantly changing designs to the oft refashioned coats of the vacillating brothers in Jonathan Swift's "A Tale of a Tub." Some village patterns, richly embroidered with the brightest threads of fancy, by no stretching of one's imagination could be mistaken as mirrors held up to nature. They reflect, to use Professor Stoll's phrasing, "the taste of the time rather than the time itself." On the other hand, some users of other community designs, thoroughly familiar with the life they sought to portray, have created pictures conforming more or less to actuality. Unlike the glorifier or the social caricaturist, they took no advantage of the high liberty of romantic convention to discolor the life they knew. A glance backward at the patterns determining the literary history of the American small town is in order here.

As is true in any new country, the American colonial era was marked by the expenditure of dynamic energies rather than by the production of artistically developed and critical creative compositions. Most of the literature of the town was in the form of histories, diaries, journals, or letters, all of which reflected village affairs but incidentally. No conscious village literature, written either purposively in defense of or against

---

[1] "Literature No 'Document,'" *Modern Language Review*, XIX, 141 (April, 1924).

the town, was the rule. Instead, religious tracts, surveying
reports, psalm books, autobiographies, and the like gave indication of the practical and theological interests of the people.
It may, therefore, be safely said that the really distinctive depiction of the colonial town followed long after the period of
actual colonial life. In 1845, for example, early Massachusetts backwoods manners furnished the theme for Sylvester
Judd's *Margaret*. J. L. Motley's *Merry Mount*, a romance of
the Massachusetts Bay Colony, did not appear until 1849.
The most significant picturing of the colonial past, of course,
is that to be found in Hawthorne's shorter pieces—one is even
called "Main Street"—and his familiar novels of somber background, *The Scarlet Letter* (1850) and *The House of the Seven
Gables* (1851). Since these works are not primarily studies of
historical background, Hawthorne has handled with careful
suppression only those elements of early Puritan village life
from which his tragedies develop. He was chiefly concerned
with producing a fitting and harmonious background for his
stories.

From Hawthorne's time to Thornton Wilder's *Our Town*
(1938) the New England village has been widely treated in
American literature. Until comparatively recent times the
mode of depiction has been mainly retrospective, with emphasis upon past backgrounds and events. The rise of the West,
resulting in the migration of some of the best of New England
stock, in later years has called forth innumerable stories, such
as those of Mrs. Freeman's warped personalities, portraying
with marked verisimilitude the passing of the older peaceful
villages and the rise of industrial towns which did much toward
blotting away traditional customs through the invasion of foreign workers with their strange languages and ways.

The moving frontier has ever captivated the writer of social
themes and backgrounds. Here, too, the village or the smaller
town has a place. Its depicters have been many: Cooper,
Bret Harte, Mark Twain, Howe, Garland, and others. Some
of these, like Mark Twain, have used the retrospective pattern
in recapturing the backgrounds for their stories. Many of the
"tales of the soil" of Garland, Howe, and other realists are
based upon actual conditions existing within the author's experiences. On the other hand, others writing contemporane-
ously with Garland and Howe fail to maintain the parallel be-

tween the actual and the literary curves. Romantic in their outlook, they have sentimentalized about the small town. They have glorified it and pictured it as the very essence of all that is good and friendly; as the very source of honest living; and as the social center from which all evil is either banished, or, if it does exist, is finally crushed by the triumphant forces of good. A Utopian place, truly, but one entirely out of joint with the economic and other trends of recent times. In many instances, such romanticists have enveloped the town with an air of Victorian nicety not altogether conformable with small town life as it has actually existed since the machine age has come to Spoon River. Assuredly, literature is no document here. With industrial expansion the genial William Allen Whites, the Tarkingtons, the Zona Gales (of *Friendship Village* days, of course), and the Margaret Delands have been opposed by the satiric forces headed by Masters and his cohorts. Theirs is a probing and critical art, sometimes truly photographic and again as exaggerated in its village caricatures as the sentimentalized pictures produced by the village defenders.

In the South the small town was retarded in development through existence of the plantation system and the dominance of the landed "aristocracy." Relatively considered, the literature of the small town, then, has, until recently, been negligible in the South. Until fairly recent times, early travel and social sketches, historical romances, and books of border humor may be said to give the fullest contemporary accounts of Southern community life. Sol Smith and fellow-itinerant actors, Northern visitors, tutors, and peddlers, and foreign travelers have left accounts reflective of the Southern life they experienced. On the whole, however, both the actual Southern town and the town of literature have been of slow growth. The really distinctive treatments, like those of Ellen Glasgow and, more recently, of T. S. Stribling and others, did not appear until the modern period. At present the much reported battle of the village has shifted from Midwestern to Southern ground. With the recent widespread criticism, favorable and unfavorable, of Stribling, Faulkner, Wolfe, and others the Southern small town has, at last, come into the limelight.

While the actual American small town of today represents a type of life far removed from that portrayed by Goldsmith and Mrs. Gaskell, the archetypes of our Gopher Prairies and

29

Spoon Rivers have contributed in various ways toward the development in American literature of a tradition of the town. The tradition of the village as embodying miraculous virtues has been radically changed by the belligerent interpreters of the twenties whose concern has been with the dullness and stupidity of small town existence rather than with the pastoral delights of an Arcadian village. In the monotony, the petty tyranny, the thinly cloaked hypocrisy, and the everlasting gossip so often associated with small town life satiric interpreters like Howe, Kirkland, Masters, Anderson, Lewis, and other more recent critics from the South have found themes of revolt. Under their variously satiric onslaughts the idols of romantic convention have fallen and crumbled; the older village life, so long poetized or idealized, has yielded to the new.

Lewis Mumford, discussing in his masterly *The Culture of Cities* (1938) the permanency and impermanency of "metropolitan economy" in America, questions : "Will life continue to ebb out of the villages and country towns and regional centers? Will urban life come to mean the further concentration of power in a few metropolises whose ramifying suburban dormitories will finally swallow the rural hinterland?"[2] Just how the continued heaping up of the disabilities and burdens of life in Megalopolis will affect countless actual towns and the fictional Gopher Prairies of the future it is too hazardous to predict. One but notes, with a well-known critic, that the present represents one of those times "when the despondent metropolitan mind turns upon the small community such a look as social reformers in Robert Owen's time cast upon America and the unshackled wilderness beyond the Alleghanies."[3] If such be true, the present, then, is an auspicious time for newer literary treatments of the small town, for newer chapters in the variously patterned story of "convention and revolt."

[2] *The Culture of Cities*, p. 223.

[3] May Lamberton Becker, "The Reader's Guide," *The Saturday Review of Literature*, VIII, 798 (June 18, 1932). Similar expressions are to be found in K. Stewart, "California's New Gold Rush," *The Literary Digest*, CXVII, 30 (March 3, 1934) ; Irving Bacheller, "Main Street Up-to-Date," *The Forum*, XCI, 185-188 (March, 1934) ; Anna Steese Richardson, "The Call of the Old Home Town," *The Forum* XCI, 173-177 (March, 1934) ; and Dorothy Roe, "Jobless Build New Town in Ozark Woods," *The Daily Times Herald* (Dallas, Texas), Jan. 31, 1932. See also R. L. Duffus, "The Small Town" in Harold E. Stearns, ed., *America Now* (New York, 1938), pp. 385-394.

CHECK-LIST FOR THE TOWN IN EARLY LITERATURE

Meager listings in the following early surveys and later check-lists indicate a noticeable lack of early delineations of American village life in both prose and poetry.

1. Samuel Kettell (1800-55), *Specimens of American Poetry with Critical and Biographical Notices* (3 vols., Boston : S. G. Goodrich & Co., 1829), lists from one hundred and twenty-five poets, now mostly forgotten, and from five hundred volumes of American poetry available at that date but seven village poems, all of which are mediocre and a few of which afford but incidental treatments.

2. Rev. George B. Cheever, *The Prose Writers of America* (New York : Hurst and Co., n.d.), lists but two nondescript prose studies of the village. The same author has an edition of poets, issued in 1829 and similar to Kettell's, or Goodrich's *Kettle of Poetry*, which I have been unable to examine.

3. *The Boston Book being Specimens of Metropolitan Literature* (Boston : George W. Light, 1841) lists but one sketch by Harriet E. Beecher and James T. Fields's negligible "The Villager's Winter Song."

4. Rufus Wilmot Griswold (1815-57), *Poets and Poetry of America* (6th ed., revised, with illustrations, Philadelphia : Carey and Hart, 1845), lists in the body of the work eighty-six authors and seven hundred poems, in addition to an appendix list, out of which about a dozen poems deal with village themes directly or indirectly.

5. Griswold, *The Female Poets of America* (2d ed., Philadelphia : Henry C. Baird, 1853), lists ninety "female" poets no one of whom shows a concern for village life.

6. G. L. and E. A. Duyckinck, *Cyclopaedia of American Literature* (New York : Charles Scribner, 1855), gives information about most of the village writers included in the above anthologies.

7. Mary Forrest, *pseud.* [Mrs. Julia Deane Freeman], *Women of the South Distinguished in Literature* (New York : C. B. Richardson, 1866), lists thirty-four women, who, though interested in plantation life and travel, evince no interest whatsoever in small town life.

8. Oscar Wegelin, *Early American Poetry, 1774-1799* (2d ed., Vol. I, New York : Peter Smith, 1930), lists but five village titles, three of which are by Philip Freneau.

9. Wegelin, *Early American Fiction, 1774-1830* (New York, 1929),

lists among many didactic and generalized titles but one village title.

10. Wegelin, *Early American Plays, 1714-1830* (The Dunlap Society, 1910), lists not a single play with a village or small town title. The same results are found in the fictional guides of Baker, Baker and Packman, Nield, and others.

APPENDIX II

YANKEE VILLAGEDOM*

From the time of Royall Tyler's Revolutionary fable, *The Contrast* (1787), the Yankee portrait has been reworked by many hands.[1] As peddler, sailor, wood-dealer, itinerant tutor, and practical joker, this "wry triumphant portrait was repeated again and again, up and down the Atlantic coast, over and over in the newly opened West, where its popularity had a quirk of oddity."[2] Plays, Western almanacs, joke books, and newspapers provided numerous ancestors for the definitely localized Yankee, a Down East village trader, who came into prominence in the early thirties.

It was from Portland, on January 18, 1830, that an uneducated, but shrewd, country youth first wrote to his Cousin Ephraim about the adventures which befell him after his departure from his native Down East village. Not so gullible as Goldsmith's Moses at the fair, this young rustic, "a sort of comic *deus ex machina* at whom one laughs while still respecting him," succeeded in selling his ax handles, cheese, and footings; went to the meeting house and the museum; lengthened his stay in Portland; and became mixed up in Maine politics.[3] Miraculously successful, this youthful trader-turned-politician speedily gained a place on President Jackson's Washington staff. From the hero's gossipy letters to his village homefolk and their full replies there comes to view a provincial Maine town, its Yankee folk, their spirit of family clannishness, their customs, and their peculiarities.

Thus began the humorous and politically significant Downing papers, for the self-seeking lad was Jack Downing (later Major Downing, adviser to the President) and the little town of the letters was Downingville. The author was Seba Smith (1792-1868), native of Buckfield, Maine ("'way down East"), who contributed the first Downing letters to the *Portland Courier* (1830-33) and continued the sketches at intervals in other publications until the Civil War.[4]

* This phase of village life has been so excellently treated by recent researchers that but the briefest mention of it is made here. For full treatment see Jennette Tandy, *Crackerbox Philosophers, etc.* (New York, 1925), chaps. ii and iii; Mary A. Wyman, *Two American Pioneers: Seba Smith and Elizabeth Oakes Smith* (New York, 1927); Napier Wilt, *Some American Humorists* (New York, 1929), Introduction and pp. 15-55; and Constance Rourke, *American Humor, etc.* (New York, 1930), chap. i.
[1] Wilt, *op. cit.*, p. vii, and Rourke, *op. cit.*, p. 16.
[2] Rourke, *op. cit.*, p. 17.
[3] Quoted matter from Wilt, *op. cit.*, p. 15.
[4] *Ibid.*

The humorous provincialism of Jack's Downingville relatives (Uncle Ephraim, Aunt Keziah, Uncle Joshua, and Cousin Nabby) furnishes a localized village background for the political career of the picaresque hero. Like Longfellow's Bungonuck, Downingville, as the Major reminiscently described it, was "a snug, tidy sort of a village, situated in a valley . . . about three miles from the main road, as you go back into the country, and is jest about in the middle of Down East."[5] A secluded village it was, founded after the Revolution by an ex-soldier, Zebedee Downing, the Major's grandfather. From Zebedee and his ten sons and daughters the settlement not only took its name but, with the increase of their families, had by Jack's day developed into a typical Maine village of the period. The activities of the villagers were typical. In addition to their routine work, the good folk of Downingville found enjoyment in singing-school exercises, sleigh-riding, militia drills, political rallies, and gossiping at the post office and stores. The greatest event of its history, however, was that when the Major wrote of President Jackson's intentions of visiting Downingville on the Fourth of July. What unwonted activity stirred the whole town as frantic preparations were made for the President's arrival! As Cousin Nabby later reported the excitement to the editor of the *Portland Courier*,

. . . such a hubbub as we were in . . . I guess you never see. Such a washing and scrubbing, and making new clothes and mending old ones, and baking and cooking. Every thing seemed to be in a clutter all over the neighborhood.[6]

Sergeant Joel, head of the militia, "flew round like a ravin' distracted rooster." The greatest "rumpus," however, was at Uncle Joshua's where the President was to spend the night. With humorous exaggeration Seba Smith creates a graphic picture of Aunt Keziah, Uncle Joshua's wife, who was "in such a pucker to have everything nice, I didn't know but she would fly off the handle." Nabby's letter continues :

She had every part of the house washed from garret to cellar, and the floors all sanded, and a bunch of green bushes put into all the fire places. And she baked three ovens full of dried punkin pies, besides a few dried huckleberry pies, and cake and a great pot of pork and beans. But the worst trouble was to fix up the bed so as to look nice ; . . . ; So she put on two feather beds on top of the bed, and a bran-new calico quilt that she made the first summer after she was married, and never put on a bed before. And to make it look nice as the New York beds, she took her red

[5] Seba Smith, *The Life and Writings of Major Jack Downing* (Boston, 1833), "My Life," p. 13.
[6] Letter of July 8, 1833.

silk gown and ripped it up and made a blanket to spread over the top. And then she hung up some sheets all round the bedroom, and the gals brought in a whole handful of roses and pinks, and pinned 'em up round as thick as flies in August.

When, after such elaborate preparations, the President failed to appear, everybody, according to Nabby, was "as mad as blazes." "Unutterable disappointment" was general.

Even though he places the strongest thematic significance on the petty bickerings of the Maine legislature and the larger political controversies of the nation, Seba Smith fashions also in his humorous sketches of Yankee villagers a new pattern for the literature of the New England village. Here are sly humor, comic exaggeration, naturally used vernacularisms, satire, and local color in a combination humorously delineative of Yankee rusticity. Pioneering with these Downing letters, Smith later brought out a collection of other Yankee stories, non-epistolary in form, in the volume '*Way Down East.*[7] Herein are other pictures of New England village life. Tavern scenes, court trials, and singing-schools, which if pictured with less humor than the Downing sketches, present, nevertheless, familiar features of village life in isolated sections of New England during the forties and fifties.

While Smith's rustic critic and satirist presented through homely phrase and provincial wisdom pictures of a localized Down East village, Lowell's *The Biglow Papers* (1848, 1862), rich though they were in contemporary political allusions and Yankee mannerisms, "had nothing of the deliberate attempt to build up a village background, ..."[8] Ezekiel and Hosea Biglow seem mouthpieces of the poet rather than individually charactered village folk. Jaalam seems a mere name and little more. Nothing of its physical features or customs remains as vivid pictures. It is, at best, just another upcountry village, the home of an indignant idealist, the upright Mr. Biglow, his relatives, and that long winded old pedant, the Reverend Homer Wilbur. It is, therefore, the political satire, rather than the village life, which looms large in *The Biglow Papers*. Village scenes yield place to satiric portraitures, the latter being in many respects "a Hogarthian company" revealing all "the gnarled fibers of the cross-grained Yankee." One must turn to the humorists of the South for further humorous sketches of localized villages.

---

[7] See '*Way Down East, or Portraitures of Yankee Life* (New York, 1854), "John Wadleigh's Trial," "The Tough Yarn," "Christopher Crochet," "Jerry Guttridge," and "A Race for a Sweetheart" for village pictures.

[8] Tandy, *op. cit.*, p. 52.

SELECTED BIBLIOGRAPHY

Adams, James Truslow. *New England in the Republic, 1776-1850.* Boston, 1926.
———. *The Founding of New England.* Boston, 1927. Vol. I.
———. *Provincial Society, 1690-1763.* Vol. III, *A History of American Life,* edited by A. M. Schlesinger and D. R. Fox, 1927 —.
———. *The Epic of America.* Boston, 1931.
Albee, John. *Remembrances of Emerson.* New York, 1901.
Alderman, E. A., and Harris, J. C., eds. *Library of Southern Literature.* New Orleans, 1909. (George Mellen, "Joseph Glover Baldwin," I, 175 ff.)
Allen, F. L. *Only Yesterday.* New York, 1931.
American Literature: A Journal of Literary History, Criticism, and Bibliography. Duke University Press, Durham, N. C., March, 1929 —.
Andrews, C. M. *Colonial Folkways.* New Haven, 1919,
Angoff, Charles. *A Literary History of the American People, 1607-1815.* New York, 1931. Vol. I.
Arber, E., ed. *Travels and Works of Captain John Smith, 1580-1631.* Edinburgh, 1910. Vol. II.
Arvin, Newton. *Hawthorne.* Boston, 1929.
Ashton, John, ed. *The Adventures and Discourses of Captain John Smith.* London, 1883.
Baker, E. A. *A Guide to the Best Historical Fiction.* London, 1914.
Baskervill, W. M. *Southern Writers: Biographical and Critical Studies.* Nashville, 1897-1903. 2 vols.
Beach, S. C. *Daughters of the Puritans.* Cambridge, 1905. (Catharine Maria Sedgwick.)
Beard, Charles A., and Mary R. *The Rise of American Civilization.* New York, 1930. One-volume edition.
Beaty, John O. *John Esten Cooke, Virginian.* New York, 1922.
Beer, Thomas. *Stephen Crane.* New York, 1923.
———. *The Mauve Decade.* New York, 1926.
Bidwell, P. W. *Rural Economy in New England at the Beginning of the Nineteenth Century.* New Haven, 1916.
Blair, Walter. *Native American Humor, 1800-1900.* New York, 1937.
Blankenship, Russell. *American Literature as an Expression of the National Mind.* New York, 1931.
Bliss, W. R. *Colonial Times on Buzzard's Bay.* Boston, 1888.
Blumenthal, Albert. *Small Town Stuff.* Chicago, 1932. (A study of Philipsburg, Montana, a mining town.)

Boas, R. P., and Burton, K. *Social Backgrounds of American Literature.* Boston, 1933.

Bott, Alan. *This Was England: Manners and Customs of the Ancient Victorians.* Garden City, 1931.

Boyer, Mary, ed. *Arizona in Literature.* Glendale, California, 1934.

Boynton, Henry W. *Bret Harte.* New York, 1903.

———. *James Fenimore Cooper.* New York, 1931.

Boynton, Percy H. *A History of American Literature.* Boston, 1919.

———. *Some Contemporary Americans.* Chicago, 1924.

———. *More Contemporary Americans.* Chicago, 1927.

———. *The Rediscovery of the Frontier.* Chicago, 1931.

———. *Literature and American Life.* Boston, 1936.

Brashear, Minnie M. *Mark Twain, Son of Missouri.* Chapel Hill, N. C., 1934.

Bridge, Horatio. *Personal Recollections of Nathaniel Hawthorne.* New York, 1893.

Bridgers, H. J. *As I Was Saying.* Boston, 1910. (Mark Twain, pp. 44 ff.)

Brooks, Van Wyck. *America's Coming-of-Age.* New York, 1915.

———. *The Ordeal of Mark Twain.* New York, 1922.

———. *Emerson and Others.* New York, 1927.

———. *The Flowering of New England.* New York, 1936.

Browne, Nina E. *A Bibliography of Nathaniel Hawthorne.* Boston, 1905.

Brownell, W. C. *American Prose Masters.* New York, 1909.

Bruce, P. A. *Economic History of Virginia in the Seventeenth Century.* New York, 1907. (First edition, 1895.)

Bryant, William Cullen. *Poetical Works.* New York, 1926.

Burr, Walter. *Small Towns: An Estimate of Their Trade and Culture.* New York, 1929. (A study of Kansas and Missouri.)

Cairns, W. B., ed. *Early American Writers, 1607-1800.* New York, 1909, 1917.

Caldwell, Erskine, and White, Margaret B. *You Have Seen Their Faces.* New York, 1937. (Pictures of Southern townspeople, etc.)

Calverton, V. F. *American Literature at the Crossroads.* (University of Washington Chapbooks), Seattle, 1931.

———. *The Liberation of American Literature.* New York, 1932.

Cambridge History of American Literature. Edited by Trent, Erskine, Sherman, and Van Doren. 4 vols. New York, 1917-21. (Quotations are from the three-volume edition, 1933.)

Canby, H. S., and others. *Saturday Papers.* New York, 1921.

Canby, H. S. *The Age of Confidence: Life in the Nineties.* New York, 1934.

Cargill, O., ed. *The Social Revolt: American Literature from 1888 to 1914.* New York, 1933.

Cestre, Charles. *An Introduction to Edwin Arlington Robinson.* New York, 1930.

Cheever, George B. *The Prose Writers of America.* New York, n.d.

Chitwood, O. P. *A History of Colonial America.* New York, 1931.

Clark, B. H., and Nicholson, K., eds. *The American Scene.* New York, 1930.

Conway, M. D. *Life of Hawthorne.* London, 1890.

Cooke, Delmar G. *William Dean Howells: A Critical Study.* New York, 1922.

Cooper, James Fenimore. *The Legends and Traditions of a Northern Country.* New York, 1920.

Couch, W. T., ed. *Culture in the South.* Chapel Hill, N. C., 1934.

Courthope, W. J. *A History of English Poetry.* London, 1910. Vol. I.

Cyclopaedia of Political Science and Political Economy. New York, 1888.

Daniels, Jonathan. *A Southerner Discovers the South.* New York, 1938.

D'Arusmont, Frances (Wright). *Views of Society and Manners in America.* New York, 1821.

De Menil, A. N. *The Literature of the Louisiana Territory.* St. Louis, 1904. (E. W. Howe and Alice French.)

Deming, Dorothy. *The Settlement of the Connecticut Towns.* New Haven, 1933.

De Quille, Dan (Wright, William). *History of the Big Bonanza.* Hartford, 1877. (Profusely illustrated.)

De Voto, Bernard. *Mark Twain's America.* Boston, 1932.

Dickinson, Thomas. *The Making of American Literature.* New York, 1932.

Dictionary of American Biography, The. Edited by Allen Johnson and Dumas Malone, New York, 1928 —.

Dollard, John. *Caste and Class in a Southern Town.* New Haven, 1937.

Dondore, Dorothy. *The Prairie and the Making of Middle America.* Cedar Rapids, Iowa, 1926.

Douglas, Paul. *The Little Town.* New York, 1927.

Drew, Elizabeth. *The Modern Novel.* New York, 1926.

Duffus, R. L. "The Small Town." *America Now.* Edited by Harold E. Stearns. New York, 1939.

Dunlap, George A. *The City in the American Novel, 1789-1900.* Philadelphia, 1934.

Duyckinck, E. A. and G. L. *A Cyclopaedia of American Literature.* New York, 1855. Revised edition, 1875.

Dwight, Timothy. *Travels in New-England and New-York*. London, 1823. Vols. I, III, and IV.

Earle, Alice M. *Stage-Coach and Tavern Days*. New York, 1900.

Eggleston, Edward. *The Transit of Civilization from England to America in the Seventeenth Century*. New York, 1901.

Ellis, H. M. *Joseph Dennie and His Circle*. Studies in English, Number 3. University of Texas, 1915.

Emerson, Edward W. *Emerson in Concord*. Boston and New York, 1890.

————. *The Early Years of the Saturday Club, 1855-1870*. Boston and New York, 1918.

Erskine, John. *Leading American Novelists*. New York, 1910.

Evans, C. *American Bibliography*. (12 vols. to date, 1639-1799). Chicago, 1903-34.

Fields, James T. *Yesterdays with Authors*. Boston, 1895. (First edition, 1871.)

Fish, Carl. *The Rise of the Common Man, 1830-1850*. New York, 1927. Vol. VI, *A History of American Life*, edited by Schlesinger and Fox.

Fisher, Dorothy Canfield. "Vermont: Our Rich Little Poor State." From *These United States*. New York, 1923.

Fisher, G. S. *Men, Women, and Manners in Colonial Times*. Philadelphia and London, 1898. Vol. I.

Fiske, John. *Old Virginia and Her Neighbors*. Boston, 1898. 2 vols.

Fitzgerald, O. P. *Judge Longstreet: A Life Sketch*. Nashville, 1891.

Foerster, Norman, ed. *The Reinterpretation of American Literature*. New York, 1928.

Foerster, N., and Paine, G. L. "A Bibliography of Books and Articles on American Literature," *Publications of the Modern Language Association*, each year in March since 1923.

Foley, P. K. *American Authors, 1795-1895, etc.* Boston, 1897.

Forbes, Allan. *Towns of New England, Old England, Ireland, and Scotland, 1620-1920*. New York, 1921. (Profusely illustrated.)

Foster, R. A. *The School in American Literature*. Baltimore, 1930.

Fullerton, B. M. *Selective Bibliography of American Literature, 1775-1906*. New York, 1932.

Glasscock, C. B. *The Big Bonanza*. Indianapolis, 1931.

Gorman, Herbert. *A Victorian American: Henry Wadsworth Longfellow*. New York, 1926.

Greenslet, Ferris. *The Life of Thomas Bailey Aldrich*. New York, 1908.

Grundy, G. B., ed. *Ancient Gems in Modern Settings, being Versions of the Greek Anthology in English Rhyme, etc.* London, 1913.

Gwathmey, E. M. *John Pendleton Kennedy*. New York, 1931.

Hagedorn, Hermann. *Edwin Arlington Robinson*. New York, 1938.

Hale, Edward E. *James Russell Lowell and His Friends*. Boston, 1899.

Halbeisen, E. *Harriet Prescott Spofford*. Philadelphia, 1935.

Hansen, Harry. *Midwest Portraits*. New York, 1923.

Harkins, E. F., and Johnston, C. H. L. *Little Pilgrimages among the Women who Have Written Famous Books*. Boston, 1902. (Alice French.)

Harrison, Oliver. *Sinclair Lewis*. New York, 1925.

Hartwick, Harry. *The Foreground of American Fiction*. New York, 1934.

Hastings, W. L. *Syllabus of American Literature*. Chicago, 1923.

Hatcher, Harlan. *Creating the Modern American Novel*. New York, 1935.

Hawthorne, Edith G., ed. *The Memoirs of Julian Hawthorne*. New York and Dallas, 1938.

Hawthorne, Julian. *Hawthorne and His Wife*. Boston, 1884.

Hazard, Lucy L. *The Frontier in American Literature*. New York, 1927.

Hicks, Granville. *The Great Tradition*. New York, 1933.

Higginson, Mary T. *Thomas Wentworth Higginson*. Boston and New York, 1914.

Holliday, Carl. *A History of Southern Literature*. New York and Washington, 1906.

Hogan, C. B. *A Bibliography of Edwin Arlington Robinson*. New Haven, 1936.

Howe, M.A. De Wolfe. *American Bookmen*. New York, 1898. (Cooper.)

Hubbell, Jay B. *Virginia Life in Fiction*. Dallas, 1922.

———. *American Life in Literature*. New York, 1936. 2 vols.

Jackson, Holbrook. *The Eighteen Nineties*. New York, 1922.

James, Henry. *Hawthorne*. New York, 1879.

Jameson, Storm. *The Novel in Contemporary Life*. Boston, 1938.

Jessup, Alexander, ed. *Representative American Short Stories*. Boston, 1923. (Full chronologically arranged lists.)

Johnson, Clifton. *New England and Its Neighbors*. New York, 1924.

Johnson, J. G. *Southern Fiction Prior to 1860: An Attempt at a First-Hand Bibliography*. Charlottesville, Va., 1909.

Jones, Howard Mumford. *America and French Culture (1750-1848)*. Chapel Hill, N. C., 1927.

———. "Longfellow." John Macy, ed., *American Writers on American Literature*. New York, 1931.

Jones, Howard Mumford, and Leisy, E. E., eds. *Major American Writers*. New York, 1935.

Kellner, Leon. *American Literature*. Garden City, 1915.

Kern, J. D. *Constance Fenimore Woolson: Literary Pioneer*. Philadelphia, 1934.

Keyserling, Count Hermann. *America Set Free*. New York, 1929.

Kirkpatrick, J. E. *Timothy Flint*. Cleveland, 1911.

Knight, G. C. *The Novel in English*. New York, 1931.

Knight, Sarah Kemble. *Journal*. Edited by G. P. Winship. Boston, 1920.

Krans, Horatio S. *Irish Life in Irish Fiction*. New York, 1903.

Kunitz, S. J. (Dilly Tante), ed. *Living Authors: A Book of Biographies*. New York, 1932.

————. *Authors Today and Yesterday, etc.* New York, 1933.

Lackey, Mabel. *New England Life in the Short Story since the Civil War*. Unpublished thesis, Southern Methodist University, Dallas, 1925.

Leisy, E. E. *American Literature: An Interpretative Survey*. New York, 1929.

Lewis, Sinclair. *Addresses by Erik Axel Karlfeldt and Sinclair Lewis, on the Occasion of the Award of the Nobel Prize*, 1931.

Link, S. A. *Pioneers of Southern Literature*. Nashville, 1900. Vol. II.

Loshe, Lillie Deming. *The Early American Novel*. New York, 1907, 1930.

Lounsbury, Thomas R. *James Fenimore Cooper*. Boston, 1910.

Lowell, Amy. *Tendencies in Modern American Poetry*. New York, 1917.

Lowes, John L. *Convention and Revolt in Poetry*. Boston, 1919.

Lyman, George D. *The Saga of the Comstock Lode: Boom Days in Virginia City*. New York, 1934. (Fully illustrated.)

Lynd, R. S., and H. M. *Middletown: A Study in Contemporary American Culture*. New York, 1929.

————. *Middletown in Transition: A Study in Cultural Conflicts*. New York, 1937.

McDowell, T., ed. *The Romantic Triumph: American Literature from 1830 to 1860*. New York, 1933.

MacGarr, Llewllyn. *The Rural Community*. New York, 1922.

McLaren, Gay. *Morally We Roll Along*. New York, 1938. (The Chautauqua influence in small towns.)

McWilliams, C. *The New Regionalism in American Literature*. (University of Washington Chapbooks), Seattle, 1930.

Macy, John. *The Spirit of American Literature*. New York, 1913.

————, ed. *American Writers on American Literature*. New York, 1931.

Manly, J. M., and Rickert, E. *Contemporary American Literature: Bibliographies and Study Outlines*. New York, 1929.

Manly, Louise. *Southern Literature from 1579-1895*. Richmond, 1895.

Martineau, Harriet. *Retrospect of Western Travel*. London and New York, 1838. Vol. II.

Mathews, Lois K. *The Expansion of New England*. Boston and New York, 1909.

Matthiessen, F. O. *Sarah Orne Jewett*. New York, 1929.

———. "New England Stories." Macy, ed., *op. cit.*

Mencken, H. L. *Notes on Democracy*. New York, 1926.

Merriam, C. E. *American Political Ideas (1865-1917)*. New York, 1921.

Merwin, H. C. *The Life of Bret Harte*. New York, 1911.

Michaud, Régis. *The American Novel To-day*. Boston, 1928.

Miller, Elva. *Town and Country*. Chapel Hill, N. C., 1928.

Mims, Edwin. *History of Southern Fiction* (in *The South in the Building of the Nation*). 1910.

Minnegerode, Meade. *The Fabulous Forties, 1840-1850: A Presentation of Private Life*. New York, 1924.

More, Paul Elmer. *The Shelburne Essays*. Boston, 1904. Vol. I.

Morris, Lloyd. *The Poetry of Edwin Arlington*. Garden City, 1923.

———. *The Rebellious Puritan: Portrait of Mr. Hawthorne*. New York, 1927.

Moses, Montrose J. *The Literature of the South*. New York, 1910.

———. *The Fabulous Forrest*. Boston, 1929.

Muller, Herbert J. *Modern Fiction: A Study of Values*. New York, 1937.

Mumford, Lewis. *The Golden Day: A Study in American Literature and Culture*. New York, 1926.

———. *The Culture of Cities*. New York, 1938.

National Cyclopaedia of American Biography. (27 vols. to date.) New York, 1892—.

Nevins, Allen, ed. *American Social History as Recorded by British Travellers*. New York, 1923.

Nield, J. *A Guide to the Best Historical Novels, etc.* Fifth edition. New York, 1929.

Overton, Grant. *The Women Who Make Our Novels*. New York, 1918. (Revised edition, 1928.)

———. *American Nights Entertainment*. New York, 1923.

Paine, Albert Bigelow. *Mark Twain: A Biography, The Personal and Literary History of Samuel Langhorne Clemens*. 3 vols. New York, 1912.

———, ed. *Mark Twain's Autobiography*. 2 vols. New York, 1924.

Parrington, Vernon Louis. *Main Currents in American Thought*. 3 vols. New York, 1927-1930.

Parrott, T. M., ed. *The Plays and Poems of George Chapman*. Vol. II. London, 1914.

Parton, James. *Topics of the Time.* Boston, 1871.

Pattee, Fred L. *A History of American Literature since 1870.* New York, 1915.

——. *Side-Lights on American Literature.* New York, 1922.

——. *The Development of the American Short Story.* New York, 1923.

——. *Tradition and Jazz.* New York, 1925.

——. *The New American Literature (1890-1930).* New York, 1930.

Patton, Julia. *The English Village (1750-1850).* New York, 1919.

Paxson, F. L. *The History of the American Frontier (1763-1893).* Boston and New York, 1924.

Pemberton, T. E. *Bret Harte: A Treatise and a Tribute.* London, 1900.

——. *The Life of Bret Harte.* New York, 1903.

Perrin, P. G. *The Life and Works of Thomas Green Fessenden.* The University of Maine Press, 1925.

Phillips, Mary. *James Fenimore Cooper.* New York, 1923.

Phillips, U. B. *Life and Labor in the Old South.* Boston, 1929.

Porter, Noah. *The New England Meeting House.* New Haven, 1933.

Quinn, A. H. *The Soul of America, Yesterday and Today.* Philadelphia, 1932.

——. *American Fiction: An Historical and Critical Survey.* 1936.

Reid, L. R. "The Small Town." *Civilization in the United States.* Edited by Harold E. Stearns. New York, 1922.

Rhea, Linda. *Hugh Swinton Legaré.* Chapel Hill, N. C., 1931.

Richards, Laura E. *Stepping Westward.* New York, 1931.

Richardson, C. F. *American Literature, 1607-1885.* 2 vols. New York and London, 1887-89.

Roberts, E. H. *The Planting and the Growth of the Empire State.* Boston, 1887.

Ross, J. F. *The Social Criticism of Fenimore Cooper.* Berkeley, 1933.

Rourke, Constance. *American Humor: A Study of the National Character.* New York, 1931.

Royce, Josiah. *California: A Study of American Character.* Boston and New York, 1886.

Rugg, H. O. *An Introduction to Problems of American Culture.* New York, 1931.

Rusk, Ralph Leslie. *The Literature of the Middle Western Frontier.* 2 vols. New York, 1925.

Sanborn, F. B., and Harris, W. T. *Memoirs of A. Bronson Alcott.* Boston, 1893. Vol. I.

Schelling, F. E. *Appraisements and Asperities.* New York, 1922.

Schlesinger, A. M. *New Viewpoints in American History.* New York, 1922.

————. *The Rise of the City, 1878-1898.* Vol. X in *History of American Life*, edited by Schlesinger and Fox, 1927 —.

Scudder, H. E. *James Russell Lowell.* Boston and New York, 1901.

Shepard, Odell, ed. *The Heart of Thoreau's Journal.* Boston, 1927.

Sherman, S. P. *On Contemporary Literature.* New York, 1917.

————. *Points of View.* New York, 1924.

————. *The Significance of Sinclair Lewis.* New York, 1922.

Simms, William Gilmore. *Views and Reviews in American Literature.* New York, 1845.

Sims, Newell. *The Rural Community.* New York, 1920.

Smith, C. F. *Reminiscences and Sketches.* Nashville and Dallas, 1908.

Smyth, J. F. D. *A Tour in the U. S. of America.* 2 vols. Dublin, 1784.

Spiller, Robert E. *The American in England during the First Half Century of Independence.* New York, 1926.

————. *Fenimore Cooper, Critic of His Times.* New York, 1931.

————, ed. *The Roots of National Culture: American Literature to 1830.* New York, 1933.

Squire, J. C., and others. *Contemporary American Authors.* New York, 1928.

Stanton, Theodore, ed. *A Manual of American Literature.* New York, 1909.

Stewart, G. R., Jr. *Bret Harte, Argonaut and Exile.* Boston, 1931.

Stowe, C. E., and L. B. *Harriet Beecher Stowe.* Boston and New York, 1911.

Sullivan, Mark. *Our Times: The United States, 1900-1925.* New York, 1926-35. Vols. II and III.

Tandy, Jennette. *Crackerbox Philosophers in American Humor and Satire.* New York, 1925.

Taylor, Walter F. *A History of American Letters.* New York, 1936. Bibliographies by Harry Hartwick.

Trent, W. P. *William Gilmore Simms.* Boston and New York, 1895.

————, and Wells, B. W., eds. *Colonial Prose and Poetry.* 2 vols. New York, 1901.

————, ed. *Southern Writers: Selections in Prose and Verse.* New York, 1905.

Trollope, Mrs. Frances. *Domestic Manners of the Americans.* New York, 1901.

Truesdell, L. E., ed. *Fifteenth Census of the United States: 1930.* Washington, 1933. Vol. III.

Turner, Frederick J. *The Rise of the New West.* (Vol. XIV, *The American Nation: A History*, edited by A. B. Hart.) New York, 1906.

30

——. *The Frontier in American History.* New York, 1920.

Twaites, R. G., ed. *Early Western Travels, 1748-1846.* Cleveland, 1904-07.

Twelve Southerners. *I'll Take My Stand: The South and the Agrarian Tradition.* New York, 1930.

Tyler, Moses Coit. *A History of American Literature during the Colonial Period, 1607-1765.* 2 vols. Revised edition, New York, 1897.

——. *The Literary History of the American Revolution, 1763-1783.* 2 vols. New York, 1897.

Underwood, J. C. *Literature and Insurgency.* New York, 1914.

Untermeyer, Louis. *American Poetry since 1900.* New York, 1923.

Vaile, R. S. *The Small City and Town.* University of Minnesota Press, 1930.

Van Doren, Carl. *The American Novel.* New York, 1921.

——. *Contemporary American Novelists, 1900-1920.* New York, 1922.

——. *Many Minds.* New York, 1924.

——. *Sinclair Lewis.* New York, 1933.

——. *What Is American Literature?* New York, 1935.

——, Carl and Mark. *American and British Literature since 1890.* New York, 1925.

Vogt, P. L. *An Introduction to Rural Sociology.* New York, 1924.

Wade, John D. *Augustus Baldwin Longstreet: A Study of the Development of Culture in the South.* New York, 1924.

Wann, L., ed. *The Rise of Realism: American Literature from 1860 to 1888.* New York, 1933.

Waring, Thomas. *The Carolina Low-Country.* New York, 1931.

Webb, Walter. *The Great Plains.* New York, 1931.

Wegelin, O. *Early American Plays, 1714-1830.* New York, 1905.

——. *Early American Fiction, 1774-1830.* New York, 1929.

——. *Early American Poetry, 1774-1799.* New York, 1930.

Wendell, Barrett. *A Literary History of America.* New York, 1900.

Wenzlick, Roy. *The Coming Boom in Real Estate.* New York, 1936.

Wertenbaker, T. J. *Patrician and Plebian in Virginia.* New Haven, 1910.

Whitcomb, S. L. *Chronological Outlines of American Literature.* New York, 1894.

Whiting, E. *Changing New England.* New York, 1929.

Who's Who in America. Chicago, 1899 —.

Williams, J. M. *Our Rural Heritage.* New York, 1925.

——. *The Expansion of Rural Life.* New York, 1926.

Wilson, Woodrow. *Mere Literature and Other Essays.* Boston, 1900.

Wilt, Napier, ed. *Some American Humorists.* New York, 1929.

Wood, L. S., and Burrows, H. L., eds. *The Town in Literature.*

New York, 1925. (A small anthology of English literary materials.)

Woodberry, G. E. *Nathaniel Hawthorne.* Boston, 1902.

————. *America in Literature.* Boston, 1903.

————. *Nathaniel Hawthorne: How to Know Him.* Indianapolis, 1918.

Wyman, Mary A. *Two American Pioneers: Seba Smith and Elizabeth Oakes Smith.* New York, 1927.

Yoder, F. R. *Introduction to Agricultural Economics.* New York, 1929.

Young, Stark, ed. *Southern Treasury of Life and Literature.* New York, 1937.

PERIODICALS

Adams, C. F., Jr. "Genesis of the Massachusetts Town." *Massachusetts Historical Society Proceedings*, VII (second series, 1891-92), 172 ff.

Aldrich, Bess Streeter. "Why I Live in a Small Town." *The Ladies' Home Journal*, L, 21 ff. (June, 1933).

Andrews, C. M. "The Theory of the Village Community." *The American Historical Association Papers.* New York, 1891, V, pts. 1-2, pp. 45-61.

Anon. "New England in the Short Story." *The Atlantic Monthly*, LXVII, 845-850 (June, 1891).

Anon. "The Village Question." *The Atlantic Monthly*, XLIV, 547 (October, 1879).

Anon. "Alarming Increase of Old Maids in New England." *The Literary Digest*, LXV, 66-70 (April 10, 1920).

Bacheller, Irving. "Main Street Up-to-Date." *The Forum*, XCI, 185-188 (March, 1934).

Baker, J. E. "Regionalism in the Middle West." *American Review*, IV, 603-614 (March, 1935). (Ruth Suckow.)

Beffel, J. N. "Fauntleroy Plague." *The Bookman*, LXVI, 135 (April, 1927).

Benét, William Rose. "The Earlier Lewis." *The Saturday Review of Literature*, X, 421-422 (January 20, 1934).

Bond, George. "Sherwood Anderson Chats at Length about Books and This Changing Age." *Dallas Morning News*, magazine section, p. 3 (October 18, 1925).

Boynton, P. H. "Willa Cather." *The English Journal* (College edition), XIII, 379 (June, 1924).

Brackett, Anna C. "The Aryan Mark: A New England Town Meeting." *Harper's Magazine*, LXXXV, 577-585 (September, 1892).

Brickell, Herschel. "The Literary Awakening in the South." *The Bookman*, LXVI, 138-143 (October, 1927).

Bromfield, Louis. "An Honest Novel." *The Saturday Review of Literature*, I, 556 (February 28, 1925). (Homer Croy's *R. F. D. No. 3*.)

Buttitta, Anthony. "William Faulkner: That Writin' Man of Oxford." *The Saturday Review of Literature*, XVIII, 6-8 (May 21, 1938).

Cabell, James Branch. "A Note as to Sinclair Lewis." *The American Mercury*, XX, 394-397 (August, 1930).

Canby, H. S. "Schmaltz, Babbitt & Co." *The Saturday Review of Literature*, IV, 697-698 (March 24, 1928).

———. "The Promise of American Life." *The Saturday Review of Literature*, VII, 301 (November 8, 1930).

Carroll, L. "Willa Sibert Cather." *The Bookman*, LIII, 212-216 (May, 1921).

Cather, Willa. "The Novel Démeublé." *The New Republic*, XXX, Literary Supplement, 5-6 (April 12, 1922).

Chapman, E. M. "The New England of Sarah Orne Jewett." *The Yale Review*, III, 160 ff. (October, 1913).

Coblentz, Stanton. "Main Street." *The Bookman*, LII, 457 (January, 1921).

Coleman, C. W., Jr. "The Recent Movement in Southern Literature." *Harper's Magazine*, LXXIV, 837-855 (May, 1887).

Cooke, Delmar Gross. "Sinclair Lewis." *Dallas Morning News*, magazine section, p. 5 (March 8, 1925).

Cooper, F. T. "Review of Friendship Village." *The Bookman*, XXXI, 79 (March, 1910).

Davidson, Donald. "The South Today: Report on Literature." *Dallas Daily Times Herald*, first section, p. 6 (July 17, 1938).

Dell, Floyd. "A Literary Self-Analysis." *The Modern Quarterly*, IV, 149 ff. (June-September, 1927).

De Voto, Bernard. "New England: There She Stands." *Harper's Magazine*, CLXIV, 405 ff. (March, 1932).

———. "Sinclair Lewis." *The Saturday Review of Literature*, IX, 397-398 (January 28, 1933).

Dickens, Byrom. "T. S. Stribling and the South." *The Sewanee Review*, XLII, 341-349 (July-September, 1934).

Dodd, L. W. "A Test Case." *The Saturday Review of Literature*, III, 330-331 (November 27, 1926). (Ruth Suckow.)

Duffus, R. L. "A Changing Nation Revealed by the Census." *New York Times*, LXXIX, section 9, p. 1 (August 17, 1930).

Earle, Alice M. "The New England Meeting House." *The Atlantic Monthly*, LXVII, 191-204 (February, 1891).

Ervine, St. John. "American Literature: Now and to Be." *Century Magazine*, CI, 578 (March, 1921).

Faulkner, William. "Sherwood Anderson." *Dallas Morning News*, magazine section, p. 7 (April 26, 1925).

Firkins, O. W. "The Return to Spoon River." *The Saturday Review of Literature*, I, 178 (October, 1924).

Frederick, John T. "The Younger School." *The Palimpsest*, XI, 78-86 (February, 1930).

———. "Ruth Suckow and the Middle Western Literary Movement." *The English Journal* (College edition), XX, 1-8 (January, 1931).

Gale, Zona. "Out of Nothing into Somewhere." *The English Journal* (College edition), XIII, 176 (March, 1924).

Graham, Pauline. "A Novelist of the Unsung." *The Palimpsest*, XI, 67 (February, 1930). (Emerson Hough.)

Gauss, Christian. "Sinclair Lewis *vs.* His Education." *The Saturday Evening Post*, CCIV, 278-281 (December 26, 1931).

Guiterman, Arthur. "Edgar Lee Masters." *The Saturday Review of Literature*, II, 903 (July 3, 1926). (A rhymed review.)

Hartt, Rollin Lynde. "A New England Hill Town." *The Atlantic Monthly*, LXXXIII, 561-574 (April, 1899).

———. "A New England Hill Town: Its Revival." *The Atlantic Monthly*, LXXXIII, 712-720 (May, 1899).

Hatcher, Harlan. "The Forces of Violence." *The English Journal* (College edition), XXIII, 91-89 (February, 1934).

Hatfield, J. T. "An Unknown Prose Tale by Longfellow." *American Literature*, III, 136-148 (May, 1931).

———. See *American Literature*, V, 377, note (January, 1934).

Hawthorne, Julian. "The Salem of Hawthorne." *Century Magazine*, XXVIII, 3-17 (May, 1884).

Henderson, Archibald. "Soil and Soul." *The Saturday Review of Literature*, I, 907 (July 18, 1925).

Herrick, Sophie B. "Richard Malcolm Johnston." *Century Magazine*, XXXVI, 276-280 (June, 1888).

Herron, Ima H. "Ruth Suckow's *The Folks*." *Dallas Morning News*, magazine section, p. 12 (September 30, 1934).

Hoagland, H. E. "Movement of Rural Population in Illinois from 1900 to 1910." *Journal of Political Economy*, XX, 913-927 (November, 1912).

Howells, William Dean. "An Appreciation." *Century Magazine*, XXVIII, 632 (August, 1884). (E. W. Howe's *The Story of a Country Town*.)

Hubbell, Jay B. "The Decay of the Provinces." *The Sewanee Review*, XXXV, 473-487 (October, 1927).

Hubbell, L. W. "New England Village." (A Poem.) *Harper's Magazine*, CLXIV, 91 (December, 1931).

Jewett, Sarah Orne. "From a Mournful Villager." *The Atlantic Monthly*, XLVII, 670 (November, 1881).

Jones, Howard Mumford. "Relief from Murder." *The Reader's Digest*, XXXIII, 9-11 (August, 1938). Condensed from *The Atlantic Monthly*, July, 1938.

———. "The Novels of Willa Cather." *The Saturday Review of Literature*, XVIII, 3-4, 16 (August 6, 1938).

Lowell, James Russell. "Longfellow's *Kavanagh*." *The North American Review*, CXLIV, 209 (July, 1849).

MacClear, Anne B. "Early New England Towns." *Studies in History and Public Law*, XXIX, Number 1, Columbia University Press, 1908.

MacLeish, Archibald. "The New Age and the New Writers." *The Yale Review*, XII, 314-321 (January, 1923).

Maurice, A. B. "Irving Bacheller's *Eben Holden*." *The Bookman*, XII, 235 (November, 1900).

Moore, H. H. "A Maine Seacoast Village." *The Outlook*, CXXV, 264 ff. (June 9, 1920).

Mott, F. L. "Exponents of the Pioneers." *The Palimpsest*, XI, 61 (February, 1930).

———. "Iowa Looks at Ruth Suckow." *Wings* (publication of the Literary Guild), X, 25 (October, 1934).

Munger, T. T. "Notes on *The Scarlet Letter*." *The Atlantic Monthly*, XCIII, 521 (April, 1904).

Nelson, W. H. "Mark Twain out West." *The Methodist Quarterly Review*, LXXII, 65 (January, 1924).

Parker, Joel. "The Origin, Organization, and Influence of the Towns of New England." *Massachusetts Historical Society Proceedings*, IX (first series, 1866-1867), 15.

Peck, Harry T. "Then and Now." *The Bookman*, XXX, 596 (February, 1910). (Notes on Harold Frederic.)

Richardson, Anna S. "The Call of the Old Home Town." *The Forum*, CXI, 173-177 (March, 1934).

St. Clair, George. "E. A. Robinson and Tilbury Town." *The New Mexico Quarterly*, IV, 95-107 (May, 1934).

Scudder, H. E. "Recent Fiction." *The Atlantic Monthly*, LV, 125-127 (January, 1885). (E. W. Howe.)

Sergeant, Elizabeth. "The Citizen from Emporia." *Century Magazine*, CXIII, 308 (January, 1927). (William Allen White.)

Shackford, Martha. "Sarah Orne Jewett." *The Sewanee Review*, XXX, 21 (January, 1922).

Shaler, N. S. "The Peculiarities of the South." *The North American Review*, CLI, 477-488 (October, 1890).

Stegner, Wallace. "The Trail of the Hawkeye: Literature Where the Tall Corn Grows." *The Saturday Review of Literature*, XVIII, 3-4 (July 30, 1938).

Sterling, John. "New England Villages." *The Atlantic Monthly*, CXXXI, 520 (April, 1923).

Stewart, Kenneth. "California's New Gold Rush." *The Literary Digest*, CXVII, 30 (March 3, 1934).

Suckow, Ruth. "The Folk Idea in American Life." *Scribner's Magazine*, LXXXVIII, 246 (September, 1930).

————. "Iowa." *The American Mercury*, IX, 39-45 (September, 1926).

Stoll, E. E. "Literature No 'Document'." *Modern Language Review*, XLX, 141-157 (April, 1924).

Thompson, Alan R. "The Cult of Cruelty." *The Bookman*, LXXIV, 477-487 (January, 1932).

Thompson, C. M. "Miss Wilkins, An Idealist in Masquerade." *The Atlantic Monthly*, LXXXIII, 665-675 (May, 1899).

————. "The Art of Miss Jewett." *The Atlantic Monthly*, XCIV, 485 (October, 1904).

Van Doren, Carl. "Stephen Crane." *The American Mercury*, I, 11-14 (January, 1924).

————. "Sinclair Lewis and Sherwood Anderson: A Study of Two Moralists." *Century Magazine*, CX, 362-369 (July, 1925).

Vinson, Esther. "Tilbury Town." *The Saturday Review of Literature*, XI, 632 (April 20, 1935).

Wann, Louis. "The 'Revolt of the Village' in American Fiction." *The Overland Monthly*, LXXXIII, 299 (August, 1925).

Wharton, Edith. "The Great American Novel." *The Yale Review*, XVI, 648 (July, 1927).

————. "The Writing of Ethan Frome." *The Colophon*, XI (1932).

Winston, Archer. "In Defense of Willa Cather." *The Bookman*, LXXIV, 634-640 (March, 1932).

Winter, Calvin. "Edith Wharton." *The Bookman*, XXXIII, 302-309 (May, 1911).

Wisewell, C. E. "An Interview with Masters." *Current Opinion*, LVIII, 356 (May, 1915).

Woolf, Virginia. "American Fiction." *The Saturday Review of Literature*, II, 1-3 (August 1, 1925).

Primary Materials

The following is a selected list of American poems, novels, short stories, plays, essays, journals, diaries, and autobiographies which variously portray life in the American small town. At times editions most accessible have been used, though ordinarily the writer has consulted first editions.

Abbe, George. *Voices in the Square*. New York, 1938. (Massachusetts small town novel.)

Adams, Andy. *The Log of a Cowboy.* Boston and New York, 1903.

Anon. *The Boston Book being Specimens of Metropolitan Literature.* Boston, 1841. (See Appendix I.)

Alcott, A. Bronson. *Concord Days.* Boston, 1888.

Aldrich, Bess Streeter. *A Lantern in Her Hand.* New York, 1928.

Aldrich, Thomas Bailey. *From Ponkapong to Pesth and An Old Town by the Sea.* Boston, 1897. (*An Old Town by the Sea,* first written 1883.)

————. *The Stillwater Tragedy.* Boston, 1907. (First edition, 1880.)

————. *The Works of Thomas Bailey Aldrich.* "Realism," Vol. I; "At the Funeral of a Minor Poet," Vol. II; "A Rivermouth Romance," Vol. IV; *The Story of a Bad Boy* (1869), Vol. VII. Boston and New York, 1913.

Anderson, Maxwell. *The Wingless Victory.* New York, 1936.

Anderson, Sherwood. *Windy McPherson's Son.* New York, 1916.

————. *Marching Men.* New York, 1917.

————. *Mid-American Chants.* New York, 1918.

————. *Winesburg, Ohio: A Group of Tales of Ohio Small Town Life.* New York, 1927. (First edition, 1919. Recently dramatized under the title of *Plays: Winesburg and Others,* New York, 1937. Contains "Winesburg," "The Triumph of the Egg," "Mother," and "They Married Later.")

————. *Poor White.* New York, 1920.

————. *The Triumph of the Egg: A Book of Impressions from American Life in Tales and Poems.* New York, 1921.

————. *Horses and Men.* New York, 1923.

————. *A Story Teller's Story.* New York, 1924.

————. *Dark Laughter.* New York, 1925.

————. *Sherwood Anderson's Notebook.* New York, 1926.

————. *Tar: A Midwest Childhood.* New York, 1926.

————. *Hello Towns!* New York, 1929.

————. *The American County Fair.* New York, 1930.

————. *Beyond Desire.* New York, 1932.

————. *Death in the Woods and Other Stories.* New York, 1933.

————. *Puzzled America.* New York, 1935.

————. *Kit Brandon.* New York, 1936. (Novel about a Virginia mountain girl who early left home to find work as a textile worker in a valley town.)

Bacheller, Irving. *Eben Holden.* Boston, 1901.

Bacon, Elizabeth. *Search the Scriptures.* Dallas, 1938. (Texas small town.)

Baldwin, C. S., ed. *American Short Stories.* New York, 1916. (Excerpts from James Hall and Mrs. Kirkland.)

Baldwin, Joseph Glover. *The Flush Times of Alabama and Mississippi.* New York, 1854. (First edition, 1853.)

Beecher, Henry Ward. *Norwood, or Village Life in New England.* Boston and Chicago, 1895. (First printed serially in the New York *Ledger*, 1867.)

Beede, Ivan. *Prairie Women.* New York, 1930.

Bird, Robert M. *Nick of the Woods; or The Jibbenainosay.* 2 vols. Philadelphia, 1837.

Bromfield, Louis. *The Green Bay Tree.* New York, 1924.

———. *Possession.* New York, 1925.

———. *Early Autumn.* New York, 1926.

Brown, Alice. *Meadow Grass.* Boston and New York, 1895.

———. *Tiverton Tales.* Boston and New York, 1898.

———. *Country Neighbors.* New York, 1910.

———. *Bromley Neighborhood.* New York, 1915.

———. *Jeremy Hamlin.* New York, 1934.

Byrd, Sigman. *Tall Grew the Pines.* New York, 1936. (East Texas locale.)

Cable, George Washington. *John March, Southerner.* New York, 1899.

Caruthers, William A. *Cavaliers of Virginia, or The Recluse of Jamestown.* 2 vols. New York, 1834-35.

———. *The Knights of the Horse-Shoe.* Wetumka, Alabama, 1845.

Cather, Willa Sibert. *April Twilights and Other Poems.* New York, 1903.

———. *The Troll Garden.* New York, 1905.

———. *Alexander's Bridge.* New York, 1922. (Written during 1911; published, 1912.)

———. *The Bohemian Girl.* New York, 1912.

———. *O Pioneers!* New York, 1913.

———. *The Song of the Lark.* New York, 1915.

———. *My Ántonia.* New York, 1918.

———. *Youth and the Bright Medusa.* New York, 1920. (Contains reprints from *The Troll Garden.*)

———. *One of Ours.* New York, 1922.

———. *A Lost Lady.* New York, 1923.

———. *The Professor's House.* New York, 1925.

———. *Obscure Destinies.* New York, 1932.

———. *Lucy Gayheart.* New York, 1935.

Catherwood, Mary H. *The Spirit of an Illinois Town.* Boston, 1897.

Clemens, Samuel Langhorne. *Roughing It.* New York, 1913. (First edition, 1872.)

———. *The Gilded Age* (with Charles Dudley Warner). New York, 1915. (1873.)

————. *The Adventures of Tom Sawyer.* New York, 1903. (1876.)

————. *Life on the Mississippi.* New York, 1899. (1883.)

————. *The Adventures of Huckleberry Finn.* New York, 1912. (1885.)

————. *The Tragedy of Pudd'nhead Wilson.* New York, 1899. (1894.)

————. *The Man That Corrupted Hadleyburg.* New York, 1900.

————. *Mark Twain's Autobiography.* New York, 1924.

Clough, Arthur Hugh. *Prose Remains.* Edited by his wife. London, 1888.

Cohen, Octavus Roy. *With Benefit of Clergy.* New York, 1935. (Southern small town jealousies and caste differences.)

Cooke, John Esten. *The Virginia Comedians; or Old Days in the Old Dominion.* New York, 1854.

Cooke, Rose Terry. "Sally Parson's Duty." *The Atlantic Monthly,* I, 31 ff. (November, 1857).

————. "Lizzy Griswold's Thanksgiving." *The Atlantic Monthly,* III, 282 ff. (March, 1859).

————. "The Ring Fetter." *The Atlantic Monthly,* IV, 154 ff. (August, 1859).

————. "Miss Lucinda." *The Atlantic Monthly,* VI, 144 ff. (August, 1861).

————. "Squire Paine's Conversion." *Harper's Magazine,* LVI, 608 ff. (March, 1878).

————. "Amandar." *Harper's Magazine,* LXI, 581 ff. (September, 1880).

————. "Mrs. Flint's Married Experience." *Harper's Magazine,* LXII, 79 ff. (December, 1880).

————. *Huckleberries Gathered from New England Hills.* Boston and New York, 1891.

Cooper, James Fenimore. *Works.* Mohawk edition. New York, 1912: *The Deerslayer* (1841), *The Pioneers* (1823), and *Homeward Bound* (1838).

————. *Notions of the Americans.* London, 1828. Vol. 11.

————. *The American Democrat.* Cooperstown, 1838. Also *The American Democrat,* edited by H. L. Mencken, New York, 1931.

————. *Home as Found.* Philadelphia, 1838.

————. *Chronicles of Cooperstown* (1838) in *History of Cooperstown and Cooper,* edited by S. T. Livermore, Albany, 1862.

————. *Correspondence of James Fenimore Cooper.* Edited by his grandson, J. F. Cooper. Yale University Press, 1922.

Cooper, William. *A Guide in the Wilderness.* Dublin, 1810.

Cozzens, J. G. *The Last Adam.* New York, 1933.

Crane, Stephen. *The Works of Crane.* Edited by Wilson Follett.

New York, 1923. Vol. III, *The Monster* (1899). Vol. XII, *Whilomville Stories* (1899).

Croy, Homer. *West of the Water Tower*. New York, 1923.

———. *R. F. D. No. 3*. New York, 1924.

Deland, Margaret. *John Ward, Preacher*. New York, 1888.

———. *Old Chester Tales*. New York, 1898.

———. *Dr. Lavender's People*. New York, 1903.

———. *Around Old Chester*. New York, 1915.

———. *New Friends in Old Chester*. New York, 1924.

Dell, Floyd. *Moon-Calf*. New York, 1920.

———. *The Briary-Bush*. New York, 1921.

———. *Runaway*. New York, 1925.

———. *This Mad Ideal*. New York, 1925.

———. *Homecoming: An Autobiography*. New York, 1937.

Downing, J. H. *A Prayer for Tomorrow*. New York, 1938. (South Dakota boom town.)

Drake, Benjamin. *Tales and Sketches from the Queen City*. Cincinnati, 1838.

Duncan, Thomas. *O, Chautauqua*. New York, 1935.

Dwight, Timothy. *Greenfield Hill: A Poem in Seven Parts*. New York, 1794.

Edgar, Day. *In Princeton Town*. New York, circa 1936. (College scenes.)

Eggleston, Edward. *The Hoosier Schoolmaster*. New York, 1871.

———. *The Mystery of Metropolisville*. New York, 1873.

———. *The Circuit Rider*. New York, 1874.

———. *Roxy*. New York, 1878.

———. *The Graysons*. New York, 1898.

Emerson, Ralph Waldo. *Complete Works*. New York, 1903-04. Vol. III, *Journals*. Vol. XI, *Miscellanies*.

———. *The Heart of Emerson's Journals*. Edited by Bliss Perry. New York, 1926.

Ethridge, Willie Snow. *As I Live and Breathe*. New York, 1937.

———. *Mingled Yarn*. New York, 1938.

Farnham, Mateel Howe. *Great Riches*. New York, 1934.

Faulkner, William. *Soldiers' Pay*. New York, 1926.

———. *Sartoris*. New York, 1929.

———. *Sanctuary*. New York, 1931.

———. *These Thirteen*. New York, 1931.

———. *Miss Zilphia Gant*. Dallas, 1932.

———. *Doctor Martino and Other Stories*. New York, 1934.

———. *The Unvanquished*. New York, 1938.

Ferber, Edna. *Cimarron*. New York, 1930. (Southwestern boom town.)

————. *American Beauty.* New York, 1931.

————. *A Peculiar Treasure.* New York, 1939.

Fisher, Dorothy Canfield. *The Squirrel Cage.* New York, 1912.

————. *Hillsboro People.* New York, 1915.

————. *Rough-Hewn.* New York, 1922.

————. *Raw Material.* New York, 1923.

————. *Bonfire.* New York, 1933.

Fleming, Barry. *Siesta.* New York, 1936. (Southern small town.)

Flint, Timothy. *Recollections of the Last Ten Years.* Boston, 1826.

Fowler, Gene. *Salute to Yesterday.* New York, 1937. (Novel about an old time editor in a small town.)

Frederic, Harold. *Seth's Brother's Wife.* New York, 1887.

————. *In the Valley.* New York, 1929. (First edition, 1890.)

————. *The Copperhead, and Other Stories of the North during the American War.* New York, 1894.

————. *The Damnation of Theron Ware.* (Published in England as *Illumination.*) Chicago and New York, 1899.

Frederic, John T. *Druida.* New York, 1923.

Freeman, Mary E. Wilkins. *A Humble Romance and Other Stories.* New York, 1899. (First edition, 1887.)

————. *A New England Nun and Other Stories.* New York, 1891.

————. *Jane Field. Harper's Magazine,* LXXXIV (May, 1892)-LXXV (November, 1892).

————. *The People of Our Neighborhood.* Philadelphia, 1895.

————. *Madelon: A Novel.* New York, 1896.

————. "One Good Time." *Harper's Magazine,* XCIV, 309 ff. (January, 1897).

————. *Jerome, A Poor Man.* New York, 1897.

————. *A Portion of Labor.* New York, 1901.

————. *By the Light of the Soul.* New York, 1907.

————. *Edgewater People.* New York, 1918.

————. *The Best Stories of Mary E. Wilkins.* Edited by H. W. Lanier. New York, 1927.

French, Alice (Octave Thanet). *Stories of a Western Town.* New York, 1893.

————. *The Missionary Sheriff.* New York and London, 1897 (o. p.). N. V.

————. *The Heart of Toil.* New York, 1898.

————. *The Man of the Hour.* Indianapolis, 1905.

Gale, Zona. *Friendship Village.* New York, 1908.

————. *Friendship Village Love Stories.* New York, 1909.

————. *Neighborhood Stories.* New York, 1914.

————. *Peace in Friendship Village.* New York, 1918.

————. *Birth.* New York, 1918. (Dramatized as *Mister Pitt*, 1926.)

————. *Miss Lulu Bett.* New York, 1920. (Dramatized, 1921.)

————. *The Neighbors.* New York, 1920.

————. *Preface to a Life.* New York, 1926.

————. *Yellow Gentians and Blue.* New York, 1927.

————. *Portage, Wisconsin, and Other Essays.* New York, 1928.

Garland, Hamlin. *Main-Travelled Roads.* New York, 1899. (First edition, 1891.)

————. *Prairie Folks.* Chicago, 1893. *Prairie Songs*, 1893.

————. *Crumbling Idols.* Chicago, 1894.

————. *Rose of Dutcher's Coolly.* New York, 1895.

————. *The Spirit of Sweetwater.* Philadelphia, 1898.

————. *Boy Life on the Prairie.* New York, 1907. (First edition, 1899.)

————. *The Eagle's Heart.* New York, 1900.

————. *Her Mountain Lover.* New York, 1901.

————. *The Captain of the Gray-Horse Troop.* New York, 1902.

————. *Hesper.* New York, 1903.

————. *The Long Trail.* New York, 1907. *Money Magic, or Mart Haney's Mate.* New York, 1907.

————. *Cavanagh, Forest Ranger.* New York, 1909.

————. *Other Main-Travelled Roads.* New York, 1910.

————. *The Forester's Daughter.* New York, 1914.

————. *They of the High Trails.* New York, 1916.

————. *A Son of the Middle Border.* New York, 1917.

————. *A Daughter of the Middle Border.* New York, 1921.

————. *Memories of the Middle Border.* New York, 1926.

————. *Trail-Makers of the Middle Border.* New York, 1926.

————. *The Westward March of American Settlement.* New York, 1927.

————. *Back-Trailers from the Middle Border.* New York, 1928.

————. *Roadside Meetings.* New York, 1930.

————. *Companions on the Trail.* New York, 1931.

————. *My Friendly Contemporaries.* New York, 1932.

————. *Afternoon Neighbors.* New York, 1934.

Gilfillan, Lauren. *I Went to Pit College.* New York, 1934. (The record of a girl's experiences in Avelonia, a Pennsylvania mining town.)

Gray, James. *Shoulder the Sky.* New York, 1935.

Griswold, R. W. *The Poets and Poetry of America.* Sixth edition. Philadelphia, 1845. (See Appendix I.)

————. *The Female Poets of America.* Second edition. Philadelphia, 1853. (See Appendix I.)

Haldeman-Julius, Anna M. and Emanuel. *Dust.* New York, 1921.

Hall, James. *Letters from the West.* London, 1828.

————. *Legends of the West.* Philadelphia, 1832.

————. *The Soldier's Bride and Other Tales.* Philadelphia, 1833.

————. *Tales of the Border.* Philadelphia, 1835.

Harris, George Washington. *Sut Lovingood: Yarns Spun By a "Nat'ral Born Durn'd Fool."* Nashville, 1867.

Harris, Joel Chandler. *Free Joe and Other Georgia Sketches.* New York, 1887.

————. *Gabriel Tolliver: A Story of Reconstruction.* New York, 1902.

Harrison, Mrs. Burton. *Belhaven Tales, etc.* New York, 1892. (First edition, 1855.)

Harte, Bret. *The Luck of Roaring Camp and Other Sketches* (1870). New York, 1899. (Cf. *Tales of Trail and Town,* 1898.)

————. *Gabriel Conroy* (1876). 2 vols. Boston and New York, 1903.

Hawthorne, Nathaniel. *The Complete Works of Nathaniel Hawthorne.* The Riverside edition, edited by G. P. Lathrop, Boston, 1883 (12 vols.) Works used : *Fanshawe* (1828). *Twice-Told Tales* (2 series), 1837, 1842. *Mosses from an Old Manse* (1846). *The Scarlet Letter* (1850). *The House of the Seven Gables* (1851). *The Snow-Image and Other Tales* (1851). *The Blithedale Romance* (1852). *A Rill from the Town Pump* (1857). *Passages from the American Note-Books* (1868). *Septimius Felton* (1872). *The Dolliver Romance* (1876). *Dr. Grimshawe's Secret* (1883).

————. *The Heart of Hawthorne's Journals.* Edited by Newton Arvin. Boston, 1929.

————. *The American Notebooks.* Edited by R. Stewart. New Haven, 1932.

Heath, E. A. *The Affairs at Tideways.* New York, 1932.

Higginson, T. W. *Malbone: An Oldport Romance. The Atlantic Monthly,* XIII (January to May, 1869).

————. *Old Cambridge.* New York, 1899.

————. *Cheerful Yesterdays.* Boston, 1899.

Higginson, Mary T., ed. *Letters and Journals of Thomas Wentworth Higginson, 1846-1906.* Boston and New York, 1921.

Hill, Clyde Walton. "Little Towns of Texas." *The Buccaneer,* I (September, 1924) ; reprinted in *The Literary Digest,* XXCII, 38 (September 27, 1924).

Holmes, Oliver W. *Elsie Venner: A Romance of Destiny.* Boston and New York, 1891. (First published in *The Atlantic Monthly,* beginning in December, 1859, as "The Professor's Story"; first edition, 1861.)

———. *The Guardian Angel*. Boston, 1867.

———. *A Mortal Antipathy*. Boston, 1886. (First edition, 1885.)

———. *The Autocrat of the Breakfast Table* (1858). Boston and New York, 1891. Vol. I.

Hooper, Johnson Jones. *Some Adventures of Captain Simon Suggs, Late of the Tallapoosa Volunteers . . . by a Country Editor*. Philadelphia, 1845.

Horan, Kenneth. *Remember the Day*. New York, 1937. (Affairs in Eastmeadow, Michigan, during the nineties as told from the viewpoint of two young girls.)

Hough, Emerson. *The Story of the Cowboy*. New York and London, 1919. (First edition, 1897.)

———. *The Passing of the Frontier*. Vol. XXVI, *Chronicles of America*, edited by Allen Johnson. New Haven, 1921.

———. *North of 36*. New York, 1923.

Howard, Sidney. *Alien Corn*. New York, 1933.

Howe, Edgar Watson. *The Story of a Country Town*. Boston, 1884. (The original copyright was issued in 1882 and the first two thousand copies printed by the author. A cheaper edition, issued in 1927 by the Blue Ribbon Books, Inc., is now available.)

———. *The Mystery of the Locks*. Boston, 1885.

———. *A Moonlight Boy*. Boston, 1886.

———. *The Anthology of Another Town*. New York, 1920.

———. *Plain People*. New York, 1929.

Howells, Mildred, ed. *Life in Letters of William Dean Howells*. Garden City, 1928.

Howells, William Dean. *Suburban Sketches*. Boston, 1870.

———. *The Lady of the Aroostook*. Boston, 1876.

———. *Dr. Breen's Practice*. Boston, 1881.

———. *A Modern Instance: A Novel*. Boston, 1882.

———. *Three Villages*. Boston, 1884.

———. *Annie Kilburn*. New York, 1891. (The story was serialized in *Harper's New Monthly Magazine*, June to November, 1888; first edition, 1889.)

———. *A Boy's Town*. New York, 1890.

———. *The Quality of Mercy*. New York, 1892.

———. *My Literary Passions*. New York, 1895.

———. *New Leaf Mills: A Chronicle*. New York, 1913.

———. *The Leatherwood God*. New York, 1916.

———. *Years of My Youth*. New York, 1916.

Hughes, Langston. *Not Without Laughter*. New York, 1930.

Hughes, Rupert. *The Old Home Town*. New York, 1926.

Irving, Washington. *Astoria*. Philadelphia, 1836. Vol. I.

———. *Selections from Irving's Sketch Book*. New York, 1910.

462 BIBLIOGRAPHY

Irwin, Wallace. *The Golden Bed.* New York, 1924.

Janvier, Thomas. *Santa Fe's Partner, Being Some Memorials of Events in a New-Mexican Track-End Town.* New York, 1907.

Jewett, Sarah Orne. *Deephaven.* Boston and New York, 1905. (First edition, Boston, 1877.)

———. *Tales of New England.* Boston and New York, 1894 and 1896. (First edition, Boston, 1879.)

———. *A Native of Winby and Other Tales.* Boston and New York, 1893.

———. *The Country of the Pointed Firs.* Boston and New York, 1927. (First edition, 1896.)

———. *The Best Stories of Sarah Orne Jewett.* Edited by Willa Cather. Boston and New York, 1925.

———. *Letters of Sarah Orne Jewett.* Edited by Annie Fields. Boston, 1911.

John, William M. *Seven Women.* New York, 1929.

Johnson, Josephine. *Jordanstown.* New York, 1937.

Johnston, Richard Malcolm. *Dukesborough Tales.* Baltimore, 1871.

———. *Old Mark Langston.* New York, 1884.

———. *Mr. Absalom Billingslea and Other Georgia Folk.* New York, 1888.

———. *Widow Guthrie.* New York, 1891.

———. *The Chronicles of Mr. Bill Williams (Dukesborough Tales).* New York, 1892.

———. *Old Times in Middle Georgia.* New York, 1897.

———. *Autobiography of Colonel Richard Malcolm Johnston.* Washington, 1900.

Judd, Sylvester. *Margaret.* Boston, 1871.

Kennedy, John Pendleton. *Annals of Quodlibet . . . By Solomon Secondthoughts, schoolmaster, etc.* Philadelphia, 1860, second edition. (First edition, 1840.)

———. *Rob of the Bowl: A Legend of St. Inigoe's.* Issued anonymously in two volumes. Philadelphia, 1838.

Kent, Louise A. *The Terrace.* Boston, 1934.

Kettell, Samuel. *Specimens of American Poetry, etc.* 3 vols. Boston, 1829. (See Appendix I.)

Kirkland, Joseph. *Zury: The Meanest Man in Spring County. A Novel of Western Life.* Boston and New York, 1887.

Kirkland, Matilda (Clavers, Mrs. Mary). *A New Home—Who'll Follow? or Glimpses of Western Life.* New York, 1839.

———. *Western Clearings.* New York, 1845.

Lane, Rose Wilder. *Old Home Town.* New York, 1935.

Lanham, Edwin. *The Wind Blew West.* New York, 1936. (A story of a pioneer Texas town—actually Weatherford, Texas.)

Larcom, Lucy. *A New England Girlhood Outlined from Memory.* Boston and New York, 1889. (A vivid picture of early factory towns.)

Lardner, Ringgold W. *The Love Nest and Other Stories.* New York, 1926.

Lee, Muna (Mrs. Luis M. Marín). "Mushroom Town." *The American Mercury*, I, 459-462 (April, 1924).

Le Sueur, Meridel. *Corn Village.* New York, 1931.

Levy, Melvin. *The Last Pioneers.* New York, 1934.

Lewis, Alfred Henry. *Wolfville.* New York, 1897.

———. *Sandburrs.* New York, 1900.

———. *Wolfville Days.* New York, 1902.

———. *Wolfville Nights.* New York, 1902.

———. *Wolfville Folks.* New York, 1908.

———. *Faro Nell and Her Friends.* New York, 1913.

Lewis, Sinclair. *Our Mr. Wrenn.* New York, 1914.

———. *The Trail of the Hawk.* New York, 1915.

———. *The Job.* New York, 1917.

———. *The Innocents.* New York, 1917.

———. *Free Air.* New York, 1919.

———. *Main Street.* New York, 1920.

———. *Babbitt.* New York, 1922.

———. *Arrowsmith.* New York, 1925.

———. *Elmer Gantry.* New York, 1927.

———. *The Man Who Knew Coolidge.* New York, 1928.

———. *Dodsworth.* New York, 1929.

———. *Ann Vickers.* New York, 1933.

———. *Work of Art.* New York, 1934.

———. *Selected Short Stories of Sinclair Lewis.* New York, 1935.

———. *It Can't Happen Here.* New York, 1935.

———. *The Prodigal Parents.* New York, 1938.

Lincoln, Enoch. "The Village, A Poem with an Appendix." Portland, 1816.

Lincoln. Joseph C. *Cap'n Eri.* New York, 1904.

———. *Partners of the Tide.* New York, 1905.

———. *Our Village.* New York, 1909.

———. *The Postmaster.* New York, 1912.

———. *Fair Harbor.* New York, 1922.

———. *Dr. Nye of North Ostable.* New York, 1923.

———. *Head Tide.* New York, 1932.

Lindsay, Nicholas Vachel. *The Golden Book of Springfield.* New York, 1920.

———. *Collected Poems.* New York, 1923.

Longfellow, Henry W. *The New England Tragedies.* Boston, 1868.

——. *Complete Poetical Works.* Edited by H. E. Scudder. Boston, 1893. Vol. VIII.

——. *Kavanagh* (1849). *Complete Poetical and Prose Works*, Boston, 1886.

Longstreet, Augustus Baldwin. *Georgia Scenes, Characters, Incidents, etc. in the First Half Century of the Republic. By a Native Georgian.* New York, 1897. (First edition, Augusta, 1835.)

Lowell, James Russell. *Prose Works.* New York, 1899. Vols. I and III.

——. *Complete Poetical Works.* "Fitz Adam's Story," pp. 411-421. Boston and New York, 1917.

Marshall, Robert. *Arctic Village.* New York, 1933.

Masters, Edgar Lee. *Spoon River Anthology.* New York, 1915.

——. *Songs and Satires.* New York, 1916.

——. *The Great Valley.* New York, 1916.

——. *Toward the Gulf.* New York, 1918.

——. *Starved Rock.* New York, 1919.

——. *Mitch Miller.* New York, 1920.

——. *Domesday Book.* New York, 1920.

——. *Children of the Market Place.* New York, 1922.

——. *The Nuptial Flight.* New York, 1923.

——. *Skeeters Kirby.* New York, 1923.

——. *Mirage.* New York, 1924.

——. *The New Spoon River.* New York, 1924.

——. *Kit O'Brien.* New York, 1927.

——. *Across Spoon River: An Autobiography.* New York, 1936.

Meine, Franklin J., ed. *Tall Tales of the Southwest.* New York, 1930.

Merz, Charles. *Centerville, U. S. A.* New York, 1924.

Meyer, John de. *Village Tale.* New York, 1938.

Milburn, George. *Oklahoma Town.* New York, 1931.

——. *No More Trumpets.* New York, 1933.

——. *Catalogue.* New York, 1937.

Mitchell, Edwin V. *American Village.* New York, 1938.

Moody, Minnie H. *Old Home Week.* New York, 1938. (Illinois small town.)

Motley, J. L. *Merry Mount: A Romance of the Massachusetts Colony.* 2 vols. Boston and Cambridge, 1849.

Nadal, E. S. *A Virginian Village.* New York, 1917.

Nathan, Robert. *Peter Kindred.* New York, 1919.

——. *Autumn.* New York, 1921.

Noble, Annette. *In a Country Town.* New York, 1890.

Norris, Frank. *The Octopus: A Story of California.* New York, 1906. (First edition, 1901.)

North, Sterling. *Plowing on Sunday*. New York, 1934.
——. *Night Outlasts the Whippoorwill*. New York, 1936.
O'Connor, Jack. *Boom Town*. New York, 1938.
Page, Thomas Nelson. *The Old South Essays*. New York, 1892.
——. *Gordon Keith*. New York, 1903.
Paillou, Emile R. *Home Town Sketches*. Boston, 1926.
Parrish, Anne. *The Perennial Bachelor*. New York, 1925.
Pattee, F. L., ed. *The Poems of Freneau, Poet of the American Revolution*. Princeton University Press, 1902. 3 vols.
Porter, William T., ed. *A Quarter Race in Kentucky and Other Sketches*. Philadelphia, 1854.
Quick, Herbert. *Vandemark's Folly*. New York, 1922.
——. *The Hawkeye*. New York, 1923.
——. *The Invisible Woman*. Indianapolis, 1924.
Reese, Lizette Woodworth. *A Victorian Village*. New York, 1920.
Richards, Caroline Cowles. *Village Life in America (1852-1872)*. Edited by Margaret E. Sangster. London, 1912.
Robinson, Edwin Arlington. *The Children of the Night*. New York, 1897.
——. *Captain Craig*. Boston and New York, 1902.
——. *The Town Down the River*. New York, 1910.
——. *The Man Against the Sky*. New York, 1916.
——. *The Three Taverns*. New York, 1920.
——. *Avon's Harvest*. New York, 1921.
——. *Collected Poems*. New York, 1922.
——. *Collected Poems* (new edition). New York, 1929.
Roopman, H. L., and Paltsits, V. H., ed. *The American Village: A Poem by Philip Freneau*. (Reprinted in facsimile from the original edition published in New York, 1772.) Providence, 1906.
Sachs, Emanie. *Talk*. New York, 1924.
Sedgwick, Catharine Maria. *Redwood*. 2 vols. New York, 1924.
——. *Hope Leslie, or Early Times in Massachusetts*. 2 vols. New York, 1842.
Sergel, Roger L. *Arlie Gelston*. New York, 1924.
Shippey, Lee. *Where Nothing Ever Happens*. New York, 1935.
Simms, William Gilmore. *Guy Rivers: A Tale of Georgia*. New York, 1855. (First edition, 1834.)
——. *Richard Hurdis: A Tale of Alabama*. New York, 1855. (First edition, 1838.)
——. *Border Beagles: A Tale of Mississippi*. New York, 1840.
——. *Beauchampe; or The Kentucky Tragedy*. New York, 1842.
——. *Charlemont, or The Pride of the Village*. New York, 1856.
——. *The Partisan*. New York, 1870. (First edition, 1835.)

———. *Mellichampe: A Legend of the Santee.* New York, 1864. (First edition, 1834.)

———. *Katharine Walton, or The Rebel of Dorchester.* New York, 1882. (First edition, 1851.)

———. *Woodcraft.* New York, 1854.

———. *The Cassique of Kiawah.* New York, 1859.

Sinclair, Harold. *American Years.* New York, 1938.

Sinclair, Upton. *King Coal.* New York, 1917.

Slosson, Annie T. *Seven Dreamers.* New York, 1891.

Smith, Seba. *The Life and Writings of Major Jack Downing of Dowingville, Away Down East in the State of Maine, Written by Himself.* Boston, 1833.

———. *'Way Down East, or Portraitures of Yankee Life.* New York and Boston, 1854.

Smith, Francis Hopkinson. *Colonel Carter of Cartersville.* Boston and New York, 1891.

Smith, Sol. *Theatrical Apprenticeship, etc.* Philadelphia, 1845.

———. *Theatrical Management in the West and South, etc.* New York, 1868.

Snell, G. D. *The Great Adam.* Caldwell, Idaho, 1934.

Spofford, Harriet Prescott. *The Amber Gods and Other Stories.* Boston and New York, 1881. (First edition, 1863.)

———. *The Elder's People.* Boston and New York, 1920.

Stevens, Barbara. *The Strongest Son.* Boston, 1938.

Stevenson, Robert Louis. *The Silverado Squatters.* Vol. VI of *The Works of Robert Louis Stevenson.* New York, 1912.

Stong, Phil. *State Fair.* New York, 1932.

———. *Stranger's Return.* New York, 1933.

———. *Village Tale.* New York, 1934.

———. *The Rebellion of Lennie Barlow.* New York, 1937.

Stowe, Harriet Beecher. *The May Flower.* Boston, 1855. (First published by Harpers, 1849.)

———. *The Pearl of Orr's Island.* Boston and New York, 1862.

———. *The Minister's Wooing.* Boston, 1869.

———. *Oldtown Folks.* Boston, 1869.

———. *Sam Lawson's Oldtown Fireside Stories.* Boston, 1872.

———. *Poganuc People.* Boston, 1871.

Stribling, T. S. *Birthright.* New York, 1922.

———. *Teeftallow.* Garden City, 1926.

———. *Bright Metal.* Garden City, 1928.

———. *Backwater.* Garden City, 1930.

———. *The Forge.* Garden City, 1931.

———. *The Store.* Garden City, 1932.

———. *Unfinished Cathedral.* Garden City, 1934.

Suckow, Ruth. *Country People.* New York, 1924.
———. *The Odyssey of a Nice Girl.* New York, 1925.
———. *Iowa Interiors.* New York, 1926.
———. *The Bonney Family.* New York, 1928.
———. *Cora.* New York, 1929.
———. *The Kramer Girls.* New York, 1930.
———. *The Folks.* New York, 1934.
Tarkington, Booth. *The Gentleman from Indiana.* New York, 1899.
———. *The Flirt.* New York, 1913.
———. *Penrod.* New York, 1914.
———. *The Turmoil.* New York, 1915.
———. *Penrod and Sam.* New York, 1916.
———. *Seventeen.* New York, 1916.
———. *The Magnificent Ambersons.* New York, 1918.
———. *Ramsey Milholland.* New York, 1919.
———. *Clarence.* New York, 1919.
———. *Alice Adams.* New York, 1921.
———. *Gentle Julia.* New York, 1922.
———. *The Midlander.* New York, 1924.
———. *Little Orvie,* New York, 1934.
———. *Mr. White, the Red Barn, and Bridewater.* New York, 1935.
The Columbian Muse: A Selection of American Poetry from Various Authors of Established Reputation. Philadelphia, 1794.
Thompson, William Tappan. *Major Jones' Courtship, with Other Scenes, Incidents, and Adventures in a Series of Letters by Himself.* Revised. New York, 1872. (First edition, 1840.)
———. *Major Jones' Chronicles of Pineville.* Philadelphia, 1843.
Tourgée, Albion W. *A Fool's Errand.* New York, 1879.
———. *Hot Plowshares.* New York, 1883.
Turnbull, Agnes Sligh. *Old Home Town.* New York, 1933.
Van Vechten, Carl. *The Tattooed Countess.* New York, 1924.
Walker, Mildred. *Fireweed.* New York, 1934.
Ward, Elizabeth Stuart Phelps. *Doctor Zay.* Boston and New York, 1899.
Watterson, Henry, ed. *Oddities in Southern Life and Character.* Boston, 1883.
Wells, Carolyn. *Ptomaine Street: The Tale of Warble Petticoat.* Philadelphia, 1921.
Wescott, Edward Noyes. *David Harum: A Story of American Life.* New York, 1898.
Wharton, Edith. *Ethan Frome.* New York, 1912.
———. *Xingu and Other Stories.* New York, 1916.
———. *Summer.* New York, 1917.
———. *A Backward Glance.* New York, 1934.

White, William Allen. *The Court of Boyville.* New York, 1899.
———. *In Our Town.* New York, 1925. (First edition, 1906.)
———. *The Old Order Changeth: A View of American Democracy.* New York, 1910.
———. *In the Heart of a Fool.* New York, 1918.
———. *Forty Years on Main Street.* New York, 1937.
White, William L. *What People Said.* New York, 1938.
Whittier, John Greenleaf. *Prose Works.* Boston, 1866. Vol. I: *Margaret Smith's Journal in the Province of Massachusetts Bay (1678-9).*
———. *Poetical Works.* Edited by H. E. Scudder. Boston and New York, 1894.
Whitlock, Brand. *The Happy Average.* Indianapolis, 1904.
Wilder, Thornton. *In Our Town.* New York, 1938.
Wister, Owen. *The Virginian: A Horseman of the Plains.* New York, 1902.
———. *When West was West.* New York, 1928.
Wolfe, Thomas. *Look Homeward, Angel.* New York, 1929.
———. *Of Time and the River: A Legend of Man's Hunger in His Youth.* New York, 1935.
———. *From Death to Morning.* New York, 1935.
———. *The Story of a Novel.* New York, 1936. First printed in *The Saturday Review of Literature,* XIII, 3-4, 12, 14, 16 (December 14, 1935); 3-4, 15 (December 21, 1935); 3-4, 14-16 (December 28, 1935).
Yenni, Julia T. *Never Say Good-Bye.* New York, 1937.
———. *This Is Me, Kathie.* New York, 1938. (Scene: a small college town in Louisiana.)

INDEX